The Past in French History

The Past in French History

Robert Gildea

Yale University Press
New Haven and London · 1994

Set in Ehrhardt by Best-set Typesetter Ltd., Hong Kong
Printed and bound in Great Britain by Biddles Ltd., Guildford and Kings Lynn

Library of Congress Cataloging-in-Publication Data

Gildea, Robert.
      The past in French history/Robert Gildea.
         p.   cm.
      Includes bibliographical references and index.
      ISBN 0–300–05799–7
         1. France—Civilization.   2. Public opinion—France—History.
      3. National characteristics, French.   4. Memorial rites and
      ceremonies—France—Political aspects.   5. Church and state—France
      —History.   I. Title.
      DC33.G48   1994
      944—dc20   93–28536
                                                                    CIP

A catalogue record for this book is available from the British Library.

For Lucy-Jean

Contents

List of Illustrations

Abbreviations

AD	Archives Départementales
AHRF	*Annales Historiques de la Révolution Française*
AIA	Association Internationale Antimilitariste
AN	Archives Nationales
APP	Archives de la Préfecture de Police
ARC	Azzione per la Rinascita Corsa
BHVP	Bibliothèque Historique de la Ville de Paris
BN	Bibliothèque Nationale
CELIB	Comité d'Étude et de Liaison des Intérêts Bretons
CFDT	Confédération Française Démocratique du Travail
CGT	Confédération Générale du Travail
CGTU	Confédération Générale du Travail Unifiée
CGTSR	Confération Générale du Travail Syndicaliste Révolutionnaire
CNT	Confédération Nationale du Travail
CODER	Commission de Développement Économique et Régional
COEA	Comité Occitan d'Études et d'Action
CSR	Comités Syndicalistes Révolutionnaires
EHR	*English Historical Review*
FAF	Fédération Anarchiste de Langue Française
FGDS	Fédération de la Gauche Démocrate et Socialiste
FLB	Front de Libération de la Bretagne
FLNC	Front de Libération Nationale de la Corse
FNSP	Fondation Nationale des Sciences Politiques

FTSF   Fédération des Travailleurs Socialistes de France

GRECE   Groupement de Recherche et d'Études pour la Civilisation Européenne

IFHS   Institut Français d'Histoire Sociale

IHTP   Institut d'Histoire du Temps Présent

ISR   Internationale Syndicale Rouge

JCH   *Journal of Contemporary History*

JMH   *Journal of Modern History*

MRP   Mouvement Républicain Populaire

NAF   Nouvelle Action Française

OAS   Organisation Armée Secrète

OURS   Office Universitaire de Recherche Socialiste

PCF   Parti Communiste Français

POBL   Parti pour l'Organisation d'une Bretagne Libre

POF   Parti Ouvrier Français

PSA   Parti Socialiste Autonome

PSF   Parti Social Français

PSU   Parti Socialiste Unifié

POSR   Parti Ouvrier Socialiste Révolutionnaire

PPF   Parti Populaire Français

PS   Parti Socialiste

RHMC   *Revue d'Histoire Moderne et Contemporaine*

RHDGM   *Revue d'Histoire de la Deuxième Guerre Mondiale*

RPF   Rassemblement du Peuple Français

RNP   Rassemblement National Populaire

RPR   Rassemblement pour la République

SFIO   Section Française de l'Internationale Ouvrière

SHPF   Société de l'Histoire du Protestantisme Français

STO   Service du Travail Obligatoire

UDB   Union Démocratique Bretonne

UNR   Union pour la Nouvelle République

UPR   Union Populaire Républicaine

Acknowledgements

First and foremost I must thank Lucy-Jean, who has been a constant support and inspiration, and for sharing in things French. This book is dedicated to her.

Financially I am indebted to the Leverhulme Trust, who awarded me a Fellowship in 1988–89, which allowed me to spend a full year in Paris completing my research there. I am also grateful to Merton College and to the Faculty of Modern History at Oxford for grants in aid of earlier trips to Paris.

The writing and rewriting of this book has been more difficult than anything I have yet undertaken. Firstly I must thank Ruth Harris for sharpening my wits and for going through the first draft of the work in its entirety. I also wish to thank Colin Lucas, Liam Smith, Martin Conway, Carol Harrison and David Berry, who saw and commented on various chapters. I am indebted also to the Past and Present conference in Oxford, the conference of the Society for the Study of French History in London, and to modern French and modern European seminars in Oxford, Cambridge and Norwich where I was able to test out some of my ideas. For tireless and faultless secretarial assistance with the various stages of the work I must thank Judith Kirby.

In Paris the staff of numerous libraries and archives offered me assistance and advice. I would like to thank in particular those of the Bibliothèque nationale, the Archives nationales, the Bibliothèque historique de la Ville de Paris, the Musée social, the Institut Français d'Histoire sociale, the Office Universitaire de Recherche Socialiste, the Institut de Recherche Marxiste, the Centre de Recherches sur l'Histoire des Mouvements sociaux et du Syndicalisme, the Archives de la Préfecture de Police, the Bibliothèque de la Fondation nationale des Sciences Politiques, and the Bibliothèque de la Société de l'Histoire du Protestantisme Français. In addition I would like to thank *L'Avenir de la Bretagne* and *La Calotte* for sending me further material after my return to this country.

Two special debts of gratitude I owe to Jacques and Antoinette Agofroy, Pierre and Alice Boyer and their families. Over more than a quarter of a century they have offered me hospitality and friendship during my long visits to France. To stay with them, the first in the Aube, the second in the Ardèche, has been to enjoy the rhythms of French village life, to gain a sense of provincial identity and of provincial history. It may be that the English will never understand the French, but these have helped me in an unmatched way on my voyage of discovery.

RNG
Oxford,
February 1993

INTRODUCTION

Writing French History

Perched on a horseshoe of hills in the Ardèche, between the Massif Central and the Rhône, is a string of gaunt hill villages. Viewing them from the village below, on my first visit to the Midi in 1975, I was told by my French friends that one of them was a Protestant village that had been put to fire and sword by Richelieu's troops in the early seventeenth century. A collective memory, which articulated a difference between the Catholic community in the valley and the Protestant community in the hills, was sustained over three hundred years, even though the hill village had first been depleted by rural depopulation, then restored by a new generation of Protestants in the form of Dutch holidaymakers.

At the time I was living in Rennes and was doing research on education in nineteenth-century Brittany. The same pattern seemed to appear as I painstakingly added my own distribution maps of support for church schools and lay schools, of the geographical origins of seminarists and *instituteurs*, to those maps already available of religious observance and political options: firm boundaries between communes or groups of communes defined attitudes that were shaped during the French Revolution and could be traced forwards to the twentieth century. To examine the impact of the Reformation as well as the Revolution on the education debate I followed a trail already blazed by British historians to Nîmes, and then, in order to test whether these continuities survived the impact of industrialisation and urbanisation, pitched camp for eight months in Lille.

Education in Provincial France, which was published in 1983, was very much at the end of a tradition. I was ten years in the wake of the brilliant cohort of pupils of Richard Cobb and John Roberts who rewrote the history of the French Revolution from the perspective of the great provincial cities, twenty years behind the French historians who had placed nineteenth-century France, and in particular the Revolution of 1848, in its departmental context. Though my work spanned three widely spaced departments it shared the same hallmarks of archival dust and obsessive localism. I feared that my findings on the continuity of patterns of belief and action were typical of slow-moving

provincial France but might have no application either for national history or
for the twentieth century. More seriously, my attention to maps might have
pleased André Siegfried, whose *Tableau politique de la France de l'Ouest* had
inspired me as an undergraduate, but it had made my handling of 'the weight
of the past' mechanical and deterministic. It allowed no space between the
actors and their past for any relation that was open, playful or in any way
problematic.

While still an undergraduate I was introduced by chance to the historian of
the French Communist party, Annie Kriegel. She treated me with courtesy but
made no concessions. 'Come back and see me', she said, 'when you have a
subject and a method.' A subject may have been forming itself in my mind, but
certainly not a method. If the word circulated in Oxford in the early 1970s it
was not in tutorials but only in the smoke-filled Balliol lecture room where the
Radical Historians met. I had invested in the compendium of the *Annales*
school, *Faire de l'histoire*.[1] I had been sufficiently inspired by Richard Cobb to
know that the people who had been taken out of history by the *Annales* historians had to be put back. Yet I was not totally convinced by the view of my
supervisor, Theodore Zeldin, that the individual was everything, the context
nothing. *Education* attempted to bridge a gap between different traditions, but
a major reconsideration of the relationship of political communities with their
past was going to take me onto very difficult terrain.

The historian of France in search of a method will be unlikely to read the
Introduction aux études historiques by Charles-Victor Langlois and Charles
Seignobos, but may discover in time that is the wall off which all other methods
bounce.[2] Langlois and Seignobos were Sorbonne professors of Dreyfusard
sympathies who tried to lay the foundations of Germanic positivist rigour in
French academic circles. 'History is written with documents', it begins, and
'documents are traces left by the thoughts and actions of men in the past.'[3]
Their first lesson was that the historian, by rigorous criticism of the documents,
must establish a firm base of historical fact. The subjective opinions of the
author of the documents, and any tradition, legend or anecdote that could not
be pinned down to time or place, were just so many obstacles that stood
between historians and their facts. The second lesson was that the mass of duly
verified facts constituted the source on which objective history must draw.
Very few clues were offered about how this account should be constructed.
All that was provided was a checklist which included 'material conditions',
'material customs', 'social customs', public institutions' and 'intellectual
habits'.[4] In any society there would be a *Zusammenhang* or consensus of these
different elements, but they would not exert a deterministic influence over
individuals. Langlois and Seignobos argued that change was initiated by superior individuals who were then imitated by the generality. It thus followed
that 'room must be made for famous people and events in the framework
of history'.[5] Their doctrine endorsed what later came to be known as
l'histoire événémentielle.

The positivism of Langlois and Seignobos was an attack on, and in turn attacked by, the Marxist school of French historiography. Its leading exponent at the turn of the century was Jean Jaurès, who used the four years he spent out of Parliament in 1898–1902 to write the *Histoire socialiste de la Révolution française* and in 1903 founded a commission to publish the economic documents of the Revolution which acted as an organising centre of Marxist historians.[6] Among the disciples of Jaurès were Albert Mathiez and Georges Lefebvre. Mathiez, like Jaurès, was a graduate of the École Normale and a socialist. He became a Communist in 1920 and republished Jaurès' *Histoire socialiste* under the auspices of *L'Humanité*, but failed to secure the chair of the history of the French Revolution at the Sorbonne in 1923 when it was vacated by his supervisor, Alphonse Aulard. Lefebvre, another socialist, by contrast had no classical education and was thus ineligible for the École Normale, but occupied the French Revolution chair from 1935 to 1945. Mathiez opened up the economic dimension of the Revolution but still ultimately approached it 'from above'; Lefebvre studied the Revolution from below, publishing his thesis on *Les Paysans du Nord* in 1924 at the age of fifty, before writing more general Marxist interpretations of the Revolution.[7] Albert Soboul, a pupil of Lefebvre at the Sorbonne and member of the PCF, completed his thesis on the Paris sans-culottes in 1958, published a standard history of the Revolution in 1962, and brought out another edition of Jaurès' *Histoire socialiste*. In 1968 he was appointed to the chair of French Revolution history at the Sorbonne.[8] He was succeeded, on his death in 1982, by Michel Vovelle, also a member of the PCF and standard-bearer of the Marxist school but also a fully fledged member of the *Annales* school.

Whereas positivist historians sanctified the autonomy of the individual, Marxists argued that men changed the world by advancing technology in order to provide more effectively for their material wants, but were then imprisoned by the economic order they had created, especially by the division between those who owned the means of production (land or capital) and those who did not. Modern history, they asserted, was a class war for control of the state first between the feudal landlords and the bourgeois capitalists and then, once the bourgeoisie had taken control of the state, between them and the proletariat they exploited. Thus the French Revolution, in Marxist historiography, was a bourgeois revolution against the feudal class supported by the absolute monarchy, with the help of the peasantry and nascent proletarian class. It offered a powerful framework of analysis for the complexities of the Revolution, and directed serious scholarship towards the economic and social dimensions of the period.

The weakness of the Marxist analysis, however, was that it tended to reduce all conflict to class struggle and all ideology to a reflection of class struggle. 'We know today', said Engels of the credo of 1789, 'that this kingdom of reason was nothing more than the idealised kingdom of the bourgeoisie . . . that bourgeois property was proclaimed one of the essential rights of man.'[9] Ideology was only a smokescreen to universalise selfish class interests. Marxists dealt effectively with politics and ideology mainly where they were prepared to bend the rules of their own system. Jaurès, for instance, said that 'our interpretation of history will be both materialist with Marx and mystical with Michelet'.[10] Lefebvre's *Grande Peur de 1789* (1932) was a study of the collective psychology of panic that owed much to the influence of his colleague at Strasbourg, Marc Bloch.[11] Soboul made a suggestive incursion into the history of mentalities with an article on the revolutionary cults of popular saints and martyrs.[12] Marx himself, when he took up his pen as a historian, was prepared to accept that ideology could exercise some constraint over and above economic conditions. 'The tradition of all the dead generations weighs like a nightmare on the brain of the living', he wrote tantalisingly in *The Eighteenth Brumaire of Louis Bonaparte*, arguing that the revolutionaries of 1848 re-enacted as farce what those of 1789 had played as tragedy.[13] Unfortunately the comment served to ridicule the revolutionaries rather than point towards a theory of history.

The third historical tradition that has dominated French historiography is the *Annales* school, which took its name from the journal of the same name founded in 1929 by Marc Bloch and Lucien Febvre, professors at the University of Strasbourg. Bloch and Febvre drew on the teachings of the sociologist Émile Durkheim, who had argued that all 'social phenomena', from economic systems to political institutions and patterns of belief were not the creation of free individuals but 'things' that existed outside individuals and exercised a coercive force over them. Durkheim's review, *L'Année sociologique*, was a focus of keen debate in the years before the First World War and eagerly devoured by young historians such as Bloch and Febvre. Through its reviews, grouped under the headings of religious sociology, legal and moral sociology, criminal sociology, economic sociology and demographic sociology, it extended an empire over all the social sciences. François Simiand, who was responsible for the economic sociology section, also dealt sharply with the historical method of Langlois and Seignobos. He argued that the analysis of society around their notion of *Zusammenhang* was arbitrary and amateur, a task that only sociology could undertake scientifically, and attacked the three 'idols' they worshipped, the chronological idol, the individual idol, and the political idol.[14]

After the death of Durkheim in 1917 and the loss of many of his pupils in the Great War, his sociological empire broke up. The torch passed to the *Annales* journal, which sought to establish, by interdisciplinary studies, if not an empire then a federation of social sciences under the aegis of history. Febvre distanced himself both from the idolatry of the individual, the event and politics and from Marxist materialism. 'Our history is neither collectivist nor individualist', he told his pupils in 1919. 'In spirit it is idealist and would remain so even if its research, against all expectation, came to prove the primacy of economics. For economic facts, like all other social facts, are facts of belief and opinion. Are not wealth, work and money not 'things' but human ideas, representations and judgements of things?'[15] Against the Marxists (and even against the sociologists) he argued that the world was not objective reality but socially constructed. The object of study must therefore be collective mentalities, the distorting spectacles through which contemporaries together viewed the world. Sources such as saints' lives had been rejected by positivists because their factual content was unreliable and by Marxists as the daydreams of the feudal class. But 'If', said Bloch, 'we consult them as to the way of life or thought peculiar to the epoch in which they were written . . . we shall find them invaluable.'[16] The concept of the social construction of reality opened up immense possibilities for future research.

The second generation of *Annales* historians, a Renaissance court presided over after 1947 by Fernand Braudel at the Sixième Section of the École Pratique des Hautes Etudes, transformed a faith into a church. *Mentalités* remained a central object of study but interest shifted more and more to the material conditions constraining everyday life. Beyond the economic systems and class structures of Marxist historians lay the demographic balance of population and resources, the geographical patterns of mountain and plain, seacoast and interior, field systems and habitat, trade routes and migration, and the ecological relation of man to his environment in the broadest sense, including climate. The study of these broad 'envelopes' of human activity led to a reformulation of the periodisation of history. What mattered to the average inhabitant of the Mediterranean in the sixteenth century, argued Braudel, was not the battle of Lepanto but the size of the next harvest. It was demonstrated that the agricultural economy, the vulnerability of the harvest to failure and the periodic decimation of the population by famine and disease was fairly constant between the fourteenth and eighteenth centuries, after which the agricultural and industrial revolutions sustained rapid population growth. Within each demographic order were shorter periods determined first by good and bad harvest cycles, then by the boom and slump of the business cycle. There were thus three hands to the *Annales* clock: one to measure the *longue durée* of the deep demographic and economic structures that set the parameters of human activity, a second to measure the cycles and crises within those structures, and a third for *l'histoire événémentielle* of kings, queens and battles that was regarded as the froth on the tidal swell that was the true substance of history.[17]

The *Annales* school set the pace for nearly forty years after the war. But the framework of analysis became increasingly rigid, and its empire declined as new areas of research opened up for which the *Annales* formula had no relevance. 'Today uncertainty seems to have overtaken us', confessed the *Annales* editorial in 1988.[18] Whole areas like the history of art, the history of science and linguistics had opened up beyond its purview. The architecture of the copybook *Annales* thesis relegated cultural factors to the attic, located demographic conditions and economic activities in the basement and put social structure and political institutions in the main part of the house. Structures and obsessive quantification had squeezed out people in what now seemed like *l'histoire anonyme*, history without people, and the *longue durée* threatened to become a changeless *histoire immobile*. It was time, said the editorial in 1989, if not to rehabilitate the event then to see society in 'a constant process of self-construction', and in terms of 'strategies, which allow the introduction of memory, apprenticeship, uncertainty and negotiation into the social game'.[19] Thus it favoured a problematisation of the relationship between action and structure, the individual and the environment, and introduced the concept of memory into the social construction of reality.

The various historiographical schools have operated in parallel, and there has always been cross-fertilisation. This was the case between the Marxist and *Annales* schools, and also between the *Annales* school and the fourth school, which subscribed to what became known as 'modernisation theory'. This was developed largely by Americans who discovered France during or after the last war. They used the basic sociological distinction between traditional and modern societies as the root of their analysis. Laurence Wylie spent a year in the field with his family for his *Village in the Vaucluse* (1957), which delighted in the Clochemerle sociability of an isolated, almost timeless rural community, without divorce, crime or unemployment.[20] In *France: Change and Tradition* (1963) Stanley Hoffman, who attended school in Nice and wrote his thesis on the Poujadist movement, popularised the idea of the 'stalemate society'. According to this view France had been slow to industrialise, and still had a large reservoir of peasants, a small, isolated working class, and a business world ruled by the family firm. The state was centralised but limited in power, an arbiter between conflicting interests. There were no mass parties as befits a modern democracy, but cliques of politicians who muddled through. Politics were locked into archaic debates such as the conflict between Church and state and the protest of declining economic groups against increasing competition and taxation. France had been overtaken by the dynamic new régimes of Stalin, Hitler and F. D. Roosevelt in the 1930s, punished for her backwardness in the 1940s, opened up to the outside world by the GIs and the Marshall Plan and finally kicked into the twentieth century by General de Gaulle.[21]

Charles Tilly, who explained the Vendée rebellion in terms of lack of integration into the market economy and centralised state, went on to investigate the impact of capitalism and state-building on patterns of collective violence in the nineteenth century. He traced a shift from 'traditional' forms of protest, such as land-occupations, machine-breaking and tax revolts, to 'modern' forms such as industrial strikes, demonstrations and election rallies, which worked within the new structures rather than resisting them.[22] Meanwhile Eugen Weber, transplanted from Romania to British public school, army and Cambridge University and thence in 1956 to Los Angeles, moved from mainstream studies of French nationalism to the question of the modernisation of rural France. In 1948 he read Roger Thabault's *Mon Village. Ses hommes, ses routes, son école* (1943). Thabault traced the modernisation of his native village in the nineteenth century in the light of notions of civilisation and acculturation that had fascinated him as an education official in Morocco in the 1920s. Weber linked theory and practice when he was put in charge of UCLA's French Center for Education Abroad at Bordeaux University in 1968–70. The result, *Peasants into Frenchmen. The Modernisation of Rural France* (1977), followed the development of a 'country of savages', ridden by priests and speaking *patois*, physically isolated and economically autarkic, into a nation of patriotic Frenchmen, thanks to the penetration of the outside world by means of roads, railways, military service and, above all, schools.

One shortcoming of this historical method has been to project the development of France as a linear process from backwardness to modernity. Yet the French were not either *patois*-speaking or French-speaking but bilingual, speaking *patois* at home or in the café, French to the schoolteacher or gendarme. One was the language of the local community, the other the language of authority.[23] Again, the French were not either superstitious or sceptical, but prepared to resort to magical rites when the harvest was in question, and anticlerical when the *curé* meddled in politics.[24] The other failing of the modernisation school has been not adequately to deal with the subject of politics and ideology. French politics may look archaic but the ongoing debate about the French Revolution is itself a matter requiring investigation. Revolution is not amenable to Tilly's statistics on collective violence, which incorporate rick-burning but blot out the Paris Commune as if it had never existed.[25] Weber argued that the French peasants were politically illiterate before the end of the nineteenth century because there were no mass parties with national programmes to vote for. He has claimed that even in 1848 politics were essentially local and managed by the educated élite.[26] To be fair, he has recognised that local events, like the 'punishment' of a village for accepting a priest who had taken the oath to the Civil Constitution of the Clergy early in the Revolution, might mark its politics for a hundred years.[27] But the point about the Civil Constitution of the Clergy is that it brought the glare of national politics to every village in France, and made the attitude of every village to its priest part of national politics. Moreover modernisers assume that by 1800 the scars of the French Revolution were healed and its spectres driven away. It would have been better for many communities, such as the Vendeans studied by Tilly, if indeed they had been depoliticised, but the memory of the Revolution was not so easy to erase.

A fifth school of historiography may be called that of English empiricism or the English miniature. It is deeply suspicious of grand theory and general laws, on the grounds that historical reality is too complex to be reduced to simple formulae. The case-study is often favoured to test a received opinion or simply to illustrate that complexity. It assumes a certain autonomy of action of individuals and often adopts the biographical approach. The 'revival of narrative' holds no surprises as the narrative style was never forsaken.

Alfred Cobban, professor of French History at University College London, mounted a decisive attack on the Marxist interpretation of the French Revolution in his 1955 inaugural lecture. He exploded the myth of the bourgeois revolution by examining the membership of the Constituent Assembly and Convention and showed that it was made up not of bourgeois merchants, financiers and industrialists but officials and professional men. At the same time he argued that the Revolution was 'not one but many'.[28] 'To know that there are theoretical assumptions behind the history we write', he said, 'is not to reduce history to the expression of a theory but to take a necessary step to its emancipation from the *a priori*, and towards really critical history.'[29] While Cobban was keen to shoot down grand theory, Richard Cobb, professor of modern history at Oxford University, merely sidestepped it. Though close to Soboul he never adopted Marxist categories of class and, from the sans-culottes of the revolutionary armies, moved on to the study of social marginals, wetnurses, prostitutes, criminals and vagabonds who seem to jump from the pages of Rétif de la Bretonne or Eugène Sue. He evoked the revolutionary mentality with brilliance but hated the global, anonymous and pseudo-scientific history of the *Annales* school. Cobb's 'sense of place' was based on the view that the fabric of social and political life was best reconstructed at the level of the city, the *quartier*, and the street. The *petit peuple* who fascinated him were not a faceless crowd but individuals with private as well as public lives, the biography of each to be lovingly reconstructed.[30] His was above all the skill of the miniaturist. Those who would wish to draw general conclusions from Cobb's approach would have to look to a historian inspired by Cobb but with grander designs. Simon Schama, introducing his *Citizens. A Chronicle of the French Revolution*, says that 'Along with the revival of place as a conditioner have come people. For as the imperatives of 'structure' have weakened, those of individual agency, and especially of revolutionary utterance, have become correspondingly more important.'[31] Schama's drama unfolded before the eyes of Talleyrand and Lafayette, and he was keen to flesh out the private lives of the actors behind their public personas. To weave events together Schama adopted the narrative. '*Citizens* returns', he proclaimed, 'to the form of the nineteenth-century chronicles, allowing different issues and interests to shape the flow of the story as they arise, year after year, month after month.'[32] Schama told a ripping yarn, but a knowing one. It was a conscious rejection of the theorising pretensions of the Marxist and *Annales* schools, but at the risk of reducing history to one senseless deed of violence after another.

While Schama did not go down well with French audiences, Thedore Zeldin took them by storm. Whether this is in spite of the fact that his *France, 1848–1945* (1973, 1977), translated as *L'Histoire des passions françaises*, went right against the grain of the French academic tradition, or because of it, is difficult to say. Zeldin started with the individual, not with groups or classes. General themes were broken down into clusters of biographies. He added that 'the more individual people are studied in detail, the more complex do they reveal themselves to be'.[33] Zeldin called his method *pointilliste*, breaking first the social mass and then individuals into an infinity of dots. He delighted in ambivalence, revealing discrepancies between the public and private lives or individuals, between their words and their deeds. He rejected determinism. 'Other disciplines may develop 'general theories' but historians fool themselves if they try to do this.'[34] The individual, he argued, acts in quite unpredictable ways which defy causal analysis. 'To talk of causes means to talk of proof and it is difficult to prove motives, character and interpretations. I prefer juxtaposition, so that the reader can make what links he thinks fit himself.'[35] From *pointillisme* we have moved on to Cubism. Here Zeldin parted company from other miniaturists. Cobb's individual is a creature of habit, by whose daily movements the observer could set a watch; Zeldin's moves at random, like a rogue electron, his intentions forever a mystery to us. Cobb's individual cannot be prised from the time and place that encrusts him; Zeldin's could pop up at any time in any place. 'I do not feel', writes Zeldin, 'that I have ceased to be concerned with the universal by studying the ideas, manners and achievements of France in such detail.'[36] Cobb has moved on to autobiography, Zeldin to the novel.

Political history, which was marginalised by the *Annales* school to a peripheral *histoire événémentielle*, has in recent years been restored to a certain primacy. Moreover, whereas politics was reduced by Marxism to a function of economic and social conflict, now its autonomy from those factors, and its power to determine them itself, have increasingly been asserted. The achievement has in part been that of political scientists, who have moved the study of politics beyond individuals to parties, associations, elections, the media and public opinion, and to issues of competition for power, the negotiation of claims, and decision-making.[37] The drawback of this approach has been a tendency to institutionalise, to reify, and to concentrate on what can be quantified. To this the antidote has been the contribution of social anthropologists. They have taught historians how to examine cultures, which may broadly be defined as the symbolic representation of concepts and values. They have also demonstrated how cultures are not given but constructed, the products of human minds. They have shown that cultures are socially constructed, elaborated by communities to represent their concepts and values to themselves and others. Moreover they have shown how cultures are not static but constantly invented and reinvented over time to serve the purposes of the group.[38]

What I intend to examine in this work is political culture. By this I mean the culture elaborated by communities competing for political power, to define themselves against competing communities, to bind together their members, and to legitimate their claim to power. In this I follow the lead of Keith Baker who has defined political culture as 'the set of discourses and practices' used by one community to articulate and enforce its claims against those of rival communities, to define 'the identity and boundaries of the community to which they belong (or from which they are excluded)', and to establish 'the authority of the principles according to which [these claims] are made binding'.[39] I do not pretend that the political cultures surveyed here constitute a comprehensive treatment of French political culture, but they are major cultures defined around the main axes of political conflict: revolution and counter-revolution, national identity and nationalism, centralisation and regionalism, and Church and State.

In particular, I wish to explore the relationship between political culture and collective memory. It will be my contention that what defines a political culture above all is not some sociological factor such as race or class or creed but collective memory, that is, the collective construction of the past by a given community. This is based on two assertions. First, that there is no single French collective memory but parallel and competing collective memories elaborated by communities which have experienced and handle the past in different ways. And second, that the past is constructed not objectively but as myth, in the sense not of fiction, but of a past constructed collectively by a community in such a way as to serve the political claims of that community.

The classic theoretical work illuminating this question is *La Mémoire collective* of Maurice Halbwachs, a pupil of Durkheim who died in a German prison camp in 1945, and published posthumously.[40] Halbwachs argued that there was no such thing as individual memory, for we need the memories of other people to corroborate our own. Memories would be only random images if the memories of others did not help to impose some order and cohesion on them. By the same token, Halbwachs continued, there is no such thing as the universal memory of the human species. Though it may be possible for a historian to write the history of the world, 'our memory rests truly not on learned history but on lived history'.[41] Collective memory is that of communities which have lived through the same experiences. That community elaborates a collective memory that is peculiar to itself and relatively impermeable to the memories of other communities. The memory of the conquered is different from that of the conquerors, that of the persecuted is different from that of the persecutors, that of the oppressed is different from that of the oppressors.[42]

Central to the process of the construction of collective memory is the act of commemoration, or remembering in common. The sacralisation of its triumphs and defeats, its heroes and martyrs, is the obvious way in which a political community defines itself, establishes consensus, and legitimates its claims. The most spectacular acts of commemoration include festivals, pilgrimages, burials and the erection of statues. But commemoration takes place in discourse as well as practice, and may take the form of explicit or coded references to cult figures and events which signal shared political assumptions. Both discourse and practice serve to define a mythical past which promotes the interest of the community that constructs it.

A great deal of work of the highest order has already been done in the field. This ranges from the study of Maurice Agulhon on the rôle of statues in public places to that of Daniel Sherman on provincial museums and that of Avner Ben-Amos on state funerals.[43] The vast and rich collection edited by Pierre Nora, *Les Lieux de Mémoire*, has examined the ritual of commemoration through festivals, monuments, flags, songs, textbooks, street-names and places of pilgrimage to proclaim the values of the French Republic and Nation and to instil the loyalty of successive generations to them.[44] If *Les Lieux de Mémoire* had a shortcoming in the earlier volumes it was to establish an archaeology of objects of memory rather than to show how collective memories were shaped and reshaped by given communities. In addition, while concentrating on the elaboration of the collective memory of the Republic and the Nation, it underestimated the struggle of other political communities—Bonapartist or royalist, federalist or regionalist, Catholic or Protestant, extreme Right or extreme Left—to gain acceptance for their version of the past, to appreciate that there is a collective memory of losers as well as winners.[45] This shortcoming has been largely remedied in the final volumes entitled *Les France*, as well as in the earlier brilliant studies by Philippe Joutard and Jean-Clément Martin of the elaboration of the collective memory of the Camisard revolt among Cévennes Protestants and of the suppression of the Vendée uprising among Catholic conservatives, and their use to develop their respective political cultures.[46] My own survey is deeply indebted to this research. But there has been as yet no single-volume general study that takes as its point of departure and general theme the rivalry of parallel political cultures and the elaboration of the collective memories that defined them.

Collective constructions of the past were not universal; neither were they objective. But they competed amongst themselves to be accepted as both universal and objective. In the first place, political communities campaigned to win universal acceptance of their interpretation of the past and to suppress interpretations which were likely to deprive them of legitimacy. 'Français, vous avez la mémoire courte', Marshal Pétain told the nation in 1941.[47] But this was usually a studied forgetfulness. As one community sought to impose a collective amnesia about certain events, rival communities sought to resurrect their memory in order to disqualify or delegitimise their opponents. Second, the same event or figure was often the subject of different constructions by different communities, each trying to privilege its own interpretation over those of others. Thus whether the French Revolution was triumph or tragedy was the object of furious debate between rival political communities, while Napoleon, Joan of Arc and Proudhon were the victims of tugs-of-war between rival political communities, each seeking to legitimate its cause by making its own presentation of these figures prevail. Third, collective memory was not set in stone, but was reworked in the light of new events. Such events presented communities with a challenge which enabled them to confer a fresh legitimacy on events or heroes who had hitherto been ill-considered, or alternatively threatened to delegitimise events and heroes who until then had commanded widespread recognition. Thus Louis-Napoleon's coup d'état of 2 December 1851 caused republicans to view Napoleon's coup of 1799 in a colder light, while on the other hand the Jacobin dictatorship of 1793 was more favourably assessed on the Left in the light of the Bolshevik Revolution.

At this point we come full circle and return to Langlois and Seignobos.

There can be no objective, universally agreed history, and even if it were possible it would be of scant interest. What matters is myth, not in the sense of fiction, but in the sense of a construction of the past elaborated by a political community for its own ends. Similarly there are only histories, mediated by different cultures, providing a multitude of viewpoints on the same events or historical figures, for the benefit of political communities, and reconstructed over time to meet their needs. French history is universal and objective only in so far as political communities have struggled to win acceptance for their own presentation of French history as universal and objective, and it is this struggle which is the subject of this book.

CHAPTER 1

Revolution

A Question of Commemoration

During the academic year 1988–9 I was lucky enough to be living in Paris, engaged on research for this book. I was able to observe the commemoration of the Bicentenary of the French Revolution as first hand. Initially, interest in the event was slow to gather momentum. But, as the weeks rolled by, the press, books and television became more and more animated. Politicians, militants and intellectuals all had their point to put across. A commemoration that was intended to adorn the Republic instead divided the nation.

The official celebrations, orchestrated on behalf of the moderate socialist presidency and government by the Mission du Bicentenaire were the most elaborate ever organised to commemorate the Revolution. The intention was to promote a consensus of opinion around what was expected to be a non-controversial aspect of the Revolution, the Declaration of the Rights of Man and the Citizen. The calendar of events focused on the achievements of 1789, when the National Assembly had steered the king towards basic political and institutional reforms. Celebrations started on 4 May 1989, anniversary of the opening of the Estates-General at Versailles; continued on 20 June, date of the Tennis Court Oath, when the deputies of the National Assembly (as it then became) defied the king's order to disperse; and reached a climax on 14 July, anniversary of the storming of the Bastille, with the Champs-Elysées parade, orchestrated by Jean-Paul Goude, and attended by a million people. The subsequent, more violent history of the Revolution was pushed to one side. The battle of Valmy in 1792, when the citizens in arms repulsed the Germanic invader to save the Republic that was proclaimed the following day, was commemorated on 20 September, but attempts were made to minimise the significance of the Terror that raged within the frontiers of France. In his speech at Versailles on 20 June François Mitterrand conceded that 'the ghastly images of Nantes, Lyon, the Carmelites and the September prison massacres flash through my mind', but argued that the reflexes of the revolutionaries, beset by internal and external war, had to be understood as well as judged.[1]

13

Instead, the official programme sought to underline the achievements of the Revolution in the realm of science and technology. Selected to have their remains transferred to the Panthéon in the Bicentenary year were Condorcet, symbol of the Enlightenment in action during the Revolution, and Monge, who transformed cannon-founding during the revolutionary wars and fathered the École Polytechnique.[2] In addition, President Mitterrand emphasised the modernity of France and its incorporation into the community of rich western democracies, leaving behind its violent origins, by overlaying the Bicentenary with a summit of the G7 in Paris, held in the gleaming new Arche de la Défense.

The official proceedings, however, were not permitted to enjoy a monopoly of interpreting the Revolution. They came under vigorous attack from both Right and Left. The Left objected to the appropriation of the principles of 1789 by the leaders of the capitalist world. Liberty, Equality and Fraternity could not be celebrated without hypocrisy by a West that was responsible for colonialism, apartheid and the debt of developing countries. 'Today, the Third Estate is the Third World', ran one slogan.[3] An alternative demonstration marched to the place de la Bastille on Saturday 8 July. In the front line were Trotskyists of the Ligue Communiste Révolutionnaire, the political bureau of the Communist Party, trade unionists of the CGT, the Fédération Anarchiste, Kanak autonomists from New Caledonia, Palestinian nationalists, Basques, Kurds, and Mgr Gaillot, the left-wing bishop of Evreux, in purple roll-neck sweater.[4] Top of the bill at the rock concert that evening was Renaud, who appeared in sans-culotte costume, and declared that the real celebrations would take place in 1993, anniversary of the popular revolution.

The Right was forced into a dilemma by the Bicentenary. On the one hand, since 1944 the major parties of the Right have subscribed to the principles of 1789. Thus the Gaullist leader Jacques Chirac, though smarting from his defeat in the presidential elections of 1988, conceded as mayor of Paris that 'the vocation of Paris is to be the capital of the Rights of Man'.[5] On the other hand, the Orleanist pretender, the comte de Paris, exploited another anniversary, the millenium of the foundation of the Capetian dynasty which fell in 1987, by bestowing the title of duc de Vendôme on his grandson Jean, and marking him out for the successsion.[6] Other dissident voices on the Right, not necessarily monarchist, seized the opportunity to mount an attack on the Revolution. At the heart of the campaign was the 15 August 1989 Association, founded in 1987 by integrist Catholics and François Brigneau, columnist of the National Front's weekly, *National Hebdo*. The Association had its own periodical, *L'Anti-89*, to expose the 'crimes' of the Revolution, notably the persecution of the Church and the execution of Louis XVI, and to build up support for an anti-revolutionary demonstration in Paris on Assumption Day, 15 August 1989, to ask God's forgiveness for those crimes. The demonstration was to gather for a mass on the place de la Concorde, site of the guillotine, and march to Notre-Dame. In the event access to the place de la Concorde was denied by the Ministry of the

Interior, and the rally, in another part of the city, fell far short of the half million envisaged. Nonetheless the notion of a consensus around the commemoration of the Revolution was exploded as a fiction.

Division over the celebration of the Bicentenary on the streets was only the most public sign of an ideological battle that raged in the media. Debates between opposing 'experts' were televised for a mass public. As with the rallies, combat was joined between three schools of intellectuals: those who formulated and supported the official view, those who criticised it from the Left and those who criticised it from the Right.

The revisionist view, which dominated the intellectual and media world at the beginning of 1989, was that of François Furet and his team. His polemical *Penser la Révolution française*, published in 1978, attacked the Marxist view of the Revolution that was based on class struggle.[7] Like-minded historians were gathered to forge and impose the revisionist interpretation at conferences held in Chicago (1986), Oxford (1987) and Paris (1988). This interpretation was passed off as the received orthodoxy in the *Dictionnaire critique de la Révolution française*, edited by François Furet and Mona Ozouf, and packaged to convert a wider public in the glossy monthly supplement to *Le Monde* during 1989, *Le Monde de la Révolution française*. The argument of the revisionist school was threefold. First, that the French Revolution was over. The principles of liberty and equality which had at first been so divisive had, since the defeat of fascism and the decline of communism, become the common currency of both Left and Right. The Revolution no longer drove a wedge into the heart of French politics, but was integrated as 'a patrimony and a national institution'.[8] Second, the Revolution was no longer to be considered as a whole for there was a plurality of revolutions. A distinction could properly be drawn between the first reforming phase of the Revolution which had been inspired by the Enlightenment and carried through by the educated and propertied, and the second phase when it skidded out of control and mob violence, revolutionary dictatorship and Terror had taken over. 'The French Revolution is not like a fixed-price menu in a restaurant', said Mona Ozouf, 'where we have to take or leave everything.'[9] 1789 was good, 1793 was bad. The experience of Soviet Russia had shown the French Revolution in a new light, and ex-Communists like Furet used revulsion at the Terror exercised in Russia by Stalin to condemn that exercised in France by Robespierre. Third, though the Revolution had been violent and had scarred French political life for a century, the exceptionalism of French history (a sort of French *Sonderweg*) was now finished. In the span from Turgot to Jules Ferry covered by Furet in his lavishly illustrated *La Révolution, 1770–1880* (1988) the Revolution was diminished in importance. Politics was now less about ideology than about management. France now functioned as a pluralist democracy, in the club of great western democracies.

The Left, which had so long been dominant in the universities, was not slow to regroup and riposte. Its exponents included Communists such as Antoine

Casanova, Claude Mazauric and Michel Vovelle, professor of French Revolutionary history at the Sorbonne, socialists like Max Gallo, former confidant of Mitterrand Régis Debray and veteran of 68 Daniel Bensaïd. Their first retort was that the Revolution was not over. Those who claimed that it was were denounced as Thermidoreans. The principles of liberty, equality and fraternity could never be put to sleep but were a constant inspiration and call to action wherever injustice and exploitation were present. Imperialism, racism and sexism could not withstand the revolutionary challenge.[10] Second, the violence of the Revolution was justified. The popular movement had been necessary from the outset in 1789 to extract the Declaration of Rights of Man from a bourgeois and aristocratic Assembly; it did not descend from the clouds in tablets of stone.[11] Moreover, the Terror itself could be amply justified. The guillotine was an improvement on the barbaric tortures and persecution of the Ancien Régime; the circumstances of war and civil war after 1792 required decisive action by revolutionaries to save both the Republic and the fatherland; and the atrocities of the counter-revolutionaries were every bit as grisly as those perpetrated by the Jacobins.[12] Robespierre was to be defended, not attacked. Third, the French Republic was not any old western democracy but a militant Republic that had constantly fought for survival against monarchists and clericals, fascists and imperialists. It had a mission and martyrs to the cause, and could not be reduced to the status of a business to be managed.[13] The Republic moreover could not be separated from Revolution; attempts had been made to do this since the Paris Commune, but the Republic was born of Revolution and was shaped by it.[14]

The revisionist school was attacked from the Right as well as from the Left; indeed, its own critique of the Marxian orthodoxy in many ways opened the door to more extreme interpretations. The right-wing view had long been powerful outside the universities; now it became academically respectable, largely under the patronage of Pierre Chaunu. In *Le Grand Déclassement* he argued that the balance-sheet of the Revolution had been disastrous, not only destroying the Church but also compromising the demographic and economic lead acquired by France in Europe in the eighteenth century.[15] Chaunu took pride in establishing the history of the Vendée, seen from the viewpoint of the victims, as a legitimate academic subject. Reynald Secher's thesis, which evaluated the destruction of lives and properties in the Vendée region by the republican armies in 1793–4, was vivaed at the Sorbonne in September 1985, something inconceivable in the days of Aulard, Mathiez, Lefebvre and Soboul. Chaunu claimed to have suggested the title of Secher's work when it was published in book form in 1986: *Le Génocide franco-français*.[16] This provoked a storm of controversy. For the Revolution-as-Rights of Man was substituted the Revolution-as-extermination.

Politicians of the Right, again forced out of power in 1988, seized this critique of the Revolution as a stick with which to beat the socialist government.

They argued first that the Revolution was the fruit of a conspiracy by secret societies and executed by a Jacobin party. The Declaration of the Rights of Man they drew up was used by the revolutionaries not to universalise rights but to exclude and terrorise those who did not agree with them. Second, they claimed that the Revolution was not part good, part bad, as the revisionists suggested, but wholly bad. It had been violent since 14 July 1789, when the Bastille had been stormed by the mob and the head of its governor cut off and paraded on a pike.[17] It reached its inevitable ghastly climax with the Terror of 1793. Philippe de Villiers, minister of culture in the Chirac government of 1986 and president of the Conseil général of the Vendée, argued further that the Terror was the model for twentieth-century terrors, 'the Nazi hell, the Gulag, the Khmers rouges, Mao's Cultural Revolution and Mengistu's state famines'.[18] By contrast, he said, the Vendean rising was in defence of liberty of conscience, and should be compared to the Solidarity movement in Poland. This flowed into the third argument, that the Revolution was unnecessary, divisive and destroyed a society that, if not perfect, had been capable of perfection had the monarchy been allowed to reform it. It was an argument that found favour with Catholics, advocates of social hierarchy, and monarchists. In 1900 Charles Maurras, the theorist of monarchism, published an *Enquête sur la Monarchie* that included the views of prominent politicians of his day. Pierre Pujo, the son of Maurice Pujo, a disciple of Maurras, published a similar inquiry in 1988. He found a good deal of unhappiness among his sixty respondents about the exposure of the presidency of the Republic to vicissitudes of party strife, although fewer agreed that a hereditary monarchy was the answer in contemporary France.[19] A survey in *Le Point* in 1987 indicated that 17 per cent of French people would accept a restoration of the monarchy along the lines of the restoration in Spain.[20] Monarchism was stronger still when only nostalgia was at stake. When Louis XVI was retried on television on 12 December 1988, defended by Maître Vergès, the advocate of Klaus Barbie, only 27.5 per cent of viewers voted for the death penalty, with 17.5 choosing exile and 55 per cent acquitting him.

The Bicentenary of the French Revolution was, counting the Fête de la Fédération of 1790, which marked the first anniversary of the Revolution, the fourth major commemoration of the event. The centenary, celebrated in 1889, and the 150th anniversary, celebrated in 1939, were racked by similar difficulties and disagreements. The 150th anniversary was celebrated as the Popular Front lay in ruins and war loomed on the horizon. The government did not agree to mounting an official celebration until three weeks before festivities were due to begin. The programme was centred on six familiar and in principle non-controversial events: the calling of the Estates-General, the formation of the National Assembly, the 14 July (intended to commemorate the Fête de la Fédération, not the storming of the Bastille), Valmy, the proclamation of the Republic, and 'intellectual developments'. Herriot, president of the organising committee, had been writing a history of the destruction of Lyon under the Terror, and in his address commemorating the opening of the Estates-General at Versailles refuted Clemenceau's dictum that the Revolution was a bloc. 'For my part', he said, 'I cannot accept that the Revolution is a bloc.'[21] Its violence could not be excused, and he was particularly grieved by the execution of the chemist Lavoisier and the poet André Chénier. The military parade of 14 July included a flypast by British Spitfires, Hurricanes and Wellingtons, which was reassuring in the light of the international situation. A podium was erected in front of the Palais de Chaillot for speeches by the president of the Republic and prime minister. But it poured with rain and the speeches were unmemorable; prime minister Daladier noted that the Fête de la Fédération of 14 July 1790 had similarly been a wash-out.[22]

As in 1989, there was no consensus about the commemoration. On the extreme Right Léon Daudet of the Action Française stirred up trouble with his *Deux Idoles sanguinaires. La Révolution et son fils Bonaparte*. Clemenceau was correct, he argued, the Revolution was a bloc, but 'a bloc of stupidity, blood and shit'.[23] In *Je suis partout*, which was very much under the umbrella of Action Française, the historian Pierre Gaxotte wrote that 'Terror is the essence of the Revolution . . . the revolution, in its final stage, was an enterprise of expropriation and extermination.'[24] A major reason for embarrassment over the festivities was that the only movement, apart from the Ligue de l'Enseignement, that was interested in promoting the anniversary was the Communist party, which had been excluded from government majority by Daladier in November 1938. The Communists, predicting that the government initiative would be skimpy and half-hearted, started their celebrations in the summer of 1938, commemorating the meeting of the three orders in the Dauphiné, which was arguably to earliest date for the beginning of the Revolution.[25] Thorez warned that Hitler, Mussolini and their agents in France had declared war on the principles of 1789, and it was up to the French people to defend them.[26] The Communists were keen to appropriate 1789, but at the Buffalo stadium on 25 June Thorez called for the rehabilitation of the leaders of the sans-culottes, Marat, Hébert and the first socialist, Babeuf.[27] On 14 July the Communists organised an alternative march of 250,000 from the Bastille to the place de la Nation.[28] The best-seller of the Revolution, *Quatre-vingt-neuf* by Georges Lefebvre, though commissioned by the official centenary committee, underlined the Communist view of the essential part played by popular movements, even in the first year of the Revolution. However the signature of the Nazi-Soviet pact on 23 August put paid to the PCF's revolutionary patriotism, and the outbreak of war on 3 September cut the official celebrations short ironically enough before the anniversary of Valmy was reached.

Celebration of the centenary of the Revolution in 1889 had been almost as painful. The government of the Republic, which was moderate, was reluctant to make much of the event. Pressure to make something of the centenary came from the radical wing of the republican party, which in particular controlled the Paris municipal council. They were supported by historians such as Charles-Louis Chassin and *Le Centenaire de 1789*, which was part academic journal and part pressure group.[29] In 1885 the municipal council founded a course (raised to a chair in 1891) in the history of the French Revolution at the Sorbonne, to which Alphonse Aulard was appointed. To mark the centenary in 1889 it also wanted a museum and a monument dedicated to the French Revolution erected in the Tuileries Gardens.

The government refused to advance any money for these projects, which would highlight the fragility of the Republic and challenge its increasingly conservative character. It was far more interested in celebrating the industrial and technological achievements of France to support its claim to stand among the advanced countries of the world, and was celebrating 1889 by a Universal Exhibition, the centrepiece of which was the Eiffel Tower. The only large republic in Europe, it was anxious not to upset visiting crowned heads (including the Shah of Persia) by indulging in a celebration of king-killing. The government focused its centenary celebrations at Versailles on 5 May, anniversary of the opening of the Estates-General, the day before the Exhibition was due to begin. But even these undistinguished celebrations were marred. President Carnot, leaving the Elysée palace for Versailles by coach, was the victim of an assassination attempt.[30] The government decided to transfer to the Panthéon the remains of Lazare Carnot, 'organiser of the victory' and grandfather of the president, and of the republican generals Marceau and Hoche, but the family of Hoche refused to release his body. The 14 July was once again wet and the military review at Longchamp was upstaged by a Boulangist demonstration on the place de la Concorde.[31] The anniversary of the proclamation of the Republic on 21 September was marked by the inauguration of Dalou's *Triumph of the Republic*. At this stage however the statue was only a plaster model, eloquent perhaps of the provisional nature of the régime.[32]

Criticism of the centenary came from both Left and Right. The radical and socialist view was that the Revolution had been hijacked by the bourgeoisie who had betrayed its principles and turned on the popular movement. It was now up to the people to conquer the Bastilles of inequality that still remained. The complication in 1889 was that many radical and socialist voters saw the best way to attack the bourgeois Republic through Boulangism. 'I continue to think that the electors of '89 were a better lot than those of today,' Jules Ferry, representative *par excellence* of the parliamentary Republic, told Charles Chassin; 'at least there were no Boulangists.'[33] On the conservative side the *Revue des Deux Mondes* complained that the Revolution had served only to create 'an indefinite state of revolution with which our country is still struggling, oscillating endlessly between all régimes, experimenting with monarchy, empire and republic in turn, without ever being able to settle'.[34] This sort of comment gave no comfort to Ferry, who wanted to establish the parliamentary Republic and bring the Revolution to a close.

Fig. 1.   Toppling the statue of Louis XIV, place Vendôme, 1792 (Musée Carnavalet)

Revolution and Ambivalence

The Revolution, for those who made it, was the construction of a new political order symbolised by the terms liberty, equality and (later) fraternity. Absolute monarchy legitimated by divine right was replaced by the sovereignty of the people with power vested in their elected representatives. The privileges of different orders, corporations, towns and provinces were replaced by the equality of citizens before the law. Fragmentation into private interests was replaced by the fraternity of all citizens, making laws in the general interest of the whole community. To begin with, these principles were compatible with the continuation of the monarchy under the formula Nation, Loi et Roi, to which oaths were taken at the Fête de la Fédération. But in time the revolutionaries concluded that the monarchy would have to be replaced by a Republic and the king executed if the Revolution were to survive. As the young revolutionary Saint-Just argued at the trial of the king, 'the Revolution begins when the tyrant ends'.[35]

The revolutionaries invented a new political culture to define and legitimate the revolutionary community of free and equal brothers. This required a veil to be drawn over the past and a totally new start to be made. So the overthrow of one king on 10 August 1792 was followed by the symbolic destruction of monarchy by pulling down the statues that all the Bourbon kings had raised to themselves: that of Louis XV erected in the place Louis XV (now Concorde) in 1763, and replaced by the symbol of Liberty; that of Louis XIV erected in the place Louis-le-Grand (now Vendôme) in 1699 [Fig. 1]; that of Louis XIII erected in the place Royale (now des Vosges), in 1639; and that of Henri IV erected on the Pont-Neuf in 1614.[36] The changing names of the squares indicated another development. Under pressure from the Paris Commune in the autumn of 1793 the Convention decided to eliminate all street names that might remind citizens of monarchy, feudalism or religion. 'When you totally rebuild a government', said the abbé Grégoire, deeply committed to the pedagogic tasks of the Revolution, 'you have to republicanise everything.' Thus the pont Notre-Dame became pont de la Raison, the rue du Roi-de-Sicile became the rue des Droits de l'Homme, the place Louis XV became the place de la Révolution, the rue du Dauphin became the rue de la Convention, and rue Montmartre became rue Mont-Marat.[37] The Panthéon, originally consecrated as a church, was redesignated a hall of fame for the heroes and martyrs of the Revolution. Thus the body of Mirabeau was laid to rest there, and late in 1794 that of Marat.[38] Festivals were organised to commemorate the sacred moments of the Revolution: 14 July, 10 August, 1 *vendémiaire*, the foundation of the Republic, which also marked the beginning of the new revolutionary calendar. That of 21 January, anniversary of the king's execution, has been called 'the impossible commemoration' by Mona Ozouf, but this did not prevent the introduction of an oath of hatred of royalty for representatives and public servants after the Directory's coup of *fructidor* Year V (September 1797) against the reviving royalist threat.[39]

To eliminate memories of the past and forge a new culture to define the Revolution and defend the Republic was no easy task. 'We, poor devils', sighed Robespierre, 'are building the temple of liberty with hands still scarred by the fetters of servitude.'[40] If the people failed to understand liberty it was, in the eyes of Robespierre, because of centuries of brutalisation by despotism or the thraldom of ignorance in which they had been kept by the Church. Those, however, who refused out of sheer greed or ambition to bend to the general will, could expect to suffer the vengeance of the people. To educate was the first task of the Republic, but those who refused to acknowledge the Republic of Virtue were excluded from it. This was the rationale of Terror, which was neither more nor less than prompt justice. The Revolution, observed Robespierre, required two blades, 'virtue, without which Terror is harmful, and terror, without which virtue is powerless'.[41] Those who conspired or rebelled against the Republic could expect no quarter.

The Robespierrist vision of the Revolution was only one possible construction of events. During the Revolution itself an alternative, counter-revolutionary construction was elaborated which saw the Revolution as violent, the fruit of conspiracy, and the destruction of an ideal political and social order. Three writers who helped to fashion this counter-revolutionary culture may be singled out. First, from the summer of 1789 the comte de Rivarol pointed out in his *Journal politique et national* that the National Assembly, sowing the wind of the foolish rhetoric of the rights of man and popular sovereignty, would reap the whirlwind of revolt by the Paris mob, the peasantry, servants and the black slaves of the colonies, claiming power and property on the basis of such theories. His perception of the Revolution was of a world violently turned upside down.[42] Second, in his *Mémoires pour servir à l'Histoire du Jacobinisme* (1797–99), the Jesuit émigré abbé Barruel argued that the Revolution had no deep-seated cause or rationale, but was planned and executed by a conspiratorial minority. He exposed the plot of *philosophes* to undermine religion, and that of freemasons to undermine the monarchy, both of which fed into the plot of the Jacobin 'sect', 'three hundred thousand strong, extended to two million hands which it manipulated the length and breadth of France, equipped with torches, pikes and all the thunderbolts of revolution', to destroy government and society.[43] Third, in 1796 Louis de Bonald, an émigré who had served in Condé's army against the Republic, claimed that if a political order were not properly constituted according to the three fundamental laws ordained by Nature—public religion, a single undivided authority, and permanent social distinctions—they would be in a state of perpetual anarchy until Nature reasserted its empire. According to Barruel, the Revolution had tried to reconstitute society according to fundamental laws, but these were not the laws ordained by Nature: 'it has a public religion, the cult of Marat, a single and general authority, that of death, and its distinct social group, the Jacobins'.[44] France, he argued, would be in turmoil until she restored Church, monarchy, and nobility.

Building on this construction of the Revolution by counter-revolutionaries, the exiled royal family sought to publicise the benefits of a restoration of the monarchy. In 1796 Louis XVIII, the king-in-waiting, issued a proclamation from Verona.

> We are persuaded that Frenchmen will support us and with redoubled loyalty will wipe away the stain that revolutionary fury has made on a name which, until then, they bore with such legitimate pride. On our side, we will forget the aberration of a people carried away by a flood of troublemakers, seduced and deceived by ambitious men who dared attack the Divinity itself. We will heed only the affection we have inherited from our ancestors for subjects who deserve such sentiments once they have been restored to themselves. Far from marking our accession by a display of vengeance like an angry monarch, we wish to show them only the tender and indulgent father who, satisfied by the repentance of his children, suspends justice in order to lavish on them the treasures of his clemency.[45]

The understanding was that the Revolution had been caused by a conspiratorial minority, and that the king was prepared to forgive and forget a national aberration, behaving like a father to his children. After a generation of

Fig. 2.   Restoration of the statue of Henri IV, Pont-Neuf, 1818 (Musée Carnavalet)

trying in vain to found a fatherless society of free and equal citizens the French were indeed happy to welcome back the king, albeit hedged about by constitutional safeguards to protect liberty. The reunion of king and people was symbolically stated. On 25 August 1818 a copy of the statue of Henri IV which had stood on the Pont-Neuf till 1792, cast in bronze and paid for by public subscription, was returned to its plinth. Eighteen pairs of oxen tired as the statue was dragged along the Champs-Elysées, and were replaced by horses. Then the people of Paris seized the traces, and pulled to shouts of 'Vive le Roi! Vive la famille royale!'. At the ceremony of inauguration the marquis de Marbois, chairman of the subscribers' committee, spoke as much of Louis XVIII as of Henri IV when he said that the latter, a 'tutelary genius', had closed a period of civil and religious war, and restored peace, property and the Church. Louis XVIII replied that the statue was 'a pledge that all parties were reunited and all mistakes forgotten'.[46] Fraternity sworn over the body of one monarch was to be replaced by reconciliation under the paternal eye of another [Fig. 2].

The right-wing view that Revolution stood for conspiracy, violence and anarchy enjoyed great success in the nineteenth and twentieth centuries. In particular, whenever the monarchy was toppled and a republic took its place, it was argued that the Republic embodied all the vices of the Revolution and could only be the Jacobin Republic of 1793, guillotining its enemies to assuage the bloodthirsty mob. Thus during the Second Republic, the revolutionaries were dubbed 'Montagnards' after Robespierre's faction, described as 'cannibals' and 'carnivors' who drank and plotted the destruction of society in clubs, mouthing platitudes about the sovereign people to stir up the social dregs, and 'shrinking from no means, nether civil war, nor Terror, nor the scaffold'.[47]

The proclamation of the Third Republic, followed almost immediately by the excesses of the Paris Commune, was grist to the mill of critics of revolution. The writer Maxime du Camp was keen to demonstate that the leaders of the Commune had modelled themselves on bloodthirsty demagogues of the Revolution, Marat and Hébert.[48] The historian Henri Wallon, turning his attention to the Tribunal révolutionnaire as the epitome of the Terror, reflected that 'we nearly experienced the reign of Terror under the Commune. The Commune had its revolutionary courts and prison massacres.' Moreover, he warned that with the rise of socialist parties, 'a régime more violent perhaps than that of 1793 is to be feared'.[49] More influential no doubt than Wallon was the historian Hippolyte Taine, whose best-selling *Origines de la France contemporaine* powerfully reworked the conservative construction of the Revolution. He argued that the Revolution had been violent not only during the Terror, but from 1789. 'Spontaneous anarchy' in the streets and in the countryside fed into the 'legal anarchy' of the Assembly.[50] He claimed that the Terror was the fruit of organised conspiracy by the Jacobin party, who rented a mob from

> the human waste that infects all capital cities, the epileptic and scrofulous *canaille* which, through inherited bad blood and its own debauchery, imports into our civilisation the degeneracy, imbecility and madness of its decayed constitution, backward instincts and deformed brain.[51]

The authority for such a portrait of the sans-culottes was not any revolutionary source but the Italian criminologist Cesare Lombroso, whose *L'Uomo delinquente* (1876) attributed criminality to regression to an earlier stage of civilisation. Thus contemporary scientific theory was used in order to discredit the Revolution of 1789 and, in the climate of bourgeois unease generated by the rise of revolutionary socialism, to discredit the Republic that embodied it.

The Bolshevik Revolution, like the Commune, was used by enemies of the French Revolution, firstly to discredit the French Revolution and secondly to attack the parties of the Left and the Republic itself, for espousing revolutionary principles that had led to Bolshevism. The historian Augustin Cochin refined the conspiracy theory of the Revolution to equate Jacobins with Bolsheviks. He argued that the French Revolution was conceived as a total ideology during the Ancien Régime in *sociétés de pensée*, which then constituted a party machine to organise elections of the Third Estate to the Estates-General and turn it into a National Assembly. During the Revolution the societies became clubs like the Jacobin Club, to determine ideology, control opinion, and purge those who did not share their revolutionary orthodoxy.[52] This updating of the conspiracy theory was taken up by right-wing historians such as Pierre Gaxotte, who also accused the revolutionaries of exercising a 'Communist Terror'. Gaxotte concluded in a phrase he was to repeat during the 150th anniversary celebrations,

> The Terror was the very essence of the Revolution, for the Revolution was not a simple change of régime, it was a social revolution, an enterprise of expropriation and extermination.[53]

The subculture of criticism of the Revolution and of the Republic goes a long way to explaining the ease with which both were done away with after the Third Republic crumbled on the battlefield in 1940. The Vichy régime replaced the Republic, if not by the monarchy, then by Marshal Pétain as head of an État Français wielding, as Pierre Laval observed, more power than Louis XIV. In addition, it swept away the sacred symbols of revolutionary France. The triad Liberty, Equality and Fraternity was replaced by *Travail, Famille, Patrie*. The Declaration of the Rights of Man was replaced by the Principles of the Community, which subordinated individual rights to the interest of the community and underlined the principles of the leader, hierarchy and the strong state.[54] Celebrations of 14 July 1942 were swamped by a 'National Revolution Week', which was given over (somewhat ironically) to the themes of national unity and continuity, and to the builders, servants and heroes of the Nation.[55] Propaganda gave Marshal Pétain all the attributes of an *ancien régime* monarch: he was at one and the same time feudal lord, receiving the oath of loyalty from diplomats, magistrates, athletes and pork-butchers; an imperial ruler, sometimes referred to as Philippe 1er; a Christ-like figure who sacrificed himself for the sake of his country; and, like Henri IV, the father of his people, travelling amongst them, sending messages to them, relieving poverty and suffering.[56] [Fig. 3]

The return of the Republic and revolutionary principles in 1944–6 commanded general support, at least overtly, in the climate of national reconciliation encouraged by the provisional government. A few, however, first privately, then publicly, asserted parallels between the Liberation and the Terror in order once again to criticise the Republic. Robert Brassillach, the right-wing intellectual and collaborator, whose early career had been assisted by Gaxotte, was drawn as he awaited the firing squad in 1945 to the young royalist poet, André Chénier, guillotined two days before 9 Thermidor. 'The resemblance between 1794 and 1944, a hundred and fifty years apart, is a bright lens through which this unique *oeuvre* and this exemplary attitude can be better contemplated and studied.'[57] Those who had served Vichy and been discredited at the Liberation

Fig. 3. Pétain, the father of his
people, receiving a provincial
delegation, Sept. 1941
(Bibliothèque nationale)

took their revenge by attacking the myth of the Liberation, arguing that it had
caused more deaths than the Terror. Their mouthpiece, appropriately, was
called *Rivarol*.

The Vendée of Memory

Of those parts of France which accepted the counter-revolutionary verdict of
the Revolution the most celebrated was the Vendée. It rose in revolt in 1793,
and felt the full force of the Terror in 1794. The revolutionaries took no
pleasure in their actions; it was on the contrary painful to admit that the
principles of the Revolution were not universally acclaimed. Thus the department of the Vendée was excised from the collective memory of the Revolution, renamed Vengé, in accordance with Barère's wish to 'throw the veil of
oblivion over the past'.[58]

Those who had suffered the Terror in the Vendée, however, and those who were keen to expose the evils of the Revolution, set about elaborating their own collective memory of the Vendée rising and its suppression. Through this myth of the Vendée the lofty ideals of the Revolution were exposed as a sham. The Revolution was redefined as an intolerant, ideological movement, which shrank from no refinements in military methods—from drowning priests in the Loire to 'infernal columns' of revolutionary soldiers putting the countryside to fire and sword—in order to destroy its enemies. By contrast the martyred and victimised Vendean region was idealised as a microcosm of Ancien Régime society, happy peasants living harmoniously under the protection of the Catholic Church, monarchy and nobility.

A central text in the elaboration of the Vendée myth was the *Mémoires* of the marquise de la Rochejacquelein, first published in 1814. The marquise, who had been brought up in the château of Versailles, left Paris after the fall of the monarchy and was successively widowed by two leaders of the Vendean insurrections. Her *Mémoires* portrayed the Vendée as the essence of a natural order that was rustic, patriarchal, hierarchical and pious. It described how the peasants were totally devoted to their parish clergy, and protected with pitchforks, scythes and guns non-jurors who said clandestine masses in the forests. It documented close relations between peasants and *seigneurs*, who would hunt and dance together, the *seigneur* elected mayor by the peasants at the beginning of the Revolution. The rising was described as a spontaneous response to oppression by the peasantry, who then prevailed upon the nobles to lead them. It characterised the leaders of the rising as Romantic heroes, particularly 'the Intrepid' Henri de La Rochejacquelein [Fig. 4], whose brother Louis she married in 1802, and Jacques Cathelineau, 'the Saint of Anjou'.[59]

At the Restoration, Legitimists and the Catholic Church developed the mythification of the Vendée as a series of shrines dedicated to sites of heroic resistance and to fallen heroes. The duchesse d'Angoulême, on a visit to the Vendée in 1823, promised money to build a chapel on the Mont des Alouettes, near Cholet.[60] The Legitimist journalist, the abbé de Genoude, promoted the cause of the family of Jacques Cathelineau, now destitute, while a statue to Cathelineau was dedicated in 1827.[61] The Church saw the virtue of stressing the martyrdom of a region the only crime of which was loyalty to Church and king. The bishop of Nantes and eighty priests officiated at the inauguration of a statue to a third Christian hero, Charette, in 1826.[62] At the funeral of the marquise de La Rochejacquelein in 1857 the ultramontane bishop of Poitiers, Mgr Pie, described the Vendean rising as a 'holy war' waged by 'the Christian army, the Catholic army', though there was little of this religious sense in the writings of the marquise herself.[63]

The myth of the Vendée in turn stimulated action, stirring up the embers of revolt in 1815, 1832 and 1870. Three generations of Cathelineaus and Charettes were involved in insurrection. Jacques Cathelineau (*fils*), who fought in 1815,

Fig. 4. The Vendée idealised: Henri
de la Rochejacquelein, 1824
(Bibliothèque nationale)

swore on the statue of his father to fight and die 'if necessary with the cross of
the martyr and sword of fidelity'.[64] The statue was destroyed after the Revolution of 1830 and Cathelineau died in the Vendée revolt of 1832. Henri
de Cathelineau, his son, responded to the invasion of 1870 by raising a corps
of Vendean volunteers under the patronage of the Virgin Mary. Though
they joined the Loire army, their commitment to the new Republic was uncertain, and the Paris Communards feared that they would head the forces of
counter-revolution ranged against Paris.[65] In the early 1880s Cathelineau presided over banquets of the mayors of the Vendée who remained faithful to
royalism and took up the story of the marquise de La Rochejacquelein that the
Vendeans lived 'under the protection of their seigneurs whom they respected
and loved', and that they had sworn 'to live for God, France and her king, or
to die'.[66]

The return of Republic and Revolution in 1870–71 served to stimulate the
collective memory of the Vendée. The attack on Church schools by the Third

Republic was discredited by parallels drawn with the persecution of the Church and clergy during the Revolution. Skeletons pointing to a new massacre were unearthed by a curé at Les Lucs-sur-Boulogne in 1874, to add more weight to the dossier of persecution. A statue of Henri de la Rochejacquelein was inaugurated in 1895 by three bishops and three hundred priests, before a crowd of 15–25,000. Stained-glass windows representing the Vendée as a religious war were set in chapels across the region, thirty-two by one craftsman alone between 1890 and 1914.[67]

The election of the Cartel des Gauches pursuing anticlerical policies in 1924 attracted to the Vendée myth outsiders in search of a cause to discredit the Republic. On 25 July 1926 Léon Daudet, an Action Française leader, addressed 60,000 Vendeans on the Mont des Alouettes. He praised them for their loyalty to the king and the Catholic religion, saying that royalists would soon be looking to them to get rid of *la gueuse* ('the whore', as the Republic was known to its enemies).[68] This rather cynical attempt by the extreme Right to play on the myth both overestimated the royalism of the Vendeans and was ill-considered by the Catholic hierarchy. Local initiatives were more significant. In 1933, following the election of another Cartel government, a review called *Le Souvenir Vendéen* was launched at Cholet. It was concerned that 'the ancestral memory is more or less lost', and that without its collective memory the distinctive political culture of the region would be eroded. Its editor, lawyer and journalist Tony Catta, began with Mgr Pie's myth of the Vendée as a holy war' and argued that if the myth were dying it should be sustained by a campaign to erect crosses or plaques where heroes had fallen, by publications for children and by popular theatre. Only this, he argued, would restore the Vendean 'soul', its traditional patriarchal, hierarchical and Catholic values and identity. Over the next seven years about thirty plaques were unveiled in the region to evoke the blood and soil of the myth, each ceremony the occasion of a mass, banquet and popular festivities.[69] Finally, in 1935, a subscription was opened to raise a monument to 'the martyred, heroic and faithful Vendée of 1793'. Two years later a huge statue of a Vendean soldier, sculpted by the royalist Maxime Real de Sarte, was inaugurated before a crowd of ten thousand. The Legitimist pretender Prince Xavier de Bourbon-Parme graced the proceedings, though Chief of Staff Maxime Weygand was put under offical pressure not to attend.[70]

Many of the conceptions of the Vendée myth-makers were echoed by those of the National Revolution, and the 150th anniversary of 1793, falling in the Vichy period, was amply celebrated. After the Liberation the struggle was more difficult, but when Catholics went onto the offensive in 1950 to demand public funding for church schools, the Vendée myth was ready to hand. Evoking the statues, the cemeteries, the chapels and the crosses, one cleric declared that 'the soil of the Vendée is an immense reliquary, an infinite memorial'.[71] At Saint-Laurent-sur-Sève 100,000 faithful demanded justice for Catholic education. Though it is impossible to assess the grip of collective memory and political culture in any scientific sense, the work of the historical sociologist André Siegfried helps to demonstrate the political consequences of the Vendéan myth. Tony Catta had been concerned in 1933 that the myth was losing its force, and had orchestrated a campaign to revive it; André Siegfried, who had first studied the Vendée for his *Tableau politique de la France de l'Ouest* (1913), returned forty years later to observe that Catholic schools and the Right were more entrenched than before.[72]

By the time the Bicentenary of the Revolution came round it might be argued that far from being marginalised the Vendée had been restored to the centre of the national debate as a blemish which apologists of the Revolution could not efface. Admittedly, the Vendée myth was still used by royalists to legitimate their cause. In 1983 the Garde Blanche, Armée Catholique et Royale, broke away from Action Française, denouncing the Orleanists as regicides, usurpers and democrats, swore to take up the guns of the Vendean rebels in the name of Prince Alphonse de Bourbon, and launched a review called *Ultra*.[73] Had the collective memory of the Vendée been monopolised by royalists it would have had no political significance. But the return to power of the socialists in 1981 encouraged conservatives more generally to revive the cause of the Vendée in order to attack the Left. It became the subject not only of academic theses defended in the Sorbonne but of popular spectaculars such as the annual Puy-du-Fou festival launched by Philippe de Villiers, minister in the 1986–8 Chirac government. Applying the term genocide to the Vendée massacres, portraying the Revolution as a totalitarian dictatorship, it proved its resilence and enduring strength as a yardstick against which to judge the Revolution and, by extension, a certain kind of Republic.

Revolutionaries and republicans, placed in the dock challenged by this myth of the Vendée, responded by creating their own version of events. If a veil could not be drawn over the whole episode, it must be presented to the French in a different way. The revolutionary version used the Vendée as a parable of counter-revolution. It was argued that the majority of Vendeans would have accepted revolutionary principles and the Republic without question, but were led astray by feudal nobles and seditious priests who had kept them ignorant and brutalised. The rising had been orchestrated, not spontaneous, and the methods used by the revolutionaries were as nothing compared to the barbarism and violence of the Vendeans themselves. Lastly, the revolt was denounced as a threat not only to the Republic but, in the face of foreign invasion, to France itself.

Michelet, professor of history at the Collège de France, who cast so many republican conceptions in the nineteenth century, from the Soldiers of the Year II and Joan of Arc to the Jesuits and the Camisards, was also largely responsible for a republican view of the Vendée which might be called that of 'the stab-in-the-back'. He pointed out that the Vendée revolt was essentially a boycott of the call to arms to save the *patrie en danger*.

At the same time as the émigrés took the enemy by the hand and opened the eastern frontier for him, on 24 and 25 August, anniversary of the massacre of Saint Bartholomew, the Vendean war, the unholy priests' war, broke out in the West. . . . The Revolution, however furious and drunk it may have been, was wild for unity. The Vendée, however democratic it may have been in form, was wild for Discord.[74]

Published in 1850, as clericals and reactionaries were taking control of the Second Republic, these volumes projected Michelet's fears for the safety of the régime onto the First Republic. He argued that now, as then, the universalism of the Revolution and the unity of the Republic was being undermined by the fanaticism of a small minority.

Accused of repression and massacre by the Vendeans, the revolutionaries seized on evidence of massacre by the Vendeans to restore legitimacy to their cause. Central to this propaganda was the cult of the republican martyr Joseph Bara. When news reached the Convention in December 1793 of the death of this thirteen-year-old soldier, Robespierre leapt up to demand that his remains be transferred to the Panthéon.

Surrounded by brigands who threatened him with death unless he shout, 'Long live the King!', he died crying 'Long live the Republic!' This child supported his mother with his pay, he divided his cares between filial love and the love of his country. A finer example or more perfect model could not be chosen to exalt love of glory, patriotism and virtue in young hearts, and to prepare the marvels that the new generation will achieve.[75]

The ceremony of Pantheonisation, designed by the artist Louis David, was due on 11 Thermidor. It never took place, owing to the fall of Robespierre, and the cult of Bara did not really flourish until the Third Republic. A statue was unveiled at Palaiseau in 1881, a magnificent canvas was commissioned by the state from J. J. Weerts for the salon of 1883 [cover], and the story became a commonplace of school history textbooks and moral and civic education manuals down to 1940.[76] In the republican temple Bara represented the divine child, who embodied the virtues of the young Republic. His martyrdom removed the stain of Terror from the Republic, cast the Vendeans as angels of darkness, brutality and reaction, and likened the Right which opposed the Republic to the Vendeans. The spirit of Bara meanwhile lived on, a vessel for the Republic's hopes for eternity.

Liberalism and Revolution

For the British or American observer one of the characteristics of nineteenth- and twentieth-century French history is the fragility of its liberal political culture. By this is meant a political society endorsing such principles as civil rights, the sanctity of private property, the separation of powers and representative government. For a liberal solution to succeed it had to be demonstrated either that the Republic was compatible with liberty, or that the monarchy was compatible with revolution. But either demonstration was incompatible with one or other of rival constructions of the Revolution. The left-wing construction of the Revolution held that liberty, equality and fraternity were incompatible with monarchy, and conjured up the spectre of counter-revolution and the Ancien Régime ever poised to destroy the principles of the Revolution and the Republic. The right-wing construction equated the Revolution with a lust for conspiracy, violence and anarchy and argued that the Republic to which it gave birth was necessarily the Republic of 1793, that of the Jacobin dictatorship, Terror and the guillotine.

'Let us try to help our fellow citizens forget the misfortunes inseparable from a great revolution; let us tell them that the past is no longer ours, but belongs to posterity.'[77] These words figured in a report by the Committee of Public Safety to the Convention on the last day of the Year II, which had seen both the Terror in full flood and the fall of Robespierre on 9 Thermidor. It was the view of a Thermidorean who wanted to forget the worst days of Revolution and ensure that they held no lessons for the future. Accordingly, the collective memory of the Revolution underwent some adjustment. The last sitting of the Convention in 1795 renamed the place de la Révolution the place de la Concorde and resolved that the guillotine as a penalty for political crimes would be abolished once peace had been secured in Europe. The remains of Marat were removed from the Panthéon. The cult of 31 May, when the Montagnards purged the Girondins from the Convention with the help of the Paris mob, was abolished, while that of the 9 Thermidor was inaugurated. The constitution of 1795 was quintessentially liberal, with a declaration of rights now accompanied by a declaration of duties, an elaborate separation of powers between two representative assemblies and an executive Directory, and high property qualifications for electoral rights.

To succeed, the new régime had to persuade the propertied classes called to exercise those rights that the Republic and liberty were now inseparable. 'To end a revolution', said Madame de Staël, daughter of the former finance minister Necker, in 1795, 'you must find a centre and a common tie. The centre we need is property, the tie, private interest.'[78] Ideological devotion to the common good was no longer enough. Benjamin Constant, her young protégé, argued that 'les honnêtes hommes' must be invited to rally to the republican government, and for that all proscriptive legislation against royalists must be shelved.[79] But Constant thereby put his finger on the problem. Royalists were regarded by most republicans as enemies of the Revolution, and the Directory met any sign that royalists might gain an electoral majority by successive coups against parliament. The Directory did not abolish celebration of the execution of Louis XVI and later prescribed an oath of hatred of royalty. For their part, therefore, royalists maintained their prejudice that liberty and the Republic were incompatible, and restored the monarchy in 1814 as a precondition of enjoying free institutions.

The restored Bourbon monarchy issued a Charter or constitution in 1814. But, granted with bad grace, it was liable to be revoked unless the monarchy now heeded the lessons of the Revolution that it had failed to heed during the first three years of the Revolution itself. When after 1820 the monarchy seemed to revert to its old reactionary practices, the young journalist and historian Adolphe Thiers took it upon himself to interpret the Revolution to the monarchy in such a way that it would be understood that one was indispensable to the other. Thus, in the teeth of the counter-revolutionary version of events, Thiers argued that the Revolution was not a conspiracy but the inevitable outcome of events. He condemned the 'excesses of the multitude' in the summer of 1789 but praised the efforts of Mirabeau, Lafayette and the Girondins who had tried to reconcile the monarchy and the Revolution and liberty with order. He rhapsodised on Louis XVI's honesty and love of his people, condemned the 'bloody anarchy' that followed the fall of the monarchy, and denounced the 'vile populace' that gathered round the scaffold to see the execution of the king.[80]

Thiers used his historical writing as a spring-board for politics. In 1829 he founded *Le National* as a liberal platform, and in July 1830 campaigned for the crown to be offered to Louis-Philippe, son of the duc d'Orléans who played a key role in the early part of the Revolution and was himself a commander of the victorious revolutionary army at Jemmapes. For Thiers, Louis-Philippe embodied the reconciliation of monarchy and Revolution, a monarchy wrapped in the tricolour flag. While the Republic of 1795 had failed to win over liberal monarchists, the monarchy of 1830 succeeded in winning over liberal republicans. On 31 July 1830 Benjamin Constant was carried sick in his sedan chair to the Hôtel de Ville to welcome Louis-Philippe. Lafayette, who was also present, informed the latter as they faced a cheering crowd, 'I am a republican, and I consider the constitution of the United States the most perfect that has ever existed', but that what France needed now was 'a popular monarchy, surrounded by republican institutions'.[81] His embrace once again conferred the blessings of 1789 on the monarchy.

'The glorious revolution which has just happened', announced *Le National*, 'completes that of 1789. That of 1789 won liberty in the civil, religious and intellectual fields, that of 1830 will be the conquest of true representative government.'[82] It was, however, an open question whether, if the monarchy had been reconciled with the Revolution, the Revolution could be contained within the monarchy. Thiers wished to take the Glorious Revolution of 1688 as a model for 1830, finally combining liberty, order and property. He wished also to stop the revolutionary clock in 1789. 'The republic served us ill thirty years ago,' he wrote in *Le National*. 'What we need is that republic concealed, under a monarchy, by means of representative government.'[83] 'We regard the republic as a generous madness', he continued, 'but madness all the same.'[84] Unfortunately for him the Revolution presented more models than that of constitutional monarchy for the appreciation of aspiring politicians. The republican Société des Amis du Peuple demonstrated outside the Chamber of Deputies during the week from 31 July 1830 to contest the settling of the crown on Louis-Philippe by a rump of parliamentarians who feared to consult the nation in new elections.[85] In June 1832 angry republicans took to the barricades and had to be put down by force. They reformed as a secret society, the Société des Droits de l'Homme et du Citoyen, whose members swore an oath to the Declaration of the Rights of Man. The Declaration, however, was not that of 1789; it was that which prefaced the constitution of 1793, inspired by Robespierre.[86]

Practising the Republic

If the Republic were to be successfully reintroduced in France, it had to be dissociated from memories of 1793: the Jacobin dictatorship, the Terror, and the guillotine. Only if it could be demonstrated that the Republic was compatible with liberty would it find supporters outside the narrow world of latter-day admirers of Robespierre. But a republic that secured a broad base of support would be open to conquest from within by non-republican parties: it risked becoming a republic without republicans. To prevent this happening republicans argued that the Republic must be constituted on revolutionary principles, and be run only by those who were committed to them. This in turn required a reconstruction of the Revolution to set it in the best possible light. The tension between the need to present an acceptable image of the Republic, and the need to constitute it on revolutionary principles, goes a long way to explaining the nature of political argument between 1848 and 1914.

'The republic we desire is not that you describe as that of 93', declared François Raspail in 1835.[87] Having been tried for membership both of the Société des Amis du Peuple and the Société des Droits de l'Homme, and declaring that since he had been born under the Republic (in 1794) he wished to die under it, he set about developing an acceptable image of the Republic through journalism. The strategy was now to campaign for universal suffrage, which would make plot and insurrection a thing of the past, and which could be formulated in terms of a demand for liberty—for all. In turn, republicans stressed fraternity, without which they would be defeated at the polls. Fraternity, the third term of the revolutionary triad, had never been given its full force during the French Revolution; now, to sell the new republic, it came into its own.

To make this republican strategy convincing, the Revolution too had to be presented in a new light, divested of its associations with conspiracy, violence and anarchy. Particularly influential in this respect were two histories which both started to appear in 1847. In the preface to the first volume of his *History*,

Jules Michelet underlined the 'profoundly pacific, benevolent character of the Revolution', and argued that 'the fraternity of love would conquer [the world], not the fraternity of the guillotine'.[88] For Michelet, the Revolution was carried forward not by a conspiratorial sect but by the mass of the people, and the people, far from being an unruly multitude, was a tidal force moved by divine breath. More successful even than Michelet's work was the *History of the Girondins* (1847), by the poet-politician Alphonse de Lamartine. Lamartine argued that it was inevitable that the Revolution should have led to the Republic, but that the Terror might have been avoided. By focusing on the Girondins he demonstrated that liberty was indeed honoured under the Republic. He considered Marat truly evil and praised Charlotte Corday, his assassin, as 'a Joan of Arc of liberty'. As for the Girondins, 'They adored liberty. They founded the Republic. . . . They died rather than permit liberty to be soiled.'[89]

The intellectuals who made the Second Republic in 1848, including Lamartine, certainly tried to make it as unlike 1793 as possible. Victor Hugo, in his address to the electors of the Seine, said that the Republic must not 'restart those two fatal machines . . . the *assignat* printing-press and the pivot of the guillotine', but be 'the holy communion in the democratic principle of all French people now, and all peoples one day'.[90] The death penalty for political crimes was in fact immediately abolished by the provisional government. Raspail, replying to the speech of the republican leader Ledru-Rollin commemorating the foundation of the First Republic, asserted, 'All your policy is based on fraternity, and the policy of a people of brothers has only to lift a finger and thrones collapse.'[91]

Ironically, Raspail's words were addressed from the prison of Vincennes. For, as he had feared, the republicans soon became strangers within the Republic itself. They were unsuccessful in all elections under the Republic, which by 1849 fell under the control of monarchists such as Thiers. When Thiers stated that the republic was, 'of all governments, the one which divides us least', he meant that it permitted Legitimists, Orleanists and moderate republicans to join forces in a party of order against the Montagnards.[92] Their majority enabled them to abrogate universal suffrage under the law of 31 May 1850, for, as Thiers, reflected, resorting to the intemperate language of his *History*, 'True republicans fear the multitude, the vile multitude who have done for all republics.'[93] In the Assembly Victor Hugo attacked the Right's attempt to detach the Republic from its revolutionary origins. 'Revolution and Republic are indivisible,' he said, 'you can no more separate 89 from the Republic than you can separate dawn from the sun.'[94] But for the moment anti-republicans had won the propaganda battle, and the Republic stood discredited as the régime of popular violence.

'Que la République était belle sous l'Empire.' Though the abolition of the Republic in 1852 created a certain nostalgia for it, the Republic would not succeed again in France until it had made itself fully compatible with liberty, and associated itself with a view of the Revolution which guaranteed liberty as well. The debate on the Revolution was given a new stimulus by the publication of a *History of the French Revolution* by the republican Louis Blanc. For the first time a major historian set out to rehabilitate Robespierre and the Montagne. He argued that while the Girondins were consumed by private interest and hot air, the decisiveness and stamina of the Montagne had saved the Revolution. Of the Terror, he wrote: 'the injustices of the past conceived it, and the prodigious struggles and unprecedented dangers of the present endangered it'. In other words, its harshness was justified by circumstances. Finally, said Blanc, in order to restore the image of Robespierre, if the Terror were identified with any one group it was with the Hébertists; Robespierre, far from embodying it, attempted to stop it without opening the way to counter-revolution.[95]

Had this view gained the day, the chances of the Republic would have been slim. Battle was therefore joined by Edgar Quinet, one of the leading republican exiles in Switzerland. His *Revolution* of 1865 argued that Robespierre converted the spontaneous anger of the crowd into the Terror as 'a permanent state . . . a principle of government', to impose the republican ideology by force. 'Imagine a storm-tossed sea suddenly changed to a motionless metallic sea. That was what terrorism meant.'[96] In the press debate that followed, the young republican Jules Ferry took the side of Quinet. He sought to discredit Blanc's praise for the Jacobin dictatorship by arguing that it led on naturally to the dictatorship of Bonaparte, and indeed that former Jacobins were the best prefects of the Empire.[97] At a time when liberals were gaining strength in the assemblies of the Second Empire and forcing concessions to be made, there was little sense in taking pride in the association of the Republic with dictatorship and Terror, for whatever reason.

When the Republic was declared in September 1870, it became associated not with dictatorship but with the popular revolution of the Paris Commune, which exercised its own form of Terror. Moreover, like the Second Republic, it was delivered by elections to the National Assembly in February 1871 into the hands of the monarchists. Adolphe Thiers, elected by the Assembly 'head of the executive power', was initially reluctant to add 'of the French Republic' to the title.[98] In a memorable speech to the National Assembly in 1872 he returned to the idea of the inevitability of the Republic. 'The Republic exists', he said, 'it is the legal government of the country; to want anything else would be a new revolution and the most fearful of all.' But he added, weightily, 'The Republic will be conservative or it will not exist.'[99]

The task of the republican opposition was twofold. On the one hand, they had to proclaim that only those who subscribed to the principles of the French Revolution could legitimately hold power in the Republic. For this reason they had to reactivate the counter-revolutionary myth, to show that monarchists, in spite of the gestures of some of them, were by nature hostile to the Revolution. On the other hand, they had to demonstrate that the Republic of the republicans stood not for dictatorship, the Paris Commune, or for Terror, but for the fundamental principles of liberal government.

In his novel, *Quatre-Vingt-Treize*, published in 1874, Victor Hugo dealt with both these problems. To revive fears of counter-revolution, he set the novel in the Vendée, and symbolised the opposition between the Vendée and the Revolution by the feudal fortress, La Tourgue, in which the rebels hold out, and the guillotine, which the revolutionary army brings up. There is, however, another opposition between the ex-priest, Cimourdin, who is committed to destroying the tower and its inmates, and his former pupil, the *ci-devant* noble, Gauvain, who advocates mercy for the rebels and is eventually executed himself.

'Liberty, Equality and Fraternity are doctrines of peace and harmony. Why give them a terrible aspect? We want to win peoples to the universal republic . . . the ideal republic . . . the absolute republic. . . . You are founding a republic of swords, I am founding. . . .' He interrupted himself: 'I would found a republic of minds.'[100]

Hugo attempted to do in fiction what Léon Gambetta, architect of the republican party, was trying to do as he stumped the country, making speeches. His brief was to dispel fears of a Republic of swords and win confidence in a Republic of minds. He insisted that republicans were not those who had written their names in fire and blood on the walls of Paris, but (carefully avoiding the concept of class) the 'new social strata' with some property and education, 'individuals in a process of rising' by dint of hard work and thrift. They were the party not of revolutionary violence but of democracy, and would come to power legally, by the conquest of a majority under universal suffrage. Gambetta was happy to claim that republicans were in the tradition of the Revolution, but insisted that the Revolution, far from being an attack on property, religion and the family, had actually upheld those institutions by giving land to the peasants, establishing liberty of conscience and instituting civil marriage.[101] Rhetoric aside, he and his allies rejected all demands from the left of the party for an amnesty for those deported or exiled as a result of the Commune, for fear of being associated with them. Not until they were safely in power, on the eve of 14 July 1880, did they concede an amnesty.[102]

In 1875 the National Assembly agreed a constitution that was clearly liberal. Whereas in 1795 republicans failed to gain the support of moderate royalists for their constitution, the constitution of 1875 was accepted by a coalition of republicans and Orleanists. The Orleanists approved a Chamber of Deputies elected by universal suffrage in exchange for an indirectly elected Senate; the president of the Republic would be elected by deputies and senators meeting together. Having won over royalists to their constitution, the task of the republicans was to win an electoral majority. For this it was necessary to discredit monarchists as counter-revolutionaries. The president of the Republic, Marshal MacMahon, a former commander of the imperial armies, played into their hands. He refused to accept the consequences of the republicans winning a majority in the first elections to the Chamber under the new constitution of 1875. On 16 May 1877 he dismissed the prime minister, a moderate republican, and replaced him with an Orleanist. He prorogued, then dissolved the Chamber of Deputies, and used all administrative pressure perfected by the Second Empire in an attempt to break the republican majority.

Three hundred and sixty-three republican deputies cried foul, denouncing irresponsible government and coup d'état. Gambetta's mouthpiece, *La République française*, set the tone for the election campaign.

> What we have before us is the great army of counter-revolution. A social war has been declared against the rebellious Tiers Etat and against emancipated workers. It is the revenge of the nobility and the clergy, a third restoration that would wipe away and atone for forty-seven years of our history. Events have precipitated the campaign, which is being led by the dukes. But who would the dukes be and what use would they be if they were not lined up behind the king?[103]

Such propaganda conjured up the spectre of a return to the Ancien Régime while caricaturing the monarchists as ridiculous die-hards. The republicans retained their majority in the elections, and took power, refusing to relinquish it, and arguing that the Seize Mai had demonstrated the refusal of non-republicans to abide by democratic decisions, which made them unfit for office. Down to 1940 only proven republicans were eligible for office, and to survive governments required not only a majority in the Chamber but a majority of republican deputies. Rather than the ideal Republic, it was the absolute Republic.[104]

By 1880 the republicans had succeeded in their double task. They had founded a liberal Republic, in which power was concentrated in the hands of the elected representatives of the people. And they had resurrected the counter-revolutionary myth in order to legitimate their monopoly of power. The symbolism of the Revolution was duly annexed to the Republic. On 30 June 1878 Paris was decked with tricolour flags and echoed to the *Marseillaise* in scenes immortalised by Manet.[105] The commemoration of 14 July, which had been banned in 1805 and remained a token of republican opposition since 1830, became the official festival of the Republic in 1880. However, it is important to note that the anniversary celebrated was not that of the taking of the Bastille (1789), which for many Frenchmen would have endorsed mob violence, but that of the Fête de la Fédération (1790), when delegates from all over France joined in communion. 'Ninety years after the first federation,' *La République française* noted, 'France will once again proclaim before all peoples its unity in liberty.'[106]

The republicans in power were now in a similar position to the Orleanists in 1830. They had annexed the symbolism of the Revolution to the régime, and hoped to preserve a monopoly of the interpretation of those symbols. But just as the Orleanists were challenged for power by the republicans, so the moderate republicans, dubbed 'Opportunists' for refusing to amnesty the Communards until the opportune time, were challenged by radical republicans. The radicals disliked the constitution of 1875, especially the Senate and the indirectly elected presidency, which they argued took power away from the people. Jules Ferry, who epitomised the Opportunist Republic, indeed had no particular love for the people, having had, as mayor of Paris in 1871, to flee the Hôtel de Ville on 18 March as barricades went up around it and generals taken prisoner by the mob were shot. Behind their criticism of the constitution lay a fear on the part of radicals that the Opportunists, with their calls for national unity and an open Republic, would sooner or later make common cause with royalists against them. In 1885 the radical Charles-Ange Laisant accused Ferry of following Gambetta as Gambetta had followed Thiers, and denounced Opportunism as 'government for the benefit of a caste' and 'Orleanism transplanted into the Republic'.[107]

Just as the republicans had used their version of the Revolution as a weapon to attack the Orleanists in the 1830s, so in the 1880s the radicals used their interpretation of the Revolution against the Opportunists. By demonstrating that the Revolution could not be contained within a parliamentary Republic, which the Revolution had never satisfactorily achieved, the radicals hoped to force consideration of their constitutional demands, and to deprive the Opportunists of legitimacy. They embarrassed the government by claiming that the glory of the Revolution was the Convention, and by pressing it to honour the heroes of the Convention. The government, which needed radical support to defeat a monarchist resurgence in the elections of 1885, and had to prevent radicals leaving it for Boulangism (as Laisant, for one, did) in 1888–9, was forced to go further to the Left in commemorating the Revolution than it would have preferred.

The municipal council of Paris, as we have seen, was at the forefront of the radical offensive. On 13 July 1883 it inaugurated a statue of the Republic, capped with a Phrygian bonnet, in the place de la République. President Grévy and Jules Ferry, the president of the council, declined to attend the ceremony. In June 1885 the council voted to republicanise sixty-three road names. Many were uncontroversial, but a proposal for a rue Saint-Just, authorised by the government, was disallowed personally by President Grévy.[108] The council was keen to erect a statue to Danton, and had the wisdom to chose a design depicting him as the champion of popular education and tribune urging on the volunteers of 1792, not that of the September massacres. This was sanctioned by President Grévy in March 1888, no doubt because to commend Danton was also to damn Robespierre.[109]

The tension between the government and the radical opposition over the centenary of the Revolution has already been discussed. After the centenary, and with the Boulangists well beaten, the government sought ways of ditching its radical allies and forming a new kind of majority with moderate royalists who were prepared to endorse the Republic. In this climate the opening of Victorien Sardou's play *Thermidor* at the Comédie française on 26 January 1891 was pregnant with political significance. An indictment of Robespierre and the

Terror, on which Opportunists and moderate royalists could agree, it provoked popular uproar in the auditorium and the government was forced to suspend performances. In the Chamber liberals like Joseph de Reinach argued that the Thermidorean critique must go on, but Clemenceau made a last stand for the radicals. He replied that he could not be made to 'peel' the French Revolution into bits he accepted and bits he wished to discard. 'Messieurs, whether we like it or not,' he added, 'the French Revolution is a bloc.'[110]

The search for a parliamentary majority of moderate royalists and moderate republicans was undertaken by royalists also. Condemnation of the Terror remained something on which they could agree. In the Senate the conservative Armand Fresneau questioned the government about a statue of Marat, depicted in his bath, which the radical city of Paris had placed in the parc Montsouris. He was worried that girls and boys playing around would fall under his spell and 'you could find yourselves, inexorably, dragged from celebrating the centenary of 1789 to celebrating the prologue of the centenary of 1793'.[111] This form of rapprochement on a symbolic level was made more concrete in 1893 when the conservative Jacques Piou launched a 'Droite républicaine'. He called for 'an open, tolerant and honest Republic' in which what he called a Tory party could hope to have influence.[112] The discrediting of the republican political class, both Opportunist and radical (including Clemenceau) over the Panama scandal of 1893 certainly increased the chances of reformed royalists obtaining office. But those opposed to such reconciliation kept their heads, arguing that royalists could not be trusted with the Republic and did not subscribe to the principles of the Revolution. 'I accept that they will suffer the Republic,' said president of the council Charles Dupuy of conservatives who claimed to have rallied to the régime; 'I am asking whether they would defend it!'[113] 'You accept the Republic, Messieurs, that's understood,' added even more pointedly the radical Léon Bourgeois. 'But do you accept the Revolution?'[114]

The closest that royalists came to securing power in the Republic was during the Dreyfus affair. Calling themselves nationalists, and joining forces with dissidents on the Left who proclaimed themselves nationalists also, they accused the government of attacking the French army and betraying the national interest. Those anxious to defend the Republic, and to gather all those from the centre to the far Left in its defence, projected their struggle as a continuation of the French Revolution. Their vanguard organisation, founded in 1898, was aptly named the Ligue des Droits de l'Homme. Édouard Herriot, later the leader of the Radical party, who joined its Lyon branch, anticipated that 'we will be fighting for the France of the Revolution'.[115] The playwright Romain Rolland returned to the myth of the Revolution to justify the position of the Dreyfusards. *Les Loups*, which opened in May 1898, transposed the debate between justice for an individual and the national interest to the French armies camped before Mainz in 1793. His *Danton*, whom he identified with courage, liberty and patriotism, was produced in 1900. *Le Quatorze juillet*, which effectively put Michelet on stage by ensuring that 'individuals are submerged in the popular ocean', opened during the election campaign of 1902.[116] The regeneration of revolutionary enthusiasm was brought to a climax on 19 November 1899, when a huge demonstration of republican and socialist Paris came to the place de la Nation for the inauguration, under the eyes of the president and government of the Republic, of the monumental and heroic statue by Dalou, entitled *The Triumph of the Republic*.[117] From that moment on, it was clear that the Republic was safe.

The resurrection of revolutionary rhetoric was exploited by the Republican, Radical and Radical-Socialist Party (to give the Radicals their full title) when it was formally constituted in 1901. Its statutes appealed to 'all the sons of the Revolution, whatever their differences, against all the men of counter-revolution'.[118] But from a party in opposition, the scourge of the parliamentary Republic, the Radicals became after 1902 the natural party of government. It would not have been surprising if, like the Opportunists, they now distanced themselves from the Revolution of 1793. In fact they accepted the Jacobin Republic as a model, in order to preserve their own identity, but reinterpreted it in a way favourable to themselves. The way was demonstrated by their in-house historian, Alphonse Aulard, professor of the history of the Revolution at the Sorbonne. First, just as Thiers had argued that the Revolution was not a conspiracy but the inevitable outcome of events, so in his *Histoire politique de la Révolution française* Aulard asserted that the establishment of the Republic was the inevitable consequence of the failure of the monarchy to accept the principle of national sovereignty. He was prepared to defend the Terror as a response to the resistance offered to the Revolution by the 'forces of the past', using methods no more violent than the Ancien Régime used against its enemies, and he denied Quinet's assertion that the Terror was a system. On the contrary, said Aulard, it was an expedient which ended after the republican victory of Fleurus diminished the danger to the régime. Republic and liberty were therefore entirely compatible.

Second, on the question of equality, Aulard argued that the Revolution had proclaimed only equality before the law, the natural consequence of which was democracy. There was no argument that revolutionary equality pointed the way to socialism.[119] In this way Aulard could be given a favourable review by Clemenceau: 'How can we understand and how can we practise the Republic to which we cling,' he asked, 'if we have no opinion of the first experiment with it of the French people, on the causes of its successes and its failings?'[120] Yet if Clemenceau had learned anything from the Jacobin Republic, it was that it had dealt harshly with the sans-culotte movement, and he was prepared to do the same with the labour movement of his day. As minister of the Interior, then president of the council, after 1906, he earned himself the reputation of 'strike breaker' and 'France's top cop'.

Third, Aulard launched a campaign to install Danton as the totem of the Jacobin Republic. This allowed him, as the Opportunists had done before, to isolate Robespierre as the architect of the Terror. Such an interpretation of the Jacobin Republic did not go unchallenged. Indeed, one of his most forceful critics was his own pupil, Albert Mathiez, who used the Revolution to justify first socialism, then communism. In 1904, while a young history master at the Lycée of Caen, he gave a lecture to the local Bourse du Travail on the social question during the Revolution, in which he argued that the Revolution was essentially bourgeois, but that the maximum and requisitions of 1793–4 were France's first experience in collectivism.[121] Far from serving uniquely to defend bourgeois radicalism, the Revolution provided justification for greater equality in society. But it was over the question of Danton versus Robespierre that Mathiez and Aulard came to blows. As Aulard from the vantage-point of the Société d'Histoire moderne praised Danton as the personification of a moderate, humane version of the Jacobin Republic, so Mathiez broke away and in 1908 founded the Société des Études robespierristes to attack what he saw as an apology for Thermidor and to rehabilitate Robespierre, still the great taboo figure. In a paper first given in 1911 on 'parliamentary corruption under the Terror' he painted Aulard's hero as corrupt and unprincipled. Mathiez's society then set about raising funds for a statue to Robespierre. The question for Mathiez was both to establish the reputation of the Incorruptible and to use Robespierre's Republic of Virtue as a stick with which to beat the Radical Republic. When Herriot, mayor of Lyon and senator of the Rhône, who had written his thesis on Madame Récamier and her circle (which included Madame de Staël and Benjamin Constant), was asked to contribute and refused, citing as a reason '1400 heads cut off in forty-seven days of which 150 between three dawns', Mathiez riposted angrily, 'Is there any task more urgent than to set against the republic of appeasement and compromise the republic of conviction and disinterest, against the pork-barrel republic the republic of principles?'[122] In the end, for Mathiez, only the Bolsheviks of 1917 held out the possiblity of a pure and exclusive Republic.

Socialism and Revolution

Just as liberal republicans regarded the Jacobin Republic with fear and loathing, so Jacobin Republicans such as Clemenceau and, before him, the Montagnards of 1849, detested any reference to the popular sans-culotte movement which might indicate they too had enemies on the Left with grievances to air. Yet there were in the nineteenth century periodic movements of the people, who felt betrayed by the refusal of Jacobin republicans to acknowledge the existence of a social question. Though the Jacobins were committed not only to the democratic Republic but beyond that to the democratic *and social* Republic, nicknamed 'la sociale', there was little evidence that they intended to call into question the sanctity of private property for the benefit of society as a whole. This point was made with devastating clarity in the June Days of 1848, when the working classes of Paris rose in defence of their social and economic rights, and were brutally suppressed by the republican bourgeoisie. Those arrested after the June Days were overwhelmingly working class, quite unlike those arrested after the demonstration of the Montagnards on 13 June 1849. These were by and large middle-class intellectuals, and were greeted in prison with insults and threats from workers who had been vegetating there since the previous year.[123]

It was necessary for those so violently excluded from the Republic in June 1848, and those converted to the primacy of the social question in the Republic, to define themselves as a political community, to compete for power within the Republic. For this a collective memory to define and legitimate their political culture was imperative. The way in which the events of 1848 politicised individuals differently, driving them into different political camps which constructed different collective memories and political cultures, may best be gauged by studying the careers of two republicans, college friends from Nantes, Charles-Louis Chassin (b. 1831) and Jules Vallès (b. 1832), who arrived in Paris in September 1848, the first to study law, the second to resit his *baccalauréat*. Both demonstrated in March 1851 when Michelet's lecture-course at the Collège de France was closed; both were traumatised by the coup of 2 December. Chassin fell under the influence of republican exiles in Switzerland, such as Edgar Quinet.[124] Vallès, by contrast, had been devastated by the sight of chain-gangs of June insurgents filing through Paris on their way to deportation. He repeatedly promised to write a history of the June Days, but so great was his emotion that he was never able to put pen to paper. The June Days, however, made him a socialist. '*Sociale!*' he exclaimed in his newspaper, *Le Cri du Peuple*, 'to be a republican is not everything, to be a Jacobin is not enough, one must be a socialist.'[125] His experience of Jacobin militants in the turmoil of 1869–71 was not good. 'All that rubbish of the legend of 93', says his alter ego Jean Vingtras (who is also writing a history of the June Days) in his novel, *L'Insurgé*, 'reminds me of a pile of frayed and faded clothes taken to père Gros, the rag man, in his draughty shop on the rue Mouffetard.'[126]

After the brutal suppression of the June Days the Paris workers were left cowed and unorganised. The only revolutionary group interested in them were the disciples of Auguste Blanqui, a theorist and practitioner of coups by armed and disciplined minorities. When not indulging in conspiracy the Blanquists tended to be long-term inmates of prisons such as Sainte-Pélagie. Their ideas were shaped by a prison culture rather then by any regular contact with the masses, but contact there must be if a coup were to trigger off a general insurrection. In 1864 Gustave Tridon, one of Blanqui's comrades from Sainte-Pélagie, published a short book on the Hébertists. In the Year II they had been the militant sans-culottes of the sections, clubs and revolutionary armies, distrustful of the politicians of the Convention, pushing the Montagne to purge the Girondins by the insurrection of 31 May 1793, advocates of market controls, de-Christianisation and Terror. Their mouthpiece had been Hébert, high up in the Paris Commune, and his scurrilous paper, *Le Père Duchesne*, until in the spring of 1794 Robespierre sent Hébert and his cronies to the scaffold.[127] Tridon called the Hébertists 'the great damned of history', uniformly reviled by other historians of the Revolution. Yet, he said,

> the revolution . . . lies in the entrails of the plebs, in the pikes of the faubourgs, in the roar of the sections, with those obscure or execrated men who were always on the move, maddening the strong, encouraging the weak . . . bringing the far too complacent *conventionnels* back to the revolutionary path, at the mouth of their cannon.[128]

Through the cult of Hébertism, Blanquists sought to gain acceptance for a radical view of the Revolution that would transform them from a conspiratorial minority into a potent revolutionary force. Their influence in the Paris Commune served as a measure of their success. Among the leaders Raoul Rigault, *procureur* of the Paris Commune, declared himself a Hébertist.[129] More important, *Le Père Duchesne* was reborn on 6 March 1870. Venting his spleen on Prussians and traitors alike, its slang and wit echoed the sentiments of the eternal sans-culotte of the popular quarters of Paris, and played on memories of the first revolutionary Commune of 1792 to fire the revolutionary Commune of 1871.

Neither the June Days nor the Hébertist experience, however, came to have the same place in the collective memory of the labour movement as the Paris Commune. This was largely because of the scale of the insurrection, which took control of Paris for ten weeks and elected a revolutionary government, and even more because of the scale of the repression, during which 20–25,000 Paris workers were killed or summarily executed, and militants imprisoned or driven into exile, not permitted to return to France until the amnesty of 1880. This repression, however, handed to the working class as it began to recover and to organise, a founding myth of the heroism, martyrdom and promised redemption of the working class that trumped all others.

Pioneers in the elaboration of that myth were the leaders of the newly formed French Marxist socialist party, the Parti Ouvrier Français (POF) of Jules Guesde. Its task was to create a working-class consciousness, in Guesde's words, 'to cut the cable which still anchors our workers in radical or bourgeois–Jacobin waters'.[130] The 'making of the working class' in France did not take place as a result of industrialisation or urbanisation but as a result of the construction of a collective memory, the myth of the Paris Commune. The French Marxists chose to do this by presenting the Paris Commune as a class war, a proletarian revolution suppressed with unprecedented violence by the French bourgeoisie. *L'Égalité*, the mouthpiece of the POF, marked the anniversary of the outbreak of the Commune on 18 March 1880 by describing it as 'a working-class revolution continuing and completing the June Days of 1848

Fig. 5.　The Commune as myth: the Mur des Fédérés from a contemporary print (Bibliothèque nationale)

and the Lyon insurrections of the first years of Louis-Philippe's reign'.[131] The main commemoration, however, was not the beginning of the uprising, but the so-called Bloody Week at the end, during which the massacre of Paris workers had taken place. *L'Égalité* urged workers to march in strength on 23 May 1880 to the Père Lachaise cementery in eastern Paris where, at what became known as the Mur des Fédérés, the Communards had made their last stand, died, and been shovelled into a common grave [Fig. 5]. Over the years the Mur was developed as a shrine to the martyrs of the Paris Commune and to the painful birth of the organised working class.

To dwell on the defeat of the rising rather than its outbreak may seem perverse, but the purpose was to project accusations of violence normally levelled against the workers onto the bourgeoisie, legitimating the proletariat as victims and martyrs, and to develop the solidarity and class-consciousness of the workers and hopes for future redemption by underlining the collective suffering they had endured. The Paris Commune was established as the revolution of the workers, the Revolution of 1789 consigned to the historical dustbin as the revolution of the bourgeoisie. Indeed, while the republicans were claiming that the social question and class divisions did not exist, and were seeking to unite the nation around the cult of the Revolution on 14 July 1880, the Parti Ouvrier ordered 'the proletarian mass' to boycott the 14 July celebrations, since for them it represented 'only a change of masters, exploitation by capital replacing exploitation by the sword . . . its Bastille, or rather Bastilles, have yet to be taken'.[132]

If the first lesson drawn from the Commune by French Marxists was that it was a class struggle, the second was that it was a violent revolution. This endorsed the insurrectionism of the Blanquists, who had provided many of the shock-troops of the Commune, though Blanqui himself was in prison. After the amnesty of 1880 allowed Blanquists to return from prison or exile, they were keen to return to their Hébertist roots. They reconstituted themselves as the Central Revolutionary Committee, in honour of the organisation responsible for the insurrection of 31 May 1793.[133] In turn the Blanquists brought their revolutionism to bear on the POF, with which they worked closely. Arguably the POF owed as much to Blanquism as it did to Marxism. But both Édouard Vaillant, leader of the Blanquists, and Jules Guesde were confronted by the dilemma posed by the existence of democratic politics in the Republic. On the one hand they denounced the Republic as bourgeois, and accused the bourgeoisie of violating the democratic rules of the game when their class domination was threatened, on the other they could not easily forego the chances offered by universal suffrage and free elections to build mass parties. Thus Vaillant was elected to the Paris municipal council in 1885, while Guesde was elected deputy of the northern textile town of Roubaix in 1893. Guesde and Vaillant nevertheless continued to speak of revolution, in effect to reinforce the doctrine of class struggle, to prevent the supporters of the Parti Ouvrier drifting off to support bourgeois parties.

The official view of Guesde and Vaillant that the Republic was essentially bourgeois, and its survival of no particular interest to the proletariat, was brought into focus by the Dreyfus affair. When republicans called for a rallying of all forces of the Left to defend the Republic against the Right, Guesde, fearing the dissolution of the socialist identity in a republican coalition and a loss of support to bourgeois parties, refused to engage his troops in what he dismissed as an internal bourgeois dispute. The crisis deepened in 1899, when a socialist was given office in the government of republican defence. In the Chamber Guesde and Vaillant resorted to the politics of class. They greeted the ministry, whose war minister had helped to suppress the Commune, with shouts of 'Vive la Commune!', and marked the 14 July by issuing a manifesto which condemned 'the so-called socialist policy of compromise and diversion which for too long has been smuggled in to replace the class and thus revolutionary policy of the militant proletariat and the socialist party'.[134] Revolutionary socialists interrupted the inauguration of Dalou's monument *The Triumph of the Republic* on 19 November 1899, by flying the red flag and singing the *Carmagnole* and the *Internationale*, which had been composed by Eugène Pottier, an exile from the Commune, in June 1871.[135] Their loyalty, they proclaimed, was not to France but to the cause of international socialism.

The revolutionary class socialism of Jules Guesde was not the only version of socialism constructed in France. Another tendency, personified by Jean Jaurès, a philosophy professor who had come to socialism from radicalism, was based on a much less doctrinaire reading of the Revolution. It understood the extent to which the myth of the French Revolution had been inculcated into the French people, so that it could not be thrust aside as irrelevant, but had to be adapted to the needs of socialism and the labour movement. For Jaurès the Republic was not simply the tool of the bourgeois class; it had been created by Revolution and, as such, was the guarantee of revolution to come. When the Dreyfus affair stirred up the enemies of the Republic he announced that 'since reaction has formed a bloc the Revolution must form a bloc'.[136] He believed that the Republic stood for liberty, which socialism was seeking to extend, and that socialists should therefore join progressive elements of the bourgeoisie against 'counter-attack by all the forces of the past . . . feudal barbarism and the omnipotence of the Church', in the defence of republican liberty and liberty of conscience.[137]

For Jaurès, the Republic stood for liberty; it also stood for democracy, and only through the channels of democracy, he argued, would socialism be realised in France. At the socialist congress of December 1899, which split the party, and at a public debate staged at Lille in 1900, Jaurès clashed openly with Guesde. Guesde argued that if the proletariat became involved in bourgeois politics it would be divided against itself, and that a socialist minister in a bourgeois government was kept as a hostage and would have to sanction the bourgeois repression of strike action. He questioned whether socialism could ever be extracted from the Republic by democratic means. If their privileges were threatened the bourgeoisie would resort to force, as in the June Days of 1848 and the Bloody Week of 1871. The proletariat could conquer power 'only in a revolutionary period, with guns blazing'.[138] Such revolutionary posturing was anathema to Jaurès. Extremely hostile to the idea of a revolutionary seizure of power and a dictatorship of the proletariat, he subscribed to the view that socialism must come to power legally, by the acquisition of a majority under universal suffrage. The advantage that France had over, for example, Germany, was a revolutionary tradition that made democratic socialism possible; to mouth revolutionary rhetoric, like the Marxists, was to expose socialism to the accusation that it would repeat the violence, dictatorship and Terror of 1793. Jaurès made a fundamental distinction, later taken up by his heirs like Léon Blum, between revolution as a means and revolution as an end. Revolution as a means—barricades and gunfire—he abhorred; what he strove for was revolution as an end, the establishment of a socialist society.

Jaurès' socialist philosophy was based on a particular reading of the French Revolution. Unlike Guesde, he did not dismiss the Revolution of 1789 as entirely bourgeois, to be abandoned for the cult of the Paris Commune. Having lost his parliamentary seat in 1898, and not reelected until 1902, he embarked on his *Histoire socialiste de la Révolution française*. He argued that the Revolution had both a material and a spiritual dimension. Political power had been used by the bourgeoisie to consecrate private property rights, liberate market forces and break up the restrictive practices of French workers. In this sense the Revolution was bourgeois. But the bourgeoisie had couched their claims against despotism and privilege in universal terms, set out in the Declaration of the Rights of Man and the Citizen. The assertion of universal rights was always open to a wider interpretation than their narrow class interest gave it, and to give force to this wider interpretation was now the task of the proletariat. In 1793 the proletariat had lacked definition and class-consciousness, but was now sufficiently developed, organised and conscious to take up the torch of Liberty, Equality and Fraternity where the bourgeoisie had left it, and to complete the Revolution by founding a socialist society.

The advantage of the liberty and democracy afforded by the Republic, according to Jaurès, was that it enabled both socialist parties to start out on the road to power, and the labour movement to build socialism within the womb of capitalist society, through the organisation of trade unions and co-operatives. In this way, society would already be partly socialised when socialists took power, and ensure the success of the socialist revolution. Once this was accepted, Jaurès was ready to rejoin Guesde in a united socialist party, the Section Française de l'Internationale Ouvrière (SFIO). Guesde was gratified by the resumption of the cult of the Paris Commune by the SFIO in 1908, following a final decision by the municipality of Paris not to use the plot against the Mur des Fédérés for private graves, and by the erection of a plaque in memory of the Commune.[139] Jaurès, for his part, was gratified by the official recognition in the *Histoire socialiste* that the Paris Commune had been a premature revolution: political power had been seized, but since no progress had been made towards building a socialist society, the Commune had been swept away.[140]

Communism and Revolution

The Bolshevik Revolution of 1917, like the Commune of 1871, offered French socialists their own revolution as a source of collective memory and collective identity. However, like the Paris Commune, it in fact divided socialists. For some, it offered a brilliant model for French socialism to follow, particularly since this seemed to have lost its direction during the war. These were keen to present the Bolshevik Revolution as heir to the French revolutionary tradition, and in this way to persuade French socialists who drew inspiration from the French Revolution that as the Bolsheviks had learned from them, so now they should learn from the Bolsheviks. Other socialists, on the other hand, who had imbibed their socialism from Jaurès, and shared his anxieties about violent, premature and dictatorial revolution, were not so convinced that the Bolshevik road was the one to follow.

Albert Mathiez, the apologist of Robespierre, was one of the first socialists to make explicit the parallel between Bolshevism and Jacobinism. And whereas the Jacobin dictatorship had long been an embarrassment to many on the Left as damaging to the image of the Republic, now the explanation of 'force of circumstances' could be seen to be justified in the light of the Bolsheviks' desperate struggle against counter-revolution and foreign intervention.

Jacobinism and Bolshevism are two dictatorships of the same order, born of civil war and foreign war, two class dictatorships using the same methods, terror, requisition and taxation, and in the last instance having a similar goal, the transformation of society.[141]

He noted that Lenin had raised a statue to Robespierre, something he had been unable to acquire support for in France. Terror was excused by the desperate circumstances in which the Bolsheviks found themselves; indeed Terror alone could prevent the Russian Revolution failing as the French Revolution had done. 'What if a Russian 9 Thermidor were to follow,' asked Mathiez, 'followed by an 18 Brumaire, executed by a more skilful Kornilov, to complete the tragedy?'[142] Pursuing the logic of his own arguments, he joined the French Communist party when it was founded.

The view of Mathiez, a historian, was shared by the socialist militant Marcel Cachin, who became one of the architects of the French Communist party over the years. Cachin, converted to socialism in 1891 as a result of the massacre at Fourmies, was sent on an exploratory mission to Russia by the French Socialist party in 1920.[143] He saw the Russian Revolution as a remake of the 'iron dictatorship of the Jacobins' in 1793, who had been forced to use energetic measures to save the Revolution from counter-revolution supported by foreign invasion.[144] He also saw it as 'the daughter of our Paris Commune', and witnessed the laying of the first stone of a memorial to the martyrs of the Commune on the square of the Winter Palace in Petrograd.[145] Finally, he saw in Bolshevism a vindication of the strategy of Jules Guesde, who had always preached that revolution would be necessary to conquer political power and found socialism.[146]

This interpretation of the Russian Revolution proved highly controversial in a French Socialist party so powerfully influenced by Jaurès. Matters came to a head at the party congress held at Tours in December 1920. The issue debated was whether the SFIO should affiliate to the newly formed Third International or Comintern founded by the Bolsheviks, which required affiliating parties to endorse revolutionary principles, condemn reformism, and call themselves Communist. Cachin repeated his view that the violence of the Russian Revolution had been imposed by the need to resist the armed might of the capitalist world, and that in doing so the Bolsheviks had drawn lessons from the French Revolution, which they understood better than the French themselves.[147]

Battle was joined by Léon Blum, the disciple, even heir, of Jean Jaurès in the same way that Cachin was the Guesde's disciple. Blum had paid homage to

Jaurès in a speech to mark the third anniversary of his death.[148] He argued that to confuse socialism and revolutionary violence was a perversion of the Marxist tradition. Like Jaurès, he insisted that there was no opposition between social-ism and democracy, and that socialists would come to power legally, by win-ning a parlimentary majority.[149] He warned that the Bolsheviks and their Guesdist imitators had fallen into the Blanquist trap of seeing revolution as the seizure of power by a gang of armed thugs, which was bound to be premature if it lacked the support of an organised proletariat, fully educated in the movement's aims. Blum reiterated Jaurès' distinction between revolution as a means and revolution as an end. Bolsheviks and Guesdists seemed to be in-terested only in the means; true socialists, however, interpreted revolution as an end, the transformation of society from one based on private property to one based on collective property.[150]

Most worrying for Blum was the Communist interpretation of Marx's con-cept of the dictatorship of the proletariat. He attacked the military command system of the Bolshevik party, the imposition of ideological uniformity, and the 'complete and radical purge of all that the socialist party has been up to now'.[151] Their dictatorship was that of a few, not that of the proletariat impersonally, and far from being temporary it was, he said, echoing Quinet on the Jacobins, 'a stable, almost regular system of government under cover of which you want to do all your business'.[152] The essence of Blum's attack was that Bolshevism meant the eclipse of liberty in the Republic. Whilst not entirely rejecting Marx's concept of the dictatorship of the proletariat, his conception of it was altogether more Girondin.

> Dictatorship, as we see it, as we will strive to realise it when the time comes, means the suspension of all legality but not the compression of all liberty. . . . It must not only tolerate but arouse, excite freedom of thought, freedom of assembly, freedom of discussion. It must be, in the words of Vergniaud [a Girondin leader], lively and clear as a flame. All individual wills must participate in it. . . . The Bolsheviks have confused dictatorship with tyranny, dictatorship with terror.[153]

The two viewpoints were irreconcilable, and at the Congress of Tours Socialists and Communists broke apart. Symbolically, the annual pilgrimage to the Mur des Fédérés also divided in 1921, on the fiftieth anniversary of the Paris Commune. The Communists claimed to be 60,000 strong at the Mur on 29 May, where Cachin argued that the revolutionary violence of the Commune had been endorsed by the Bolshevik Revolution.[154] The So-cialists processed to the Mur the week before, and Blum restated the view that to raise the red flag on the Hôtel de Ville was not enough to make social revolution.[155] Socialists ensured that Jaurès was canonised as the official face of socialism, his remains translated to the Panthéon in 1925, after the victory of the Cartel des Gauches, and twenty-seven monuments raised to his name between the wars, mostly in the 1920s as socialist municipalities were elected to office.[156]

Fig. 6.   Popular Front leaders at the Mur des Fédérés. This shot is of 24 May 1936 (Roger-Viollet)

A further concern of socialists, and of the population in general, was that the PCF took its orders from Moscow, was not patriotic and was indifferent to the fate of the Republic. When the parliamentary Republic was threatened by the rioting of the extreme Right in Paris on 6 February 1934, the initial response of the Communists, echoing the response of the Guesdists in the Dreyfus affair, was that the democratic bourgeoisie and the fascist bourgeoisie were equally despicable. 'Between cholera and the plague there can be no choice', said Maurice Thorez, secretary-general of the PCF, who would always loyally follow Moscow's line.[157]

In May 1934, however, Moscow changed its line. After the triumph in Germany of the Nazi party, with its loudly proclaimed anti-Soviet designs, Stalin sought allies among the western democracies. For the first time, the PCF could serve two masters—Moscow and the French Republic—without fear of contradiction. Moreover, since they could never win a majority at the polls, they could influence policy only as members as a broad coalition of the Left. French Communists were instructed by Moscow to build this coalition, first combining with Socialists and reuniting the proletariat that had divided in 1920, then seeking an electoral alliance with the Radical party.

In July 1934 Thorez paid homage to the memory of Jaurès by inviting the Socialists to a joint commemoration of the twentieth anniversary of the leader's death.[158] On 19 May 1935 Communists and Socialists marched together, for the first time since the schism, to the Mur des Fédérés, 200,000 strong.[159] [Fig. 6]

To extend the coalition to the Radicals was more difficult. In order to achieve it the Communists presented themselves less as the disciples of the Communards than as the true heirs of the French Revolution and the Enlightenment, challenging the Radicals on their own territory for the mantle of 1789. In November 1934, trying to prise the Radicals out of the government and into the Popular Front coalition in which the Communists claimed the leading rôle, Thorez deftly inserted the Communist party into the classic revolutionary tradition:

> We claim the spiritual heritage of the great French Encyclopedists of the eighteenth century, whose writings opened the way to Revolution and whose profound and refined materialism was at the root of historical materialism, at the root of the brilliant doctrine of Marx and Lenin. . . . We claim the heritage of the Jacobins, in Lenin's words 'the best example of democratic revolution and of resistance to the counter-revolutionary coalition of the monarchs'.[160]

At a mass meeting at the Buffalo stadium on 14 July 1935, organised to celebrate the Rassemblement populaire of all democratic forces against fascism, Jacques Duclos, another leading Communist, signalled the return of the Communists to the revolutionary mainstream by proclaiming the cult of 1789 in all its integrity. He saluted the tricolour as well as the red flag, and the crowd responded by singing the *Marseillaise* as well as the *Internationale*. The socialist press was happy to draw a parallel between the Buffalo stadium meeting and the demonstration of the united Left around Dalou's *Triomphe de la République* in 1899.[161]

The Radical party was torn two ways over the formation of the Popular Front. The right wing, under Herriot, was minded to stay in government, the left, under Daladier, wanted to leave the government and join the opposition to campaign in a Popular Front alliance for the elections of 1936. Significantly, at the Paris congress of the Radical party in 1935, Daladier chose to justify his policy by invoking the precedent of 1789. By casting the Radicals in the leading rôle of the Third Estate, he hoped to assuage fears that the Communists would be the dominant partner in the coalition. Moreover, he warned that a divided Left ran the risk of defeat by reaction. 'The Popular Front is the alliance of the Third Estate and the proletariat', he said. 'United, the Third Estate and the proletariat are capable of 1789, 1793, 1848 and 4 September [date of the proclamation of the Third Republic in 1870]. . . . Divided, they suffer Thermidor, Brumaire and 2 December.'[162] The Radicals responded to the appeal and left the government to join the Popular Front early in 1936.

On the Popular Front's triumph at the polls in May 1936 the Communist party decided to remain outside the government. It did not, however, stir up the masses against the Popular Front government and continued, by its enthusiasm for the cult of the French Revolution, to present itself as the guarantor of the legitimacy and continuity of the Popular Front coalition and of France's leading rôle in the struggle against international fascism. To refine this image, the party and the CGT commissioned Jean Renoir, who had made a propaganda film for the Communists' election campaign, to make a film on the French Revolution. *La Marseillaise*, released in February 1938, dramatised the march of the patriots of Marseille to Paris to secure the Revolution, found the Republic, and defend France against the international forces of reaction. The great set pieces of the film were the attack on the Tuileries palace on 10 August 1792, toppling the monarchy, and the battle of Valmy. Speaking of the crowds, Renoir told an interviewer that 'it is considered good form to portray them as dirty, rough and loud-mouthed', but insisted that 'our revolutionaries will be as clean as you or I'. Renoir's revolutionaries, cast as heroic freedom-fighters, were modelled on the People of Michelet rather than the atavistic mob of Taine or the caricature of the Communist as the man with a knife between his teeth.[163]

The Communists' cult of the Revolution was not without its contradictions. On the one hand they expressed their full enthusiasm for the cult of 1789, taking, as we have seen, a pre-eminent rôle in the celebrations of the 150th anniversary of the Revolution. This was necessary in order to gain access to the mainstream of republican politics. On the other, they wanted to keep one hand free to criticise the Radicals, who increasingly sought to abandon the Popular Front and to form a new majority, with the parties of the centre and centre-right, against the Communists. Thus the Communists resumed the cult of Robespierre inaugurated by Mathiez, to suggest disapproval of the return of the Republic of compromise and corruption. Jacques Duclos, elected deputy of the Paris suburb of Montreuil in 1936, managed to have a street and therefore (according to administrative procedure) a metro station named after Robespierre.[164] In this way they proclaimed the sanctity of the pure, incorruptible and militant Republic against what they saw as the Republic of appeasement with the Right and Nazism.

The Nazi–Soviet Pact of 1939, however, took the wind sharply out of the Communists' sails. Stalin's opportunistic foreign policy forced French Communists, now banned and persecuted as traitors, to vent what remained of their revolutionary spleen on warmongers and imperialists in their own country and Great Britain. But on Hitler's invasion of the Soviet Union in June 1941, the French Communists threw themselves into the Resistance and resumed the cult of the Revolution of 1789 and of revolutionary patriotism in a bid to establish hegemony over the internal Resistance. The cult of the Revolution took on a new significance under the Vichy régime, which abolished the Republic and rejected the principles of the Revolution. For a population shattered and atomised by defeat, and denied the usual means of expression, the commemoration of 14 July became a statement of defiance against the government and the occupant. *L'Humanité*, which was published clandestinely, called for demonstrations and strikes on 14 July 1941, flying the tricolour and singing the *Marseillaise*, 'as sung by our fathers of the French Revolution and by French people who want to liberate France from Hitlerian oppression'.[165] The PCF guerilla organisation, the Francs-Tireurs et Partisans Français, resurrected *Le Père Duchesne*, with its familiar slang, 'to express the fury, disgust and shame of the French people. . . . Every day the Père Duchesne was "bloody angry", which is why he must be reborn, because France needs to be "bloody angry" '.[166] In 1942 the Communists revived the commemoration of the Commune at the Mur des Fédérés. The Père Lachaise cemetery was to be occupied by the Gestapo and the French police, but *L'Humanité clandestine* assured its readers that flowers would nevertheless be laid, 'to tell our illustrious dead that their sons continue the struggle for liberation, that the revolutionary patriots of 1942 know how to fight and die like their fathers in 1871'.[167]

If the Communists had really wished to launch a violent revolution in France, and to establish a dictatorship of the proletariat, no time would have been more appropriate than the high summer of 1944. They were the key elements in a network of liberation committees thrown up by the Resistance at the local, departmental and national level. They controlled the revolutionary courts, the *comités d'épuration*. They had their own police force, the *milices patriotiques*, and guerilla organisations, such as the Franc-Tireurs et Partisans Français, one of the constituents of the Forces Françaises de l'Intérieur. Why, then, they did not attempt to seize power needs to be explained. Part of the answer lies in the international configuration after Yalta, the division of Europe into spheres of influence which put France beyond the range of Stalin. Any revolution on the part of the Communists would have been immediately dealt with by the American forces on French soil. Part, however, lies in the Communist party's decision to translate its leading rôle in the Liberation of France, in which it claimed to have lost 75,000 martyrs, and the success of its appropriation of the collective memory of the French Revolution, into the foundation of the new Republic and experiment with the democratic road to socialism. Communists were represented in the provisional government of de Gaulle and emerged as the largest parliamentary party, with 26 per cent of the vote and 150 seats in the two Constituent Assemblies of 1945 and 1946.[168]

On the other hand, if the Communists endorsed the idea of the Republic, they were keen to ensure that the Republic was organised to their taste and not to that of the Right. At the end of 1944, Jacques Duclos told the Consultative Assembly that 'it [was] time to return to the wild fervour of the Committee of Public Safety' in the purge of Vichy traitors, not to allow them to slink back to control the new Republic.[169] At their 10th Party Congress in June 1945, Thorez called for 'the rejuvenation of the Republic, the perfecting of democracy', but André Marty made it quite clear that they wanted no limits on the powers of the assembly elected by universal suffrage. Their model was the Convention Parliament of 1792, although references to it were avoided as too controversial. Instead, the principle of the sovereignty of the people laid down in the Declaration of the Rights of Man was said to require an assembly emanating directly from it, and attention was drawn to the frustration of reform by the

Senate of the Third Republic.[170] As if to make their point, in 1946 the municipality of Paris renamed the place du Marché-Saint-Honoré the place Robespierre (though the name was changed back in 1950). But despite a march of one and a half million people from the Bastille to the Nation on 1 May 1946 in support of the Communist vision, the constitution providing for a single chamber was rejected by referendum.

The Communists nevertheless accepted the verdict of the French people on the second constitution put to them, which provided for a two-chamber parliament. They still believed that they could benefit from universal suffrage, and indeed secured 29 per cent of the vote in the legislative elections. Thorez thereupon demanded the right to form a government. In an interview to *The Times* he underlined 'the national and democratic character of the French Communist Party', and its commitment to a French path to socialism, independent of the Soviet or East European model.

> The progress of democracy through the world, in spite of rare exceptions which serve only to confirm the rule, permits the choice of other paths to socialism than the one taken by the Russian Communists. In any case, the path is necessarily different for each country. We have always thought and said that the French people, who are rich in great traditions, would find for themselves their way to greater democracy, progress and social justice.[171]

That Thorez was not himself able to form a government in 1946 was explained mainly by the opposition of the Christian Democratic MRP. They had to be content with holding portfolios in coalition with the SFIO and MRP. However, the Cold War was brewing and in May 1947 Communist ministers were unceremoniously ejected from the government. Interestingly enough, though forced into a political ghetto, the PCF did not relax its cult of the Revolution of 1789, which served as its lifeline to the mainstream of republican politics. It continued to mark the 14 July, marching on 14 July 1947 under the slogan, 'Union to defend the Republic!'. Steadfast in their loyalty to the Republic, the Communists were the only left-wing party ten years later to be uncompromising in their defiance of 'the military and fascist dictatorship' of de Gaulle. Similarly they opposed his revision of the constitution in 1962 in the name of the 'great princples of 1789' to be reaffirmed in 14 July demonstrations and 'the union of republicans'.[172]

To increase their electoral weight at the Liberation, the Communists approached the SFIO with a proposal of creating a single proletarian party, to be called the Parti Ouvrier Français. Jacques Duclos warned that the revolution made at the Liberation was being hijacked by bourgeois parties, in the same way as in 1830, and that it was the responsibility of revolutionary parties to stand together.[173] This was rejected by the SFIO at its 37th congress in August 1945. The strategy of merging Communist and Socialist parties was one that the Communists would put to good effect in the Peoples' Democracies of Eastern Europe. Moreover, the reasons for the schism at Tours in 1920 had not been forgotten. Communists still aroused suspicion as the party of violent revolution and the dictatorship of the proletariat, and one that operated under instructions from Moscow. Léon Blum, returning from prison in Germany, argued that unity would not be possible until the Communists committed themselves not only to democracy inside and outside the party, but to the respect of individual liberties and the verdict of the electorate in free elections, and demonstrated that they were not at the beck and call of Moscow.[174] Likewise, in his notes for that party congress, Vincent Auriol, formerly Blum's finance minister in the Popular Front government and shortly to be elected president of the Fourth Republic, insisted that they did not want rule by 'a committee of all-powerful individuals or a totalitarian government. The social revolution is not dictatorship. It is the definitive victory of true liberty, true equality, true fraternity.'[175] The reservations of the Socialists seemed to be borne out by the behaviour of the PCF after 1947, at the height of the Cold War: the cult of Maurice Thorez; the purges of members who had been prominent in the French Resistance (as Thorez had not); the defence of Stalinism, even when Stalinism was denounced at the 20th congress of the Communist party of the Soviet Union in 1956, and the approval of the Soviet invasion of Hungary, which flouted the notion of separate roads to socialism.

The SFIO itself was not without problems of its own after the Liberation. In its relationship with the Communists it was in the same position as the Orleanists relative to the republicans after 1830, the Opportunists relative to the radicals in the 1880s, and the Radical party relative to the socialists after 1900. It wavered between an alliance with the Communists, building a political community on the Left legitimised by the cult of the French Revolution, and fighting shy of the Communists, given the climate of the Cold War, to seek an alliance with parties of the centre. Neither was its rôle in the Fourth Republic entirely happy. The Socialists reconstituted themselves at the Liberation as the 'great republican, democratic and revolutionary force of the Nation'.[176] But they were both closely associated with the chaos into which the Republic sank during the Algerian war, and compromised themselves by supporting General de Gaulle's coup against the Republic.

Guy Mollet, mayor of Arras, was the Socialist leader who typified this loss of direction. He challenged the established leadership around Léon Blum, disciples of Jaurès, intellectuals, and linked by the Resistance, by arguing that the SFIO must compete for support on the same territory as the Communists and thus set out the same Marxist ideology of class struggle and revolution. At the party congress of 1946 Mollet was elected secretary-general of the party: it was the revenge of the Guesdists.[177] Resorting to the Guesdist tactic of refusing to authorise socialists to hold office in bourgeois cabinets, he distanced himself from Blum (who formed a government in December 1946) and the ministerial socialists. Yet his own strategy was entirely incoherent. While proclaiming a Marxist dogmatism to prevent seepage of support to the Communists, he tried to govern with the centre parties against the Communists. In 1956 Mollet headed a Republican Front government with the Radicals, but insisted that there was 'no question of a Popular Front' with the Communists.[178] Almost at once he involved France in the Algerian war. In 1958 he approved of de Gaulle's seizure of power as the only way of saving France from the colonels, and entered de Gaulle's government to help revise the constitution.[179]

The renaissance of socialism required the recognition of two principles. First, that the Republic was nothing without liberty, and second, the socialists should seek a united front of the Left, together with the Communists, appealing to the French Revolution for inspiration. That renaissance came from two sources. The first source was the Parti Socialiste Autonome (PSA, later unifié, the PSU), which broke away from Mollet's SFIO under Édouard Depreux, an admirer of Blum and linked to the Resistance leadership, who asserted that 'socialism compromises with any form of military despotism only on pain of death', and that 'socialism can be conceived only in, by and for liberty'.[180] He attacked Mollet as 'Robespierre', and saw himself as continuing in the steps of Jaurès which had been so rudely flouted. Auriol copied his letter of resignation from the SFIO to Depreux, adding that he had joined the party at its outset in 1905: 'All my activity has been mingled with the life of this party of Jaurès. . . . Today I see everything falling apart.'[181] One notable recruit to the party was the former Radical premier Pierre Mendès-France, who said that extending the principles of 1789 had taken him, like Jaurès before him, along the road from republicanism to socialism. He told Depreux that socialism, 'to succeed in France, should be inspired by the humanist tradition of Jean Jaurès and Léon Blum'.[182]

Depreux believed in drawing closer to the Communists, who in his view represented only the most radical manifestation of the revolutionary tradition, and had the courage to defend democracy against the personal power of de Gaulle.[183] This strategy was held to by the second source of the regeneration of socialism, a movement of clubs and associations which took shape outside the ambit of the established parties, in such little esteem did they hold their leaders. The Convention des Institutions républicaines was formed in 1964 by François Mitterrand and Charles Hernu. Mitterrand had served in several governments of the Fourth Republic, including that of Mollet, but claimed to have been reborn by the experience of 'republican resistance' to de Gaulle.[184] Charles Hernu had founded a Jacobin Club in 1951 to rejuvenate the Radical party and had gloried in the brief ministry of the Radical Pierre Mendès-France in 1954–5, but had become disillusioned with the Radicals after the victory of the Thermidoreans in the party in 1957.[185]

The Convention built a bridge to the SFIO and Radical party in the Fédération de la Gauche démocrate et socialiste (FGDS), a Jacobin alliance of the non-Communist Left, with Communist support. The Fédération ran Mitterrand as the single candidate of the Left against de Gaulle in the presidential elections of 1965, and relied on Communist votes at the second ballot in the legislative elections of 1967. However, it had to battle against a rival tendency in the SFIO which detested the Communists and sought to lead a centrist coalition without and against them. This tendency was represented by the deputy-mayor of Marseille, Gaston Defferre, who ran in the 1969 presidential elections with centre-party support. Dialogue with the Communists had broken down after the Soviet invasion of Czechoslovakia in August 1968; the SFIO plumped for Defferre, who signed up Mendès-France as a running-mate and conducted a very anti-Communist campaign. In the event Defferre polled a mere 5 per cent of the vote, against the 22 per cent of the Communist Duclos. This fiasco effectively destroyed the old SFIO and opened the way to the foundation of a new socialist party, the Parti Socialiste, at the congress of Épinal in 1971. The Parti Socialiste rejected the centrist tactic and committed itself to the 'union of the Left' as its 'normal axis'.[186] Negotiations were begun with the PCF, and in 1972 the common programme was agreed. The first condition for the renaissance of socialism had been achieved.[187]

The second condition was the unequivocal commitment of socialism to liberty in the Republic. The reconstituted Socialist party pursued a double strategy. On the one hand, it opted to reconstruct the unity of the left, in alliance with the Communists, and played on the collective memory of the Revolution; on the other, in engaged in a drawn-out struggle with the Communists for the votes of those on the Left, predicting that success would go to whichever party projected itself most successfully as the defender of democracy and liberty. As the PCF reeled under the impact of the publication of Solzhenitsyn's *Gulag Archipelago* in France, Mitterrand set off briskly for the moral high ground of Blum and Jaurès. He argued that 'the true heirs of the Declaration of the Rights of Man and the Citizen are the French socialists. For them, a repressive society cannot be socialist.' Making it clear that he was opposed to the dictatorship of privileged economic groups, he also insisted, 'I recognise no other mission for socialism than organising society to liberate the individual.'[187] He quoted Léon Blum's attack on Marcel Cachin at the Congress of Tours for erecting terror into a system of government, and thus in the same breath echoed Jaurès' attack on Guesde and Quinet's attack on Jacobinism.

For the elections of 1978, Mitterrand was sold as no less than the heir of Jaurès. 'But, Jean Jaurès, there is no longer any need to fear for liberty in France,' Mitterrand congratulated himself in *Demain, Jaurès*, 'the Socialist party is there as its guarantor.'[188] The espousal of democratic socialism paid off. In the first round of the elections of 1978 the Socialists won more of the popular vote than the Communists for the first time since the war. Playing on the slogan 'La Force tranquille', Mitterrand was elected president of the Republic as the candidate of a united Left on 10 May 1981 and immediately held fresh elections to secure a majority of the Left in the National Assembly. On 21 May, following his inauguration, he climbed the steps of the Panthéon alone to lay a red rose on the tomb of Jean Jaurès; he sent an aide to lay another on that of the more controversial Léon Blum.[189] The right-wing press attempted to discredit the Socialists meeting in congress in Valence in October 1981 by calling it the 'tranquil Terror', suggesting that 'it resembled the September massacres', with delegates calling for heads to roll, and characterising Paul Quilès as 'Robespaul' or 'Robespierre in a suit'.[190] But it was on the Communists, not on the Socialists, that accusations of Jacobin dictatorship would now stick.

While the Socialists projected themselves as the defenders of liberty in the Republic, the Communist party was beginning to suffer the electoral consequences of its adherence to the doctrines of violent revolution, class struggle and the dictatorship of the proletariat. To be fair, after the mass strikes and demonstrations of 1968 and under pressure from the Socialists to negotiate a common programme, the Communists did start to revise some of their old doctrines. Engels was pillaged for a ruling that 'the time for armed coups, for revolutions carried out by small conscious minorities at the head of the unconscious masses is over'.[191] Blanquism was discredited, and the rigid Marxist view of class struggle required adaptation. The movement of students, teachers and workers forced the PCF to recognise that those oppressed by monopoly capitalism now included not only the working class but 'engineers, technicians, researchers, teachers, artisans, shopkeepers, and small peasants', who made up 'two thirds of the active population'. The breadth of this social constellation offered the possibility of a majority being achieved under a democratic system, leading to what the PCF called a first stage of 'advanced democracy'. The next stage of socialist revolution might yet be achieved by 'pacific means', as democratic assemblies were put under pressure by 'the diverse mass actions of the working class and the broadest strata of the people'. But there was still talk of a 'revolutionary leap', and the possibility of violence was not excluded if the dominant classes used force to defend their privileges.[192] Most important, it was not until the 22nd congress of the PCF in 1976, meeting under the slogan 'A democratic path to socialism', that the party abandoned the doctrine of the dictatorship of the proletariat. Dictatorship, Communists conceded, was a term in bad odour after the Nazi experience. 'At each stage,' clarified secretary–general Georges Marchais, 'we will respect and ensure respect for the choices of our people freely expressed by universal suffrage.'[193]

This evolution did not resolve the Communist party's problems. If it were to participate in the mainstream of republican politics, it had to commit itself to a legal and democratic, not violent, path to power, and to the principle of a plurality of parties alternating in power according to the verdict of the electorate, not refusing to relinquish it once they had won power. But it also needed to maintain a specific revolutionary identity in order to distinguish itself from the Socialist party, to provide a platform from which to criticise it, and to ensure that its supporters continued to think along class lines. The contradiction between these two positions was revealed by the attitude of the PCF to the collapse of Communism in Eastern Europe and Russia, and in the incoherence of its handling of the collective memory of the Revolution.

For the benefit of a wider public, Georges Marchais gave the impression that the PCF would learn lessons from the collapse of Communism in the Eastern

bloc: 'Any socialist country that falls behind in the necessary renewal of socialist society taking into account changes not only worldwide but also changes at
home, will pay the price sooner or later.'[194] Likewise he noted that changes in
Eastern Europe went 'in exactly the same direction' as the French Communist
conception of socialism.[195] Nevertheless, he used every means in his power in
the PCF to keep down Communist reformists, led by Charles Fiterman, who
had held office in the 1981 government, and who argued that the PCF had
entirely failed the challenge of democratisation in both its outlook and internal
organisation. Not for nothing did Marchais earn the reputation as the last of the
Mohicans or the last Stalinist in Europe, surviving even Ceaucescu.

The incoherence of the Communists party's handling of the Revolution for
its own political purposes could be traced back to the 1930s, but by the 1980s
the dilemma looked insoluble. On the one hand, the Communists adopted the
cult of 1789 to stay in the mainstream of republican politics, and to maintain the
possibility of an alliance with other parties of the Left. On the other, they
prioritised the period of the Jacobin dictatorship and mobilised the memory of
working class revolutions as a weapon to attack the Socialist party for its
abandonment of revolutionary policies and its strategy under the premiership
of Michel Rocard of seeking an 'opening' to the centre and offering portfolios
to centrist politicians.

Thus the 24th party congress of 1982 inaugurated a Communism 'in the
colours of France', those of 1789, the tricolour, and liberty.[196] But in 1984,
mortified by the hegemony of the Socialist-led government in which they were
very much junior parties, they left the government and tried to prise away from
the Socialists what they considered to be the disillusioned working-class vote
by reviving the tactic of 1920s of the 'united front from below'. To this end,
they highlighted the problem of unemployment and appealed to the Marxist
doctrine of class struggle.[197] The approach of the Bicentenary of the French
Revolution only served to sharpen the dilemma. At the Fête de l'Humanité in
September 1988, the centre-piece was an exhibition of the tricolour in French
painting, with a programme prefaced by Georges Marchais recalling the moment in 1935 when the Communist party hailed the tricolour as well as the red
flag, the *Marseillaise* as well as the *Internationale*. However, reproductions of
the bust of Saint-Just by David d'Angers did a roaring trade, supported by a
pamphlet urging 'Réhabiliter Saint-Just'. On 14 July 1989 the cover of
L'Humanité represented the folds of the tricolour, and the editorial of Georges
Marchais paid homage to the Declaration of the Rights of Man. But the main
story, the campaign to reinstate ten sacked Renault workers from Billancourt,
developed the rhetoric of class war. Morever, in his book seductively entitled
Démocratie, published in 1990, Marchais insisted, 'Yes, the class struggle is still
with us . . . I doubt that the French bourgeoisie is "the most stupid in the
world", but I am sure that it is one of the most savage and ruthless.' This he felt
was evidenced by the massacres it perpetrated in Lyon in 1831, in Paris in June
1848 and May 1871, and in numerous colonial wars.[198] This is not to say that

handling of the collective memory of the Revolution by republicans, radicals and socialists had not been complex before. But the PCF could no longer wave the spectre of counter-revolution, as in the 1930s, because its main enemy was not the Right, but the Socialist party. And to fall back on the heroes of 1793 and the rhetoric of class war was to retreat to a position that had been marginalised by politicians, the media and revisionist historians alike.

The contention of this chapter is that struggles between Left and Right in French history may be understood only in the light of their appeals to the Revolution to define, bind and legitimate contending political communities. The task of each political community was to develop an interpretation of the Revolution that sustained its goals, and to universalise that interpretation while attacking the legitimacy of rival interpretations. Movements and régimes which did not subscribe to the principles of the Revolution, such as ultra-royalism or Vichy, were delegitimised and rejected. There were, however, two basic problems about recourse to the Revolution for legitimacy. First, the Revolution could be used to defend any movement from liberal to Communist, every régime from constitutional monarchy to popular dictatorship. A liberal régime that appealed to the principles of the Revolution but attempted to harness them in defence of moderation, gave a hostage to radical movements which would accuse it of Thermidoreanism, of betraying the Revolution, and in turn use the Revolution to sanction more extreme political solutions. Successive revolutions in 1830, 1848, 1871, 1917 and 1944 paid homage to the great Revolution but reinterpreted it in order to legitimate more radical political ends. The revolutionary slogan equality, for example, might be limited to civic or political equality, or else be used to justify social equality. To make a hero out of Mirabeau or Condorcet implied quite different political choices from making one out of Robespierre or Hébert. Second, however, if the Revolution were constructed not as a set of principles found out by reason but as the purveyor of violence, Terror and dictatorship, it could be turned against those who subscribed to its principles by those who wanted the Revolution to stop or wished that it had never started in the first place. Thus the Right, by focusing on revolutionary violence and the Vendée in particular, sought to discredit the Left which preached a utopian vision of the Revolution. Within the revolutionary tradition, moderates accused radicals of justifying the Terror of 1793 in order to discredit them and prevent the political process lurching to the left. And successive waves of radicals were torn between cultivating the more extreme phases and leaders of the Revolution in order to define themselves against the moderates and establish their revolutionary credentials, and the risk being deprived of legitimacy as apologists of the Terror.

CHAPTER 2

Bonapartism

Shaping the Bonapartist Myth

Throughout the day of 18 June 1990 a large replica of an early radio set erected at the place de la Concorde broadcast the appeal that General de Gaulle had made to the French nation from the BBC in London on 18 June 1940. The following day the text of the appeal, engraved in bronze, was unveiled at the Arc de Triomphe by President Mitterrand.[1] The fact that in 1940 few people had heard the original broadcast, as the French had fled before the advancing German army, did not seem to matter. The Gaullist moment had been constructed as a myth almost from the beginning. It was significant also that homage was paid to de Gaulle by his former political enemy, François Mitterrand. It was a tribute to the power of the Gaullist myth to command universal recognition, and in particular to its ability to draw selectively on the culture of Bonapartism, appropriating its positive aspects while freeing itself of its negative connotations.

The Gaullist myth was constructed on three pillars. First, de Gaulle was presented as a charismatic and providential figure who had saved France in her hour of need in 1940, and restored national integrity, popular sovereignty and the Republic. Second, he was credited with re-establishing the unity of the nation after four years of division and civil war. Third, he was held to be responsible, if not at the first attempt, for freeing French political life from the anarchy of parties and parliamentary government, and for the strengthening of the French state under a presidential constitution.

The relationship of the Gaullist myth with Bonapartism was ambivalent. It developed the myth built around Napoleon I and Napoleon III of the saviour of the nation, chosen by the people, architect of a strong state and national unity over and above the divisiveness of party. It also, however, struggled to shake off the taboos that had blighted the Bonapartist tradition, and handicapped and finally doomed the Bonapartes themselves. For while the legacy of Bonapartism was glorious, it also nourished fears—of the illegal seizure of power by coup d'état, of the destruction of the Republic and the usurpation of monarchical authority, of the extinction of liberty under despotic rule, of siding with the cause of counter-revolution against the Revolution, and of leading France to national disaster at Waterloo or Sedan. To succeed, in short, Gaullism was required to reconstruct the collective memory of Bonapartism in order to render it beneficial rather than harmful to its cause. The skill of de Gaulle was to give France the elements of the Bonapartist system which inspired the French people, while laying to rest the nightmares that tormented them.[2]

Napoleon Bonaparte may be seen as one of the revolutionary brothers of the 1790s who founded the fraternal association of the Republic, but who was not content with his equal share of sovereign power. After a fratricidal struggle, he seized power by the coup d'état of 18 *brumaire* Year VIII (9 November 1799) against the parliamentary institutions of the Republic, and set himself apart with supreme powers as First Consul under constitution of the Year VIII (1800). The coup of *brumaire* was not regarded at the time as a political offence that deprived him of all legitimacy. Between 1795 and 1799 the Directory which Bonaparte displaced had organised several coups against parliament when elections returned or threatened to return majorities hostile to it. More-over, the revolutionary principle of the sovereignty of the people was not violated but formally endorsed by dispensing with a constituent assembly and submitting a new constitution directly to the people for approval by plebiscite. Finally, as Napoleon explained in the *Memorial* dictated in exile on St Helena, 'the fact is that without us the country was done for and we saved it'.[3]

The problem of legitimacy was nevertheless central to Bonapartism. As a general thrown up by the Revolution, Bonaparte could legitimate his power only by reference to a popular mandate. Yet that popular mandate was un-stable, and the Bourbon dynasty, supported by the coalition of France's en-emies, kept the threat of monarchist restoration constant. Gingerly, therefore, Bonaparte constructed a monarchy for himself. Napoleon Bonaparte became Napoleon I. Firstly, in 1802, he became consul for life. Then in 1804 he boldly assumed the royal robes of the deposed dynasty, and became hereditary em-peror. His assumption of the crown was doubly problematic. It was denounced as usurpation by those faithful to the Bourbons, a crime far worse than his coup against the assembly, and as the assassination of the Republic by those who looked on him as the saviour of the Revolution. As hereditary emperor Napoleon still claimed to be a delegate of the sovereign people, in that the hereditary law was put to a plebiscite (a score of under 3 millions being massaged up to 3,578,898). The instrument of the Senate, which defined the formula for official texts on 28 *floréal* Year XII, suggested that the Republic was still intact, referring to 'Napoleon, by the grace of God and the constitutions of the Republic, Emperor of the French'.[4] Briefly, divine right was balanced by democratic right. But divine right superseded democratic right at Napoleon's coronation in Notre-Dame on 2 December 1804, as he stood in the presence of the pope adorned by the regalia of Charlemagne (in replica, the originals having been sold in 1798). From now on Napoleon referred to the French as his subjects rather than as citizens. The *Imperial Catechism* which replaced all diocesan catechisms in the Empire stated that the Emperor was to be obeyed 'because God, who creates empires and arranges them according to his will, by showering our emperor with gifts in both peace and war, has made him our sovereign, minister of his power and his image on earth'.[5] In order to gain access to the international cartel of legitimate monarchs and establish an imperial succession, Bonaparte divorced Josephine, the former mistress of his revolutionary patron Barras, and in 1810 married Marie-Louise, the daughter of the Austrian emperor. The birth of a male heir, given the title 'Roi de Rome', seemed to assure the future of the hereditary empire.

If one dilemma faced by Napoleon and his heirs was that of legitimacy, a second was the place given to liberty. 'In the last fifty years', Bonaparte wrote to Talleyrand in 1797, 'we have clearly defined only one thing, the sovereignty of the people, but . . . the organisation of the French people has scarcely even begun.'[6] The revolutionaries clearly established the theoretical principle that power derived from the people. But in Bonaparte's eyes they failed to move successfully to the next stage, the organisation of that power. After the experience of monarchy, the revolutionaries had a deep fear of executive power and concentrated all power in the legislature; the Committee of Public Safety had been merely a committee of the Convention parliament. Similarly, they argued that democracy required that all offices be elective, and all elected officers should be responsible to the sovereign people. Bonaparte distinguished between formal sovereignty and the organisation of power. He strengthened the executive at the expense of representative bodies, and developed a bureaucracy in which offices were appointive and officers responsible to their hierarchical superiors.

At the summit of his power in Europe, Napoleon exercised what was in effect a dictatorship. The police force was developed and refined, soldiers sat alongside civilian judges in the courts, press censorship was tightened, representative institutions ceased to meet, constitutions issued to satellite states remained on paper, and states with autonomous governments were brought under the direct rule of Paris. Napoleon earned himself the enduring hostility of the political class. But as his military power crumbled after the invasion of Russia, the political class took its revenge. The Legislative Body and the Senate for the first time showed signs of life and deposed the emperor. The Restoration was as much a restoration of liberty as of the Bourbon monarchy. Though Louis XVIII rejected the constitution proposed by the Senate, he was constrained to grant more power to representative bodies in the Charter he himself issued. On his return from Elba in 1815, Napoleon was obliged to accommodate the political class, and with the Charter under its belt, it would not compromise on free institutions. He therefore invited the liberal leader Benjamin Constant to the Tuileries. 'Let me have your ideas', he invited Constant. 'Free elections, public discussions, responsible ministers, all that I want. Especially the liberty of the press: to stifle it is absurd.'[7] With Constant's help, Napoleon drew up the

Additional Act to the constitutions of the Empire, which defined a more liberal, parliamentary Empire, and put it to a plebiscite.[8] More significant, given the swift intervention of Waterloo, was the effort to create the myth that Napoleon was a champion of liberty. The conversation with Constant, relayed by Constant in his *Mémoires sur les Cent Jours*, published in 1819, was eagerly taken up and quoted verbatim by Napoleon in his *Memorial*, in order to rebut charges of dictatorship repeatedly made against him by liberals.

A third claim put forward by Napoleon on St Helena was that he healed the divisions wrought by the French Revolution and restored union and harmony to the French nation. The Emperor was a consummate politician: he judged that republicans and royalists could not be reconciled within a representative system, for free elections encouraged a climate of civil war, and rigged elections, coups and purges provoked insurrection by the aggrieved party. Reconciliation therefore took place under an authoritarian system in which offices, honours and symbolic gestures were distributed equitably to each side without any concession of attendant political power. Both republicans and royalists were appointed prefects, bishops and generals under what Napoleon called his 'system of fusion'.[9] Emigré royalists were amnestied and allowed to return, and the festival of 21 January, anniversary of the King's execution, and the oath of hatred of the monarchy were abolished in an attempt to weaken memories of regicide in the Revolution. At the same time, the comte de Provence, brother of Louis XVI and the future Louis XVIII, was told bluntly, 'You should not hope to return to France; you would have to walk over 100,000 corpses.'[10] Likewise, Napoleon endorsed the principles of 1789, retained the festivals of 14 July and 21 September (date of the proclamation of the Republic) and enshrined the abolition of privilege in the Code Civil of 1804. But he would have nothing to do with the cult of 1793 and dealt severely with revolutionaries who challenged his political power. He blamed Jacobins and anarchists for an attempt to blow him up on Christmas Eve 1800, in order to execute or deport batches of them, even though the attack was unquestionably mounted by counter-revolutionaries.

In fact, it was almost impossible for Napoleon effectively to marry revolutionary and counter-revolutionary. The fault-line in French society ran too deep. Those who shared the Emperor's revolutionary origins were alienated by his grasping for personal power and ultimate abolition of the Republic. When he made himself consul for life, one of his councillors of state, Thibaudeau, told Josephine, 'the more power he receives, the more he will alienate his true supporters, the men of the Revolution'.[11] When he became emperor, Thibaudeau asked, 'Was it to go backwards that the Nation launched itself into a new path which it soaked with its purest blood? Are we no more than slaves in revolt who have been forced to reforge with our own hands the chains that we broke?'[12] A republican general, Moreau, who described himself as a 'brother-in-arms' of Bonaparte, was so incensed by such betrayal that he threw in his lot with royalist conspirators.[13] Evidence of Bonaparte's sense of guilt is manifest in that while he was keen to see the royalists executed, he commuted Moreau's sentence to banishment, and Moreau went to live in the United States.

There is, however, little evidence to suggest that those who regretted the Revolution rallied in large numbers to the Napoleonic régime. Though Napoleon as emperor established a court and an imperial nobility, most of the old nobility shunned the court and refused to exchange their Bourbon titles for imperial ones. In the *Memorial*, destined for a royalist audience, Napoleon expressed his regrets that he had not been able to stop the Revolution sooner, but pointed out that the tide of revolutionary opinion had been too powerful. He blamed Talleyrand for preventing him from consummating his marriage with the old nobility of the faubourg Saint-Germain. As a pledge of his commitment to royalism, he recalled that at the end of his reign he had plans to convert the Madeleine from a Temple de la Gloire to a chapel to house the remains of Louis XVI and Marie Antoinette.[14]

The impossibility of building a bridge between revolutionary and counter-revolutionary elements was never more obvious than during the Hundred Days. As Napoleon landed at Cannes and marched through Grenoble and Lyon to Paris, he encountered massive support among soldiers and peasants who feared the restoration of feudal dues and tithes and regarded the emperor as the implacable enemy of privilege.[15] He told Benjamin Constant that

> the people, or if you prefer, the multitude, wants none but me . . . I am not only as has been said, 'the soldiers' Emperor', I am the Emperor of the French peasants and plebeians. See the people come back to me in spite of what has happened . . . the popular fibre answers my own . . . I have only to make a sign, or rather avert my gaze, and the nobility would be massacred in every province. . . . But I do not wish to be the king of a *jacquerie*.[16]

This latent support was given some articulation in May 1815 by the spontaneous formation of units of *fédérés* who sought to infiltrate the National Guard. Swearing fidelity to the Emperor and the Empire, they set out to prevent a second restoration of the Bourbon dynasty, together with the old nobility, feudalism, tithes and a state church. They regarded the Empire as the instrument by which the Revolution had been consolidated and wanted Napoleon to take on the profile of a revolutionary Emperor. In some parts of France, the *fédérés* were overwhelmingly middle class, but in Paris the 14,000 *fédérés tirailleurs* of the city were drawn from the popular classes. Fearful of a *jacquerie*, Napoleon was reluctant to arm them and the National Guard remained responsible for public order in the capital. Though the *fédérés-tirailleurs* were his most fervent supporters in the capital, and defended the fortifications they had built against the oncoming Allies, Napoleon refused to use them for a final coup against the assemblies, and abdicated instead.[17]

The flaw in Napoleon's position was thus exposed. An emperor of the people only in theory, he was concerned above all to reconcile the republican and royalist halves of the propertied and educated class. 'Bonaparte has rallied the landowning and educated class against the multitude', wrote a future speaker of the Legislative Body in 1802.[18] Yet the propertied and educated class now espoused the monarchy as the guarantor of its liberty, and though Napoleon persuaded parliament to proclaim his son Napoleon II, they did so only as a means to remove him from the country and to bring back Louis XVIII. If the popular fibre responded to that of Napoleon, it was only on the battlefield and in the occasional plebiscite. It was not Napoleon but his nephew, Louis-Napoleon, who was to realise that it was necessary fully to exploit the popular appeal of Bonapartism, that it was unwise to play fast and loose with the gains of the Revolution, and that true national union was to be achieved not at the level of the propertied and educated class but in the bosom of the masses.

After the death of Napoleon II in Austrian captivity in 1832, the mantle of Bonapartism was taken up by Louis-Napoleon, son of Napoleon's brother Louis, king of Holland, who assumed the position of heir. His early writings, in support of somewhat rash actions, amounted to a major reshaping of the Bonapartist myth, designed to appeal to the republican opposition to the July Monarchy, presenting the emperor as a true man of the people and one who reconciled the nation without betraying his revolutionary origins.

In 1836, when he tried to raise the Strasbourg garrison in revolt, Louis-Napoleon issued a proclamation to the French people. Like the republicans, he argued that the French people who had made the Revolution of 1830 had been betrayed; parliamentary intriguers had stitched up a monarchical settlement without consulting the nation. But he went on to argue that Napoleon was the people's choice and that the pact between the people and Napoleon and his heirs made by the plebiscite of 1804 was still intact. If power had ever been usurped it was not by Napoleon but by the monarchists of 1830. Louis-Napoleon therefore offered himself to the nation 'the will of Napoleon in one hand and the sword of Austerlitz in the other'.[19] The fact that Napoleon had gone on to make himself a hereditary monarch, affirmed Louis-Napoleon, in no sense invalidated his popular mandate. As emperor, Napoleon remained 'the elect of the people, the representative of the nation', and his fibre had answered to that of the people.[20] For himself, his principles were 'entirely republican', but 'if, in my projected constitution I prefer the monarchical form of government, it is because I think it suits France best, in that it would give more guarantees of peace, order and liberty'.[21]

Louis-Napoleon was keen to dispel the view that that Napoleon had betrayed the Revolution, arguing that he was a truly national figure but was always faithful to the Revolution. He quoted Napoleon telling his Conseil d'Etat, 'To govern through a party is to become dependent on it sooner or later. No one will get the better of me that way: I am national.' Louis-Napoleon was particularly keen to demonstrate for the benefit of those who criticised Napoleon for his courting of royalists that 'everything he did to undertake a general fusion was done without renouncing the principles of the Revolution'.[22] The Catholic

Church and the émigrés were reconciled without calling into question liberty of conscience and sold *biens nationaux*, and titles of nobility were granted without restoring privilege.

The most difficult task faced by Louis-Napoleon was to persuade doubters that Napoleon was the friend of liberty, and his heirs likewise. It was a point to which he constantly returned. 'The Emperor Napoleon has done more than anyone else to accelerate the reign of liberty', he stated baldly in *Des Idées napoléoniennes*.[23] 'If one day peoples are free, they will owe it to Napoleon,' he wrote in 1832. 'Do not hold his dictatorship against him: it was leading to liberty, as the iron ploughshare making furrows prepares the fertility of the land.'[24] Arguing that mammoth tasks imposed by constant war had prevented Napoleon from conceding as much liberty as he would have wished, he added that

If he had been victorious, we would have seen the Grand Duchy of Warsaw become the Polish nation, Westphalia become the German nation, the viceroyalty of Italy become the Italian nation. In France a liberal régime would have replaced the dictatorial régime; everywhere there would have been stability, liberty and independence, instead of incomplete nations and transitory institutions.[25]

Louis-Napoleon attacked those who felt that liberty was well provided for under the constitutional monarchy by pointing out that it was the liberty of the few; suffrage was restricted, and the people would not be free until they all had the vote. Liberty was thus equated with universal suffrage, of which he was a champion.

In 1840 Louis-Napoleon tried to repeat his uncle's 'Vol de l'Aigle' of 1815 by landing at Boulogne with a few supporters. But Boulogne was not Cannes and Louis-Napoleon was captured, tried and imprisoned. The popular appeal of the Bonapartism he refined was manifested not through madcap adventures but legally, after the establishment of universal manhood suffrage by the Second Republic in 1848. Following the election of the National Assembly at Easter 1848, Louis-Napoleon stood in by-elections in four departments (Seine, Yonne, Charente-Inférieure, Corsica) in June 1848 and was elected to the Assembly. The completion of a constitution that provided for the election of the president of the Republic by direct universal suffrage gave him an unri-valled opportunity for achieving power, and on 10 December 1848 he was elected president with 5.5 million votes, nearly 75 per cent of the votes cast.[26]

Marx attributed this landslide to the backwardness and illiteracy of a suddenly enfranchised peasant population.[27] But the mass of the population which had been excluded from political life since 1815 had no reason to vote for monarchists or republicans who represented the same political class. His appeal to the masses was based in part on the concrete proposals of *The Abolition of Poverty*, which he had written in prison, announcing that 'today the reign of castes is finished, you have to govern with the masses', and arguing that the working classes must be allowed to organise themselves in order to acquire property.[28] The socialist Pierre-Joseph Proudhon, who was elected to the National Assembly for the Seine in a by-election on the same day as Louis-Napoleon, recognised the importance of this text.

> The abolition of poverty means the emancipation of the proletariat; it means the right to work, society turned upside down. In a word, Bonaparte has done no more than Raspail or Ledru-Rollin [the two left-wing candidates] to win votes, he has turned into a socialist. That is what the peasants and workers who gave their votes to Louis-Napoleon have understood.[29]

There was, however, another explanation for the popular appeal of Louis-Napoleon: that he was portrayed as the revolutionary Napoleon of the people who had been the idol of the *fédérés* of 1815. Enthusiasm for the name of Napoleon was the same in 1848 as it had been in 1815, and often in the same areas, such as the Dauphiné or Burgundy. After the by-election victory in the Yonne a republican newspaper asked,

> What mysterious genie had breathed this illustrious name into the ears of our rural population while they slept? . . . Their minds have focused on the memory of the Emperor, whose name is still worshipped in our cottages.[30]

Louis-Napoleon exploited this popular appeal at the moment of his coup d'état against the Assembly on 2 December 1851. The Assembly had opposed both his scheme to revise the constitution to permit him to run for a second term in office, and to abrogate the law it had passed on 31 May 1850, disfranchising three million of the poorest electors in a bid to check the tide of Montagnard by-election victories. Louis-Napoleon dissolved the Assembly, but at the same time proclaimed the restoration of univeral suffrage and gave power back to the people to ratify or reject a new constitution. Though this coup was denounced as a violation of the constitution by republicans and liberals, and a republican representative of the people, Baudin, who died on the barricades, was at once declared a martyr to the republican cause, it was in many ways a popular move. The coup dissolved an Assembly dominated by monarchists who had abolished universal suffrage. Louis-Napoleon claimed that he was defending the Republic against monarchist plots, not attacking it, and he re-established universal suffrage not only to allow the people to judge between the Assembly and himself, but as the means of electing future legislative assemblies, something which had not been conceded by his uncle. Prominent politicians were arrested but Victor Hugo, waving his representative's scarf from a carriage window on the place de la Bastille, met with no response.[31] The working-class suburbs of Paris welcomed the restoration of universal suffrage and took no small pleasure in the discomfiture of the politicians. Some historians have pointed to insurrection in the south-east of France as evidence of popular opposition to the coup.[32] But an alternative explanation asserts that risings in departments such as the Drôme and the Ardèche were *in support* of

Louis-Napoleon and against the politicians who were locally trying to frustate his victory.[33] Moreover, the plebiscite on the heads of the constitution on 20 December 1851 was endorsed by 7.5 million voters. It showed a decline in conservative support for Napoleon but a strengthening in left-wing, democratic socialist departments.[34]

The new constitution provided for a head of state with a ten-year mandate, like the first consul under that of the Year VIII. At this point Louis-Napoleon confronted the question of the succession that had tormented his uncle. To restore the Empire and the Bonaparte dynasty was perhaps a less serious business than to found it in the first place, but he was careful to lay the groundwork for restoration. He spent the summer of 1852 on a provincial tour, encouraging manifestations of support for a Second Empire. He was warmly greeted by the textile workers of Reims, the miners of the Loire, and the silk–workers of Lyon, though as often as not he was met with coolness from the bourgeoisie. The Empire was established by an instrument of the Senate, which was received from a delegation of senators to the palace of Saint-Cloud, where Napoleon had himself received a similar delegation in 1804. But to preserve the formality of popular sovereignty, it was put to a plebiscite on 21–22 November 1852, and approved by almost eight million votes. According to the Bonapartist fetish for symbolic dates, the Empire was proclaimed on 2 December, anniversary of Napoleon's coronation and of Austerlitz, which the coup of 1851 had already marked.

Like Napoleon, Louis-Napoleon was anxious to present himself as a national leader, beholden to no particular party. Since the Republic had been re-established in 1848, it was important in his early campaigns to give firm guarantees of his republicanism. Newspapers that supported him in the by-elections of June 1848 carried such titles as *Napoléon républicain* and *L'Aigle républicain*. 'I have never believed and will never believe,' he stated, 'that France should be the apanage of one man or one family. . . . Nothing has changed in France, there is just one more republican.'[35] Proudhon argued that Louis-Napoleon wielded enormous authority over the Montagne. 'Louis-Napoleon put the democratic and social republic into his pocket,' he argued after the presidential election of 10 December 1848. 'In three days he became more powerful than his uncle, the Emperor, had been made by fifty victories.'[36]

Louis-Napoleon was, however, also presented as a guarantor of property and stability, particularly after the working-class insurrection of the June Days, 1848. He was proffered as the candidate of those who opposed the Republic of February, and one who could combine the votes of the competing royalist camps, Orleanist and Legitimist. Later in the campaign, he took votes from his main rival, the republican Cavaignac, who had crushed the June insurrection, on the grounds that he was not conservative enough.[37] He was backed by the 'party of order', steered by the Committee of the rue de Poitiers, of whom the leading figure was Adolphe Thiers.

As president of the Republic, Louis-Napoleon was nevertheless kept under control by the party politicians. Thiers dismissed him as 'a cretin whom we will manage'.[38] 'From the first days after the election,' recalled Louis-Napoleon's close collaborator Persigny, 'M. Thiers spun his web around the Emperor's nephew.' He had to accept ministers from the Orleanist, Legitimist and republican parties; his first prime minister, Odilon Barrot, was Louis-Philippe's last. 'The only aim of M. Thiers', continued Persigny, 'was to make the victor of the 10 December dependent on the Assembly, to garrotte him with an iron parliamentary collar.'[39] This was all the easier after the legislative elections of May 1849, which returned a royalist majority. In danger of becoming a slave of party, Louis-Napoleon appealed over the heads of the politicians to the country. He had no party base of his own. The short-lived Society of 10 December was dissolved on his orders after the presidential election. He set out to project himself as the focus of national unity, over and above political parties, and in the summer of 1849 he made a tour of the provinces. He opened railway lines and visited great industrial and commercial centres such as Rouen, Le Havre, Nantes and Lyon to develop the theme of prosperity as a factor of reconciliation in a divided France. At Sens, chief town of the Yonne, he thanked the electors for their support the previous year, and for their understanding that 'as a stranger to all parties I was hostile to none of them, and . . . could serve as a rallying point when the parties seemed to be tearing each other apart'.[40]

In the end, Louis-Napoleon was obliged to break the grip not only of party, but of parliament as well. Like his uncle, he saw that free elections only exacerbated the conflict between royalists and republicans, and that a strong and independent executive was required to hold the ring above faction. Promulgating the new constitution on 14 January 1852, he asked, 'Since France has functioned for the last fifty years only by virtue of the administrative, military, judicial, religious and financial organisation of the Consulate and Empire, why do we not also adopt the political institutions of that period?'[41] This was a somewhat naïve and rhetorical question, because while there had been a general consensus since 1815 among both royalists and republicans about the institutions of the centralised state, there was no consensus as to how political power should be organised. Moreover, the constitution of 1852 was designed explicitly to weaken the political class, republican or royalist, which required a free press, free political meetings, free elections and ministers responsible to parliament, none of which obtained. Since no Bonapartist party existed, it was the task of prefects to manage elections by fair means or foul to secure the return of official candidates, who were selected as far as possible from outside the ranks of professional politicians, for instance among the business community.

There was, however, a limit to how authoritarian the régime could be. 'You can suppress a riot with soldiers and make an election with peasants,' observed the former Orleanist statesman, François Guizot, 'but soldiers and peasants are not sufficient to govern. You need the support of the upper classes, who are the natural governing classes.'[42] So long as the political class was divided, between republican and royalist, Napoleon III could defy it and ignore its liberal demands. But in 1863 a Liberal Union was formed between Orleanists, Legitimists and republicans, obliging Napoleon to concede a freer press and public meetings. As a result, in 1869 the opposition sharply reduced the official majority in the legislative elections. The question now was whether the Empire could become more parliamentary or liberal without falling into the hands of the royalists on the one hand, or the republicans on the other. Towards the end of that year Napoleon asked Emile Ollivier, a republican who had accepted the form of the Empire but wished to liberalise its content, to form a ministry. A liberal constitution, echoing the Additional Act, was drafted, and a plebiscite on 8 May 1870 endorsed it with 7.35 million votes. 'The Empire is stronger than ever,' confessed Gambetta.[43] The main problem, however, was that it was difficult to translate the mass of unorganised opinion in the country into a coherent ministry or a reliable parliamentary majority. Orleanists resigned from the ministry because they regarded the constitution as insufficiently parliamentary. Hard-line Bonapartists like Granier de Cassagnac fought rearguard actions against what they saw as creeping parliamentarism. To present himself as a national leader, Napoleon III was obliged to eschew the formation of a Bonapartist party. As a result there was no majority for the ministry in the Legislative Body. The only issue that commanded majority support in the house was war against Prussia.

The defeat of France at Sedan destroyed the Second Empire as Waterloo had destroyed the First, and almost destroyed Bonapartism. Only nineteen Bonapartist deputies were returned to the National Assembly in 1871. But the Bonapartist press, spearheaded by *Le Pays* of Paul de Cassagnac, returned to the issue of legitimacy and argued that Bonapartist claims were still intact. Just as Louis-Napoleon had argued that the pact of the emperor with the people in 1804 had survived the usurpations of 1814–15 and 1830, so Bonapartists now argued that the pact with the people of 8 May 1870 was still in force. The republicans had perpetrated a coup d'état on 4 September 1870, and the National Assembly, elected in 1871 to ratify the peace with Germany, had usurped powers to which it had no right to make a constitution.[44] If this argument were not accepted at face value, then another plebiscite should be held, and the choice between monarchy, republic or empire put squarely to the popular vote. A Comité de l'Appel au Peuple was founded by the Bonapartists in 1872 to campaign for this solution.[45]

The argument that only the Empire could reconcile a divided France had some force in the early years of the Third Republic, when republicans and royalists were at daggers drawn and the survival of the régime remained uncertain. Napoleon III died at Camden House, Chislehurst, in 1873, and speaking there on the first anniversary of his death his son, the prince imperial, stated that a plebiscite would open the way to 'a great national party, composed neither of victors nor of vanquished, rising above everyone to reconcile them'.[46] But the very success of the Bonapartists in by-elections for the National Assembly in 1874–5, betraying the persistent force of latent Bonapartism, drove the political class together. Moderate republicans and Orleanists combined in the Assembly to vote a constitution that was above all anti-Bonapartist. The president of the Republic would be elected not directly by the people, as in 1848, but indirectly by the Senate and the Chamber of Deputies meeting together, presumably a seasoned politician from their own ranks. Moreover, he would not be able to dissolve the Chamber, as in 1851, without the authorisation of the Senate.

Bonapartists thrived on the disunity of the political class. The new-found unity of the political class in the elaboration of a parliamentary constitution had the effect of exposing the fact that Bonapartism, though it may have articulated a consensus in the bosom of the nation, was divided at the level of party politics into a left and a right. Each wing had a quite different view of what the Empire stood for. The right wing, led by Paul de Cassagnac, placed the dynasty above all else, had nothing but contempt for the Republic and advocated an alliance with the royalists to stop the republicans taking power.[47] When on 16 May 1877 President MacMahon looked to the Senate for authorisation to prorogue the republican Chamber, Bonapartist senators gave the president the majority he needed.[48] Bonapartism was once again compromised by identification with what was a coup d'état against the spirit if not the letter of the constitution.

This alliance with royalists and sanction of a coup d'état appalled the left wing of Bonapartists. Insisting that 'the Empire is not conservative', they argued that the elections of 1876 (which returned only ninety-four Bonpartists) should be interpreted as a plebiscite that endorsed the Republic.[49] For them, the way ahead was not to support the Empire or bust, but to accept the republican régime while seeking to win over republicans who were disaffected with the parliamentary system in order to form a majority in favour of the revision of the constitution. This shelving of the imperial principle and commitment without ambivalence to the authority of popular sovereignty was a turning-point in the history of Bonapartism. It dissociated the important issue of whether France should have a liberal or an authoritarian constitution from the more contentious issue of whether France should be a Republic or a hereditary Empire. In doing so, it gave the left wing of Bonapartism a flexibility and resourcefulness that the right wing could not match.

It was nevertheless one thing to deal with the question of heredity in theory, as a question of policy, and another to cope with the Bonaparte family. The prince imperial died in 1879, trying to establish a military reputation fighting the Zulus. After his death it would not be unfair to say that the Bonaparte family was an embarrassment to the cause. The head of the family was now Jérôme-Napoleon, son of King Jérôme of Westphalia and cousin of Napoleon III. He declared his hand in a manifesto of 15 January 1883, in which he asserted the principle of popular sovereignty and 'the right of a people to appoint its leader'. But in the same breath, he announced that he was the heir of Napoleon I and Napoleon III.[50] The candidacy of Jérôme-Napoleon was anathema to conservative Bonapartists who regarded him as an anticlerical, even a radical, as well as a playboy. Paul de Cassagnac, who declared that he was a Catholic and a monarchist before he was an imperialist, led a conservative revolt to assert the candidacy of Jérôme-Napoleon's nineteen-year-old son, Victor, scarcely out of military school, but named by the prince imperial in his will as his successor. In addition de Cassagnac founded a new paper, *L'Autorité*, under the slogan 'for God, for France', and built an alliance with other royalist groups in the Union des Droites in a bid to replace the Republic by 'a modern monarchy, under the folds of the tricolour'.[51] The reaction of the republicans to this sort of posturing was to expel the leading members of the former French ruling families, including the Bonapartes, from French soil in 1886.

The division in Bonapartist ranks was exposed dramatically during the Boulanger affair. Revision of the parliamentary, 'Orleanist' constitution of 1875 was on the agenda not only of Bonapartists but of discontented radical-nationalist republicans such as Paul Déroulède, leader of the Ligue des Patriotes. These radicals particularly resented the check on universal suffrage imposed by the Senate, and wanted a strong president of the Republic directly responsible to the people. They had taken to the streets at the end of 1887 when it appeared that Jules Ferry, the candidate of the moderate republicans, might be elected president of the Republic. General Boulanger, who had been briefly minister of war in 1886 and had then been dropped by the republican establishment as too hot to hold, became a focus for the aspirations of all opponents of the parliamentary Republic.

Boulanger occupied a position similar in many ways to that of Louis-Napoleon in 1848. He stood as candidate in a series of by-elections in 1888, rallying support in one department after another, resigning his seat in order to run again, holding a rolling plebiscite in favour of the dissolution of parliament and the revision of the constitution. He was backed by a Republican Committee of National Protest which included Déroulède, but had also been introduced to Jérôme-Napoleon at his Swiss residence by a Bonapartist journalist, and commanded interest among the supporters of Prince Victor. The Bonapartists saw that Boulanger could enable them to step over two problems that had confronted Louis-Napoleon. First, that if he created a majority of deputies in favour of revision, it would be possible to avoid recourse to a coup d'état, which tended to cost them dear. Second, that it was more likely that the revision of the constitution towards the direct election of the president of the Republic would go through if it were dissociated from the dynastic question of restoring the Empire. A Bonapartist prince would not step forward until the first presidential elections were to be held, when he could hope to repeat the landslide of 10 December 1848.

At this point, however, left-wing and right-wing Bonapartists diverged. Left-wing Bonapartists, working closely with Déroulède and the Ligue des Patriotes, and calling themselves republican Bonapartists, swore that they would never question the existence of the Republic. At a banquet in November 1888 they called for 'a truly national Republic . . . a strong and united France on the republican basis of the absolute sovereignty of the people'.[52] Replying to the Bonapartist committee of the Nièvre on the fateful date of 2 December 1888, General Boulanger declared that it would be foolish to renew the mistakes of 1851. Rather than use the term 'plebiscitary', which had anti-republican connotations, he called for 'a new, national Republic, open to all honest men and every progress, made by the people and for the people'.[53] Right-wing Bonapartists, however, saw the establishment of direct presidential elections as only the first step to the restoration of the Empire: 1848 would be followed by 1852. These in turn divided between those who wanted the imperialists to go it alone, and those, under Paul de Cassagnac, who favoured an alliance with the monarchists.[54] Once Boulanger had shot his bolt at the beginning of 1889 and the chance of direct presidential elections receded, the only feasible option for conservative Bonapartists was an alliance with the monarchists to win an anti-republican majority in the elections of October 1889. Monarchists threw their weight and their coffers behind Boulanger, but treated the Bonapartists as inferior coalition partners, allowing them to run unchallenged only in seats that were unwinnable by monarchists.[55]

Each time two steps were taken forward in projecting Bonapartism as a system of government, standing in particular for the principle of a directly elected president, the eruption of dynastic issues forced the debate one step back. The death of Jérôme-Napoléon in 1891 simplified matters somewhat. But real progress could not be made until the dynasts had been marginalised by the left-wing Bonapartists, reinforced by nationalist republicans who hated the parliamentary Republic, and might be attracted to a Bonapartist viewpoint, provided that it did not call the Republic into question. To win them over, left-wing Bonapartists revived the argument developed by Louis-Napoleon in the 1830s that Napoleon had been the continuator of the Revolution, not its grave-digger, and that his system had been the natural conclusion of the Republic.

In 1894 the Bonapartist deputy Gustave Cunéo d'Ornano published a book called *La République de Napoléon*. He focused not on the Empire but on the Consular Republic of 1800–1804 which, he argued, had maintained the democratic traditions of the French Revolution. The constitution of the Year VIII, he claimed, had been put to the popular vote in the same way as the constitutions of 1793 and the Year III, whereas in 1875 parliament had usurped this constitution-making function and failed to consult the people. Cunéo d'Ornano took over the *Petit Caporal* in 1895 to campaign for 'the democratic, plebiscitary Republic', suggesting that a plebiscitary congress be called, under the chairmanship of the irreproachably republican Paul Déroulède. Déroulède was re-elected deputy of Angoulême in 1898 with the slogan, 'Down with the parliamentary Republic! Long live the plebiscitary Republic!', and reconstituted the Ligue des Patriotes which had been dissolved after the Boulanger affair. Since a congress of both houses of parliament which had the authority to revise the constitution would clearly not have a majority for such a course of action, Déroulède resorted to the alternative of the coup d'état. At the state funeral of President Félix Faure in February 1899, he tried to harness the support of the army to march on the Élsyée. In his pocket he had a proclamation abrogating the 'usurping' constitution of 1875, and forming a provisional government until a constituent assembly could be summoned. 'The parliamentary republic has had its day,' it concluded, 'Long live the plebiscitary Republic!'[56]

Arrested, Déroulède was tried by the Assize Court of the Seine, which sought to discredit him by projecting onto him its fears of another *Brumaire* or 2 December. In his defence, Déroulède denied that he had mounted a coup; there had been 'a popular revolution supported by the army'. He continued to denounce the usurpation of 1875, which had established a monarchist constitution without the king, and called for the sovereign people to be empowered to elect the president of the Republic directly. Moreover, he argued that to avert another coup of 2 December the president should be indefinitely re-eligible.[57] Acquitted by the Assize Court, Déroulède was tried by the Senate sitting as a High Court and banished in January 1900. In his absence, the Bonapartists tried to increase their influence in the Ligue des Patriotes. Cunéo d'Ornano prevailed upon Prince Victor to give it funds for the election campaign of 1902, and for a time the Ligue renamed itself the Ligue des Patriotes Républicains Plébiscitaires.[58] But the suffering imposed by exile, the more sturdy international showing of the Republic after 1905, and above all fatigue with the resolute refusal of his enemies to believe that the reforms he envisaged were intended to strengthen, not to undermine, the Republic, drove Déroulède to abandon his plebiscitary position. Returning to France at the end of 1905 he told his troops, 'We still prefer the Republic without plebiscite to the plebiscite without the Republic.'[59]

Meanwhile, the question of whether Bonapartists accepted or rejected the Republic came to a head. This reflected a struggle for power within the Bonapartist organisation and for the ear of Prince Victor between Paul de Cassagnac and the allies of Cunéo d'Ornano. Cassagnac did not want to be involved with Déroulède's direct presidential elections, on the grounds that they would be open only to those who professed total loyalty to the Republic he so much despised; he would accept only an 'integral plebiscite' choosing between an emperor, a king and the republic.[60] Nor did he have any time for the notion of Consular Republic so dear to the republican Bonapartists; for him, the apogee of Bonapartism was the imperial monarchy. 'You would have dropped Napoleon I on the eve of his coronation,' he ranted at one of them as the centenary of the Empire approached, 'and not got as far as Austerlitz.'[61] Cassagnac had advocated the plebiscite to break the hold of the Republic, but he was ultimately a defender of the Empire as a hereditary monarchy rather than an office that the people could confer and take away. He detested the idea of Prince Victor running in a presidential election with no more claim than 'the nephews of Thiers or Grévy, the sons of MacMahon, Carnot or Loubet'.[62] He would rather stand by the duc d'Orléans, who was not prepared to prostitute his hereditary rights before the sacred cow of democracy, and who would uphold religion and order. Cassagnac had often been accused of working for the Orleanist pretender, and when he died, in 1904, a representative was sent by the duc d'Orléans, but not by Prince Victor. His obsession with the dynastic principle had finally taken him into the royalist camp.

The argument was won by those who defended a plebiscitary or consular Republic. Yet the presence of a Bonapartist family which continued to assert its claim to rule fostered an ambiguity about the Bonapartist cause that undermined even strictly republican Bonapartists. Prince Victor himself did nothing to dispell that ambiguity. In 1911 he published a manifesto claiming that 'plebiscitarians' appealed to 'all French people who recognise the sovereignty of the people and the need for a strong national authority'. Their policy was an alternative to the corrupt parliamentarianism. 'It is, in a word, the policy of the Consulate.' For himself, he insisted, 'I do not lay claim to any dynastic right; I am a son of modern France and remain faithful to the traditions embodied by the French Revolution.' But he added, 'The name of Napoleon is a programme in itself.'[63] And the very fact that Prince Victor was a Bonaparte cast the shadow of hereditary charisma, if not hereditary right. The birth in 1914 of an heir, Prince Napoleon, was welcomed even by the plebicitary Bonapartists as 'a link added to the Napoleonic tradition'. Fears among republicans that Bonapartists intended not only to revise the constitution but also restore the imperial family were not allayed by the collective memory of the Bonapartists themselves, which was sustained by the commemoration of the sacred moments of the Napoleonic epic. The anniversaries commonly celebrated by Bonapartists were 9 January, the death of Napoleon III, 1 June, the death of the prince imperial, and 10 December, date of the presidential election of 1858. With the exception of the latter, they represented an imperial martyrology. The Bonapartist students or 'jeunesse plebiscitaire' went so far as to insist that 'there was no date in the life of Napoleon I or Napoleon III which should be passed over in silence'. They regularly celebrated 2 December and 18 *Brumaire*, which served only to remind republicans, if they needed reminding, that Bonapartists had forgotten nothing about the practice of coups d'état.[64]

The Bonapartist Parti de l'Appel au Peuple continued in the inter-war period. Its weekly, *La Volonté nationale*, appeared sporadically in the 1920s, and in 1930 a new paper, *Brumaire* was launched and published down to 1940. Support for Bonapartism, however, dwindled to a hard core of professional nostalgics. Only a dozen self-professed Bonapartists were elected to the

Chamber in 1919. The victory of the Republic in 1918 convinced many Bonapartists that the régime did not perhaps merit the scorn that they had previously poured on it. After all, the Republic had succeeded on the battlefield where the Empire had twice failed. Paul de Cassagnac *fils* claimed that his family had always served principles, not princes, defending the authoritarian Empire, for example, but attacking the Liberal Empire. The liberal Republic had been a disaster but the advent in 1917 of Clemenceau and Foch, the one political authority, the other military authority, incarnate, had changed everything. 'That day,' he concluded, 'I stopped hating the Republic.'[65] In 1928 he put the weight of *L'Autorité* behind Poincaré, another war hero, in the belief that he would strengthen the executive power. Similarly Pierre Taittinger, who had been president of the Jeunesse Plébiscitaire of Paris in 1913, and had fought in the trenches for the Republic, became after the war leader of the Jeunesses Patriotes, the youth wing of the republican revisionist organisation founded by Déroulède, the Ligue des Patriotes. Though he abandoned any interest in the Bonaparte family, the lessons that he had learned from Bonapartism on constitutional revision were not forgotten. The reformed constitution he proposed in 1928 was almost a replica of the Consular Constitution of the Year VIII.[66]

Defusing the Bonapartist Myth

On the death of Prince Victor-Napoleon in 1926, Charles Maurras commented that 'the reign of Napoleon V' had offered no new ideas since 1884 and certainly no radical alternatives to republican governments.[67] His heir, Prince Napoleon, who celebrated his majority in 1935, was a perfectly honourable pretender and said to resemble the prince imperial, but he had not the mercurial and adventurous qualities of his namesake. But if the dynastic incubus of Bonapartism was fast becoming a thing of the past, its ideas on constitutional revision were never more relevant. The inter-war period in France was dominated by debate on *la réforme de l'Etat*. Though the Republic had survived the Great War there was no evidence, as storm clouds gathered once again, that, with its parliamentary centre of gravity and weak executive, it would survive another ordeal. Plans to strengthen the executive sprouted like mushrooms in the 1930s, and the Bonapartist solution, as the established alternative to parliamentarism, was the obvious one. However, because of the political taboos associated in the Republic both with the Bonaparte family and with the Bonapartist movement, the Bonapartist solution was likely to be adopted only if it originated both outside the Bonapartist family and outside the Bonapartist camp. Ultimately, it was delivered by General de Gaulle, but before that supporters of the Bonapartist solution nailed their hopes to the hero of Verdun, Marshal Pétain.

C'est Pétain qu'il nous faut! was the title of a controversial pamphlet which appeared in 1935, when Pétain was minister of war in the Doumergue government, a post that Boulanger had held fifty years previously before his meteoric career. After the Liberation, the pamphlet was used as evidence that Pétain's rôle as providential man in 1940 had been carefully prepared.[68] But what has scarcely been explored is the classical Bonapartist programme which under-pinned the propostion that Pétain should become president of the Republic. Its protagonist was Gustave Hervé, who had made his reputation before 1914 as a violent antimilitarist and antipatriot but was transformed by the war into an equally outspoken militarist and nationalist.[69] In 1926 he advocated an 'authori-tarian Republic', admitting that it was 'simply the rejuvenated programme of the plebiscitary Republic for which Déroulède battled all his life'.[70] At the beginning of 1935 Hervé renewed his campaign in his paper, *La Victoire*, announcing that they had not needed to go to Italy or Germany for a model; they had found it 'at home, in the idea of that plebiscitary Republic which is a combination of the Bonapartist formula and the republican spirit'.[71] He envis-aged the election to parliament of a majority in favour of revising the constitu-tion, which would establish the direct election of a national leader with enhanced powers. The strategy planned was that the Bonapartist pretender should make way for Marshal Pétain: Prince Napoleon had not proved himself, Pétain had. He adapted Napoleon's phrase to argue that Pétain's 'illustrious name will not ruffle the republican fibre, which despite its disgust for the parliamentary régime is fairly well developed in the heart of the French people'.[72] Finally, Hervé was also fairly clear that a republican democracy 'did not want to leave the task of finding a national leader to the blindness of the hereditary principle'.[73]

Pétain indeed emerged as a providential figure as France collapsed before the onslaught of the German armies in June 1940. He was appointed president of the council by the president of the Republic according to constitutional form. Whether he subsequently undertook a coup d'état was hotly debated. On 10 July 1940 a revisionist majority in parliament abdicated to Pétain full powers to make a new constitution. Immediately issuing a constitutional act, he declared himself head of state, deposing the incumbent president of the Republic at the stroke of a pen, and another act concentrating all executive, legislative and constituent powers in his person. At his trial in 1945, it was argued both that the assembly was subjected to military pressure, and that the powers it granted were immediately abused to undertake a coup d'état.[74]

Clearly, in the hour of catastrophe, Pétain touched the fibre of the nation. François Mauriac captured the moment for *Le Figaro*.

> The words of Marshal Pétain, that evening of 25 June, had an almost timeless quality. It was not a man who spoke to us; rather we heard the appeal of the great nation, humiliated, rise from the farthest depths of our History.[75]

But the relationship between Pétain and the French people remained purely mystical. In three major respects the régime established at Vichy diverged from the Bonapartist model. First, there was never any ratification of his powers by a popular vote, a procedure that would have been a formal requirement of

Bonapartism. True, he made no attempt to revert to the hereditary principle. But he abolished the Republic, replacing it by something called the État
Français, and gave orders to remove the busts of Marianne from town halls,
which did ruffle the republican fibre. Second, the Bonapartist model stipulated
a reform of the constitution that would strengthen the executive power. Pétain
dissolved the Chamber of Deputies and the Senate and concentrated power in
his own hands. Although three different constitutions were drafted by Pétain's
advisers (none of which provided for the direct election of the head of state),
none was ever finalised, let alone put to the people for ratification. Moreover,
the strengthening of the French state was only in respect of the domestic
situation, and of part of the country. The writ of the Vichy government ran
only in the zone not occupied by the Germans in 1940, and internationally the
sovereignty of the French state was heavily curtailed by the Third Reich.
Third, though indisputably the mass of the French people accepted the armistice in the summer of 1940, and France was described as counting 40
million Pétainists, so much did the marshal embody the fragile hopes of the
French people, that the Bonapartist rhetoric of reconciliation rang increasingly
hollow. Far from bringing together the revolutionary and counter-revolutionary, Pétain ruthlessly sacrificed the former to the latter. Those who clung
to the principles of 1789 and who believed in the Republic were driven inexorably into opposition to the Vichy régime. By the early months of 1944,
France was in the grip of civil war.

    In June 1940, however, there emerged a second providential figure, Charles
de Gaulle. Whereas Pétain looked to save France by concluding an armistice
with Germany before it was totally overrun, de Gaulle claimed that suing for an
armistice of itself disqualified the Pétain government. In the event, de Gaulle
succeeded where Pétain failed, and made the Bonapartist vision of popular
legitimacy, a strong state and national union a reality. But he had to sidestep
accusations of coup d'état, dynastic ambition, dictatorship, counter-revolution
and defeat, all elements of the spectre of Bonapartism in the republican mind.
In short, he had to defuse the Bonapartist myth. This he achieved after three
attempts to secure his power, in 1940, 1944 and 1958.

    'I, General de Gaulle, French soldier and leader, am conscious of speaking in
the name of France.'[76] So said de Gaulle in his second broadcast from London,
on 19 June 1940. The hubris was of Napoleonic proportions: a claim that the
popular fibre responded to his own. It was more outrageous because in 1940 de
Gaulle was no Bonaparte, just another general who had briefly held office in
1940 as under-secretary of state for war (perhaps more important than might
be thought in the light of the experience of Boulanger and Pétain). In January
1941 he repeated his claim, speaking of 'an immense silent plebiscite' which,
given the impossibility of a formal plebiscite, endorsed his actions.[77] This set
alarm bells jangling in the ears of French exiles in London, particularly those of
a parliamentary background. 'De Gaulle is pulling on the boots of Napoleon,'
the socialist deputy Félix Gouin reported back to the imprisoned Léon Blum in

October 1942. 'He will do anything to institute personal power, and the republicans who back him are likely to fall victim one day to their good faith or naïveté.'[78]

De Gaulle, however, was too skilled to allow such accusations of Bonapartism to stick. He avoided the booted, military image of a Napoleon, paid repeated homage to the sovereignty of the people and never called into question republican legality. He did not enter Algiers or Paris as a victorious commander at the head of his tanks but followed his commanders as the liberator, striding down the boulevards on foot, making contact with the cheering crowds and taking his legitimacy from them.[79] He told the Consultative Assembly when it opened in Paris in November 1944 that he had assumed authority as a measure of public safety but intended to return it to the people.

> We believe that we have preserved the treasure of the sovereign nation's rights in order to restore it intact. This respect and protection of republican legitimacy has justified and justifies our exercise of power to lead the country in war . . . and give[s] us the capacity to assume the prerogatives of state at home and abroad.[80]

De Gaulle's ambition was to heal the wounds of civil war and achieve national reconciliation as quickly as possible. His own background was Catholic and conservative; at one point, he had dallied with the Action Française. But he realised that the driving force to liberate and renew France was republican, even revolutionary, and he placed himself at the head of this movement. He argued that France had been betrayed by its élites who put the defence of their privileges above the defence of the country. 'We believe that a roaring and a cleansing wave must rise from the depths of the nation', he told an audience in the Albert Hall on 15 November 1941, 'to sweep away pell-mell the causes of the disaster and the structures erected on capitulation.'[81] No insults were bad enough for the Vichy régime. But with victory in sight he tried to limit the revolutionary drive of the Liberation and the extent of the purge of the guilty. He told the provisional Consultative Assembly at Algiers that the provisional government had 'no intention of suddenly sweeping away the great majority of servants of the state', and later blamed only 'a handful of wretches'.[82] From liberated Paris he remarked that 'as the abominable tide goes down, the nation breathes the air of victory and liberty. In her depths is revealed a marvellous unity.'[83] The bridge between Resistance legitimacy and national unity was not in fact easy to sustain. The rhetoric of Resistance divided the French into good and bad, patriots and collaborators; the rhetoric of unity meant making peace with Vichyist elements in French society. When de Gaulle in 1948 called Pétain 'a great leader of the Great War', and then suggested that it was cruel to keep a ninety-five-year-old in prison, supporters of Pétain credited de Gaulle with the wartime nostrum that France needed two strings to its bow, that of Pétain as well as his own, the shield alongside the sword. This stretched the bridge too far. De Gaulle was forced publicly to distance himself from such a view, by condemning Vichy's strategy of capitulation and collaboration with the enemy.[84]

After national unity, de Gaulle's obsessive concern was to restore the authority of the state. At the beginning of 1945, his collaborator Michel Debré wrote that the old régime of parties must not be allowed to resurface: 'the only chance for French democracy is, if the term may be used, a republican monarch'.[85] Both de Gaulle and Debré would have preferred a referendum on the heads of a new constitution—the tool of Louis-Napoleon in 1851—rather than the election of a Constituent Assembly with sovereign powers, on the analogy of those of 1789, 1848 and 1871. This idea, however, was fought tooth and nail in the summer of 1945 by the Consultative Assembly, which feared that a Bonapartist plebiscite would give rise to a Bonapartist constitution.[86] Marcel Plaisant, a centre-left politician and one of the minority to vote against giving Pétain full powers in July 1940, told the Assembly,

> I am not doing de Gaulle the wrong of comparing him to Louis-Napoleon Bonaparte, no more than I shall do the memory of Louis-Napoleon Bonaparte the graver wrong of comparing him with Adolf Hitler. What I want to say is that dictatorships always arise from similar conditions.[87]

At this point, de Gaulle was not able to have his way with the constitution. Centainly the parliamentary system of the Third Republic had been discredited and there was little support, even among politicians, for a return to them. But the comparison of Louis-Napoleon to Hitler was knowing. Liberal democracy had been eclipsed in France under the Occupation, and for most French people the Liberation stood for the return of liberal institutions. The Republic had acquired a new sheen, old politicians discredited by the vote of full powers to Pétain were replaced by new ones coming up through Resistance organisations, and the political parties were rejuvenated. A compromise was therefore reached between de Gaulle as head of the provisional government and the Consultative Assembly. He conceded that a Constituent Assembly would be elected and that this would elect the head of government; they conceded that the Assembly would be limited in both duration and powers, and that the constitution it drafted would be subject to a referendum.

The Constituent Assembly elected (by women as well as men) in October 1945 was dominated by three mass parties, the Communists, the Socialists and the newly formed Christian Democratic MRP. De Gaulle was elected head of government but his rival Félix Gouin became president of the Assembly. The parallel with the deadlock between the president of the Republic and the National Assembly of 1849–51 was impossible not to see, and fears that the outcome might be another 2 December were not absent from the minds of politicians. On this occasion, however, the politicians had their way, riding on a tide of support for representantive government. De Gaulle meanwhile was not the elect of the people but the elect of an Assembly he sought to control.

Though his room for manoeuvre was limited by the ministers he had to draw from the parties, including Communists, and though he hated the parliamentary constitution they were set on, there could be no question of a coup against the Assembly. On 20 January 1946 he resigned as head of government, and was replaced by Félix Gouin. He criticised the constitution from the sidelines and appealed to the people to reject it, but the people endorsed the constitution (at the second attempt) and rejected the general.

De Gaulle had expected to be back within a week by force of popular demand. In the event, he waited twelve years. At this stage there was no question of his considering a coup against the Fourth Republic. At Nice in 1948, greeted by a rapturous crowd shouting 'Au pouvoir!', he replied, 'No, I am not Bonaparte! No, I am not Boulanger! I am General de Gaulle!'[88] Despite his distaste of parliamentarism and political parties, he foreswore the Bonapartist tradition, accepting the rules of parliamentary democracy by founding a political party, and trying to build an electoral majority against the constitution. The Gaullist party he formed in 1947 was called the Rassemblement du Peuple Français (RPF) and pretended not to be a party at all. It was to embody national unity, but was limited on the one hand by opposition to Communists—denounced as 'separatists' by de Gaulle—and on the other by accusations from the Right, that he was a tool of the Communist party. This was indeed the view of *La Victoire*, the mouth-piece of the late Gustave Hervé, revived to fight the elections of 1951 and counting former Bonapartists such as Paul de Cassagnac and Pierre Taittinger on its staff. Far from being Gaullist, it defended the memory of Marshal Pétain.[89] The RPF emerged as the largest, though still a minority, party in the legislative elections of 1951, but de Gaulle refused power unless he could revise the constitution, affected surprise that some of his deputies were keen to take office unconditionally, and then dissolved the RPF lest it become more entangled in the 'games, poisons and delights of the system'.[90]

Only when the parliamentary institutions and political parties of the Fourth Republic had become as discredited by crisis and catastrophe as those of the Third Republic was de Gaulle able to return to power. When he did so it was with the greatest political calculation and finesse. He needed to achieve a coup of Bonapartist dimensions in the knowledge that if accusations of Bonapartism levelled against him persuaded the electorate, he was doomed. His strategy was thus guided by four main considerations. To begin with, though a military coup in Algiers in defence of French Algeria made his return possible, he maintained sufficient distance from the military conspirators to avoid being tarred with the brush of *Brumaire* or 2 December. Then, while playing on the threat of military violence if the system did not bend to let him in, de Gaulle was careful always to observe legal and constitutional forms, to respect republican legality and the verdict of the people. Next, once in power, he was prepared to take his time before proposing the ideal constitution, rather than the best practicable constitution, to the people. Finally, he never allowed his desire to reform the constitution to be overtaken by the question of the succession and, in particular, by dynastic issues.

The riots in Algiers and the coup of the officers on 13 May 1958 was followed on 15 May by the cry of 'Vive de Gaulle' by General Salan to the crowd massed on the Forum of Algiers. De Gaulle replied somewhat ominously, 'I hold myself ready to assume the powers of the Republic.'[91] *L'Humanité* was quick to denounce the 'coup de force' and called for a republican union to 'block the road to de Gaulle and the military and fascist dictatorship'.[92] The bandwagon of republican defence against another *Brumaire*, 2 December, 6 February 1934 or 10 July 1940 began to roll. But the distance between the military in Algiers and de Gaulle in his country retreat at Colombey and the hidden nature of any links encouraged the view that far from being an accomplice of the coup, de Gaulle was the only person who could impose discipline on the army and prevent it striking in metropolitan France. The socialist leader Guy Mollet, who accepted office in the government of Pierre Pflimlin to strengthen it in the crisis, soon took the view that the choice was between 'a de Gaulle government or a colonels' *pronunciamiento*'.[93] A similar view was taken, influentially, by Hubert Beuve-Méry, the founder-editor of *Le Monde*.[94] De Gaulle was perceived not as mounting a coup against the Republic, but ensuring its survival. On 27 May, as if to reward this trust, de Gaulle instructed army officers to fall into line under their hierarchical superiors.

It is important to underline that for a fortnight after 13 May there was still a regular government in Paris, that of Pflimlin. In the Assembly, Pierre Mendès-France, among others, called on the government to stay firm, reminding his audience that 'the Conventionnels did not compromise either with the supremacy of the civil power, or with the indivisibility of republican authority. Let us take inspiration from their lessons to ensure the rule of law.'[95] De Gaulle had a bruising interview with Premier Pflimlin in the night of 25–6 May, but Pflimlin refused to resign. The government received a massive vote of confidence on 27 May and, the following day, 500,000 people demonstrated in Paris in defence of the Republic. On 19 May de Gaulle was forced to give ground and admit that 'the powers of the Republic, when they are assumed, can only be those delegated by the Republic itself'.[96] The way to power was eventually opened by Pflimlin's resignation and a summons to form a government from the president of the Republic, René Coty, who must bear a heavy responsibility in the matter. After that it was possible for de Gaulle to assume power by constitutional means. He went to the Assembly to request a vote of *pleins pouvoirs* to re-establish order and union, and to draft a new constitution which would be submitted for the approval of the people by referendum. The resolution of the major parties was undermined. De Gaulle was deemed preferable to either soldiers or Communists. Socialists, Radicals and MRP split down the middle and gave de Gaulle the majority he needed on 2 June. The analogy was less with 2 December than with 10 July, although de Gaulle, as always, was careful to demonstrate respect for republican legality. Symbolically, to allay fears that he might tamper with the Republic, he presented his constitutional project in the place de la République on 4 September 1958, anniversary of the proclamation of the Third Republic in 1870.[97]

De Gaulle continued to play his constitutional hand close to his chest. For the Fifth Republic, he initially proposed a constitution that was deliberately not Bonapartist, providing for the election of the president of the Republic not directly but by an electoral college of parliamentarians and local councillors. A system that empowered notables rather than the masses was seen by political commentators to be reminiscent more of Orleanism than of Bonapartism.[98] The new constitution was voted on 28 September 1958 by 17.7 million to 4.6 million, and de Gaulle was elected president of the Republic on 21 December. His ultimate goal was to remove the headship of state from the gift of parliamentary politicians and restore it to the sovereign people by way of direct election. But he waited his moment. In 1962, with the Algerian war ended, and playing on fears aroused by an attempt on his life, de Gaulle published his plan for direct elections to the presidency of the Republic.

The outcry was extraordinary. In the first place, de Gaulle was accused of violating his own constitution by proceding with constitutional reform without consulting parliament. Guy Mollet, who had pulled the SFIO behind de Gaulle in 1958 and helped to draft the new constitution, now became one of the most outspoken opponents of revision. The Bonapartism of the gesture was immediately recognisable. De Gaulle now proposed the course from which he had shrunk in 1944: to exclude parliament from the revision process, and to appeal directly to the sovereign people for a sanction. Direct elections to the presidency of the Republic had not been tried since the election of Louis-Napoleon in 1848, and with cause. The socialist press juxtaposed texts of de Gaulle demanding a 'yes' vote with menaces of 'après moi le déluge' with similar texts of Louis-Napoleon before and after the coup d'état of 1851.[99] Maurice Thorez campaigning for a 'no' vote told car workers at Boulogne-Billancourt that 'the Constituants of 1848 made the mistake of allowing the election by universal suffrage of a second Bonaparte. They opened the way to the Second Empire, which led to Sedan, just as the First had led to Waterloo.'[100] Jacques Duclos began work tracing the roots of Gaullism, which appeared in 1964 as *De Napoléon III à De Gaulle*. François Mitterrand joined the attack with *Le Coup d'État permanent*, also published 1964. Even so, though the result was less clear-cut than in 1852, the referendum of 28 October 1962 endorsed direct presidential elections by 13 million votes to 8 million.

De Gaulle's success was explained by the fact that he had exorcised the demon of Bonapartism. He borrowed its lessons on the organisation of power, but warded off accusations of coup d'état by his observance, for the most part, of constitutional form, and where he played fast and loose with the constitution, by his obeisance to the sovereignty of the people and his respect for the intangibility of the Republic. He had no dynastic ambitions of his own which might undermine faith in his republicanism. This is not to say that the accusation of dynasticism was not laid at his door. The socialist *Populaire de Paris* suggested that de Gaulle would either stand aside for the comte de Paris, or found his own dynasty, designating his own son, Philippe de Gaulle, to succeed him.[101] There was a spate of books with titles such as *Le Couronnement du Prince* and *De Gaulle Ier. La Révolution manquée*.[102] The only smear not made was that de Gaulle might open the way for the Bonapartist pretender, Prince Napoleon. But then the latter was not in fact a challenger, having been awarded the Legion of Honour by de Gaulle for his rôle in the Resistance, and living quietly in France under the assumed name of the comte de Montfort.

Yet de Gaulle knew only too well that the issue of the reform of the state, the establishment of a strong, popularly accountable government, had to be divorced from the question of heredity. To confuse the two had wrecked the Bonapartist enterprise; to separate them would be the Gaullist achievement. De Gaulle inaugurated a Fifth Republic, the roots of which were in the national republic of Boulanger, the plebiscitary, consular republic of Déroulède, the authoritarian republic of Gustave Hervé, so long kept at bay by the parliamentary republic of the party politicians. But the Republic as such was never called into question. The succession had to be organised in a different way, through the acceptance of the un-Bonapartist principle that a political party would be required to ensure a parliamentary majority committed to protect his constitution. Legislative elections on the same day as the referendum on direct elections secured a majority for the new Gaullist party, the Union pour la Nouvelle République (UNR), and its allies the Républicains Indépendants. What had always eluded the Bonapartists—a parliamentary majority to back up the plebiscitary majority—had finally been achieved. Whereas in 1945–6 the political parties were in a position to dictate to de Gaulle, now he had the means of dictating to them.

De Gaulle's triumph was not without its flaws. He was inclined, especially in later years, to a certain Napoleonism, losing some respect for the will of the people, an air of dictatorship, the elision of the fate of the Republic with the fate of a party. The legitimacy conferred by plebiscite came to matter less than his own belief that he matched the fibre of the nation personally, at some metaphysical level. In 1960 he referred to 'the national legitimacy that I have embodied for twenty years', as if to ignore the referenda and elections that had gone against him.[103] In the presidential elections of 1965, he dismissed François Mitterrand as the candidate of political parties; he, de Gaulle, was the candidate of History.[104] Whereas de Gaulle had repeatedly dismissed accusations that he sought personal power, asking journalists in 1958 whether they thought that 'at the age of 67, I am going to begin a career as a dictator?', in 1964 he declared that 'the indivisible authority of the state is entrusted wholly to the president by the people who have elected him'.[105] Though he had claimed to stand above parties to arbitrate between them or to reconcile them, as a president with a presidential majority, de Gaulle threw his weigh behind one half of the political spectrum. He came to argue that the very existence of the Fifth Republic depended on the survival of the presidential majority. Thus in the 1967 legislative elections he warned that a 'majority of deputies hostile to the Fifth Republic', which repeatedly censured governments appointed by the president, would 'plunge France into the upheavals that were inherent in the old régime of parties'.[106] This was tantamount to ruling out pluralist democracy.

The effect of this rigidity and authoritarianism was to drive opposition onto the streets, which exploded in May 1968. This represented a massive loss of legitimacy for one who swore by the verdict of the people, and de Gaulle almost lost his nerve. First he promised a referendum, then he visited French troops stationed in the Federal Republic of Germany, provoking fears that tanks would be brought onto the streets of Paris. On 30 May, insisting that he was still 'the keeper of national and republican legitimacy', he announced that he was dissolving the National Assembly and would go to the country.[107] This cunning move split opposition politicians, who immediately looked to the electoral campaign, from their troops, who were committed to direct action. De Gaulle won the gamble, his presidential majority holding by a small margin. However, he failed to grasp the consequence of the crisis, which recalled those of 1815 and 1870, and dictated that the liberal opposition should be placated by a shift to a liberal Empire. The reform of the Senate and the reform of regional government which was put to a referendum in April 1969 was in no sense an adequate response to demands for liberalisation and participation, and de Gaulle lost the vote by 10.9 million to 12 million. What can be said, however, is that *in extremis* he remained committed to observe the will of the sovereign people, and left the Élysée quietly by car.

Napoleon I had said that a constitution was the work of time. The greatest compliment that can be paid to de Gaulle and the constitution of the Fifth Republic is that it has survived a number of tests and showed itself to be both tough and adaptable. The conservative majority constructed by de Gaulle ensured the succession of the Fifth Republic better than any heir, and remained intact for twelve years after his fall. But the doubts always remained as to whether the victory of an opposition majority would destroy the new Republic. Giscard d'Estaing, who continued the rule of the right-wing majority in 1974, saw that 'alternation is the property of advanced democratic societies' such as the United States or West Germany, but he regretted 'the pointlessly dramatic character of the political debate in our country'. He believed that political life in France was not yet mature enough for pluralism, but hoped that economic growth and the death of ideology would ultimately permit it to take place in France.[108]

The threats and menaces were nevertheless unnecessary. The victory of the Left in 1981 was the fruit of an ideological struggle, but it demonstrated that one majority could alternate with another within the framework of the Republic without weakening its structure. François Mitterrand had launched a scathing attack against the Bonapartist system in his *Coup d'État permanent*, and promised in the election campaign of 1981 to reduce the presidential term from seven years to five, or deny a second term. However, he settled happily into the structure left by de Gaulle and Giscard when he took office. 'France's institutions were not made for me,' he observed, 'but they suit me well enough.'[109] He immediately dissolved the National Assembly to produce a parliamentary majority and thus a government of the Left that reflected the new presidential majority. When he ran again in 1988, however, Mitterrand was careful to minimise partisanship. In true Bonapartist style he put himself forward as 'the president of all French people', to whom he addressed an open letter, and declared himself in favour of 'la France unie'. He argued that he stood for 'the impartial state' against the 'RPR state' which, he argued, was represented by Jacques Chirac.

Although de Gaulle failed to push through liberal reforms, there was a case, after the crises of 1958 and 1968, for allowing the Fifth Republic to become imperceptibly less presidential and more parliamentary and liberal. Giscard d'Estaing began his mandate lunching in the homes of ordinary people, but ended it ridiculed for his monarchical pretensions. Mitterrand styled himself the father or grandfather of the nation and won the affectionate nickname 'tonton'. This shift was partly the effect of circumstance. Whereas prime ministers before the Mitterrand era had tended to be the poodles of the president, between 1986 and 1988 Mitterrand had to endure 'cohabitation' with Jacques Chirac, a prime minister of an opposing majority. He survived largely by confining the presidency to foreign policy and 'arbitrating' on behalf of minorities, whilst allowing the government to take responsibility for failures of policy. In the 1988 presidential elections Mitterrand made a virtue of necessity, observing 'I believe and I hope that whatever future majorities govern France there will be a return neither to the absolute president of the early Fifth Republic, the effective master of all power, nor to the impotent president of the Fourth Republic, who had no power.'[110] Chirac riposted that 'France does not need a leader who pretends to do nothing. You don't set a course for the future by putting on carpet-slippers.'[111]

The defeat of Jacques Chirac in the presidential election of 1988 seemed to indicate that the electorate preferred a somewhat attenuated form of Bonapartism to that suggested by the more obvious Bonapartist or Boulangist candidate. Ironically, however, a faction emerged in the RPR in 1990, challenging the leadership of Chirac, demanding the renovation of Gaullism, and candidly appealing for inspiration to Napoleon III. The driving force behind this movement was Philippe Séguin, mayor of Épinal and deputy of the Vosges. To regain its lost empire, Séguin believed that the Gaullists had to win back voters from the Front National on the Right and win over a popular constituency disillusioned with a decade of socialism in power. Gaullism had to recover a popular mandate in support of a more powerful presidential régime and national cohesion.[112] To make his point, Séguin published a major study entitled *Louis-Napoléon le Grand*, in which he argued that for both Louis-Napoleon and for de Gaulle there had to be a head of state who embodied the authority of the state and had full executive power, drawing his legitimacy from the people by means of direct election and the plebiscite, standing for the unity of the nation above party.[113] On 13 June 1990 he spoke, along with Jacques Chirac, and in the presence of Prince and Princess Napoleon, at the inauguration of the place Napoleon III in Paris, until then the place de Roubaix opposite the Gare du Nord. He argued that Napoleon III, so much disparaged, was one of the greatest heads of state France had ever known, and looked forward to the day when his remains would be brought back to France from their exile in Farnborough.[114] Whether in fact the spectre of Bonapartism is so far faded as to make the cult of Napoleon III a profitable exercise for the Gaullist party remains to be seen.

The Cults of Napoleon

In 1847 a grenadier of the Grande Armée, who had served Napoleon on the island of Elba, commissioned the sculptor Rude, creator of the warrior-maiden of the Arc de Triomphe, *La Marseillaise*, to execute a statue in bronze of the Emperor. Erected on a Burgundian hillside outside Fixin, it cast Napoleon as 'the Christ of modern times, a new messiah'. Above an eagle, broken upon a craggy rock, the waking Emperor, eyes still closed, raises himself on one arm and with the other parts the shroud which envelopes him. The scene, unmistakably, is one of resurrection.[115] [Fig. 7]

The religious metaphor should not surprise us. For what is suggested by the cult of Napoleon, if not a religion? Its god had returned once, as if from the dead, to redeem his people, when in 1815 he landed from Elba at Cannes; there was no reason why he should not return again. The cult of Napoleon had its priesthood, the poets, painters, dramatists and story-tellers of the Napoleonic legend, and a hard core of faithful in the veterans who had followed him across Europe and the *fédérés* who swore during the Hundred Days to resist the restoration of the Bourbons. It had its sacred texts, such as the *Memorial of St Helena*, dictated with such powers of hindsight by the Emperor to the scribes in his last exile. It had its own shrines and monuments, raised to his own memory during his reign, such as the column in the place Vendôme, and its calendar of festivals, such as his birthday on 15 August and 5 May, anniversary of his death, when pilgrims gathered to pay homage to his name.

Like most religions, however, the cult of Napoleon was divisible into many denominations. There was broadly not one cult, but three. First, there was the official cult. This, promoted by Napoleon and his heirs, portrayed the Emperor as a charismatic leader, the saviour of the nation and, in particular, as a war hero, the architect of unrivalled military greatness. Second, there was the popular cult of Napoleon, which also paid homage to him as a war hero, but as a leader of men rather than as a triumphal emperor. But it also had a political

Fig. 7. Statue of
Napoleon at Fixin, by
Rude, 1847 (Conway
Library, Courtauld
Institute of Art)

dimension. It remembered Napoleon as a revolutionary emperor, whose power
was sanctioned by the people, and who defended the gains of the Revolution
against the kings, priests and nobles who wanted to dismantle it. The cult of
Napoleon here merged into Bonapartism, and was used, at least down to the
emergence of socialism, as a stick to beat political régimes which excluded
the masses, whether property-owning monarchies or republics of notables. The
third cult, that of the political class itself, was more problematic. The political
class was, as we have seen, the sworn enemy of Bonapartism, regarding it as a
menace to liberalism. It developed the 'black legend' of Napoleon as a dema-
gogue, usurper, dictator, warmonger and foreigner to boot. Yet even those
who held this view were forced to concede that Napoleon was a military genius
who had restored the greatness of France. Thus there was a fundamental
ambivalence at the heart of the political class, a love-hate relationship with the
Emperor. Moreover, régimes controlled by the political class, which fought
Bonapartism, Boulangism and Gaullism, nevertheless resorted to the cult of

Napoleon in order to consolidate popular support and appropriate for themselves the lustre of military greatness.

The cult of Napoleon was, in the first place, of Napoleon's own making. Jean Tulard has pointed out that the legend of Napoleon began not on St Helena after 1815 but on the plains of northern Italy, where the young general on campaign in 1796 commissioned news-sheets both to maintain the morale of his troops and to push up his stock in France.[116] A young pupil of Louis David, Antoine-Jean Gros, crossed the Alps with Napoleon in 1796 and created the image of a messiah or deliverer in his portrait of Bonaparte with sword and flag, leading the assault at the bridge of Arcola. Later, he was commissioned to record the Egyptian expedition, and painted *The Plague at Jaffa*, in which Napoleon is portrayed touching the sick as if to heal them, and *The Battle of the Pyramids*, which articulates Napoleon's words to his troops, 'Soldiers, consider that from the top of those pyramids forty centuries gaze at you.'[117]

Napoleon ran a police state, with tight censorship of the press, picture-prints and the theatre, but his rule, in Madame de Staël's words, was 'a chattering tyranny'.[118] In other words, Napoleon was a dictator who was skilled in the use of propaganda. The manufacture of the myth reached its height after Napoleon's coronation with a succession of large-scale victories beginning at Austerlitz. The *Bulletin de la Grande Armée*, issued as a regular four-page broadsheet throughout his campaigns, conjured up scenes and slogans that captured the imagination. Number 30, dated 12 *frimaire* Year XIV, pictured the Emperor riding in front of his waiting troops as the sun rose, with the command, 'Soldiers, we must finish this campaign with a thunderclap which confounds the arrogance of our enemies', to be greeted by shouts of 'Vive l'Empereur!' from soldiers waving their shakoes on the end of their bayonets. Also recorded were the words of the Emperor after the battle, 'Soldiers, I am proud of you.'[119]

To surpass the pomp and pagentry of monarchy, Napoleon cast himself as a triumphant Roman emperor. Two triumphal arches to the glory of the armies were commissioned in 1806. The first was inaugurated on the place du Carrousel in 1808. The second, on the place de l'Étoile, was held up by a dispute between the architects, and only a mock-up of the Arc de Triomphe was in place for the solemn entry into Paris of Napoleon and his new bride Marie-Louise on 2 April 1810. In the place Vendôme, where previously a statue of Louis XIV had stood, a column was built from twelve hundred bronze cannon captured from the Austrians and Russians at Austerlitz. A statue of Napoleon in imperial costume was commissioned from the sculptor Chaudet, and the monument was inaugurated on the Emperor's birthday, 15 August 1810. The name of Austerlitz was given to a new bridge in front of the Jardin des Plantes, while another new bridge in front of the Champ de Mars was dedicated to the victory over the Prussians at Jena.[120]

The official cult of Napoleon was nevertheless fragile. It was sustained only by his run of victories, and when he was defeated for the first time in 1814 the very material of the myth was demolished. Royalists tried to pull the statue from the Vendôme column, but in vain. The founder was then obliged to remove it on pain of the firing squad, and it was melted down to be used for the statue of Henri IV which was replaced on the Pont-Neuf.[121] When Napoleon was driven out again after Waterloo, the Prussians mined the pont d'Iéna, and were prevented from blowing it up only by the intervention of the other Allies. It was renamed the pont des Invalides, while the pont d'Austerlitz was renamed the pont du Jardin du Roi.

The dismantling of the official cult, however, was only a sign for the launch of the popular cult of Napoleon. Effectively this dates from the summer of 1815. The peasant masses, which had by no means been spoiled by Napoleon until then—consulted by plebiscite but otherwise excluded from political life, subject to conscription and police repression—suddenly turned to Napoleon as their deliverer after their first experience of Restoration, and constructed him as the revolutionary emperor of the people. The second coming was for them more wonderful than the first. And the exile of Napoleon to St Helena after Waterloo only stimulated hopes of a third coming. The countryside was swept by rumours that Napoleon had beed sighted in Spain, Italy, Toulon, Grenoble or Lyon; he was said to have returned at the head of a vast army of Americans or Turks. Sedition inflamed by the name of the Emperor increased during the subsistence crisis of 1816–17, and in the wake of news of Napoleon's death in 1821, the fact of which popular opinion stubbornly refused to accept.[122] Veterans who had left their communities with the greatest reluctance and complained every step of the way (hence the term *grognards*) now gave to the Napoleonic period in their yarn-telling the glow of a golden age. Harvests had been good, work plentiful, nobles and priests and the despots of Europe had been put in their place. Above all, the campaigns in Italy, Egypt, Germany and Russia were an epic of desert and snowfield, in which the common soldier had been a companion-in-arms of the Emperor, and the Emperor the little man in the cocked hat who lent his fur to the cold, shared his flask with the thirsty, and was at their side when the gunshot began to fly. This was the Napoleon of the people, a construction differentiated boldly from either the Roman emperor of official orthodoxy or the ogre of the black legend.[123]

The Napoleon of the people was no fairy tale. It was developed under the Restoration as an energetic criticism of the monarchy and the political class it returned to power. The government used equally energetic measures to stamp it out. Representations of and references to Napoleon were prohibited by the authorities, and writers and artists resorted to symbol and metaphor to evade not only censorship but fines and prison terms that were frequently meted out. The term 'L'Homme' or simply 'Lui' sufficed to evoke the Emperor. The column praised by the popular song-writer Emile Debraux in 1818 was the Vendôme column, and hence Napoleon.[124] *Le Vieux Drapeau* exalted in 1820 by another song-writer, P.J. Béranger, was the tricolour, not the white flag of the Bourbons, and thus the glory of the revolutionary-Napoleonic period contrasted with France's current inferiority.[125] The *Grenadier of Waterloo*, depicted protecting a fallen comrade and the tricolour in a lithograph of 1818 by Nicolas-Toussaint Charlet, who had himself fought as a National Guardsman at the Clichy gate of Paris against the advancing Allies in 1814, expresses the ethic of comradeship and sacrifice to a higher cause and criticism of a society based on self-interest and materialism.[126] Auguste Barthélemy seems to have escaped the censor with his epic poem of 1828, *Napoleon in Egypt*, which opened with the words, 'Console our century, glory's orphan!', and repeated Napoleon's famous line, (subtracting a thousand years for the metre) 'Trente siécles debout contemplent notre armée'.[127] But when he returned from Vienna the following year, having tried to present a copy of the poem to Napoleon's son, now known as the duc de Reichstadt, and published another called *Le Fils de l'Homme*, the metaphor caught up with him and he received a prison sentence.

At moments of crisis, such as the July Revolution of 1830, the political content of the popular cult of Napoleon could manifest itself as Bonapartist opposition. The inauguration of the duc d'Orléans was marred by Bonapartists shouting 'No more Bourbons!' and for the next two years until the death of the duc de Reichstadt, crowds gathered in the place Vendôme on 5 May to pay homage to the imperial family. However, the popular cult of the revolutionary emperor was often difficult to distinguish from republicanism, which re-emerged as a dynamic expression of political opposition after 1830. Moreover, many of those who subscribed to the cult of Napoleon, including former servants of his régime, *fédérés* and indeed Béranger himself, concluded that their interests would best be met by rallying to the July Monarchy.[128] The Monarchy itself, as we shall see, was not alien to the cult of Napoleon.

The ambivalence of the political class with regard to Napoleon was increasingly exposed under the Restoration. The collapse of the Empire for the first time in 1814 was the sign for liberals to open up their attack on Napoleon. He was denounced as a warmonger, usurper, tyrant and foreigner-Buonaparte. In a word, he was attacked as the enemy of the French who had cynically and brutally used them to further his own personal vainglorious ends. Chateaubriand, who had broken with Napoleon after the kidnapping and execution of the young Bourbon prince, the duc d'Enghien, was obsessed by the usurpation and condemned Napoleon as a foreigner who saw France only as a source of plunder and 'cannon fodder', raising five billion in taxes and sending five million people to their deaths.[129] Madame de Staël, living in exile in Germany, attacked Napoleon in her posthumously published *Considerations on the French Revolution* (1818) as a tyrant who was guided by three maxims: 'to satisfy mens' interests at the expense of their virtues, to corrupt opinion by specious argument, and to divert the nation towards war and away from liberty'.[130]

Benjamin Constant, Madame de Staël's protégé, argued that 'a monarch approaches the throne nobly; a usurper slides towards it through slime and blood'. Further, 'Illegality pursues him like a ghost', forcing him to put on pageant after pageant and to stagger from one victory to the next for 'he is never satisfied with his house that is built on sand'. Constant's rhetoric even ran to comparisons with Genghis Khan and Attila the Hun.[131] Constant, however, was soon disappointed by the restored Bourbon monarchy. The liberties it granted under the Charter were at the pleasure of the king. A powerful lobby of nobles and clergy was pressing for the revival of many aspects of the Ancien Régime. And the sight of the court making hell-for-leather for the northern frontier as the Emperor landed in the south seriously tarnished its image. And so within days of Napoleon's return Benjamin Constant accepted an invitation to the Tuileries to advise on the construction of a liberal Empire. In Constant, the ambivalence of liberals with regard to the Emperor was revealed at an early stage.

The political class was not cured of its disillusionment with the Bourbon monarchy after the second restoration. The monarchy suffered the handicap that it had been brought back, as the expression went, in the baggage-train of the foreigner. It was as small in European terms as the Empire had been great. The Bourbons had been welcomed initially as champions of the liberty that Napoleon had so ruthlessly stifled, but constitutional and representative government came to be at risk no less from the monarchy, especially that of Charles X. Even among royalists it became possible to look more favourably at the experience of the Empire. The Emperor's death in 1821 made his cult safer, and was followed by a powerful piece of advertising from the grave, the *Memorial of St Helena*, which sought to purvey the view that Napoleon had been but a reluctant revolutionary and had wanted nothing better than to make peace with royalists.

Victor Hugo, born in 1802 was a new convert in the royalist camp to a warmer appreciation of the Emperor. His early hatred of the Emperor was inseparable from a hatred of his father, a general in the Napoleonic armies, whom he knew only as a distant, unfaithful and tyrannical figure. By contrast, he was very close to his mother, a Vendean and a royalist, and after Waterloo wrote 'Vive le Roi!' in his Latin grammar. A year later, he declared, 'I want to be Chateaubriand or nothing.'[132] His early poems included an ode to the duc de Berry, assassinated in 1820, and an ode to the coronation of Charles X, which he attended. His ode on 'Buonaparte' in 1822 repeated all the clichés about usurpation, despotism and conquest. But around 1823 there came a change of heart. He wrote an ode to his father which acknowledged his rôle as a warrior and his part in the military glory of the Empire. With recognition of his father came recognition of the Emperor. It is known that Hugo read the *Memorial of St Helena* soon after its publication. The smallness of France was then brought sharply into focus for him by the treatment of Napoleon's marshals, most of whom had rallied to the monarchy. In 1827 the Austrian ambassador in Paris on

Metternich's orders ceased to recognise the titles of those marshals which recalled Austria's defeats: the duke of Dalmatia (Soult), the duke of Reggio (Oudinot), the duke of Tarento (MacDonald). For Hugo, it was an unaccept-able humiliation: at least under Napoleon marshals had worn their honours with pride. His response was an ode *To the column of the place Vendôme*, an echo of the poem of Debraux a decade earlier, and the point of Victor Hugo's conversion to the cult of Napoleon.

Balzac was another convert from royalism. The son of an imperial civil servant, he espoused legitimism after the fall of Charles X, but was fascinated by the popular cult of Napoleon. Through Balzac, the popular myth was reworked for a more educated public. In his *Médecin de campagne*, which went through six editions between 1833 and 1846, the story-teller in one scene is an old soldier, Goguelat, who is pressed by his audience, gathered in a barn one evening, to tell them about the Emperor.

> What good times they were! Colonels became generals in the twinkling of an eye, generals marshals, and marshals kings . . . Napoleon carried the true sword of God in his scabbard. The soldier had his respect, and he made the soldier his child. He was concerned that you had shoes, linen, overcoats, bread, cartridges. He kept his majesty, for his job was to rule. But it made no difference! A sergeant, even a common soldier, could say to him, 'Mon Empereur', in the same way you sometimes say to me 'my good friend'. He answered our grumbles, slept in the snow like the rest of us, and almost had the air of an ordinary man.[133]

The construction of the story is one of eavesdropping by the notables, for Goguelat and his audience are being listened to from the hayloft by the coun-try doctor and his officer friend. Similarly, Balzac is eavesdropping on the Napoleon of the people for the educated classes.

Meanwhile the artist Auguste-Marie Raffet was in the process of developing a certain vision of the Emperor. A pupil of Gros and Charlet, he made his name as a lithographer, producing a series of albums in the 1830s which celebrated the devotion of the soldiers of the imperial armies to the Emperor, often depicted as a far-off but vigilant presence, watching over his troops. In addi-tion, Raffet illustrated a number of texts celebrating Napoleon, such as the songs of Béranger, the poetry of Barthélémy and Méry, and Thiers' *History of the French Revolution*. His work was executed in microscopic detail, but his masterpiece, *La Rêve Nocturne* (1837), suggested the fantastic side of the Napoleonic myth. Its subject was a ghostly review of the Grande Armée, in the mists over the Champs-Élysées, taking place at midnight under the gaze of the Emperor.[134]

The cult of Napoleon which was developed among the popular classes was taken up by the educated élite, while being carefully separated from its political connotations. Under the July Monarchy, moreover, it virtually assumed an official status. The precondition was that Bonapartism as a political force be effectively silenced. The funeral of Napoleon's Marshal Lamarque, a hero of Wagram, on 5 June 1832, provided the spark for a popular insurrection in Paris, admittedly more republican than Bonapartist, but this was ruthlessly suppressed by the government. In addition, 1832 saw the death of Napoleon's son, the duc de Reichstadt, a prisoner of the Austrians. The July Monarchy, which was far from being in a position militarily to burst the shackles of the treaties of Vienna, saw the benefits of living vicariously off the prestige of the Empire for much-needed political stability and consensus. The cult of the Emperor would provide a veneer of military greatness for the bourgeois monarchy. Accordingly, in 1833 the statue of Napoleon was replaced on the Vendôme column, not this time as a Roman emperor but a Napoleon of the people, designed by Seurre, in greatcoat and cocked hat.[135] The Arc de Triomphe, unfinished at the death of Napoleon, was completed in 1836. The pont du Jardin du Roi and the pont des Invalides reverted to their original names, the pont d'Austerlitz and the pont d'Iéna, while the rue Saint-Germain-des-Prés became the rue Bonaparte. When the château of Versailles was opened as a museum in 1837, rooms were dedicated to the achievements of the Revolution and Empire.

Above all in 1840, by popular request, the remains of Napoleon were brought back from St Helena to lie in the Invalides. This was a risky business, particularly in a year when France suffered diplomatic humiliation at the hands of Great Britain, and the new pretender of the imperial family, Louis-Napoleon, imitated his uncle's landing at Cannes by landing at Boulogne. But the depoliticisation of the cult was admirably expressed by the sentencing to life-imprisonment of Louis-Napoleon by a chamber of peers thick with Napoleon's marshals, while the government of Marshal Soult and François Guizot presided over the return of the Emperor's remains. It should be said that the latter occasion was deliberately played down by the authorities. The convoy travelled from Le Havre not overland but up the Seine, to minimise demonstrations; from the bridge of Neuilly on 15 December 1840, the procession moved to the Arc de Triomphe and down the Champs-Élysées, the coffin hidden in the funeral carriage; and at the Invalides it was received without pomp by Louis-Philippe. 'A great memory, a great occasion, nothing more,' reflected Guizot, 'and friends of the régime of peace and liberty had reason to believe that the imperial régime was buried in the Emperor's coffin.'[136]

It was no doubt naïve of those like Guizot who thought that the cult of Napoleon could be sanitised, depoliticised and harnessed for the purposes of a régime that excluded the masses from the vote and put down civilian discontent by armed force. When the Second Republic was proclaimed and universal suffrage established, the popular cult of Napoleon, as we have seen, was immediately translated into Bonapartism and the election of Louis-Napoleon as president of the Republic. Louis-Napoleon repaid the compliment by endorsing the Napoleon of the people; in 1850 he paid homage to the monument to the Emperor at Fixin with which we began this section. It is likely that the cult of the Emperor among the popular classes made easier the path towards the re-establishment of the Empire in France. While Louis-Napoleon was at Bordeaux in the autumn of 1852, announcing that 'l'Empire, c'est la paix', one of his aides, Adolphe Granier de Cassagnac, took time off to visit his brother, a *curé* in the Pyrenees. There a cobbler gave him, for Louis-Napoleon, a pair of boots richly adorned by pictured of the Emperor's battles and marshals, picked out in different coloured leathers.[137] When the Empire was finally proclaimed, an old *grognard* in Alsace declared, 'Didn't I say that the Empire and the Emperor would return? It's the most wonderful day of my life. I was fond of his uncle but I don't like the nephew any less.'[138]

Once in power, Louis-Napoleon endeavoured to translate the popular cult of Napoleon into the official orthodoxy of the régime. While still prince-president, he began negotiations with Austria for the return of the remains of the Roi de Rome, Napoleon II, which lay in a Capucin crypt in Vienna with those of other members of the Habsburg family. Negotiations dragged on until 1853, but without success.[139] The housing of the tomb of the Emperor in the crypt of the Invalides, designed by the architect Visconti, was completed in 1861, his victories commemorated in the mosaic around the tomb and campaigns by winged figures supporting the vault. In addition, his peaceful achievements and institutions from the Code Civil to the Concordat were also marked by bas-reliefs around the gallery.[140] In keeping with new imperial dignity, the Seurre statue of Napoleon on the Vendôme column in greatcoat and cocked hat was moved in 1863 to the Paris suburb of Courbevoie, on the Seine opposite Neuilly where the body of the Emperor had landed in 1840, and replaced by a statue in the style of a Roman emperor, by Dumont, based on the original (1810) statue by Chaudet.

The rebuilding of Paris by Baron Haussmann after 1858 offered immense scope for the cult of the Emperor, and Napoleon III was keen on broadening it to include the imperial family as a whole. The Étoile, which was then only a crossroads, was developed to include eight more avenues. These were named in 1864, interlacing victories with the family photograph, and moving clockwise from the Champs-Elysées: avenue de Joséphine, avenue d'Iéna, avenue du Roi de Rome, avenue d'Eylau, avenue de l'Impératrice, avenue de la Grande Armée, avenue d'Essling, avenue du Prince Jérôme, avenue de Wagram, avenue de la Reine Hortense, and avenue de Friedland. Between the avenue du Roi de Rome and the avenue Joséphine, parallel to the Seine, was built the avenue de l'Empereur. Also in the same year the rue Militaire, which had run inside the fortifications built around the twenty Paris *arrondissements* by Thiers, and were now demolished, was renamed after nineteen of Napoleon's marshals, from Bessières to Victor.

The attitude of the educated and political class to the official cult of the Emperor was, as usual, ambivalent. Louis-Napoleon had consolidated his régime by trampling on the free institutions which protected the political class. At the same time, the pursuit of military greatness, which was taken up by Napoleon III in the Crimea and Italy, continued to exercise its seductive power.

Having said that, there was clearly a revival, this time mainly in republican quarters, of the black legend which condemned Napoleon as a warmonger who, because he was not himself a Frenchman, had had no qualms about sacrificing France and the French to the realisation of his own ambition.

Adolphe Thiers and Victor Hugo, two men who were both literary figures and politicians, illustrate the first, ambivalent, attitude. For Thiers, Bonapartism combined the twin evils of despotism and demagogy. 'The wretched multitude', he said in 1850, 'has surrendered to every tyrant the liberty of every republic', and he was happy to see universal suffrage abrogated.[141] Between 1840 and 1862 he was engaged on a *History of the Consulate and Empire* in twenty volumes. He argued in 1845 (vol. 5) that Napoleon had overreached himself by grasping the imperial crown, and at the end of the work he drew the lesson that 'you should never hand over a country to one man, whoever the man, whatever the circumstances'.[142] But the bulk of his history was devoted to the Emperor's military achievements. And far from being another lesson about overreaching oneself, Waterloo was yet another example of a 'giant' and 'genius' at work, brought low by the incompetence of a single general, Grouchy, who happened to be in the wrong place at the wrong time.[143]

Victor Hugo was no less divided against himself by the cult of Napoleon, seeing greatness on the one hand, despotism and militarism on the other.[144] The coup d'état of 2 December had a devastating effect on him. It was a violation of Louis-Napoleon's oath to uphold the constitution, a crime, no less, followed by the massacre of innocent people on the streets. Until 1851, the black legend had dwelt on the questions of usurpation, despotism and war-mongering rather than on the coup of *Brumaire*. Now, for Hugo, the coup of 1815 was central and cast a shadow over that of 1799. The behaviour of Napoléon-le-Petit had a retrospective impact on perceptions of Napoléon-le-Grand. 'The 18 *brumaire*', said Victor Hugo, 'is a crime whose stain on the memory of Napoleon has been spread by 2 December.' And yet Hugo seemed able even then to keep separate the crimes of Napoleon from 'the dazzling curtain of glory'.[145] He visited the battlefield of Waterloo in the summer of 1861 'to confront', as he put it, 'the legend with the reality'.[146] For him it represented the high point of the Napoleonic epic, and in 1862 he opened the second part of *Les Misérables* with a pageant of the battle.

The approach of the fiftieth anniversary of Waterloo in fact was the occasion of a heated debate on the Emperor's achievement. Views diametrically opposed to those of Thiers and Hugo were expressed by republican exiles in Switzerland. Lieutenant-Colonel Charras, briefly minister of war in 1848, argued that responsibility for defeat at Waterloo had to be laid firmly and squarely at the door of the Emperor. Napoleon's ambition he argued, had cost France dear. 'Personally,' he said, 'I am perfectly dry-eyed about Napoleon chained to his rock in the middle of the ocean; I reserve my tears for those who were the victims of his ambition', the thousands of soldiers littering the battlefields of Europe.[147] His friend, Edgar Quinet, expressed a similar view in another study of the campaign of 1815. Quinet, in addition, revived the argument of the black legend that Napoleon had used France as the instrument of his ambitions in a way that was inconceivable to Richelieu or Louis XIV, because he was not French but Italian.[148]

The interpretation of Napoleon as a warmonger and enemy of the people was taken up by the popular novelists Emile Erckmann and Alexandre Chatrian. Dismissed by Flaubert as 'two old chaps with somewhat plebeian souls', their *Romans nationaux* nevertheless expressed the aspirations of ordinary people liberated by the Revolution but betrayed by Napoleon, whom they characterised as an over-ambitious dynast, bent on conquest, using the people merely as cannon-fodder.[149] Their *Story of a Conscript of 1813* (1864) is told from the viewpoint of a young apprentice from Alsace, conscripted for the German campaign of 1813. Left for dead on the battlefield of Lützen, he dreams of his loved ones and the thirty or forty thousand other families who would receive the worst tidings from the battlefield. At Leipzig, the soldiers see the little man in the grey coat and cocked hat, and cheer 'Vive l'Empereur!', but 'he didn't hear us . . . he paid no more attention to us than to the fine rain that hung in the air'.[150] The legend of the sun of Austerlitz, of the Emperor carried forward by the roar of his troops, was replaced by that of a flock led astray and sacrificed to one man's lust for power.

Whereas the Napoleon of the people survived Waterloo and even flourished because of it, the defeat of Sedan dealt a sharp blow to the popular Napoleon as well as the official one. In the first place, the criticism to which the cult of Napoleon had been subjected percolated down to the revolutionary leaders and militants. In February 1871 Jules Vallès attacked Adolphe Thiers, then head of the executive of the Republic, for taking 'ten years to regild the coat on the shoulders of the Caesar defeated at Waterloo and buried on St Helena . . . and [giving] the bandit of the coup d'état a little cocked hat to suckle in'.[151] Secondly, however, the Empire gave way not to the monarchy but to the Republic, and in Paris the popular classes seized power in the Paris Commune. Napoleon was now seen as an enemy of revolution, not as the revolutionary Emperor. Accordingly, the statue of the Napoleon of the people by Seurre, moved to Courbevoie, was thrown into the Seine. The Roman Emperor on top of the Vendôme column, and the column with it, was brought crashing to the ground by the Paris Commune. [Fig. 8] 'If ever a man landed us in the shit,' raged *Le Père Duchesne* over the rubble, 'then it was certainly that bugger Bonaparte the first. Not only by war, when he had so many people massacred, but by a host of tricks that stopped the Revolution and strengthened tyranny.'[152]

The politicians who came to power in the Third Republic had been effectively excluded from power by the Second Empire. Some had been hounded, imprisoned or driven into exile by the coup d'état of 2 December. As republicans, they subscribed to the doctrine of the sovereignty of the people but were both horrified and fascinated by the way in which Louis-Napoleon had used it

Fig. 8. Destruction of the statue of Napoleon, place Vendôme, by the Communards (Bibiothèque historique de la Ville de Paris)

to his advantage for nearly twenty years. Though Napoleon III had fallen, and Paris had toppled the statue of Napoleon I, they were constantly vigilant lest there should be a revival of Bonapartism. In 1874, indeed, there was a series of Bonapartist victories in by-elections which confirmed that the threat was still present. At Auxerre, in the Yonne, Gambetta warned that Bonapartism was not democracy but pseudo-democracy. 'Caesarism', he said, 'means corrupting democracy, debasing and degrading it into a low demagoguery, the more fearsome because people believe that they will find peace and prosperity by surrendering to a master, while in fact there is only dishonour and catastrophe.'[153] Republicans were driven into the arms of Orleanists to pass a constitution that was quintessentially anti-Bonapartist, and would render impossible a repeat of the coup of 2 December 1851.

The dramatic success of Boulangism, attacking as it did the cosiness of the parliamentary Republic, was feared by republican oligarchs as new manifestation of Bonapartism. As we have seen, General Boulanger carried the hopes of the imperial family from one electoral success to another, although the movement was far from being controlled by Bonapartists. For Jules Ferry, in many ways the parliamentary Republic incarnate, Boulangism revived painful memories of the aftermath of the coup d'état of 2 December 1851 when, as a student, he had witnessed the shooting of innocent passers-by on the boulevards of Paris by 'corrupted and possibly bribed soldiers'. It was doubly painful for the architect of the education reforms of the Third Republic, who had dedicated himself to drilling the French people in the virtues of republican citizenship, to see them once again throwing themselves at the feet of a Caesar. Ferry was unable to explain the phenomenon except as a kind of madness. 'What is this legend', he asked, 'that generates spontaneously and spreads suddenly, this sudden infatuation, this need to create an idol and to acclaim a master, other than the return . . . of the old national disease which has twice in one century handed over the country to dictatorship?'[154] At the end of the Boulangist episode Ferry gave less credence to the Napoleonic legend and incorporated contemporary scientific thinking about hysteria and hypnosis. He attributed Boulangism to 'a hypnotic trance of the masses . . . there was more sickliness than Caesarism at the outset of this adventure'.[155] In either case, his verdict betrayed a fear of the republican élite that universal suffrage, while being central to their political catechism, was also a monster of Frankenstein over which they had little control.

The politicians of the Republic were, however, as susceptible as those of the July Monarchy to appropriating some of the glory of the First Empire to give a veneer of greatness to the régime. The defeat of 1870 had been catastrophic and it was a long time before the Third Republic was able to register any military successes. The cult of Napoleon was revived to inspire sentiments of French greatness, although in a rather selective way. The First Empire was presented as a culmination of the glories of the revolutionary wars and the later, bloodier campaigns of the Empire were no longer celebrated. The First Empire was sharply distinguished from the Second Empire, which merited only contempt, as did the dynasticism of the Bonaparte family. Thus a week after the Commune had toppled the Vendôme column, the National Assembly decided to re-establish it, and the Dumont statue, duly restored, resumed its place in 1875. Around the Étoile, avenues were renamed in a most calculated way. References to the imperial family disappeared. The avenue de l'Impératrice became the avenue du Bois-de-Boulogne in 1875. The avenues Joséphine, du Roi-de-Rome and de la Reine Hortense took in 1879 respectively the names of revolutionary generals who, significantly, had died before establishment of the First Empire: Marceau (d.1796), Hoche (d.1797) and Kléber (d.1800). Some of Napoleon's bloodier battles were forgotten. The avenue d'Essling was renamed Carnot in 1880, and the avenue d'Eylau renamed after Victor Hugo in 1886. But the avenues celebrating the great decisive victories of the Empire (Iéna, Friedland, Wagram) and the Grande Armée retained their names. The question of the rue Bonaparte was more tricky, since it suggested both military greatness and a political system that was anathema to most republicans. An extract from a debate in the Paris municipal council in 1885 illustrates the closed circle of divergent views:

Marius Martin: Even if you don't like the 18 *brumaire* you can't forget that
Bonaparte filled the universe with his name, his glory. . . .
M. Chautemps: And with corpses.
M. Cattiaux: He sowed ruin everywhere.
Marius Martin: The council cannot deny respect for the name of the victor
of Marengo, Austerlitz, Wagram. . . .
M. Mayer: And of *Brumaire*.[156]

The majority on the council voted by forty-one to twenty-four to change the
name of the rue Bonaparte to the rue du Luxembourg, but was overruled by the
Opportunist government which, though violently anti-Bonapartist, interpreted
this homage as part of the cult of Napoleon.

As at the end of the Second Empire, those who found it possible to combine
anti-Bonapartism with the cult of the Emperor were rivalled by those who
subscribed to and encouraged the black legend. A key figure in this respect was
Hippolyte Taine. In an article published in the *Revue des Deux Mondes* in 1887,
which became the substance of his analysis of Napoleon in *The Origins of
Contemporary France*, Taine took up the notion dear to Chateaubriand and
Quinet that much was to be explained by Bonaparte's Italian origin, and
compared him to 'the little Italian tyrants of the fourteenth and fifteenth
centuries', like the Sforza of Milan. He was characterised as a man without
spirituality or humanity, an engineer by training who applied the same cold
scientific methods to matters both military and political. And he was criticised
as an egoist who 'instead of placing himself at the service of the state, placed the
state at his personal service', and bore responsibility for nearly four million
deaths in the French Empire.[157]

Taine's interpretation, though influential, did not carry the day. The period
after 1890 saw a tremendous flourishing of the cult of Napoleon in France. As
under the July Monarchy, both domestic and international conditions were
favourable. As the July Monarchy had dealt with the political threat of
Bonapartism, so the parliamentary Republic defeated Boulangism. There was
to be no plebiscitary dictatorship and no war of revenge against Bismarck.
Peace and political liberty were the order of the day. On the other hand, what
survived looked to many observers scarcely more appetising. Peace and liberty
from another angle looked like the corruption of parliamentary government and
the failure of France to keep up in the great-power race with Great Britain,
Germany and Russia. Behind that failure was still felt the pain of defeat in 1870.
The approach, after the centenary of the Revolution, of the centenary of the
great dates of the Consulate and the Empire, focused the collective mind on the
gulf between the glorious past and the prosaic present in which France seemed
so insignificant. As in the 1830s, there was a conversion of the educated class to
the cult of Napoleon. Now as then, he was resurrected not as the imperial ruler
of the official cult, nor as the Napoleon of the people, the revolutionary emperor elected by the people to defend the gains of the Revolution—that was the

Fig. 9.　Edouard Détaille, *The Dream*. Salon of 1888 (Musée d'Orsay)

task of the Republic—but as military leader who had brought greatness to France and in whose greatness France could vicariously bask anew. He was presented as a charismatic leader and war hero, and for the first time the private Napoleon was also explored. Particularly popular too was the interpretation of the Napoleonic episode as epic, legend, even as fantasy, a distant dream-world that continued to haunt and inspire.[158]

The most significant media for the revival of the cult of Napoleon were those of fine art, the theatre, and imaginative literature. *The Dream*, the most famous painting of the military artist, Édouard Détaille, exhibited in the Salon of 1888, depicted a row of soldiers in the war of 1870 sleeping by their bivouac fires, while in the night air a ghostly apparition of Napoleon's Old Guard gallops by to inspire and protect them. [Fig. 9] Seurre's statue of Napoleon, the little man in the cocked hat that had once stood on the Vendôme column, was fished out the Seine where it had been left by the Communards and found a last resting place in 1911 in the Cour d'honneur of the Invalides.

In the theatre, the Napoleonic legend was a box-office success. *Madame Sans-Gêne* by Victorien Sardou was first performed in Paris at the Vaudeville theatre in 1893. Based on the true story of the daughter of an Avignon cloth-merchant who dressed as a man and fought in the revolutionary and

Napoleonic armies, it cast the heroine as a washerwoman, risen to become the wife of Marshal Lefebvre and duchess of Danzig, and staged comic dialogues between herself and the Emperor. *Le Figaro* praised its portrayal of an 'intimate, dressing-gowned Napoleon' and of characters who appeared to have walked out of a picture by Meissonnier or Raffet.[159] Even more fantastic was *L'Aiglon* of Edmond Rostand, which opened in Paris in 1900 with Sarah Bernhardt in the title-rôle. The legend was approached through the dreams of 'little eagle', the duc de Reichstadt, held captive in the Austrian court, and pictured as 'a French Hamlet' by the *Figaro* critic. The extent to which republican politicians had no difficulty reconciling hostility to Bonapartism and militarism with dabbling in the cult of Napoleon is illustrated by the fact that the opening night was attended not only by imperial celebrities like Prince and Princess Murat but also by René Waldeck-Rousseau, head of the government of republican defence, his education minister Georges Leygues, and other republican politicians including Léon Bourgeois and Louis Barthou.[160]

Among the fictional works of the period the novels of Georges d'Esparbès were particularly popular. These were set in the twilight moments of the Empire, when the greatness of the Napoleonic epic was already a thing of the past, yet the hardened veterans who survived from the giant armies profess undying loyalty to the emperor, while the emperor, reviewing them, knows their every act of courage.[161] Nostalgia was being created before the eyes of the public. Meanwhile in *Les Déracinés*, published in 1897 by Maurice Barrès, who had a great following among young men who had cut their political teeth on Boulangism, Napoleon was held up as a source of inspiration. Barrès describes *bacheliers* from the provinces, pursuing their careers in Paris, but seeing the Republic corrupted and dessicated by big business and official phiosophy, making a pilgrimage to Les Invalides to seek guidance at the tomb of Napoleon, 'professor of energy'.[162]

The educated public was not satisfied with the Napoleon of legend and fantasy. In the 1890s there was a lively market for memoirs of Napoleon's contemporaries, which claimed to evoke the authentic person of the emperor, but generally contributed to the myth of his military genius or leadership. The memoirs of General Baron Marbot, originally written in 1816, and published in 1891, revived the old myth of 'the magical power that Napoleon exercised over his troops, so that his presence and a few words were enough to hurl them into the greatest of dangers'.[163] Also published in 1891 were the popular *Notebooks of Captain Coignet*, the autobiography of a genuine *grognard* who, as an orphan, looked on the imperial Guard as his family and on the Emperor as his father.[164] More hostile to the Emperor were the memoirs of Napoleon's private secretary, Bourrienne, who was sacked in 1806. First published in 1829, they were republished with greater success in 1899.[165] Napoleon's aide-de-camp, General Baron Gourgaud, who had saved the emperor's life from a Cossack's lance in 1814 and shared his exile on St Helena, had in 1823 published a military history down to 1801; in 1899 it was his private diary, recording the day-today life and table-talk of the court of exiles at St Helena, that was published and in demand.[166]

For the first time, however, the Napoleonic period was the subject of serious academic history. These accounts were certainly scholarly, but were also a further elaboration of the Napoleonic myth. For these historians, who had experienced the traumas of 1870, the Napoleonic epic offered some clues as to how to recover greatness in the most testing circumstances. Henry Houssaye, himself a veteran of 1870, switched attention from the overarching ambitions of Napoleon to the campaigns of 1814 and 1815 when, after all, Napoleon had defended *French* soil to the last drop of blood.[167] Albert Vandal, in his study of the alliance of Napoleon and Alexander in 1807, sought to show how the Emperor had escaped diplomatic isolation, and had anticipated the Franco-Russian alliance of 1891–2.[168] Frédéric Masson looked to meet the popular demand for studies of the private person of Napoleon and, in particular, his relationships with women. But he found himself using the unpublished youthful correspondence of Bonaparte to lay to rest the myth of the Corsican ogre woven by Taine, while his work on Napoleon's family argued that they were largely responsible for his downfall and concluded that he was 'the incarnation of a national strategy as old as France itself; he was its last soldier, and indeed its martyr'.[169]

The cult of Napoleon flourished among the educated classes in a climate of peace and liberty. Threats to peace and liberty might be expected to make them less comfortable with the myth and restore the black legend to favour. The Dreyfus affair, which raised the spectre of Bonapartist revival and military conspiracy, might easily have rendered the cult impolitic. The Great War shattered the illusion of the colourful and heroic nature of war that the Napoleonic myth had helped to sustain, and invited reconsideration of the Napoleonic wars as a series of massacres which prefigured the modern war of the trenches. In the event, the cult of Napoleon, reworked in the light of new challenges, proved surprisingly resilient.

The Dreyfus affair occurred during the run-up to the centenary of the birth of Victor Hugo (1902). In many ways the range of sentiments that was expressed during the Dreyfus affair mirrored the ambivalence of Hugo's views on Napoleon, and Hugo was variously appropriated as an enemy of coup d'état and champion of the army. Émile Zola, who denounced the framing of Dreyfus by the military hierarchy, constructed the affair as a struggle between liberty and despotism, light and darkness. In his *Letter to France* he evoked Victor Hugo on 2 December: 'I saw the shadow of the sabre falling across the wall. France, if you do not take care, you will end up under a dictatorship.'[170] On the other hand, Henri Houssaye, that great admirer of Napoleon, set out to present Hugo, who had vented his spleen on Louis-Napoleon in *Napoléon-le-Petit*, as the apologist of Napoleon I. He placed an advertisement in the *Écho de Paris* for a limited edition of texts from Victor Hugo gathered under the title *Napoléon-le-Grand*. The frontispiece, it was announced, depicted the emperor, in a cloud of smoke at the head of his cavalry, stopping his horse to salute the coffin of Victor Hugo as it lay in state under the Arc de Triomphe. Though the collection was never published, the intention to reclaim Hugo for the cult of Napoleon was serious.[171] Victor Hugo's ambivalence towards Napoleon, and through the prism of Hugo, the ambivalence of the French people, was appreciated by Charles Péguy in *Notre Patrie* (1905). Writing after the first Morocco crisis, which has often been seen as the point of take-off of the French nationalist revival, Péguy explained that 'the people want to make fun of the army, to insult and revile the army which is, if you like, one way of making fun of it; and to dream of wars . . . Hugo, like the people, is at once for and against war, for and against the military . . . Victor Hugo the poet never shook off the cult of Napoleon'.[172]

Whether the First World War would be favourable to the cult of Napoleon was also an open question. Clearly, the mobilisation of the nation in a protracted military struggle for survival encouraged the French to turn to the Napoleonic myth for inspiration. Yet, the Great War corresponded little to the popular image of the flair and swiftness of Napoleon's campaigns. There was a danger that the cult of Napoleon would provide ammunition for those who wanted to attack him as a warmonger who had presided over massacres and brought ruin to France.

The centenary of the Emperor's death, which fell on 5 May 1921, exposed these rival interpretations. Whereas victory had hitherto lain outside the experience of the Republic, it was now something it had in common with the Empire. Just as the victory of the Republic dealt a mortal blow to Bonapartism, so it enabled it to consider the achievements of the Empire without any sentiment of inferiority and to establish the cult of Napoleon safely as part of the national heritage. The president of the centenary committee, Édouard Driault, told an audience assembled in the Sorbonne on 4 May 1921, that 'the Republic is by definition "the thing of all" and should honour with the same piety all the glories of France', including Napoleon's victories.[173] However, speaking on the morning of 5 May 1921 at the Arc de Triomphe, in the presence of the president of the Republic, Louis Barthou, the minister of war, proclaimed, 'For our part, we do not want war, we have a horror of war, conquests, annexations and imperialist ambitions.'[174] That afternoon, in the chapel of the Invalides, Marshal Foch praised Napoleon's understanding of the art of war, but suggested that he had neglected the nation, and declared, 'above and beyond war, there is peace'.[175] The Communist party took the view that the experience of trench warfare had done little for the Napoleon of the people, and was angered by the coincidence of the centenary with the mobilisation of the class of 1919 to service French ambitions in the Ruhr. 'To revive chauvinist ideas, the spirit of conquest abroad and authority at home,' wrote Marcel Cachin in *L'Humanité*, 'those who used to vilify the Empire now try to glorify it.'[176] At an anti-war demonstration of 100,000 on 8 May the police charged, killing one and wounding fifty.

To combat a resurgence of the black legend that attacked Napoleon as a war-monger, a new image of the Emperor was presented in the 1920s, that of peacemaker, visionary and pioneer of a federal Europe. This rested on some of the more extravagant claims made by Napoleon in the *Memorial of St Helena*, that he intended to gather the nations of Europe into nation-states and thence into a European federation, which seemed perhaps less extravagant after the Treaty of Versailles. The art historian Élie Faure described Napoleon as a poet and discovered the 'spiritual character' of his imperialism. He quoted the emperor to the effect that 'war is an anachronism; one day victories will be achieved without cannon and without bayonets', and argued that his ultimate aim had been to found 'universal democracy'.[177] In his *History of France*, published in 1924, Jacques Bainville attributed to the Revolution and its con-tinuator, Napoleon, an 'attempt to realise a dream, that of the universal Repub-lic, under the presidency of the French people'.[178] The ideas became common currency in Abel Gance's epic film, *Napoleon*, in 1927. At the end of the film the young Napoleon Bonaparte, about to lead the army to Italy, is visited by the ghosts of Danton, Saint-Just and Marat, who ask him what his plans are. 'The liberation of enslaved peoples,' replies Bonaparte, 'the reconciliation of great Eurpean interests, the abolition of frontiers and . . . the universal Republic.'[179]

The federalist idea was at the heart of the Institut Napoléon, founded in 1932 to sustain the cult of the emperor. When a pilgrimage was made to the field of Waterloo in June 1935, the tomb of King Albert of the Belgians, who had so bravely defended his people in 1914–18, was also visited. Relations were good with the Czechs, who had gained their freedom from the collapse of the Austrian Empire in 1918 and were at the centre of France's East European Entente. A Napoleonic congress was held in Prague in 1933 and in 1936 a delegation of the Napoleonic society of Brno brought a gift of soil from the battlefield of Austerlitz, sited on Czech territory, in an urn of black Bohemian crystal, to lie in the Invalides.[180]

Whereas France approached the First World War with a certain confidence, she approached the Second with very little confidence at all. If the cult of a military Napoleon had confirmed sentiments of her own greatness in the first instance, in the second the cult of a peaceful Napoleon served to underwrite the system of collective security. But the breakdown of collective security, and France's sense of her own weakness, particularly after the reoccupation of the Rhineland by Germany in 1936, opened the way to the revival of the black legend according to which Napoleon had done France nothing but harm. In 1937 Charles Maurras took up the story from Chateaubriand and Taine. He attacked Napoleon as a son of the Revolution who had destroyed the natural order of society under the 'the steam-roller levelling of the Year VIII'. Napoleon was accused of establishing equality before the law and rigid cen-tralisation in order to reduce the French nation to servitude, and attacked as a foreigner who wanted only to use and abuse France for his own ambition. Maurras argued that the Emperor had thrown away hard-won frontiers by impatiently seizing power from the monarchy in 1815, and had provoked German nationalism and unification. He was accused of engendering Bismarck, and by implication, Hitler.[181]

Hitler himself sported with the cult of Napoleon in order to demonstrate the destruction of French greatness and the end of its influence in Europe. Since the centenary of the death of the Roi de Rome in 1932, a campaign had been mounted in France for the return of his remains from Vienna. A committee had been set up under Prince Joachim Murat and the consent of the fallen Habsburg family obtained. The Austrian government, however, refused to co-operate. The deadlock was broken by the *Anschluss* and the defeat of France. To set the seal on the policy of collaboration inaugurated by the handshake of Pétain and Hitler at Montoire, Hitler decided to present France with the remains of the duc de Reichstadt. On the night of 14–15 December 1940, a century to the day since the return of Napoleon's remains from St Helena, the coffin was brought by train from Frankfurt to the Gare de l'Est and by gun-carriage with an escort of German officers to the Invalides, where it was received by Admiral Darlan. Marshal Pétain wisely declined to make the journey from Vichy to receive the remains. The gesture for the Reichschancellor only served to symbolise the reversal of the humiliation inflicted on the German nation by Napoleon and again in 1918.[182]

It might be imagined that the cult of Napoleon would have been ripe for the picking by General de Gaulle, to associate his own bid to restore the honour and greatness of France with the enterprise of Napoleon. The Fifth Republic might have inaugurated an official cult of the emperor like the First or Second Empires, or at least like the July Monarchy and Third Republic. In fact the relationship of de Gaulle and the cult of Napoleon was more distant and more ambiguous, and it never acquired any official status under the Fifth Republic. Just as he sought to avoid accusations of Bonapartism, so he was wary about the cult of Napoleon, first lest he become a victim of the black legend of militarism and war-mongering and, second, lest popular opinion make comparisons between his Napoleonic stature and Bonapartist ambitions.

De Gaulle was certainly exposed to the revival of interest in Napoleon at the turn of the century. Born in 1890 and brought up in Paris, he would sometimes be taken on Thursday half-holidays to the Arc de Triomphe or the tomb of Napoleon at the Invalides, like the *Déracinés* of Barrès, while in 1900 his birthday treat was to attend *L'Aiglon* of Rostand.[183] As a lecturer at the miltary college of Saint-Cyr after the Great War, he expounded on Napoleon's campaign of 1805, the surrender of the Austrian army at Ulm and the victory of Austerlitz. He argued that Napoleon's technical mastery was adorned by 'a prestige, an authority and an energy whose renown made the Emperor a fabulous personage'.[184] When de Gaulle began to organise the Free French forces in Africa in 1941, he made a speech in Cairo which recalled the Egyptian expedition of Bonaparte, and he followed in the path of Bonaparte when he entered Syria and Lebanon with the Free French in June of that year.[185] In 1945 the First French Army crossed the Rhine, occupied Baden-Wurttemberg, and went on, for reasons as much symbolic as strategic, to take Ulm on the Danube.[186]

For de Gaulle the inspiration of Napoleon nevertheless remained qualified and was never central. He shared the concern of Taine that Napoleon was merely a technician, a global chess-player whose imperialism lacked any spiritual dimension. De Gaulle's own creed was that France was not just a great military power but the bearer of liberty and civilisation in the world. Further, his nationalism was eclectic: Napoleon had a place in the hall of honour but other architects of French greatness shared it with him. Thus his wartime speeches appealed to Joan of Arc, Louis XIV, Danton and Clemenceau, as well as to Napoleon. His Cairo address of 1941 paid homage not only to Bonaparte but also to St Louis and Ferdinand de Lesseps, and to the 'religious, moral, technical and economic activities' of the French in Egypt over the centuries. As he marched down the Champs-Élysées on 26 August 1944, he wrote in his *Mémoires de Guerre*, the associations conveyed by the monuments of Paris included the victories commemorated by the bridges across the Seine, the military reviews witnessed by the triumphal arch of the Carousel and the chestnut trees of the Champs-Élysées dreamed of by Rostand's Aiglon. These, however, were overshadowed by the nodding statue of Clemenceau, the dome of Louis XIV's Invalides, sheltering the tombs of Turenne and Foch as well as that of the Emperor, the statues of Joan of Arc and Henri IV, the palace of St Louis, who (unlike himself) had never returned from the sands of Africa, the hill dedicated to St Geneviève, who had saved Paris from Attila the Hun, and the place de la Concorde, where Louis XVI and Marie Antoinette had perished.[187] Finally, in de Gaulle's commonplace-book for 1946 there was only one quotation from Napoleon, and a line from Lamartine reflecting ungloriously that 'the reign of Napoleon was nothing but a harsh discipline imposed on the nation'. There were, however, three quotations from Barrès, four from Péguy, and no less than nineteen from the mortal enemy of Napoleon, Chateaubriand.[188]

De Gaulle may have been felt relief that he fell from power before he was obliged to confront the Napoleonic legend on the bicentenary of the Emperor's birth at Ajaccio on 15 August 1969. Nevertheless, he confided his sentiments to André Malraux who came to interview him in his retirement at Colombey. He was still of the opinion that 'spirituality was always foreign to Napoleon', and accused him of being too ambitious, particularly after 1811.[189] He returned to the tomb of Napoleon before which crowds felt as nowhere else 'the thrill of greatness', and to Barrès' notion of the 'professor of energy', though he felt that Napoleon had been much more of a 'professor of ambition'.[190] De Gaulle was also sensitive to the fantastic side of the Napoleonic legend. 'One of his remarks has always troubled me', he confessed, 'because it is magnificent and incomprehensible: "I make my plans with the dreams of my sleeping soldiers." '[191] There was more than a whiff of Raffet and Detaille about de

Gaulle's Napoleon. Malraux himself ventured to the general that his predecessor in France was in fact Victor Hugo.[192]

The speech that de Gaulle had been due to give at Ajaccio was in the event given by his successor as president, Georges Pompidou. Where de Gaulle's Napoleon was that of Barrès and the revival of his boyhood, that of Pompidou was the vision of the *Memorial of St Helena*, taken up in the 1920s and appropriated once again to sanction the development of the European Community. 'The spirit of conquest has been attributed to Napoleon quite wrongly,' Pompidou insisted. 'The maritime supremacy achieved by England literally forced him repeatedly to attack and win.' He quoted Napoleon's project of national states federated in a 'great European family', and concluded that 'the genius of Napoleon dominates our history as it prefigures the future of Europe'.[193] This Napoleon, recast as Jean Monnet, visionary of the Common Market, resurfaced again in 1992 during the referendum campaign on the Maastricht treaty. The socialist government, to add weight and legitimacy to the case for European integration, resurrected the little man in the cocked hat with the slogan, 'Napoléon ler aurait voté pour Maastricht.'[194]

While the cult of Napoleon was not taken up in any official sense by the Fifth Republic, the popular cult was certainly not dead. The Commumist party, which had immediately denounced the advent to power of de Gaulle as a coup and attempted to discredit him by comparing him to Napoleon III, nevertheless did not eschew the cult of Napoleon. Naturally this was a revolutionary Napoleon, sent to protect the achievements of 1789 and 1793. The Communist historian Albert Soboul, paying homage to Napoleon in *L'Humanité* on the occasion of the bicentenary, introduced him as a Jacobin, a protégé of the Robespierre brothers, arguing that whatever his personal ambition, he could not triumph over dialectical materialism.

> The reign of Napoleon is bound to the revolutionary period by a profound unity. Whatever his genius, it was not within the power of an ambitious general to return to the past or to step outside the limits traced by History. Napoleon's will to power was not able to win the day: the new dynasty, a European empire, everything disappeared. Nothing remained but what was in keeping with the revolutionary heritage, and with the grain of History.[195]

As for the cult of the political class, it has been sustained by two major institutions. The Institut Napoléon, founded in 1932 and headed successively by the historians Edouard Driault (1932–6), Philippe Sagnac (1936–47), Marcel Dunan (1947–73) and Jean Tulard (since 1974), has promoted historical research into the Empire in the best scholarly traditions, but with a certain nostalgia for its greatness. Tulard regretted that the 'new history' gave short shrift to the events of 1789–1815, but noted in 1988 'the astonishing vitality of research into Napoleonic history'.[196]

Alongside the Institut is the Souvenir Napoléon. This was founded in Nice in 1937 by Eugénie Gal, a great-great-niece of Louis-Gabriel Suchet, duke of

Albufera, who converted to the cult of Napoleon by reading Victor Hugo. It gathers within its ranks amateur and professional historians, the *fine fleur* of imperial families such as the princes Murat and the counts Walewski, and a general public dedicated to the cult of Napoleon. Its style is theatrical and hagiographical. In 1965, for example, it marked the 150th anniversary of the return from Elba by staging a reconstruction of the landing at Cannes by fifty *grognards* in period costume, the emperor played by Albert Dieudonné, who had immortalised Bonaparte in Abel Gance's film nearly forty years before.[197] The president since 1983 has been Baron Napoleon Gourgaud, the great-great-nephew of the Baron Gourgaud who had saved Napoleon from a Cossack's lance and had been his aide-de-camp on St Helena. In 1987 the Souvenir was renamed the Fondation Napoléon after the legacy of a millionaire businessman, Martial Lapeyre, equipped it with impressive premises in the rue de Monceau, Paris VIII, and provided it with substantial working capital. Celebrations to mark the fiftieth anniversary of its foundation were held in September 1988. These were attended by Jacques Chirac and Prince and Princess Napoléon, despite the embarrassment to the former of attempts in his own party to revive the Bonapartist myth and the long-suffering of the latter, for thirty years the patron of the fanatics of the cult of Napoleon.[198] Thus while the official cult of Napoleon fell into disuse, the educated and political class abandoned the black legend and took up the popular cult, while purging it of its revolutionary connotations.

CHAPTER 3

Grandeur

Constructing Greatness

'France cannot be France without grandeur.' So wrote Charles de Gaulle in his *Mémoires de Guerre*.[1] But de Gaulle prided himself on articulating the profoundest sentiments of the French, and the phrase might have been uttered by any national leader from the time of Louis XIV onwards. Each régime, monarchy, republic or empire, undertook the task of defending the honour of France, both to match the precedent set by previous régimes and indeed to win the necessary popularity to ensure its own survival. 'The rôle of France is to retain its rank.' Again, this might have been said by de Gaulle, or Marshal Foch, or even Napoleon, but in fact it was proclaimed at a press conference in 1989 by François Mitterrand.[2] He was at pains to point out that France was the third military power in the world, the fourth or fifth economic power, and that as a cultural force her place was without equal. In order to assert its claim to influence world affairs, France has constructed a national political culture based on the notions of greatness, honour and her rank in the league-table of nations.

And yet the history of France has been punctuated by a series of national catastrophes. France was invaded and occupied in 1814, 1815 and 1870, survived the Great War only at the cost of a million and a half lives, and came perilously close to extinction as an independant power under the German occupation of 1940–4. It may be argued that the main impulse to develop a myth of national greatness has been precisely the fact that the collective memory of defeat and humiliation has been too painful to bear. A number of strategies was adopted to ensure acceptance of this myth. First, individual defeats were subsumed in what has been asserted as a continuity of French greatness, going back to the earliest periods of the French monarchy, if not to the Roman inheritance. Second, even in the midst of defeat individual heroic actions or slogans were found to preserve the honour of France as a nation of combatants. Third, the blame for defeat was levelled at particular régimes in order to exculpate opposing régimes; thus it was claimed that the Republic was

112

incapable of greatness, or that empires led to defeat as water to the sea. Fourth, France directed her urge for supremacy away from a Europe dominated by her rivals to other parts of the world in the hope of recovering rank by indirect means. Fifth, it was argued that defeat and national mourning rather than victory were conducive to sentiments of national solidarity, and that it was in the crucible of collective suffering that renewed greatness was forged. Sixth, a collective amnesia tended to overtake the French, who inclined to persist in the cult of their own national greatness even when all objective grounds for it had ceased to exist. Napoleon III's General Trochu was indeed perceptive when he observed in 1867, 'we have a special talent for explaining and justifying our defeats'.[3]

When the Revolution replaced the monarch by the nation as the seat of sovereign power, conquest and domination were rejected as the pastime of dynastic rulers who sacrificed their people to their lust for glory, but hardly the concern of a free people. 'The French nation renounces the undertaking of all war with a view to conquest,' stated the constitution of 1791, 'and will never use its strength against the liberty of any people'.[4] Revolutionary, then republican France, it seemed, would adopt an entirely different strategy towards other peoples. However, the revolutionaries, though they had formally renounced conquest, were anxious to equal, if not to surpass, the military brilliance and power of the race of kings they had deposed. They, too, therefore began to expand the frontiers of France, albeit under the cover of the recovery of France's 'natural frontiers', the 'consent' of foreign territories to annexation, and the disguising of satellite states as 'sister republics'. Louis XIV had presided over France's Grand Siècle, but the Republic matched this with the rhetoric of the Grande Nation. Thus on the death in 1797 of Lazare Hoche, commander of the Sambre-et-Meuse army and conqueror of the Rhineland, Marie-Joseph Chénier wrote an elegy in his honour which concluded:

La grande nation à vaincre accoutumée
Et le grand général guidant la grande armée.[5]

The claim to power of Napoleon Bonaparte was based on his military prowess, furthering the influence of the Republic under the Directory in Italy, Egypt and Syria. As First Consul, after Marengo, he appropriated the glory of Louis XIV by having the body of Louis's great commander Turenne transferred to the Invalides. By instituting the Empire in 1804, Napoleon attempted to match the greatness both of the Bourbons he had displaced and the Habsburg, Hohenzollern, Hanoverian and Romanov dynasties which challenged his power. The Roman trappings of the consulate were blended with claims to universal monarchy legitimated by the cult of Charlemagne. 'Sirs,' he told churchmen still doubtful about his pretensions in 1811, 'you want to treat me as if I were Louis the Pious? Do not confuse the son with the father. In me you see Charlemagne. I am Charlemagne . . . yes, I am Charlemagne!'[6] Moreover, through the Empire Napoleon sought to combine dynastic greatness with the greatness of the nation. Norman Hampson has argued that the notion of honour, to which the aristocracy in the Ancien Régime had subscribed, but which had been replaced by probity in the domain of private morality by the revolutionaries, was transferred under Napoleon to the nation-state as an essential attribute.[7]

The claim to imperial greatness had to be sustained by ever more extraordinary feats of arms. Ancient dynasties could afford to lose a war, a usurper was doomed if he so much as lost a battle. Three European coalitions were constructed against Napoleon, and the last brought him to his knees at Waterloo. After Waterloo the restored monarchy adopted a two-pronged approach to international relations. On the one hand, it sought to convince the Allies that the mania for conquest was a property only of the Republic and the Empire, and that it could be trusted to act as a reasonable power and admitted as a partner to the Congress System which had, in the first instance, been established to check French ambitions. On the other, it could not ignore the challenge of greatness of the Empire, Republic and indeed of the Ancien Régime monarchy before it. France would have to recover something of its former rank as a great power if the monarchy were to retain sufficient popular support to survive.

The augury was not good. While the restoration of the monarchy in 1814 had been a brilliant affair, in 1815 the royal family had been forced to leave in a hurry for Ghent and returned to Paris, as the expression went, in the baggage-train of the Allies. Under the treaties of Vienna, France lost territories gained since 1792, had to pay a massive war indemnity and suffer at its own expense for seven years an army of occupation 150,000 strong. The foreign minister, the duc de Richelieu, believed that if the occupation lasted more than three years the Bourbon dynasty would again be expelled, just as the Stuarts had been diminished by financial and military dependence on Louis XIV, and been deposed in 1688.[8]

Given the constraints on the European stage and its own inherent weakness, the restored monarchy attempted to recover a semblance of glory in theatres where the susceptibilities of the Allies would not be ruffled. The colonisation of Algeria was begun by the Bourbons in 1830 in a fruitless attempt to acquire international prestige. But Charles X never matched the glory of the Ancien Régime monarchy and this inferiority was as important a factor as its hostility to liberalism in explaining his downfall. The July Monarchy inherited a French foothold in Algeria and was caught between the need to recover great-power status and the interminable struggle in which it became trapped to defeat the Algerian Arab empire of Abd-el-Kader. General Bugeaud, governor-general of Algeria, who thought the whole Algerian enterprise a mistake, concluded only that France must make the best of a bad job. 'Great nations, like great men,' he reflected, 'must make mistakes with grandeur.'[9] He argued that 'if we maintain 40,000 men in Algeria our army at home will remain too weak to keep up the rank that belongs to France in Europe'. The only way to benefit from this was to use Algeria as a training ground for the French army, imitating the way the British used India.[10]

In the absence of a glorious foreign policy, borrowed glory had to suffice. Both the restored Bourbons and the July Monarchy attempted to convince their subjects that their régimes shared in a continuous heritage of French greatness. In 1816 the government ordered twelve sculptures to adorn the pont-Louis XVI, including those of Bayard and Duguesclin, Turenne and Condé, and the naval hero Dugay-Trouin. The project, however, came to nothing.[11] The July Monarchy was somewhat more accomplished in the art of presentation. In 1833 Louis-Philippe decided to convert the château of Versailles into a museum dedicated, in the words that appeared on the pediment, 'A toutes les gloires de France'. The intention was to express the continuity of French glory, and glory as a national asset. Glory, the argument ran, was to be found whatever the régime in power. The July Monarchy, as a genuinely national monarchy, situated where the monarchical and republican traditions converged, was supposed to be able to draw on both sources of greatness. The hall of battles inaugurated in 1837 thus commemorated on vast canvases great French victories from Tolbiac in 496, via Fleurus in 1794, to Wagram in 1809. Delacroix provided the battle of Taillebourg (1242) but the most commissioned artist was Horace Vernet. Vernet was a genuinely national painter whose picture of the defence of the Clichy gate had been refused by the Salon of 1822 because of the number of tricolurs flying. He then executed an equestrian portrait of Charles X. For the hall of battles, he painted the battles of Bouvines (1214), Fontenoy (1745), Jena, Friedland and Wagram. Alongside the hall of battles, Louis-Philippe commissioned a special '1792 room'. This housed studies of the departure of the Paris National Guard for the army in September 1792 and the battles of Valmy and Jemmapes in 1792.[12] Having been present at Jemmapes, Louis-Philippe was keen to focus attention on the participation in the myth of 1792 of the future king of the French.

That France's claims to great-power status were as much a façade as the pediment of the château of Versailles was demonstrated by the crisis of 1840. The July Monarchy was keen to recover the influence of Napoleon in Egypt and Syria, but given her shortage of troops and fears of antagonising the other powers, she chose to do it by proxy. While Great Britain and Austria defended the integrity of the Ottoman Empire, France gave her support to the rebel pasha of Egypt, Mohammed Ali, who wanted to be recognised as the hereditary ruler of Egypt and was trying to conquer Syria.

The cause was a popular one in France. It recalled in a rather incoherent way Napoleon's expedition of 1798. It raised popular expectations that France was about to throw off the shackles of the treaties of Vienna and resume its march to greatness. The coalition of great powers that formed against France and Mohammed Ali and the British bombardment of Beirut only served to incense patriotic opinion. *Le National* appealed to the heritage of French greatness:

France, noble France, awake! . . . resume your task, the task of 89 and 1830, and since you are forced to draw the sword of Fribourg and Marengo, France, draw the sword! The time has come. Think of supreme mission and the grandeur of your destiny . . . March on the Rhine, tear up the treaties of 1815, tell Germany, Italy, Spain and Poland that you carry the magnet of civilisation at the tip of your weapons . . . whether France will retain its rank in the world or not is at stake.[13]

In the event, popular expectations were dashed. France was forced to climb down and to forfeit its claims to rank and greatness. The humiliation of 1840 recalled the pain of defeat in 1815 for the Romantic generation born at the turn of the century, which grew up amid the military glories of the Empire, only to find them dissipated when it reached manhood. Edgar Quinet, the son of a military administrator in the revolutionary armies, remembered as a boy, stationed in Germany, meeting the heroes of Austerlitz.[14] But when the July Monarchy was inaugurated he asked, 'Where are our virile robes? You have clothed us in grief and loathing. And if that were not all, we have no hope in our hearts.'[15] The humiliation of 1840 reopened for Quinet the wounds of 1815.

The Revolution surrendered its sword in 1815; we believed that the Revolution would take it up again in 1830, but it was nothing of the sort . . . the chains of 1815 were suddenly fastened again . . . As if she had lost the battle a second time France was reliving the day after Waterloo.[16]

The July Monarchy, he concluded, had failed in its mission. Because it was a bourgeois monarchy which refused to give power to the people, he argued, it could never be the genuine national monarchy of which Louis-Philippe had dreamed. Only a democracy (another term for the republic), in his opinion, could articulate popular patriotism for the greater glory of the nation.[17] Quinet's model of the powerful, patriotic republic was that of 1792. Those brought up on Montesquieu, however, were more sceptical of the potential of republics for greatness. The orthodoxy of Montesquieu was that monarchies were characterised by honour, democracies by virtue, and were therefore incapable of greatness. Alexis de Tocqueville, an admirer of Montesquieu, shared this view. 'Until now,' he wrote in *Democracy in America* in 1835, 'there never has been a great democratic republic. To call by that name the oligarchy which ruled over France in 1793 would be to insult republics.'[18]

Such conflicting views on the potential of republics for greatness were fully exploited by Lamartine, the *doyen* of Romantics who became foreign minister in the Second Republic of 1848. In his address to foreign powers of 2 March 1848, Lamartine was anxious to assert that the Republic was indeed capable of the greatness achieved by that of 1792, but that this in no sense meant that it was about to launch its armies across Europe and provoke a new coalition of European powers against France. 'The treaties of 1815 have no legal standing in the eyes of the Republic,' he declared. He proclaimed that the principles of liberty, equality and fraternity applied to foreign policy meant 'liberating France from the chains that weigh on its principle and its dignity; recovering the rank that it must occupy among the great European powers; and declaring alliance and friendship with all peoples'. Lamartine threatened French military action to protect the independence of the Swiss and the aspiration of the Italians to national self-determination. However, he said nothing about liberating the Poles, and was prepared to accept the territorial settlement of 1815 as the basis of relations with other nations. Finally, to lay old ghosts to rest, he asserted that 'To return after fifty years to the principle of 1792, to the idea of conquering an empire, would be to go not forwards but backwards in time.'[19]

Radical republicans, however, were driven by the desire to repeat the successes of 1792, without qualification. For them, the war of liberation was a model to imitate, not a reef to be avoided, and they were incensed by the government's lack of action. On 15 May 1848 they invaded the National Assembly, and Blanqui, leaping to the rostrum, warned, 'the people expects [it] to remember the glory of its predecessor', the Convention. The Assembly, he taunted, 'knows that all the obstacles erected by diplomacy could be brushed aside by resolute will alone, supported by a French army on the Rhine, and the Poland of 1772 reconstituted within its old frontiers'.[20] The response of the government was to round up the radicals. A year later it sent forces into Italy not to assist the patriots, but to restore Pope Pius IX to Rome, whence he had been ejected. The radicals denounced this violation of the constitution, article 5 of which reiterated the promise of the constitution of 1791 not to undertake wars of conquest and never to use force against the liberty of any people. 'Here are men,' protested the Montagnard leader Ledru-Rollin, 'who are the sons of the victors of Rivoli, of the victors of Lodi, of the victors of Castiglioni, who are now going to fight not for peoples or for their liberties, but against peoples, tarnishing the glory of their fathers!'[21] On 13 June 1849 the Montagnards attempted an insurrection against the government in defence of the constitution, but were soon put down.

Louis-Napoleon presided over the unfortunate intervention in Rome as president of the Republic; as emperor he saw to it that France took more decisive steps towards recovering great-power status. The challenge of his uncle was there to meet; the birthmark of Napoléon-le-Petit to be erased. 'My gaze shall be upon you,' he told troops bound for Russia in 1854, 'and soon, when I see you again, I will be able to say: they were worthy sons of the victors of Austerlitz, of Eylau, of Friedland and the Moscowa. Go forward! God speed you!' The resounding victories of Napoleon I's armies were missing in the Crimea, but so too were the disasters. When the troops returned at the end of 1855, Napoleon III told them that they had 'recovered for France the rank that is its due'.[22] He had learned his lessons well. He was bent on tearing up the treaties of 1815, but equally careful to do it within the framework of the Congress system. Whereas France had been entirely isolated in 1840, in 1853 she managed to bring at least Britain with her into the war against Russia. Napoleon was alert to the first signs of any coalition against him. He began talks with Russia well before the end of the Crimean war. When he intervened against Austria in Italy in 1859, he told the army that 'as you pass Mondovi, Lodi, Rivoli, Castiglione, Arcola, you will be marching on a sacred road, amid glorious memories'.[23] But his message to other powers was that he was embarking not on conquest but on a 'policy of nationalities', to liberate Italy and help her on the path of national self-determination. When the Prussians began to think that Napoleon III's next stop might be the Rhineland, they ordered a mobilisation and, rather than face an Austro-Prussian coalition, Napoleon concluded a truce with the Austrians at Villafranca, even though they still held Venetia.

The danger of the cult of grandeur was that myth was soon taken for reality. French success in Italy in 1859, and the acquisition of Nice and Savoy from Piedmont in recognition of her help, gave an illusion of effortless superiority. 'Be proud', Napoleon told his army after Villafranca 'to be the cherished sons of that France which will always be the *grande nation*.'[24] But a Prussia that had been smarting from humiliation by France since Jena, if not since the treaty of Westphalia (1648), now had the industrial and military means to exact its revenge. Its defeat of Austria at Sadowa in 1866 and extension of influence over most of Germany was a rude awakening for the French. Suddenly it appeared that they were being toppled from the pedestal of top nation. The effect, however, was not a return to realism but a fit of pique and a blind trust in France's traditional superiority to carry her through. The Legislative Body which mangled Napoleon III's plans for military reform in 1867, defending bourgeois exemptions from military service to the last, bayed in July 1870 for Prussian blood. The new chief minister Émile Ollivier, aware that war was the only issue on which he could secure a majority, asked deputies whether Sadowa did not mark 'an intolerable decline which they had to obliterate', and warned that 'France had lost its rank and would have to prepare for a struggle in order to recover it'. Adolphe Thiers, almost alone, argued that France should not declare war 'capriciously' for 'matters of pride', but was shouted down by cries of 'Remember 1840'.[25] That honour, rank and grandeur were at stake was no mean thing. The people of Paris, meanwhile, nourished on legends of greatness, demonstrated in favour of war with shouts of 'Vive la France!', 'Vive la Guerre!', 'A bas la Prusse!', 'A Berlin!'.[26] 'No war was ever embarked upon', wrote Arthur de Gobineau the following winter, 'with such a swelling of pride, such an intense delight in going out to inflict harm, or a more absolute certainty in military superiority . . . blindness had never been pressed to such limits.'[27]

Pride preceded a sudden and dramatic fall; in a matter of weeks, the Second Empire had collapsed at Sedan. The immediate task of the provisional government of the Third Republic was not to end the war but to prove that from a standing start, as it were, it could lay claim to the glory that the Empire had, after two decades of boasting, so dismally forfeited, and demonstrate beyond all doubt that the Republic was capable of defending the honour of France. 'The eternal honour of the Republic', announced minister of war Gambetta as French forces forced their way out of Paris towards the Marne, 'will be to have restored to France a belief in herself, and having found her degraded, disarmed, betrayed and under foreign occupation, to have brought back honour, discipline, arms and victory.'[28]

Gambetta was in favour of war to the knife against Prussia and worked tirelessly to mobilise the nation, but his claims to greatness also turned out to be hollow. In January 1871 the Republic, having failed to expel the occupier, was forced to sue for an armistice. The peace terms repeated many of the provisions of 1815 and went some way to reversing the Treaty of Westphalia: an indemnity, an army of occupation, and the loss of Alsace and much of Lorraine. Those who argued that the Republic was constitutionally incapable of greatness seemed once again to have been vindicated. Ernest Renan, in his call for the *Intellectual and moral reform of France* (1871) argued that 'the republic could have neither army nor diplomacy; the republic would be a military state of a rare insignificance'. For him the French nation had been created over centuries by the Capetian dynasty and 'the day France cut off the king's head, it committed suicide'.[29] Not until its defeat of Germany in 1918 was the Republic able effectively to lay claim to great-power status.

The effects of the defeat were paradoxical. The defeat of 1870 probably inflicted more pain on the French nation than any other defeat in its history, even that of 1940. The defeat was sudden, unexpected, incomprehensible. Yet, as if the pain were too great to endure, there was a collective refusal on the part of the French to confront the reality of the disaster and indeed a pretence that it had not happened. Almost at once, the symbols of military glory were flourished. On 29 June 1871, a military review of 120,000 men in the Napoleonic style took place before the crowds at Longchamp. Taking the salute was one president of the Republic, Thiers, who had opposed war and sued for peace, and leading the march-past was a future president, Marshal MacMahon, who qualified for fame as commander of the French army at Sedan.

If France's rank had been lost, and her grandeur was in tatters, then the most that could be expected was that honour should be saved. One way in which this done was to argue that the French had been overcome by sheer force of numbers, but that acts of courage and heroism by individuals and small groups redeemed France's military reputation. As General Trochu had remarked in 1867, the French were able to 'console [themselves] by the memory, faithfully retained from age to age, of some chivalric action or words, which is always to hand to ennoble or poetise the struggle, whatever the outcome'. Of Waterloo, the only popular memory was *La garde meurt et ne se rend pas*, while of Fontenoy the only memory was the order, *A vous, Messieurs les Anglais*.[30] The war of 1870 was poetised in similar fashion by the *Chants du soldat* of Paul Déroulède and

Fig. 10.   Alphonse de Neuville, *Champigny*. 1870 (Sterling and Francine Clark Art Institute, Williamstown, Massachusetts)

the paintings of his friend and fellow war veteran, Alphonse de Neuville. In *Vive la France* Déroulède set the tone of this interpretation:

Oui, nous savons encor mourir, sinon combattre.
Et puis, nous n'avons pas toujours été si bas:
Froeschwiller est l'assaut d'un homme contre quatre,
Et ces assauts-là les Prussiens n'en font pas![31]

Similarly Alphonse de Neuville depicted not large-scale actions but packets of men cornered in isolated buildings or cemeteries, offering resistance to the end. 'His military paintings', wrote Déroulède on the death of the artist in 1885, 'are like so many admirable ex-votos hanging on the wall of the Temple of the Fatherland, in gratitude for the miracles of energy that saved our Honour.'[32] [Fig. 10]

   The defeat of 1870 established Bismarck's domination of Europe, a domination he sought to perpetuate by a system of alliances of which Germany was the centre. A second round, as a result of which France might recover lost territories and status, was out of the question. Revenge against Germany was talked about after 1870, but only to maintain the illusion of French greatness, never as a viable option. Instead, as after 1815, France tried to compensate for her weakness in Europe by concentrating on the race for colonies, where she might recover some prestige. France, in the words of one republican statesman, 'failing direct revenge . . . wanted at least to deploy her armies, to demonstrate that they retained their strength'.[33] She lost her stake in Egypt to the British but gained Tunisia, started to open up Black Africa, and consolidated her hold on Vietnam, then a vassal-state of China.

This strategy was vigorously opposed by Paul Déroulède and his Ligue des Patriotes, founded in 1882. They pointed out that it was clearly in Bismarck's interest that France should remove her troops to far-flung parts of the globe and forget about the incorporation of Alsace-Lorraine into the Reich. The purpose of the Ligue des Patriotes was precisely to keep the lost provinces of Alsace and Lorraine at the forefront of French concerns and to prepare the young generation of French people physically and mentally for revenge.

Déroulède's first option was to obtain a war of revenge by supporting General Boulanger, first as minister of war in 1886–7, then as candidate for president of the Republic in 1888–9. When Boulangism failed, Déroulède concentrated on battling against the collective amnesia of 1870, fixing in the popular memory the enormity of the defeat of 1870, in the hope that the memory of collective suffering would strengthen national solidarity and the will to fight. In this sense the Ligue des Patriotes acknowledged the teaching on nationhood of Ernest Renan who, lecturing at the Sorbonne in 1882, said,

> The nation, like the individual, is the end-product of a lengthy past of effort, sacrifice and dedication. . . . A heroic past, great men, glory (by which I mean the genuine article) is the social capital on which the national idea is based. [Yet] we love in proportion to the sacrifices we have agreed to and the pain we have suffered . . . indeed, collective suffering unites more than joy. Mourning is more important for national memory than triumph, for it imposes obligations, it demands a collective effort.[34]

So the Ligue des Patriotes made collective mourning into a patriotic religion. Each year throughout the 1890s, they made pilgrimages to the battlefields and other symbolic sites of the war of 1870 as if they were stations of the cross: on 14 July to the allegorical statue of Strasbourg, now in German hands, on the place de la Concorde; on 21 September, anniversary of the Republic, to the Lion of Belfort at Denfert-Rochereau, in memory of the city and garrison that did not surrender in 1870; around 27 October to Le Bourget, site of a failed sortie from beleaguered Paris; on 30 November to the battlefield of Champigny, where an offensive had died out; on 27 December to the plateau of Avron, which had been bombarded by the Germans; and on 19 January to Buzenval, the site of a catastrophic mass sortie to the west of Paris, which effectively settled its fate.[35] In the patriotic religion, as in the Christian, suffering was to be followed at some time in the future by redemption.

Another way to deal with the defeat of 1870 was to subsume it into what was presented as an unbroken history of French greatness. 'Before the disasters of 1870,' said Paul Déroulède at the funeral of the historian Henri Martin, the first president of the Ligue des Patriotes, 'the young people of my generation studied virtually nothing in our history other than the pages of our immortal Revolution.'[36] After 1870 there was a marked revival in historical interest in France's national past, led by two historians born in 1842, Ernest Lavisse and Albert Sorel, and two born in 1853, Arthur Chuquet and Gabriel Hanotaux. Their contribution was to underline the continuity of French national history, and to absorb the occasional set-backs into a seamless story of French greatness which was calculated to stimulate a rebirth of national sentiment and self-confidence.

In his *Souvenirs* Lavisse, a native of Picardy, noted that he had no memory of the coup d'état of 2 December 1851, but that his grandmother had passed on to him the traumatic events of her youth, namely the Russian occupation of northern France after 1815. 'I discovered that the past is short', he wrote, 'you would not need a long chain of people, no more than thirty or so octogenarians, to get back to the birth of Jesus Christ.'[37] In his school textbook, first published in 1876, he reduced the last war and the loss of Alsace-Lorraine to a single episode in the struggle between France and Germany for the central strip of Lotharingia, which had been going on since the division of the Carolingian empire in 843. He implied that the outcome of the war of 1870 could in no sense be considered definitive, because the natural frontiers of France since ancient Gaul had been the Rhine, the Alps, the Mediterranean, the Pyrenees and the Atlantic.[38]

Albert Sorel, a civil servant in the foreign ministry, was seconded to the delegation of the provisional government at Tours during the war of 1870, and was devastated by the collapse of the French armies.[39] After the war, he was appointed on the advice of Taine to the chair of diplomatic history at the new École Libre des Sciences Politiques. His great achievement was to set the diplomacy of the revolutionary and Napoleonic periods in a thousand-year tradition, and to show how close beneath the surface of the revolutionaries' rhetoric about self-determination and liberation were the old obsessions about natural frontiers (in particular the Rhine), the struggle between France and Austria/Germany over the Burgundian lands, and the recreation of Charlemagne's empire and the *pax romana*.[40]

The principles of continuity and greatness were underpinned by further publications. Arthur Chuquet, educated at the Lycée of Metz before the city was surrendered to the Germans in 1870, and a pupil of Sorel, threw himself into a study of the revolutionary wars on the eastern frontier, with General Hoche a particular hero, and special attention paid to French triumphs in Belgium, Alsace and in the Rhineland.[41] Gabriel Hanotaux, who later became foreign minister, passed his *baccalauréat* at Saint-Quentin during the Franco-Prussian war, and from 1878 shared long afternoons in the Quai d'Orsay archives with Sorel while he was working on Cardinal Richelieu.[42] He set out to revise the image of the clerical despot popularised by Hugo's *Marion Delorme* and to present Richelieu as a statesman, the architect of France's national unity and greatness. 'If this book gives those French people who read it a new opportunity to have confidence in their country,' he wrote in the preface, 'if it helps to demonstrate the efficacy of a tradition to the statesmen of the Republic, if it sheds light on the factors which have made the greatness of France in the past and will assure it in the future . . . it will have surpassed my wishes.'[43]

During the period between 1894 and 1898 when Gabriel Hanotaux was foreign minister, France had regained a new confidence as a result of the conclusion of the Franco-Russian alliance which freed her from the diplomatic and military isolation in which Bismarck had kept her. In the hope that it would be more permanent a fixture than Napoleon's Russian alliance, a bridge dedicated to Tsar Alexander III was built opposite the Invalides. However, the Republic's confidence was established on a fragile base, and its ability to defend the honour of France was called into question by two events, the Fashoda incident and the Dreyfus affair. In the autumn of 1898, a French garrison was forced to withdraw from Fashoda, on the head-waters of the Nile, by British troops moving up from Egypt and the Sudan, putting paid to French ambitions of an equatorial empire from the west coast of Africa to the east. This coincided with a campaign against the army and for the retrial of Captain Dreyfus, who had been condemned by court martial and imprisoned for selling military secrets to Germany. For French nationalists, the two events were connected: the Republic, they argued, was in the hands of Jews, Protestants, Freemasons and foreigners who attacked the army by reopening the Dreyfus case and betrayed French national interests.

Charles Maurras and the Action Française led the attack on the Republic as incapable of preserving French greatness. Maurras claimed that he had not been born a royalist but had been converted first by a visit to Greece, when he realised that France entirely lacked influence in the Mediterranean, and second by the Dreyfus affair, 'an affair of state which blew up in a country that had virtually no state.'[44] His royalism was rational not sentimental, based on the argument that all the great powers were currently monarchies and that if France wished once again to be a great power, she would have to restore the monarchy. He took up Renan's argument that France had committed suicide when she executed her king and inquired,

What are Pavia or Rosbach . . . compared to Sedan or Waterloo? Revolutions have succeeded revolutions. The state is bankrupt. Three times foreign invaders have occupied Paris. We have had two civil wars. We have witnessed the making of Italian unity and German unity and the enormous expansion of the double Anglo-Saxon empire. Never has political France been so small. And since then she has accomplished her masterpiece of smallness. She has turned herself into a Republic, in other words she has deliberately chosen to be weak and defeated.[45]

To attack the Republic for failing to sustain France's mission of national greatness was to attack it at its most vulnerable point. Fortunately for the Republic, other nationalists, while critical of the parliamentary Republic, nevertheless accepted it as a régime. Déroulède, as we have seen, flirted with Bonapartism, and attempts were made by royalists to colonise the Ligue des Patriotes, but both ultimately remained faithful to the Republic.[46] Maurice Barrès, another nationalist, and member of the Ligue de la Patrie française, from which the Action Française split in 1901–2 because of its alleged woolly liberalism, challenged Maurras in a public debate. 'I do not count only the last century of French history,' he stated, 'but I cannot ignore its most recent periods.'[47] In other words, though he did not hold that French greatness began with the fall of the monarchy, plenty of greatness had been achieved after it. What was great was not any particular régime but the French nation, which had been variously represented by the Consulate, the Empire, the restored monarchy, the July Monarchy, the Republic of 1848, the authoritarian Empire, the Liberal Empire and the Third Republic. 'I love the Republic,' concluded Barrès, 'but armed, glorious, organised.'[48]

After 1905, it appeared that Barrès' vision was a possibility. France sank her differences with Great Britain and now had two allies on whom she might count. With the backing of her allies, she stood up to German provocation in the Morocco crises of 1905 and 1911. In 1913 the French parliament elected to the presidency Raymond Poincaré, who had more authority and international presence than the usual run of French presidents, and at once set about re-arming France. When the socialist Marcel Sembat advised 'make a king, if not, make peace', Charles Maurras took the opportunity to attack 'those hybrid animals called militarist republicans' and urged, 'make a king'.[49] But Charles Péguy, who had progressed from Dreyfusism to patriotism and was soon to die on a Champagne battlefield, argued that the debate between monarchy and republic was a false one.

> All this French history is so simple. Louis XVI was not kingly enough and was displaced by a more kingly Republic. A *roi fainéant*, he was displaced by the young Republic, just as the last Merovingians, who had become *fainéants*, were displaced by the young Carolingians, and as the last Carolingians, become *fainéants*, were displaced by the young Capetians. The Republic was the fourth dynasty, in the vigour of its youth.[50]

The argument about the viability of the Republic was settled on the battle-fields of France in the autumn of 1914. At the outset of war, the German armies drove all before them. Paris was threatened and the French government evacuated to Bordeaux without pausing, as in 1870, at Tours. 'There is no real comparison', wrote Barrès on 4 September, 'between our position in 1870, when the siege started, and the present moment.'[51] Unfortunately, the com-

Fig. 11. Statue of Wilhelm I at Metz, overturned Dec. 1918 (Roger-Viollet)

parison was only too obvious, and self-confidence looked likely to give way to humiliation, as in 1870. On 4 September, however, commander-in-chief Joffre ordered a general offensive which within a few days stopped the Germans on the Marne. 'The Barbarians are turning back', exclaimed Barrès on 13 September, 'as once the duke of Brunswick and Attila turned back.'[52] The demon of 1870 was at last exorcised. The Third Republic for the first time earned legitimate comparison with the Republic of 1792. Arthur Chuquet marked the occasion by publishing a book entitled *From Valmy to the Marne*. 'In 1914, as in 1792,' he proclaimed, 'the Prussians met defeat on the plains of Champagne.'[53]

After their victory in 1918, the French were keen both to erase all evidence of the defeat of 1870 and to establish continuity with the revolutionary-Napoleonic period when France controlled both the left and right banks of the Rhine. Until the French reoccupied Alsace-Lorraine in 1918, the practice of the occupant had been to leave intact the symbols of the occupied nation's glory. Thus after 1870 the Germans not only left the statue of the French revolutionary general Kléber in Strasbourg, his native city, but also in 1909 permitted the patriots of Le Souvenir Français to erect a monument on their territory at Wissembourg, in honour of the French soldiers killed there in 1705, 1744, 1793 and 1870. But when the French armies reoccupied Metz in 1918, they stamped their authority on the city and destroyed outward manifestations of German domination by overturning the statue of Kaiser William I. [Fig. 11]

Meanwhile the statue of Kléber at Strasbourg was still erect to take the salute generals of Foch and Castelnau at a military parade.[54]

Barrès, who replaced Déroulède as leader of the Ligue des Patriotes on the latter's death in 1914, and visited the recovered provinces of Alsace-Lorraine in the wake of the French, articulated the nationalist French view that in the interest of both status and security France must recover the strong presence on the Rhine that it had exercised in the revolutionary-Napoleonic period. He pressed not only for France to annex the left bank of the Rhine but for an autonomous Rhenish state on the right bank that would serve as a diminutive Confederation of the Rhine. At this point, however, the requirements of French greatness came up against its relative loss of international ranking as a result of the intervention of the United States in the war. The United States did not want to recreate the problem of Alsace-Lorraine on the other side of the Rhine, neither had it put down one ambitious continental power to raise up another. France was therefore forced to accept an alliance treaty as a guarantee against German aggression together with the right to occupy the Rhineland for fifteen years, while withdrawing her demands for a Rhine frontier and an autonomous Rhenish state.

The failure of the United States Senate to ratify the Versailles treaty in 1920 made the offer of an American alliance worthless, and served to increase French regrets that they had not managed to recover the Rhineland on a permanent basis. Before they left the Rhineland, ahead of schedule in 1930, the French established a symbolic presence, at least. Bas-reliefs designed in 1800 for an obelisk at Weissenthurm commemorating Lazare Hoche, the commander of the Sambre-et-Meuse army who had dreamed of a Cis-Rhenan republic, were fitted and inaugurated before the Rhine army on 14 July 1928.[55] Meanwhile Clemenceau and Foch, the premier and generalissimo, who together had taken France to victory in 1917–18, savagely attacked each other for the loss of the Rhineland from their death-beds. Foch said that his doctrine in 1919 had been that 'the only solid frontier is the Rhine', and that the Rhineland would have been separated from Prussia as a buffer-state if Clemenceau had listened to him.[56] 'I can see', retorted Clemenceau sarcastically, 'that Marshal Foch took it upon himself to achieve what Napoleon had failed to do. But before I yield I would like to know why Napoleon, so rich in victories, was unable to realise his military dream on the Rhine, or anywhere else.'[57]

The Great War demonstrated that the Republic could be armed, glorious and organised, fit to preserve the honour of France. It also reasserted French greatness. The cost of greatness, however, was frightful: a million and a half dead, for no cast-iron guarantees of French security. The victory was pyrrhic; indeed, whereas the French had a special talent for pulling victory from the jaws of defeat, in this instance they showed a tendency to regard victory as defeat. Eloquent on this point were the *monuments aux morts* erected in virtually every town and village in France after the war, inscribed with the roll-call of the commune's dead. A survey of these monuments reveals that a small proportion

Fig. 12.   Ossuary of Douaumont (Roger-Viollet)

are triumphalist, surmounted by a cock, portraying winged Victory crowning a *poilu*, or bearing such inscriptions as 'Gloire à nos héros'. The majority, however, express the notion of sacrifice for the survival of the fatherland or the grief of bereaved families. Thus a soldier, killed in action, sinks into the flag which becomes his shroud, while children, a wife or a mother, kneel before a helmet lying in the mud. A few, finally, bear pacifist inscriptions, such as 'Guerre à la guerre' or 'Maudit soit la guerre'.[58] The battlefield of Verdun, where 400,000 Frenchmen and 600,000 Germans had died, was commemorated not as a glorious victory, but as a symbol of the resilience of the French spirit before months of mechanised onslaught. Close by, at Douaumont, an ossuary of vast proportions was built by public subscription and inaugurated in 1932. [Fig. 12] When thousands of veterans of many nations made the pilgrimage to Douaumont for a vigil on 12 July 1936 to mark the twentieth anniversary of the high point of the battle, it was in the name of the horror of war and to safeguard the future peace.[59]

It was perhaps ironic that in the summer of 1940, when France went down to a catastrophic defeat before the German military machine, an armistice was sued for by Marshal Pétain, the victor of Verdun. But Pétain, born in 1856 and older than Maurice Barrès, was admirably equipped to employ the strategies used after 1870 to reconstruct grandeur out of defeat. He told the French on 23 June 1940: 'Our flag remains spotless. Our army has fought bravely and loyally. But inferior in arms and numbers it was obliged to request an end to hostilities.'[60] Courage had been demonstrated in the midst of defeat, and so honour was saved. 'Let us dedicate ourselves to France,' he urged on 12 July, 'she has always carried her people to greatness.'[61] Thus the defeat of 1940 was swept up in the continuity of greatness ensured by the genius of the French nation itself, and Pétain, as we shall see, was soon drawing parallels between himself and Joan of Arc. The Republic was blamed not only for the defeat but also for bellicism and the folly of embarking on war before France was prepared either materially or morally, and the trial of republican leaders at Riom in 1942 was designed to demonstrate this truth. While three-fifths of metropolitan France had been occupied, the Empire, which Pétain described as 'this finest jewel in the French crown', remained intact. Charles-Robert Ageron has argued that the Empire was never more popular in France than during the war, when it survived as an earnest of French greatness.[62] Pétain followed the teaching of Renan that collective suffering could enhance national solidarity when he observed that 'the renaissance of France will be the fruit of this suffering'.[63] As in 1870, the commander who had lost at Sedan, General Huntziger, was appointed to high office, in this case as minister of war. And Pétain invited the French to share in a collective amnesia when he claimed that 'For the present they are certain to show more greatness by admitting their defeat than by protesting against it by vain words and illusory projects.'[64]

This, of course, was an indirect attack on the strategy of General de Gaulle. De Gaulle, in London, faced by the total collapse of France as a military power and independent nation, appealed to the myth of French honour, greatness and rank in the world in order to persuade the French to continue fighting. At the very moment that French greatness ceased to exist as a reality, it had to be recreated as a myth to give the French a sense of obligation to their own history. Calling on French forces to rally to him on 22 June 1940, he concluded, 'Long live free France in honour and independence!'[65] On 2 July, when the British were threatening to sink the French fleet in North Africa—lest it fall into German hands—he asked his countrymen whether the great wartime leaders of France—Joan of Arc, Richelieu, Louis XIV, Carnot, Napoleon, Gambetta, Poincaré and Foch—would have handed French arms over to the enemy so that they could be used against her allies.[66] After Pétain shook hands with Hitler at Montoire on 24 October 1940 to set the seal on Franco-German collaboration, de Gaulle issued a manifesto from Brazzaville in West Africa calling to action those French men and women who wanted to 'restore the independence and greatness of France'.[67]

French honour was saved at the Liberation, and in a broadcast on 31 December 1944, de Gaulle as head of the provisional government announced, 'the year of the liberation gives way to the year of greatness . . . mark my words, victory will find France armed and in the first rank'.[68] Whereas after 1870 France had had to live for forty years in the shadow of defeat, in 1944 the war was not over, and she had the chance of recovering her greatness and rank without delay. Fears that the ghosts of 1870 might return to haunt them nevertheless dictated the way in which the French fought the campaign of 1944–5 against Germany. French forces under General Leclerc liberated Strasbourg on 23 November 1944 only to receive the order from the Allied commander Eisenhower, in response to the Battle of the Bulge, to fall back on the Vosges. General de Lattre de Tassigny, after consulting with General de Gaulle, disobeyed the order, telling his superior that 'Strasbourg is a symbol of the resistance and greatness of France. The liberation of this city was the ultimate sign of the national resurrection of France. To abandon it would undermine French confidence in victory . . . military honour and the prestige of our armies is at stake.'[69] For the next fortnight, the French withstood the German assault and held onto Strasbourg and Alsace. The statue of Kléber, which had been demolished in 1940 by the Germans, who had learned from the French how to treat the national monuments of their enemies, was restored to its plinth, and the mayor of Strasbourg paid homage to Leclerc as a modern incarnation of the revolutionary general.[70]

Meanwhile France was keen to ensure that she did not repeat the mistakes of 1918, letting Germany off the hook and allowing her the means to reassert herself as a great power. De Gaulle insisted that the peace should provide for 'the definitive presence of French forces from one end of the Rhine to the other [and] the separation of the territories of left bank of the Rhine and the Ruhr basin from what will be the German state or states'.[71] The French First Army crossed the Rhine on 31 March 1945 and occupied Karlsruhe and Stuttgart. It then moved on to Ulm, where the Austrian army had surrendered to General Mack in 1805. 'You wanted our colours to fly at Ulm, to renew the victory of the Grande Armée', de Lattre de Tassigny told his troops. 'You have rediscovered the tradition of French greatness, that of the soldiers of Turenne, of the revolutionary volunteers and the *grognards* of Napoleon.'[72]

In *The Edge of the Sword*, published in 1932, de Gaulle argued that after victory in the Great War, the condition of France was much more akin to that after 1815 than to that after 1870. In other words, as in 1815, it had learned to hate war and looked forward to a long period of peace. By contrast, 'After the disaster [of 1870], France was certain that one day she would confront the opportunity to efface it and therefore the élite of her youth furnished the army with the pleiad of great commanders who subsequently led her to victory.'[73] It is no coincidence that this work was republished in 1944. De Gaulle was eager that, in spite of becoming victors in 1945, the French should react as they had after 1870, putting to use the collective suffering imposed by the defeat of 1940 and the German occupation by sharpening their swords and nourishing military ambitions, not by turning them into ploughshares and hoping for peace and mediocrity. 'In the last hundred and forty years,' de Gaulle reminded the French in 1945, 'France has been invaded on seven different occasions. Paris has been occupied four times by the enemy. No other state in the universe has been subjected to as much.'[74] For de Gaulle, the collective memory of invasion and Occupation made it imperative that France reclaim its status as a great power, and also provided her with the incentive to do so.

To recover French greatness was one thing; to recover her former rank in the world rather different. For the liberation of France and the extension of her power in Europe and the world was very much the fruit of the goodwill of France's allies. The United States had been slow to abandon Vichy and to recognise the legitimacy of de Gaulle's government-in-waiting. Without the support of the United States, Great Britain and, indeed, Soviet Russia, France would not have been liberated, nor have acquired a zone of occupation in Germany, nor have started to recover her Empire. After 1945 the status of France as a great power was thrown into doubt. When the United Nations was set up in September 1944 a Security Council was formed of the United States, Great Britain, Russia and China, but not France. When the 'big three'—Roosevelt, Churchill and Stalin—met at Yalta in February 1945 to discuss the post-war settlement, de Gaulle was not invited. 'I was not at Yalta' became an obsessive refrain. This relationship of dependence on the great powers and of exclusion from major decision-making provoked a mood of resentment and a compensating flaunting of France's independence and importance. In Paris at the end of January 1945, de Gaulle told the American envoy Harry Hopkins that the United States had let France down in 1920 and 1940, and 'did not seem to appreciate that the very fate of France was tied to [her] vocation of greatness'.[75] Roosevelt, pausing at Algiers on his way back from Yalta, invited de Gaulle for talks, but de Gaulle refused the invitation on the grounds (as he subsequently told French journalists) that it was not the business of a foreign head of state to extend invitations from French sovereign territory, and that he did not want to be seen endorsing decisions that had been made without him.[76]

De Gaulle's attitude to the United States after the war was very much conditioned by the way he felt he been handled by Eisenhower and Roosevelt during the war. His insistence on an independent foreign policy after 1958 was very much a reaction to the position of dependence he had been forced to endure before 1946. 'The need for allies is obvious in the period of history where we find ourselves,' he said in 1963. 'But free self-determination and the means to fight to keep it is a also a categoric necessity for a great people.'[77] De Gaulle set immense store by the acquisition of an independent nuclear deterrent. Once France had the bomb, there could be no question of the Americans telling her when she could or could not use it, and in 1966 de Gaulle removed France from the military command of NATO. He not only insisted on the autonomy of France in international relations; he also regularly attacked American imperialism. In 1966, for example, he made a speech in Phnom Penh endorsing the neutrality of Cambodia and, while glossing over France's colonial interest in Indochina, he denounced the war inflicted on Vietnam by the United States. This uncompromising stance was later echoed by Mitterrand's condemnation of the American invasion of Grenada in 1982, and refusal to allow US planes to enter French air space on the Libyan raid of 1986.

To counterbalance the hegemony of the United States, France cultivated a special relationship with the Soviet Union. On the eve of Yalta, in December 1944, de Gaulle went to Moscow to conclude a treaty of alliance and mutual assistance with Russia. He returned there in 1966, announcing that 'no fundamental difference ever opposed them, not even at the time of "War and Peace" or Sebastopol'.[78] Neither the Cold War nor the Soviet Union's record on human rights was allowed to come between them. The French government did not change course as a result either the invasion of Czechoslovakia in 1968 or the invasion of Afghanistan in 1979. Brezhnev visited France in 1974 and Giscard d'Estaing returned the compliment in 1979. When other powers were imposing sanctions on the Soviet Union in 1980, Giscard sought to maintain a lifeline to Brezhnev. François Mitterrand dismissed Giscard as Brezhnev's 'little telegraph boy' in the presidential election campaign, and criticised the Soviet record on human rights when he visited Moscow in 1984, but relations with the reformer Gorbachev were never particularly good.[79] Mitterrand was for some time inclined to accept the verdict of the miltary coup against Gorbachev in August 1991. In general, the French government did better business with Brezhnev than with Gorbachev, as indeed it had fared better with Alexander III than with the Tsar liberator Alexander II.

One way for France to recover her status as a world power was to reassert control over her Empire. For the Free French, the Empire had provided a launch-pad from which the liberation of metropolitan France was alone possible. But the weakening or collapse of the European empires in Africa and Asia, followed by the collapse of Japan's Greater East Asia Co-Prosperity Sphere, left a vacuum for the development of national liberation movements and the assertion of their claims to independence. The French, though bound by the Brazzaville Declaration of 1944 and the constitution of 1946 to support the self-determination of peoples, were also driven by the contrary desire for greatness to re-establish control in their colonial possessions. Thus in the summer of 1945 French forces crushed demonstrations by autonomists in Algeria, leaving 6,000–8,000 dead, moved back into the pre-war French mandate of Syria-Lebanon, and undertook a coup in Saigon to ensure that the power was not seized after the departure of the Japanese by the Communist Vietminh.[80] It was not by chance that the high commissioner in Vietnam, the monk-turned-admiral Thierry d'Argenlieu, kept a bust of Cardinal Richelieu on his desk.

In the event, France was not able to retain its grip on the Empire. She abandoned Vietnam after the defeat of Dien Bien Phu in 1954 and Algeria in 1962. De Gaulle, who had been hoisted to power in 1958 in order to defend

French Algeria very soon embarked on the road to self-determination. The man who claimed to have saved the honour of France was now accused of betraying it by French Algerians and partisans of a French Algeria. Pierre Lagaillarde, a young deputy of Algiers put on trial for organising the 'Week of Barricades' in January 1960, told the court, 'Messieurs, honour has been cheated.'[81] Jacques Soustelle, who had been at de Gaulle's side in the Resistance and again at Algiers in 1958, called the abandonment of Algeria 'a crime against France, which is dishonoured'.[82] In this instance, de Gaulle demonstrated that he had the same talent as other French statesmen to explain that France's honour and greatness was in no sense called into question by losing an empire. 'We do not believe', he told a press conference in 1961, 'that the interest, honour and future of France is now in the least connected with maintaining domination over populations most of whom do not belong to her people and who are and will increasingly be driven towards emancipation and self-government.'[83] Five years later, in his speech at Phnom Penh, de Gaulle congratulated the French for releasing Algeria after 130 years 'without her prestige, her power or her prosperity suffering—quite the contrary!'[84]

Though France lost an empire, no time was lost while she found a rôle. Territorial domination was quickly replaced by the civilising mission, undertaken by French teachers, doctors, engineers and industrialists. For the notion of empire was substituted that of the Third World, of Africa, Asia and Latin America, where French influence would be promoted at the expense of that of the United States. Returning from a state visit to Mexico in 1964, de Gaulle stopped at Guadeloupe to review the situation. 'I concluded, everyone concluded,' he said, 'that the international standing of our country is more brilliant, more assured than ever. We are a great nation.'[85] In the event, France's greatness was not maintained by civilisation alone. In Black Africa, for example, as French garrisons withdrew after 1960, military or defence agreements were made with a score of newly independent nations, under with France continued to provide training, equipment and even troops. France was also the only European country to deploy a rapid action force to come to the aid of its allies, which it used in Beirut in 1982 and Chad in 1983.[86] Though on a smaller scale than a century earlier, the glove of the civilising mission concealed a mailed fist military presence.

'No more Reich!' declared de Gaulle in 1948, opposing the formation of a federal Germany.[87] There was, however, even less question after the Second World War than after the First, that Germany would be eliminated as a power in order to satisfy the French desire for revenge. The United States promoted the Federal Republic of Germany as a strong frontline state within NATO and part of a European army. Moreover, while de Gaulle remained a champion of the 'Europe des patries', the dominant parties of the Fourth Republic felt that the time had come to solve the eternal Franco-German problem within a framework of European co-operation.

When he returned to power in 1958, de Gaulle modified his attitude to Europe. He realised that it could serve as a power bloc to counter American pretensions, and also as the instrument of French hegemony in Europe. The claim of France to exercise that hegemony was underpinned by historical precedents which de Gaulle was keen to summon up. In 1959 he visited Italy and recalled how France had helped to liberate her at the battle of Solferino exactly a century before.[88] In 1962, when Chancellor Adenauer came to Paris, de Gaulle said that European union had been the dream of Charles V, Louis XIV and Napoleon, and was now the goal of France and Germany, bringing with them Italy, Holland, Belgium, Luxemburg and one day, perhaps, Great Britain.[89] It was nevertheless the Napoleonic model that was at the forefront of de Gaulle's mind. His Europe was a new edition of the Continental System, a Europe under French influence and including a divided Germany, but directed against Britain, which was refused entry in 1963. President Pompidou, who negotiated the entry of Great Britain into the Common Market in 1972, admitted that 'England could no longer put up with the Europe of Six, which must have reminded her of Napoleonic Europe and the continental blockade'.[90] Fifteen years later, President Mitterand, in the face of the reluctance of Great Britain to play a full part in Europe, said that he 'did not exclude' a new treaty on economic and monetary union without her.[91]

The illusion of a Europe dominated by France continued until the collapse of the Berlin Wall and the reunification of Germany in 1989–90. The speed of developments took the French government by surprise, but it insisted that it could do nothing to stop reunification and had no objections so long as it was 'democratic and peaceful'.[92] In addition, it looked to contain a united Germany within a Europe that was both knitted more closely and expanded to include Eastern European countries newly freed from the Communist yoke.[93] Outside government circles, opinion was much less sanguine. The reunification of Germany inevitably stirred up memories of 1870 and 1940 and fears of a new Reich. The former Gaullist minister Edouard Balladur warned of 'the presence in the centre of Europe of a Germany with eighty million inhabitants, freed to all intents and purposes from the constraints of both the Warsaw Pact and NATO'.[94] Likewise, the weekly *Le Point* carried an interview with Franz Schönhuber, the leader of the German Republican party and former soldier of the Waffen SS. 'There can be no question of a Fourth Reich,' he declared.[95] But memories of defeat and occupation were too vivid in the minds of many French people for them to take him at his word.

'The French have no more national ambition,' reflected de Gaulle in his retirement. 'No longer do they wish to do any more for France.' And yet, he said, 'I will not be able, for a third time, to seize France by the hair at the last moment.'[96] These words, conveyed in private to André Malraux, reveal a significant paradox. On the one hand, the French have cultivated the discourse of honour, greatness and rank, in spite of a record of successive defeat, invasion and occupation. The collective memory of defeat has itself served as a crucible of national solidarity and national revival. And yet it can be argued that the myth of French greatness, constructed for each generation with such care by French statesmen, politicians, publicists and intellectuals, is also a burden from which the French want nothing better than to escape.

The Soldiers of the Year II

Nobody likes armed missionaries ... such an invasion would awake the memory of the scorched-earth policy pursued in the Palatinate [in 1674 by Louis XIV's commander Turenne] and of past wars more readily then it would sow the seed of constitutional ideas. . . .

War is good for army officers, for men of ambition, for speculators who profit from those kinds of events; it is good for ministers who then conceal their actions behind a dark and almost sacred veil; it is good for the Court; it is good for the executive power whose authority, popularity and influence is thereby increased; it is good for the coalition of nobles, intriguers and moderates who run France, who can place their own heroes and cronies at the head of the army. A commander who would otherwise detest the idea of betraying the fatherland might be induced by cunning politicians to use force against the most patriotic citizens, [for] the destruction of the patriot party is the prime object of all their plots. Why have we not answered these facts by expounding on the dictatorship of the Romans and the parallel between Caesar and our generals? (Robespierre, 2 Jan. 1792).[97]

One section of our people will fly to the frontiers, another will dig fortifications, a third, with pikes, will defend the interior of our cities. Paris will support this enormous effort. The *commissaires* of the Commune will solemnly invite citizens to arm and march to the defence of the fatherland. . . . The tocsin that will be rung will sound not an alarm but the charge against the enemies of the fatherland. To defeat them we need daring, more daring and still more daring, and France will be saved (Danton, 2 September 1792).[98]

These two speeches, both drawn from the *annus mirabilis* of 1792, illustrate two very different perspectives on the question of war and revolution. For Robespierre, war begot militarism and was thus a threat to Revolution. First, it played into the hands of the military and executive power, provided an excuse to suspend liberty, and would result in despotism. Second, the revolutionary armies which might drive beyond the borders of France would be no different from the armies of the Ancien Régime which had ravaged Europe for plunder and conquest; they would turn *peoples* as well as their rulers against the French. For Danton, on the other hand, war was necessary to defend the Revolution against the massed battalions of reaction. The Revolution had invented the 'Nation' as a community of citizens with equal rights, replacing a society of privileged orders and corporations; it had also established France as the 'patrie', in the sense of the home of liberty. The Revolution, by creating equal rights for all citizens, imposed a duty on the whole nation to defend it; while the acquisition of liberty generated the will to safeguard the 'patrie'. The army of the Revolution would thus be quite unlike the unwilling conscripts and hired mercenaries who had done the work of the dynasts of the Ancien Régime. It would be the nation-in-arms, the body of citizens flying with patriotic fervour to the defence of Revolution and fatherland.[99]

Danton had no illusions about those who conspired against the Revolution within France as well as without. The answer was not, however, as Robespierre advised, to concentrate on the enemy within, but to divide the armed citizenry between those who marched to the frontiers and those who remained on the home front to eliminate that menace. The volunteers who converged on Paris to commemorate the anniversary of the Revolution on 14 July 1792, and helped to overthrow the monarchy on 10 August, included those who drove back the Prussian invader at the battle of Valmy on 20 September 1792 and those who purged royalist prisoners in the so-called September massacres. The patriotism of the soldiers of the Year II did not distinguish between the Revolution and France, its home; indeed it was on the anvil of revolution that French patriotism was forged.

A final dimension of the Dantonist view of the revolutionary war was that of the war of liberation. The constitution of 1791, as we have seen, stated that 'the French nation renounces the undertaking of all war with a view to conquest, and will never use its strength against the liberty of any people'.[100] But the ideology of the Revolution did not easily lend itself to a philosophy of live and let live. French revolutionaries considered that all men were naturally free and equal in rights, and that if they consulted their reason they would establish laws that consecrated liberty and equality. France had shown the way and was now the home of liberty, but there was no reason why the new gospel should stop at the frontiers of France. If despots and privileged orders prevented other peoples from realising liberty and equality, then the French had an obligation to take up arms on their behalf and present them with the laws that would ensure their freedom. The end-product would be a universal community in which liberty was enjoyed by all. In November 1792 the Convention declared 'in the name of the French nation that it will provide fraternity and aid to all peoples who seek to recover their liberty'.[101] The constitution of 1793 affirmed that 'the French people is the friend and natural ally of all free peoples'.[102] These principles were dispensed to the French revolutionary armies by a political education which included revolutionary festivals, clubs, newspapers and songs. A verse from one of the most popular marching-songs, *Le Chant du Départ*, composed in 1794 by Marie-Joseph Chénier, illustrates this revolutionary patriotism:

Fig. 13. Thomas Couture, *Enrolment of Volunteers in 1792*. 1848 (Giraudon)

> Sur le fer, devant Dieu, nous jurons à nos pères,
> A nos épouses, à nos soeurs,
> A nos représentants, à nos fils, à nos mères,
> D'anéantir les oppresseurs.
> En tous lieux, dans la nuit profonde,
> Plongeant l'infâme royauté
> Les Français donneront au monde
> Et la paix et la liberté.[103] [Fig. 13]

The gospel of liberation came to be so persuasive that it blinded French revolutionaries to the possibility that other peoples might see things differently, desire freedom in their own way and, in particular, wish to assert a right of national self-determination against the French.[104] What is remarkable about this ideology is how durable it proved, in the face of all facts to the contrary.

While the view of Danton had great power as a myth, that of Robespierre was more prophetic. The revolutionary authorities relied increasingly on the military and the military repaid the trust with coup d'état and Caesarism. The volunteers of 1792 thought in terms of a single campaign and had to be supplemented in 1793 by a *levée en masse*. In 1798 the Republic went over to a system of regular conscription and the massive army that invaded Russia in 1812 was less like the citizen army of the Year II than the cosmopolitan army of unwilling conscripts and hired mercenaries that had served the ambitions of Ancien Régime dynasts. Moreover, it was made possible only by mobile military columns tracking down draft-dodgers and deserters in the French countryside.[105] The revolutionary wars were received by European peoples not as wars of liberation but as wars of conquest. Wars of liberation after 1812 were fought not by the French on behalf of oppressed peoples but by those peoples against their French oppressors. The French had sown the wind of revolution and reaped the whirlwind of nationalism.

The standard view in governing circles after 1815 was that war generated revolution and provoked a reign of terror against those deemed to be its enemies. For the ruling class, the enduring memory of September 1792 was not the victory of Valmy but by the massacre of royalists by a frenzied mob in the prisons of Paris. The way to prevent another such disaster was to avoid a large-scale European war, indulging at most in limited colonial wars, and to use the army primarily as a force to maintain internal order. This required an army which, far from expressing the revolutionary dynamism of society, existed to contain it. Reforms of 1818 and 1832 established a small, professional, long-service army, inculcated with what was known as the *esprit militaire*, insulated from civilian life and trained to fire on rioters and insurgents where necessary.[106] There was ample scope, therefore, by the middle of the century, for the development of a powerful antimilitarism which blamed a praetorian army for colonial brutality, the massacre of the Parisian working class, and coup d'état. The epitome of such an army's commanders was General Bugeaud. He was responsible for the massacre of innocent civilians in the rue Transnonian, Paris, in April 1834, during the mopping-up of an insurrection ordered by the minister of the interior, Thiers. In 1840 he was appointed governor-general of Algeria, where he presided over the massacre of 500 Algerian tribesmen, smoked out of the Dahra caves in which they had taken refuge. Even in 1844, this atrocity provoked an outcry in the press and parliament.[107] In February 1848 Bugeaud was back in Paris as commander-in-chief of the Paris army and National Guard, but the government realised that the presence of such a hard man could be counter-productive and removed him in a vain attempt to hold onto power. Even so, the Algerian connexion provided a series of men of order during the Second Republic. General Cavaignac, who served in Algeria for most of the July Monarchy and was its governor-general in February 1848, was given almost dictatorial powers by the Assembly as minister of war to put down the insurrection of June. General Saint-Arnaud, who had served in

Algeria since 1837, was eased into the control of the Paris military in the summer of 1851 by President Louis-Napoleon and master-minded the coup of 2 December.

As if there were no connection between the practice of the military and the ideology surrounding it, the myth of the soldiers of the Year II and France's universal mission was at the same time being elaborated and sustained by the French Left. Central to its elaboration was the historian Jules Michelet. In his *Introduction to Universal History* (1831), Michelet announced that France was 'henceforth the pilot of the vessel of humanity'. Even when ostensibly engaged in a war of conquest, he argued, the real purpose of the French was to remake the world in her own image.

> Each of our armies has withdrawn to leave behind another France. Our language rules in Europe, our literature invaded England under Charles II, Italy and Spain in the last century; today it is our laws, our liberty, so strong and so pure, that we are going to share with the world.[108]

This theme was amply developed in *Le Peuple* (1846), where he described France as 'much more than a nation; she is fraternity made flesh'.

> When France remembers that she was and must be the saviour of the human race, when she gathers her children about her and teaches them France as faith and religion, then will she rediscover her vitality and be as firm as the globe. . . . Only France has the right to project herself as a model, because no people has merged its own interest and destiny with that of humanity more than she.[109]

In the third and fourth volumes of his *History of the French Revolution* (1850), Michelet narrowed the focus of his interpretation, and painted an exquisite picture of the soldiers of the Year II at the battle of Valmy as the nation-in-arms, inspired by their revolutionary ideals as with a religious fervour. The new phenomenon is seen through the eyes of the Prussian general, the duke of Brunswick.

> The Prussians were so blissfully unaware of those they had to deal with that they imagined that this army of *vagabonds, tailors and cobblers*, as the émigrés described it, had hurried to take refuge in Châlons or Reims. They were astonished to see them boldly stationed at the windmill of Valmy. . . . This army, in part composed of National Guardsmen, endured an ordeal worse than any combat: immobility under fire . . . Brunswick oriented his spyglass and beheld an amazing, extraordinary sight. Following the example of Kellerman, the French all raised their hats on the points of their sabres, their swords, their bayonets, and uttered an immense shout. . . . The cry of thirty thousand men filled the valley, like a cry of joy, but wondrously prolonged; it lasted fully a quarter of an hour. When it was finished it went up again, louder still; the earth trembled. . . . It was 'Vive la Nation!'[110]

The ideal of the citizen army and the liberating mission of the French was not confined to the pages of Michelet. It inspired Blanqui and the radical republicans who invaded the National Assembly on 15 May 1848 to demand the liberation of Poland and Italy, castigating the government for its inaction. It was held up by Montagnards under Ledru-Rollin when he launched the insurrection of 13 June 1849, accusing the government of violating he constitution of 1848 (copied from that of 1791) by sending troops to put down the Roman Republic.

Governments might put down the rebels who supported the liberating mission, but they were well advised to heed the argument. Thus Louis-Philippe dealt sharply with republican opposition, but at dawn on 20 July 1836 the Arc de Triomphe was unveiled to reveal the magnificent relief of Rude, *The Genius of War*, a Marianne going into battle, and popularly known as *The Marseillaise*. W. H. C. Smith has argued that Napoleon III's 'politique des nationalités', in so far as French military might was put at the service of emergent nationalities, was forced on him by the popular vitality of the rhetoric of liberation.[111] When, after the defeat of Austria by Prussia in 1866, Napoleon tried to reorganise the French army, the republicans were vociferous in their demands for a citizen army. 'We must mingle the army with the nation,' said Henri Brisson, 'and make soldiers citizens.'[112] Calling for the replacement of the standing army by a Swiss-style militia, Jules Simon said, 'the only cause that renders an army invincible is liberty!'[113] The Empire ignored their calls, but in 1870, after the plebiscite of May, the régime was more, not less dependant, on the popular will. And the popular will, as manifested in the streets of Paris on the nights of 13, 14 and 15 July 1870, was in favour of war. 'You would have to go back to 1792 and 1793,' said one police report, 'to get some idea of the national enthusiasm.'[114] At the outset of the war of 1870, the Empire was obliged to authorise the singing of the *Marseillaise*, which it had banned, in order to tap that enthusiasm for its own benefit.

The popular myth of 1792 received explicit sanction from the Third Republic which rose from the defeat at Sedan with a monumental struggle on its hands. The republican generation of 1848 was quick to draw the parallel between 1870 and 1792. Victor Hugo, returning from exile, commanded, 'Let the lion of 1792 draw itself up and bristle.'[115] 'If the Republic of 92 triumphed over peril,' echoed Edgar Quinet, 'hasn't the Republic of 1870 likewise guarantees of victory?'[116] The provisional government saw the myth as a way both to legitimate the new régime and to stir up spirit for the fight. 'The Republic was victorious over the invasion of 1792', ran the first proclamation of the Government of National Defence. 'The Republic is proclaimed.'[117] Gambetta, as minister of war, set about recreating the army of the Year II. 'Let us rise up *en masse* and die rather than undergo the humiliation of dismemberment,' he cried as, imitating the Convention's decree of August 1793, he requisitioned all able-bodied men.[118]

The strategy of the government did no more than endorse the revolutionary patriotism manifested in Paris. The Blanquists brought out a paper which echoed one of the slogans of 1792, *La Patrie en Danger*. The Paris members of the International Working Men's Association cited article 121 of the constitution of 1793—'the French people never makes peace with an enemy occupying its territory'—and told the Germans to get back over the Rhine.[119] This was much to the chagrin of Marx, who trusted that members of the International in France, building on Robespierrist antimilitarism, would call for peace between French and German proletarians.

The main threat of revolutionary patriotism, however, was to the generals and to the government, which appeared more interested in using the army to contain internal disorder than to mobilise the masses to repel the invader. To those generals, the nation-in-arms was none other than the people-in-arms, and they were haunted by old fears that war would lead to revolution. Danton had urged volunteers to the frontier but had also sanctioned the September massacres, and who was Gambetta if not a reincarnation of Danton? Moreover, many of the regular army's commanders, who were men of the Empire, had no particular brief to defend the Republic. On 11 October 1870 Marshal Bazaine, the commander-in-chief of the Rhine army now besieged at Metz, enquired of the government whether

> at a time when society is threatened by the attitude taken by a violent party in Paris . . . the army placed under his command was not destined to become the palladium of society. The military issue appears to be resolved; the German armies are victorious, and H. M. the King of Prussia would scarcely value the sterile triumph that would be his if the only force that could control anarchy in our unfortunate country were dissolved.[120]

On 28 October Bazaine surrendered to the Prussians with 179,000 men. This served only to provoke the people of Paris, 250,000 of whom were mobilised in the National Guard, to attempt to seize power from the Government of National Defence on 31 October. As the Prussians laid siege to Paris, pressure built up among the National Guard for sorties to break the encircling ring. But General Trochu, the military commander in Paris, criticised Gambetta for espousing 'the military tradition of 1793', and saw the swollen National Guard as nothing but 'armed demagogy'.[121] He refused to lead it on sorties outside Paris, and provoked a second attempt by the Paris militants to seize power (22 January 1871), after which he was removed from office.

Gambetta was, however, increasingly isolated within the Government of National Defence, losing influence to Adolphe Thiers who wanted to end the war and demobilise the people as quickly as possible. His way to power would be paved by peace and order. An armistice was therefore concluded on 28 January, a National Assembly was elected to endorse peace terms, and Thiers, now chief of the executive power, looked to disarm the Paris National Guard and restore order in the capital. The National Guardsmen, however, revolutionised by the radical press and the revival of political clubs, were in no mood to lie down. Blanqui's *La Patrie en danger* denounced 'the open alliance of Reaction with Bismarck'.[122] The model for the Paris militants was now the Paris Commune of 1793, which had challenged the Convention and forced purges in the frontier armies and the establishment of revolutionary armies of sans-culottes to silence the enemy within. 'If the Loire army had been commanded by the republican generals we had in 1793,' argued the militants of the Club Favié at Belleville, 'Paris would have been relieved. That is why we need the Commune. It will bring us back 93 and 93 will bring us victory.'[123] The Paris Commune elected after the insurrection of 18 March 1871 was complex and built bridges to a number of political cultures, which are examined elsewhere in this study. But one strand was the myth of 1792 as revolutionary patriotism, the coexistence within that tradition of both the patriotic and the revolutionary reflex, and the shift, in the desperate circumstances of siege and betrayal, from the model of 1792 to that of 1793.

The suppression of the Paris Commune, however, at the cost of 20–25,000 Parisian lives, thousands of deportations and the flight of surviving militants into exile, punctured for the moment the myth of 1792 and provoked a revival of Robespierrist criticism of the military. Indeed, antimilitarism was a popular cause exploited by socialism and the labour movement to broaden their support. For most of the Third Republic socialists blamed the army for the repression of popular movements, for coups d'état, and for wars of conquest in the colonies. Only the issue of war with Germany caused socialists and trade unions to fall back on the myth of 1792 and made possible a rapprochement with the government and the military, which then rediscovered the power of myth.

The antimilitarists' first argument was that the French army, unable to win on the battlefield, was of use only to prevent social revolution, if necessary to crush the French people in civil war. The military reform of 1872 was designed to eradicate all memories of the soldier of the Year II and to reinforce the *esprit militaire*. Thiers, who continued to be an admirer of Bugeaud and for whom the nation-in-arms meant 'putting a gun on the shoulder of every socialist', established a small, professional army constrained to five years of military service.[124] Romantic republicans were incensed. 'What is proposed for us?' asked Edgar Quinet. 'Not that the nation will give its spirit to the army but the that army will give its spirit to the nation.'[125] In the absence of an effective police force popular demonstrations and strikes were contained by the military, and all too regularly crowds were fired upon. On May Day 1891 demonstrators campaigning for an eight-hour working day in the northern woollen town of Fourmies were gunned down by troops. The future Communist leader Marcel Cachin argued that aged twenty-one he was converted to socialism by this brutal use of armed force by the bourgeoisie.[126] Louis Lecoin, twenty years younger, who while at school was a chauvinist of the school of Déroulède, refused orders while doing his military service to break the railway strike of

1910. Court-martialled, he argued that he sympathised with the strikers and 'had always considered that the rôle of the army was not to underpin capitalist privileges'. After six months in prison he was converted to a lifelong career as an anarchist and antimilitarist.[127]

A second line of antimilitarist attack was to denounce colonial wars as wars of aggression. Jules Ferry provided the argument that colonialism was a natural extension of capitalism, but antimilitarists dismissed the capitalist rhetoric of 'peaceful penetration'. In his *Colonialisme* (1905) the socialist Paul Louis argued that 'European domination, implanted by force, is maintained only by force'. Indigenous populations were massacred, taxed, expropriated, driven into a precarious cash-crop economy and subjected to forced labour services that scarcely differed from slavery. The scramble for colonies, he continued, engendered the arms race and the domination of the military caste and brought Europe to the brink of war.[128]

A third argument of the antimilitarists was that the army was not reconciled to the Republic but exposed it to the threat of coup d'état. According to Gambetta's files, in 1874–5 88 per cent of divisional generals owed loyalty to the monarchy or Empire.[129] In 1879, when the republicans took power, there was an enquiry into whether the army had planned to seize power by military coup after the Seize Mai crisis of 1877, confronted by another republican electoral victory.[130] The Dreyfus affair stirred passions because it highlighted the army as an institution isolated from French society, with its own system of justice, patronage and values, and thus as a possible danger to it. Though the army remained *la grande muette*, it came close to being harnessed for a coup d'état by Déroulède and his nationalist militants in 1899.

A problem facing antimilitarists was the popular image of the army. The glamour and glory, symbolised by the annual military review on 14 July, with spurs jangling and pennants fluttering, was the outward and visible manifestation of the army. Some attempt to expose the pretence of this glorious image was made by a popular new genre, the antimilitary novel. Both its writers and audience were created by the introduction in 1889 of universal military service, which for the first time in the century effectively ended the exemption of the sons of the middle class and initiated them into the brutality of army life. The antimilitary novel presented facets of military life other than the glamour of the review and the privileged existence in exotic locations. It also portrayed the army not as the force and vigour of the nation but as a source of corruption and decay within it. *Sous-offs* (1889) by Lucien Descaves was publicised as a laboratory analysis of military life in French cities, and portrayed barracks as dens of brutality, drunkenness, prostitution and venereal disease within the body politic. The war ministry brought proceedings against Descaves and his publishers for 'outrage to good morals', but they were acquitted by the Assize Court of the Seine in 1890, and by 1892 the book was into its thirty-sixth edition.[131]

In the decade before the First War, antimilitarism developed as an organised movement in its own right, and also served as a recruiting ground for the labour movement and socialist parties. The International Antimilitarist Association (AIA), set up at Amsterdam in 1904, had important propagandists in France, including the anarchist Miguel Almereyda, CGT leader Georges Yvetot, editor of *La Voix du Peuple*, and the socialist Gustave Hervé, who launched *La Guerre sociale* in 1906. Whereas the aim of militarists was to isolate the army from the nation and cultivate the *esprit militaire*, the aim of the antimilitarists was to maintain links between conscripts and civilian life, injecting into the army the spirit of the nation, and more specifically working-class consciousness. The poster aimed at the new class of conscripts in October 1905 urged that

> when you are ordered to fire on your brothers in poverty, on workers, on those who will be soldiers tomorrow,—as happened at Châlon, in Martinique, at Limoges—Shoot, but not at your comrades. Shoot at the braided mercenaries who dare give you such orders. When you are sent to the frontier to defend the strong-boxes of capitalists against other workers who are abused just like you, refuse to march. All war is criminal. Answer the mobilisation order by an immediate strike and by insurrection.[132]

The government clamped down on the AIA, twenty-eight of whom were sent for trial in December 1905. Hervé, Yvetot and Almereyda were all sent to prison. But there were new powerful waves of antimilitarism in 1906–8, when mass strike action was met with military force by the Clemenceau government, and in 1913 when the government restored the three-year military service that had been cut to two in 1905.

The international crisis of 1914, however, provoked a resurgence of the Dantonist myth of the Year II in socialist and labour circles. Robespierrist antimilitarists preached countering the outbreak of European war by general strike and insurrection, and they were prepared to sacrifice the nation to the triumph of the proletarian revolution. But here they parted company with majority opinion on the Left, and hardened antimilitarists were themselves given cause to question whether antimilitarism also entailed antipatriotism. The fact that the Left fell into line behind the war effort should not be attributed to the incompetence of labour leaders, nor to the failure of socialist nerve after the assassination of Jaurès, nor to a surge of atavistic nationalism in the breasts of the French people. What spoke for them was their own tradition of revolutionary patriotism, the myth of the soldiers of the Year II, who engaged in a defensive war, not only for the soil of France but for the principles of the Revolution, and in particular liberty.

A few antimilitarists stuck to their guns. Louis Lecoin was arrested for waving a banner inscribed 'Désertez' at the antimilitarist demonstration on the Pré Saint-Gervais in November 1912, and spent most of the Great War in prison. Gustave Hervé, on the other hand, emerging from prison in 1912, performed an astonishing somersault. He rejoined the mainstream of the SFIO and confessed that he had built a little hastily on the doctrine of class struggle. Overwhelmed by the myth of the Revolution he now 'returned to the revolutionary patriotism and the concept of national defence that since 1793 had always been honoured in France by both bourgeois democracy and working-class socialism'.[133] His paper, *La Guerre sociale*, was duly renamed *La Victoire*.

Even more significant for the Left was the attitude of Jaurès. He announced as early as 1893 that 'we will defend to our last breath the patch of land where republican liberty was born, and the seed of social justice is beginning to open'.[134] In his *Histoire socialiste de la Révolution française* he struck a fine compromise by praising the energy with which Robespierre opposed the war while there was still a chance to prevent it, and the energy with which he pursued it once it had been unleashed.[135] He managed to praise both Robespierre's speech of 2 January and the 2 September speech of Danton, to whom he likened Gambetta. His masterpiece of reconciliation in terms of policy, to link both the hatred of the Left for a professional army run by a military caste that might support coups d'état, fire on workers or start a war of conquest, and the reflex of the Left to defend France where liberty and justice stood the best chance of flourishing, was the Armée Nouvelle. This he described in terms echoing Quinet and Michelet as 'the people itself, the people-in-arms, the people organised, forming its militias, electing its leaders, and the leaders themselves alive to science, to democracy and involved in modern life'.[136] At his graveside on 4 August 1914, Léon Jouhaux, the trade-union leader, served as a mouthpiece. 'The working class,' he said, 'which has always been nourished by revolutionary traditions, remembers the soldiers of the Year II going out to carry liberty to the world. . . . We will be the soldiers of liberty conquering liberty for the oppressed, to create harmony between peoples.'[137]

As in 1870, the government of the Third Republic endorsed the myth of the Year II in order to win over the working classes and the Left to war; unlike in 1870, it stuck to its guns to minimise the risk that a war that mobilised eight million men would degenerate into violent revolution against traitors to the fatherland. The war was projected as a defensive war against Germanic barbarism on behalf of little oppressed peoples such as Serbs and Belgians. The CGT congress of August 1915 gave its assent by voting a resolution of Jouhaux which denied that France was engaged in a war of aggression and conquest. Only a minority of delegates supported the rival motion of the engineers' leader, Alphonse Merrheim, to the effect that

THIS WAR IS NOT OUR WAR . . . it is claimed that this war is being fought to liberate oppressed peoples, but every government is claiming to bring a definitive liberation to those peoples who were oppressed before the war . . . The congress is convinced that one day history will show that the lust of these nations had only one object: to satisfy the appetites of each respective national imperialism.[138]

There was a moment of panic when mutinies broke out at the front between April and June 1917. Over 3,500 soldiers were punished, of whom 629 were executed. Generals feared a political link between the Russian Revolution, strikes in Paris, political opposition and mutiny. General Franchet d'Esperey reported that the indiscipline had 'a political character and was linked to Paris'.[139] Officers closer to their men, however, explained the mutinies in purely military terms: hostility to wasteful offensives such as that launched by chief of general staff General Nivelle on 16 April 1917 which resulted only in massacre; and a demand for an organised system of leave.[140] The replacement of Nivelle by Pétain, who favoured a return to defensive warfare, helped to calm the discontent. Well treated, the *poilu* accepted a defensive war which required him, dug into the trenches of northern and eastern France, to protect not only French soil but the graves of comrades who had fallen alongside him.[141]

The myth of the soldiers of the Year II was extended from the notion of a defensive war to that of the universal mission of France to confer freedom on subject peoples. Arguably, the Versailles settlement was the crowning glory of the war of liberation and the 'politique des nationalités', as Poles and Czechs, Romanians and South Slavs were freed from the old empires and gathered around France in the Little Entente. But the concept of the universal mission began to wear thin after the conclusion of hostilities in Europe, when French military might became committed to imperialism and conquest in the Rhineland, Ruhr and Russia. The Russian case was particularly difficult, since the Russian people, like the French a century before, had overthrown their oppressors by revolution. Yet French and British ships were now sent to the Black Sea to blockade Russia, support the White Russians in the Ukraine and stifle the Revolution. In the socialist weekly *La Vague*, Pierre Brizon asked,

> What happened to the time in the Revolution when French armies claimed to bring not fire and sword to the left bank of the Rhine but liberty? Today they bring Reaction. French reaction on the banks of the Rhine. French reaction in Russia. French reaction in France.[142]

Bolshevik propaganda added its weight to French propaganda, reminding French forces of their own revolutionary tradition. At Easter 1919 the French Black Sea fleet, which had instructions to bombard Odessa, mutinied, and the mutineers demonstrated onshore at Sebastopol. Order was restored by court martial. Five death-sentences were later commuted and 28 soldiers and 102 sailors were given a total of 630 years of prison or hard labour.[143]

Support for the Russian Revolution, opposition to the use of French arms to crush it, and the campaign launched to amnesty the Black Sea mutineers, were major preoccupations among those who founded and developed the French Communist party. While socialists such as Léon Blum had been converted to the official doctrine of France's civilising mission, Communists exposed the hollowness of the myth of 1792. Marcel Cachin, a majority socialist who had supported the war when he believed it to be one of defence and liberation, now accused the government of putting 'the rifle of liberation' in the hands of French soldiers to 'smother the Soviets' revolution of workers and peasants', and became a Communist.[144] He played a prominent part in the campaign to amnesty the Black Sea mutineers, such as André Marty, who was sentenced to twenty years' hard labour, and joined the party on his release in 1923.

Communists denounced French foreign policy both in Europe and the colonies as barefaced plunder for the benefit of large-scale capitalism backed up by France's military machine. When the Ruhr was occupied by French forces in January 1923, Marcel Cachin travelled to Essen to attack the use of armed force to obtain German coal for Schneider and Wendel of the Comité des Forges, and called for an international general strike. On his return, he was deprived of his parliamentary immunity, tried and imprisoned. In 1925 the Communists attacked French intervention in Morocco in the so-called Rif war, and Cachin ironised on Marshal Lyautey's refusal to hang the Declaration of the Rights of Man in public buildings there: 'to speak to the Moroccans of 'resistance to oppression' would clearly be illogical for the French government'.[145] When opposition to the French in Indochina became organised and violent after 1930, and the French government responded with bombing raids and the guillotine, the Communists defended the right of the Vietnamese to fight for their liberation, and sent a message of support to Ho Chi Minh.[146]

The strategy of French Communists was determined not by themselves but by the Comintern. In the 1920s the Comintern was committed to a policy of anti-imperialism and 'class against class'. After 1934, however, its strategy was not to denounce western capitalism as imperialist but to manoeuvre the Communists into Popular Front alliances with socialist and bourgeois parties in western democracies in order to swing them into a military alliance with the Soviet Union against the Third Reich. This reversal of strategy posed no great difficulties for French Communists: on the contrary, the 'class against class' line imposed by the Comintern had lost them supporters and votes, and the switch to Popular Front alliances and national defence could readily be justified by appealing to the myth of 1792. To build a bridge to the French middle classes, so recently their implacable enemies, they cast the Nazis and their fascist imitators in France as partisans of the Ancien Régime, and summoned the bourgeoisie to join the proletariat in a revolutionary-patriotic alliance against them. Thorez announced that

> The Communists—'these Jacobins of the proletarian revolution'—claim the heritage of the revolutionary energy of the Jacobins of 1793 and the Communards of 1871. They claim the heritage of the sans-culottes of the Year II and the soldiers of Valmy . . . and they summon the middle classes, as their ancestors did, against the White Reaction, against aristocrats like

Colonel de La Rocque, president of the Croix de Feu, and the descendant of the Coblentz emigrés.[147]

It was important for the French Communists to extend the same interpretative framework to Spain, where civil war broke out in July 1936. Stalin and the Comintern were keen to take on the enemies of the Soviet Union as far away from its frontiers as possible, but Soviet aid to Spain could only too easily be interpreted by anti-Communists as the lever of international Communist revolution. The French Communist party, which campaigned energetically for the French government to intervene in support of the republican government against Franco, presented the popular rising on the republican side as a new edition of the revolutionary wars. After a visit to Spain in August 1936 André Marty enquired,

> Does it not stir the emotions to see this general arming of the people which recalls the *levée en masse* of 1793 in the Great French Revolution? Don't these workers' militias, leaping from the soil of the Republic, recall the Convention hurling its fourteen popular armies to every frontier and at the Vendée and other territories held by insurgent royalists who stretched out a hand to the foreigner while trying to stab the young Republic in the back?[148]

Unfortunately for the PCF, the strategy of Comintern was always subordinate to the diplomatic and military interests of the Soviet Union. When, therefore, the Soviet Union concluded a non-aggression pact with the Third Reich in August 1939, and when Great Britain and France declared war on Germany, the PCF found itself obliged to take the side of Germany. It was immediately dissolved by the French government, but in a clandestine series of *L'Humanité*, returned to the anti-imperialism of the 1920s. 'Down with the imperialist war!' shouted the Communists, arguing that war had been foisted on the reluctant French people by the bankers of the city of London and arms dealers like Schneider.[149] Whereas the SFIO had been converted from anti-imperialism to patriotism in 1914, the Communist party in 1939 was driven the other way.

The French war effort of 1939–40, compared to that of 1914–18, was lamentable. One element of explanation may be that the strength of the myth of the Year II in the one case was matched only by its weakness in the second. The celebrations due to take place at Valmy on 20 September 1939 as part of the programme of the 150th anniversary of the Revolution were cancelled because France was at war, but the problem went deeper than that. An examination of the myth of 1792 in each of three departments—the defence of the home of liberty, the war on enemies of the Revolution, and the universal liberating mission—finds them all wanting in 1939–40.

First, as in 1792 and 1914, France was committed to a defensive war. Prime minister Daladier declared, 'it is not the French who will get up and invade the territory of a foreign state. Their heroism is that of defence, not that of conquest.'[150] But a war in defence of the home of liberty provided precious little inspiration for the departing soldiers. The defence of the First Republic in 1792, revenge by the Third Republic in 1914, might inspire, but the defence of the corrupt Republic of ageing *camarades* did little to fire the troops of 1940. After the massacres of Verdun and the trenches, the notion of defence was caked in too much mud and gore and, as a result, the Robespierrist tradition was noticeably stronger on the Left than the Dantonist tradition. It was Robespierre who justified pacifism for the left-wing Ligue internationale des Combattants de la Paix. Georges Michon, a member who was an authority on Robespierre in his own right, not only restated Robespierre's position, but argued (against Jouhaux's interpretation of 1914) that his was the authentic socialist attitude sanctioned by Jaurès.

> With a prophetic clairvoyance he was able to sense the peril, foresee the hostility of other peoples, the exhaustion of the country and military dictatorship. He campaigned against the war for five months with a series of speeches in the Jacobin Club remarkable for their eloquence, penetration and wisdom ... which won the admiration of Jaurès.[151]

Second, it made no sense to work up a revolutionary-patriotic crusade against the enemy within as well as the enemy without. An ideological war, cast as an anti-fascist crusade, was ruled out by last-ditch attempts to keep Mussolini's Italy out of the war against France. Moreover, the French Right had with few exceptions abandoned appeasement by the summer of 1939 and adopted a bellicist position. If there was an enemy within in 1939, it was not the fascists but the Communists, and in so far as there was any national unity, it was constructed against the Communists. The fact that the myth of the soldiers of the Year II had been sustained above all by the Communist party made it unpopular with other parties which were waging an anti-Communist crusade, and after August 1939 the Communist party too abandoned the myth.

Third, the idea of the war of liberation was redundant 1n 1939. France had spent the last few years trying to wriggle out of her obligations to small nation-states threatened with absorption by the Third Reich. She betrayed Czechoslovakia at Munich, and while accepting war over Poland, did nothing to help it. 'Occasionally,' reported *L'Intransigeant*, 'we hear absurd theories aired in some parts of Paris: France is the champion of liberty across the world ... she looks to come to the aid of oppressed minorities ... she wishes to recall certain ideas ... No, France is saving her skin.'[152]

The revolutionary-patriotic sentiment that had been so obviously wanting in 1939–40 made a dramatic recovery by 1944. It was reforged by the movements of opposition and Resistance that asserted themselves against the Vichy régime and the German occupant. In so far as Vichy was seen to be reactionary and in collaboration with the enemy, so the myth of the Year II was seen as a potent force to define and legitimate Resistance.

In 1940 as in 1870, there was a feeling in some quarters that France's generals were not only incompetent but lacking in martial determination, and concerned more to preserve the army in order to maintain internal order than to defeat the enemy. Weygand, the commander-in-chief of the armed forces, declared Paris an open city as the German advance crossed the Seine and the government took the familiar route west via Tours to Bordeaux. His motive was perceived to be less safeguarding the sites and monuments of the capital than preventing the warming of a revolutionary cauldron within the beleaguered city. There is evidence that Weygand was obsessed by fear of another Paris Commune. On 13 June 1940, when the government was fleeing west to Bordeaux and met in cabinet at the château of Cangé near Tours, Weygand announced that there had been a Communist coup at Paris and Thorez was at the Élysée. This, it soon became apparent, was a spectre of his own imagination. Pétain himself, the hero of Verdun, taken on as deputy premier by Paul Reynaud in mid-May 1940 to restore confidence in the war effort, was secretly committed to an armistice. It is possible that he feared that panic seizing the retreating troops would provoke rebellion worse than that of 1917; certainly he looked to the armistice as a means to take power, and to open the way to a new counter-revolutionary order in France. The analogy with 1870 was certainly not lost on contemporaries. Weygand and Pétain were quickly pilloried as reincarnations of Bazaine. *L'Humanité clandestine* applied the term first to Weygand, then asserted 'the new Bazaines must be punished'.[153] The historian Marc Bloch, demobilised and withdrawing to the Limousin, noted the twist to the story: 'in 1940, Bazaine succeeded'.[154] Just as full of irony was Daladier, put on trial by the Vichy régime at Riom in 1942 with other leaders of the Popular Front. 'You might well ask', he said, 'whether today Gambetta is not in prison and Bazaine in the government.'[155]

The myth of the Year II was the more potent, because the regular army and the ruling élites were seen to have failed. Moreover, those élites were seen to be collaborating with the enemy and rooting out revolution. What myth was there to bind and inspire those citizens who took up the struggle against the oppressors and traitors other than that of the nation-in-arms that had saved France and the Republic in 1792? In a France atomised by defeat, and in which regular political organisations were banned, the anniversaries of the revolutionary moment provided a focus for latent protest. The clandestine Communist party, the bane of the nation since the Nazi–Soviet Pact, resorted once again after Hitler's invasion of Russia in June 1941 to the myth of 1792 to place itself at the centre of the revolutionary-patriotic struggle. *L'Humanité* called for demonstrations and strikes on 14 July 1941, flying the tricolour and singing the *Marseillaise*.[156] Communists had more than their share of martyrs, as the German authorities demanded that scores of Frenchmen be shot for every German assassinated, and the Vichy régime selected Communists for the purpose. At Riom Léon Blum recalled reading that a Communist labour leader he knew had died singing the *Marseillaise*, that *Marseillaise* which in spite of everything we had taught the workers to sing once again, not perhaps the official *Marseillaise* of state processions and railway platforms, but the *Marseillaise* of Rouget de l'Isle and the volunteers of the Year II, the *Marseillaise* of Rude's statue, the *Marseillaise* of Hugo, 'winged and flying among the bullets'.[157]

The chance offered by the 150th anniversary of the battle of Valmy on 20 September 1942 did not escape the Communists. Despite the curfew imposed by Pierre Laval on the Paris region, the Communists went ahead, calling the celebrations 'an appeal to combat against the invader and against the traitors'.[158] Finally, in the autumn of 1943, after Stalin's dissolution of the Comintern, the Communists rewrote their past to erase the anti-imperialism of 1939–41 and give themselves a continuous record of revolutionary patriotism. A document was produced, dated 6 June 1940, purporting to have been a message to the Reynaud government. It called for the immediate arrest of enemy agents in Parliament, the government and the general staff, the release of labour and Communist deputies and militants, a *levée en masse* and the transformation of the war into 'a national war for independence and liberty'.[159]

The ideology of a war of liberation was not a monopoly of the Communists but the common currency of the Resistance. De Gaulle, therefore, despite his regular army background and right-wing sympathies, had to subscribe to the myth of 1792 if he were to outbid the Communists and establish his hegemony over the Resistance. 'It is a revolution, the greatest in its history', he declared in the Albert Hall in 1942, 'that France, betrayed by its ruling élites and privileged minority, has begun . . . France in revolution, proclaiming and applying the Declaration of the Rights of Man, always prefers to heed Danton than to fall asleep to the drone of yesterday's platitudes.'[160] De Gaulle used similar language in order to wrest control of the French Empire from Vichy and make it into a spring-board for the liberation of France. His address to colonial governors invited to a conference at Brazzaville early in 1944 said that the Empire would be replaced by a federation, and the countries within it guided through moral and material progress to greater self-government.[161] This perspective on what became the French Union achieved official status in the constitution of the Fourth Republic. After repeating the formula of the constitution of 1791 that France would never undertake a war of conquest or use force against the liberty of any people, it declared,

> Faithful to her traditional mission, France intends to guide the peoples for whom she has taken responsibility to freedom of self-administration and the democratic management of their own affairs. Rejecting all systems of colonisation based on arbitrary rule, she guarantees equality of access to public office to all and the individual or collective exercise of the rights and liberties proclaimed or confirmed above.[162]

As she emerged from defeat and occupation France was intoxicated by the ideology of liberation, both on the Continent and overseas. But she was also, as we have seen, obsessed with recovering *grandeur*. The programme of the Conseil National de la Résistance, which co-ordinated the parties and movements of the Resistance, looked to reinstate both the universal liberating mission and the greatness of France. The contradiction between the two ideals were soon made manifest. France became involved in a series of bloody colonial wars in order to reassert her domination in Asia and North Africa. For a minority, this represented a betrayal of her mission, and indeed a violation of the constitution, launching wars of conquest and using force against the liberty of other peoples. What is extraordinary, however, is that the myth of the universal mission of France to bring liberation to oppressed peoples was upheld and considered to have the sanctity of tablets of stone even at a time when France was resorting to massacre and torture to maintain her colonial rule.

Nowhere was this more obvious than during the Algerian war of 1954–62. The political class actually believed that in pacifying Algeria and keeping it within the French Union it was preserving for Algeria the benefits of French liberty and civilisation. The fact that the government in 1956 was headed by the socialist Guy Mollet made things not better but worse. Mollet belonged to the 'République des professeurs' which held it as axiomatic that France was the bearer of universal values of liberty, equality and fraternity; that it was her mission to bestow freedom on the benighted peoples of the world through the rights of man and democratic constitutions; but that she should ensure that they first reached a given threshold of moral and material civilisation. According to this view, Islamic peoples such as the Algerians clearly had a long road to travel to civilisation. If the peoples who were to be guided to freedom rebelled against the French and, worse, if they killed and mutilated the bodies of their oppressors, then this served only to confirm the prejudice that they were not yet ready for freedom.

In the ideological battle that marked the Algerian war the language of liberation, civilisation and even the defensive war was blithely appropriated by those who had no answer in the short term other than the 'policy of pacification'. A manifesto signed among others by Jacques Soustelle and the president of the Ligue de l'Enseignement, Albert Bayet, denounced 'the instruments of theocratic, fanatical and racist imperialism' (by which they meant that of the Algerians), and asked 'who, if not the *patrie* of the rights of man, [could] clear a human way to the future' for the populations of Algeria?[163] Another manifesto, signed by professors of the Sorbonne, condemned 'the injustice of repudiating, out of either ignorance or passion, the benefits of a undertaking pursued for 125 years'.[164] President Coty exalted 'la patrie en danger' although there was no foreign invasion, only internal disorder. Speaking at Verdun in 1956, he claimed that conscripts had been 'called to arms by the Republic to counter abominable violence by French force, which is inseparable from French generosity'.[165] For Coty, French arms could never be used in aggression, and were always at the service of a higher cause.

The major parties of the Republic were troubled but endorsed the strategy of the government. The Communist party might easily have fallen back on the anti-imperialist rhetoric it developed in the 1920s. But it had been forced into a political ghetto since 1947, denounced as Stalinist and the tool of Moscow. With Guy Mollet in power, it saw the chance of a building a united front with the SFIO, perhaps of gaining a few portfolios, and the opportunity to return to the national mainstream by defending the French Union. Thus it voted special powers to the Mollet government to handle the Algerian crisis in March 1956, gave no support for conscripts protesting against their recall to arms, and prohibited Communist students from attending a mass rally against the war in October 1960.[166]

The SFIO was even more embarrassed, given the responsibility of the Mollet government for prosecuting the war. At its congress at Lille in July 1956, Robert Lacoste, the minister resident and architect of pacification, was attacked by the veteran militant Marceau Pivert who likened the execution of insurgents to the repression by the Versaillais of the Paris Communards, and quoted the view of Jaurès that colonialism was conquest that would lead to revolt, repression, lies and betrayal.[167] Édouard Depreux spoke of Robert Lacoste as 'a parliamentary reactionary from the Dordogne' like Marshal Bugeaud, who had 'elevated devastation to the level of a doctrine'.[168] Depreux duly broke with the SFIO over the Algerian war and helped to found the PSU.

Those dissident party members, intellectuals and students who opposed the Algerian war were keen to demonstrate that the values of liberation and civilisation were not defended but entirely betrayed by the French establishment. Matters reached crisis point when it became known that French paratroopers and police were using torture against native Algerians. France, which had fought to liberate Europe from concentration camps, torture and totalitarianism, was now committing the same sins as its former oppressor. Among the works of protest published by François Maspéro in this period was *Le Refus* by Maurice Maschino. Maschino, who had gone to teach in Morocco, learned of torture being used by the police. 'Everything fell apart,' he wrote. The education he had received at the lycée had equipped him with the standard myths.

France, 'symbol of liberty' (*Liberté, liberté chérie*), 'land of the rights of man' (*French* values), 'cradle of democracy', finally 'eldest daughter of the Church (*Catholique et français toujours*). Didn't the history of the last few years confirm what we had been taught at school? Wasn't the victory of 1945 that of (*French*) civilisation over (*foreign*) barbarism? At the Liberation I heard about 'German brutality', Nazi horrors, death-camps, torture by the Gestapo: *boche* and *executioner*, *Frenchman* and *avenger* became synonomous. . . . The day I learned that in their turn the French were behaving like the Germans, that they tortured as well, that the same year they were denouncing German crimes they were committing their own, just the same, that even in 1830 there were hundreds of Oradour at Algiers, that the civilising mission of France was rubbish, that day I discovered colonialism.[169]

The breakthrough by the opposition to the Algerian war was both to deny the universalism of French values and to expose them as humbug. The offical view of France's mission was exposed as colour-blind and culturally chauvinist. Critics argued that France had no monopoly of the doctrine and practice of liberation, and must openly embrace the right of all peoples to self-determination. She must recognise the values of other peoples as different but no less the constituent elements of civilisation. In a word, they took sides with Robespierre against Danton. The right to refuse to take up arms against the Algerian people was endorsed in 1961 by a manifesto signed by 121 intellectuals including Simone de Beauvoir, André Breton, Marguerite Duras, Daniel Guérin, Henri Lefebvre, Françoie Sagan, Nathalie Sarraute, Jean-Paul Sartre, Simone Signoret, François Truffaut and Pierre Vidal-Naquet. 'Fifteen years after the destruction of the Hitlerian order,' they wrote, 'French militarism . . . has succeeded in restoring torture and once again institutionalised it in Europe.' 'The cause of the Algerian people,' they concluded, 'which contributes decisively to undermining the colonial system, is the cause of all free people.'[170]

It might be imagined that the Algerian war finally destroyed the myth of the Year II and exposed French ambitions for what they were. But this was not the case. The language of liberation and civilisation seemed to have a life of its own, and to coexist with a reality that was entirely different. Let one last example suffice. The Gaullist manifesto of 1984, with a preface by Jacques Chirac, included a passage on the Third World which rehearsed an argument about France's influence that was only too familiar.

The impact and influence of France abroad are far greater than its economic or demographic weight in the contemporary world. This is probably due to the radiance of our culture, but it can certainly not be separated from the fact that we are the land of the Declaration of the Rights of Man. In the domain of policies towards the Third World perhaps more than in any other, 'France oblige'.[171]

And yet, within four years, at the high point of France's struggle with one of the last fragments of its Empire, New Caledonia, French forces under the orders of Prime Minister Chirac were sent to massacre Kanak rebels who had taken refuge in caves. The contradiction between the rhetoric and the reality was as stark as that under the July Monarchy between French forces burning Algerian rebels out of the Dahra caves on the one hand, and on the other, Michelet's gospel of liberation and the bas-relief of Rude on the Arc de Triomphe, *The Genius of War*.

Joan of Arc

Joan of Arc is the French national heroine. But she is not the idol of a national religion, around whom a national consensus can be constructed. It may be argued that there is no such national religion in France, unless it be the cult of the greatness of the *patrie* itself. Not even the commemoration of 14 July or the cult of Napoleon commands universal applause.

The problem of the cult of Joan of Arc, as with the cult of Napoleon, is that there is not one cult but several. Joan has been imagined in various ways by rival political cultures each anxious to assert its version as the orthodoxy to be accepted by all, in order to conquer a national legitimacy for themselves. Broadly speaking, there have been four Joans: first, the Voltairean Joan, invented to discredit the Catholic Church; second, the Joan of Michelet, spiritual rather than either anticlerical or clerical, popular, patriotic and republican; third, the Catholic and royal Joan, sent by God to save Church and king; and fourth, the national Joan, Catholic, republican and patriotic. The last was the patron saint of France. But against the consensus postulated by this fourth cult pulled the particular cults constructed by the three rival political cultures. And against this particularism the consensual Joan could not stand.

Voltaire's Joan of Arc enjoyed a good deal of popularity in the late eighteenth and early nineteenth century among those who contested the claims of the Catholic Church to assert or reassert its influence in state and society. His poem *The Maid of Orleans* was already circulating in manuscript and pirated editions before he published an official edition in 1762, and went through 125 editions between 1755 and 1835 before it fell from grace.[172] His Maid was no simple, innocent country girl.

> Trente-deux dents d'une égale blancheur
> Sont l'ornement de sa bouche vermeille,
> Qui semble aller de l'une à l'autre oreille,
> Mais bien bordée et vive en sa couleur,
> Appétissante et fraîche par merveille.
> Ses tétons bruns, mais fermes comme un roc,
> Tentent la robe, et le casque, et le froc . . .[173]

Rather, she was something of a sex-symbol, and the drama of the poem is whether she can preserve her virginity both from the English, whose main occupation is raping nuns, and from amorous French knights. On this, and on nothing else, hangs the fate of France.

This was clearly a bid to make play with the purity of Joan of Arc, so important to the Church. However, Voltaire's sharpest barbs came in his article on Joan for the *Dictionnaire philosophique*. Here he questioned whether she was sent by God. She believed she was inspired, her judges believed she was a witch, and the French captains used her to exploit the superstition of the soldiers. He denounced her judges, nine doctors of the Sorbonne and thirty-five other priests and monks presided over by Bishop Cauchon, vicar-general of the Inquisition in France, for the trickery they used and for condemning her to the stake merely for wearing men's clothes. 'It is difficult to conceive how we dare to call any other people *barbarous*', concluded Voltaire, 'after the innumerable horrors of which we ourselves have been guilty.'[174]

Under the July Monarchy the Romantics presented a different version of Joan of Arc. To taunt a bourgeois monarchy that did nothing to further the national mission of France, they portrayed her as a popular heroine, champion of the masses and the architect of national redemption. For evidence they relied more on the retrial of 1456, which rehabilitated her than on the trial of 1431 which condemned her, and were indebted to the scholar Jules Quicherat, who was working on a new edition of both trials.[175]

The trail was blazed by Michelet in his *History of France* (1841). 'What was required', said Michelet, 'was the Virgin descended to earth, a popular, beautiful, gentle and daring virgin.' His Joan was a simple peasant girl, brought up on the war-torn border of Lorraine and Champagne. She was moved in her woman's heart by the 'grande pitié qui était au royaume de France', of which St Michael spoke to her, and she came to embody the aspirations of the people for freedom and national independence. Michelet described her campaigns in terms that might have evoked the wars of the Year II. He called the march to Reims, after the liberation of Orléans, to have the king crowned, the 'irresistible surge of a pilgrimage or crusade. In the end the indolent young king was picked up by this popular wave, this great tide which rose and pushed northwards.'[176] To explain her trial, Michelet set the inspired Joan against the forces that had raised her up and now betrayed her. In his eyes there was a clash between the inner God revealed to her and the Church hierarchy, which would brook no challenge to its dogma and authority of the Church, while the king did nothing to save her. Michelet's Joan, unlike Voltaire's, had a fervent spirituality, though she was ripe for adoption by anticlericals, while her disagreements with the monarchy could be seized upon by republicans.

Michelet's popular view was reinforced in more secular and less mystical terms by Henri Martin in his popular *History of France* (1844). Martin was more sceptical about Joan's religious inspiration, saying that 'she thought she heard a voice'; news of the 'grande pitié' in France was imparted by 'spirits'. Joan was cast as a liberator, dedicated to 'the national cause' and only at Reims did 'this celestial figure . . . appear to be an angel directing the resurrection of the fatherland'. Finally, Martin did not qualify his anticlericalism, blaming the Inquisition and its princes of darkness for condemning and burning her.[177]

It was not until the mid-nineteenth century that the Catholic Church launched an offensive to reclaim Joan for itself. The monarchy had never been enthusiastic about the cult. A monument was erected at her birthplace of Domrémy in 1820, but when Charles X was crowned at Reims, where Joan had brought Charles VII, no reference was made to the Maid, who was felt by the royalist establishment to be altogether too plebeian.[178] The main forum of the Catholic Church was the cathedral of Orléans, where a panegyric to Joan of Arc was delivered by a leading Catholic orator annually on 8 May, anniversary of the liberation of the city.[179] The custom had been revived in 1759, but lapsed during the Revolution and between 1831 and 1840. After 1840 the Catholics hit back with major restatements by the abbé Pie, future bishop of Poitiers (1844), the abbé Freppel, future bishop of Angers (1860, 1867) and Bishop Dupanloup of Orléans (1855, 1869). The Catholic interpretation was first, that Joan was miraculous, sent by God on a providential mission; second, that her mission was to save France but above all to save the Church of which France was the eldest daughter and the French the chosen people; third, that her death at the hands of the Church was not a problem for the Church, for martyrdom was the standard fate for all redeemers. Interpretation, however, was not enough. To reclaim Joan of Arc irrevocably for the Church she would have to be canonised, and to this effect a campaign was launched in 1869 by Bishop Dupanloup.[180]

The campaign of Dupanloup was given decisive support by Henri Wallon, professor of history at the Sorbonne. His immensely popular *Joan of Arc* was published in 1860 and went through four full and six abridged editions before 1880. It was used by Dupanloup to promote the cause of beatification, and praise from Pope Pius IX was inserted in the 1876 edition. Wallon's interpretation was profoundly Catholic. He rejected all explanations of Joan's voices (sickliness, hallucinations, the spirit of the age) other than that she received a divine visitation for a divine mission. He argued that Joan was indeed a martyr and a candidate for beatification but exculpated the Church for any part in her downfall. The villains of the piece were the English, who demanded the trial, set it up and paid Pierre Cauchon, bishop of Beauvais, to condemn her. On the other hand, he did nothing to defend the behaviour of the monarchy. Thus while reclaiming Joan for the Church, Henri Wallon attempted to build a bridge to republicans, provided that they did not consider Catholicism an impediment to their republicanism. Wallon's was the first attempt to make Joan into a Catholic, republican and national figure. His taste for consensus was confirmed by his 'amendment' of 1875, which established the basis of a constitution of the Third Republic that was acceptable to both republicans and Orleanists. As if to underline that Joan of Arc was eligible to become the force that linked Catholics, republicans and patriots, in the same year Frémiet's magnificent statue of Joan of Arc on the place des Pyramides was inaugurated to a poem by the republican patriot Paul Déroulède. [Fig. 14]

The cocktail of Catholicism, republicanism and patriotism was not easy to mix, however, particularly after the republican party came to power. 'Le cléricalisme, voilà l'ennemi' was the war-cry of Gambetta who sought to discredit the Catholic Church by arguing both that it wanted to restore the monarchy in France and, more loyal to Rome than to France, that it was prepared to embroil France in another war with Germany in order to restore the papal states to the papacy. In this battle with the Church it was necessary

Fig. 14. Barrès, Déroulède and the Ligue des Patriotes at the statue of Joan of Arc, 14 July 1912 (Roger-Viollet)

to explode the myth that Joan had been sent by God to restore the Church and to establish the version of Voltaire that the Church had burned her. The centenary of Voltaire's death, celebrated in the Théâtre de la Gaîté on 30 May 1878, coincided with the anniversary of the execution of Joan of Arc and gave anticlerical republicans an opportunity not to be missed. Émile Deschanel asked, pointing the finger at Catholics, 'if Voltaire insulted Joan of Arc, who burned her?' In reply Catholic partisans of Joan of Arc tussled with police in an attempt to lay wreaths at Frémiet's statue and organised an anti-Voltaire pilgrimage to Domrémy.[181]

No possibility of a consensus around Joan of Arc could be considered until Catholics accepted the Republic and republicans ceased persecuting the Church. The threat posed by organised labour and socialism, and the need for the state's colonial enterprises to be supported by the Church, began to push republicans and Catholics together in the 1890s, and reopened the possibility of a national cult of Joan of Arc. In January 1893 Pope Leo XIII declared her 'venerable', the first post on the road to canonisation. The following year Joseph Fabre, who as a senator of the Aveyron had an interest in demonstrating that Catholicism and republicanism were compatible, introduced a bill to make 8 or 30 May a national festival. Fabre had written a history of *Joan of Arc. Liberator of France* in 1884, which tried to sell Joan to the republicans by going back to Michelet and arguing that she stood for liberty of conscience against the theologians and patriotism against the English. Indeed, the link he drew between Joan of Arc and the soldiers of the Year II was quite explicit.

> When democratic France rose up in 1792 to drive back the cohorts of monarchical Europe, it burned with the same sacred fire that animated the Maid when she drove back the English. The greatness of Hoche, Kléber, Marceau and their like has interpreted to the world the greatness of this virgin of whom they were the spiritual sons.[182]

Joseph secured the assistance of Henri Wallon, who supported his bill in the Senate. For the benefit of Catholics, Wallon underlined that Joan had dedicated herself to France and had been 'a fifteenth-century liberator of the territory', as Thiers had been in their own time. For the benefit of anticlericals he argued that Joan of Arc had been condemned not by the Church but by one bishop and the doctors of the University of Paris who had all been in the pay of the English. On the contrary, the Church had rehabilitated Joan and had a legitimate claim to sanctify her.[183]

Even in the favourable climate of the *Ralliement*, it proved impossible for Fabre and Wallon to achieve any consensus. The anticlerical and free-thinking wing of republicans was determined to keep up the myth of Joan of Arc burned alive by the Church as a stick with which to beat the Church Intolerant. On 30 May 1894 freemasons turned up at her statue on the place des Pyramides with a wreath inscribed, 'To Joan of Arc, abandoned by the monarchy and the priests, victim of the clergy'.[184] On the other hand the rise of anticlericalism and the 'godless school' made the Catholics even more defiant in their insistence that Joan of Arc had been sent by God to restore the Church, through the resumption by France of her obligations as the 'eldest daughter of the Church' which had been inaugurated on the battlefield of Tolbiac by the baptism of Clovis.[185]

The Dreyfus affair made reconciliation around the figure of Joan of Arc even less possible as Catholic, republican and patriotic positions were driven apart. Catholics denounced republicans who took up the cause of Dreyfus as a cosmopolitan fifth column which was betraying the fatherland. Republicans, for their part, took up the old accusation that Catholics were the enemy of the republican régime and devoted to Rome rather than to France. Leading Dreyfusards, while denying that they subscribed to a hard-line Voltairean position, tried to pluck Joan of Arc from the Catholic camp. Anatole France argued that Joan's mysticism was explained partly by hysteria and partly by the intensely religious climate of the waning Middle Ages. He claimed that she stimulated a budding national sentiment, and pointed out that the doctors of the University of Paris who had handed her over to the Inquisition had been Dominicans, an order which specialised in the persecution of heretics.[186]

Nationalist movements which sprang up during the Dreyfus affair were, however, keen to discredit their opponents as insulters of Joan of Arc in the Voltairean tradition. Amédée Thalamas, who taught in a major Paris lycée, was alleged to have denied to his class both the divine mission and the virginity of Joan of Arc. Thalamas replied that the rôle of the historian was to establish the facts, not to speculate about miracles or the hand of God in human affairs. And the facts for him were that Joan had been a perfectly rational 'peasant Socrates', 'a brave and good daughter of France of the stock of the heroes of Valmy who would have sung the *Marseillaise* with them under the folds of the tricolour', who was 'abandoned by the great [and] martyrised by the priesthood'.[187] However, the nationalists were in no mood to let Thalamas off the hook. When he was invited to lecture at the Sorbonne in the winter of 1908–9, nationalist students headed by the Camelots du Roi of the Action Française demonstrated weekly in an attempt to disrupt the lectures. Their poster of 10 February 1909 argued that his lectures continued 'because Jews, Freemasons and foreigners are the absolute masters of the republican state. That is what Joan of Arc is up against: the state and the foreign horde that exploits it.'[188] On 16 May 1909, Action Française celebrated Joan of Arc's feast-day at her statue in an obvious bid to appropriate her patronage for the extreme Right.

The beatification of Joan of Arc in April 1909—the second post on the road to canonisation—provided another incentive for consensus to be reached on her cult. The calming of clerical and anticlerical passions after the Separation of Church and state and the revival of national sentiment after 1905, renewed the possibility of constructing a Catholic, republican and patriotic Joan of Arc. On 8 May 1909 Paul Déroulède, president of the Ligue des Patriotes, marked the beatification by speaking at Orléans 'as the Christian patriot I have always been and the Catholic republican I always will be'.[189] He acknowledged for the benefit of Catholics that Joan had indeed been sent from God, but he insisted that her main task had been to kick the English out of France, and that if she were present now she would be kicking the Germans out of Alsace-Lorraine.

Charles Péguy made another attempt to encourage a consensual Joan of Arc. A native of Orléans, he had always nourished an interest in her, and took a year away from his studies at the École Normale between 1895 and 1896 to write his first piece about her, which was reminiscent in many ways of Michelet.[190] Péguy espoused socialism at the École Normale, and was a passionate Dreyfusard, but after 1905 he moved to a more Catholic and patriotic position. His second study of Joan, *The Mystery of the Charity of Joan of Arc* (1910), dealt not with the public Joan of Arc but with private debate within Christianity about ways to salvation. The argument attributed to Joan was that to claim not to understand the ways of God and passively to accept suffering was not enough; charity was worthless if it did not lead to action to save the world.

Péguy's interpretation might have been seen as another attempt, after Michelet, to oppose an inner, inspired view of the Christian position to the official teaching of the Catholic hierarchy. To the Right, however, Péguy, simply by writing about Joan of Arc, was repudiating his earlier Dreyfusism and returning to his ancestral roots and the 'traditional discipline' of the Catholic Church.[191] Péguy protested in *Notre Jeunesse* that his Dreyfusism and devotion to Joan of Arc were incompatible only at the level of politics. His Dreyfusism stood for 'the temporal salvation of the people and of the race' while his Christianity stood for 'the eternal salvation of our people, the eternal salvation of our race'.[192] And what was the mission of Joan of Arc, if not the temporal and eternal salvation of France? Péguy wanted to save Joan of Arc from the fate of being a hostage of the Right. But he had also to confront those on the Left who continued to insist that the fate of Joan of Arc was a massive indictment of the Church which it must never be allowed to forget. The philosopher Alain, writing in 1912, shared his view that Joan had an inner spirituality that was quite different from the official orthodoxy, but drew the conclusion that this made agreement about her impossible and undesirable.

> There is the faith of Joan of Arc and the faith of those who burned her . . . I see two Gods locked in combat, a God who is matter and a God who is spirit. . . . A new prayer; inner revelation; a new God. An insult to order, to plans, to interests, to intrigues, to captains, kings, priests. First they killed the new God. And when he was safely dead they recognised him and believed they adored him. That is why it is important that Joan of Arc should divide us.[193]

The establishment of a national festival of Joan of Arc and her canonisation were ultimately made possible by the Great War. To begin with, the Republic needed a myth with a spiritual dimension that might protect and inspire France in her hour of need. The myth of Valmy and the soldiers of the Year II was a potent one, but was perhaps too secular to satisfy soldiers and civilians in a war of mass destruction. Running counter to this was the fact that Catholics now expressed their solidarity with the Republic in the *Union sacrée*, and became concerned for the survival of France as a nation in its own right, not only as 'the eldest daughter of the Church', the chosen vehicle of God's will.

The check inflicted on the German advance in September, the 'miracle of the Marne', was seized upon by partisans of the cause of Joan of Arc as evidence that her presence still inspired the French and that she must be acknowledged both as national heroine and patron saint. Maurice Barrès, who had succeeded Déroulède as president of the Ligue des Patriotes, hailed victory on the Marne 'the eternal French miracle, the miracle of Joan of Arc', and introduced a bill to establish an official festival in her name.[194] He argued that whether the French were royalist, Bonapartist, republican or revolutionary, they all had their cult of Joan of Arc and all needed her, because she was 'that mysterious force, that divine force from which hope springs'.[195] The fact that the patriotism of Joan of Arc had been directed against the English and the English so often blamed for her burning did not worry Barrès. He argued that the next mission of Joan, once the English had been expelled from of France, would have been to ally with them in defence of Christianity and civilisation, against among others barbarian and pagan Germany.[196] On 16 May 1915, therefore, an English delegation was welcomed at the place des Pyramides to lay a wreath at Joan's shrine.

On the same day Mgr Baudrillart, rector of the Institut Catholique of Paris, led prayers to Joan of Arc in Notre-Dame, that French soil might be liberated. The miracle of the Marne was a sign for Baudrillart that 'Joan has come down again amongst us; now and more than ever she is our patron saint of the fatherland'. 'Blessed Joan, remain with us and crown your work!' he continued. . . . 'Help us to win the victory!'[197] Later he described Joan as 'the incarnation of French soil and of the French peasant'.[198] Just as the war gave the Republic a spiritual dimension, so also it served to bring the Church down to earth. Though for the Church, Joan of Arc's mission had been to restore France to her Catholic vocation, she could not ignore France if her very existence was threatened. Thus the Church rediscovered Joan as the 'liberator of the territory'. It was perhaps not by chance that the bishop of Verdun was one of the prime movers in the setting up of the feast of Joan of Arc as a national festival.

The argument that the victory of Catholic France against Protestant or pagan Germany also safeguarded the Catholic Church and the pope's authority was nevertheless still used in Rome to ensure that Joan of Arc was duly canonised on 16 May 1920.[199] The first national festival dedicated to Joan of Arc was held on 8 May 1921, eclipsing somewhat the celebrations dedicated to Napoleon three days before. The president of the Republic was present both for the wreath-laying at the statue in the place des Pyramides, and at the ceremony in Notre-Dame. The prime minister, Marshal Foch, Mgr Baudrillart and the bishop of Verdun were among those present. Republic, nation and Catholic Church were finally reconciled in the cult of Joan of Arc, who had come to represent the national sentiment of the whole French nation. The festival of 1921 was reinforced in 1931 by five days of military and ecclesiastical junketing at Rouen on the 500th anniversary of Joan of Arc's death. This marked the high point of the establishment's control of the myth. In his thanks to the organisers, Marshal Pétain noted that 'Joan of Arc embodies patriotism in its most complete sense. Not only did she vanquish the foreign enemy and liberate the territory of the nation, but she pacified discord within which threatened the existence of the country'.[200]

Nonetheless, it was difficult to preserve consensus around the official cult of Joan of Arc. It articulated a particular moment in French history, that of the victory of 1918 and the triumph of social defence immediately after the war. But it failed to establish a monopoly interpretation. Too many factions had an interest in the triumph of their particular vision, to legitimate their own cause and, as political conflict increased, so did the fragmentation of the cult of Joan of Arc.

Militants of Action Française used the occasion of the 500th anniversary of the liberation of Orléans in 1929 to claim Joan of Arc for the royalist cause. Angered by what looked like the appropriation of the cult by the Republic, Charles Maurras asserted that 'official orators have agreed amongst themselves to leave out one essential point: that to undertake the liberation of the father-land, Joan had to go directly to the Dauphin Charles, acknowledge the right of his royal blood, and have him crowned and acclaimed on the cathedral square of Reims'.[201] Joan of Arc, he insisted, was a royalist, even 'somewhat Action Française', for she understood that the monarchy was even more important than the Church in the revival of France and therefore followed the Action Française maxim, 'politics first'.

This bid to seize control of the memory of Joan of Arc by the extreme Right was contested in 1936 by the extreme Left. The Communists not only used the myth of the French Revolution to seduce the republican middle class into the Popular Front, but they also used the myth of Joan of Arc to further their policy of the 'outstretched hand' to Catholic workers. In order to do this, they revived Michelet's Joan of Arc, presenting her as the third daughter of a Lorraine peasant, who rose up to expel the enemy from the fatherland only to be betrayed by her king. Thus argued the Communists, Joan belonged not to the royalists, let alone to the fascists, but to the people. Moreover, for the sake of the Catholics they were wooing, they did not call the Church to account for the trial and execution of Joan.[202]

The fragmentation of the cult of Joan of Arc was completed by the defeat of 1940 and the French civil war of 1940–4. A battle for the ownership and in-terpretation of the myth took place between the Vichy régime and the Resist-ance. As the solidarity engendered by the First World War paved the way to the establishment of a national cult, so the divisions engendered by the Second broke up the cult into rival denominations. The Catholic, republican and national Joan of the Great War was split into Joan, the symbol of national suffering and redemption, on the one hand, and Joan, the rebel and freedom fighter, on the other.

Marshal Pétain, assuming power in occupied France, presented himself to the French people as a Providential leader sent to protect France in her hour of need. Comparisons with Joan of Arc, however ridiculous at first sight, were not discouraged. The 'sublime child of seventeen' and 'the glorious, providential old man of eighty-four' seemed to one writer to be 'two French miracles'.[203] Pétain, like Joan, was said to have sacrificed his person for the redemption of France, and to stand for traditional, rural, Catholic values associated with Joan of Arc.

The cult of Joan of Arc, adopted by the régime, was not unproblematic. After all, Joan had liberated French soil, while Vichy had entered upon a strategy of collaboration with Germany. One solution was to present Joan of Arc as the scourge of the English, not of foreigners in general. Admiral Darlan, vice-president of the council and foreign minister, meeting Hitler at Berchtesgaden on 11 May 1941 to further Franco–German collaboration, announced hopefully, 'Today is the festival of Joan of Arc, who drove out the English.'[204] Another solution was to draw a moral rather than a military lesson from the story, to see Joan above all as a model for moral rearmament and the enemy of the rottenness that had brought France to its knees in 1940. This was the style of the official commemorations of Joan of Arc in the unoccupied zone on 10 May 1942. The key slogans imparted to 20,000 young people drawn up on the place Bellecour at Lyon were 'restoration', 'redemption' and 'resurrection', in the sense of a moral purification, not a call to arms.[205] Pétain's message, read at Limoges and Chambéry where new statues of Joan of Arc were unveiled, betrayed his concern about internal discord rather than an enthusiasm for liberation. He urged that the people should 'unite, discipline themselves, stop questioning their leaders' and 'close their ears to foreign propaganda'.[206]

The myth of Joan of Arc was developed in the theatre under Vichy. The oratorio of the Catholic poet Paul Claudel, *Jeanne d'Arc au Bûcher*, with music by Arthur Honneger, first performed at Rouen in 1939, was taken on tour in the unoccupied zone in the summer of 1941 and broadcast from the Salle Pleyel on 9 May 1943. This dispensed with the Voltairean myth of the Church Intolerant by portraying the judges as a pig, a sheep and a donkey, and suggested that the doctors of the Sorbonne included Anatole France; it attacked Michelet's version by attacking the people as drunkards who relished the burning of a saint.[207] More ambiguous was *Jeanne avec nous* by Claude Vermorel, which was performed at the Comédie des Champs-Elysées in the spring of 1942 and at the Théâtre Pigalle that summer. Certain lines, such as 'How sweet is the word *patrie* when it is joined to the word revolt, to the word youth!', may have suggested Resistance. But the play could easily be interpreted as anti-British, and it was both subsidised by the Vichy régime and met the approval of the German censors. Not until it was revived at the Théâtre Verlaine in December 1945 was it produced with an anti-German message, with the occupiers clicking their boots and fingering their gauntlets.[208]

The Vichy régime was unable to establish a monopoly of the cult of Joan of Arc. Opponents of the régime and of its policy of collaboration were not slow to see that the myth could serve their purposes just as well, if not better. The Communists, seeking the widest possible national legitimation after June 1941, espoused the myth not only of the soldiers of the Year II but that of Joan of Arc as well. In May 1942 *L'Humanité clandestine* revived Michelet's Joan of Arc and claimed that the Communists were her heirs.

In the fifteenth century France, at war for a century, divided and devastated, fell under the foreign yoke. Then, as now, there was a party of treachery, in the pay of the invader. . . . But the masses burned with patriotic faith . . . and a humble peasant girl of Domrémy, Joan of Arc, put herself at the head of the party of resistance, fought the climate of resignation that surrounded the Dauphin, and set a courageous example in the freedom struggle that finally drove all foreign troops from the soil of the Fatherland. . . . Communist and other patriots who are fighting to deliver the country, who are gunned down by the Hun and their lackies, are in the tradition of Joan of Lorraine, while the 'collaborators', the men of Vichy, Laval, Pétain, Darlan and Co., are in the tradition of Bishop Cauchon.[209]

At the Liberation, Joan of Arc was firmly located in the camp of the Communists and Charles de Gaulle, who marched together in procession to her statue on 12 May 1945. Literature at the Liberation tended to reflect the image of Joan the freedom fighter and to return to Michelet and Péguy for inspiration. In *L'Alouette* (*The Lark*) by Jean Anouilh, first performed in 1953, Joan believed herself to be inspired, but scorn was poured on the idea that God was there to protect the French. Bishop Cauchon confessed to the charge of collaboration with the English but defended it as 'the only reasonable solution in the chaos'. Joan's father and the Inquisitor evoked the debate in Péguy that Joan should merely have prayed to God to save France, but Joan is shown frankly to enjoy the clash and camaraderie of war.[210] Similarly the cineast Robert Bresson, defending his *Procès de Jeanne d'Arc*, made in 1962, explained that Joan was neither a naïve peasant girl nor a pure and obedient saint, but a young woman of 'magnificent insolence', who loved royal finery and powerful horses.[211]

After the war, however, the Left increasingly lost its grip on Joan of Arc. Catholic bishops delivering the annual panygyric in Orléans cathedral took the coincidence of the date of the liberation of Orléans and VE day, 8 May, to be confirmation of the divine protection of France and the divine inspiration of Joan.[212] Every second Sunday in May traditionalists headed by Action Française processed to pay homage to the statue of Joan of Arc in the place des Pyramides. François Mitterrand attempted to reclaim the cult on 8 May 1982, when he not only laid a wreath at the tomb of the unknown soldier under the Arc de Triomphe, but also went to Orléans at the invitation of the Giscardian mayor to take part in the festival of Joan of Arc. He cited Michelet in an attempt to place the stamp of the Left on the ceremony, but none were more embarrassed than the socialist politicians obliged to attend an event dominated by the clergy and military.[213]

Nothing was more embarrassing for the Left, however, than the appropriation of the cult of Joan of Arc by the Front National of Jean-Marie Le Pen. The Front National made its début in 1984 in the traditional procession (13 May), but subsequently organised a separate demonstration on 1 May. In 1988 it sang 'Catholiques et Français toujours' at an immense mass in the Tuileries Gardens for the benefit of its integrist supporters. But the goal in 1989 was to attract workers away from the 'red' Labour Day to a labour day of the 'popular, social and national Right'. Michelet was accordingly dusted off and then stood on his head. Le Pen's Joan of Arc was a popular peasant heroine and liberator, but having expelled the English, her next task was to expel illegal immigrants. Her mission was to 'give France back to the French by expelling the foreigners who were occupying it' and, as the European elections approached, to check the slide into 'a cosmopolitan Europe, a multiracial Europe'.[214] So long as the Right retained a relatively distinct interpretation of Joan of Arc, there was still some hope of the Left presenting its own interpretation, but the synthesis of conservative and populist images by the Front National poisoned the ground that had nourished Joan the liberator and effectively closed it off to the Left.

Defining a national community was not easy in France, because the cult of the Revolution cut across that of the nation. This gave rise to national mythologies which were specific to Left or Right. Though the Left repeatedly tried to define Joan of Arc as a popular national heroine, she was in the end secured by the Right as the embodiment of Catholic France. The myth of the soldiers of the Year II was developed to discredit the Right as antipatriotic as well as counter-revolutionary, but also served as a model to offset the alternative culture of antimilitarism and antipatriotism on the Left, in 1914 if not in 1940. The patriotism of the Left was nothing if not full of contradictions. It was developed as a revolutionary patriotism which renounced wars of conquest in the name of the rights of peoples to self-determination; but it was also keen to imitate the cult of greatness entertained by the French monarchy. To resolve this contradiction, revolutionary patriots developed the notion of the war of liberation, which championed liberty but also brought greatness. Thus the programme of the Committee of National Liberation, which spearheaded the French Resistance, in March 1944, was to 're-establish the power, grandeur and universal mission of France'.[215] Those contradictions were cruelly exposed when the French took it upon themselves to crush revolutions and movements for self-determination in other parts of the world, such as Bolshevik Russia, Indochina and North Africa. But they had for so long cultivated the myth of the war of liberation that they were blinded to the reality of the war of conquest. By contrast, the cult of French greatness, far from being undermined by repeated national catastrophe, fed off it as if it needed disaster to reach fruition.

CHAPTER 4

Regionalism

The Struggle for Republican Federalism

In his *Ancien Régime et la Révolution* (1856) Alexis de Tocqueville argued that the process of administrative centralisation bequeathed to the French by Napoleon was begun not by the French revolutionaries but by the monarchy of the Ancien Régime. In seeking to establish this view, he exposed those who held the Revolution responsible for the strait-jacket of centralisation as the dupes of two myths. The first myth, created by the revolutionaries themselves, was that provincialism was the essence of the Ancien Régime, and was subsequently defended by counter-revolutionaries who had lost their local power-bases as a result of the Revolution's administrative reforms. The second myth, created by counter-revolutionaries, was that the Ancien Régime had been a golden age of provincial liberties, and that these had been rudely violated by the Revolution, which brooked no opposition to the ideological despotism it sought to impose on France.

Tocqueville presented himself as an objective historian whose task it was to reveal the reality behind the myth. Equally important, however, is the development of these myths by rival political cultures, the revolutionary and the counter-revolutionary, to define themselves and legitimate their claims to power.

The third element of the revolutionary triad-fraternity indicated the obsession of the revolutionaries with the principle of unity. This meant, in the first place, political unity. On 17 June 1789 the deputies to the Estates-General declared themselves to be the National Assembly. The principle of absolute monarchy, whereby all political decisions emanated from the person of the king, was thereby challenged by the representatives of the sovereign nation. What was retained, however, was the notion of the unity of the sovereign power, in the words of Sieyès, 'a one and indivisible representation' of the nation.[1] Nothing was more alien to the French political tradition than the perceived British system of divisive party politics. Great was the consternation therefore on 20 June when, expelled from their hall and meeting in the Tennis

Fig. 15.   La Fête de la Fédération, 14 July 1790 (Bibliothèque nationale)

Court to swear never to separate until they had fixed a constitution for the kingdom, a single deputy refused the oath.

The cult of unity was best symbolised by the Fête de la Fédération on 14 July 1790. [Fig. 15] Before fourteen thousand National Guardsmen elected from the eighty-three departments and drawn up on the Champ-de-Mars, Lafayette proclaimed the oath: 'We swear to remain forever faithful to the Nation, Law and King, to defend with all our strength the constitution decreed by the National Assembly and accepted by the King . . . to stay united to all Frenchmen by the indissoluble ties of fraternity.'[2] Before long, however, it became clear that the division of sovereignty between nation and king under a constitutional monarchy was unsatisfactory, and the monarchy was replaced by a republic. Nevertheless, France went straight from a unitary monarchy to a unitary Republic, without any experiment with federal ideas. Montesquieu and Rousseau had taught that republics were suited only to small states; in large states a republic would have to be federal. However, the Conventionnels decided that in the face of secessionist movements a federal structure would court division, and weaken the French state in its struggle with the European monarchies. Curiously, in the light of their later espousal of federalism, it was the Girondin deputies who pressed most vigorously the advantages of a unitary

Republic. 'Federative government does not suit a great people', declared the Marseilles deputy Barbaroux, 'because of administrative delays and the profusion and confusion of the machinery.'[3] So on 25 September the Republic was proclaimed, One and Indivisible.

As they were committed to the unity of the sovereign power, so the revolutionaries were committed to administrative reform. The purpose of this was twofold. First, the perfection of the power of the centralised state required the elimination of rival centres of power. Thus on the night of 4 August 1789, under the pressure of popular revolt, not only the seigneurs who exercised feudal rights in their manors but also towns, cities and provinces enjoying liberties in matters of taxation and self-government surrendered their privileges to the nation. Second, the new political class that was in the process of making the Revolution was keen to displace the old élites who occupied positions of power in the corporative state. The easiest way to do this was to abolish the judicial and administrative institutions they controlled and the practice of the sale of offices which kept them entrenched, and to establish new institutions and elective offices.

The National Assembly therefore divided France into 40,000 communes, the taxpayers of which elected a municipal council and mayor. Above the municipalities was an intermediate level of elective government, the district. Above the districts France was divided into eighty-three departments, each run by a *conseil-général*, elected by primary and secondary assemblies, and by the departmental directory or executive the *conseil* in turn elected. Royal supervision over the councils was ensured by a *procureur-général syndic* in each department, but administrative centralisation was not fully developed until the Jacobin dictatorship and, more permanently, by the law of 28 *pluviôse* Year VIII (17 February 1800), passed by Bonaparte as First Consul. The effect of this measure was virtually to eliminate the elective principle in local government. The prefect who ran each department, the sub-prefect in each *arrondissement* (which replaced the district) and the mayor in each commune, were agents of central government, whom it hired and fired. The main function of the representative bodies at the different levels—the *conseil général, conseil d'arrondissement*, and municipal councils—was to levy taxes, and prefects having extended powers to overrule the decisions they might make.

In order to justify these reforms, the revolutionaries endeavoured to discredit the provinces they had abolished as mainstays of the Ancien Régime, if not centres of counter-revolution. The idea of provincial counter-revolution was a myth which suited the revolutionaries well, but it has been argued that the province itself was either a very recent construction in 1789, or actually invented by the Constituent Assembly in the course of its administrative reforms. It is clear that the province was not the natural focus of loyalty of the French people before 1789. They were answerable to a large number of jurisdictions—fiscal, judicial, military and religious—all of which overlapped and few of which corresponded to a province.[4] Their natural loyalty, if there were such a thing, was to the *pays*, a unit far smaller than the province, centred perhaps on the local market town, or characterised by a certain geographical coherence. The monarchy of the Ancien Régime did little to encourage the provincial spirit. Provincial estates—which in any case represented only the nobility, upper clergy and urban oligarchies—were largely eliminated by the end of the seventeenth century, with the exception of those of Brittany, Burgundy, Languedoc and a few tiny ones at the periphery of the kingdom. Provincial sentiment may have increased as an accidental by-product of administrative centralisation under the monarchy, as royal intendants imposed some sort of unity on their *généralités*. In this way, it has been argued, the reawakening of Gascon feeling in the eighteenth century was explained by the formation in 1716 of the intendancy of Auch from those of Montauban and Bordeaux.[5] But the revival of provincial sentiment was generated above all by the need of the monarchy to increase taxes and to go back to representative institutions in order to gain consent for them. To associate landowners with the raising of a land tax in 1787, the monarchy created provincial assemblies of landowners in the central areas of France that did not have provincial estates. This, argued Albert Soboul, generalised the term and conferred a provincial identity over and above the sense of belonging to a *pays*.[6] This movement was reinforced by the 'révolte nobiliaire' of 1788 against the government's plans of taxation and centralisation, one aspect of which was the revival of long-dormant provincial estates, such as those of Franche-Comté and Provence. Paradoxically, however, the province was not defined as the administrative unit of the Ancien Régime until the Constituent Assembly set about its administrative reforms in 1789. At that point, Destutt de Tracy, deputy of the nobility of Moulins, proposed that the Assembly 'define what was meant by the word *province*, before moving on to the new administrative division'.[7]

Neither the unity of sovereign power nor administrative centralisation satisfied the revolutionaries' quest for unity. In addition, they came to claim that religious and linguistic uniformity were also central to the survival of France and the Republic. The papal enclave of Avignon and the Comtat Venaissin were frequently used by Louis XIV to put pressure on the Papacy on ecclesiastical matters. The Constituent Assembly employed the same technique, using the demand of Avignon patriots for union with France, to press the papacy to accept its reform of the Church, the Civil Constitution of the Clergy. The papacy's refusal to accept reform, and the armed resistance of the Union de Saint-Cécile of the Haut-Comtat around Carpentras to annexation by France in 1791, forged in the revolutionary mind a link between Catholicism, counter-revolution and separatism that became difficult to dislodge.[8]

Links between other languages, counter-revolution and separatism were also drawn by the revolutionaries. Invading armies in 1792–4 lent a hand to peripheral areas which wanted to protect their provincial liberties. Support was provided by Austrians in Flanders, by Prussians in Alsace, by Sardinians in the county of Nice, which France was trying to annex, by Spaniards in the Pyrenees, and by the British fleet off the coast of Brittany. The danger of disintegration drove the Committee of Public Safety to demand religious and linguistic uniformity as well as political unity and administrative centralisation. In a word, they not only insisted on the One and Indivisible Republic, but they also required that the French all be assimilated into one nation. Whereas in the early years of the Revolution the assemblies had translated their laws and decrees into the minority languages of the French periphery, the persistence of these languages was now seen as a political challenge to the Revolution. Reporting to the Convention for the Committee of Public Instruction early in 1794, Bertrand Barère, examining conditions in Brittany, Alsace, Corsica and the Pyrenees, argued that 'federalism and superstition speak Lower Breton, emigration and hatred of the Republic speak German, counter-revolution speaks Italian and fanaticism speaks Basque. Let us destroy these damaging and mistaken instruments'.[9] The abbé Grégoire extended the argument from minority languages to much more widely dispersed *patois*. This, he argued, offered a toe-hold for institutions that had been formally abolished: the feudal aristocracy and provincial divisions. Citizens of the Republic had all to speak French, otherwise the practice of liberty, eqality and fraternity was doomed.[10]

While the revolutionaries came to portray any manifestation of provincial sentiment as a threat to the Revolution, counter-revolutionaries constructed a rival myth of the Ancien Régime as the golden age of provincial liberties. According to this view, France had been put together like a mosaic, piece by piece. Provence had been incorporated in 1487, Brittany in 1532, Béarn and Lower Navarre in 1620, Alsace in 1648, Artois and Roussillon in 1659, Flanders and Franche-Comté in 1678, Lorraine in 1766, Corsica in 1768. Whether they had been acquired by inheritance or conquest, contracts had been drawn up guaranteeing the customary liberties of the cities, duchies and suchlike in matters of taxation and representation. Though some counter-revolutionaries remained critical of Louis XIV, who was driven by the demands of war to violate tax privileges and to suspend provincial estates, in general they painted a rosy picture of the harmonious coexistence of monarchy and provinces which remained one of the glories of the French constitution until the outbreak of revolution.

Two examples of this myth-making will suffice. In 1791 the comte de Botherel, *procureur-général-syndic* of the Estates of Brittany which were abolished at the Revolution, who had played a leading part on the 'révolte nobiliaire' in Brittany when the Parlement at Rennes was closed in 1788, claimed the existence of a virtually autonomous duchy of Brittany. 'Under its constitution Brittany is self-governing,' he argued. 'We swore to see to the preservation of Brittany's institutions recorded in its ancient contracts, of its franchises and liberties endorsed by all contracts passed by the king's commissioners at each session [of the Estates] to the effect that no new law contrary to them would be introduced.' Since he considered that the assault on Breton liberties had been harsher under the Revolution than under the monarchy of the Ancien Régime (not that the monarchy had treated the Parlement and the Estates with kid gloves), the comte de Botherel joined the counter-revolutionary movement, in league with the British, in the hopes of reconstituting this mythical Brittany.[11] In Franche-Comté, meanwhile, the approach of war prompted some discontented noblemen to look to the House of Austria to support their claims to greater autonomy. This had been conquered after two wars by Louis XIV in 1678, but many Franc-Comtois nobles retained a nostalgia for Burgundian and (after 1477) Habsburg rule. In May 1791 one, an émigré in Switzerland, appealed to the Emperor Leopold II to advise him that, 'If the Emperor has plans for Franche-Comté, it could be his in very little time. He would be strongly supported by a part of the nobility who miss the rule of the kings who preceded him. This part of the nobility would be supported in such a plan by a people already tired of the anarchy into which it has been plunged.'[12]

The notion of a monarchy gracefully respecting provincial liberties under the Ancien Régime stood up to little scrutiny, and hopes among the displaced élites that the restored monarchy would also restore provincial liberties were sadly misplaced. For the advantages of a centralised administration were plain to every régime, Consulate or Empire, Republic or Monarchy. There was no question that after 1814 the Bourbon monarchy would restore the provinces of the Ancien Regime, whatever they were, let alone their liberties. It was happy to inherit the centralised system perfected in 1790 and 1800. At this point, the monarchy came into conflict with the provincial nobility who saw that the collapse of central government in 1814 indeed provided a unique opportunity to revive provincial institutions. Thus the royalist leader of Franche-Comté, the comte de Scey-Montbéliard, who had fought in the émigré armies, organised a small force of nobles and appealed to the protection of the commander of the invading Austrians. 'This province, which was once a part of the German Empire,' he said, 'might become the appanage of a prince of that illustrious house. Its one desire is to remain *comtois*.'[13] In the first quarter of 1814 Scey-Montbéliard acted as unofficial governor of Franche-Comté, alongside the official Austrian governor, who happened to be his cousin. When the Bourbon monarchy re-established itself, Scey-Montbéliard transferred his allegiance to it. But as the Austrians left, the Bourbons restored the grid of three departments that made up Franche-Comté, and offered Scey only one of them, as prefect of the Doubs. Ousted during the Hundred Days, Scey was one of the royalist extremists who was not offered his post back at the Second Restoration; the monarchy was committed to the departmental system, and to a team of moderates to run the administration.[14]

The suspicion of counter-revolution and separatism that hung over all claims to decentralise the administration in France made defining a position both decentralist and republican extremely difficult. But the presence of Paris as both a political and administrative centre, and as the hot-bed of radical revolution, served to complicate the simple equation of revolutionary and centralist, provincialist and counter-revolutionary. The vulnerability of Paris to a seizure of political power by a revolutionary mob, who then found to hand the system of administrative centralisation that enabled them to impose their revolutionary will on the country, provoked moderate revolutionaries to look to some form of administrative decentralisation in order to protect France and indeed the Republic against the excesses of revolutionary despotism.

In the spring of 1793 the Girondin deputies of the Convention, who were moderate revolutionaries, were increasingly concerned over the growing popular movement in Paris, the pretension of the Paris Commune to dictate to the departments, and the Montagnard deputies who were prepared to side with the radical movement to impose their will on the Convention. On 31 May the Girondins were purged from the Convention, and responded by organising federalist resistance and revolt in many cities and departments, particularly in the Midi. 'Let us unite under the same banner,' Marseille addressed the other departments, 'and inscribe on it these words: "Unity of the Republic, respect of persons and property".'[15] The federalists argued that they were defending the true principles of the Revolution—the liberty and equality of the 83 departments within the One and Indivisible Republic—against the 'anarchists' who were trying to impose the revolutionary dictatorship of Paris on the rest of France. They constituted the revolutionary political class which had been brought to power in the new municipalities and departments of 1790, but a class endowed with property and education. Save in a few exceptional circumstances, they had no relations with the provincial counter-revolutionaries. Barbaroux, one of the leaders of the federalist revolt in Marseille, had been at the forefront of the suppression of counter-revolution in Arles in 1792 and, as we have seen, had campaigned for the unitary Republic. Yet the Montagnards in Paris had no hesitation in denouncing the federalists as provincial counter-revolutionaries and collaborators with foreign invaders, the more exclusive to make their own version of the One and Indivisible Republic and the harder to hit any dissent from it.

A fundamental tension governing the issue of centralisation can be observed here. Fear of red revolution in Paris was a crucial factor determining hostility to centralisation, not only among those nostalgic for the lost provinces but also among those *within* the revolutionary and republican tradition who looked to the department and its administration—a creation of 1790—to guard against the revolutionary despotism of Paris. However, from this point in French history any demand for administrative decentralisation or questioning of the unitary state was rapidly discredited as lying *outside* the revolutionary and republican tradition and as a threat to it. To establish the political space for decentralisation within the revolutionary and republican tradition required freeing it from the smear of counter-revolutionary provincialism and separatism and rewriting the history of the federalism of 1793 as a sober and republican enterprise.

The reassertion of provincial claims tended to wait upon two events: the weakening of political power at the centre, or the upsurge of radicalism in Paris, or both. The 1830 Revolution was triggered off by popular revolt in Paris but successfully hijacked by the notables. But those politicians displaced by the July Revolution, and forced to return to their estates, espoused Legitimism and gambled on the weakness of the new régime. Attempts at insurrection took place in the West and Midi, but were quickly suppressed. After that Legitimists resorted to opposition that was non-political, or at least clothed in non-political forms. One strategy was to cultivate popular support in the provinces to which they had returned by asserting the distinctive identity of the provinces against the interference of the centralised state. The elements of this identity were defined as a separate language where it existed, a popular culture expressed in that language which was not that of polite and civilised society, a religious faith that was insulated from anticlericalism and revolutionary ideas by that language, a rural economy and rustic population that was not corrupted by urban life and labour, the whole wrapped up in a particular vision of the provincial past which glorified tradition and denigrated change. How this provincial sentiment was encouraged in the Breton case will be examined in the next section.

The threat of popular revolution was more serious in 1848 than in 1830. The Revolution ushered in the Republic, then unleashed working-class insurrection. This revived old fears of red revolutionaries seizing power in Paris and imposing their will on the provinces by the centralised administrative machine. The problem of Paris had not been dealt with by any attempt at decentralisation, but (under the law of *pluviôse* Year VIII) by depriving it of all self-government and placing it under the control of the prefect of the department of the Seine and the prefect of police. To remedy this shortcoming, the National Assembly set up a commission to look at administrative decentralisation for France as a whole, and a reform of 3 July 1848 permitted the election of mayors by municipal councils in communes of fewer than six thousand inhabitants. But the commission fell prey also to the recurrent fear that decentralisation would play into the hands of reaction. 'Don't touch the sub-prefects,' it argued, 'they are our surest guarantee against the return of feudalism.'[16]

A barrage of criticism opened up from *La Revue provinciale*, a journal launched in September 1848 by comte Louis de Kergolay, a legitimist who had been arrested for his part in the conspiracy of the duchesse de Berry in 1832 and who later became secretary of the Association bretonne, and Arthur de Gobineau. 'A handful of men, a single coup are enough at a given moment . . . to overthrow the government and rule France by means of the telegraph,' they announced.[17] In their attempt to restore federalism to the agenda, Gobineau argued that it had nothing to do with feudalism or the Ancien Régime, but was within the revolutionary and republican tradition. The Girondin Brissot, he said, was 'the first federalist. Everything was new in the doctrine of this revolutionary innovator. There was no question for him of restoring the old provinces which had just been destroyed by the Constituent Assembly . . . those who speak of federalism as a terrifying nightmare have no idea what it is, or what it was.'[18] Even so, Kergolay's study of the provincial estates of the old monarchy betrayed a certain nostalgia for the Ancien Régime and neither he nor Gobineau was happy with the thesis of Alexis de Tocqueville (of whom Kergolay was a distant cousin and Gobineau *chef de cabinet* at the Foreign Ministry in 1849) that the Revolution was not wholly responsible for administrative centralisation in France and that some part of the blame had to fall on the Ancien Régime monarchy.[19] Indeed, Tocqueville traced back to the pre-1789 monarchy both the centralisation of administration and the concentration in Paris of political activity, population and industry which made revolution possible.[20]

The Legislative Assembly of 1849, which was dominated by royalists and conservative republicans, was prepared to make some concession in the direction of decentralisation. It appointed a commission which came out in favour of giving departmental *conseils-généraux* greater financial powers and permanent executive commissions to limit the power of prefects. However, its work was interrupted by the coup d'état of Louis-Napoleon, whose authoritarian régime made prefects into local despots and removed the right of all municipal councils to elect mayors.[21] Under the Second Empire, two distinct movements of opposition defined themselves. The first claimed to have no ambition to resurrect the province as a political entity, nor any separatist intention, but it looked to revive the identity of the lost province in terms of a distinctive provincial history, religion, language and culture. The second also claimed to have no political ambition, but started from the administrative framework established in 1790, and called for greater local democracy and less interference from the central administration. In this sense, it took up the campaign initiated by the federalists of 1793 while hoping to avoid their fate.

Examples of the first movement may be found in the former Habsburg territories of Flanders and Franche-Comté. In 1864 the *Annales Franc-Comtois* were launched by abbé Louis Besson, head of the Catholic college of Besançon and later to be promoted as bishop of Nîmes. 'Religious struggles have begun again,' he announced in response to Napoleon III's switch to a more anticlerical policy. It was time to fall back on the defence of Franche-Comté, which had once been called by Montalembert, who represented it in the Legislative Assembly, the 'Christian Mountain', standing against the 'Red Mountain' of the Assembly.[22] For abbé Besson there was no question of disloyalty to the French state, but resources existed in Franche-Comté which should be used as insulation against its anti-religious policies. 'France is a mother whom we must love and serve,' he said; 'Franche-Comté is an ancestor of whom we have only the portrait, but whose free, proud and generous blood still flows in our veins.'[23]

To the north, Flanders had the additional advantage of a distinct language to reinforce its provincial identity. This was reasserted after 1853 by the Comité flamand de France. Its task was not to defy the French state, which was regarded as the second fatherland after Flanders, but to redeem the Flemish language, and thus to etch the Flemish identity more sharply within France. Charles de Coussemaker, president of the Comité, argued that 'for the people the maternal language is a heritage more precious than rank or fortune; loyalty, honesty, love of work, domestic virtues and the Catholic faith—the maternal language represents all these for the Flemings of France'.[24] The central government was attacking the Flemish language, but one correspondant of the committee was confident that 'decrees cannot transform a country whose inhabitants have soaked the soil with their blood and sweat'.[25]

The second, federalist, movement gathered momentum in the cities and departments as part of the growth of liberal opposition to the Empire. Indeed the five republican deputies who sat in the Legislative Body by virtue of having taken the oath of loyalty to the emperor were at the front of the campaign for what they saw as local democracy. One of these, Jacques-Louis Hénon, deputy of the Rhône, told the chamber in 1863 that Paris and Lyon should be granted 'an elected and independent municipal council' which would be fully accountable to the electorate.[26] Two years later, in 1865, a group of municipal and departmental councillors of Nancy published a plan of decentralisation which was endorsed by liberals of all shades, legitimist (Berryer, Falloux), Orleanist (Barrot, Guizot, de Broglie), Catholic (Montalembert) and republican (the three Jules: Ferry, Favre and Simon). They expressed fears of red revolution in Paris, pointing out that 'it is easy to pinch a throne when all you have to do to mount it is take control of the Hôtel de Ville of Paris', but added that for the moment 'centralisation is submerging us less by the omnipotence of Paris than by the abusive interference of the bureaucracy in our affairs'. They denied that they wanted to 'resurrect an independent Lorraine or Franche-Comté' and for the moment they did not press the case for the election of mayors directly, or even by municipal councils, since the mayor was an agent of the central government as well as representative of the commune. But they launched the slogan, 'emancipate the departments', and demanded for the *conseils généraux* more financial powers, permanent executive commissions and a departmental administration.[27]

Pressure was kept up by a congress of the provincial press at Lyon in September 1869, and the Liberal Empire ministry of Emile Ollivier, formed on 2 January 1870, gave ground by creating a commission on administrative decentralisation, chaired by Odilon Barrot. Barrot told the first meeting of the commission that decentralisation was the best guarantee against revolution and the bewildering succession of political régimes witnessed since 1789, because participation in local affairs would civilise the political habits of citizens.[28] The commission voted narrowly for the election of mayors by municipal councils, but the government refused to give up its right of appointment. It also decided that *conseils-généraux* would have permanent executive commissions, and that the task of the prefect would be to execute its decisions, but progress on this front was interrupted by the war.[29]

As in 1814–15, decentralisation could only be achieved by default, when the iron cage of administrative centralisation cracked under the impact of war and defeat. Lyon reclaimed its municipal autonomy, forming a committee of public safety which for some time kept Challemel-Lacour, the envoy of minister of the interior Gambetta, a virtual hostage in the Hôtel de Ville. A municipal council displaced the committee of public safety after municipal elections on 15 September, and Hénon was elected mayor. Fighting red revolution as well as administrative centralisation, Hénon's municipality foiled an attempt on 28 September by the anarchist Bakunin to take over the Hôtel de Ville. Departments were also quick to renew the federalist experience. Alphonse Esquiros, a Montagnard of 1848 and a Jacobin enemy of decentralisation by temperament, was sent by Gambetta to serve as prefect of the Bouches-du-Rhône. But under local pressure on 18 September 1870 he put himself at the head of a Ligue du Midi of thirteen departments, which took control of the regional administration and military.[30]

All these movements were federalist in inspiration, and opposed to the red revolution that reached its apogee in Paris after 18 March 1871. The 'bourgeois' mayors elected in each *arrondissement* on 5 November 1870 did not satisfy the revolutionaries' demand for a unitary, autonomous, elected municipality. The provisional government refused to give ground, and eventually the revolutionaries launched an insurrection in Paris and organised elections to a Paris Commune. The Paris Commune of 1871 modelled itself on that of 1792 but differed from it substantially. It not have access to the levers of administrative centralisation, and in any case the dominant sentiment in it was anarchist, hostile to state power, subscribing to a concept of federalism that was quite unlike the property-owners' federalism of 1793 or the Nancy programme. Its declaration to the people of France of 19 April announced that the communes of France (some of which, at Lyon, Marseille, Le Creusot, Saint-Étienne, Narbonne and Toulouse had proclaimed revolutionary communes of their own) were henceforth autonomous, free to undertake their own reforms without let or hindrance from the central government, and that unity would no longer be imposed but that they were free to federate by voluntary union.[31] 'For federalism,' said James Guillaume, a disciple of Bakunin and stalwart of the First International, 'there is no longer a nation, no national or territorial unity. There is only an aggregate of federated communes. Neither is there any longer a state, no more central power higher than other groups and imposing its authority on them.'[32]

This anarchist federalism, however, was not to the taste of provincial cities like Lyon and Marseille which wanted a federalism and municipalism that was legal and respectful of property. These mobilised the National Guard and appealed to the military to put down the communes in their back yards. It was even further from the views of the National Assembly, some of whose members cherished a provincialism that had been honed on fears of red revolution in 1848 and were adamant that it should not succeed this time, even at the cost of civil war. On the other hand, both these elements were determined to claim their reward for extinguishing revolution in the form of measures of administrative decentralisation. The president of the Republic, Adolphe Thiers, was clearly indebted to these forces. Yet in a year when France had almost broken up under the strain of foreign invasion, revolution and civil war, decentralisation from his point of view was ill-timed. A compromise was therefore found. Large towns had shown themselves vulnerable to revolutionaries, and Thiers insisted in retaining the government's right of appointment of mayors in all towns with a population of over twenty thousand. In the departments, however, which had once again served as a rampart against revolution, *conseils-généraux* were accorded the permanent executive commissions they had demanded since 1848 and, while not assuming a political rôle, now became important assemblies with a good deal of influence in matters of education, transport and the economy.[33]

In its struggle to obtain power within the Republic the republican party had committed itself to furthering local democracy. In power, it was responsible for the law of March 1882 which finally restored to municipal councils the right to elect mayors. Conversely, republicans, like any other wielders of political power, soon became aware of the usefulness of the centralised state as a means to control their opponents. The law of April 1884 conferred more freedoms on municipal councils but did not release them fully from the tutelage of prefects. Moreover, chastised as much as the royalists by the experience of the Paris Commune, republicans refused to concede a mayor for Paris. As the moderate Waldeck-Rousseau put it in 1884, 'In Paris riot or insurrection hold sway, and revolution in Paris provokes revolution or counter-revolution in the whole of France.'[34] Fear of another Paris Commune was never hidden very deep among men of property. Henri Wallon, architect of the parliamentary constitution of 1875 and campaigner for the cult of Joan of Arc, published a book in 1886 on the Montagnard revolution of 31 May 1793 and the federalist response. He argued that 'the revolution of 31 May was the triumph of the Paris Commune over the national parliament', and the beginning of the Terror aimed at Girondins who championed local liberties. 'These events which took place nearly a century ago,' he continued 'have the merit of interesting us as if they happened only yesterday.' For Wallon the Paris Commune of 1871 had threatened the national parliament and local interests in exactly the same way, and what had happened twice could easily happen again. 'What would France do, I ask . . . today, if the vanguard of the Jacobins (for there are always Jacobins), if the *anarchists* as people said in 1793, if determined revolutionaries, using methods which have become classic in their history . . . seized power?'[35]

The revival of federalist and regionalist sentiment in the Third Republic owed much to fear of another Paris Commune. This was compounded by the frustration of the Right which after 1871 never won a national legislative election, while the governing republicans perfected the system of using the centralised administration to confer contracts, jobs and public works on constituents and thus ensure their repeated re-election. The fact that the Right came close to regaining power in 1885, through Boulanger, under Méline, and during the Dreyfus affair, only to see victory slip from its grasp, encouraged it to blame the twin evils of the parliamentary régime and the centralised state, and to search for alternatives. Moreover, the displacement of moderate republicans by radicals in 1895–6 and after 1898, together with the growing power of socialist parties in local and national elections after 1892 and their periodic alliance with radicals, gave even some moderate republicans cause to question the virtues of the centralised régime, lest it fall into the hands of extremists.

As under the Second Empire, there were two basic strands of opposition to the centralised régime. One was republican and federalist in the tradition of 1793 and the programme of Nancy; the other criticised the department as the basic unit of administration and was thus provincialist or regionalist. As during the French Revolution, the champions of the centralised, unitary Republic were keen to discredit any projects of decentralisation as counter-revolutionary and separatist. For their part decentralisers strove to throw off these accusations by placing themselves in the republican and federal tradition, which was legitimate for some of them, but more questionable for others. A minority had the courage of their convictions and put their provincialism under the banner of monarchist restoration.

Campaigners of the Left who retained the early republican commitment to local democracy proposed schemes of decentralisation. In 1890 the radical-socialist deputy Abel Hovelacque introduced a bill to establish regional councils, but he also wanted to abolish the senate and presidency of the Republic. In 1896 another radical-socialist Henri Michelin introduced a scheme to give full powers to *conseils-généraux* through their executives, called departmental directories, but the main purpose of his bill was to give administrative autonomy to the Ville de Paris.[36] With these exceptions, however, radicals subscribed to the Jacobin view of the centralised unitary Republic. 'Question these ardent "decentralisers",' urged Clemenceau in 1904, 'and you will soon discover that their plan is to decentralise not liberty but reaction.'[37] Supporters of decentralisation in the republican camp tended to be moderates by persuasion. Their view tended to be that the law on *conseils-généraux* of 1871 and the municipal law of 1884 were only a beginning. 'To return to the maxims of 1789, while repudiating those [of the Montagnards] of 1793, that is our programme,' stated the Progressist Paul Deschanel.[38] Joseph Paul-Boncour, private secretary to Waldeck-Rousseau during the ministry of republican defence, regretted in 1903 that 'the truth was that decentralisation has been cast aside as a wild dream, fine for the opposition, inhibiting for those in power, which must be relegated with the election of judges and the abolition of the president of the

Republic among the juvenilia of radicalism'.[39] André Tardieu, another protégé of Waldeck-Rousseau, concurred that 'If, like Paul-Boncour, we believe that decentralisation is not incompatible with the Republic, we think that it is incompatible with radical-socialism . . . Nothing is more hateful than this historical diversity to the Jacobin mind that is now in charge of France.'[40]

These moderates were firmly within the republican tradition and had no wish to tamper with the departmental structure of France. Others, however, attacked the department as the basic unit of the system of administrative centralisation, which they saw in turn adapted to the electoral needs of the parliamentary oligarchy. To assert their allegiance to the province was to court the accusation of counter-revolutionary; they therefore tended to prefer the term 'region' and developed scientific reasons to explain its superiority to the department. Lastly, while most of them loudly proclaimed their republicanism, one wing ventured to argue that only the monarchy could ensure satisfactory decentralisation.

Maurice Barrès, the grandson of an Auvergnat officer in Napoleon's armies who had retired to Lorraine, embraced Boulangism and was elected deputy for Nancy in 1889, but after his defeat in 1893 he took up the cause of federalism to criticise the parliamentary Republic. His federalism was firmly republican. 'From 1789 to 1793 the Revolution was federalist,' he declared in a lecture of 1895 to socialists of Bordeaux. 'It was the Jacobins who, in June 1793, centralised us decisively', he continued, 'to confront momentary crises in the Vendée and on the Rhine.' Yet, he asserted, 'the federalist doctrine conforms to the underlying tradition of France and the Revolution.'[41] In his novel *Les Déracinés*, published in 1897, Barrès elaborated his attack on the centralised parliamentary régime. Parliamentary politicians, he argued, far from pursuing the general good, deceived the electorate through a partisan press, and were themselves corrupted by private business interests. The subordination of public to private in the parliamentary Republic left it divided and rudderless.[42] The politicians, meanwhile, used the centralised state to secure their re-election by satisfying the private concerns of their constituents. Even worse, however, they used the centralised school system of the Republic to prise the youth of France away from the influence of home and province and to impose their own partisan, secular ideology on them. His criticism, nevertheless, was of the practice and ideology of the Republic, not of the Republic itself.

Barrès argued that his regionalism was republican; he also demonstrated that it was the opposite of separatist. He placed the region at the service of France. For him, the process of regeneration would be effected not by abstracting individuals from their past and environment, and exposing them to the glare of universal reason, but by rooting them there more firmly. Here Barrès paraded his scientific apparatus. The collectivity, he argued, was greater than the individuals who composed it. 'There are no personal ideas,' he said.[43] Moreover, the collective consciousness (or collective unconscious) was determined by two powerful forces, the heritage of ancestors, and the milieu or region in which people grew up—blood and soil, *la terre et les morts*. Once this determinism was accepted, it was not difficult to rebuild the 'moral unity' of France. This theory in turn enabled Barrès to side-step claims that he was a reactionary. For the moral unity of France could not be reconstituted by a return to monarchy or to the Church, both of which institutions divided the French or ceased to be relevant. It would be rebuilt by the cult of ancestors and provinces. Cemeteries, especially those in which soldiers who fell in the war of 1870, together with the grave of his mother, were the high altars of this cult.[44]

If Lorraine was one source of regionalist thinking, Provence was another. They were, however, a Lorraine and a Provence refracted through Paris. Just as Barrès, pursuing his career in Paris, became a professional regionalist, Charles Maurras was alerted to his Provençal roots only by life in the anonymous capital and, as his mother reminded him, learned his Provençal in Paris.[45] Maurras joined the Félibres, who campaigned for the revival of the Provençal language, and later claimed that their leader, Mistral, was 'the doctor of our traditions'.[46] But he soon came to believe, first, that their preoccupation with Provençal language, tradition and folklore had to be subordinated to a clear demand for political autonomy and, second, that it was necessary to reach out from Provençal particularism to other autonomists in France. Maurras was one of the young generation of Félibres who subscribed to the manifesto read at the Café Voltaire in Paris on 22 February 1892 for which they were expelled from the movement.

> We are fed up with keeping quiet about out federalist intentions. We can no longer confine ourselves to demanding the rights and duties of freedom for our language and writers; that freedom will not achieve political autonomy, but will flow from it. . . . We demand liberty for our communes. . . . We want to release from their departmental cages the souls of provinces whose names are still used everywhere by everyone: Gascons, Auvergnats, Limousins, Béarnais, Dauphinois, Roussillonnais, Provençaux and Languedociens. We are autonomists, we are federalists, and if somewhere in northern France a people wants to march with us, our hand is out-stretched. . . . We want sovereign assemblies in Bordeaux, in Toulouse, in Montpellier, in either Marseille or Aix. These assemblies will run our administration, our courts, our schools, our universities, our public works.[47]

The demand for sovereign provincial assemblies was a challenge to the unitary nature of the state. And in that these resembled nothing more than the provincial estates of the Ancien Règime there was a challenge to the revolutionary tradition. It was some time, however, before Maurras took the manifesto to its logical conclusion. In his *Idea of Decentralisation* (1898) he criticised the Bourbons for not restoring provincial and communal traditions in 1814, and accepted that Louis XIV had done as much damage to 'flourishing federative France' as the Revolution and Napoleon.[48] But by 1900 he concluded that the restoration of provincial liberties required the restoration of the monarchy. He recreated the myth of the Ancien Régime as a golden age, in which the monarchy achieved a perfect balance of authority and liberty, leaving the communes and provinces the freedom to order their own internal affairs while it concentrated its energies on furthering the national greatness of France. Moreover, Maurras exposed with clinical precision the link between the parliamentary Republic and administrative centralisation. Whereas under a monarchy, he argued, positions of power had been filled by heredity or the representation of territorial or professional interests, in the Republic all responsibilities were elective, and to ensure its survival the government had to step in to 'make' the elections. 'The more bureaucrats a central power which is elective has at its disposal,' he said, 'the more chance it has of retaining its electors, since bureaucrats are the most precious intermediaries between itself and the electorate.'[49] Thus, paradoxically, democracy and centralisation were on one side of the coin, monarchy and decentralisation on the other.

Not all the young 'political' Félibres were convinced by Maurras' monarchism. In particular, Jean Charles-Brun, a Montpellier academic, feared alienating a growing body of opinion that was opposed to radical Jacobinism but was still republican. In 1900, to link up decentralisers of all political persuasions and from all parts of France, he did not opt for the monarchy but founded the Fédération Régionaliste Française. The minimum programme of 1901 proposed was administrative decentralisation, 'management of the affairs of the commune by the commune, of the region by the region, and of the nation by the state'; regional control of economic life and a regional perspective in education, arts and sciences.[50] The Federation was particularly concerned about the damage done to regional life by the concentration of government and population in Paris and hoped to use the newly reformed regional universities to generate interest in regional life. The use of the term 'region' rather than 'province' was intentional. To rehabilitate the province would invite criticism that the Federation, like the Maurassians, wanted to restore the Ancien Régime. The region was developed deliberately as a scientific concept, reflecting an economic, geographical or historical reality. The Federation drew on the work on the geographer Vidal de la Blache, who used the concept of nodality to construct his map of regions which would be articulated around regional centres such as Bordeaux, Toulouse, Nantes and Rouen.[51] The province was set aside as merely a historical unit, and a unit that was frequently as irrational in its outline as the department.

One goal of Charles-Brun was the establishment of regional assemblies. The form such assemblies might take was a matter for debate; but there was general agreement that representation would be corporative, of interests rather than of individuals. This was both because economic questions would be at the top of the agenda, and because successive legislative elections in 1906, 1910 and 1914 returned increasing numbers of socialists. The spectre of red revolution was no longer barricades in Paris but a dictatorship of the proletariat using the levers of centralised administration to impose collectivism on France. At a regional

congress at Angoulême in 1913, a local deputy and brandy magnate, Jean
Hennessy, who admired the work of Charles-Brun, launched the idea of 'the
profession represented in the organised region'.[52] In April 1915 he introduced
a bill to provide for the representation of professional groups in regional
assemblies and became chairman of a parliamentary commission looking at
administrative reorganisation.

As in other wartime situations, the Great War reopened the debate on the
administrative structure of France. Some regions, like northern France, caught
on the wrong side of the front line and isolated from Paris, had to fend for
themselves. The problem of post-war reconstruction was posed during the war
itself, and Jean Hennessy argued that the national parliament would be so
overloaded with business that the rebuilding of regional economies should be
made a responsibility of the regions themselves. A third problem outlined by
Hennessy was posed by the possible reintegration of Alsace and Lorraine, and
whether it would be reasonable, or indeed possible, to extend to them without
modification the system of administrative centralisation obtaining in the rest of
France.[53]

The programme suggested by Hennessy received short shrift at the hands of
his parliamentary colleagues. His commission would have nothing to do with
regional assemblies drawn from interests outside their own. Its expectation was
that if regional assemblies were to be introduced, they should be elected by
conseillers-généraux: the notion of pluralism of office was central to the determination of the political class to retain a monopoly of power.[54] The only
measure taken towards regionalisation was confined to the economic sphere
and, while leaving the political class unscathed, empowered existing economic
élites. After 1917 the minister of commerce Clémentel pressed chambers of
commerce to organise themselves into economic regions, to be based on regional economic capitals. By 1921 twenty-eight economic regions had been set
up. Little consideration was taken of the aspirations of the chambers of commerce of Metz and Nancy, Strasbourg, Colmar and Mulhouse. Though they
wanted separate economic regions for Alsace and Lorraine, the government
imposed a joint economic region of Alsace-Lorraine.[55]

The question of Alsace-Lorraine set the regionalist movement off on an
entirely new tack in the inter-war period, that of autonomism. France refused
to compromise on the unitary Republic and administrative centralisation when
it reincorporated the lost provinces. It restored to the banks of the Rhine the
sign that had stood there in the revolutionary period—'Ici commence le pays de
la liberté'—while seeking to impose uniformity in the French language and the
secular ideology of the Republic in a way reminiscent of revolutionary intransigence. [Fig. 16] Regionalist opposition to republican centralism had
hitherto taken two forms: the cultivation of regional languages by conservative
élites excluded from power in an attempt to broaden their popular electoral
base; and the cultivation of regional languages by the Catholic Church in an
attempt to protect the Catholic religion from revolutionary ideology. Of course,

Fig. 16. 'Ici Commence le Pays de la Liberté': sign re-erected at the Kehl bridge over the Rhine, 1918
(Roger-Viollet)

the Catholic Church could be defended without recourse to regional languages, but some clergy felt that to preach and catechise in those languages conferred immunity against modern secular ideas. In 1882 the archbishop of Cambrai had announced that 'Flemish [was] the language of heaven.'[56]

The defence of regional languages, however, could lead to demands for administrative and political autonomy, because the imposition of French as the only official language excluded from public employment those who were not well versed in the language, and attracted from outside French-speaking bureaucrats who tended to treat the local population with disdain. Those who wished to argue the case for autonomy now considered that their position was legitimated by the principle of national self-determination endorsed by the treaties of Versailles. The multi-national empires had been broken apart in its name, independent nation-states had been set up from Ireland to Poland, and provision made for the protection of national minorities within sovereign states. In search of similar goals a Vlaamsch Verbond van Frankrijk or French Flemish League was set up in 1926 and autonomist parties were set up in 1927 in Corsica, Alsace and Brittany The last two will be examined as case studies in the second part of this chapter.

After 1930, and particularly after the triumph of the Nazi party in Germany and the victory of the Popular Front, a new extremism developed among autonomist movements. As legal, parliamentary methods of achieving their ends brought no success, so direct action seemed more attractive. The most resolute of the autonomists adopted the trappings of fascism: élitism, the cult of the leader, paramilitary organisation, commitment to violence, racism and separatism. Moreover, the extremists looked increasingly to war and a further crisis in the French state to liberate their homeland: the example of the Sudeten Germans was a powerful inspiration.

The French government did not look on passively. A decree-law of 25 May 1938 criminalised all attempts to undermine the territorial integrity of France. Breton and Alsatian autonomists were brought to trial at Rennes and Nancy and autonomist organisations were broken up. The outbreak of war made the crackdown even sharper: an Alsatian autonomist was convicted of high treason by a military court and executed early in 1940. But by June 1940 the state had collapsed more dramatically still than in 1793, 1814 or 1870. The prospect suddenly opened for French separatists of autonomy under the patronage of the Third Reich. In the new world order, France would be reduced to a rump and the oppressed minorities would float free.

In the event, French autonomists were gravely disappointed. German strategy was determined by strategic considerations which included relations with the French state at Vichy, firm control of the Channel and Atlantic littoral of France, the administration of French Flanders from Brussels and the reannexation of Alsace and the Moselle. As the autonomist extremists were marginalised by the Germans, so the way was cleared for regionalists who had themselves been squeezed out since the 1920s. Instead of looking to Germany to catapult them to power, these regionalists looked to Vichy and tried to take advantage of the new climate of National Revolution.

The moment was well chosen. Marshal Pétain had shared most of Barrès' assumptions concerning the evils of the centralised parliamentary Republic. Fears that that Republic might fall into the hands of red revolutionaries had been realised by the Popular Front victory of 1936 and the general strike that followed it. Paris had been declared an open city in June 1940 lest another siege by the Germans provoke another Paris Commune. Pétain was looked to as a regionalist head of state and indeed made a series of declarations which were music to the ears of regionalists. On 13 November 1940 he declared his wish to divide France into about twenty regions, according to geographical character- istics, and to place a governor at the head of each; the rôle of prefects would be drastically reduced.[57] A month later, he paid homage to Mistral on the 110th anniversary of his death, calling him 'the sublime evocator of the new France that we want to found'.[58] The Conseil National of notables, who were planning that new France under Pétain's authority, sprouted a number of commissions, including one on administrative reorganisation, which met from May 1941 under the chairmanship of Lucien Romier, a former editor of the *Figaro*. A member of the commission was Jean Charles-Brun, president of the Fédération Régionaliste Française. He had been trying to broaden the appeal of his regionalist projects by invoking the heritage not only of Mistral but also of Proudhon, who became in his reinterpretation not an anarchist but a defender of the family, trade, soil and province, a believer in liberty and authority, property and patriotism.[59] By August 1941 the commission had sanctioned the project of Pétain and Romier for governors, appointed by the head of state, who would, like military chiefs, superintend a grand strategy for the regions, weakening the prefects, advised by provincial councils in which 'territorial', 'economic', and 'spiritual' (familial, social and intellectual) interests and values would be represented.[60]

There was, however, a sense in which the Conseil national and its commission floated in a dream-world above the realities of government under Vichy. Though Maurras had argued that democracy and administrative centralisation were two sides of the same coin, Vichy was far more interested in dismantling democracy, which had assured the political class of the Third Republic sixty years of unchallenged power, than in tampering with the structures of administrative centralisation. A law of 16 November 1940 abrogated the municipal democracy of 1884 by reverting to the appointment of mayors in all communes of more than two thousand inhabitants; another, of 12 October 1940, replaced elective *conseils-généraux* by appointed administrative commissions. The suspension of democracy and the link-up of central bureaucrats and local notables were in some sense reminiscent of the First Empire.[61] The crown of the centralised edifice was the system of regional prefects established under the law of 19 April 1941. Like Pétain's projected governors, the regional prefects had a certain Ancien Régime air about them, but where the governors were military in style and somewhat ornamental, the regional prefects were all-powerful civilian administrators, like the intendants of Louis XIV.[62] No provincial councils came into being alongside them, much to the distress of *conseillers-nationaux* like Charles-Brun.[63] 'Should we admit,' he asked a training school of Vichy cadres in 1943, 'that the region, as the Fédération régionaliste française defined it, must merely fulfil the rôle of myth . . . that the vision may sustain regionalists but that its perfect realization is doubtless impossible?'[64]

Though the reforms of Vichy were inspired by a fear of revolution and a hatred of democracy, revolution and democracy soon returned to claim their due. The Communist-dominated Resistance set up a revolutionary Comité de Libération in Paris which was in touch with other *comités de libération* set up in other towns and departments of France. Communists were also dominant in the Resistance militia, the Forces Françaises de l'Intérieur, and the revolutionary police, the *milices partiotiques*. The task of the provisional government of the Republic under de Gaulle was both to clear up the remnants of the Vichy order and to prevent France falling prey to red revolution in the manner of 1871. Initially, the provisional government fell back on the regional division of France sanctioned by Vichy as the framework for its *commissaires de la République*. These were moved into France ahead of the liberation of Paris to establish control of and dismantle the revolutionary authorities. But there was no intention of letting the *commissaires* become regional bosses independent of the central government. Minister of the interior Tixier told them in September 1944,

> The period of regional administration is finished. The central government has been installed in Paris. It intends to govern. You are its representatives, you must execute its decisions. . . . You must re-establish the unity of France: first unity of the law . . . [then] unity of the administration, unity of justice, unity of the police, unity of the army. . . . In a word you must found the One and Indivisible Republic of the Liberation.[65]

De Gaulle would have been happy with the unitary Republic and his regional *commissaires de la République*. The Liberation, however, was not only the restoration of the state; it was also the restoration of the politicians and their political parties. The party politicians were used to bending prefects to the purposes of their re-election, but regional officials were beyond their reach.[66] The return of democracy in the guise of the political class brought in its wake the return of administrative centralisation articulated around the department. After the departure of de Gaulle in January 1946, the Constituent Assembly duly abolished the *commissaires de la République*.

The aftermath of the Liberation marked a very low point for regionalism. The unity and independence of France that had been betrayed by Vichy had been recovered after four years of struggle, and no sympathy was due to those who were seen to have impaired it. Autonomists were discredited as separatist and collaborationist, if not as downright Nazis, and were punished either by the death penalty (a number of which were pronounced *in absentia*) or by long periods of hard labour. Harmless regionalists were attacked as no better than autonomists and the new constitution explicitly reiterated that France was a One and Indivisible Republic.

If regionalism were to make its way back onto the political agenda, it had first to construct a non-political case for its claims and, second, to avoid antagonising the newly ensconced political class. One argument it turned to was the danger of the demographic and economic preponderance of Paris. The key text here was *Paris et le Désert français*, published by Jean-François Gravier in 1947. Gravier, who had run a training school for Vichy propagandists, argued at that time that 'the national renaissance will be a function of provincial and local renaissances' and supported the notion of a return of populations to the soil.[67] At the Liberation, he was employed as a geographer by Raoul Dautry, the minister of reconstruction and town planning, and couched his proposals *couche* in less ideological and more scientific terms. Gone was the obsession with Paris as a hot-bed of red revolution; Paris was now criticised as a black hole into which the population of France disappeared and whose massive surplus of deaths over births largely accounted for the demographic and, hence, military inferiority of France. 'It is clear', Gravier said, 'that a France of 70 million inhabitants [like Germany in 1939, instead of 42 millions] would most probably have been spared war and invasion in 1914, as in 1939.'[68] For this, he blamed the centralisation of administrative, intellectual and business activity in Paris, which was reinforced by the radiation of all railways from the capital, and demanded a regional economic policy to develop and diversify the regions. In 1942 he had criticised the French state as an apartment block of which only the ground and sixth floor were inhabited, in which the state and the individual confronted each other unmediated, and urged that the communities represented by the other floors be adequately represented.[69] In *Fédération*, a review to which he contributed, he suggested a hierarchy of cantonal, departmental and regional councils, crowned by a national council, each to be to furnished by deputies from the rung below.[70] But in *Paris et le Désert français*, his ambitions were limited to regional *economic* councils, which would not disturb the political class in place.[71]

Gravier's work undoubtedly influenced the regional economic planning that developed in France in the 1950s. Some initiatives were local: a Comité d'Étude et de Liaison des Intérêts Bretons (CELIB) was founded in 1950 under René Pleven, president of the *conseil-général* of the Côtes-du-Nord and former prime minister. A self-styled 'estates-general of the Breton economy', it devised ways of coping with the relative backwardness and poverty of Brittany and the rural depopulation that resulted. These included the elimination of the small-field *bocage* system, the development of dairy and meat co-operatives, the construction of a tidal power-station across the Rance estuary, and broadening the industrial base of the peninsula.[72] The main impulse behind regional policy was, however, the Commissariat au Plan. Decrees of 1954 and 1955 gave it responsibility for approving regional expansion committees and regional plans, and for organising public and private finance for regional development companies. In 1963 the regional aspects of the Commissariat au Plan were hived off by Prime Minister Pompidou and entrusted to a Délégué à l'Aménagement du Territoire et à l'Action Régionale. 'L'aménagement du territoire' was a technocratic term, the idea behind which was to modernise as quickly as possible those parts of France that lagged behind. It was a regional policy to do away with regionalism. The first *délégué*, Olivier Guichard, believed that the reason for the regionalists' obsession with their own language and history was backwardness, and that the economic revolution would dissolve these old–fashioned sentiments.[73]

The hostility to regionalism of the government of the Fifth Republic was underlined by the nature of the regional authorities that they were prepared to put in place. Regional economic development was used as an excuse in 1964 to install regional prefects, a reincarnation of the *commissaires de la République* and the regional prefects of Vichy. Each was to be advised by a *commission de développement économique régional* (CODER), but no challenge was offered to the existing political class and business leadership. The commissions would be responsible only for economic questions, and would be drawn half from business organisations, a quarter from mayors and *conseillers-généraux*, and a quarter appointed by the prime minister.

After the events of 1968, an attempt was made to modify this structure in favour of greater 'participation'. De Gaulle proposed a system of regional councils, alongside a reform of the Senate, to be put to the people in a referendum on 27 April 1969. But this was hardly an advance on the CODER. To representatives of the municipalities, the *conseils-généraux* and economic and professional organisations were added the parliamentary deputies of the region. The councils had no political power and could deal only with economic, social and cultural matters. They met only twice a year, had no permanent commission, no permanent staff and next to no budget. Above all, they were strictly under the control of the regional prefect who prepared the agenda of the council, chaired it and executed its decisions.[74] The proposal was called 'singularly disappointing' by Jean-François Gravier.[75] It was rejected by the electorate and brought about the departure of de Gaulle. Yet the alternative of President Pompidou, enshrined in the law of 5 July 1972, was if anything a step backwards. The power of the regional prefect remained unchallenged. Economic and social affairs were hived off from the regional council to a *comité économique et social* which had only consultative powers. Meanwhile the regional councils were handed over lock, stock and barrel to the political class. Packed half with delegates from the municipal councils and *conseils-généraux*, half with the deputies and senators of the region, they gave a new twist to the practice of the pluralism of mandates held by the political class.[76]

The attempt to dissolve regionalism by an economic miracle and by providing another slice of patronage for the political class was not enough to satisfy the regionalists. Regionalism indeed returned with a vengeance in the 1960s, in some cases traditionalist, but in general consciously adopting a new rhetoric which protected it from being identified with movements discredited by association with Vichy and the German occupation. The great stimulus to a revival of regionalism was the disintegration of the French Empire, and in particular the Algerian war. Some of the new regionalists were converted as a result of being conscripted to fight the Algerians; all were impressed by the war of liberation successfully waged by Algerian nationalists against the French state. Strategies of imperial domination and assimilation undertaken for over a century in the French Empire were shown to have failed, and the experience of the French Empire was compounded by movements of decolonisation in the British, Belgian, Dutch and American empires. The language of anti-imperialism and decolonisation was now firmly harnessed to the regionalists' cause. To the traditional regionalism of the Right was now added a regionalism of the Left.

Regionalists applied to metropolitan France the left-wing critique of colonialism as exploitation by adopting the concept of internal colonisation. They argued that the development of the Common Market had opened a division between the rich north and east of France and the poor south and west. These were described as colonies, which were maintained in a state of enforced underdevelopment by bureaucrats, technocrats and capitalists in order to provide primary materials, cheap labour and markets for the industrialised zones, playgrounds for holidaymakers and bases for the military. The response to this economic imperialism, as in developing countries, it was argued, was the collectivisation of 'foreign' assets and the establishment of a balanced economic base in the regions. This programme had much in common with socialist politics, but was distinguished from it by the national question. Here again, however, nationalist rhetoric moved with the times. Concepts of national and racial superiority had been discredited by association with movements of the Right, with collaboration, and ultimately with the Holocaust. But the concept of the ethnic group, derived from anthropology and used to suggest an endangered species, was attractive to the Left. Regionalists now cast their claims in the language of the rights of ethnic minorities asserted against the domination of national majorities. Guy Héraud, university professor at Strasbourg, argued that while the Universal Declaration of the Rights of Man of 1948 protected individuals from discrimination, it offered no such protection for minorities. The answer, in his view, was to provide them with autonomy within a 'European federation of ethnic groups'.[77] Official sanction was given to such efforts by the encyclical of Pope John XXIII, *Pacem in terris* (1963), which stated that 'there is nothing truer to justice than public action to improve the living conditions of ethnic minorities, especially so far as their language, culture, customs, resources and economic activities are concerned'.[78]

Pressure for change was nevertheless building up, and becoming increasingly violent. In 1957 Corsica was presented with a regional plan of action which concentrated on the promotion of wine monoculture and tourism by two large development companies. A hostile response came from the Front Régionaliste Corse, which set out to protect agricultural land, the coastline, and Corsican language and culture from the wave of speculators who soon interlocked with the island's political clans. More nationalist and less socialist was the Azzione per la Rinascita Corsa (ARC) which broke away in 1974 to demand 'internal autonomy' and the recognition by the French state of a distinct 'Corsican people'.[79] As it took to direct action so President Giscard d'Estaing and his minister of the interior, Michel Poniatowski, responded with force. Dissolving the ARC, they landed troops on the island and used *barbouzes* or secret police to infiltrate the nationalist networks. The effect was to provoke the formation of the Front de Libération Nationale de la Corse (FLNC), which modelled itself on the Basque separatist movement ETA, founded in 1959, and was committed to attain its goals by terrorism. The Giscard government only increased repression, and four Corsican militants were sent to prison early in 1981 by the Cour de Sûreté de l'Etat.

Corsican nationalism nevertheless provided the hard case that eventually forced a reconsideration of the question of administrative centralisation. The Socialist opposition opted for a more accommodating approach. During the presidential election campaign of 1981, François Mitterrand visited Corsica and promised the island 'special status'. The new Socialist government could not swallow the term 'Corsican people', and so diluted it to the more acceptable 'Corsican people, a constituent part of the French people'.[80] Corsica was duly granted a directly elected regional assembly in 1982, and the autonomist Union du Peuple Corse contained with little more than ten per cent of the vote.

The Socialist government of 1981 followed through with the most important measure of administrative decentralisation since the Revolution. The principle underlying the law of 2 March 1982 was that 'communes, departments and regions [were] freely administered by elected councils'.[81] The great innovation was the introduction of direct universal suffrage for the election of regional councils. In addition, the regional prefects, now renamed *commissaires de la République* or *commissaires de la République en région*, were much weakened in relation to presidents of the *conseils-généraux* and presidents of the region who were now elected, with their own executive, from their councils. An attempt was made to limit the pluralism of the political class by making deputies, senators and mayors of communes of over twenty thousand inhabitants ineligible for regional councils. A whole range of duties was shifted to the region, from regional and town planning, transport and the environment to housing, health, education, training and culture.

The federalist solution to the French state had at last been found. Four elements enabled this reform to find a place within French political culture. In the first place, regionalism, which had been associated with political reaction from the Revolution to Vichy, had elaborated a left-wing discourse during and as a result of the process of decolonisation. This made it possible for a socialist government to accommodate at an ideological level a major law of decentralisation. Indeed, the onus on those who proclaimed themselves the friends of liberty was to begin to dismantle the worst features of the centralised state.

Secondly, the fear that decentralisation at the level of Paris would invite the formation of a new Paris Commune was now dissipated. 'You can only govern against Paris', observed Thibaudet in *La République des professeurs*.[82] The events of May 1968 had again raised the spectre of revolution, but since the Second War Paris had become a stronghold of the Right. Even the Communist 'red belt' in the suburbs was not stable. In 1975 President Giscard d'Estaing reinstituted the office of mayor of Paris, abolished after the Revolution, and the mayoralty fell into the hands of his Gaullist ex-premier, Jacques Chirac. That Paris was dominated by Gaullists who were also centralists freed up the question of decentralisation for the rest of France. And though the coexistence of a socialist government and a conservative administration of Paris might be unsatisfactory, Mitterrand would not call it into question. 'Let us take care', he warned, 'not to be accused of being Versaillais against the Commune, by going back on what M. Giscard d'Estaing granted Paris.'[83]

Thirdly, the reform was clearly within the republican and federalist tradition of 1793 and represented a triumph beyond the grave for the Girondins. It is significant that its sponsor was Gaston Defferre, mayor of Marseille, that bastion of federalism in 1793 and 1870. Concerns about the risk to the territorial unity of France and to state power were voiced by the Gaullists, who were now the chief defenders of Jacobin centralisation. However, at a reception for French mayors in September 1981, Defferre informed Jacques Chirac: 'France will remain a One and Indivisible Republic.'[84] The doctrine of the One and Indivisible Republic was indeed written into the constitution of 1958, so that limits to what the Socialist government could do were imposed by the Conseil constitutionnel, the watch-dog of the constitution. For example, the concept of 'free administration' which replaced that of administrative tutelage by the prefects in the socialist law was subsequently modified by the Conseil constitutionnel to require the 'control of the legality' of the acts of regional councils by the central government. Moreover, the law recognising 'the Corsican people, a constituent part of the French nation', finally passed in April 1991, was adjudged incompatible with the notion of the One and Indivisible Republic by the Conseil constitutionnel. Bertrand Barère would have been delighted to learn that the unity of the French state still entailed the uniformity of the French nation.

Fourthly, the law was negotiated openly between Left and Right and the interests of the political class were respected in the moderation of the solutions to pluralism, and in the time accorded to politicians to resign conflicting offices. There was precious little in the law for regionalists and autonomists who were struggling for their own regional identity and home rule. This was confirmed by the fact that in the elections to regional councils it was the established political parties, especially those of the Centre and Right, who benefited rather than the regionalists and autonomists. In the elections of March 1986 the Centre and Right won control of twenty of the twenty-two regional councils. In those of March 1992 the socialists secured only 18 per cent of the vote as against 33 per cent for the Gaullist–Giscardian bloc, the Union pour la France. Moreover, the regionalist parties were totally eclipsed by the Front National, which obtained 9.7 per cent of the vote and 137 regional councillors in 1986, and 13.9 per cent of the vote and 239 regional councillors in 1992.[85] Thus, though the law of 1982 was republican and federal, in the end it was the Right which benefited from decentralisation, as the French revolutionaries had feared.

Defining the Region

The law of 1982 revived the republican, federalist version of French administration first proposed in 1793. It did not address, and did not satisfy, regionalists who sought not only administrative decentralisation but also some degree of political autonomy for the regions and contested the view that citizenship of the French state necessarily implied national uniformity.

To define themselves and legitimate their claims against the state, regional-ists had to construct a specific regional identity. In some cases, like the Breton, they claimed that they were not only a distinct region but a distinct nation. The basis of this identity was usually said to be a separate language, a separate religion or a separate ethnic grouping. In addition, the collective memory of an historical struggle against the French state or of the prior existence of a state was also central to the construction of a regional or national identity. Of the three regions to be placed under the microscope here, one, Alsace, had a history of belonging to two states; the second, Brittany, claimed to have been an independent state until 1532; and the third, Occitanie, had never been a state but played on the historic opposition between northern and southern France.

Those who defined regional cultures had to be prepared to defend them-selves against two accusations levelled against them by champions of the cen-tralised nation-state. One was the accusation of separatism, the other that of political reaction. To confront the first, regionalists tended to claim that their identification with the region in no sense detracted from their loyalty to the French state or to the French nation. They argued that it was quite natural for regionalists to articulate a hierarchy of loyalties, first to France but also to their region, even that their love of the fatherland grew out of their love for the region. This will be demonstrated in particular with regard to Alsace. In addition, there were always gradations of regionalist opinion, some activists seeking only to establish a cultural distinctiveness, others arguing that ad-ministrative decentralisation, even political autonomy, were required if the identity of the region were to be preserved. To confront the second accusation, that of being reactionary, regionalists developed, alongside or instead of the conservative rhetoric of regionalism, a republican or socialist rhetoric of re-gionalism. This was more explicit in some regions than others, in Occitanie more than in Brittany, for example, and it took on a new significance in the era of decolonisation, a process with which, as we have seen, many regionalists identified themselves. Thus though the goals remained the same the language used to formulate regionalist demands was fluid, and capable of drawing on alternative banks of collective memory.

Alsace

Alsatians regarded themselves as French patriots. There was no more eloquent symbol of this myth than the much-reproduced first rendition of the *Marseillaise* as the battle-song of the army of the Rhine on 26 April 1792 by the captain of engineers, poet and composer Rouget de l'Isle to the piano accompa-niment of the mayor of Strasbourg, baron de Dietrich.[86] At the same time, Alsatians were passionate in the cultivation of their specific Alsatian identity. This was characterised first by deep religious conviction, whether Catholic, Protestant or Jewish; second, by a French-German bilingualism and the existence of an Alsatian dialect; and third, by the cult of self-government, sustained by the provincial and municipal liberties Alsatians had enjoyed in the Ancien Régime.

Few regions of Europe have had so tortured a history. Part of the Holy Roman Empire before its annexation by France in 1648, it was shuttled four times between France and Germany in the period 1870–1945. 'Change of nationality!' a retired Alsatian teacher confided to his diary in February 1945. 'How many times does that make now? And for how long? Let us not anticipate.'[87] Alsace was a frontier region, repeatedly disrupted by war. Alsatians yearned for peace, and saw the ideal situation in neutrality. At the end of 1870, the comte de Gasparin, a Protestant liberal, published a pamphlet entitled *The Neutral Republic of Alsace*. He dreamed of 'an independent republic whose existence and neutrality would be placed under the guarantee of Europe'.[88] Alsatians were the original Europeans, who understood that Franco-German rapprochement would turn them from the cockpit of Europe into its turntable.

Not all Alsatians were cast in the same mould. A basic distinction had to be made after 1871 between those who remained in Alsace after its annexation by Germany and those who chose to leave for France. Those who stayed generally accommodated themselves to their new situation, while those who left set themselves up as ultra-patriotic champions of the return of Alsace-Lorraine to France. Initially, for those who stayed, things were not easy. French administrators were replaced by Prussians, the Catholic Church was persecuted during the *Kulturkampf*, and local government was reduced to a weak, indirectly elected territorial committee. The majority of Alsatian deputies returned to the Reichstag in the early years protested against annexation. In time, however, the situation improved in the three fields of language, religion and self-government. The similarities between Alsatian dialect and High German meant that there was no language problem, except for the French-speaking bourgeoisie. Alsace-Lorraine was insulated from the lay laws and the separation of Church and state in France, and in 1902 the German government conceded a Catholic faculty at the University of Strasbourg. In 1909 Alsatians were permitted to erect a monument to the dead of the four battles of Wissembourg (1705, 1744, 1793, 1870) fought under the colours of France. In May 1911 Alsace-Lorraine was given a popularly elected Landtag and full status within the German Confederation with the right to send three delegates to the Bundesrat. In June 1917 the president of the Landtag, Dr Ricklin, pressed for full autonomy within the Confederation on the lines of the grand duchy of Baden or kingdom of Bavaria, and in November 1918 Ricklin set up a provisional government to negotiate the terms of their return to France.[89]

There was always, in Alsace, a minority who maintained a staunch anti-German position. The cartoonist Hansi illustrated a brilliant *History of Alsace for Children* (1912) which linked Alsatians to the 'great Gallic and Celtic people' and the French revolutionary tradition, and portrayed the Germans as barbaric, drunk, and stupid.[90] In some senses Alsatians never felt more French than when under German rule. But the main *revanchard* thrust came from

Alsatian exiles in France or French patriots. In Alphonse Daudet's short story *La Dernière leçon* (1872) the French *instituteur* tells his class not to forget the most beautiful language in the world when he has gone, for 'when a people is enslaved it possesses the key to its prison so long as it possesses its language'.[91] This was clearly a French view, for the attempt to Gallicise Alsace down to 1870 had met with little success.[92] Though the Ligue des Patriotes met ritually at the statue of Strasbourg on the place de la Concorde, evidence from the educational establishment shows that concern with Alsace-Lorraine declined from the 1870s until 1905, when it was reawakened by French antagonism with Germany over Morocco.[93] Not until 1905 did the federation of French Alsace-Lorraine societies receive permission to erect a statue in memory of the Alsatian and Lorrainer dead of the war of 1870 outside the Gare de l'Est.[94] And when interest was expressed in the recovery of the lost provinces, it was invariably couched in the somewhat nationalist or imperialist terms of how Alsace-Lorraine, the symbol of French national unity, could make the nation whole again, rather than in terms of what France could do for Alsace-Lorraine.

Maurice Barrès was the outstanding representative of this attitude. A Lorrainer by birth, he had as a child during the war of 1870 seen his father and uncle taken prisoner by the Germans. Having pursued a muti-faceted career in Paris, after 1905 he became a professional Lorrainer, but with Alsace-Lorraine always placed at the service of France. He argued that Alsace and Lorraine should be restored to France to counterbalance the radical and socialist politicians of the Midi who formed the Bloc des Gauches and were imposing their wicked policies on the rest of France.[95] In his cycle of novels *Les Bastions de l'Est*, he rejected the hypothesis of the Germanness of Alsace-Lorraine, portraying it as a Gallo-Roman and Catholic outpost against a Germany untouched by Roman civilisation and now Protestant if not pagan. Sacred shrines within that outpost were Mont Sainte-Odile in Alsace, where a convent headed by St Odile in the seventh century had preserved the Latin and Christian tradition intact, and the city of Metz, 'an illustrious Gallo-Roman and Catholic city founded to suffer and make war on Germany eternally'.[96] And he also used Alsace-Lorraine as a key example of his theory of 'la terre et les morts'. Both its landscape and its history were impregnated with French patriotism, and its people only had to listen to its lessons to be galvanised in French nationalism. Thus in his novel *Colette Baudoche*, the annual pilgrimage to the cemetery of Chambières, maintained in memory of the dead of 1870 by the women of Metz, and the annual mass for their souls in the cathedral, for which the women of Metz made wreaths, persuades Colette that she must break off her engagement to the German schoolmaster Asmus.[97] Finally, when France recovered Alsace and Lorraine and occupied the left bank of the Rhine, Barrès did not hesitate to convert the provinces into bases for France's civilising mission. Speaking at the newly Gallicised University of Strasbourg in 1920, he argued that 'France must act in such a way on the Rhine that she makes Rhinelanders aware of a spiritual, political and social ideal that turns them away once and for all from the

Germanism of Berlin, and restores them to closer contact with Latin culture and our western mind.'[98]

Barrès betrayed the basic thinking of Frenchmen 'of the interior' that there was no middle way between being French and being German. This view was shared by a proportion of the Francophile bourgeoisie, politicians and clergy of Alsace who moved to France at the outbreak of war. It was also shared by the French authorities, who carefully screened Alsatian POWs, refugees and even long-term residents in France, and interned those whose loyalty appeared suspect.[99] The attitude of Alsatians who had remained in Alsace was quite different. The Great War tore them apart. Soon after it began the schoolteacher Philippe Husser wrote,

> It inflicts both physical and mental pain on the Alsatian. He loves Germany yet cannot bring himself to hate France. He feels like a child who loves both his parents and suffers to see them not only getting on badly but beating each other and then separating. He is entrusted to his father, a stern, harsh and authoritarian figure. He manages well, copies his example, respects and loves him. But he cannot forget his pretty mother, who is such a charming woman.[100]

Alsace became a war zone in 1914–18. Though Alsatians who stayed put professed loyalty to Germany in 1914, they were regarded with suspicion by the German authorities, often treated brutally by the German military or sent before the courts for anti-German attitudes, espionage or defeatism.[101] When the French reoccupied Alsace-Lorraine in 1918, tricolours were hung out and cockades worn. Alsatians were proud to reassert their French identity. Here, however, they parted company from the French. The latter restored to the banks of the Rhine the sign that had stood there in the revolutionary period, 'Ici commence le pays de la liberté.' [Fig. 16] But they had not modified the revolutionary view that the language of liberty was French and that their mission in Alsace-Lorraine was not only to liberate it but to assimilate their lost sisters to French civilisation.

Alsatians affirmed their patriotism but they also wanted to cultivate their Alsatian identity, expressed through their religion, their bilingualism, and their tradition of self-government. The French paid no regard to their feelings in all these departments. The provisional government was ignored by Clemenceau and Poincaré when they visited Alsace in December 1918, and there was no question of holding a plebiscite on whether Alsatian-Lorrainers wished to return to the French state. Alsace-Lorraine was reintegrated into the French system of centralised administration. Germans were expelled, Alsatians with inadequate French were either dismissed or sent for retraining, and Alsatians 'of the interior' or French officials were imported to staff the higher levels of the bureaucracy. Though Husser began to write his diary in French, he insisted that 'since we have indeed become French, we want to be fully French, as before 1870, with respect for and the preservation of our language, without which our people would suffer a cultural impoverishment'.[102] Thus Alsatians created an image of French rule before 1870 as a golden age, when the strategy of assimilation had not been enforced with such rigour. Neither were the French prepared to recognise the special status that Alsace-Lorraine had obtained with regard to the lay laws and the separation of Church and state. A Catholic League of Alsace was set up in 1921 to protect Catholic schools, under the patronage of Mgr Ruch, the bishop of Strasbourg and supported by the Catholic party, the Union Populaire Républicaine (UPR). Matters came to a climax with the election of the anticlerical Cartel des Gauches in 1924 and moves to impose schools of all religions. 'Let us tell the fatherland,' said Mgr Ruch, 'that you have no son more loving or more devoted . . . but you have no claims against our religious faith. To the fatherland what is the fatherland's. To God alone what is God's.'[103]

French intolerance provoked the formation of an autonomist movement, organised around a weekly paper, *Die Zukunft* (May 1925) and a league, the Heimatbund (May 1926). Strongly supported by the teachers' unions led by Catholic Joseph Rossé and the Strasbourg Workers and Peasants' Congress led by the Communist Charles Hüber, they won over autonomists from another generation such as Dr Ricklin. *Die Zukunft* complained about discrimination against Alsatians in the civil service and demanded 'the right to enjoy our particularism without interference. We want our language and our civilisation to be respected.' The Heimatbund demanded recognition for 'the imprescriptible and inalienable rights of the people of Alsace-Lorraine' and 'complete autonomy within the framework of France'. This meant both administrative and political autonomy, with an elected parliament and executive at Strasbourg, taking responsibility for the affairs of Alsace-Lorraine, while the parliament and government of Paris would deal with matters of general interest to France.[104]

This was a manifestation of *Landesbewustssein* or regional consciousness, and a bid to recover within France the autonomy that had been enjoyed within the Second Reich before 1918. The French government, however, was unable to see these developments except as evidence of a separatist conspiracy, orchestrated and funded by German agents. After the formation of an autonomist Landespartei in 1927, and the election of four of its candidates (including Ricklin and Rossé) in the legislative elections of 1928, the government sent a batch of autonomists for trial at Colmar for plotting against the security of the state. The prosecution showed the usual failure to comprehend the Alsatian mind. Questions asked of Ricklin as to how often he wore an officer's uniform and whether he celebrated the Kaiser's birthday under the Reich were calculated to show that he was a German at heart. For his part, Ricklin rejected all accusations of separatism. He had been an autonomist ever since his student days at Regensburg, and wanted to make Alsace into another Bavaria. Now that they were part of France 'no one in Alsace thinks of being restored to Germany', he said, but 'we we do not want to be assimilated or have the distinctive features of our country tampered with'. 'We do not hate the German people with whom we are united by race,' he added. 'We are pacifists and believe reconciliation with Germany necessary. Union between these two nations would permit them to march at the head of the civilisation of the whole world.'[105] His defence lawyer, a Corsican, attempted to explain the Alsatian mentality in the words of Napoleon, 'Let the Alsatians speak their *patois*, they still charge like Frenchmen.'[106] The only grain of understanding shown by the French government was to pardon Ricklin after the court had sentenced him to a year's imprisonment.

In the 1930s a far more extreme form of autonomism developed in Alsace. The goals were much the same—hostility to French assimilation and exploitation, demands for autonomy to defend the Alsatian national character—but the means were different. From the Landespartei sprang the paramilitary Jungmannschaft under its Führer Hermann Bickler, sporting brown uniforms with black armbands and a werewolf motif, singing *Treu dem Elsass sollst du bleiben*. By 1934 it became a separate Elsass-Lotharingische Partei, as the constituent elements of the old autonomist party, including the Catholic UPR and the autonomist Communists, fell away in disgust.[107] The French government had no hesitation in clamping down on these autonomists as separatists and Germanophiles, claiming links between Bickler and Konrad Henlein of the Sudetendeutsch Partei, executing one of the leaders and imprisoning the others in Nancy at the outbreak of war. But they were no more successful in obtaining autonomy from the Third Reich than from the Third Republic. In 1940 the Moselle was attached to the Sarre-Palatinate under one Gauleiter, Alsace to Baden under another. Hitler demanded the return of the Alsatian autonomists under the terms of the armistice, but kept them in prison until they had signed a request for 'the integration of their Heimat within the great German Reich'.[108] They were brought out on ceremonial occasions, such as the renaming of a Strasbourg street after Dr Ricklin; otherwise they were integrated into the German system of government and mass mobilisation in Alsace-Lorraine. Bickler joined the Nazi party, became an SS colonel, and in 1943 headed one of the sections of the Sicherheitsdienst in Paris.

For the majority of Alsatians, the situation was much worse after 1940 than after 1870. Again they had to choose between staying or fleeing to France. In France they were blamed for causing the war. 'Let the Germans keep Alsace-Lorraine and leave us alone', was one common response to Alsatian refugees.[109] But none were more mortified by the war than the Alsatians. Philippe Husser, who stayed, now had one French and one German grandchild, for two of his daughters had married two French brothers, and a third daughter had married a German. He wrote in his diary,

> Ah! if only my childhood dream could come true, if Germany and France could reach an understanding, if no frontier separated the two peoples with their refined civilisation and flourishing economy any longer, if I could see

and embrace my little grandchildren, my gracious Annemay and my darling Frank, when I wanted.[110]

Meanwhile, conditions under the Germans deteriorated. No manifestations of French civilisation were permitted, from French names to the *béret basque*. Another *Kulturkampf* was launched against the Catholic Church. Under the ordinance of 25 August 1942, the Germans resorted to force to conscript 130,000 young men into the Wehrmacht to fight on the Eastern Front. Of these 25,000 died in the war and another 10,000 never returned from Russia.[111]

After their reincorporation into France in 1945, Alsatians were far more explicit about the complexities of their situation. They felt it necessary to explain that they were indeed patriots, but that they resented the way in which their identity had been trampled underfoot by the French after 1918. Two crucial texts from this period were *Situation de l'Alsace* by Émile Baas, and *Psychanalyse de l'Alsace* by Frédéric Hoffet. Baas warned against a new wave of Jacobinism which failed to distinguish between unity and uniformity, and argued that

> The only way to prevent autonomist extremism will be to give Alsace every political liberty that is compatible with national sovereignty . . . all aspects of our Alsatian originality—language, literature, history, economic life—must be publicly recognised both institutionally and in education.[112]

He suggested that Alsace be made the site of a 'sociological test' in regionalism, which could then be applied to the rest of France. In a somewhat more penetrating analysis, Hoffet wrote that 'the Alsatian's great fear is to be what he is', that is, an amphibious creature, neither French nor German but both. Under French rule they were not allowed to express their German identity, under German rule they could not express their Frenchness. If anything, they fared better under the Germans, because the French paraded their cultural excellence and made them feel inferior, whereas under German rule, particularly between 1870 and 1918, they were able to project their slowness, pedantry and respect onto the Germans, laugh at their bald, square heads and monocles. 'Next to these absurd Germans they suddenly felt themselves the bearers of every French superiority that had once crushed them . . . at last, they felt French!'[113]

The experience of the Second War did not necessarily make it easier for French and Alsatians to understand each other. Many Alsatians felt that the French had done nothing to defend them in 1940, and many French people felt that the Alsatians had gone along with the Germans during the war. Matters came to a head in 1953 when Alsatians who had been conscripted into the SS regiment *Das Reich* were put on trial in Bordeaux for their part in the massacre in the the French village of Oradour-sur-Glane in 1944. Alsatians were identified with Germans and worse, the SS, while they tried to argue that they had been conscripted by force, and that their families would have suffered if they had dodged the draft. The issue provoked a resurgence of Alsatian autonomism, headed by the Mouvement Populaire Alsacien and its mouth-piece, *La Voix d'Alsace/Elsässische Volksstimme*. But two factors combined to ensure a decline in autonomist feeling after the war. The first was that while the French were slow to concede regional institutions, they did not resort to the same degree of assimiliationism as after 1918. This may have been because they listened to explanations of the Alsatian complex, but more likely because the Catholic democratic MRP, which took over in Alsace from the UPR, was also one of the ruling parties in the Fourth Republic. Notwithstanding the lay constitution of the Republic, the MRP was able to confirm the 'special status' of Alsace-Lorraine with regard to confessional schools and the Concordatory Churches, and to negotiate for more flexibility on the teaching of German in schools.[114] The second factor was the reconciliation of France and Germany within the European Community. This eliminated not only the frontier that ran between France and Germany but also the frontier that ran within each Alsatian. His parents reunited, the Alsatian could feel whole again. Moreover Alsace-Lorraine was situated not at the margin of Europe but at its centre. It could not pretend that it was a colony, for it lay in the heartland of European prosperity; moreover, Strasbourg became the home first of the Council of Europe, then of the European Parliament.

Autonomism was not entirely moribund. Movements sprang up from time to time to demand full bilingualism in education and political autonomy on the model of the German Länder.[115] A direct action group called the Black Wolves took exception to French celebrations of the 300th anniversary of Turenne's victory at the battle of Turckheim in July 1975, first daubing the commemo-rative column in red and white paint, then in 1980 attempting to blow it up.[116] But the vast majority of Alsatians was happy with the new situation and autonomism declined to a minority concern.

Brittany

Regionalism was often perceived as a counter-revolutionary movement, but the overlap between the two was far from being exact. *Chouannerie*, the guerilla war fought in Brittany against the Revolution, had little to do with regionalism. Similarly, the notion of a separate Breton identity was initially put at the service of Napoleonic imperialism rather than counter-revolution. A Breton soldier, La Tour d'Auvergne, nicknamed by Napoleon 'the first grenadier of the Re-public', postulated that France had once been the cradle of the Celtic people, who subsequently colonised England, Scotland, Ireland, Spain, Portugal, Italy, Illyria, Germany, Hungary, Scandinavia and Muscovy. The French had been called Scythians by the Greeks, Gauls by the Romans, while Franks was simply the Celtic word for 'free'.[117] This theory, which became the orthodoxy of the Celtic Society, founded in 1805, was attractive to Napoleon since it legitimated his growing empire as a reincarnation of the empire of the Celts.[118]

Parallel to this official, French-speaking celebration of the Celtic past, however, ran a retrieval of Breton language and literature that was opposed to the Revolution and all its works. Jean-François Le Gonidec, a noble who narrowly escaped the guillotine in 1793, and learned Breton while in hiding, dressed as a peasant and sheltered by Breton families, published a Breton grammar in 1807 and a Breton-French dictionary in 1821. At his death, he was working on a French-Breton dictionary which was completed in 1847 by another Breton noble, the vicomte Hersart de La Villemarqué, who himself published a collection of Breton poems, *Barzaz Breiz*, in 1839. This, the latter claimed, was the authentic voice of the Breton soul, as sung by the bards, legends of Breton saints and heroes who battled against the French.[119] It was a challenge to French cultural imperialism and a riposte to the prejudice that Brittany was backward and uncivilised.

The usefulness of defending Breton identity and interests was not lost on a local nobility and clergy who after 1830 suffered the effects of the liberal, anticlerical July Monarchy. One of the virtues of the Breton language for Le Gonidec and La Villemarqué was to have protected the religious faith of the Bretons from Protestantism and Voltaireanism. An infrastructure of publicly funded elementary schools threatened to carry these scourges to the heart of every village. The fact that French had also been the vehicle of the Counter-Reformation was not allowed to cloud the argument. In 1846 the bishop of Quimper intervened with a Lenten message denouncing the 'civilising mission' of the education system.

> That you need to be polished by the modern civilisation of this century we do not contest, but take care lest by polishing you civilisation wears you out, weakens you, erases the imprint of your religious character. . . . That is why we are genuinely happy to see you uphold your old customs, your old costumes, your old language. . . . We speak . . . as a bishop convinced by experience and reason of the tight link that exists between a people's language and its beliefs, between its customs and its morals, between its habits and its virtues.[120]

The Association Bretonne was a third area of elaboration of Breton identity, beyond scholarship in language and literature and the defence of Breton religion. Founded in 1843, its purpose was to combine the improvement of agriculture and literary pursuits. Jules Rieffel, one of its prime movers, had set up a farm-school and was one of the pioneers of agricultural science and education. A large number of its members was, however, drawn from the Breton nobility, claiming the heritage of the previous agricultural society founded by the Estates of Brittany, and the Breton flag was flown with the motto *kent merwel*, 'rather die'.[121] The most important aspect of the Association was its archaeological section, which was concerned with the preservation of Breton monuments, including art, musical instruments and costumes, and research into Breton language, literature and history. Arthur de La Borderie, an historian who was to make his mark on the association, argued that Brittany had become a nation-state under Nominoë in the ninth century, and had successfully resisted the Frankish power of Charles the Bald.[122] When the Association was dissolved by the Second Empire in 1853 as a hot-bed of Legitimism, La Borderie continued his historical publications in the *Revue de Bretagne et de la Vendée* (1857–87). He explored the national identity of the Bretons, describing them in 1867 not as a trading people like the English or Carthaginians, nor as a martial people like the Romans, nor as an intellectual people like the Greeks, Italians and French, but a resistant people, who alone had defended their liberty against the Franks, as in Great Britain the Celts had defended theirs against the Anglo-Saxons.[123]

The Association's Bretonism was never overtly political. Though it might serve as a substitute for the Estates of Brittany in the same way that the Polish Agricultural Society fulfilled the rôle of the Polish Sejm on the eve of the insurrection of 1863, it never included political autonomy on its agenda. This would have been impossible under the Second Empire, so that political opposition was transposed into cultural opposition. But even under the Third Republic, Bretonists such as Arthur de La Borderie showed little taste for active politics. Elected to the National Assembly in 1871, La Borderie gave up his seat at Vitré in 1876, aged forty-nine, to concentrate on promoting the cult of Breton saints.[124]

The triumph of republicans within the Republic, however, and the failure of the Right to win any general election after 1871, opened the way to the political exploitation of Bretonism. Some Breton royalists saw the potential of the myth of the Breton nation as a way to rally popular support behind the defence of conservative interests. The formation of the Union Régionaliste Bretonne in August 1898 may be seen as a response to the victory of the Radicals at the polls the previous May, and to fears that the Republic was falling into the hands of extremists. The Union set up five different sections, to look at questions of Breton administrative decentralisation, economic life, history, language and literature, and the arts.[125] At the congress of 1904, attended by Breton and Welsh bards, with many of the notables in national costume, the president, the marquis de l'Estourbeillon, deputy of the Morbihan, observed that 'our Brittany, profoundly attached to its traditions, its customs, its faith and its language, cannot live without an ideal, nor draw life and strength from any other source'.[126] Before long, however, it became clear that the marquis' ideal was electoral success on the back of the Breton idea, and in 1911 the Union broke in two. Those opposing the marquis' authoritarian behaviour and his subordination of the Union to conservative political interests separated off to form the Fédération Régionaliste de Bretagne, which vowed to have nothing to do with politics or religion.[127] After the Great War, when the issue of regional reorganisation resurfaced, de l'Estourbeillon pressed for 'the moral and administrative autonomy of the regions', with the establishment of regional assemblies and regional governors.[128] The historian Henri Hauser, a promoter of the government's scheme of economic regions, dismissed de l'Estourbeillon and his associates as 'aspiring politicians, particularists, let us be candid: more or less avowed "reactionaries" who would have liked to shield their provinces from the democratic and secular legislation originating from the Revolution'.[129]

More sincere than the Union Régionaliste in its commitment to the Breton language and religion was a movement of the lower clergy, led by the abbé Jean-Marie Perrot, who in 1911 took over the editorship of the review, *Feiz ha Breiz Faith and Brittany*, and in 1912 founded an organisation called Bleun-Brug (Heather Flower). It was a response to the Radical government's offensive against the use of Breton by the clergy in the pulpit and to teach catechism, and was provoked by the traditional revolutionary view that Bretons would not be fully republicans until they spoke nothing but French.

Unlike the Union Régionaliste, Perrot's movement was not controlled by notables and acquired a genuine popular base. Bleun-Brug also claimed a certain independence from the Church hierarchy. In 1913 the five bishops of Brittany described the province as 'the last rampart of Catholic resistance'.[130] But they did not share Perrot's view that the Breton language had a peculiar force in the preservation of religious faith, and they certainly feared the political overtones of such a movement. These became more explicit after the Great War, as Perrot (who had served as a stretcher-bearer) started to defend the claims of national minorities. The statutes of Bleun-Brug were revised in 1925 to include 'the pursuit and achievement of an autonomous régime, which will permit Brittany to develop her personality without hindrance, and to safeguard her interests in all spheres'.[131] Just as the bishop of Strasbourg steered his clergy and his flock away from Alsatian separatism, so the bishop of Quimper intervened to warn Perrot of the dangers of separatism. Perrot replied that

> When you have suffered what we suffered in the Great War, when you see the terrible sight of our most sacred liberties cut down by the lay laws and our oldest traditions pulverised by revolutionary laws, then you stop dreaming and want to act. So a few of us have sworn to sacrifice everything to save the disparate elements of our Breton nationality, if there is still time.[132]

The following year the bishop instructed the clergy to abandon Bleun-Brug. Despite his ardour, Perrot inclined to the rules of the hierarchy, and withdrew.

The drift of Bleun-Brug towards autonomism may be partly explained by the challenge of a new, explicitly autonomist movement in Brittany in the wake of the Great War. This grew out of a regionalist review, *Breiz Atao* (*Brittany for Ever*), and the Union of Breton Youth, founded in 1920. Its leaders were too young to have fought in the war, but were nevertheless traumatised by it. France had lost its mystique for them in the mudfields of Flanders, and the sacrifice of 250,000 Bretons, one in fourteen of the population, was seen as just another episode in the exploitation of Brittany, as cannon-fodder. The leaders were inspired by the movements of national liberation stirred up by the war, particularly by the Easter Rising of 1916 in Dublin. Their response to the

Breton question was overtly political, but they had no time for the aged reactionaries of the Union Régionaliste. Two of the leaders, Maurice Marchal and
Olivier Mordrelle, were students at the École des Beaux-Arts at Rennes, while
a third, François Debauvais, worked in a Rennes pharmacy. They were
Maurrassian by temperament, did not see why Catholicism should be a defining characteristic of Bretons, and despaired of the subservience of clerical
regionalists to the hierarchy. They were prepared to defend the Breton language, and Bretonnised their names (to Morvan Marchal, Olier Mordrel, and
Fransez Debauvais), but they were natives of Upper Brittany, which did not
speak Breton.[133]

The movement's autonomism was thus not concealed behind the defence of
language or religion, but cast in clearly historical terms. 'We are for our
ancestors against our parents,' Debauvais was accustomed to say.[134] The argument constructed by the autonomists was not only that France was a nation
distinct from the French nation, but that under the treaty of 1532 by which it
had been incorporated into the French state its internal autonomy was guaranteed. The *Appeal to Breton Youth* of 1922 suggested that the lies of conventional history had to be exposed.

> Your books do not tell you this, because at the Revolution France tore up this
> treaty, 'like a piece of paper', and in spite of her promises, and in spite of
> Breton protests, she annexed Brittany and carved it up into five shapeless
> and stupid departments, the better to possess and destroy it.[135]

This view of history inspired the transformation of the Union of Breton Youth
into the Breton Autonomist Party in 1927. Its Châteaulin declaration asserted
that while they were not separatist or anti-French, they demanded a federal
reorganisation of France, with 'administrative and political autonomy' for
Brittany, realised in a Breton parliament, to which a Breton executive drawn
from it would be responsible.[136]

In the 1930s, as in Alsace, the autonomist movement grew more extreme.
The Autonomist party divided between those, like Morvan Marchal, who saw
the solution within a federal reorganisation of the whole of France, and those
who were committed only to Breton interests. These, under Debauvais and
Mordrel, formed the Breton Nationalist party in 1931. The nationalists
sprouted a terrorist wing, Gwenn ha du (Black and White—the Breton colours), led by Célestin Laîné, a student of the École Centrale in Paris. During
the night of 6–7 August 1932, on the 400th anniversary of the treaty of 1532, it
blew up a monument, set into the façade of the Hôtel de Ville of Rennes in
1911, which depicted the duchesse Anne de Bretagne kneeling before her
betrothed, the king of France.[137] [Fig. 17] Ideology and organisation became
increasingly fascist, and Debauvais and Mordrel established contacts in Germany, thinking that only a wartime catastrophe would effectively liberate
Brittany.[138] After the outbreak of war they fled to Germany, hoping to win
support for the formation of a Breton state. After the Armistice they returned

Fig. 17.   Speech of the Mayor of Rennes, Jean Janvier, inaugurating 'the Union of Brittany and France', 29 Oct. 1911 (Roger-Viollet)

to Brittany and at Pontivy on 3 July 1940 set up a Breton national council which declared the independence of the Breton state.[139] However, the Breton nationalists were gravely disappointed. German strategy included firm control of the Channel and Atlantic coasts and the maintenance of relations with the French state at Vichy. The German authorities refused to recognise the Breton national council, and in December 1940 Mordrel handed over the Breton Nationalist party to a moderate who was at least prepared to negotiate with Vichy.[140]

Those who benefited from Vichy were not the nationalists but the conservative regionalists, who sought to exploit Marshal Pétain's florid speeches on the virtues of regionalism. In November the Association Bretonne and the Union Régionaliste Bretonne petitioned Pétain for certain concessions to Brittany, including a provincial assembly and the teaching of Breton in schools. Such concessions, they argued, would undermine the case of the separatists and were themselves wholly compatible with 'the indivisibility of France and the necessary and sovereign action of the central government'.[141] Support for this move was provided by a new paper, *La Bretagne*, edited by Yann Fouéré, who was sub-prefect of Morlaix in 1940 but a convert to Breton regionalism.

Though little came of the project of Vichy's Conseil national for provincial assemblies, and though the establishment of regions for regional prefects in 1941 detached the Loire-Inférieure from the Breton region to attach it to that of the Loire, one concession was made to Brittany in the form of a Comité Consutatif de Bretagne, set up in October 1942. Representatives were appointed from key Breton pressure groups such as the Association Bretonne, the Union Régionaliste, Bleun-Brug (abbé Perrot), the Collège des Bardes and the Institut celtique. It was to meet three times a year, had a permanent commission of seven and a secretary-general, who from January 1944 was Yann Fouéré. Its competence was purely advisory and limited to 'questions of culture, language, folklore and in general anything that might interest Breton traditions and intellectual life'.[142] Although this was the first all-Breton representative institution since the pre-1789 Estates of Brittany, comparisons with that august assembly were painful for the new delegates. At its second session, therefore, in January 1943, the marquis de l'Estourbeillon, on behalf of the Comité, presented the regional prefect with a draft statute for Brittany. This included a provincial assembly with financial and legislative powers, a Breton executive, official bilingualism, and the reconstitution of the integral Brittany of five departments (to include the Loire-Inférieure once again). Endorsed though it was by 230 communes and 1,000 Breton notables, the regional prefect refused even to submit it to the Vichy government.[143]

The Comité Consutatif de Bretagne was derided by the Breton Nationalist party as a ploy to 'stifle the activity of Breton organisations and ensure control of the most docile ones by the regional prefecture while smashing the unanimity of the Breton movement'.[144] But autonomists who refused to look to Vichy for concessions were left only with the German forces of occupation, and these were engaged in increasingly bitter fighting against a swelling Resistance. At the end of 1943, Célestin Laîné broke away from the Nationalist party to form a group of active collaborationists who called themselves the Bezenn Perrot—after abbé Perrot of Bleun Brug (himself killed by the Resistance on 12 December 1943)—and wore the uniforms of the Sicherheitsdienst.[145] Such collaborationists were a small minority among autonomists, but all autonomists were dealt with severely at the Liberation. Debauvais died in 1944 and in 1946 Laîné and Mordrel were sentenced to death *in absentia*. Fouéré was sentenced to a year in prison and ten years' exile. Regionalism was discredited as pro-Vichy, autonomism was discredited as separatist, collaborationist, even Nazi.

It was a long time before Breton regionalism was able to reassert itself. Its first manifestation in the Fourth Republic, the Comité d'Étude et de Liaison des Intérêts Bretons (CELIB), founded in 1951, was confined to the economic sphere, established within the framework of government planning, and entrusted to the established political class. Yann Fouéré, formerly secretary-general of the Comité Consutatif de Bretagne, returned from exile to address students at Rennes in 1956. 'It is illusory to think', he said, 'that the cultural

liberties of Brittany will be guaranteed or that its economic interests will be
protected, if a minimum of political and administrative liberties are not granted
to it.'[146] Fouéré placed his demands in the context of the growing federalism of
Europe, but his nostalgia for the Vichy period betrayed him. In 1957 he
launched the Mouvement pour l'Organisation de la Bretagne to press for a
'Statute for Brittany', recalling that drafted in 1943, which argued that the 1532
treaty of union gave Brittany the right to manage her own internal affairs, and
demanded an elected regional assembly and regional administration.[147]

One method of reasserting the claims of Breton autonomism was to use the
discourse of decolonisation. If the struggle of colonies for self-determination
were legitimate, then so was the struggle of France's internal colonies. The
militants who founded the Union Démocratique Bretonne (UDB) in 1964 were
shaped by the Algerian war and depicted Brittany as 'a colony' or 'underdevel-
oped country', exploited by monopoly capitalism and the centralised state,
controlled since the Revolution by the French bourgeoisie. Breton workers
were doubly proletarians, first as workers, and second as Bretons. 'The solution
to the Breton problem is through socialism,' it proclaimed.[148] This Marxist
approach was ridiculed by Olier Mordrel, who returned from exile in Argen-
tina in 1972. 'We are no longer debretonised but alienated,' he scoffed, 'no
longer oppressed but exploited. We are fighting not French domination but
capitalism.'[149] There is no evidence that the UDB listened to Mordrel, but after
the failure of the Left in the legislative elections of 1978, a UDB congress
decided that 'autonomist demands, which have always been implicit in the
party's position, must now be highlighted and made credible for Breton
workers'.[150]

The Front de Libération de la Bretagne (FLB), which began terrorist attacks
in 1966, shared the anti-colonial rhetoric of the UDB but believed that change
could only be achieved by revolutionary action. 'The French imperialist state
has only ever accepted the liberation of its colonies by being forced to do so, and
after trying to steep them in blood,' stated a communiqué in December 1968,
'and there is no evidence that any of this has changed today in France.'[151] But
when eleven FLB militants were brought before the Cour de Sûreté de l'Etat
in October 1972 the depth of the collective memory that informed their
struggle was impressive. Yves Gourvès, a young doctor, insisted on speaking
Breton, in spite of repeated reprimands by the president of the court, and
praised the work of Le Gonidec, who had systematised the Breton language in
the early nineteenth century. Jean-Yves Gaultier, a typographer, launched into
a speech on French violation of the treaty of 1532 and the glories of Breton
resistance, from the *Bonnets rouges* of 1675 onwards. Maurice Drouin, a
plumber, admitted blowing up a statue of the republican general Hoche at
Quiberon earlier that year, claiming that 'people poke fun at Bretons to the
extent of erecting statues to their executioners'.[152]

Under Giscard d'Estaing, as at the Liberation, the sins of the extremists
were visited on the moderates. Yann Fouéré spent five months in La Santé

prison in 1974–5 for alleged membership of the dissolved FLB and possession of explosives. He considered himself worse treated than at the Liberation, when at least he did not have to wear handcuffs.[153] In 1978 Fouéré once again floated his bid for 'special status' for Brittany. Again it included an internal autonomy to be assured by a directly elected regional assembly, for which existing deputies and senators would be ineligible, regional tax-raising powers and a regional executive responsible to it.[154]

The regional reform of 1982 was quite inadequate for the needs of Breton regionalists. They considered themselves a nation, not a region like any other. What they required was a special political status, on the Corsican model, which could be secured simply by reactivating the treaty of 1532. Moreover, the continued exclusion of the Loire-Atlantique from Brittany under the 1982 reforms brought Breton demonstrators onto the streets of Paris.[155] Yann Fouéré commented,

> Socialists or not, the leaders of France, its techno-bureaucracy and its political classes, have a terrible fear of giving back to peoples and to citizens the rights and liberties they gradually took from them to monopolise them for their greater gain . . . regionalism is worthless unless it is seen, as it must be seen, as the antechamber of federalism.[156]

Far from giving up the struggle, Breton autonomists immediately formed a Party for the Organisation of a Free Brittany (POBL), to press for what it now called 'national autonomy.' It repeated the claim that it had been a nation-state until 1532, and had almost recovered that status in 1788. It called for a Breton democracy, since 'the democratic idea is incompatible with generalised Jacobin practice, and with the narcissistic ideology of the bloc of Parisian interests'.[157]

The break-up of the multinational states of the USSR and Yugoslavia, together with the struggle of the Kurds, gave hope to Breton autonomists that the French state might take the same course. Yann Fouéré pointed out that François Mitterrand's nightmare of a Europe of fifty sovereign states held no fears for him, and suggested that if the president wished to reform the con-stitution he could start with abrogating the principle of the One and Indivisible Republic.[158] But when the socialist party held its congress in Rennes in March 1990 and the POBL demanded audiences with socialist ministers to put their case, their demonstration was broken up by riot police. The regional elections of 1992, moreover, exposed the weakness of the Breton autonomists at the polls. For these, the POBL formed an electoral pact with the UDB and two other Breton parties. The traditional goal of a regional assembly elected by universal suffrage had been granted in 1982, so the main plank of the au-tonomists was that the assembly should be given more resources and more powers. Additional demands included recognition of the existence of the Breton people and the reconstitution of the historic Brittany of five depart-ments, the recognition of Breton as an official language, and the economic development and ecological protection of the region. In the event, the autonomists were able to register only 2 per cent of the popular vote.[159] Though coherent, the political culture of the autonomists was clearly marginal, while the political class and the traditional parties demonstrated their ability to reap the benefits of administrative decentralisation.

Occitanie

If the tragedy of Alsace was to be torn between two states, and the regret of Breton autonomists was to have lost their own state, then the problem of those living in the south of France was not to be able to look to the shadow of a former state at all. Until its conquest in the thirteeth century by the French crown, what was later called Occitanie was divided between the houses of Aquitaine, Toulouse and Barcelona. Toulouse appeared so well integrated into the French state that, unlike Bordeaux, Lyon and Marseille, it played no part in the federalist revolt of 1793. To construct a national or even regional identity was difficult: in the twentieth century the characteristics of language, race and colonial status were all tried with varying success, but the only binding force that could be agreed on was the historical one of having been at the receiving end of the Albigensian Crusade in the thirteenth century. Moreover, two distinct versions of Occitanism were elaborated. The first, launched by Frédéric Mistral was conservative and cultural, offering no threat to the unity of the French state. The second, inspired by Louis-Xavier de Ricard, was radical, political and in search of a genuine federalist solution.

Frédéric Mistral was the leading light of the revival of regionalist sentiment in the Midi in the second half of the nineteenth century. Born (he claimed) into a solid peasant family in the Provençal village of Maillane, near Saint-Rémy, and a student of the Collège Royal of Avignon, he was seventeen when the 1848 Revolution broke out. Though he worshipped Lamartine as both poet and statesman, he was horrified by the triumph of Jacobinism in the Republic and the Bonapartist centralisation that followed the coup d'état of 1851. 'It destroyed all the illusions I had about the future federations of which the Republic in France might have been the cradle,' he later wrote.[160] Mistral's response, however, was not political. In 1854 he gathered around him a coterie of Provençal poets who called themselves the Félibres, sometimes rendered as men of free spirit, and orchestrated a revival of Provençal language and poetry to undermine the cultural hegemony of the French Academy. His first great Provençal poem, *Mirèio* or *Mireille* (1859) sang the praises of a simple, rooted, pre-industrial community, and used the heroine as a metaphor for the beauty, innocence, passion and faith of Provence. Though he never openly identified the Félibres with a political movement, he was hostile to the Jacobinism, anticlericalism and urbanism of the Third Republic. 'The Félibrige can only be Girondin, federalist, religious, liberal and respectful of traditions,' he told a colleague in 1870, 'otherwise it would have no further *raison d'être*.'[161] He set Catholic Provence against the Voltairean and progressive ideology of northern

France, which was rather different from Barrès' later view of the red and anticlerical Midi.[162] He looked back to the golden age of the troubadours, 'the true representatives of poetry, gallantry, civilisation and liberty in Europe,' which implied a criticism of the philistinism, egalitarianism, materialism and despotism carried by the French language.[163]

Mistral refuted all claims that he was a separatist. He favoured *enracinement*, was convinced that the prohibition of 'patois' in the schools of the Republic was a major reason for the drift to the cities, and argued that the particularism of each of France's sister provinces were so many roots which strengthened the national tree.[164] Though language in the nineteenth century was often used as a characteristic of nationality, Mistral refused to equate the Provençal language with any defined political unit. Either he was interested in Provençal and thus Provence, or he spoke of the poetry of the troubadours, which he claimed originated in Provence but was heard in Languedoc, Gascony, Limousin, Auvergne, Dauphiné, Catalonia, Castille, Portugal and Italy. This led him to such dreamy concepts as the 'Latin idea' and 'the Empire of the Sun'.[165] It is therefore not surprising that some who originated in the Félibre camp, such as Charles Maurras and Jean Charles-Brun, felt the need to define the federalist idea more rigorously. Not having an obvious former state to look to, like the Bretons, and presented only with the notion of a linguistic or cultural unit by Mistral, they grasped at schemes that would fit Provence into an all-French federalist scheme, whether based on the provinces of the Ancien Régime under monarchical rule or modern geographical and economic regions and the principle of subsidiarity.[166]

A lesser-known figure, that of Louis-Xavier de Ricard, should be placed back-to-back with Mistral as a pioneer of southern regionalist thought. Thirteen years Mistral's junior, he was brought up in the suburbs of Paris, and his formative federative experience was the Paris Commune. After the Commune, he fled to Switzerland and discovered the Félibrige only when he settled in Montpellier in 1874. In his work *Le Fédéralisme* he argued that Latin peoples, including the French, were 'ethnically and historically destined for federation', by which he meant the linking up of independant cities and provinces.[167] According to Ricard, the Latin idea of the Roman Republic was quite different from the Caesarian idea of Imperial Rome, which then combined with the Catholic Church to invent and impose the unitary state.

> This bourgeois, royal, unitary France, as it was made, was made not by the Midi but actually against it. . . . Unfortunately northern France crushed our hopes of political liberty as it crushed the religious liberty of the Albigensians and the Reformation.[168]

Ricard parted company with Mistral at a number of points. He tried to persuade Mistral of the virtue of the federalist Republic, citing Switzerland and the United States as models.[169] He argued that the Catholic Church was despotic, the enemy of freedom of thought, and declared himself to be a 'Huguenot of the will'.[170] Ricard believed that the *langue d'oc* would only survive if the country where it was spoken acquired statehood, arguing that Portuguese would have disappeared if Portugal had remained a province of Spain. 'It is absolutely necessary', he told Mistral, 'to acquire or conquer our political and national autonomy.'[171] Lastly, while he hoped to realise Mistral's 'Latin idea' as a 'Latin alliance' of Mediterranean states, he resented the narrowness of Mistral's attachment to Provence. 'To counterbalance the reactionary Félibrige which Provencalised and Papalised in Avignon,' he said, 'we asserted ourselves, somewhat roughly, to be freethinkers, republicans and Languedocians.'[172]

In the twentieth century there was rivalry for the leadership of Oc between the vision of Mistral and that of Ricard, between that of Provence and that of Languedoc, between that of the Right and that of the Left. Three examples will suffice: the winegrowers' revolt of 1907, Vichy and the Resistance, and the high point of the Occitan movement in the 1960s and 1970s.

In 1907 the winegrowers of southern France rose in revolt against falling prices and what they perceived as fraudulent overproduction in the wine market. Massive demonstrations took place across Languedoc-Roussillon in May and June 1907: 100,000 at Narbonne, 150,000 at Béziers, 172,000 at Perpignan, 250,000 at Carcassonne, 250,000 at Nîmes, 800,000 at Montpellier. The leader of the peasants was Marcellin Albert, a winegrower of Argelliers, near Narbonne, while political focus was provided by the radical-socialist deputy-mayor of Narbonne, Ernest Ferroul. In their attempt to give meaning and legitimacy to the movement, they turned to the vision of Ricard. At Carcassonne on 26 May Ferroul likened the industrial barons of northern France, the sugar-beet producers who were a rival source of alcohol production, to the feudal barons who had invaded and ruined the Midi in the thirteenth century. Marcellin Albert took up the theme:

> As at the time of the Crusades, when the Albigensians came to defend their country and their faith under the walls of Carcassonne, so the army of winegrowers has come today to camp at the foot of the ancient city of the Carcassès. The cause is just as noble, just as holy! Our thirteenth-century ancestors died like heroes to defend it.[173]

A message of fraternal greeting to the winegrowers of Languedoc was received from Frédéric Mistral, but Ferroul's hopes that he might assume the head of the movement were dashed. Mistral wanted nothing more to do with a movement that was so clearly revolutionary, so clearly Languedocian. The movement was crushed by Clemenceau's troops, who fired on the crowd at Narbonne. Six years later when Raymond Poincaré, the great Lorrainer, was elected president of the Republic, Mistral, the great Provençal, met him off the train at Maillane and received him for lunch.[174] There was no contradiction for Mistral between the cult of Provence and the unity of the French state.

Mistral's lifelong campaign for the cultural revival of provincial life achieved its apotheosis under the Vichy régime. Commemorating the 110th anniversary of Mistral's birth, Pétain spoke of Mistral as 'the sublime inspiration of both the new France we wish to institute and the traditional France we wish to re-establish'. What appealed particularly to Vichy was the limitation of Mistral's project to the cultural sphere, his reluctance to address the political question of provincial reorganisation, and the ammunition his world-view provided for an attack on the values of the Third Republic. Pétain was keen to establish

> that attachment to the small *patrie* in no way detracts from love of the large, but actually increases it by providing an insuperable resistance to all that seeks to downgrade us, to level us, to uproot us.[175]

This mobilisation of Mistral to endorse the Révolution Nationale was nothing less than the kiss of death for conservative Occitanism. Within a short space of time, moreover, the fortunes of Ricard's vision were revived by the Resistance. The zone unoccupied by the Germans until November 1942 and under the control of Vichy was very broadly the France of the *langue d'oc*; but after 1942 it was also the site of the Maquis and some of the most effective movements of Resistance. Several Félibres such as Robert Lafont argued that the time was ripe to dissociate the culture of Oc from its Mistralian incubus. A number of the *Cahiers du Sud* in February 1943 which was devoted to reassessing 'le Génie d'Oc' argued that the Albigensians rather than the troubadours should be the source of their inspiration. They needed to look no further then the historical landscape of Languedoc. From Béziers and Agen north to Montségur (Gironde) 'one can see the ruins of castles which resisted Simon de Montfort's crusaders, while in the city of Carcassonne may be found the remains of the Inquisition that persecuted the Cathars and the Vaudois'.[176] Mistral now came in for concerted criticism. Robert Lafont accused him of failing to draw any political conclusions from his Provençal concerns, of having no interest in the people except garbed in Provençal costumes, of shifting to legitimism and the defence of the papacy, of paving the way for Maurras and Pétain, and of making nothing of the Albigensian crusade. 'You will never find a single anti-French adjective under Mistral's pen,' he concluded.[177]

In 1962, at the end of the Algerian war, Lafont founded a Comité Occitan d'Études et d'Action (COEA) to give some structure to the Occitan renaissance. The central problem with Occitanie, as he later observed, was that it was

> a space without power. . . . The misfortune of Occitanie was not to have had time to establish itself on its territory as a more or less unitary state. . . . Let us be frank: Occitanie never was a nation-state.[178]

There was no clear answer to what defined Occitanie, other than a profound sense of the opposition of southern to northern France, even to those who asserted its peculiar identity and its right to control its own destiny.

Lafont and the COEA suggested that Occitanie was in a neo-colonial situation with regard to northern and eastern France and the heartland of industrial Europe. Lafont attacked 'the alliance of centralised authoritarianism and an expansionist economy, which [had] smashed regional economies' under the system of central planning.[179] Lotharingia had reappeared on the map as a political and economic power, and French capital was combining with German and American capital to reduce the south of France to an economy of tourism, wine monoculture and oil refineries. 'The colonial war is now in France', asserted Lafont, and therefore 'regional decolonisation is an important form of the struggle against imperialism.'[180] Or as the COEA put it in their *Petit Livre sur l'Occitanie*:

> socialism, the only way to decolonise effectively; regionalism, the only democratic guarantee of this decolonisation; occitanism, alone capable of giving socialist, decolonising regionalism its full development, which is also cultural.[181]

The strength of the argument was to develop the notion of internal colonisation and to relate the regional struggle for decolonisation to the socialist class struggle. The weakness was that the specific Occitan dimension to the struggle would be washed away. To underline the cultural dimension was not easy. Lafont argued that 'there could be no Occitanie without the *langue d'oc*, which gave it the only definition possible', but there were in fact several *langues d'oc*, together with a hybrid language, *francitan*.[182] The main defining characteristic of Occitanie for COEA remained historical, the reaffirmation of the collective memory of oppression by the north and of Occitanie's struggles for liberation. In *Le Petit Livre de l'Occitanie* it was argued that Occitanie was originally Visigothic, that it had been conquered by the Franks and laid waste by Charles Martel, subjugated as a result of the Albigensian crusade and the persecution of Protestants, but that it had fought back as the 'Midi rouge' in the communes of 1871, the winegrowers' revolt of 1907 and the Popular Front victory of 1936.[183]

Those seeking to create an Occitan regional identity could choose to emphasise either the socialist or the cultural component, echoing either Ricard or Mistral. The Poble d'Oc, formed in 1971, achieved notoriety in 1973 during its campaign to defend the land of the peasantry of Larzac against a planned military and nuclear base. While arguing that Occitans were an ethnic group which was suffering 'cultural genocide', Poble d'Oc also called for the liberation of the Occitan people by means of direct democracy, self-management, a federation of the communes and regions of Occitanie and the collective appropriation of the means of production. As well as adopting the language of anarchism, it adopted that of the emerging ecological movement, demanding the reconsideration of technological progress and the protection of the environment against 'ecological aggression' or pollution. Collective memory of revolt in the Midi rouge was nevertheless crucial to define and sustain the goal of an 'Occitan revolution', which looked for inspiration to the winegrowers' revolt of 1907, the Popular Front victory of 1936 and the events of 1968.[184]

A movement, by contrast, that developed the cultural and national rather than the socialist component of Occitanism was the Parti National Occitan, founded by François Fontan in 1959, and a rival of the COEA. Fontan made a gallant attempt to argue that Occitans constituted an ethnic group, and that even if they had never had a state they should have one now. 'More than proletarian classes,' he asserted, 'there are proletarian nations.'[185] The examples of Yugoslavia and the Soviet Union demonstrated for him that socialism was no guarantee against the imperialism of a dominant nation. Proletarian nations suffered 'physical genocide' or 'cultural genocide' at the hands of stronger nations. The fact that they may have been all but assimilated by a dominant nation only served to underline their right to their own language, territory and state. Fontan was accused by COEA of national-socialism, Third Worldism and a total lack of realism, but he was keen to point out that what he called 'ethnism' was 'nationalism of the Left, patriotism of the Left', and that not unlike de Gaulle he thought in terms of a 'Europe des patries'.[186] It is significant, however, that though Fontan theorised a great deal about ethnic groups in general, he did little to prove that the Occitans constituted one. Instead he used the notion of genocide to highlight the historical experience of the Occitans and returned once again to the Albigensian crusade.

> For us the most important event in the history of the French state is the conquest of Occitanie. This 'Crusade against the Albigensians' was without doubt the greatest attempt at genocide perpetrated in Europe for a thousand years.[187]

The example of Occitanie demonstrates the difficulty of constructing a regional identity in the absence of obvious linguistic or ethnic characteristics, and above all in the absence of state at some point in its history. These weaknesses contributed to the elaboration of rival regional identities, some heavily tinged by socialism on the left, others seeking to invent some kind of national coherence. The collective memory of persecution and victimisation, carefully sustained by Occitan regionalists, nevertheless remained the common denominator of the different Occitan regional cultures.

CHAPTER 5

Catholicism

Revolution and Catholicism

In 1864 the Church of Rome published the *Syllabus of Errors*, condemning liberalism, secularism, nationalism and modern civilisation in general. In 1870 the Republic was founded in France for the third time in eighty years, but immediately came under threat from the election of a royalist majority to the National Assembly at Versailles and from the Paris Commune. The republican leader Léon Gambetta, speaking at a banquet in November 1871, attacked the propagation of the *Syllabus of Errors* as

> the greatest danger that the society of 89, of which we are the heirs and representatives, could run. The main objective of the society of 89 is to derive the political and social system from the idea of reason rather than that of grace, from the idea that the status of citizen is superior to that of the slave. . . . For eighty years these two systems have confronted each other. They have divided opinion and maintained an antagonism, a relentless war, in the heart of society, which is why, for want of unity in our education system, we roll without hope of stability from revolt to repression, from anarchy to dictatorship.[1]

This speech touched on three recurrent themes of anticlerical discourse. First, there was the accusation that the Catholic religion stood for revelation against reason, dogma against free thought, tradition against progress, darkness against light. Second, the Catholic Church was attacked as inimical to the revolutionary principles of 1789 and to the Republic that followed from it, since it had always defended divine right monarchy and welcomed the alliance of throne and altar. The only way for anticlericals to guard against this threat was to ensure that the future citizens of the Republic were educated in revolutionary principles, and therefore not by the Church but by the state. The third point, however, was that conflict over religion and education resulted in both political and social upheaval. In could indeed be argued that conflict over religion was a safer alternative to political or social conflict. But anticlericals set limits to how far they wished to persecute the Church. Their main preoccupation was the stability of the régime and the unity of the country. Their attacks on the obscuranticism of the Catholic religion served to legitimate their attacks on the Church. But beyond that anticlericals cared about social stability and recognised the part played by the Church in its provision. They therefore tended to attack the Church not in general but only certain exposed outworks, such as the Jesuits, teaching congregations or the clerical party. Thus even under the Republic periods of conflict with the Church alternated with periods of compromise, and the rhetoric of anticlericalism coexisted with the practice of accommodation.

Two painful collective memories that were elaborated and sustained served to nourish the obsessions of anticlericals. The first was of the struggles of Enlightened thought against the intellectual despotism of the Church which in the Ancien Régime had claimed a monopoly of correct opinion and had relied on the state to enforce uniformity. In a word, Catholicism was identified with the Inquisition. The second was of the Revolution's inability to deal satisfactorily with the Church. Whether it tried to reform it, destroy it or disregard it the Church came back to haunt the Revolution, to oppose it and ultimately to destroy it. Any future Republic would have to take care lest the Church conspire against it once more.

The question of whether the Church was compatible with the Republic, and Catholicism with the Revolution, was posed again when the Second Republic was proclaimed in 1848. On 25 February 1848, on the Montagne Ste-Geneviève in Paris, a liberty tree donated by the Dames de Sacré-Coeur was blessed by a Catholic priest. Writing about this incident the following year in *L'Enseignement du Peuple*, Edgar Quinet asked, 'What is the difference between the Revolution of 1789 and that of 1848? The first believed that it could save the world by its own spiritual energy. . . . The second believed that it could only save the world with the support of the priest. This led necessarily to the Roman expedition.' Here Quinet referred to the Republic's sending troops to restore Pope Pius IX to Rome. He feared that the Republic lacked the confidence and resolution to deal with the Catholic Church, yet was convinced that the two were irreconcilable. The Church was a monarchy. 'How can you deduce a political republic from a religious monarchy?' he asked, 'How from absolutism can you deduce liberty?'[2] The son of a Calvinist mother, though he was himself brought up a Catholic, he argued that it was unfortunate that France had not had a religious reformation before her political revolution. Protestantism was much more compatible with liberty, as Great Britain and the United States demonstrated. The attempt by the French Revolutionaries to democratise the Church had been a fiasco. The Papacy had rejected the reforms of the National Assembly and the Church fell back on the monarchy, aristocracy and Vendean rebels to defend itself. Dechristianisers had tried to destroy the Catholic religion, but had been opposed for fear of a counter-revolutionary backlash by revolutionary leaders such as Robespierre. Robespierre himself had proposed a new religion—the Cult of the Supreme Being—but instead of persisting with it to displace the Catholic Church, he had re-established the free exercise of religions which had allowed the Church to destroy the Cult of the Supreme Being.[3] Under the Concordat of 1802 Napoleon had restored the Church under the strict control of the state, but Quinet wanted the abolition of the Concordat, the separation of Church and State, with the Church reduced to a private institution. In addition, he demanded the separation of Church and school, the exclusion of the Church from the responsibility of teaching the future citizens of the Republic.

The Revolution of 1848, however, drove such radical thoughts from the minds of the governing class. The Legislative Assembly elected in 1849 had a conservative majority which was keen to use the Church to check the upsurge of revolution, and the Church was more than happy to see the lifting of restrictions placed on Catholic teaching congregations by the revolutionary authorities and Napoleon. A bill to promote Catholic schools was sponsored by the royalist education minister, the comte de Falloux, which prompted Victor Hugo to intervene with a masterpiece of anticlerical invective.

> Your law is a masked law. (*Bravo*!) It says one thing and will do another. It has the look of liberty and the intention to enslave. That is your custom. When you forge a chain you say: Here is a liberty!
>
> Yes, we know you! We know the clerical party. It is an old party that has a record of service. (*Laughter.*) It is the sentinel at the gate of orthodoxy. (*Laughter.*) It has found these two excellent props for truth, ignorance and error. It forbids knowledge and genius from venturing beyond the missal and wants to cloister thought in dogma. Every step made by the European mind has been made in spite of it. Its history is written in the annals of human progress, but it is written on the reverse side. (*Astonishment.*)
>
> So, you wish to be given peoples to educate. Fine. Let us see your pupils. Let us see your products. (*Laughter.*) What have you done to Italy? What have you done to Spain? . . . Spain has lost the secret of strength that she held from the Romans, the artistic genius she held from the Arabs, the empire that she held from God. And in exchange for everything you have lost for her, you have given her the Inquisition. (*Agitation.*)
>
> Everywhere, to avoid Torquemada, people will prefer Robespierre. . . . And those who, like myself, fear anarchic change for nations as much as priestly stillness, must shout a warning.[4]

This speech was a powerful expression of the mid-nineteenth century polemic against Catholicism as obscurantist and reactionary. The image conjured up was that of the medieval Church or the Counter-Reformation, symbolised by the Spanish Inquisition. On the other hand, the notion of a clerical party, a secret organisation within the Church given to conspiracy, exempted from attack the generality of clergy and Catholic faithful. Moreover, the fear expressed of a popular and dangerous de-Christianising backlash, should the

Church be allowed to reassert itself in the public domain, suggested a preference for accommodation between Church and Republic.

The guerilla war waged against the Republic by royalists in league with the
Church, and the final blow administered to it by Louis-Napoleon Bonaparte,
who also initially enjoyed the Church's support, forced republicans to reconsider the rôle of education in the strengthening of a future republic. This was
made more necessary by the restoration of universal suffrage by Louis-
Napoleon and the popular support commanded by his rule. Jean Macé, who
went to Beblenheim in Alsace to teach after the coup of 2 December, came to
the conclusion that no republic would ever survive in France unless those
empowered to vote under universal suffrage were properly educated as citizens.
He devoted himself to the task of popular education by writing educational
books and founding public libraries in Alsace. In 1866 he set up the Ligue
de l'Enseignement as a pressure group campaigning for free, compulsory
elementary education for all. Shortly after the defeat of France by Prussia a
third article was added, that of *laïcité*, to demand free, compulsory and lay
elementary education for all. The separation of Church and school was now
officially regarded as complementary to universal education, and was the subject of a massive petition delivered to the National Assembly in 1872.[5]

Free, compulsory, lay education in state primary schools was adopted as the
programme of the republicans and duly enacted by Jules Ferry after they came
to power, in 1881–2. In addition, at the Théâtre de la Gaîté in Paris in 1878,
anticlericals commemorated the centenary of Voltaire's death to mark what
they saw as the triumph of reason over prejudice, tolerance over dogma. They
also inaugurated the cult of a martyr to the liberty of conscience that the
Catholic Church was alleged to have trampled underfoot. Victor Hugo, always
a vigilant watchman on the barricade of the anticlerical Republic, made a
speech on the devastating irony of Voltaire's smile, recalling the story of one of
the philosopher's *causes célèbres*, the chevalier de la Barre. The chevalier, a
young man of nineteen brought to trial by the Church, was judged by the local
Parlement in 1766 for singing a guard-room song on a bridge at Abbeville one
stormy night when a cross fell from it. Accused of blasphemy and of knocking
the cross into the river, the young man was punished by a horrific execution: his
hand was cut off and his tongue ripped out before he was burned at the stake.
Voltaire had taken up the cause to clear the chevalier's name and in order to
demonstrate the Church's barbarity and wickedness; Victor Hugo saw the
opportunity of reviving the accusation by taking up the chevalier's cause.[6]

Republican anticlericalism was, however, more complicated than this. The
cult of the chevalier de la Barre was part of a vigorous polemical war against the
Church; on the other hand, anticlericals were careful not to attack the Church
as a whole, and to reach some working compromise with it. Paul Bert, one of the
leading republican educationists, who attempted to devise a code of morality
for teaching in schools that did not rely on religion for a sanction, summed up
his anticlericalism as 'peace to the *curé*, war on the monk!'[7] By this, an echo of

the 'peace to the cottages, war on the châteaux!' of the revolutionary armies, he meant that the teaching congregations, and above all the male ones, should be expelled from the state school system, but that secular clergy should be left free to teach the catechism in their own sacristies.

Jules Ferry, minister of education and architect of the Republic's lay laws, also developed his anticlericalism on a number of registers. He insisted that the elimination of religious instruction from state schools was a condition of the survival of the Republic and of revolutionary principles.

> This neutrality is a neutrality that matters for the security of the state and for the future of republican generations. It matters to us that the supervision of schools and the definition of the doctrines that are taught there do not belong to prelates who declare that the French Revolution was deicide, or, like the eminent prelate who I have the honour to see before me [Mgr Freppel] . . . that the principles of 89 are the negation of Original Sin.[8]

However, he inclined to focus his attacks on the Jesuits, whom he accused of indirect theocracy and of orchestrating the clerical party. Moreover, he was eager to head off popular anticlericalism which resorted to violence and the grotesque and pressed for such measures as the separation of Church and state. In 1878, for example, the miners of Montceau-les-Mines in dispute with the pit-owner who forced them to send their children to the schools of nuns and Marist brothers that he subsidised, celebrated the feast of the Assumption in typically iconoclastic fashion by blowing up a statue of the Virgin Mary and setting fire to the nuns' chapel and school.[9] In 1885 radicals on the Paris municipal council demanded that all street-names which included the prefix 'saint' be laïcised.[10] But Ferry was a practical politician who understood that the majority of Catholics was prepared to accept the Republic if compromises were reached. Thus Ferry allowed Catholics to run private schools without state funds, accepted that a Catholic education might be entirely suitable for girls, who were not future citizens, and argued that to break the Concordat and separate Church and state went entirely against the grain of popular sentiment and would provoke 'a war of religion'.[11]

When, however, the Republic was held to be in danger, those who were anxious to squeeze the Church even more tightly seized the opportunity to reinforce its image as the enemy of free thought and ally of reactionary régimes. During the Dreyfus affair, when the army and its system of justice came under attack, the Dominican père Didon told a school prize-giving assembly that if the country fell into the hands of sectarian and factious politicians who were campaigning to reopen the Dreyfus case, the army should be called upon as a last resort to impose justice.[12] The Radical Camille Pelletan lost no time in explaining that, let down by the monarchy, the Church had joined forces with the army—'the holy alliance of the habit and the plume, the sabre and the holy-water sprinkler'—and using the history of the Dominican order to heap Gothic horrors on the clerical party.

We read in amazement the furious speech in which the père Didon addressed to the military chiefs a summons to coup d'état. The monk is worthy of the habit he wears. He is the true heir of the ferocious *dévots* whose order was founded to massacre heretics, who, in the Middle Ages, put the Midi to fire and sword, and until the beginning of this century, made the name of the Spanish Inquisition odious to the civilised world.[13]

But the very moderate head of the government of republican defence, René Waldeck-Rousseau, saw it as his business to narrow the target of clergy to be punished to a few congregations which had never been properly authorised rather than ride on the tide of anticlericalism. His claim that 'sometimes we really see in this country too many conspiratorial monks and too many business monks', was a veiled reference to the Assumptionists and distillers of Chartreuse, who were his main targets. Accused by the Right of sectarianism, Waldeck insisted, 'we remain faithful on this point as on every other to the republican tradition, which we have resumed, and far from abandoning the Concordat we are returning to it'.[14] The separation of Church and state was no part of his agenda. Waldeck-Rousseau was responsible for the Associations Law of 1901 which gave the government powers to close down unauthorised congregations, in private as well as public education. But he had no intention of applying it indiscriminately, and in particular wished to leave nuns' schools well alone, for the republican paterfamilias was in general happy with a convent education for his daughters. However, he was replaced after the elections of 1902 by the Radical Émile Combes. Combes was something of a monomaniac, his anticlericalism honed on several years' teaching in the Assumptionist College of Nîmes in the 1850s, and known to Herriot as 'Robespierre in carpet-slippers'. In pursuit of his goal of ridding France of all religious congregations, female as well as male, he rode on a swell of popular anticlericalism, especially from his native Midi, but came into conflict with Waldeck-Rousseau and moderate republicans, as well as with Catholics and Catholic republicans.[15]

The conflicts over religion at the time of the Dreyfus affair stimulated free-thought societies, a popular offshoot of freemasonry, to develop the cult of the chevalier de la Barre that Victor Hugo had launched. The French Section of the International Free-Thought Federation persuaded the Paris city council in 1904 to erect a statue to the chevalier opposite the basilica of Sacré-Coeur, arguing that if the statue were denounced as a blow to religious beliefs, then the Sacré-Coeur, erected on one of the strongholds of the Paris Commune, was a blow to freedom of thought and an insult to republicans by the forces of reaction.[16] [Fig. 18] And to press home the enormity of the punishment the inscription read, 'Supplicié à l'âge de dix-neuf ans pour ne pas avoir salué une procession'—for not having doffed his hat before a passing Capuchin procession. Until the statue was removed during the German Occupation, anticlericals had their martyr to liberty of conscience cast in bronze, a constant reminder of the Church Intolerant.

Fig. 18.   Statue of the Chevalier de la Barre (*La Calotte*/Deborah Elliott)

In the inter-war period the temperature of religious disputes diminished significantly, for a number of reasons. First, the anticlerical agenda of the republicans was completed by 1905. The lay laws attained the status of 'republican' or 'intangible' laws, and were held to be the bedrock of the republican régime and French unity. The only outstanding question after 1918 was whether to extend the lay laws to newly incorporated Alsace-Lorraine, where the lay laws had not been applied, and schools were therefore still Catholic, Protestant or Jewish. Second, the Catholic Church no longer had any official status after the separation of Church and State under pressure from the socialists in 1905. The state stopped funding the secular clergy, as it had stopped aiding Catholic schools, and the Church became nothing more than a private corporation. As a result, any claims it had to impose its doctrines had to compete in the market-place of ideas with all other doctrines and ideologies. Third, the Great War ushered in the Union Sacrée and the Catholic Church effectively became the national Church, the French people at prayer, symbolised as we have seen by the institution of a national festival dedicated to Joan of Arc.

Anticlericalism was of no interest to the various Centre-Right governments that held power in the inter-war period. Only when the Radical party abandoned its moderate allies and came to power at the head of the Cartel des Gauches in 1924, was it obliged to heed anticlerical pressures from the SFIO, which supported it in the Cartel, and to make some gesture towards rectifying the anomalous status of the Church in Alsace-Lorraine. The SFIO put itself forward as the champion of *laïcité* and at the SFIO congress of 1935 at Mulhouse Alsatian socialists complained that they were an oppressed minority and demanded their liberation by the entry of the 'democratic and lay Republic' into Alsace-Lorraine.[17] But when the SFIO came to power at the head of the Popular Front government in 1936 it was confronted by threats from an extreme Right which had no obvious relationship with Catholicism (indeed Action Française had been condemned by Rome in 1926), while the Communist party was actually extending an outstretched hand to Catholic workers in the hope of winning their vote. Anticlericalism was not part of the programme of the Popular Front.

This is not to say that anticlericalism withered away. It was certainly relegated to the margins of political life. But it remained a coherent political culture, elevating the struggles and champions of the heroic period of the nineteenth century to mythic status, a passionate commitment for those militants who were converted and committed to the cause.

The review *La Calotte* was one of the most consistent vehicles of popular anticlericalism. It was founded by André Lorulot, a Parisian who was 'very pious' at the age of ten when he took his first communion. But he could not accept the idea of God as a merciless gendarme, punishing evil, and never went back to Church after being punished for giggling while the priest took his time hearing a lady's confession. During the Dreyfus affair he had been shocked by the persecution of a Jewish friend at school by boys who had all received a Catholic education. He was carried by his libertarian spirit through socialism to anarchism, and after six months in prison for antimilitarism, threw himself into the free-thought movement.[18] In 1930, incensed by what he saw as the repeated attempts by the Church to exploit the Union Sacrée to reassert its influence in state and society, he founded *La Calotte*, which adopted the witty, satirical tone that had been Voltaire's hallmark. It denounced the Church's alliance with capitalism and militarism (the monarchy having gone for good), and attacked the clergy as rich, lazy and immoral. Lorulot was one of those present at the inauguration in 1905 of the monument to the chevalier de la Barre, and made a special point in his review of defending it against reactionaries who wanted to dismantle it.

Anticlericalism was revived as a serious force under the Vichy régime and at the Liberation became once again a party political issue. The genuflection of the French episcopate before Marshal Pétain, attacks on the lay system of schooling for producing corrupt and godless citizens, permission to teach catechism in state schools and the restoration of public funding of private Catholic schools gave anticlericals the opportunity once again to argue both that Catholicism was opposed to progress and reason, and that the Republic and the Church were indeed incompatible. When Mgr Baudrillart, rector of the Institute Catholique of Paris, blessed the Ligue des Volontaires Français contre le Bolchévisme, calling them the twentieth-century crusaders for the faith, André Lorulot argued that he had 'put religion and the Church fully at the disposal of the Nazis'.[19] Lorulot was also keen to denounce the Church as the enemy of progress and reason. Relaunching *La Calotte* in 1945, he attacked the clergy who now buzzed round de Gaulle as they had round Pétain, asking his readers, 'Have you shaken off the tyranny of German battlegrey only to fall under that of Their Graces of the Candle-Snuffer [a metaphor for reactionary clergy since the Restoration], the apostles and possible continuators of the Holy Inquisition?'[20]

The Liberation nevertheless complicated the debate on the influence of the Church because if the hierarchy had by and large endorsed the Vichy régime, this was far from being the case for all Catholics. Catholics had played a leading rôle in the Resistance and now formed a Christian Democratic party, the Mouvement Républicain Populaire, which was one of major parties of the Fourth Republic. The SFIO recognised this difficulty. Its congress of November 1944 restated that it was a party of *laïcité*, committed to the neutrality of state education in the name of liberty of conscience. But it affirmed that

> the Socialist Party does not forget the friendships that many of its members have formed during the clandestine struggle for freedom with enthusiastic believers, who are also enthusiastic republicans. It does not confuse these brothers-in-arms with those who used the Vichy régime to try to establish clericalism in France; for it knows . . . that true believers do not confuse faith with clericalism.[21]

The Communist party, on the other hand, which had stretched out a hand to Catholics before the war, now vied with the SFIO and the Radicals for the honour of being the leading party of *laïcité*. The Communist Georges Cogniot chaired the education commission of the Consultative Assembly which decided to abolish the grants that Vichy had given to Catholic schools. He demanded a return to 'the republican legality of 1939', and quoted Paul Bert to the effect that priests should remain in their sacristies.[22] In 1946 the Communists campaigned vigorously against the MRP for the constitution to describe France as 'an indivisible, lay, democratic and social Republic', which in the end it did, and to legitimise their bid they commemorated the work of Jean Macé.[23]

A new wave of battles over religion and education, however, was only just beginning. The MRP also enjoyed republican legitimacy and had the electoral clout to ensure that public funding for private Catholic schools be reconsidered. Against the Catholic lobby, Macé's Ligue de l'Enseignement was revived to defend the anticlerical position. The run-up to the 1951 elections was particularly intense. The Ligue's Paris circle was addressed by Prosper Alfaric, who had been active in the Ligue since he had been appointed professor in the Arts faculty of Strasbourg in 1918. Born in a small village in the Catholic Aveyron, Alfaric had risen in the Catholic Church and taught successively at the Grands Séminaires of Bayeux, Bordeaux and Albi before the Papal condemnation of the 'modernist' movement, which believed in subjecting the traditional teachings of the Church to critical linguistic and historical analysis, drove him out of the Church in 1910. Discovering that the Church would brook no questioning of dogma, Alfaric went to the opposite extreme and appropriated the nineteenth-century discourse of anticlericalism which attacked the Church as intolerant and counter-revolutionary.[24] In 1935 he republished Victor Hugo's speech of 1850 against the loi Falloux.[25] He argued that 'every clerical [was] by a natural tendency and internal logic a monarchist', while 'the laic, simply by following his reason founded on experience, [was] drawn naturally to opt for the republican régime'.[26] He told his Paris audience in 1950 that the Catholic tradition was 'that of counter-revolution', and that even now in the 'chouan country' of the west of France the Church relied on reactionary mayors, squires and rich bourgeois to dragoon the local populations into its schools.[27]

During the same campaign Albert Bayet, president of the Ligue de l'Enseignement, who remembered having played with Alfred Dreyfus' children at Berck-Plage, presided over a rally of 5,000–6,000 faithful of the Ligue who had made a pilgrimage to Saint-Dié in the Vosges—the home town of Jules Ferry—which, to gain inspiration, had erected a statue in Ferry's honour. Bayet, happier with the battle-lines of the Dreyfus affair, ignored the fact that many Catholics had fought in the Resistance, and argued that the Church's collaboration with collaborationist Vichy made it unfit to educate the young of France and the Republic. 'To the reviving spirit of Montoire [where Pétain had shaken hand with Hitler in 1940], we oppose the spirit of Saint-Dié,' he proclaimed. 'We keep our faith in liberty, the Republic and France intact and burning, and we come here to say, Pétain will not defeat Jules Ferry.'[28]

The Fourth Republic, under pressure from the MRP, introduced a small measure of state funding for private Catholic education under the Marie and Barangé laws of 1951. Accommodation between Catholicsm and the Republic seemed easier than under the Third Republic. When the Fourth Republic collapsed and de Gaulle took power in 1958, Catholics rallied to his side and were rewarded by more systematic state funding under the loi Debré of 31 December 1959. Again anticlericals fought the measure, waving all the spectres that had been invented in the nineteeth century. They denounced it as a new edition of the loi Falloux. In the Senate the Communist Jacques Duclos announced that 'M. Michel Debré is today in the tradition of M. de Falloux', and quoted from Victor Hugo's speech against the law.[29] His colleague Georges

Cogniot made a powerful speech in the Vendée, also quoting Hugo's diatribe against the loi Falloux, and condemning 'the alliance of bishop-politicians with factious officers'. He claimed that 'The Church [had] linked itself zealously with the establishment of authoritarian government', supporting de Gaulle's plebiscite in return for payment for Catholic schools. Like Hugo, he argued that the Church wanted to turn France into Spain, only this time it was the Spain of General Franco.[30] In the Senate Cogniot updated his references in the light of the Second World War. 'They invoke peace between schools and think only of a war of extermination,' he said of the clericals. 'Their language is pluralist, their intention totalitarian.'[31]

In his Vendée speech Georges Cogniot called for a mass campaign in favour of lay education in the tradition of Jean Macé. A campaign was in fact already under way, co-ordinated by the Comité National d'Action Laïque. The Comité organised a petition against the Debré law which collected nearly eleven million signatures. On 19 June 1960, the anniversary of the date in 1872 when Jean Macé had delivered his petition for free, compulsory and lay education, a rally of over 300,000 supporters was held in the Bois de Vincennes, prior to the delivery of this petition.[32]

The Comité was unable to shift the loi Debré so long as the Right was in charge of the Fifth Republic. But in 1972 they restyled their policy, calling for the nationalisation and democratisation of the education service, and were gratified when François Mitterrand, campaigning for the presidency in 1981, promised 'a great public, unified and lay national education service'.[33] After the triumph of the Left in 1981, the Comité National d'Action Laïque organised another demonstration of 300,000 at Le Bourget on 9 March 1982, to mark the centenary of Ferry's lay laws. But the anticlericals neglected that Ferry had been a man of compromise rather than of conviction. Alain Savary, the education minister in 1982, was no different. Addressing the crowd, he pointed out the tension in the mind of the republican fathers who founded the lay school between the desire to 'develop free men' and the desire to 'forge a national spirit'. Lay public education safeguarded the liberty of conscience of non-Catholics and protected the Republic, but others including Catholics also had the right to their culture and beliefs. 'It is still important for us to know that the Republic is one and indivisible', he continued, 'but we have become more aware of the diversity it embraces . . . and *laïcité* means in fact the recognition by the state of all cultural diversity, beginning with those of the linguistic minorities.'[34] It was a tension at the heart of liberalism, that education to dispel prejudice could lead to uniformity, while respect for liberty of conscience might legitimate religious and cultural pluralism.

The government made clear that it sought a compromise with the Catholic establishment. It proposed only to reorganise public funding for Catholic schools, not to abolish it. Again the anticlericals protested. None was more more furious than the editor of *La Calotte* since Lorulot's death in 1963, Henri Perrodo-Le Moyne. Perrodo had served as a curé in the Seine-Maritime for twenty years until he joined the Resistance (where his code name was Le Moyne), and he was appalled by the hierarchy's collaboration with Vichy. The last straw for him was the elevation in 1948 to become primate of Normandy of Bishop Martin, whom had been happy to bless the Miliciens of Vichy.[35] Now, early in 1984, he denounced Savary's accommodation with the Catholics in terms that echoed Victor Hugo and Camille Pelletan.

> The only independent school is the state school, the lay school. The Catholic and God-bothering school is the school of intellectual and moral slavery, the school of superstition, of confessional brainwashing and, above all, the school of intolerance. It is the school that has always championed the sabre and holy-water sprinkler.[36]

The government's moderate bill went before the Assembly in May 1984. A coup by anticlerical socialist deputies inserted an amendment that had the effect of confining state funding to state schools. 'For the state school, state funds, for the private school, private funds', insisted Pierre Joxe, citing a principle first laid down in 1886.[37] Prime Minister Mauroy was prepared to accept the amendment, and dragged Alain Savary with him. But the Catholic camp mobilised, organising a massive demonstration on 24 June. Mitterrand, a Waldeck rather than a Combes, compromised with the Catholics and scandalised the anticlericals. He appeared on television to announce that the bill was being withdrawn, leaving Savary to resign, followed by Mauroy. Arbitrating between conflicting forces, Mitterrand ensured that the Fifth Republic, even under a socialist president, was compatible with the Church.

Catholicism and Revolution

Revolution as Punishment

Summoning Catholics to a mass demonstration on the place de la Concorde to protest at the commemoration of the bicenary of the French Revolution, the 15 August 1989 Association declared:

> Recalling that the French Revolution was essentially and above all anti-Christian, and became anti-monarchical only after Louis XVI refused to go further with anti-religious measures;
> Recalling the systematic killing by the guillotine or drowning of several thousand priests and nuns, and the deportation of tens of thousands of others;
> Recalling the massacres committed all over France, especially in the Lyonnais and the Midi, the deportation of the population of several Basque villages, and above all the massive genocide of the Vendée and the western provinces . . .

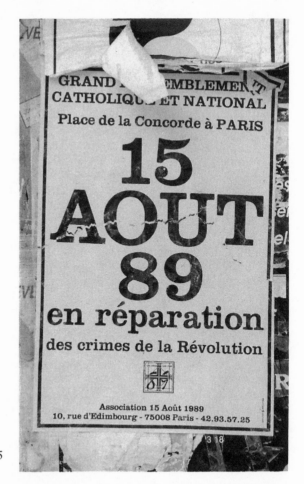

Fig. 19. Poster of the Association of 15
August 1989 (Iain Pears)

Observing that by claiming to found society on the dualism of the individual
on one side and the state on the other, according to the Declaration of the
Rights of Man and of the Citizen, the Revolution set a course for totalitarianism . . .

The Association of 15 August '89 summons all Catholics and all nationalists
to meet on the place de la Concorde on Tuesday 15 August 1989 at 9 a.m.,
on the feast of the Assumption of the Holy Virgin Mary, patron saint of
France, to celebrate the Holy Mass in order to atone by fervent prayer for the
innumerable crimes committed on our soil by the Revolution of 1789 and to
render to God our Creator and Saviour all honour and glory.[38]

This manifesto, and the demonstration to which it rallied the Catholic
faithful, was indicative of a Catholic construction of the French Revolution
which dated back to the Revolution itself. [Fig. 19] Its first contention was that
the Revolution was essentially anti-religious, and perpetrated the massacre of

France's Most Christian king, of a large number of the secular and regular clergy, and of thousands of ordinary believers who were prepared to fight to defend the Church. But it implied, secondly, a Providential view of history, whereby the crimes of the Revolution could be atoned for and God's protection of France recovered by the act of 'fervent prayer'.

The view that the Revolution was 'anti-religious . . . satanic' was propagated in 1797 by Joseph de Maistre, a Piedmontese subject who had fled to Switzerland when the French armies invaded Savoy, and became regarded as one of the architects of the counter-revolutionary mentality.

> Look at its great set-pieces! Robespierre's speech against the priesthood, the solemn apostasy of priests, the profanation of liturgical objects, the proclamation of the goddess Reason . . . it is all beyond the scope of ordinary crimes and seems to belong to another world.

De Maistre explained that 'we are all attached to the throne of the Supreme Being by a supple chain that restrains without enslaving us'.[39] Each nation, like each individual, was given a mission to fulfil by God. That of France, since the baptism of Clovis, was to further and protect the Church. France had betrayed that mission at the Revolution by attacking the Church and de-Christianising France. But the Revolution was also portrayed by de Maistre as divine punishment for the sins of France. 'Punishment rules the whole of humanity,' he wrote, 'punishment protects it; punishment watches over it while human guards are sleeping. The whole race of men is kept in order by punishment.'[40] France could avoid further punishment by two courses of action, 'either by wiping out the crime that had made it necessary, or by prayer, which has the power to avert punishment or mitigate it'.[41] In other words, she could be redeemed either passively, by prayer, or actively, by counter-revolution. Such a vision of the Revolution goes a long way to explaining the Catholic revival at the beginning of the nineteenth century, the restoration of the alliance between throne and altar, and the bid to recover France's providential mission as 'eldest daughter of the Church'.

Other national disasters tended to reinforce the Maistrian model of fall, punishment and redemption, both as a way of explaining events and as a justification for the Church extending its empire over state and society. The defeat of 1870 was explained by Louis Veuillot, editor of the Catholic *Univers*, as a punishment inflicted by God on France for her straying from the ways of religion and onto the paths of materialism, liberalism and secularism during the nineteenth century. These crimes led to the abandonment of Rome by French troops, sent out in 1849 to protect the Holy See against revolution. The instrument of God's wrath was Prussia which, in accordance with providential irony, France had herself converted to atheism in the eighteenth century. 'Its second founder, after Albert of Brandenburg, the apostate,' observed Veuillot, 'was Frederick the atheist. The principal minister of Frederick, to deceive and

Fig. 20.   Massacre of Carmelite priests, 1792
           (Musée Carnavalet)

Fig. 21.   Massacre of Hostages, 24 March 1871
           (Bibliothèque nationale)

corrupt opinion, was Voltaire.' 'Prussia is the sin of our fathers,' he continued, 'and is also our own.'[42] So senseless was the blasphemy of the French, said Veuillot, that they were actually erecting a statue to Voltaire while Prussia was beating them on the battlefield.

Veuillot interpreted the Paris Commune as the climax of the de-Christianising trends of the century, as the bloodthirsty mob 'planted its dagger where the revolution of intellectuals had thrown most ink', massacring Dominican priests in a ghastly repetition of the September massacres of 1792. [Figs 20 & 21] But the flames that consumed Paris were a holocaust, like the Terror, in which the Revolution destroyed itself and created the martyrs by whom redemption could be achieved.[43] The years after the Commune saw both renewed attempts to restore the monarchy in France and a revival of the Catholic religion, centred on the expiation of the crimes of the century and in particular those of the Commune. Catholics subscribed to build the basilica of the Sacré-Coeur on one of the strongholds of the Commune, the hill of Montmartre, went on pilgrimages in droves by courtesy of French railway companies, and campaigned to restore the Pius IX to the Papal States.

When France was defeated again in 1940 and Paris was threatened by a repetition of the Paris Commune, the Catholic clergy were on hand to resurrect the Maistrian view of sin and punishment, which necessitated a return to the ways of God. 'Let us not forget', said one Catholic newspaper, 'that what has just collapsed so lamentably is a house that people tried to build without God.'[44] Though not himself a practising Catholic, Marshal Pétain gave his authority to a secular version of fall, punishment and redemption.

I hate the lies that have done us so much harm. . . . Our defeat is explained by our laxity. The pleasure principle destroys what the principle of sacrifice has built up. It is to an intellectual and moral rectification that I urge you first of all.[45]

For Pétain, France had failed to rearm not only materially but morally. She had been undermined by socialism, pacifism, individualism, laicism and all other corrosive ideologies of the primary schools of the Third Republic. Punishment had come in the shape of the armies of the Third Reich, sweeping away the Third Republic and its vices, and opening the way for the redemption of France.

The ecclesiastical establishment saw Vichy as a guarantee against revolution and desired that the redemption should be above all Catholic. The bishops were quick to flatter Pétain and attempt to convert him to their cause. Cardinal Gerlier, archbishop of Lyon, informed Pétain in November 1940 that 'France needed a leader to take it towards its eternal destiny. God enabled you to be there. Pétain is France, and France today is Pétain.'[46] The Vichy régime did much to restore the Church's influence in education and the period saw another revival of pilgrimages calling for God's blessing on France. In addition, the Church took more active measures to stimulate counter-revolution. Cardinal

Baudrillart, rector of the Institut Catholique in Paris, blessed the Legion of French Volunteers against Bolshevism who went off to fight Communism on the Eastern Front. He had been eleven years old at the time of the Paris Commune, and feared that the war of 1940 would bring Communism as that of 1870 had brought the Commune. For him, the war was a struggle between Christian civilisation and the latest manifestation of revolution.

> Placed at the front line of this definitive combat, our Legion is the living example of medieval France, the France of our revived cathedrals. And I say, because I am sure of it, that these soldiers are laying the foundations of the great French renaissance. This Legion is truly, in its own way, a new order of chivalry. These legionaries are the crusaders of the twentieth century.[47]

Revolution as Plot and Persecution

If one Catholic version of the Revolution was punishment for revolt against God and the betrayal of his special mission for the French, a second was that the Revolution was a plot by a party or sect to seize power and to persecute all those who did not share their revolutionary ideology. While the Providential view of history could easily be mocked in the name of reason, it started from the first principles of the Revolution and turned them against the revolutionaries. Though Catholics were not entirely happy with the concept of liberty, which for revolutionaries meant liberty of conscience to defy the Catholic Church, in time they became seduced by the idea. They reasoned that the Revolution, while proclaiming liberty, gave no liberty to Catholics to practise their religion or educate their children in the principles of the Church. They also argued that accusations of intolerance and persecution levelled against the Church by the revolutionaries could equally be levelled against the Revolution by Catholics. And just as anticlericals tried to win over the generality of Catholics by blaming only a minority of clericals, so Catholics tried to win over the generality of republicans by blaming only a party or sect, be it of Jacobins, Freemasons, Protestants or Jews.

In 1878 Mgr Freppel, bishop of Angers, attacked the republican leader Gambetta for a recent speech which envisaged banning religious instruction and religious congregations from state schools in the name of the state's neutrality. He put it to Gambetta that it was not the Church, but the republican party, that was the enemy of liberty.

> It is rich of you to speak of 'general enslavement', you who in your speeches talk of purging anyone who doesn't think like you from the magistrates' bench, the bureaucracy and the army. That is the despotism you plan to establish in France, and you dare to utter the word liberty! The word has no sense in your mouth. . . . What you promise is persecution, and in short order. What else do you call the abolition of religious orders and termination of recruitment to the priesthood? You and the violent party of which you are

the leader constitute yourselves the guardian and defender of our national history! You who date that history from 1789 or 1793 and see beyond it only a string of horrors and vile deeds.[48]

The centenary of the Revolution gave Mgr Freppel the occasion to develop the nation that the massacre of the French clergy was a 'natural product of the despotism of the state' and to reflect, 'Don't we find a century after 1789 exactly the same expressions in the mouths of those who claim the heritage of the purest traditions of the Revolution?'[49]

The Catholic contention that those who favoured persecuting the Church were always a minority party or sect was popularised during the Dreyfus affair. Catholics, like nationalists, hammered away at the idea that the Republic was in the hands of a syndicate of Jews, Protestants and Freemasons who were betraying the interests of France. When Waldeck-Rousseau was accused by a Catholic royalist of sectarianism, he defended his action against teaching congregations not only in terms of the 'republican tradition that we have resumed' but also in terms of the 'liberal tradition', on the grounds that the legislation of the 1880s against religious congregations had been voted by both houses of parliament.[50] But republicans were finding it increasingly difficult to retain a monopoly of the term 'liberal'. In 1901 the Catholic opposition under comte Albert de Mun founded a political party it called Action Libérale. It propounded the view that liberalism was represented not by the Waldeck-Rousseau government but by the Catholic opposition. As Albert de Mun announced, 'We want to defend religion persecuted by sectarians, the fatherland threatened by cosmopolitans, liberty trampled underfoot by Jacobins, and finally the people deceived by those who abuse their confidence.'[51]

In 1924, when the Cartel des Gauches announced its intention to apply the legislation of the 'republican tradition' to Alsace-Lorraine, Catholics once again mobilised their arguments against the despotism and intolerance of a sectarian minority. The archbishop of Rennes informed the archbishop of Strasbourg that the abrogation of its special status 'would put Alsace in a position far more odious than Germanic oppression'.[52] General de Castelnau, who launched the Fédération Nationale Catholique in 1924 as a mass movement to fight the government's plans, put the blame firmly at the door of the 'masonic sect' that pulled the strings of government and planned 'the dictatorship of freemasonry in France'. The masonic plan was 'the de-Christianisation of France, the most lively and active rampart of Christian civilisation'. The programme of federation, by contrast, was to 'restore the Christian social order'.[53]

After the Liberation in 1944, Catholics resumed their campaign for *la liberté de l'enseignement* against those parties of the Left which wanted to reassert the principle of the neutrality of the state and abolish the public funding of private Catholic schools that had been sanctioned by Vichy. The Christian democratic MRP campaigned to have the principle of *la liberté de l'enseignement* included in the constitution of the Fourth Republic. Like the anticlericals, Catholics skilfully adapted the language of the Second World War to reinforce their case against victimisation. Pierre-Henri Teitgen, one of the founders of the MRP, told the Constituent Assembly that the state monopoly of education 'looked singularly like a hangover of fascism or totalitarianism . . . if you are looking at ways of restoring French unity, it is towards pluralism—which, despite appearances, is not a paradox—that you should turn'.[54] Catholics failed to secure this amendment to the constitution, but did not give up their campaign for public funding for Catholic schools. On 23 April 1950 nearly a quarter of a million Catholics demonstrated at huge meetings throughout the west of France, playing liberally on the myth of the Vendée and stories of republican oppression past and present.[55] Like the MRP, the French episcopate updated accusations of despotism and oppression by denouncing the totalitarianism of parties that defended the state monopoly. In April 1951 the plenary assembly of the French episcopate appealed to the Universal Declaration of the Rights of Man of 1948 in defence of the right of Catholics to choose their school, and to the principle of social justice to obtain state funding of Catholic schools. It concluded that 'the moral unity we are seeking with all our strength will be realised only by the mutual respect of consciences, and not by a totalitarian unification against which the genius of our race will always rebel'.[56]

The loi Debré of 1959 sanctioned the public funding of Catholic schools that the bishops desired, and this settlement continued down to the return of the Left to power in 1981. The Church made representations to the socialist government and persuaded it that if *laïcité* meant respect for liberty of conscience, tolerance and pluralism, then Catholic schools should be not only tolerated but assisted. When the government bill was amended by socialist deputies effectively to restore the principle of state funding only for state schools, the Catholic reaction was swift and concerted. Cardinal Lustiger, archbishop of Paris, regretted that the compromise achieved by the loi Debré had been destroyed. He argued that the debate on education had moved on and that the anticlericals had learned nothing and forgotten nothing.

> All important issues in our society focus on youth. All their difficulties—employment and training, racism and the diversity of cultures, repect for liberty and learning to live together—accumulate in the education system. It is senseless to shy away from this real debate and regress to positivist ideology, which has anyway been abandoned in all but a few circles which are heir to M. Homais, to an anticlericalism as outdated as the electoral banquets on which it fed. It is too late to imitate 1905.[57]

The marginalisation of anticlericals as replicas of Flaubert's caricature, trapped in another age, was skilfully done. But Catholics displayed more than purely rhetorical power. On 24 June 1984 over a million Catholics, with the full support of the hierarchy, demonstrated on the place de la Bastille.[58] *La Croix* argued that it was a response to the crowds who had greeted the election of Mitterrand to the presidency on 10 May 1981.[59] *Le Monde* compared it to the campaign of the Fédération nationale catholique in 1924.[60] The symbolism of Catholics occupying the privileged space of revolutionary culture was certainly eloquent. On this occasion, moreover, the Catholic interpretation of liberty was the one that convinced the president of the Republic.

Catholicism and Liberty

To take up the concept of liberty was to combat the Revolution on its own terrain. But for two hundred years this project was only attractive to a minority in the Catholic community. More numerous and more vocal were those who presented an uncompromisingly negative view of the Revolution. This may be demonstrated first of all by looking at the fortunes of the abbé Grégoire.

On 12 December 1989 the remains of the abbé Grégoire, who had died in 1831, were ceremonially transferred from Montparnasse cemetery to the Panthéon. Though this may have appeared as homage paid to a leading churchman, Mgr Lustiger, archbishop of Paris, refused to be involved with the ceremony. For him, Grégoire had violated the liberty of the Church by promoting its reorganisation by the state; neither could he sanction the transfer of the body to a monument which had once been a church but now housed the remains of Voltaire and Marat.[61] The mayor of Emberménil, the Lorraine village where the abbé Grégoire had been curé before the Revolution, had a monument erected and a square renamed in his honour, but an official of the *conseil-général* of Meurthe-et-Moselle confessed that he was 'relatively ill-considered and ill-loved in the region'.[62]

The Church's rejection of the abbé Grégoire symbolised its rejection of those in its midst who were prepared to accommodate the Revolution. Grégoire had been one of the *curés patriotes* of the First Estate who had argued that the clergy should abandon their privileges and join the Third Estate to establish a National Assembly. He had believed that the Catholic Church ought to be reformed in the name of liberty, and had been an architect of the Revolution's reform of the Catholic Church, the Civil Constitution of the Clergy, which included the election of priests and bishops by the citizen body. Grégoire himself was duly elected bishop of Blois. But he had also believed that the Revolution should be Christianised. The Declaration of Rights of Man could be deduced from the gospel, but the Christian ethic of justice and love was necessary to sustain the revolutionary principles of liberty, equality and fraternity. He attempted to have the Constituent Assembly add a declaration of duties to the Declaration of Rights, though without success.

Subsequently the abbé Grégoire became increasingly isolated between revolutionaries and Catholics. There is some question as to whether he actually signed the death-warrant of Louis XVI, but it was certainly held against him at the Restoration. When, during the de-Christianising charades of 1793, pressure was put on Grégoire to resign the priesthood, he told the Convention that 'Catholic by conviction and by sentiment, priest by choice, I was chosen by the people to be a bishop, but I hold my mission neither from it nor from you.'[63] He continued to sit in the Convention, robed in purple, alone on his bench, and spoke in favour of the freedom to worship. Under the Directory he tried in vain to revive the constitutional Church. On his death-bed the archbishop of Paris refused to absolve him unless he retracted his constitutional oath. He refused, and the last sacrament was administered to him illicitly.[64]

Shunned by the Church, Grégoire's memory was cultivated rather by republicans and partisans of *laïcité*. A crowd of twenty thousand, mostly students and workers, turned out for his funeral in 1831. A statue was raised to him in the Lorraine town of Lunéville in 1885, the period of the lay laws. The membership of the Société des Amis de l'Abbé Grégoire, founded in 1931, the centenary of his birth, interlocked with that of the Ligue de l'Enseignement.[65] During the bicentenary, he was praised most of all for his essay of 1788 demanding equal civil and political rights for Jews, and his advocacy, during the Revolution, of the cause of the slave population of the French colonies.[66]

The exclusion of Grégoire from the Church's bosom served as a lesson for all Catholics who subsequently argued that there was room for an understanding between the Church and the Revolution. These formed a first culture within Catholicism. They made repeated initiatives in the nineteenth and twentieth centuries to break the Church's traditional alliance with reactionary régimes. They argued that revolutionary principles could be justified by the gospels, but that any revolution—democratic, socialist or communist—should be Christianised, that worldly liberty, equality and fraternity should be sanctioned by spiritual freedom, justice and love. In short, they proposed a revolutionary Christianity or Christian democracy. Given the experience of the Revolution, however, the Catholic hierarchy tended to condemn such initiatives. In the first place, they were seen to defy the Church's authority, since revolution was generally interpreted as substituting the will of man for that of God, and God's will was held to be realised in the dogma of the Church. In the second place, any revolutionary challenge to the existing political and social order was feared by the Church, which assumed that its survival as an institution required political and social order.

A second culture may be described as that of liberal Catholicism. This inclined to accept the liberal, capitalist order that emerged from the Revolution in the nineteenth century. It favoured civil, political and economic freedom, but also demanded religious freedom. It required of liberal institutions that they respect the institutional freedom of the Church. It was happy that Catholicism should compete in the market-place of ideas with other ideologies, but on equal terms.

There were, however, Catholics who argued that there could be no compromise with any order that arose from the French Revolution. This third Catholic culture was intransigent or counter-revolutionary. Those who subscribed to it insisted that the Church should reject the liberal or democratic bourgeois order and replace it by a Christian social order that was based on an idealised vision of the Ancien Régime, when society had been organised on Catholic principles of order, authority and hierarchy. Whether these latter-day crusaders could convince the hierarchy to give its blessing to their vision was another question.

It was in fact possible for any one individual to move between different Catholic cultures. A liberal Catholic could become a Christian democrat, as could a counter-revolutionary Catholic. In some sense, Christian democracy and counter-revolutionary Catholicism, both of which sought to revolutionise the world, had more in common with each other than with liberal Catholicism, which tended to accept the world as it was.[67]

The extraordinary career of Félicité Lamennais can serve to illustrate the way in which an individual at different times could espouse all three Catholic cultures. Born in 1782, Lamennais was one of the young generation of priests who at the Restoration spearheaded the Catholic revival. In his *Essay on Indifference* (1817), he followed an impeccable line by denouncing the Revolution as a revolt against the authority of God by men who took themselves to be gods, arguing that 'true religion', the basis of all order and society, was defined by the dogma of the Catholic Church. He entered more dangerous ground in 1825 when he reasoned that if the Revolution had been a disaster for the Church, the alliance of throne and altar was no better. The state was 'atheistic' in that it did not establish Roman Catholicism as the state religion, only as that of the majority of French people, and in addition it violated the Church's independence. The subordination of Church to state in France, Lamennais pointed out, dated back not to the Revolution but to the Gallican controls imposed by Louis XIV in 1682. He looked to the Pope to maintain the necessary discipline, stating that he should be allowed full independence. 'Without the Pope there can be no Church, without the Church there can be no Christianity, and without Christianity there can be no religion and no society.'[68]

Lamennais' insistence that the Church should reclaim its liberty from monarchical absolutism propelled him down the road to liberalism. In 1830 he launched *L'Avenir* under the motto 'God and freedom'. Not only the government but also the Church, he argued, should be detached from despotism and allied with liberty. In Ireland, Belgium and Poland, liberty was claimed not in the name of Voltaire to attack the Catholic Church but on behalf of a Catholic Church suffering persecution. 'All the friends of religion must understand that they need only one thing, freedom. Its strength lies in the conscience of peoples, not in the support of governments.'[69] At this point, Lamennais came into conflict with the papacy. For the papacy had no intention of supporting revolution against the established political order. When Catholic Poland rose in revolt against tsarist autocracy, Lamennais took the side of Catholicism and liberty, while the papacy sanctioned the suppression of revolt by Russian armies. *L'Avenir* was condemned by a papal encyclical in 1832. When support for revolution was met by papal condemnation, Catholics had to decide between obedience to the Church or open revolt against it. Most of Lamennais' liberal Catholic friends, such as Lacordaire and Montalembert, bowed to the papal ruling. Lacordaire said, 'I would rather throw myself into the sea with a millstone around my neck than maintain a centre of hopes, ideas, even charitable works, outside the Church.'[70]

Lamennais' reaction was to abandon dogma and look to the gospels for illumination. In *Les Paroles d'un croyant* (1833), he discovered Jesus the carpenter and claimed that the gospels both taught and Christianised the principles of liberty, equality and fraternity.

> Heed well how you become free. To be free you must first love God. For if you love God you will do his will; and the will of God is justice and love, without which there is no liberty! . . . Liberty is destroyed by injustice . . . love preserves it.[71]

The Church now feared that Lamennais was a republican and a socialist. He assured the archbishop of Paris that though he now identified himself with the suffering of the poor, the poor would never achieve liberty if they violated private property.[72] But he now confronted the dilemma inherent in Christian democracy as to whether to put the Church first or the people first. The Church felt that he was putting the people first and his work was duly condemned by another papal encyclical in 1834. Lamennais was now effectively outside the Church. He committed himself fully to the democratic cause. He did not abandon Christianity, but placed it at the service of a utopian vision which would ensure the moral improvement and spiritual fulfilment of the people, as well as their political and material emancipation.

> Far off in the future we glimpse the happy period when the world will form a single city under the same law, the law of justice and charity, equality and fraternity, the future religion of the whole human race, which will salute in Christ its supreme and final legislator.[73]

As the Revolution of 1830 threw down the challenge of liberalism, so the Revolution of 1848 threw down that of democracy. The Republic, as we have seen, was not initially hostile to Catholicism, and Catholicism was prepared to give the Republic a chance. But Catholics who embraced democracy nevertheless feared that it would unleash the greed of the majority or degenerate into the de-Christianising Republic of 1793. Lacordaire, who had re-established the Dominican order in France, the abbé Maret of the Paris theological faculty, and Frédéric Ozanam, together launched a paper called *L'Ère nouvelle*, with the aim of Christianising democracy. 'Let the peoples understand', it underlined, 'that above their arbitrary wills there is an eternal law of reason and justice, an expression of the divine order and the necessary base of rights and duties.'[74] At this point, the editors confronted a tension at the heart at the Christian democratic position between the cause of the people and the cause of religion. For Lacordaire, the main purpose of the paper was less to go along with the popular will, smoothing its rough edges, than to check anything that smacked of popular disorder or socialism. 'This revolution, which has become that of the bourgeoisie,' it stated, 'must not be overthrown within two years by a revolution of workers, followed in its turn by a revolution of peasants.'[75] The June Days, in which the workers of Paris rose up and killed the archbishop of Paris, convinced Lacordaire that the Church was powerless to Christianise revolutionaries and must throw its weight behind the forces of order, which alone could safeguard the Church. He therefore abandoned *L'Ère nouvelle* to Maret and Ozanam.

Maret and Ozanam held the alternative view that Christian democrats should not abandon the people at the first whiff of class war. They blamed the June Days on the 'materialism' of the bourgeoisie, the market forces worshipped by their economic liberalism which had created exploitation, unemployment and poverty rather than on socialist agitators. The masses were not agents of de-Christianisation; they had never been Christianised. To Christianise them was a priority, but simply to convert them for the Catholic Church's peace of mind would not work. 'The working class', they observed, 'will only accept religion with its consolation and hope so long as religion is full of concern for its poverty and just towards its legitimate wants.'[76] Frédéric Ozanam reinforced this point in his *Origins of Socialism*:

It is time to reclaim our own, by which I mean those old and popular ideas of justice, love and fraternity. It is time to demonstrate that we can plead the cause of the proletarians, dedicate ourselves to the relief of the suffering classes, pursue the abolition of poverty, without condoning the preaching that unleashed the tempest of June, whose dark clouds still hang over us.[77]

Maret and Ozanam's radical position was very isolated, rejected by the Catholic hierarchy and by such heavyweights of the Catholic laity as Montalembert, who argued that Christian democrats

confuse[d] socialism with democracy, and democracy with Christianity. The strong sympathy towards the poor and weak proclaimed and inspired by Christianity should not be taken as the same principle as democratic government; that would be to make the same mistake as to deduce the doctrine of absolute monarchy from the respect enjoined by the gospel for the authority of Caesar.[78]

Montalembert pointed out that Christian doctrines of charity did not enjoin Catholics to overturn the existing political and social order. Neither, on the other hand, did the doctrine of 'render unto Caesar' require Catholics to submit to absolutist régimes. Montalembert was the quintessential Catholic liberal. Favouring freedom in state and society in the shape of representative government, private property and the free market, he insisted on freedom for the Church as well. 'Liberty suits the Church on one condition,' he told Cavour, the chief minister of Piedmont, 'that it enjoys liberty itself . . . the Church free in a free state, that is my ideal.'[79] And the spiritual freedom of the Church, he warned Cavour, required the temporal freedom afforded the papacy by the papal states.

The weakness of the liberal Catholic position, for many Catholics, was that it sanctioned a compromise with a bourgeois liberal order that had been created by the Revolution. And the combination of political freedom and capitalism honoured by liberalism unleashed the forces that could create social revolution. Just as the Revolution of 1789 had generated Lamennais' early intransigent views, so the proclamation of the Republic and the Commune of 1871 forged those of comte Albert de Mun. De Mun symbolised the revival of the Catholic counter-revolutionary position after 1870. Captured at Metz in 1870 as a young army officer, and interned at Aachen, he became familiar with Christian social ideas fashionable in the Rhineland which blamed the bourgeois cult of market forces for much of the working classes' sufferings. The Paris Commune had a dramatic effect on him. On his release from Germany, he served in the general staff of General Gallifet during the suppression of the Commune, but saw the long-term solution to social crisis in the building of a Christan social order, inspired by an idealisation of the Middle Ages, as a monarchical, hierarchical, Christian society.

De Mun began a crusade to win the working classes back to the Church by organising them into Catholic circles. During a pilgrimage made with some members to Chartres he argued that the liberty proclaimed by the Revolution had been heaven for the bourgeoisie but hell for workers. Economic liberalism had resulted only in exploitation and poverty for the workers, and driven them to revolt. To those who accused him of socialism, he said,

> No, no, we are not and will never be socialists! (*Applause.*) Socialism is the negation of God's authority, and we are its affirmation; it is the affirma-tion of the absolute freedom of man, and we are its negation. (*Applause.*) Socialism is the logic of revolution, and we are the irreconcilable counter-revolution. There is nothing in common between us, but between these two terms there is no longer any room for liberalism. (*Loud applause.*)[80]

De Mun went on in the Chamber of Deputies to trace liberalism back to the Revolution which 'claimed to found society on the will of man rather than founding it on the will of God'. Stating his desire to restore a Christian society that was based on God's law, he rejected the accusation that this was simply the Ancien Régime.[81]

De Mun's was an extreme view, which not only lost him his seat in the Chamber of Deputies but was disavowed by the leader of the Legitimist royal-ists, the comte de Falloux, who accepted liberal parliamentary institutions. Neither was it altogether to the taste of the new pope, Leo XIII, who believed that accommodation with the Third Republic was necessary and possible if it relaxed its anticlerical legislation and committed itself to social reform. De Mun followed the lead offered by Leo XIII, which took him from a counter-revolutionary position eventually to a liberal one. In the first place, he accepted the Pope's call that royalists should rally to the Republic and work within it to ensure that the Church's liberties were respected. Secondly, he was inspired by the papal encyclical *Rerum Novarum* of 1891, which condemned economic exploitation and urged Catholics to become involved in the organisation of labour in the interests of social justice and social peace. In 1901 De Mun founded a party, the Action Libérale, in order to gather Catholics, royalists who accepted the Republic, and moderate republicans who disagreed with the re-vived anticlericalism of the government. But the need to gather forces which were politically and socially conservative drove him to set aside interest in the social question. He had become, like Montalembert, a classic Catholic liberal, who accepted liberal institutions and capitalist society, provided that they respected the institutional liberties of the Church.[82]

In the late nineteenth and twentieth centuries, Christian democrats made new attempts to break the traditional alliance of the Catholic Church and reaction. These endeavours differed from those of liberal Catholicism in that they criticised liberalism and capitalism, which they saw as only increasing inequality and exploitation. They were inspired by a vision of a more just and more Christian society.

Christian democrats could take one of two routes. The first of these was to undertake programmes of social reform designed to innoculate society against socialism and Communism, themselves also a response to inequality and ex-ploitation, and thus ended up defending the social order against revolution. In addition, they remained obedient to the Church hierarchy, necessary if they were clergy, useful if they were laity. Alternatively, they took at face value socialist and communist criticisms of society, and accepted the principle of class struggle and social revolution. Their task, as Christians, was to add a moral and spiritual dimension to a revolution they saw as essentially material, following the example of Lamennais. But they ran the greater risk that Chris-tianity would be revolutionised rather than the revolution Christianised. This provoked condemnation from intransigents who wanted, like the Christian democrats, to transform society, but in a counter-revolutionary direction. More important, this kind of Christian democrat risked anathematisation by the hierarchy and by the Papacy, both because threatening the social order was seen as threatening the Church as an institution, and because embarking on their revolutionary course would be seen to be defying the Church's authority. The first route was that of the *abbés démocrates*, the Parti Démocrate Populaire, *L'Aube*, the Mouvement Républicaine Populaire and the Centre Démocrate/ Centre des Démocrates Sociaux; the second was that of the *Sillon*/Jeune République, *Esprit* and the worker-priests.

The *abbés démocrates* led what has sometimes been called the second wave of

Christian Democracy in the 1890s. They were particularly strong in areas like Flanders and the tip of Brittany, where the influence of large landowners was weak and the lower clergy commanded a great deal of popular support. Like Lamennais, they believed that the association of the Church with political and social reaction was unnecessary, and a basic cause of popular hostility to the Church. Some *abbés démocrates* were elected to parliament against candidates of the traditional Right. In 1893 the abbé Lemire, who taught at the local *petit séminaire*, beat the conservative Catholic General de Frescheville, who enjoyed the support of the archbishop of Cambrai, in the Flemish constituency of Hazebrouck.[83] In 1897 the abbé Gayraud, a former Dominican, defeated the candidate of the conservative nobility, comte Louis de Blois, at Brest.[84] Critical of liberalism and capitalism, they were guided by Leo XIII's encyclical *Rerum novarum* in their crusade to promote social justice and peace. They were committed to the interests of the masses, but deeply opposed to socialism and class war. Mixed unions of employers and workers and various forms of social insurance were seen as steps along the way to a Christian social order, a harmonious society under the aegis of the Church. 'At the head of our pro-gramme,' announced the abbé Naudet at the launch of his paper, *La Justice sociale*, 'we place religion, the Family and Property.'[85] They also had a tendency to be anti-Semitic, as they blamed the Jews rather than the bourgeoisie as a whole for the progress of liberalism and capitalism in the nineteenth century. An anti-Semitic banquet at the Christian democratic conference of 1896 was addressed by Édouard Drumont, author of *La France juive*.[86]

Robert Cornilleau, a lay Catholic who had worked on *La Justice sociale*, and subsequently biographer of the abbé Naudet, founded a newspaper, the *Petit Démocrate de Saint-Denis*, on the eve of the Great War which embraced the Republic provided that it respected the Catholic religion, and proclaimed that 'just as we repudiate religious war, so we repudiate the social war and all its violence'.[87] Cornilleau was a founder in 1924 of the Parti Démocrate Populaire, which declared itself republican in mind and heart so long the Republic could distinguish *laïcité*, the neutrality of the state, from *laïcisme*, the persecution of religion. Its task was to provide moral and religious guidance for democracy. Although it did not consider itself a Catholic party, it was clearly in touch with elements of the hierarchy and defended Church interests. Politically, it placed itself between Left and Right, and in the run-up to the 1928 elections, Cornilleau published a series of articles in *Le Petit Démocrate* entitled 'Pourquoi pas?', floating the idea of an alliance with the socialists. This invited an attack on the popular democrats as 'red Christians'.[88] But the term 'popular' signified an organic rather than individualistic or class-based conception of society, which praised the family, commune, region and class co-operation, as a thinly secularised version of the Christian social order. Increasingly, moreover, popu-lar democrats were elected with the support of the right-wing Fédération républicaine, and in 1936 they fought against the Popular Front coalition.[89]

L'Aube, edited by Francisque Gay, was launched in 1932 as a journalistic attempt to detach Catholicism from the Right. It accepted the *laïcité* of the state provided this meant impartiality between religions and not official irreligion, and even hoped to prise the Radicals out of the Cartel with the socialists to make a new centre coalition. But it counted wrongly on the waning of anticlericalism, and made no impression on the Radicals. It cast itself as Catholic and subject to the directives of the Church, but not clerical. But in its fear of appearing clerical, it lost the support of many Catholics to reactionary organisations such as Castelnau's Fédération Nationale Catholique and de la Rocque's Croix de Feu.[90] Its social policy was equally indecisive. It was committed to 'social progress' and to 'everything that can promote the understanding, mutual comprehension and collaboration by which fearful social conflicts may be pacified'.[91] In 1936 the paper campaigned in the centre when no centre ground existed, and though not part of the Popular Front had enough sympathy for the strike movement of May–June 1936 to encourage Action Française and General Castelnau to lobby Rome to ban it. Gay's only response was to declare that they were 'Catholiques d'abord' and throw himself on the pope's mercy.[92]

Over half the 204 deputies of the Mouvement Républicain Populaire elected to the Constituent Assembly in 1945 had belonged to the Parti Démocrate Populaire. Emerging at the Liberation, the MRP made explicit its commitment to the Republic, but looked to defend the interests of the Catholic Church. The Catholic hierarchy was so discredited by its association with Vichy that it had no alternative to blessing the movement. Like the PDP, the MRP placed itself at the centre of the political spectrum, refusing both laissez-faire capitalism and socialist collectivism. It believed that 'both collectivism and liberalism [led] to human enslavement' and stood for a 'true economic democracy . . . nationalisation without state control or confiscation, respectful of freedom of initiative and personal responsibility'.[93] On the other hand, with the right-wing parties eliminated at the Liberation, the MRP was looked to by many electors as a barrier against Communism, making it in the words of Jean-Marie Mayeur, 'a left-wing policy with a right-wing electorate'.[94] The MRP strove valiantly to 'break the mould' of extremist politics and to mark out a centre ground that it could control. When de Gaulle founded his RPF in 1947, the MRP drifted to the Right in order to check the flight of Catholic voters to Gaullism, but in 1962 it broke with de Gaulle over the issue of direct presidential elections.

Jean Lecanuet, mayor of Rouen and a former president of the MRP, attracted the hopes of the centre when he stood as a presidential candidate against both de Gaulle and Mitterrand in 1965, and in 1966 replaced the moribund MRP by the Centre Démocrate. The Centre Démocrate, however, found it as difficult as the MRP to control the centre ground between the left-wing and Gaullist parties. It lost MRP heavyweights such as the Europeanist Robert

Schuman to the Gaullists and the likes of Robert Buron, deputy for the Mayenne, to the socialists.[95] A faction that supported de Gaulle's successor Pompidou, rather than the centrist Poher, in the presidential elections of 1969, broke away. Fearing the rise of a united Left, Lecanuet made a deal with Jean-Jacques Servan-Schreiber's Radicals in 1973 on the basis of a vaguely moralising *Projet réformateur*, but went on to back Giscard d'Estaing in the presidential elections of 1974. The Centre Démocrate and its breakaway faction were reconstituted as the Centre des Démocrates Sociaux in 1976, but swung between participation in the Chirac government of 1986, heeding the 'opening' to the centre of Rocard's socialist government in 1988, and running its own list in the European elections of 1989, when it collected a meagre eight per cent of the popular vote. To retain a grip on a centre-ground occupied also by the Radicals, it had to make itself less and less Catholic, but in doing so risked losing the support of Catholics to the large parties of the Right.

As they became less and less overtly Catholic, the various Christian Democratic parties placed themselves beyond the range of the Catholic hierarchy. But in any case, despite some progressive flourishes they favoured class cooperation rather than class war, and served as a rampart against socialism and communism. The experience of those Catholics who were seriously concerned with the grievances of the masses, and who understood the challenge of socialism and communism, whilst arguing that only Christianity could provide the moral and spiritual force that those doctrines lacked, was somewhat different. Time and again the hierarchy and the papacy came down on their initiatives, as if to warn that the path on which Lamennais had lost himself was now closed to other travellers.

Marc Sangnier, founder of the Sillon movement in the wake of the Dreyfus affair, was almost as extraordinary and isolated a figure as Lamennais. He had no qualms about the Republic as a régime, but equally saw that the Dreyfusard revolution had driven it into the arms of cold-blooded anticlericals. He claimed that 'democracy thirst[ed] for Christianity', and indeed that the Rousseauist subordination of the individual's particular interest to the general interest of society could only be ensured by Christian notions of justice, truth and love.[96] But concern for equal rights and the collective interest led beyond the confines of the Catholic community and from 1906 Sangnier was recruiting liberal Protestants and even tolerant free-thinkers into his movement.[97] Neither was Sangnier afraid of socialism. In a public debate with Jules Guesde in 1905, he argued, like Jaurès, that social revolution would have to be accompanied by moral and intellectual emancipation if it were not to go awry.[98] He claimed the heritage of the revolutionaries of 1789 and 1848, with their vision of an ideal city, declaring that this spiritual dimension had been destroyed by the scientific socialism of Marx. He told a Sillon conference in 1908,

There has been a deviation from traditional French socialism, and I myself am convinced that if the glorious dead of 1789 or even those wrapped in the shroud of their own utopia—I mean the Saint-Simonians and the Fourierists—rose from their tombs, they would embrace us, their Christian brothers, but nevertheless their brothers in a common ideal.[99]

This kind of language attracted the arrows of almost the entire Catholic world. It looked like a hijacking of Christianity for revolutionary purposes and worse, a Christian blessing for revolution. Charles Maurras, though himself an atheist, took up the cause of counter-revolutionary Catholicism elaborated by intransigents such as Albert de Mun in his early years. Reasoning that the Catholic Church stood for order, authority and hierarchy, he urged Catholics, if they felt betrayed by 'Christian anarchists' like Sangnier, to look to the Action Française to defend their cause. To reassure them as to his intentions, he praised the *Syllabus of Errors* and hung a portrait of Pius X, the scourge of modernism, in his office.[100] Maurras undoubtedly had a hand in provoking the Papacy's condemnation of the Sillon in 1910. 'The breath of the Revolution has passed that way', said Pius X, accusing Sangnier of 'ignoring the directions of ecclesiastical authority' and placing authority in the people instead.[101]

Charged with revolt against the Church, Sangnier had to submit or leave. Like Lamennais, he decided to leave. He continued his movement outside the Church's jurisdiction, in the form of Ligue de la Jeune République. Launched in 1912 and revived after the war, it counted on the decline of anticlericalism to inject the moral and social ideals of the Christian gospel into the Republic, and at the same time aimed to 'extract Catholicism from the shell of the old conservative policy'.[102] Catholic parties, said Sangnier, even the Parti Démocrate Populaire, were 'always, whether they like it or not, on the Right'; his Ligue was decidedly on the Left.[103] It took part in the Rassemblement populaire of 14 July 1935 and at its Montrouge congress of November 1935, alone of the Catholic parties, it committed itself to the Popular Front.[104]

In the 1930s Emmanuel Mounier was a prime mover in accepting the challenge of the revolution at the same time as attempting to Christianise it. Born in 1905, he had been inspired by the philosophy of Charles Péguy, who had been killed in 1914, which believed that at a mystical level it was entirely possible to reconcile Christianity, republicanism and socialism; only when politicians began to attack each other were they driven apart. In consultation with Péguy's son Marcel, Mounier published *The Thought of Charles Péguy* in 1931, and founded the review *Esprit* in 1932. He followed Péguy's hostility to the separation of material and spiritual spheres and the subordination of the latter to the former. In particular, he disliked the way spiritual values had been harnessed by the Right and put at their service, as in 'the bloc: property-family-country-religion', while revolutionary ideas had been defined by Marxists in a purely materialistic sense.[105] He wanted to replace individualism, which defined people in a material sense and related them contractually, with personalism, which made them whole by releasing them from material concerns and rela-

ted them to each other spiritually. 'First we could have the collectivist revolution with the communists,' he wrote, 'then we will have our personalist
revolution.'[106]

Mounier was anxious to reach a wider audience than the Catholic community and accepted an invitation from the Communist Paul Nizan to speak at a
Popular Front meeting in June 1935. Action Française began to campaign in
Rome for a condemnation of 'Catholicisme de gauche'. In April 1936, just
before the elections, the Communist leader Maurice Thorez proclaimed the
policy of the outstretched hand to Catholic workers. The Church of Rome
papacy reacted sharply: there could be no question of Catholics and Communists meeting half way. In May 1936, it condemned *Esprit*. This was followed
up in March 1937 by the encyclical *Divini Redemptoris* which stated that
'Communism is intrinsically wrong, and no one who would save Christian
civilisation may collaborate with it in any way whatsoever.'[107]

Mounier was briefly seduced by the priority given by Vichy to France's
moral regeneration. He received permission to revive *Esprit* in November 1940
and applied himself to 'arm the French soul against Nazi contamination'.[108] He
also taught at the school set up to train the new Vichy élite at Uriage, near
Grenoble. Whilst he hoped to develop the ideas on spirituality and
communality of the Révolution Nationale, he soon realised that the authorities
were intent on imposing their own doctrines without discussion.[109] He disagreed with many of Vichy's doctrines, notably its anti-Semitism and bid to
hijack his mentor Charles Péguy for its own ends. Marcel Péguy ingratiated
himself with the authorities by writing in 1941 that 'my father's racism is
essentially Christian and his Christianity is essentially racist.'[110] Mounier was
dismissed from Uriage and *Esprit* was banned in the summer of 1941. He drew
close to the Catholic wing of the Resistance, was arrested, tried and acquitted.
At the Liberation, he thought the moment had arrived for Catholic revolution
and attempted to come to terms with Communism, which had played such a
vital part in the Resistance and had emerged as the largest party in France at the
Liberation. When he revived *Esprit*, Mounier undertook a survey among young
people on their attitude to the PCF, discovering that 'in France in 1946 the
Communist party ha[d] the confidence and the strength of the immense majority of the working class and especially its most dynamic part'. He accepted
that Communists dismissed religious values as essentially bourgeois, but took
heart from the Communist preoccupation with the political and technical side
of the initial revolution. This left the spiritual dimension free for a moral
revolution directed by *Esprit*. And he felt sure that so long as Communism did
not, like the Church, develop its own rigid clericalism, and 'held out the same
signs of internal liberty, a large proportion of the reservations it provoked
would fall away'.[111]

If the war drove the Catholic hierarchy and the masses further apart, there
was one experiment that brought select clergy closer to workers. Under the

forced-labour system imposed by the Germans in 1943 (the Service du Travail Obligatoire, STO), some 700,000 French workers were conscripted for work in Germany. The German authorities refused Cardinal Suhard, the archbishop of Paris, permission to send an official chaplaincy, but twenty-six priests went incognito and at great personal risk with the deportees. One of these, a Jesuit named Henri Perrin, was caught, and shared a prison cell with a Communist building worker. It was a great revelation. 'What he wants', wrote Perrin in his diary, 'is not massive upheaval, nor subordination to Moscow, nor the abolition of property, but the abolition of too glaring social inequalities, more dignity and comfort for the proletariat, and state control of industry.'[112]

After the war, Perrin became involved in the Church's mission to deprived areas, initiated by Cardinal Suhard in the wake of a shocking report of 1943 on the de-Christianisation of the working class. The mission's novelty, drawing on the STO experience, was that the priests were to abandon clerical trappings and live and work in working-class communities. Perrin soon realised that the working class had not abandoned the Church; the Church had abandoned the workers. In the centenary year of the 1848 Revolution, he turned for inspiration to Frédéric Ozanam's *Origins of Socialism*, regretting that the Church had repeatedly sided with the rich and powerful. Experiencing at first hand the oppression and alienation of factory life, he was forced to conclude that

> it can no longer be a question of 'educating the working class', only of justice and the struggle of the proletariat for its liberation. . . . It is easy to call [the proletariat] materialist. But I have found more than enough proof [to the contrary] in the Communists' tireless faith, the anarchists' desire for love and liberty, the fraternity of the bars and the songs that express it.[113]

In 1949 the Church of Rome once again condemned Catholic and Communist collaboration. Henri Perrin and other worker-priests were driven to abandon the rôle of missionary, and joined the workers in their struggle for justice. Perrin left the Jesuit order, went to work on a hydro-electric scheme in the Alps, joined the Communist-dominated trade union, the CGT, and became involved in strike action to improve wages and conditions. After a wave of strikes in August 1953, the Church authorities decided that the experiment of worker-priests had to come to an end. It suspected that some were not only flirting with Communism but had also become Communists. About fifty worker-priests defied the hierarchy and stayed on as workers, risking excommunication. Perrin obeyed, but only after signing with a number of others a communiqué which protested in language that betrayed their conversion.

> We do not think that our life as workers has ever prevented us from remaining faithful to our faith or calling. We do not see how in the name of the gospel priests can be forbidden from sharing the condition of millions of oppressed men and expressing solidarity with their struggle.[114]

A few months later he died in a motor-bike accident which had the appearance of suicide.

For over a century and a half after the Revolution, the Catholic Church in France was organised as an absolute monarchy. It opposed all doctrines emanating from the Revolution and brought swiftly into line, or expelled from its bosom, those who sought some compromise with revolutionary principles. But in 1962 Pope John XXIII convened the Second Vatican Council to re-examine the fundamental notions of authority and uniformity that had governed the Roman Catholic Church for so long. The conclusions of the Council were far-reaching. The Church now defined itself as 'the people of God', rather than 'the faithful' guided by a clerical élite. It was organised on a collegial rather than a monarchical principle, and the freedom of other religions was conceded alongside the Catholic faith. The Church allowed liberty within its own structures, and recognised liberty as more than its own independence and authority. This was seen in many quarters as a victory for liberal Catholicism. Marcel Prélot, a founder member of the Parti Démocrate Populaire and senator of the Doubs, published an anthology of texts entitled *Le Libéralisme catholique*, arguing that fundamental precepts of liberal Catholicism had been adopted by the Vatican Council. At a festival in 1970 to mark the centenary of the death of Montalembert, liberal Catholicism's figurehead, Prélot regretted only that Jean Lecanuet's Centre Démocrate had not paid Montalembert the tribute due to him.[115] Meanwhile the events of May 1968 found Catholic students on the same side of the barricade as other students, questioning once again the traditional alliance of the Church with capitalism and authority. Unlike in 1848 and 1870, the archbishop of Paris was not martyred by the Revolution. He was wise enough not to anathematise revolution baldly, declaring on the contrary that 'God is not conservative' and that 'Christians should not be astonished by criticism of the consumer society and materialism, in both East and West'.[116]

This shift by the Vatican and a good proportion of the episcopate to more liberal ideas did not go unchallenged. Intransigents who took the line sanctioned by the papacy that there could be no deals with revolution, and who were encouraged by Rome's position during the Cold War that only a rigid Catholic orthodoxy, purged of 'progressive' heresies, could stand up to the threat of Communism, now felt themselves marginalised. They claimed that the Church was being infiltrated by Marxist revolutionaries who were steadily conquering not only the outworks but the very hierarchy itself. Their response was to defend what they saw as Catholic truth and the values of Christian civilisation against the hierarchy and, if necessary, against the papacy itself. Like their predecessors, they felt that the only answer was to recreate the Christian social order they presumed to have existed in the Middle Ages.

Within a year or so of the Liberation, a network of organisations was set up in the Catholic Church to winkle out Communist fellow-travellers from the Church, and more generally to defend Christian civilisation against Communism. Dear to them all was the concept of Christ the King, symbolising the goal of establishing the Kingdom of Christ on earth. The Pax Christi movement, inaugurated in 1946 at Vézelay, that centre of the medieval Church in Burgundy, took the form of an anti-Communist crusade for 'the salvation of souls, the propagation of the Catholic and Roman faith, the triumph of Christ the King'.[117] Jean Marial (a pseudonym of Jean Ousset), who launched *Verbe* in 1946, insisted that France remain the vehicle of Christian civilisation, the 'eldest daughter of the Church, still streaming from the baptism of Reims', and he looked forward to 'the triumph of Christ the King, through Mary, Queen of Heaven and Queen of France'. He took as his models the intransigents of the nineteenth century—de Maistre, Bonald, Mgr Pie, bishop of Poitiers, and Louis Veuillot, who had defended the Word against all compromise with the Revolution.[118] Among the popes to whom the intransigents were devoted were Pius X, the scourge of modernism, and Pius XII, a cult figure after his death in 1958, the embodiment of anti-Communist rectitude. That others accused Pius of knowing about, and doing nothing to stop, the Holocaust only sharpened the polemics. Jean Madiran, who launched *Itinéraires* in 1956, spoke of Pius XII as a 'universal genius' who should be canonised. Arguing that the Soviet Union had also established concentration camps before, during and after those of Hitler, he denounced 'the closed world of lies which consider[ed] progress the liberation of Christian and Jewish communities, only to hand them over to Communism'.[119]

For the intransigents, Pius XII's death marked the opening of the flood-gates to Communism. With Vatican II and the opening of the Church to 'contestation', they claimed that they alone occupied the high ground of orthodoxy, while Rome and the bishops had gone over to the other side. Mgr Marcel Lefebvre, who had spent most of his active life running the Church's mission in Africa, founded an élite of traditionalist priests, the Sacerdotal Fraternity of St Pius X, based at the seminary of Écône in Switzerland. He believed that allowing the principle of liberty of conscience to displace that of orthodoxy and uniformity was to court self-destruction. His position was outlined in a lecture of 1969:

> Throughout the nineteenth century Catholics . . . believed that there could be a compromise or understanding with the principles of Protestantism, with the principles of the Revolution. That was the history of liberal Catholicism. . . . The successors of this liberalism were the Sillon, modernism, and today neo-modernism . . . If we do not build on the rock of Catholicity [however], the corner-stone of which is Our Lord Jesus Christ, we will start to tergiversate and through liberalism and neo-modernism find ourselves at the door of Communism.[120]

Preaching at Lille in 1976, he claimed that 'what the Revolution had done was nothing beside what the Second Vatican Council had done. Nothing.' He roundly condemned 'the adulterous union of the Church and the Revolution', which could only produce 'a bastard rite . . . bastard sacraments . . . bastard priests'.[121]

Traditionalists in the Church had their allies in the political world. The defeat of the classic right-wing parties after 1981 gave a boost to the extreme right-wing National Front and to Catholic traditionalists, who were linked in a somewhat unholy alliance. At a meeting in support of Mgr Lefebvre in 1976, Romain Marie, a traditionalist close to the National Front, declared that 'our worst enemy is liberalism . . . it tries to pass itself off today as the only rampart against Bolshevism, the better to throw Christendom to it'.[122] He founded the Christendom-Solidarity committees, stating that 'with a few exceptions, all the French bishops are socialists', and was elected to the European Parliament in 1984 and 1989 on the National Front list of Jean-Marie Le Pen.[123] Jean Madiran, who continued to edit *Itinéraires*, became director and political editor of the right-wing Catholic paper *Présent*, which had a certain political affinity with the National Front. He rediscovered and republished Maurras' condemnation of the Sillon, *La Démocratie religieuse*, to recall the good old days when Rome had stamped on modernism instead of encouraging it.[124] The faithful were leaving the Church, he believed, 'because they no longer had confidence in priests who are open friends of socialist-communists', and he praised the 'militantly Christian anti-communism' of Mgr Lefebvre.[125]

The traditionalists denounced the revolutionary principles condemned by the Catholic Church in the past but with which it was now prepared to make some limited transaction. More seriously, although they proclaimed the Church's authority in theory, in practice they contested its right to stray from the orthodoxy, which had a more ancient foundation. Accordingly, Mgr Lefebvre was excommunicated in June 1988. Jean Madiran was left writing to John Paul II to condemn the 'enemy party that occupies the Church', and calling for an intellectual and moral reformation that would appeal to the heritage of Louis Veuillot, Cardinal Pie and Charles Maurras.[126] Traditionalists were nevertheless unhappy that their defence of orthodoxy should lead them into conflict with the papacy, and increasingly they fell into line within the Church.

The history of attempts by the Church and by Catholic parties and movements to come to terms with the challenge thrown down by the Revolution has not been a happy one. The Church has long maintained that the Revolution was in essence anti-Christian, a punishment inflicted on France for straying from the ways of God, a plot hatched by the enemies of the Church, and resulting in the persecution and massacre of Catholic priests and laity. To be sure, Catholics learned in time to use the language of liberty sanctioned by the Revolution to justify demands for the freedom for Catholics to run their own schools. But such freedom was demanded to secure the institutional liberty of the Church, in other words, its authority. The Church was reluctant to tolerate initiatives by Catholics to come to terms with the Revolution. This was essentially because it was unable to forget the crimes committed against it by the Revolution, and because, according to its view, the Revolution, which sanctified the will of man, challenged its own authority to interpret the will of God. In time, the Church acknowledged the culture of liberal Catholicism, not least because it did not question the existing social order. In the 1960s, it even began to liberalise its own institutions. It also came to accept some forms of Christian Democracy, provided that in the end they offered a barrier to socialism and communism. Catholics also, however, made radical attempts to meet revolution on its own terms, to sympathise with its arguments, and to move with its current, with the proviso that its material goals be tempered by spiritual ones derived from Christianity. The abbé Grégoire, Lamennais, Ozanam, Sangnier, Mounier, and the worker-priests were all examples of this impulse. And all, in the end, were condemned by the Church. These cases, no matter how unrepresentative they were, must in the last resort gauge how far the Church was able to come to terms with the Revolution and its shock-waves.

Protestantism and Revolution

The collective memory of the French Protestant community has revolved around the commemoration of two fundamental events. The first was the Revocation of the Edict of Nantes in 1685, the high point of religious persecution by the absolute monarchy of Louis XIV. The second was the Camisard revolt of Protestants in the Cévennes against the régime of Louis XIV during the War of the Spanish Succession. However, these two events did not have equal status in the Protestant collective memory: the commemoration of the Camisard revolt, a powerful and heroic act if ever there was one, was subordinated in Protestant political culture to the tragedy of the Revocation, which ushered in a century of persecution, with the breaking up of peaceful religious meetings by armed force in the 'Desert' of the Cévennes and the condemnation of Protestant preachers and militants to prisons and galleys.

There are several reasons for this imbalance. First, the identity of the Protestant community—both geographically (concentrated in the Cévennes) and mentally—was essentially forged by persecution, and persecution gave Protestants the historical legitimacy of victims and martyrs.[127] Second, martyrdom brought hope of redemption, and Protestants were fond of demonstrating that even if they had been defeated physically by persecution, spiritually they had not been and could not be broken. Third, to establish a cult of the Camisard revolt was to teach that persecution justified armed resistance. There was some reluctance to endorse this view, especially since the revolt had been a ragged sort of rising by a common sort of people. It was altogether safer to concentrate on the Revocation, which made Protestants the privileged bearers of the principle of liberty of conscience, which they considered the fount of all other civil and political liberties. Fourth, since heresy in the Ancien Régime was seen to be as much a challenge to royal power as to the Church, Protestants were vulnerable to the accusation of being rebels. To revolt during a war fought with Protestant powers, Britain and Holland, led to accusations that they were the enemy within. And when France was defeated it was only a step to accusing Protestants of a stab in the back.

It was not before the middle of the nineteenth century that the cult of the Camisards began to take shape. Samuel Vincent, the leading Protestant minister of Nîmes at the Restoration, in the process of republishing the account of the Camisard war by the eighteenth-century pastor Antoine Court, who had done much to rebuild the formal structures of the Protestant church, had little time for the rebels. He drew the lesson that a people could not be converted by force, but also that if an oppressed people were deprived of its ministers by persecution and fell under the influence of ignorant prophets and visionaries, then it could be led into an orgy of fanaticism and violence, like the Camisard war. In the wake of another eruption of persecution and violence, the White Terror, Vincent said that his purpose in republishing Court's history was not 'to envenom painful memories . . . but to demonstrate that the true interests and duties of everyone, under the Charter [of 1814] [were] to live in peace in the religion they [had] chosen, and to accept alongside them other religions which [could] do them no harm'.[128]

The History of the Pastors of the Desert by Napoléon Peyrat was the first passionate defence of the Camisards. Peyrat cast himself not as an observer or critic but as a descendant of the Cévenol heroes who had learned from the cradle the hymns and stories of the Camisard tradition. Like Vincent, he believed that the Cévenols 'proved that evangelism by the sword is powerless to convert souls', but he dignified the Camisards with the name they gave themselves, 'the children of God', and portrayed them as Cromwell's New Model Army or the Covenanters of Walter Scott's *Old Mortality*. 'The children of God', he wrote, 'therefore formed a military theocracy, in other words a society of soldiers governed by prophets who said they were inspired by the heavenly spirit.'[129]

It is significant, however, that this positive view of the Camisards was taken up by Jules Michelet rather than by other Protestants. Michelet met Peyrat in 1857 and corresponded with him. He was keen to use the Camisard legend as more ammunition to indict the Catholic Church and French monarchy. The raping of women and the kidnapping of children by the dragoons he deemed worse than the Terror of 1793. He saw another occasion to denouce the Catholic Church's inquisitorial practices, particularly in the person of the *grand vicaire* Du Chayla, who commanded the Catholic militias and 'enjoyed himself torturing people in his own cellar'. He described Protestants as sober and hardworking, but driven to fight by persecution. The Camisard movement was 'absolutely democratic and popular. Nobles took no part in it. It was national. The Cévennes received no help from abroad.'[130] Michelet cleared the Protestants of the accusation that they were un-French, and argued that in their proclamation of the right of resistance and their struggle for liberty, they blazed the trail that led to the French Revolution.[131]

The latter part of the century saw a renewal of Protestant interest in the 'Desert', which became sanctified as a place of Protestant pilgrimage, although the focus of Protestant celebrations remained not revolt but the Revocation of the Edict of Nantes which had victimised and martyrised them. The bicentenary of the Revocation, which fell in 1885, triggered much activity. The Society for the History of French Protestantism, founded in 1852 but scarcely active until 1865, held its first annual general meeting outside Paris in 1883, when it travelled to Nîmes. It visited the Tour de Constance, where female prophets had been imprisoned in the eighteenth century, and inspected the macabre graffito *Résistez*, etched in the wall by one of the prisoners. They went to the Mas Soubeyron, the house of the Camisard leader Roland in the Cévennes, purchased by the Society in 1881, to study his Bible; but they also heard lectures on Paul Rabaut, one of the great pastors of the 'Desert', and on Admiral Coligny, victim of the St Bartholomew massacre.[132]

In 1887 the centenary of the edict of toleration was celebrated by the erection of a monolith at Font-morte, in the high Cévennes, on the site of a Camisard battle. However, Pastor Viguié of the Paris Theological Faculty seemed more inspired by Samuel Vincent than by Michelet when he told the crowd of six thousand that

> these Camisards, passionate as they were, are not quite to the taste of our more calm and rational generation. They were not popular in their own time . . . they were and still are called rebellious, demented, frenzied, fanatical . . . I call them martyrs, because they went to their death freely, for liberty . . . the idea, passion, dream of liberty of conscience swept them along and they rose up to die for it.[133]

Though they were still described as rebels, they were rebels for a cause, that of liberty of conscience, and they were sanctified by martyrdom. Like Vincent again, he did not exalt the struggle but drew the lesson of the horror of religious war and called for mutual understanding between Catholic and Protestant. The inscription on the monument read:

> On the centenary of the Edict of Tolerance
> the Sons of Huguenots
> On the Site of Ancient Battles
> Have Raised this Monument
> To Religious Peace and the Memory of Martyrs.[134]

External events helped to rework the collective memory of Protestants. The Dreyfus affair, though it implicated a Protestant rather than a Jew, revived in the Protestant mind memories of persecution. Raoul Allier, another academic from the Paris Theological Faculty, immediately saw the parallel with the Calas

affair, which had so exercised Voltaire. Calas, a Protestant merchant in Toulouse, had been executed in 1762 for allegedly murdering his son who had
converted to Catholicism. It took five years for the case of Dreyfus to be
reopened, as it had taken three years to rehabilitate Calas. The same obstacles,
suggested Allier, stood in the way.

> First there was the instinctive and mindless opposition of those whose peace
> and quiet would be interrupted and digestion upset by such an
> initiative.... Several people who in France would be called *dévots* an-
> nounced that it was better to break an old Calvinist on the wheel rather than
> oblige eight Languedoc magistrates to admit that they had made a mistake.[135]

Protestants were among the first to campaign to reopen the Dreyfus case, only
to find the inertia and ill-will of the establishment before them. Auguste
Scheurer-Kestner, a Protestant of Alsace, who had grown up among republicans exiled after the coup of 1851, and was himself briefly imprisoned in 1862,
put his weight as vice-president of the Senate behind the campaign from the
summer of 1897. This cost him his re-election to the vice-presidency and his
health, and he died in 1899.

The Dreyfus affair demonstrated once again to Protestants the evils of
religious intolerance and persecution. It was also the occasion of a revival of the
myth of the Protestant as the enemy within, ready to stab France in the back.
Nationalists denounced the campaign to reopen the Dreyfus case as a cosmopolitan conspiracy against French interests by a syndicate of Protestants, Jews
and Freemasons which had taken over the Republic by stealth. A new wave of
anti-Protestantism gathered momentum alongside that of anti-Semitism.
Protestants were accused of exploiting their financial and intellectual advantages to carve out a position of political dominance in the Republic. From there
they were said to have pioneered the lay laws to take revenge on the Catholic
Church. The Monod family, headed by Gabriel Monod, editor of the *Revue
historique* was singled out by Charles Maurras as a state within a state, whose
cosmopolitan connections brought it closer to Germany and Great Britain than
to France. Protestants in general were accused of being a fifth column which
had betrayed France since the Wars of Religion, of supporting Prussia in the
war of 1870 and Britain over Fashoda.[136]

The anti-Protestant polemic reached from the world of Paris reviews to the
smallest Cévenol village. Before the elections of 1902, the predominantly
Protestant canton of Saint-Agrève in the Ardèche was moved from the second
Tournon constituency to the first to strengthen the chances of the republican
candidate. The latter, however, still failed to dislodge the conservative, and the
night the result was known, the tocsin rang in several communes and angry
Catholics armed with axes, knives and guns with the blessing of their curé, set
upon the Protestants. 'You would have thought that the Wars of Religion were
over,' said *La République des Cévennes*, 'you would have thought that everyone
today shuddered in horror to think of the atrocities once committed for the

same motives, but there are still people who want to revive those terrible times and go back to the dark ages.'[137]

The renewal of the Wars of Religion sharpened the Protestant community's awareness of its past. In 1911 Roland's house at the Mas Soubeyron was made into a Museum of the Desert by the Société de l'Histoire du Protestantisme français, and a date early in September was fixed for an annual gathering there of the Protestant community. At the opening of the museum, Frank Puaux, the president of the society, indulged in what was to become a classic obeisance, reference to the oral transmission of the Protestant tradition. He recalled how as a child he had listened at his father's knee to the 'wonderful epic of the Camisard war'. His father had also related 'the glorious martyrdom of the preachers of the Desert', and which prompted Puaux now to ask,

Is there an example in history of a faith as strong as that of those poor persecuted people, whose defeat seemed certain as kings, priests, soldiers and judges combined against them? Who would not bow to these great defenders of the most sacred of liberties, freedom of conscience?[138]

The emphasis was still on persecution, martyrdom, the powerlessness of force against spirit, and devotion to the cause of liberty. The banner over the entrance to the village read, 'To the martyrs of freedom of conscience'.[139]

The Great War undoubtedly served to reintegrate Protestants into the national community. Maurice Barrès, who as a nationalist had no love for 'cosmopolitans', recognised that the youth of Protestant families such as Monod or Allier had sacrificed themselves as much as any other of the spiritual families of France for the fatherland and for the recovery of Alsace, which was almost as Protestant as it was Catholic.[140] The rise of fascism, like the Dreyfus affair, however, provoked renewed fears of persecution, particularly given the sufferings of the churches in Nazi Germany. In 1935 André Chamson, a young Protestant writer, and André Philip, a Protestant academic lawyer and SFIO militant in Lyon, were among the signatories of a manifesto of the 'Protestant university group for the defence of freedoms of conscience'. This asserted that the individual could not fulfil himself without 'freedom of conscience and the public liberties which flow from it', and condemned 'religious, anti-religious or political oppression whatever its origin', but particularly the new German paganism.[141] Chamson, addressing Protestants at the Musée du Désert that September, took his theme from the graffito at the Tour de Constance, 'Résistez'. Significantly, however, he noted that 'to resist is doubtless to fight, but it is also to do more: to refuse in advance to accept the law of defeat'.[142]

Though some elements of the Protestant establishment were initially attracted by Vichy's promise to regenerate spiritual values, its strategy of exclusion and persecution inclined Protestants generally to oppose Vichy in the name of freedom of conscience. As during the Dreyfus affair, Jews were more vulnerable to persecution than Protestants, but Protestant Cévenols were in an excellent position, both geographically and psychologically, given their own experience of refuge from persecution, to hide persecuted Jews. Jews were bussed in as 'false pilgrims' to the annual gathering at the Musée du Désert in September 1942 and subsequently dispersed among Protestant families for protection.[143]

The armed Resistance movement was also fairly active in the mountainous regions of the Midi, and Protestants, alongside Catholics, were heavily involved. This offered the opportunity to refashion the Protestant collective memory, and to recast the Camisard war in a better light, supplementing the virtues of silent suffering and martyrdom by the virtues of struggle for a cause. André Ducasse, who taught at the Lycée Périer in Marseille, and escaped the STO to become involved with the Maquis on Mont Aigoual, wrote a history of the Camisard wars in which he noted that 'the old cévenols have never been more present; their madness has never seemed wiser. The Camisard war continues.'[144]

Curiously, there remained among Protestants a reluctance to esteem the Camisard revolt above memories of persecution, which privileged freedom of conscience. The Lyon pastor Roland de Pury, a friend of André Philip, arrested in his pulpit in 1943 for alleged links with the Resistance, wrote in his diary, 'It is actually better to suffer injustice than to commit it.'[145] Philip himself, who joined the Resistance in London, was eager to stress the spiritual value of the struggle. Its purpose, he said, was to defend the 'sacred character of the individual . . . unknown in Antiquity, denied by today's totalitarian systems in which race, nation and blood are the new barbaric gods to which the individual is sacrificed'.[146] André Chamson, returning to the Musée du Désert in 1954, referred back to his last address on Resistance, which he had made 'without knowing that this word would become our motto during four years of ordeal'. He praised the story of the Camisards, which had been handed by word of mouth from generation to generation, as 'our chanson de geste, our Iliad, our Odyssey and our golden legend'. But he insisted, echoing André Philip, that 'this civil war, this war of religion, this bloody clash between two ways of serving and adoring God, was not just a war. It was the affirmation of the most sacred, fundamental and essential principle, that of freedom of conscience and, through freedom of conscience, of mutual respect between man and man.'[147]

This unwillingness to exalt the myth of the Camisard revolt above that of persecution and perseverance was evident in Chamson's later works. In *La Superbe* (1967) and *La Tour de Constance* (1970) he took two loci of the persecution of Protestants, a galley of King Louis XIV (*La Superbe*), and the tower in which the prophetesses had been imprisoned between 1723 and 1768. For Chamson, the effect of the Second World War was to remind him not of the heroism of the Camisard war but that 'the persecution of man by man, totalitarian madness, the total war in which a whole people is sacrificed, which we now call a subversive war and if we look at it from the other side is also called genocide, the universe of concentration camps, finally', had existed long before 1945 in the sufferings of Protestants.[148] The lessons to be learned were that freedom of conscience was a fragile conquest, always at risk, and that liberty would not be safe until present generations escaped from the burden of history. *La Tour de Constance* finished with a reminder that (with a few counter-revolutionary exceptions) the Protestants and Catholics of the Cévennes had federated in defence of the French Revolution.[149]

The hatred of persecution and violence that helped to shape Protestant political culture also shaped the Protestants' construction of the Revolution. Their attitude was highly ambivalent. They were indebted to it for consecrating liberty of conscience and for giving them the range of civil and political rights they had not hitherto enjoyed. But they also suffered from the uniformity imposed by the Jacobin dictatorship which was little different from the uniformity imposed by the absolute monarchy. Equally, they found that they had nothing to gain from the cycle of revolution and counter-revolution, Red Terror and White Terror. The key elements of the wider political culture formed by Protestants in the light of the Revolution were pluralism rather than uniformity, and fraternity rather than conflict. Briefly, they favoured the Revolution of 1789 and 1790, not that of 1793 or 1815.[150]

A study of major Protestant public figures from Guizot to Rocard demonstrates this enduring concern for liberty and justice and fear of violence and division. François Guizot, who passes as a cerebral and rather bloodless statesman, was in fact torn apart by his experience of the Revolution at Nîmes. The Revolution had set against each other his father, a Girondin, who in 1793 joined the federalist revolt against the Montagnard seizure of power in Paris, and his father's father-in-law, who headed the Montagnard administration of the Gard. Guizot's father went to the guillotine in April 1794, when the boy was six. 'Overwhelmed and shattered by grief,' his mother wrote to a friend in 1797, 'for three years neither time, nor reflection, nor my two sons could draw anything from me.'[151] She took her sons to Geneva, where Guizot was educated until he went to Paris in 1806 to study law and, after 1812, to embark on an academic and political career. Guizot's memoirs say nothing of this. 'I entered political life only in 1814,' he begins, 'having served neither the Revolution nor the Empire. My age distanced me from the Revolution, and my convictions from the Empire.'[152] Nothing was said about his early life; neither, among all his historical writings, did he ever tackle the Revolution. The Revolution was too terrible to behold directly, and thoughts about it he simply repressed.[153]

Guizot welcomed the Charter of 1814 which he saw as affording liberty under the monarchy, in the same vein as the constitution of 1791. He blamed the Hundred Days, which sparked the White Terror, for re-igniting 'the old quarrel that the Empire stifled and the Charter sought to extinguish, between traditional France and new France, that of the emigration and that of the Revolution'.[154] When he was approached by radicals in 1820 he replied,

I consider the Revolution of 1789 to be over and done with. All its interests and legitimate wishes are guaranteed by the Charter. I am not afraid of counter-revolution; we have the force of both law and fact against it. . . . What France needs now is to do away with the revolutionary spirit that still torments it, and make use of the free institutions it now has.[155]

His lectures of 1828–30 dealt with the history of civilisation in France and Europe between the fall of the Roman Empire and 1789. They were studies across time of the achievement of liberty and equal rights by the Third Estate or bourgeoisie, under the auspices of the crown. Sudden jumps and violence were ironed out as history drove its inevitable course. Guizot's priorities in 1830 were of the same order. 'We did not choose a king,' he wrote, 'but negotiated with a prince we found next to the throne and who alone could, by mounting it, guarantee our public law and save us from revolutions.' 'Our minds', he admitted, 'were guided by the English Revolution of 1688, by the fine and free government it founded, and the wonderful prosperity it brought to the English nation.'[156]

The July Monarchy was a golden age as far as Protestants were concerned. The immediate cause of its fall was Louis-Philippe's refusal to withdraw his confidence from Guizot. Protestants could gain little from the Revolution of 1848, and it is significant that the Protestant Odilon Barrot was one of the politicians who tried to maintain an element of continuity and stability in 1848. Four years younger than Guizot, his view of the Revolution may have been coloured by the fact that his grandfather had been killed by a royalist band in his native Lozère. Barrot was a leader of the 'dynastic' or would-be official opposition to the July Monarchy which during the banqueting campaign against the government used the slogan, 'A reform, to prevent revolution!', and insisted that a toast be drunk to the constitutional king. After Guizot's dismissal, Louis-Philippe turned first to the comte Molé, then to Thiers and, finally, to Barrot to form a ministry to save the situation. On the king's flight from the Tuileries, Barrot tried to establish a regency for his grandson, the comte de Paris. He went to the Chamber with the young count and his mother, the duchesse d'Orléans, and pleaded with the deputies,

Be united in one sentiment, to save the country from the most hateful scourge, that of civil war. . . . In the name of liberty, in the name of order, and above all to preserve our unity in such difficult times, I implore you and ask my country to rally round this woman and this child, noble representatives of the July revolution.[157]

At this point, on 24 February, it was too late for order and unity. After ten months of turmoil, however, Barrot was back, as Louis-Napoleon's first minister, the choice of the Orleanist men of business. A typical Protestant man of compromise and conciliation, prime minister on the last day of the July Monarchy, he thus became first prime minister under the constitution of 1848.

The Second Empire, which played fast and loose with constitutional rules and free institutions, was not to the taste of leading Protestants. They were likely to be found in the liberal opposition to the Empire, associated in particular with the Liberal Union of both royalist and republican liberals which made a breakthrough in the legislative elections of 1863. Prominent among them were Edmond de Pressensé, pastor of the chapelle Taitbout in Paris and leader of the Free Evangelical Church, and Lucien Anatole Prévost-Paradol, leading light of the liberal *Journal des Débats*, married to a Protestant and close to Protestants like Edmond de Pressensé, though not actually a Protestant himself—'a political Protestant', according to his biographer Pierre Guiral.[158]

The Third Republic, which gathered liberal royalists and liberal republicans around the constitution of 1875, was a régime in which Protestants were much more at home. It is significant that when a republican president of the Republic, Jules Grévy, was finally installed in 1879, five of the nine ministers of his ministry were Protestants. All these, moreover, were members of the Senate, which generally represented middle-of-the-road opinion.[159] The latter regretted the polarisation of the Republic after the 16 May crisis and advocated an 'open' Republic which would win over its former adversaries. 'It is up to us [republicans] to go half or three-quarters of the way, since we are strongest,' said the Protestant minister Freycinet in 1878, '[and] it is up to us to bring about reconciliation.'[160] To secure the Republic, Protestants tended to favour persuasion rather than persecution. Francis de Pressensé wrote of his father Edmond that he was 'ready to support Jules Ferry [who joined the Waddington cabinet as its tenth member and education minister] in his great work of establishing lay, free and compulsory education, but had a pronounced antipathy for vulgar Jacobinism and above all for coarse anticlericalism which was sometimes more illiberal than clericalism itself.'[161]

That Protestantism flourished under the July Monarchy and Third Republic was explained in part by its bourgeois social and political leadership. Socialism preaching class conflict and denouncing religion as middle-class mystification presented a challenge, but Protestantism, like Catholicism, developed a wing that believed that the gospels required a separation of Church and capitalism in the name of social justice, while religion was required to provide a moral and spiritual ideal for socialism.

In 1888 Tommy Fallot, a Lutheran pastor from Alsace, broke with the French and German Marxists with whom he was linked and founded a Protestant Association for the Study of Social Questions. He told Edmond de Pressensé that he wanted to found a Protestant socialism as bold as any other, but would have to begin by winning the confidence of the largely bourgeois Protestant churches.[162] The vice-president of the association, the economist Charles Gide, accordingly proposed a middle way between capitalism and collectivism through the co-operative movement, which would allow the gradual, non-violent emancipation of the working class.

If one task was to revolutionise the Protestant churches, a second was to convince the working classes that religion was a necessary spiritual compliment to their material emancipation. In 1908 a Union of Christian Socialists was founded by Protestant members of the SFIO who called themselves 'socialists because Christians' but were offended by socialist attacks on Christianity. The cover of their review, *L'Espoir du Monde*, portrayed David and Goliath with the explanation:

> The Philistine (*Capitalism*) advanced, his shield-bearer (*the Enslaved Proletariat*) before him . . . David (*the Organised Proletariat*) said to the Philistine: You come to me with sword, spear and javelin (*the Forces of Social Conservation*) and I come before you in the name of the Eternal (*Immanent Justice*).[163]

In *L'Avant-Garde*, another review of Protestant pastors and laity founded in 1929, a contributor wrote, 'I have no more faith in capitalism, yet I fear for the Revolution, which like war increases human suffering.' He and his colleagues were 'convinced that revolutions [were] powerless unless they [were] accompanied by a moral revolution which [could] be inspired only by the gospel'.[164] This kind of thinking was shared by André Philip, who published a work entitled *Socialisme et Christianisme* in 1934 and, elected an SFIO deputy for the Rhône in 1936, served in the Popular Front government and was responsible for steering through the law on the forty-hour week.[165]

Protestantism did not sit easily with Communism. In 1927 a Protestant pastor Henri Tricot, who had in fact begun his career in the Catholic Church, founded Union Communiste Spiritualiste with a review, *La Terre Nouvelle*. Tricot believed in the necessity of the proletarian revolution, but that 'a new society will never be built without new men'.[166] The Union opened its ranks to Catholics, and took part in Popular Front demonstrations with the emblem of the hammer and sickle superimposed on the cross, but provoked the wrath of the Protestant and Catholic Churches alike, as well as that of the Communist party (because, rather than in spite, of the *main tendue*) alike.

Protestants understood that civil and political liberties gained could only be safeguarded by the rule of law and by the reconciliation of warring parties. In order not to offend Catholic sensibilities, those who entered politics rarely declared their religious affiliation, but the Protestant passion for reconciliation was nevertheless clear. Three examples may suffice: those of Gaston Doumergue, Gaston Defferre and Michel Rocard.

Gaston Doumergue, a Protestant from the wine-growing country south of Nîmes, was elected deputy for Nîmes in 1893, and senator of the Gard in 1910. In December 1913 he became prime minister as someone who could placate the Radical party, but whose solid patriotism would not put the Three-Year military service law at risk. In 1924 he was elected president of the Republic as favourite of the Senate and on a 'republican union' ticket against the candidate of the Cartel des Gauches. On the expiry of his mandate in 1931 he retired, but after the right-wing riots of 6 February 1934 and the counter-demonstrations of the Left, he agreed at the age of seventy to form a government of national unity. 'I ask all French people', he said, 'to forget their quarrels and old divisions caused for the most part by differences of temperament or by mutual incomprehension . . . Forget all of that. Unite. Believe me and hear my appeal . . . A divided nation means the suicide of the nation.'[167]

Gaston Defferre was also of the middle ground. A Protestant of the Hérault, he was on the right of the SFIO as Doumergue had been on the right of the Radicals, and was mayor of Marseille from 1953 till his death in 1986. In the presidential elections of 1965, his ambition was to create an alternative to the union of the Left, a bridge from the socialists to the Radicals and MRP in the shape of a grand federation against de Gaulle and the Communists. 'France has suffered for over a century', he said, 'from a chronic political instability which has led it periodically to witness the replacement of the democratic régime by personal dictatorships . . . To participate in future developments France needs a régime both stable and democratic.'[168] He attacked the 'revolutionary verbalism' of the SFIO and argued that the party would have to learn to manage capitalism. 'To confuse the victory of progress with the crushing of a social category is to deny oneself the taking of power by any other means than force,' he explained.[169] The Communists, who stood for economic catastrophe, totalitarian dictatorship and subordination to Moscow, were to be marginalised unless they were prepared to treat with the federation on its own terms. In the event, the plan for a federation was scuppered by the leadership of the MRP and the SFIO, but Defferre remained a man of compromise to the end. His funeral, an ecumenical service held in the Catholic cathedral of Marseille, was seen as symbolic of the 'cohabitation' of Left and Right recently embarked upon in the government.[170]

The last example, Michel Rocard, also reflects a distancing of the Socialist party from the Communists and a readiness to co-operate with the centre. Though the triumph of 1981 was a victory for the united Left, the Communists did not stay in power for long, and after his re-election in 1988 Mitterrand turned to the Protestant Michel Rocard to head the government. Though a former leader of the Parti Socialiste Unifié, which broke with the SFIO over Algeria, Rocard was less a revolutionist than a manager. He presided over the 'opening' of the government to centrist parties in 1988, in an attempt to give it more of a national foundation. And his comment on the bicentenary of the Revolution was quintessentially Protestant. 'Among the many results of the great Revolution,' he said, 'one is important, that it convinced many people that revolution is dangerous, and if you can get by without one, you are no worse off.'[171]

CHAPTER 6

Anarchism

In 1871 Benoît Malon, a refugee in Switzerland after the suppression of the Paris Commune, published a work entitled *The Third Defeat of the French Proletariat*. It looked back on three popular risings—of the Lyon silk-weavers in 1831, of the Paris workers first in June 1848 and again in March 1871—and on their suppression by the French state. The sense of this work is that the French proletariat as a political community was shaped not by a socio-economic process of industrialisation or urbanisation, but by violent repression on the part of the bourgeois state.[1]

Recent research has confirmed this view that the politics of the working classes in France as in Great Britain and elsewhere is to be explained not in terms of working-class formation, for working classes remained highly fragmented according to level of skill, diversity of production unit, sex, religion, region or ethnic background, but rather in terms of their interaction with the state.[2] Conflict with the state provoked the working classes to develop a political culture which defined their identity, established their solidarity and legitimated their aspirations. What brought workers together and generated some form of class consciousness was not factory production or economic exploitation, but the growing sense that working people were excluded from power in the state, despite the doctrine of the sovereignty of the people and conditions of universal suffrage, and were liable to violent repression if they attempted to organise themselves to improve their lot.

The First International

Workers, especially skilled workers such as printers, were at the forefront of the 'people' in the 'Trois Glorieuses'. They took strike action in opposition to the press ordinance of Charles X, then manned the barricades. They felt, nevertheless, that the Revolution was hijacked by the parliamentary politicians who patched together a political settlement that suited their interests, and that the revolutionary rhetoric of liberty, equality and fraternity that enticed

them onto the streets soon rang extremely hollow. When they demonstrated and sent delegates to the government to press their own claims for
improved working conditions, they were threatened with prosecution for illegal
coalition, since collective action was denied to workers under the Le Chapelier
law of 1791. To voice their frustration, the Paris printers launched *L'Artisan.
Journal de la classe ouvrière*. It argued that they had made the Revolution, yet
were its first victims. They had fought for liberty but liberty had done nothing
for them. A sense of betrayal by the bourgeoisie served to define their identity
as a part of a working class with both grievances and a growing sense of its own
importance.

> The most numerous and useful social class is without doubt the working
> class. Without it capital has no value and there can be no machines, no
> industry, no commerce. . . . Yet it lives in poverty and enslaved to monopoly
> without being aware of it, silently suffers all kinds of humiliation from those
> whose wealth it creates, and is not surprised to be persecuted by the authori-
> ties. Is that truly as it should be?[3]

The obvious way forward for disgruntled workers was to join the republican
opposition. Republicans angry at the taking over of the Revolution by monarchists had formed the Society of Friends of the People, later the Society of the
Rights of Man.[4] But another way could be attempted. If they were beginning to
define themselves as a working class, as likely to be tricked by middle-class
republicans as by middle-class monarchists, the alternative was to take economic action, to organise as workers in pursuit of their collective goals. William
Sewell and Tony Judt have shown how, though the workers' corporations of
the Ancien Régime had been abolished by the Revolution, their ghost helped to
inspire new generations of organisation: first, under the Restoration, mutual aid
societies; then, after 1830, associations which took on the functions of trade
unions, and producers' associations or co-operatives.[5] Though these associations were illegal according to the letter of the law, workers considered that they
represented legitimate economic action and trusted that the state would observe a studied neutrality and arbitrate fairly between the conflicting interests
of workers and employers.

Organised workers soon learned that they were as unwise to trust the state on
the question of class neutrality as they were on that of political liberty. In Lyon
silk-weavers or *canuts* organised themselves into a Society of Mutual Obligation
to press their case for a revised 'tariff', the agreed rate payable by the silk-
merchants for their cloth. Unable to bring the latter to the negotiating table, the
weavers appealed for justice to the prefect of the Rhône, who brought merchants and workers' delegates together to agree a tariff. The merchants, however, appealed over the prefect's head to the government of Casimir Périer for
a ruling that the rate was not binding and to have the prefect removed. At this
point, the workers took matters into their own hands. On 21 November the
canuts went on strike and marched down from the suburb of La Croix-Rousse

to demand the enforcement of the tariff, flying the black flag and shouting, 'Vivre en travaillant ou mourir en combattant.'[6] According to the silk-workers' account, *L'Écho de la Fabrique*, the merchants then 'mobilised . . . the first legion of the National Guard, of which they formed the majority', and met the demonstrators with gunfire.[7] The workers rose in revolt and occupied the Hôtel de Ville, trying to force the prefect's hand. After order was restored by the military, the latter was dismissed and the tariff abrogated. It was now clear to the workers, if it had not been before, that the state was the arm of the bourgeoisie and, as the National Guard, the armed bourgeoisie. The bourgeois state naturally applied bourgeois law, by trying workers' leaders under the Penal Code and making working-class organisation virtually impossible under the Associations law of 28 March 1834.

Since the formation of labour organisations was deemed to be political, it seemed reasonable for workers to look to a political solution for their troubles. Some turned to the Society of the Rights of Man, which for its part was looking for popular support and prepared to add a social dimension to its demand for universal suffrage. The alliance, however, was not ideal. The Jacobins of the Society of the Rights of Man remained essentially bourgeois in their outlook. A worker who joined the Society declared himself 'opposed to the absolute and abusive right of property, the cause of all social inequality and obstacle to all fraternal reconciliation among workers'. But, he continued, 'It would be impossible to describe the tempest I unleashed in that meeting, made up though it was of workers deprived all worldly property.'[8] The workers gained nothing from hitching their cause to that of professional revolutionaries who were fighting the battles of Robespierre. Indeed, in April 1834, they found themselves caught in the cross-fire between government and republicans. In Lyon the working classes, not least the silk-workers, bore the brunt of the casualties and arrests when the insurrection was put down.[9]

Confronted by a régime that was committed to defend the interests of the possessing classes and concluding that political opposition led them to disaster, the working classes began to think once again about an economic solution to their ills. At this point, the aspirations of the labour movement and the ruminations of those bourgeois intellectuals who came to be known as utopian socialists converged. In 1840 Louis Blanc published *The Organisation of Labour*, the title of which was itself a programme. He argued that competition was ruinous for the bourgeoisie and was 'a system of extermination' for the people, driving wages down and unemployment up. He proposed the setting up of 'social work-shops', financed by capital raised on the money markets by the government, which would attract both employers and workers and eventually substitute association for selfishness.[10] This work was an inspiration to a working class seeking a way forward. A labour journal, *L'Atelier*, confirmed the view that the political road was blocked by two parties, conservative and radical, which represented only the political class.

Fig. 22. Insurgents of the June Days 1848 (Bibliothèque nationale)

The majority, it must be said, is of no party; for the moment it is indifferent and passive . . . it is horrified of everything that looks like *politics*; the word frightens it, if not the thing. It has witnessed many revolutions and gained virtually nothing apart from tax increases; it has constantly spilt its blood for the fatherland yet harvested nothing . . . it interprets the word *revolution* as deception, trickery, lies, a new form of exploitation with the help of grand words, a change of men but rarely one of principles.[11]

For *L'Atelier* labour had to rely on the strength that could be drawn from collective action, building up mutual aid societies and 'industrial associations' or co-operatives. However, even this road could not side-step politics altogether and the journal realised that little could be done so long as the Associations law remained on the statute book.

The flaw in the positions of Blanc and *L'Atelier* was that although they preached economic action, the government's assistance was still required and the government was in the hands of the bourgeoisie. The Revolution of 1848 seemed, with the introduction of universal suffrage, to make the sovereignty of the people into a concrete reality. Those who believed in a political solution to economic ills, through the democratic and social Republic, seemed vindicated. The peers of the realm were cleared out of the Luxembourg palace to make way for a commission on social questions chaired by Louis Blanc, which introduced among other reforms national work-shops for the unemployed. However, elections to the Constituent Assembly demonstrated that the political class was able to manipulate universal suffrage as it had manipulated limited suffrage. Apostles of socialism were scant in the Assembly and only thirty-four working-class deputies were returned. As the climate grew more inhospitable to social reform, Louis Blanc resigned from the commission. Having asserted its supremacy at the ballot-box, the political class asserted it on the streets. The national work-shops, which were increasingly seen to be dens of idleness and revolutionary conspiracy, were closed down, provoking a massive working-class insurrection in the eastern districts of Paris, the so-called June Days. The rising was ruthlessly suppressed by the National Guard and regular forces under General Cavaignac, and gave way to a period of bourgeois dictatorship.

After the suppression of the Lyon risings, that of the Paris workers in June 1848 was proof if ever it was required of the reality of class war behind the democratic rhetoric of the bourgeoisie. For some militants, it finally demonstrated the bankruptcy of political action as a means of advancing the cause of the working classes, and the need to devise a strategy of economic action that *at no point* would require recourse to the state. This impasse was at the origin of the elaboration of an anarchist political culture, the father of which was Proudhon.

Pierre-Joseph Proudhon, editor of *Representant du Peuple. Journal des travailleurs*, had himself been seduced by the possibility of political reform and was elected to the Assembly in a by-election early in June. But the June Days entirely changed his outlook. 'The memory of the June Days will leaden my heart with an eternal remorse,' he wrote. It was a 'disastrous apprenticeship' both for the rebels and for him. 'Fighters of June!' he reproached them. 'In March, April and May, instead of organising yourselves for labour and liberty . . . you ran to the government, asked it to provide what you alone could give yourselves, and postponed the revolution by three stages.'[12] His paper, like so many others, was closed down. *Le Peuple*, which he launched in the autumn of 1848, devoted itself to the question of the organisation of labour and credit, and envisaged workers taking control not only of small work-shops but also of large enterprises, landed estates, canals, railways and mines. This was to be achieved not only without the state but also against the state. 'We no more want the government of man by man,' he concluded, 'than the exploitation of man by man.'[13]

In the presidential elections of 10 December 1848, Proudhon backed Raspail as most resembling a socialist, dismissing Ledru-Rollin as 'that political rust'.[14] He had no time for the Jacobin Montagne, which claimed, 'Give us the right of life and death over your persons and property and we will make you free! . . . Kings and priests have been telling us the same thing for six thousand years!' Proudhon warned that workers could expect as little from a democratic republic as from absolute monarchy, a view that was confirmed by the two years he spent in the prison of Sainte-Pélagie under the Second Republic between 1849 and 1851. In *L'Idée générale de la Révolution*, written in prison, he argued that the Ancien Regime, based on divine right, had been held together by authority and faith. But democratic society, by substituting the divine right of the sovereign people for the divine right of God, only perpetuated the doctrines of authority and faith. What was required was a society based on human right which dispensed with authority and faith. Society would be an economic society, the warp and weft of which would be the organisations of labour. 'Between the political order and the economic order, between that based on laws and that based on contracts,' he asserted, 'there can be no compromise: you have to choose.'[15] Under the notion of contract, individuals would not alienate all their sovereign power, as the Rousseauistic or Jacobin model required them to do, resulting in a centralised state. They would retain at least as much sovereignty as they alienated to the commune, province and nation, which would give rise to a federal ordering of society.[16] The balance between autonomy and federation was central to Proudhon's new order.

Proudhon's anarchist ideas would be of no consequence unless the labour movement could be won over to them. Nothing could flourish under the authoritarian Empire, but after 1860 the government of Napoleon III began to relax labour legislation in the hope of prising the working class away from the republican opposition. A law of 25 May 1864 ceased to deem coalition a criminal offence, except where the 'freedom to work' of others was infringed and, after March 1868, trade unions were tolerated *de facto*, if not fully legalised. Unfortunately, the Parisian working class, though it had discovered the futility of following bourgeois republican leaders, was not yet convinced of the futility of political action. Faced by a Paris by-election in 1864, a committee of workers decided to run their own labour candidate, an engineering worker named Tolain. Proudhon intervened to dispense a few home-truths. Workers, he told them, should have no truck with electoral politics. Parliament was controlled by a 'conspiracy of old parties', which were themselves backed by powerful financial, industrial and press interests. Social justice would never be achieved by that route. 'Separate off', he advised, 'as the Roman people once separated from the aristocracy. By separation you will conquer; no representation, no candidates.'[17] This advice Proudhon developed in *De la Capacité politique des classes ouvrières*, which was published posthumously in 1865. The 'legal capacity' given to workers by universal suffrage was of little use to them, for it would always be manipulated by the political class. What they must define and articulate was their 'real capacity', which required consciousness of their value, dignity, and strength as a class.[18] His message was both that the working class could rely only on itself for its own emancipation, and that it should refuse all political action which served only to legitimate the state. Even if the state were conquered by the working class, he insisted, as required by Louis Blanc, it would be no improvement, a 'communist, governmental, dictatorial, authoritarian, doctrinaire system'. 'In my system,' said Proudhon, 'the worker is no longer a state serf, swallowed up in the communitarian ocean; he is a free man.'[19]

How far Proudhon's ideas penetrated the labour movement may be gauged by examining the International Working Men's Association, founded in 1864, and what may be considered in part an achievement of the International, the Paris Commune. The International declared that 'the emancipation of the working class must be achieved by the working classes themselves'. It was a meeting-ground of organised workers from Great Britain, Belgium, Germany, France, Switzerland and Italy which recognised that international capitalism had to be fought by an international labour movement. But it was also a battleground in which competing political cultures—anarchist, Marxist and republican—fought for influence. The congress held in Geneva in 1866 was described by the local professor of economics as 'Proudhon's tail', so much was it dominated by the Paris delegation under Tolain, who had been converted to anarchism.[20] Karl Marx recognised the same influence, but was even less complementary.

The heads of Messieurs the Parisians were filled with the most hollow Proudhonian rhetoric. They talk of science and know nothing. They poured scorn on all *revolutionary* action, that is originating in the class struggle, and on every social movement that is centralised and can therefore also be realised by political means ... *Under the pretext of liberty* and anti-governmentalism, or of anti-authoritarian individualism, these people—who for sixteen years have accepted and still so peacefully accept the most abominable despotism—in fact preach a vulgar bourgeois régime that is simply idealised in the Proudhonian way.[21]

For Marx, the Proudhonists failed on two counts. First, they tinkered with social organisation but refused the 'communist' programme of collectivising private property and were thus still bourgeois instead of revolutionary socialists. Second, they foreswore political action and thus for all their economic organisation had to accept the political régime in place. Marx's ambition was to convert the International to political action, either revolutionary or electoral, under central direction, in order to seize control of the state, and to collectivise the means of production in order to expropriate the expropriators and emancipate the proletariat. At the congresses of Brussels in 1868 and Basle in 1869, to which German and Belgian delegates were shipped in force, Marx was able to have his own way. But having defeated the Proudhonians he now had to face the émigré Russian anarchist Bakunin, who founded an Alliance of Social Democracy in 1868. Bakunin developed the anti-authoritarian message of the

Proudhonians in a revolutionary direction and, building up support in Geneva, Naples and Barcelona, used the alliance as a trojan horse to challenge for influence in the International.

In France the government, which had originally given the International a helping hand in order to undermine the republicans, soon realised its mistake and clamped down on it with two bans and three trials of its militants between 1868 and 1870. Such repression had the effect to giving the labour movement more definition, solidarity and radicalism. Tolain, a moderate Proudhonian, was replaced as torch-bearer of the International by Benoît Malon and Eugène Varlin, who were more extreme and more active. Malon later wrote of those Internationalists who were elected to the Paris Commune that

> these workers all knew each other; they had shared the same struggle, shared the same imperial prisons; they were a group of friends. Their federalist sympathies, their socialist convictions, their organisational and administrative experience distanced them from the empirical terrorism of 1793.[22]

A wave of industrial strikes at the end of the Second Empire enabled these militants to experiment with economic action, urging striking workers to organise and to affiliate to the International, either as trade unions or sections of the International. At Le Creusot, for example, there was a strike of metalworkers in January 1870, followed by the miners in March. Both Varlin and Malon went to the town to organise a section of the International, and drummed up subscriptions through the radical press to sustain the strike.[23] In December 1869 Varlin gathered sixty trade unions in Paris into a Chambre fédérale des sociétés ouvrières, twenty of which affiliated to the International, and in April 1870 had a central part in forming a Fédération des sections parisiennes of the International, which protested vigorously against the outbreak of the Franco–Prussian war.[24]

During the siege of Paris, the capital was left without effective government and became a cauldron of revolution. Members of the International not only had a significant presence in the revolutionary institutions thrown up in Paris, but they also printed their own federalist patterns onto them. Vigilance committees sprang up alongside mayors in each *arrondissement* (Varlin in charge in the sixth, Malon in the seventeenth) to keep the mayors on the revolutionary straight and narrow; a central committee for the twenty *arrondissements* was set up which included about fifteen members of the International.[25] Internationalists were probably responsible for grouping the National Guard battalions in a federal organisation, and 16 of the 38 members of the central committee of the National Guard Federation, which was responsible for seizing power on 18 March 1871, were members of the International.[26] When the Paris Commune was elected, 32 of the original 92 councillors were members of the International, but after the resignation of moderates and by-elections on 16 April this figure rose to 42 out of 78, a majority.[27]

The significance of these developments did not go unnoticed in anarchist circles. James Guillaume, apostle of the Jura Federation of sections affiliated to Bakunin's alliance, declared from Geneva:

> The Paris revolution is *federalist*. . . . *Federalism*, in the sense given to it by the Paris Commune and a good many years ago by the great socialist Proudhon . . . is above all the negation of the *nation* and the *state*. . . . But one should not imagine that having abolished states and nationalism federalism leads to absolute individualism, isolation, or egoism. No, federalism is socialist, that is to say that under it *solidarity* is inseparable from *liberty*. . . . Let the French people . . . be the initiator of the *federative and social Republic* in 1871 as it proclaimed the rights of man in 1793.[28]

Some of the Commune's key measures did indeed reflect Proudhon's teaching on the organisation of labour and federalism. A decree of 16 April handed over work-shops abandoned by their owners to the workers formed into co-operative associations. At the same time, the Commune showed a Proudhonian deference to private property, refusing to house slum-dwellers in the abandoned homes of the rich, while Charles Beslay, a disciple of Proudhon, was given an armed guard to protect the vaults of the Banque de France, if only to ensure that the National Guard was paid.[29] The Commune's manifesto of 19 April to the people of France dismissed fears that it intended to impose a Terror on the rest of France by proclaiming the 36,000 French communes liberated from the tutelage of centralised administration. But it also countered fears that it wanted to break up the nation by inviting them voluntarily to federate.[30]

The Paris Commune, however, was neither the first proletarian revolution, nor simply an expression of the Proudhonist International. While the main rivals of the Proudhonists in the congresses of the International had been the Marxists, in the Paris Commune they were also Blanquist and Jacobin republicans. Jean Allemance, a Communard, thought the Commune 'more Jacobin than anarchist'.[31] Blanquists and Jacobins believed in revolutionary political action and in the One and Indivisible Republic. This was demonstrated on 1 May as government forces closed round the city and the Jacobins called for the establishment of a Committee of Public Safety over and above the Commune. They carried the vote against the Internationalists, who protested in no uncertain terms. Gustave Courbet protested against the irrelevance of the language of the first French Revolution, but behind the complaint about language lay a fear of the revival of the Terror and political purges.

> I wish that all titles and words that belong to the Revolution of 89 to 93 were applied only to that period. Today they do not have the same significance and cannot be used with the same accuracy and the same meaning. Terms like *Salut public*, *Montagnards*, *Girondins*, *Jacobins* cannot be used in the socialist republican movement . . . we are like plagiarists, and we are estab-

lishing to our cost a terror that is not of our time. Let us use terms that our own revolution suggests to us.[32]

Unlike in 1793 the dissidents were not purged and returned to take their seats. Unlike in 1793, equally, the Revolution was crushed in a matter of weeks. Some Internationalists such as Varlin died in the blood-bath; others fled into exile in Switzerland or England. The International continued on a European plane, the battle for supremacy continued not by the Proudhonists but by Bakunin and his disciple James Guillaume of the Jura Federation. Guillaume challenged the organisation of the International that Marx, based in London, was seeking to establish, developing an argument that was also transparently about the nature of the future socialist society. The circular sent by the Jura Federation meeting at Sonvillier to the other federations of the International in November 1871 demanded

> the maintenance of the principle of the autonomy of sections which hitherto has been the basis of our organisation. . . . The unity that some want to establish by centralisation and dictatorship we wish to realise by the free federation of autonomous groups.[33]

Guillaume was sent by the Jura Federation to the congress of the International at The Hague mandated to defend the federal principle and abolish the general council and all authority in the International. He was admitted to the congress only to be solemnly expelled. 'I told you so,' he riposted, 'you are authoritarians. You think you have built a Church that is infallible, with a pope commanding total obedience, who hurls excommunications at those who do not share his beliefs.'[34] Like the fourteenth-century Church, the International suffered its own schism. The Jura Federation became the centre of a rival anti-authoritarian International, with support among Italian and Spanish delegates, which was federalist in structure and insisted on a policy of direct action—not political action—on the grounds that the latter only legitimated and reinforced state power. Opposing the German Social Democratic party, the anti-authoritarians clarified their strategy in a motion submitted to the universal socialist congress of Ghent in September 1877:

> We hold it our duty to fight all political parties, whether they are called socialist or not, in the hope that the workers who still march in the ranks of those various parties, enlightened by experience, will open their eyes and leave the political road to take that of *anti-governmental* socialism.[35]

The Battle with Socialism

The repression of the Paris Commune, in which twenty to twenty-five thousand died, was an unambiguous demonstration of state terror. That it was ordered by the president of a democratic Republic strengthened the argument that political action was fruitless, even in a régime based on universal suffrage. The threat of a monarchist restoration momentarily increased the popular standing of the republican party, but after its electoral successes in 1876 and 1877 the party revealed itself to be as bourgeois as any other.

The anarchist response to state repression was direct action to eliminate all forms of authority. Jean Grave, a shoemaker who voted for the only time in the elections of 1877, joined forces with some former Communards to form an anarchist group based in the popular fifth and thirteenth *arrondissements* of Paris. He launched a paper called *Le Révolté*, telling a labour conference in 1880 that dynamite was preferable to the ballot-box.[36] Dr Paul Brousse, an anarchist and member of the International who had been involved in a wave of municipal revolutions in the first Spanish republic, and had tried to seize control of the town hall of Barcelona, saw the socialist future in terms of a federation of communes and workers' organisations. He campaigned vehemently to expose, in the light of the Commune, the fiction of popular sovereignty and the uselessness of universal suffrage. He told the workers that if they were elected to parliament like Tolain, like him, 'you would have to observe the massacre of your brothers, the murder of your friends, impassive on your bench'.[37] 'Don't forget', he warned voters during the election campaign of 1877, 'that among those you would elect to office will be those whom your brothers elected in 1870 [*sic*], and those men massacred or endorsed the massacre of your brothers in May 1871!'[38]

The labour movement, smashed after the Commune, gradually began to recover with national workers' congresses in Paris in October 1876, in Lyon in February 1878 and in Marseille in October 1879. The rules laid down were that only working men were permitted to speak and vote, and there would be no discussion of politics. The memory of the defeat of the Commune was in every delegate's mind, but no direct reference was made to it until the congress of 1879. At Lyon Bellèle, delegate of the Paris shoemakers, denounced the bourgeoisie, saying that 'the time had come to break openly and underscore the division by exercising ourselves as producers, as wage-workers, as proletarians and as dispossessed, quite determined to pursue the task of Revolution'.[39] One of the achievements of the Lyon congress was to launch a paper entitled *Prolétaire* (renamed *Prolétariat* in 1884).

Repression had served to give French workers a collective identity as an excluded proletariat. The issue for anarchists, however, was whether they could steer the workers away from political action to direct action. James Guillaume was pleased to note after the Paris congress that 'this movement is anti-governmental, anti-*étatiste*'.[40] At the congress of Lyon in 1878 Ballivet, the engineers' delegate, speaking for the French federation of the International, reiterated the illusory nature of democracy in a bourgeois state. 'The day the workers look like laying a finger on their economic privileges,' he said, 'there is no law they will not break, no vote they will not fiddle, no prisons they will not

build, no witch-hunt they will not organise, no massacre they will not plan.'[41]
The majority of the congress nevertheless felt that in the new Republic they
should not pass up the chance to elect working-class candidates, and this they
endorsed, to the chagrin of James Guillaume.

Guillaume's opinion of the Lyon congress, that it was 'decidedly reactionary', betrays what would become a common view among some anarchists, that
the labour movement was too confined to its own immediate concerns to be
susceptible to anarchist propaganda.[42] It also betrays an inability on the part of
anarchists to distinguish in the labour movement a hatred of oppression and an
acceptance of authority and law. Government repression in 1871 was one thing,
but the opportunity presented by universal suffrage in a democratic republic
was generally considered by workers to be quite another. Moreover, Marxists
were observing the re-emergence of the French labour movement with antici-
pation, hoping to gain acceptance for the formation of a workers' party. At the
congress of Marseille Jean Lombard, a jeweller, said,

> What we must consider first and foremost is the foundation of a workers'
> state. The Fourth Estate must free itself and replace the Third Estate which
> today is so powerful. The usefulness of organising a workers' party, which
> would be entirely separate from all the political parties, and would bring
> together all proletarians . . . is thus demonstrated and proven.[43]

The Parti Ouvrier was sold to the Marseille congress on behalf of Jules Guesde,
who was not a delegate and did not speak to it. Guesde himself was a former
anarchist who had been secretary to the Sonvillier congress of the Jura Federation which had so roundly condemned Marx's position. Converted to Marxism
by German émigrés in Paris in 1876, he had been sensitive enough about the
anarchist view of politics to present the argument that though the Parti Ouvrier
sought political power in a workers' state, the means by which it operated had
none of the self-seeking and trickery of bourgeois parties, and was therefore not
in that sense political. 'Against the political parties', Guesde said, 'it is necessary, indispensable even, to create a workers' party that is *not political but
socialist*, which will cast aside those ambitious for office and seek practical ways
of improving the producers' lot.'[44]

Marx kept himself very much in the background, confiding to a friend, 'I do
not have to tell you—for you know French chauvinism—that the hidden
strings which have set the leaders in motion have to remain *between ourselves*.'[45]
But Guesde's trip to London in May 1880 to draw up an election manifesto for
the Parti Ouvrier with Marx and his son-in-law, Paul Lafargue, did not go
unnoticed. Just as Guesde had been converted from anarchism to Marxism, so
Paul Brousse was forced to reconsider his position on political action if he were
to stand any chance of preventing the Parti Ouvrier becoming committed to
wholesale nationalisation, which would reinforce the power of the state, and
subordinated to centralised direction from London. Brousse argued that if the

autonomy of communes could be obtained and socialists were elected to social-
ise municipal services, electoralism would be justified as 'propaganda by deed'
in the shape of model socialist municipalities.[46]

Brousse was also intent on challenging Guesde on the organisation of the
party itself. At the Reims congress of the Parti Ouvrier in 1881, he managed to
win a majority for the autonomy of each regional federation of the party and the
right of constituency parties to draft their own manifestoes.[47] Guesde and
Lafargue refused to accept this, and writing in *Égalité* accused Brousse of
opportunism and 'possibilism'. The show-down came at the Saint-Étienne
congress of the party in 1882. Echoing Guillaume's anti-Catholic rhetoric,
Brousse attacked 'Marxist authoritarianism' and spoke of the Guesdists as 'the
ultramontanes of socialism' . . . adding, 'the Marxists cannot obey the party's
decisions because their leader is in London'. They were 'the Marxist
Capuchins of the socialist workers' state'.[48] A motion was passed to expel
the Guesdists on the grounds that 'they have tried to impose on the party the
specific programme, type of organisation and strategy of a coterie, for the
benefit of the same "Marxist" domination that disrupted the International'.[49]
The Guesdists left for Roanne to found the Parti Ouvrier as an orthodox
Marxist party, while the Broussist majority christened their party the
Fédération des Travailleurs socialistes de France (FTSF).

The road of electoralism was a slippery one, however, even for socialist
parties. Brousse's party met with success, winning nine seats on the Paris
municipal council in 1887, and two seats in Paris in the legislative elections of
1889. But to win seats, it had to agree to second-ballot deals with bourgeois
parties, and therefore sinned on the question of class struggle as well as on that
of political action. Though the Broussist politicians argued that such alliances
were required to defend the Republic against the threat of Boulangism, militants who felt abandoned by the politicians were quick to wheel out the myth
of the Commune in order to discredit such a betrayal of principles. Jean
Allemane, who in many ways embodied the conscience of the Commune, called
for an end to alliances with bourgeois parties and a return to class struggle,
'those ideas of the emancipation of the workers by the workers themselves'.[50] At
the FTSF congress of Châtellerault in 1890, he insisted that if the political road
were still to be followed, socialist politicians had to be disciplined by the
imperative mandate, a ban on office-holding, and the possibility of recall not by
the constituency party but by the regional federation. For this intransigence,
Allemane and his friends were expelled from the Broussist party and founded
the Parti Ouvrier Socialiste Révolutionnaire (POSR). But in the long term, the
Allemanists sought to abandon political action for direct action, and began to
feel their way towards the position that for the labour movement the ideal
strategy was not the stick of dynamite but the general strike.[51]

The year 1891 compounded the experiences of 1831, 1834, 1848 and 1871 in
the annals of the Terror of the bourgeois state. On May Day of that year, ten
textile workers demonstrating in the northern textile town of Fourmies were

gunned down by the military. At another demonstration that day at Clichy, anarchists unfurled the black flag and the police opened fire. The sentencing of the Clichy anarchists provoked a wave of anarchist attacks and violent repression by the government. Ravachol, as François Koenigstein was better known, who tried to blow up the apartments of the judges in the Clichy trial, was executed in July 1892, and at once became a folk hero. Auguste Vaillant, who threw a bomb into the Chamber of Deputies on 9 December 1893, was executed the following February. Émile Henry, a student who bombed a restaurant in the Gare Saint-Lazare, was executed in May 1894. A month later Sadi Carnot, the president of the Republic, was stabbed to death in his carriage in Lyon by an Italian anarchist.

The anarchist movement was not only composed of bomb-throwers. There was a flourishing underground anarchist press. Jean Grave launched *La Révolte* in 1887. Sébastien Faure, the Jesuit-educated son of a Bordeaux merchant, joined the Parti Ouvrier in Bordeaux, but converted to anarchism when he moved to Paris in 1888 and became a leading theorist of anarchism. It was to Faure that Vaillant entrusted his daughter for guardianship before his execution.[52] Émile Pouget, the orphan of a highways official in the Rouergue who as a boy had been greatly moved by the trial of the Narbonne Communards in Rodez, espoused anarchism in Paris and launched the scurrilous *Père Peinard*, modelled on the *Père Duchesne*, in 1889.[53] These intellectuals also felt the weight of government repression, as a series of bills was hurried through in 1893–4 to criminalise anarchist propaganda and associate anarchist publicists with anarchist attacks.[54] Sébastien Faure and Jean Grave were among those put on trial in the notorious 'Procès des Trente' in August 1894, while Pouget escaped to London. The trial, however, was a fiasco. The accused were acquitted and the only result was a renaissance of the anarchist press. Grave founded *Les Temps nouveaux*, Faure launched *Le Libertaire* with Louise Michel at the end of 1895, while Pouget returned to start up *Père Peinard* in 1896.

For the moment, the anarchist sub-culture remained independent of the labour movement. Guesde's Parti Ouvrier was able to gain effective control of the textile unions of northern France and of the central organisation of category federations, the Fédération Nationale des Syndicats, set up in 1886. Guesde regarded the trade unions as an extension of the party, and as a way of corralling working-class votes for the higher political goal of the conquest of power. He dismissed Vaillant's bomb attack as 'quite monstruous. The act of a madman . . . socialism will succeed only by law and the peacefully expressed will of all peoples.'[55] Neither did he approve of strike action, which smacked of the autonomy of the labour movement. Rather, from 1890 he organised May Day demonstrations, which had been popularised by the American Federation of Labour and endorsed by the two Internationals that met in Paris in 1889. Street demonstrations appeared to be an excellent means of propaganda in the labour movement, which thus remained under the control of the party.[56] Guesde's strategy seemed to pay off. In the local elections of 1892 socialists gained a majority on twenty-three municipal councils while in the parliamentary elections of 1893 they won forty-eight seats; Guesde himself was elected in the textile town of Roubaix.

The labour movement, however, was a long way from being under the overall control of Guesde. The Bourses du Travail, clusters of unions of all trades in the same town and formally labour exchanges, quickly became local centres of trade-union activity which were much more resistant to the orders of the Parti Ouvrier.[57] In 1890 the Allemanists took control of the Paris Bourse and in 1892 gathered ten Bourses, mostly from the south of France, into a Fédération des Bourses du Travail. At their congress of 1891 they continued to endorse political action as a means of agitation and propaganda but placed much more emphasis on direct action. 'It is necessary to envisage the possibility of a vast rising of workers who, through the general strike, both national and international, will sanction partial strikes and assert more energetically their right to life'.[58]

In the same year Bourses were founded at Nantes and Saint-Nazaire by Guesdists who, at the grass-roots, did not share the same hostility as their leader to strike action. Fernand Pelloutier, the young Guesdist at the Bourse of Saint-Nazaire, who had been expelled from a seminary for writing an anticlerical novel and was election agent to Aristide Briand (then an extremist) in the 1889 elections, became a leading organiser and ideologist of the Bourse du Travail movement. He understood that the rôle of the Bourses was not only to unionise workers and support strikes but also educational, to realise Proudhon's teachings of *séparatisme ouvrier* and *capacité politique*, acquainting the proletariat with 'la science de son malheur' and enabling it to take its place in the future socialist society. His father, a post office worker, was moved to Meaux and then Paris to interrupt his son's revolutionary activities, but this only served Fernand's career; in 1895 he was elected secretary-general of the Fédération des Bourses du Travail.[59]

The Allemanists, having consolidated the Fédération des Bourses, sought to wrest the Fédération Nationale des Syndicats from the Guesdists. Their secret weapon was the general strike, which they considered to be the modern strategy of revolution, but which was anathema to Guesde and his notions of political action and party control. The argument that electoral success was illusory if the bourgeoisie resorted to force the moment its economic privileges were threatened was reinforced by the government's sudden closure of the Paris Bourse du Travail in July 1893, a month before the elections. Victory came at the Nantes congress of the Fédération Nationale des Syndicats in September 1894, when the motion in favour of the principle of the general strike was carried by 63 votes to 36. Guesde's federation was destroyed and replaced in 1895 by a new organisation of category federations, the Confédération Générale du Travail (CGT). Pelloutier kept the Fédération des Bourses separate from the CGT but provided guidance for the whole movement with his pamphlet *Ou'est-ce que la grève générale?* in which he demonstrated the fruitlessness of political action, either electoral or insurrectionary, and argued that a general strike would both paralyse the capitalist economy and swamp the military.[60]

Having shaken off the control of Guesde's Parti Ouvrier, the rising stars of the labour movement seized the opportunity to bring the anarchists, champions of direct action, into their midst. Pelloutier addressed a letter to anarchists in Grave's *Temps nouveaux*, arguing that they should abandon dynamite and look to the unions for support for their ideas. The unions, once regarded as nurseries of aspiring deputies, now felt so betrayed by their deputies that they were turning away from political action. They were not only, Pelloutier told the anarchists, the new levers of revolution, they were the schools of the proletariat and the cells of the libertarian society of which anarchists dreamed.

> Suppose that the day revolution breaks out almost all producers are organised into unions. Would it not constitute a quasi-libertarian organisation ready to take over from the present system, effectively abolishing all political power. . . . Would it not be 'the free association of free producers'?[61]

If anarchists needed a prompt to become involved in the labour movement, and resume the struggle against the Marxists, it was provided by their expulsion from the Second Socialist International, which was dominated by the Marxist German Social Democratic party. The Zürich congress of the International in August 1893 voted the exclusion of all groups who did not subscribe to political action, in other words, anarchists. This ruling was reaffirmed at the London congress of the International in July–August 1896. The anarchist Paul Delesalle, who had been brought up at Issy on stories of the Paris Commune and had worked on Grave's *Temps nouveaux*, was a witness of the proceedings. In terms reminiscent of Guillaume and Brousse, he described the domination of the congress by 'Marx's Family', which included Aveling in London, Bebel and Liebknecht from Germany and Lafargue from France, and the struggle between 'authoritarian Marxists and revolutionary socialists' in the French delegation, which resulted in the expulsion of the latter.[62]

Pelloutier was not able to cause the mouths of all anarchists to water. Some, like Sébastien Faure, continued to see trade unions as the bureaucratic tools of a labour aristocracy serving only their material interests, not the vehicle of universal liberation. Others were convinced. Delesalle became assistant secretary to Pelloutier at the Fédération des Bourses in 1897 and continued under the anarchist Yvetot when Pelloutier died in 1901. Victor Griffuelhes, general secretary of the CGT, was a Blanquist with anarchist leanings; its treasurer, Albert Lévy, was an Allemanist. Pouget became editor of the CGT paper launched in 1900, *La Voix du Peuple*, which paid homage to Proudhon by taking its name from Proudhon's paper of 1849–50.

Having taken such a strong position in the labour movement, anarchists, or as they were now called, anarcho-syndicalists, had to fight to keep the movement independent of political parties and in particular of the Socialist party. This was no easy task at the time of the Dreyfus affair, when anarchists like

Sébastien Faure were throwing themselves into the Dreyfusard campaign in order to attack the crimes of the military, and the Guesdist and Jaurésist tendencies of socialism, initially divided by the affair, began to find their way to unity and to political power in the ruling republican coalition. Pelloutier wrote a second letter to anarchists in December 1899, warning them of the danger of unions falling under the yoke of a socialist party that was becoming more parliamentarian, even counter-revolutionary. He urged anarchists who believed in

> the revolutionary mission of the enlightened proletariat to pursue more actively, more methodically, more obstinately than ever the work of moral, administrative and technical education necessary to make viable a society of free men.[63]

The achievement of Pelloutier, who died tragically young in 1901, was not only to bring anarchist militants into the labour movement but to put at the movement's service the mythic power of Proudhon and the First International. He reactivated Proudhon's memory, and urged that working people should be educated in the science of society if they were to preserve freedom, once obtained, from the will to power of politicians and the state. Moreover, since the Second International had shown itself to be authoritarian and centralised, a coalition of national socialist parties, he held up the First International, in the anti-authoritarian and decentralised version constructed by the Proudhonists and Bakunists, as a model for the organisation of the French labour movement. Delesalle wrote poignantly of Pelloutier in his obituary that 'he was haunted by the beautiful workers' movement that was the *International*, he dreamed of reorganising it, making it stronger, more powerful, pure of the filth and compromise of politics, with its own existence, by and for the workers'.[64]

Pelloutier was dead, but the power of this myth served to shape the future development of the CGT. His continuator in the first instance was Émile Pouget. Pouget was initially sceptical of the ability of the 'unconscious' and 'human zeros' of the labour movement to grasp anarcho-syndicalist principles. But at the Congress of Bourges in 1904 he achieved two victories. First, to ensure the supremacy of an enlightened minority so dear to the anarchists, he established the rule of one union, one vote against the proportional representation demanded by the large reformist unions, empowering small, dynamic unions against the bloc vote for conservatism. Second, he committed the CGT to the principle of the general strike in the teeth of the Guesdist textile unions, which still opposed it. The eight-hour day was chosen as the object of a general strike scheduled for 1 May 1906, leaving ample time for revolutionary propaganda and organisation. 'Direct action', he said, 'is not just giving work to glaziers. It is the affirmation that from now on workers intend to count on themselves alone, and not on some messiah from without, to improve their condition and stride towards their complete liberation.'[65] Pouget was in no doubt about why the congress had followed his lead. 'The congress', he wrote, 'came out in favour of counting only on the energy and vigour of the workers, inspired by the precepts of the *International Working Mens' Association*.'[66]

The endorsement of the principle of the general strike was a sharp defeat for the Socialist party. It seemed to be legitimated in 1905, when the Russian Revolution took the form of a general strike. 'Direct action and general strike in Russia,' proclaimed Kropotkin in *Les Temps nouveaux*.[67] When the general strike was due in France on 1 May 1906, the Guesdists argued that since a general election was scheduled for 6 May it would be more sensible to wait for a few days and take political power at the polls, without loss of blood.[68] But the general strike went ahead, its brutal repression by the soldiers of Clemenceau only serving to reinforce the argument that the labour movement should have nothing to do with politics or politicians. The CGT thus formally affirmed the independence of the trade-union movement at the congress of Amiens in October 1906. A text drafted by Griffuelhes established that while individual trade unionists were free to vote in elections, the trade-union movement as such declared its independence of political parties. This resolution, known as the Charter of Amiens, subsequently acquired mythical status in the labour movement. The Socialist party meeting at Limoges the following month was much put out. Guesdists accused anarchists of undertaking anti-socialist propaganda in the unions. But Gustave Hervé wisely reminded the congress, 'Alongside the socialist current there is an anti-parliamentarian, federalist, libertarian or anarchist current that dates from the beginning of the International, and which will continue, because it is not a matter of doctrine but one of temperament.'[69]

It was not only those involved in the movement who claimed the authority of Proudhon and the First International for the separatism of the labour movement. Others, writing for the approaching centenary of Proudhon's birth in 1909, contributed to the elaboration of a cult status for Proudhon. Eugène Fournière, an early collaborator of Jean Grave, said that 'the International was the work of the worker-disciples of Proudhon as much as it was the authentic expression of his thought'.[70] Édouard Droz, university professor at Proudhon's native Besançon, stated that 'the time has come completely to *resurrect* Proudhon, whose thought, so French, is better adapted to our labour movement than that of Marx'. Pelloutier had been inspired by Proudhon, and 'the Confédération Générale du Travail was for the most part created by Proudhon himself and by his disciples'.[71]

The homage payed to Proudhon by both the labour movement and historians had the effect of attracting a new generation of anarchists to the CGT. Pierre Monatte, the son of an Auvergne blacksmith who became a printer and fell under the spell of Pouget, was brought by Pouget onto the Comité confédéral of the CGT. Monatte observed that 'it was not very difficult to crush the poor Guesdists of the Nord' at the congress of Amiens, but his task was then to convince an anarchist congress at Amsterdam that the place of anarchists was in the labour movement.[72] He found himself pitted against the veteran anarchist Malatesta who argued that trade unions were bureaucratic and conservative, and that in any case it was the task of anarchists not just to emancipate one class in one way, but all of humanity, economically, politically and morally. Monatte asserted that the labour movement had reached its present revolutionary syndicalist position by virtue of the work and inspiration of the anarchists of the First International, and that anarchists could not now abandon it.

> The motto of the International, you remember, was: 'the emancipation of the workers will be the task of the workers themselves',— and it is still the motto of all of us, advocates of direct action and enemies of parliamentarism. The ideas of autonomy and federation so much in favour among us once inspired all those Internationalists who rebelled against the General Council's abuse of power and openly took Bakunin's side after the congress of The Hague. Even more, the very idea of the general strike which is so popular today was an idea of the International, which first understood the force contained within it.[73]

In 1908 Monatte collaborated with anarcho-syndicalists such as Pouget, Delesalle and Griffuelhes on a paper called *Action Directe*. The following year he founded a fortnightly review, *La Vie ouvrière*, which was intended to serve as an organ of debate and education for anarchists and trade unionists who subscribed to revolutionary syndicalism. James Guillaume, now aged 65, re- turned from long years of silence to contribute to the enterprise. Since the anti- authoritarian International had dissolved in 1878, he had accepted the patronage of his Swiss friend Ferdinand Buisson and lived as a scholar, helping with the *Dictionnaire de Pédagogie* and then editing the archives of the Comité de l'Instruction publique for the commission publishing the documents of the French Revolution. The return of the labour movement, as he saw it, to the principles of the International, persuaded him back into the world of anarchist debate, to impart his reading of the International to the rising generation of anarcho-syndicalists. 'I am delighted by the harmony that is so close between the ideas of militants of two different generations,' he told Pouget.[74] He was welcomed as 'the ghost of the time of Proudhon and Bakunin, just as Buonarotti was the ghost of the time of Babeuf'.[75] 'Once again we saw him in our groups', wrote one anarchist, 'the ancestor, who had departed; we heard his clear and warm words in our meetings, and found his signature in our papers and reviews.'[76]

Guillaume's most substantial contribution was to publish four volumes of documents on the First International between 1905 and 1910. In the final volume he paid homage to the present labour movement. 'What is the Confédération Générale du Travail', he asked, 'if not the continuation of the International?'[77] Again, he said in a letter to Monatte, 'true syndicalism (that is to say, that of the CGT, *which is that of the old International*), is *all-inclusive* and *self-sufficient*.[78] In addition, Guillaume contributed to a broad debate in the period before the First World War on the anarchist heritage of anarcho-syndicalism, and thus to the redefinition of its collective memory and political culture. He was keen to rehabilitate Eugène Varlin, the apostle of the International who came to be portrayed as the precursor of trade-unionism and prophet of the new libertarian society; his martyrdom in the Commune and his bearded portrait conferred a Christ-like symbolism on him.[79] He did much for the reputation of Bakunin, writing an introduction to his works in 1907.[80] The centenary of Bakunin's birth in 1914 was given full coverage in *La Vie ouvrière*.[81] Lastly, Guillaume campaigned with other anarchists and anarcho-syndicalists to rehabilitate Proudhon, and in particular to underline his anti-authoritarian position. In an exchange of letters with Monatte in 1911, he quoted Proudhon's maxim that 'Between the political and economic order, between the régime of laws and that of contracts, there can be no compromise'; and he reasserted that 'Proudhon was an anti-authoritarian, anti-statist communist, a federalist communist'.[82]

The Battle with Communism

Penetration of the labour movement by anarchist ideas was remarkably successful before 1914. The collective memory of anarcho-syndicalists, shaped by repeated repression by the bourgeois state, paid homage to their founding fathers, Proudhon and Bakunin, Varlin and Pelloutier. The experience of the Great War undermined much of this achievement. Anarcho-syndicalists who saw in the CGT the reincarnation of the First International were bitterly disappointed by its performance in August 1914. Instead of launching a general strike to stop the war and overturn capitalism, the CGT rallied to the defence of the state and co-operated with employers to ensure the war effort. The CGT was under pressure from both above and below. In return for its renunciation of the general strike the government withdrew the order to arrest those leaders who were filed in the interior ministry's Carnet B, and equally the CGT managed to retain its influence over the masses. 'If the CGT had wished to stand in the way of the war or refused to participate in national defence', Alphonse Merrheim told the congress of Lyon in September 1919, 'the Parisian working class, carried away by a massive attack of patriotism, would not have waited for the gendarmes but have shot us all on the spot.'[83]

The consequence of this was twofold. Anarchists who had always harboured suspicions about the revolutionism of the labour movement had their prejudices confirmed, and persisted with well-tried forms of direct action. Conversely, anarcho-syndicalists who had achieved influence in the CGT before 1914 now lost it, first to the reformists who had followed the governmental line, then to the Communists who launched a second Marxist offensive within the labour movement. They clung to their collective memory of the First International and the Charter of Amiens, but the political culture based on it looked increasingly rigid and irrelevant.

Individualist anarchists went their own way, not without scornful backward glances at the CGT. Louis Lecoin, released from prison and ordered to join up, refused and paid a visit to Gustave Hervé, renegade socialist and leading chauvinist, to shoot him, only to find he was out.[84] A certain Cottin, who tried to assassinate the warmonger Clemenceau in 1919, at least fired and missed. *Le Libertaire* of Sébastien Faure (on which Lecoin returned to work after another spell in prison) was scathing about the CGT's performance.

> Where are the Varlins of yester-year? . . . What would Bakunin think? . . . Can we without anger compare support for the capitalist war, Jouhaux's speech of 4 August 1914, and close collaboration with the government . . . with the class struggle, direct action and the general strike, those tactics of the revolutionary CGT of 1st May 1906?[85]

Those who converted to anarchism in this period were impatient with the trade-union movement. René Michaud, a young worker who experienced his first strike in the Paris munitions industry in 1917, and found Marcel Cachin's *L'Humanité* too tame, started to read the anarchist press. 'While trade-union activity made it possible to dispute conditions of work,' he wrote, 'it was confined in the short term to this world [and] was not enough to satisfy my aspiration towards a better world.'[86] In the great demonstration of 1 May 1919 [Fig. 23] Michaud left the red flag of the shoemakers' union for the black flag of the anarchists, which provoked a police charge; he found his way back to the headquarters of *Libertaire* and joined the Jeunesses anarchistes. 'All victims of authority deserved our solidarity', he believed, including those court-martialled during the war and the Black Sea mutineers.[87] He flourished among anarchists who were 'fiery, impatient to do something to stir up the crowd', and took Ravachol, Vaillant, Henry and Cottin as his models.[88]

Of course, the CGT was not united in its wartime espousal of nationalism and class collaboration in the Union sacrée. Its deviation from historic principles provoked attacks on the leadership from assorted minorities seeking to develop their influence in the labour movement. While the CGT betrayed them, they took inspiration from revolutionary events in Russia, which they constructed in their early stages not as the triumph of the Bolshevik party over the working class, but as a libertarian or anarcho-syndicalist revolution. There was some evidence for this interpretation of events. Captain Jacques Sadoul, who was attached to the cabinet of Albert Thomas, the socialist minister of munitions, was sent to join a French military mission in the Russian Republic in October 1917. 'More and more I discover here some of the essential ideas advocated for many a long year by some French trade unionists', he wrote to Thomas in January 1918.[89] Forty-six years later, at a conference to mark the centenary of Proudhon's death, Georges Gurvitch, who spoke as one of the organisers of the Russian soviets in 1917, affirmed

Fig. 23.   Police charging demonstration of May 1, 1919 (Roger-Viollet)

The first Russian soviets were organised by Proudhonians, drawn from the Left SRs or from the left wing of Russian social democracy. They could not have taken the idea of a revolution by grass-roots soviets from Marx, because that is an essentially, exclusively Proudhonian idea.[90]

This sort of interpretation was taken up by dissident elements in the CGT, who were eager to build a bridge to libertarians and to mount a challenge to the CGT leadership. Early in 1917 Raymond Péricat set up a Comité de Défense Syndicaliste to campaign for a general strike in response to the strikes in Russia to demand an immediate peace. He launched *L'Internationale* (later renamed the *Internationale communiste* in February 1919) and renamed his committee the Communist party (French Section of the Communist International) the following May. After the peace, Péricat's aim was to present a libertarian interpretation of the Russian Revolution, and to convert the strike movements of the spring of 1919 into a general revolution. On both counts, however, he failed.[91]

The anarcho-syndicalists grouped around *La Vie ouvrière*—Pierre Monatte, Alfred Rosmer and Maurice Chambelland—were equally desirous to construct the Russian Revolution as a revolution that legitimated their doctrines. Monatte had been called up, and resigned from the Comité confédéral of the

CGT in December 1914. Rosmer, a militant in the public employees' union, became involved in preparations for the Zimmerwald congress in 1915, favouring not just peace but revolutionary defeatism, like Lenin.[92] Meditating on the failure of the trade union bureaucracies at the bottom of a trench in 1917, Monatte decided that the regeneration of the labour movement would have to come from 'a minority clear-sighted before it claimed to be active', which would educate itself and then organise militant cells within each union. This strategy of enlightened militants operating within the labour movement seemed to be legitimated by events in Russia. 'What is the Russian Revolution then if not a revolution of a syndicalist nature?' asked Monatte and his comrades, as they admired the factory committees, trade unions and soviets thrown up by a series of general strikes.[93] Events seemed to disprove the Marxist thesis that revolution must be undertaken by a political party. 'The Bolshevik coup d'état in November was only the last touch required to switch power from the hands of the organisations of the bourgeoisie to those of the workers,' affirmed *La Vie ouvrière.*[94]

While CGT leaders continued a policy of class collaboration and governmentalism, and clung to the remnants of the International that had gone up in flames in 1914, those who seriously wanted revolution replied to the formation of Moscow-based Comintern by setting up a Comité de la IIIe Internationale. Though led by hardline socialists, it included anarchists like Péricat and revolutionary syndicalists like Monatte and Rosmer. Monatte made no excuse for trying to undermine the International from which they had been expelled on the orders of Marxists in 1896. 'We revolutionary syndicalists', he said, have forgotten nothing.'[95] They certainly hoped that the Third International would revive some of the promise of the First, which they held so dear.

The revolutionary syndicalists' plan was to secure a majority within the CGT and affiliate it to the Comintern or, more precisely, to its trade-union wing, the Internationale Syndicale Rouge (ISR) that was established at Moscow in July 1921. They perfected the art of entryism, forming Comités Syndicalistes Révolutionnaires (CSR) within the major unions from the summer of 1919 to push them towards a more revolutionary strategy. A wave of strikes gripped France in the spring of 1920, but did not tip the country into revolution, largely because the grass roots movement was resisted by the union bosses and the CGT leadership. Monatte was arrested for threatening the security of the state and sent for trial. *La Vie ouvrière* characterised the trial as 'the trial of the great strike of May 1920 and the trial of communism and the Third International' and divined revolutionary portents. 'On the eve of every revolutionary upheaval,' it warned, 'trials of this kind have multiplied. There was a whole series in the last years of the Empire. The Paris section of the International endured three of them.'[96] Monatte was thus cast in the rôle of a Varlin or a Malon, and France was said to be on the eve of another Commune.

This was not to be. The showdown at the Lille congress of the CGT in July 1921 did not go their way. The executive wanted to deal with the revolutionaries and expel those unions affiliated to the CSR. Monatte riposted that 'thanks to its present executive and its present policies, the CGT has turned its back on revolution' and in terms reminiscent of Pouget he defended the CSR as 'groupings of yesterday's clear-sighted and active minorities, the force that can electrify our unions'.[97] He went on to declare that the CGT should not affiliate to the Second International based at Amsterdam, denouncing it as 'nationalist Amsterdam, class-collaboration Amsterdam, the politicians' Amsterdam'.[98] He further stated:

> What we want is an International that does better than the two Internationals, and particularly the trade-union International, did on 2 August 1914. . . . The International we need, the trade-union International, can have its headquarters nowhere other than Moscow. . . . We intend to go there, we hope to go there, we are sure to be going there (*Applause*) while retaining our revolutionary syndicalist idea.[99]

For all their efforts, Monatte and his followers failed to gain a majority in the CGT (1,348 votes to 1,556), and the CGT divided, with Monatte and other opponents of the leadership forming the Confédération Générale du Travail Unifié (CGTU).

Although the formation of the CGTU was precipated by Monatte's actions, it became a battleground for supremacy between revolutionary syndicalists and Communists who wanted to impose an orthodox Marxist-Leninist line on the labour movement. And whereas the struggle in 1904–6 was won by the revolutionary syndicalists, in 1921–3 victory went to the Communists.

Monatte and his friends were keen to affiliate to Moscow as the epicentre of the triumphant international proletarian revolution. But they failed to see that the initial confused phase of the Russian Revolution had now given way to the stern imposition of Bolshevik party control over the organised working class. In June 1921 Monatte republished a text of Guillaume, written in 1876, in which he described the future socialist society as a federation of both communes and groups of production.[100] But the Bolsheviks had no time for this kind of idealism. The first congress of the Internationale Syndicale Rouge, held in Moscow in July 1921, established that the ISR would be subordinated to the Comintern and trade unions subordinated to Communist parties. When the French delegation under Rosmer protested, they were criticised by Zinoviev for coming 'in 1921 with the same perspective as in 1906'.[101] Trotsky wrote to Monatte, appreciating the traditional aversion of the French labour movement to parties and politics but insisting that the future revolution in France required strong political leadership. 'The true avant-garde of the French proletariat', he explained, 'must form a coherent whole in order to accomplish its historical task, the conquest of power, and pursue its strategy in the unions, which are the basic and decisive organisation of the whole working class, under this flag.'[102] Monatte, who continued to think that the ISR might change its rules replied that in France 'syndicalism . . . is big enough to lead itself, and recruits its leaders from the once and future clear-sighted and active minorities, who include all revolutionary workers whatever their political label. . . . It will not follow those leaders who want to revive Guesdism and proclaim that the Party is the eyes and head of a blind body, meaning the unions'.[103]

The ISR kept up the pressure, warning the revolutionary syndicalists that if it fought separetely from the Communist party they would be beaten separately.[104] Monatte initially gave ground, leaving *La Vie ouvrière* for a post on *L'Humanité* at the beginning of 1922, and finally joined the Communist party in October 1923. He was happy with the decision of the CGTU at the Saint-Étienne congress of July 1922 to affiliate to the ISR. But increasingly it became clear that the Russian Communist party was completely in control of both the Comintern and the ISR. At the CGTU congress of Bourges in November 1923 the Communists passed a motion rejecting 'the thesis of entirely self-sufficient "trade-unionism above everything"' and insisting that 'trade-unionism must work together with all other revolutionary forces [that is, the Communist party] to accomplish its mission'.[105] The independence of the trade-union movement, a sacred principle to anarcho-syndicalists, was finished. Monatte left *L'Humanité* and distanced himself from the ruling group of the French Communist party, though he remained a member. In the summer of 1924, he was invited to the congresses of the ISR and Comintern on the grounds that he was 'the only leading French Communist who had not yet visited Soviet Russia', but he turned down the invitation.[106] As a result, Monatte and Rosmer were marginalised by the PCF leadership, accused first of being on the Right, then of '*ouvriérist* neo-gauchism'. In reply Monatte and Rosmer attacked the Bolshevisation of the party.

> From top to bottom of the party cascades a torrent of slogans which has to be obeyed without understanding and above all without murmuring anything but the ritualistic, 'Aye, aye, Captain'. . . . It is said that the party must be an Iron Column, [yet] what is being formed is not an Iron Column but a regiment of slugs.[107]

Monatte, Rosmer and Chambelland were expelled from the party in December 1924 and, having lost control of *La Vie ouvrière*, launched a new monthly, *La Révolution prolétarienne*. Nevertheless, they remained within the CGTU trying to recover support for an independent trade-union movement. In the sense that they went with the drift of the revolutionary movement while trying to safeguard principles dear to them, they differed from those who placed purity of principle above everything else and withdrew into sectarianism rather than compromise. This was the case of Pierre Besnard, who had been active in the Comités Syndicalistes Révolutionnaires, who parted company with the CGTU after its first congress in the Bourse du Travail of Saint-Étienne in 1922. He opposed affiliation to the ISR as incompatible with complete trade-union autonomy and, after the defeat of his motion, his supporters shouted, 'Long live Pelloutier, anyway!'[108] Besnard was wedded to the heroic past of the First International, the pre-war CGT and revolutionary general strike. He worshipped at the shrine of Fernand Pelloutier, to whom a monument was erected in the cemetery of Sèvres in September 1924. Around him he gathered unions which shared his views, binding them in the Confédération Générale du Travail Syndicaliste Révolutionnaire (CGTSR), and drafting a charter for them at their founding congress of Lyon in 1926. He quoted the Congress of Amiens to the effect that trade unions were not only instruments of resistance but would also be the basic units of the new socialist society, having eliminated capitalism by a 'general expropriating strike'. The CGTSR affiliated to the Association Internationale des Travailleurs which was now based in Berlin, proclaiming 'that this International is the logical continuation of the First International, just as the CGTSR is the continuation of the CGT of 1906, following the failure of the two other CGTs'.[109] This point was underlined by adopting for its newspaper, *Le Combat syndicaliste*, the motto of the First International, 'the emancipation of the workers will be the task of the workers themselves', and drawing on the authority of Bakunin and Guillaume for legitimacy.[110]

The fragmentation of the trade-union movement continued until the growth of the Rassemblement populaire after 1934. Trade-union unity was seen to be a natural concomitant of the electoral alliance of Socialists, Radicals and Communists. The concern of many trade unionists, however, was that trade-union unity would facilitate the extension of Communist hegemony from the CGTU to the newly united CGT. Pierre Besnard, for one, refused to come down from his perch. He was urged by a former member of the CGTSR to bring his anarcho-syndicalists back into the CGT: 'You spoke of Bakunin, of the old Jura Federation, of the manifesto of the First International, telling us they were the charter of the AIT and the CGTSR.' 'But', he added, 'the French trade union movement is steeped in them and we remain in agreement with the thought of Bakunin and James Guillaume.'[111] Besnard was less sanguine, and refused the invitation. In the run-up to the congress of Toulouse of March 1936, which reunited CGTU and CGT, Maurice Chambelland urged that 'Toulouse must not disfigure the trade-union movement in this country . . . It must continue Amiens. It must prolong Amiens.'[112] At the congress itself, he warned against the trade unions endorsing the Popular Front programme of the political parties. The trade unions must remain independent, he said, 'until the moment when, according to the expression of Proudhon, the workshop replaces the government'.[113] Not only did he stick by the independence of the labour movement, he also reiterated, true to Proudhon, his distrust of political action and his dream of a stateless society.

The congress of Toulouse formally endorsed Amiens by voting to ban the holding of CGT office by any officer of a political party. This was aimed in particular at the Communist party. Nevertheless, the ex-CGTU militant Benoît Frachon, an engineer from the Loire department (who incidentally had been an anarchist down to 1920), though he formally resigned his posts on the Central Committee and Political Bureau of the PCF, continued to lunch with party leaders and enabled the PCF effectively to extend its grip over the CGT.[114] Evidence of this can be gauged by the editorial policy of *La Vie ouvrière*, which became a CGT review. Paul Delesalle, once the deputy of Pelloutier and Yvetot, who was full of praise for the portrait of Varlin shown at the exhibition of the Commune in Saint-Denis in 1935, was invited to write four articles for *La Vie ouvrière* on the First International in the period 1867–70. Instead, the review printed an article by Delesalle on the First International during the Commune, and then articles on 1848, the June Days, and the first Guesdist demonstration at Père Lachaise in 1880. What began as a celebration of the First International and direct action became a celebration of political action and Marxism.[115] Pierre Monatte was right to cry out in 1937 that 'the trade unionism of 1906 must not die . . . Woe betide workers who do not keep a ceaseless vigil'.[116]

Anarchists, revolutionary syndicalists and anarcho-syndicalists were extremely concerned to keep their ideological powder dry, but this in no sense helped them to take advantage of the explosion of labour discontent when it occurred. The wave of strikes and factory occupations that swept France in May–June 1936 was the greatest manifestation of working-class direct action since 1906. It was essentially spontaneous in origin, a response to the victory of the Popular Front at the polls, and revolutionaries were quick to point out its significance. The anarchist *Libertaire* applauded the return of direct action, and for once looked favourably on the labour movement, quoting Pelloutier's *Lettre aux anarchistes* of 1899 on the need for anarchists to improve their position in the trade unions.[117] From October 1936, it published a one-sheet supplement entitled *Libertaire syndicaliste*. Pierre Besnard of the CGTSR saw that direct action by the workers removed decision-making from the hands of the politicians and interpreted the factory occupations as a dress-rehearsal for the 'real seizure' of the means of production by the proletariat.[118] Pierre Monatte compared the strikes to the general strike of 1 May 1906, with the gloss that the strike of 1906 had been planned for two years whereas this was 'immediate and spontaneous'.[119] 'And then Wham!' as one of his colleagues put it more sharply, 'revolutionary syndicalism is once again the thing of the moment.'[120]

Whether the strikes of May–June 1936 indeed represented the revival of revolutionary syndicalism is a matter for debate. The demands of the strikers tended to fairly traditional: improved wages, better conditions, the recognition of trade-union rights and collective bargaining. The displacement of employers from the work-place was highly symbolic, but the articulation of demands for workers' control was rare. Moreover, the strikers did not rule out political action in any doctrinaire way; after all, the moment they had chosen was the triumph of the Popular Front parties. For their part, neither the CGT nor the parties of the Left (with few exceptions) were interested in turning a crisis into a revolutionary situation. The main concern of Jouhaux, the CGT leader, who confessed that 'the movement broke out without us really knowing how and where', was to steer the trade unions towards negotiation with the employers and the government in order to secure concrete concessions such as collective contracts and a forty-hour week.[121] Maurice Thorez, the Communist leader, meanwhile, far from supporting the strike action, told workers on 11 June that they must 'know when to end a strike once satisfaction had been obtained'.[122]

The outbreak of revolution in Spain was seized upon by anarchists, with more justification than when they had considered the Russian Revolution, as a largely anarchist revolution. Franco's *pronunciamiento* against the Spanish Republic was met by a popular insurrection, in which both anarchists and anarcho-syndicalists of the CNT took a leading rôle.[123] 'The Spanish Revolution is our revolution!' proclaimed *Le Libertaire* without hesitating.[124] Anarchists immediately began to hold meetings, collect subscriptions and send militants to Spain. But here the opportunity provided by a world-historical event was wasted by the insistence by some anarchists that the doctrines of *séparatisme ouvrier* and direct action could not be negotiated. Thus when Sébastien Faure of the Union Anarchiste began to share platforms with members of bourgeois parties and movements ready to join an anti-fascist Front révolutionnaire, just as he had campaigned in a broad Dreyfusard front, purists in the Union broke away to form the Fédération Anarchiste de Langue Française (FAF), which worked closely with Besnard's CGTSR. More trouble came when Spanish anarchists confronted the dilemma as to whether to accept power in the Republic in order to save it, or whether to stick to their principles and repudiate all political action. The Spanish anarchists decided to accept office in both the Catalan and central governments, throwing French anarchists into more turmoil. Faure's Union anarchiste accepted the decision, but Besnard's CGTSR and, above all, the FAF condemned the CNT for taking the wrong road and for a gross violation of anti-authoritarian principles. While the Union anarchiste was prepared if necessary to make a choice between evils, and to accept that power might on exceptional occasions have to be used in defence of a wider liberty, the purists, while keeping their principles spotless, ended up by having next to no influence on events.[125]

One reason for insisting on principle was to avoid absorption by the Communist party. Communists were always committed to political action, keen to drag bourgeois parties behind them into anti-fascist fronts, and in Spain engaged in a shooting-war behind the republican lines with anarchists and anarcho-syndicalists who did not accept the orthodoxy of the subordination of the organised working class to the party. This problem surfaced again at the Liberation in France, when the Communist party emerged as the largest party at the polls, until 1947 collaborated in government with the SFIO and MRP, and renewed its rivalry with the reformist Jouhaux to establish its hegemony in the CGT. Anarchists and anarcho-syndicalists again fell back on their sacred heroes and traditions to construct an identity that would keep the labour movement safe from seduction by Communism. But again the danger was that they were preserving a cult for its own sake, and would find themselves with less influence than before in the labour movement.

Sébastien Faure had died during the war but the Union anarchiste's *Le Libertaire* reappeared in 1945 to repeat warnings about political action. It campaigned for abstention in the municipal elections, arguing that 'liberty does not lie in the ballot box', and again in elections to the Constituent Assembly, since no French constitution had ever abolished capitalism. 'No constitution! Social revolution!' was its slogan.[126] Without confining themselves to propaganda in the labour movement, the Union Anarchiste insisted that the trade-union movement remain in the tradition of Proudhon and Bakunin, and denounced Jouhaux as 'the most active agent of the liquidation of the syndicalist ideal that was defined by its founders, from Pelloutier to Griffuelhes'.[127]

The return of the Union anarchiste to strict direct action and anti-authoritarianism made possible a merger with the FAF in October 1945, to become the Fédération Anarchiste. Alongside it Besnard revived the CGTSR as the Fédération Syndicaliste Français/Section Française de l'AIT. Then in December 1946, taking to its conclusion his admiration of Spanish anarcho-syndicalists, and drawing on the help of Spanish anarchists in exile, he relaunched it as the CNT. He remained a purist, totally hostile to the Communist attempt to enslave trade unionism, committed to the 'general, insurrectional and expropriating strike' and upheld the Aragonese model as 'the first syndicalist society'.[128] He died prematurely in April 1947 but the CNT republished his 1926 Charter of Lyon word for word as the Charter of Paris (1947), and revived his newspaper, *Le Combat syndicaliste*, with its motto, 'The emancipation of the workers must be the task of the workers themselves'.

Pierre Monatte, on the other hand, was still going strong. He relaunched *La Révolution prolétarienne* in April 1947 and endeavoured to pass on the gospel in two 'Letters from an elder to a few young trade-unionists without stripes'. He warned them that reformism had led to collaboration with every government from the Union sacrée to Vichy and Gaullism, and that Russia, in spite of what Communists told them (and in spite, no doubt, of his own brief membership of the Communist party), was 'no more the country of socialism than Napoleon's France was still the country of the Revolution'; instead, it was controlled by 'the red fascism of Stalin'. He explained that the touchstone of French trade unionism, anathema though it was to Communists, was the Charter of Amiens, which 'embodies separation from the bourgeoisie, from the state and from parties' and 'calls for the integral, real emancipation of labour'.[129] Pelloutier was held up as an inspiration, and Monatte quoted his letter of 1899 to anarchists, urging them 'to pursue more doggedly than ever the task of moral, administrative and technical education to make a society of free men viable'.[130]

The CGT nevertheless once again fell under the domination of the Communists, with a reformist wing that Jouhaux struggled to maintain intact. Under the Communists, direct action was entirely subordinated to political needs: when the PCF wanted a strike, the CGT acted as its transmission belt; when it did not, the CGT opposed action. Crisis arose in April and May 1947 when a wave of strikes in the nationalised industries began at Renault. Renault was a bastion of the CGT, but the CGT was opposed to strike action because the Communist party was part of the Tripartite government. The strike at Renault was thus organised not by the union but by a strike committee. Trotskyists were the leading activists and the strike was supported by anarchists, the CNT and *Révolution prolétarienne*. In May the Communists were expelled from the government and began their long period in the ghetto. Their attitude to strike action changed accordingly and in November 1947 they orchestrated their own strike wave.

This cynicism precipitated the break with Jouhaux's reformists who formed a separate federation, Force Ouvrière. In 1949 Force Ouvrière began to publish the *Cahiers Fernand Pelloutier*, not because Jouhaux had ever been a great supporter of Pelloutier, but because Pelloutier symbolised resistance to Marxist domination. Communist manipulation also outraged anarchists and revolutionary syndicalists. 'When will the lads from Renault, the Marseille dockers, the Pas-de-Calais miners, the Lyon weavers, the state engineering workers realise that the CGT is now only a colony of the Communist general staff, a branch of the Russian headquarters?' asked *Le Libertaire*.[131] Monatte attacked the political purpose of the Communist strikes. 'Strikes to protest at Thorez leaving the government, strikes to annoy Ramadier, strikes to annoy Washington, strikes against accepting the Marshall Plan. . . . All this is far too complicated for an old chap like me who is used to strikes for workers' demands.'[132] And, he might have added, wedded to the principle of the independence of the trade-union movement, however, grim the reality might seem. Commemorating the half-century of the Charter of Amiens, Monatte asked, 'Will there be enough workers in 1956 to restore life to the Charter of Amiens of 1906 and to that of the First International? Let us hope so.'[133]

1968

The events of 1968 demonstrated a curious paradox: the explosion of anarchist forces in French society while anarchist theory and organisation remained only a marginal political culture. The movement involved both workers, as in the previous events of 1906, 1920, 1936 and 1947, and students as well. But unlike the *jeunesse des Écoles* who had traditionally sought to use working-class discontent for political ends, the students of 1968 rode at the head of the movement, showing the way. The key to the movement was spontaneity, action preceding reflexion, an orgy of intellectual experiment and improvisation. The student leader Danny Cohn Bendit noted that 'the students' position became radicalised only in the course of the struggle because any commitment to action generates a political awareness'.[134] '*Every* opinion was expressed by the students', wrote one of their teachers, Henri Lefebvre, a sociology lecturer at Nanterre. 'They began the great questioning [*contestation*], that of society as a whole, its institutions and its ideologies.'[135] Conventional relations of power were overturned as the forces of order temporarily withdrew, and students occupied administrative blocks and lecture-halls and reclaimed historic walls for graffiti, all in the name of 'a libertarian, anti-authoritarian, communitarian and spontaneity-endorsing counter-utopia'.[136]

The May events started on 22 March with the occupation of the administrative building of the overspill university of Nanterre in the Paris suburbs. A meeting and demonstration at the Sorbonne on 3 May was broken up by the police and the Sorbonne and Nanterre were closed down. The clash with the police and closures drove the demonstrations onto the streets and brought the lecturers' union and main teaching union onto the side of the students. During the night of Friday–Saturday, 10–11 May, barricades were thrown up in the streets of the Latin Quarter, and the violence brought together the unions of students (UNEF), lecturers (SNE-Sup) and teachers (FEN), with the Communist CGT and the non-Communist CFDT and FO, to organise a one-day general strike and mass demonstrations on Monday, 13 May. In Paris 800,000 demonstrators marched from the place de la République to Denfert-Rochereau behind banners reading 'étudiants, enseignants, travailleurs solidaires'. The demonstration sparked off a wave of strikes and factory occupations that spread from the car and aircraft industries to public transport, government offices, large stores and schools. Even so only the teachers' union, on 20 May, officially called a general strike. The electric charge ran directly from the students to the shop floor, bypassing the union bureaucracies, often through the medium of young workers. One worker, brought up by his grandmother on the crushing of the Paris Commune, and seeing the same repression applied to students, reported that he 'went to see the guys at their machines, even the foremen. And the guys said, "No, no, it's not on; blokes are being clubbed in Paris. . . ." It was out of solidarity. We thought about it later. If the guys went on strike all the same it was out of solidarity with the students.'[137]

Comités d'action sprang up in the universities, factories, even in localities. They concretised the spontaneity and direct action preached by the student leaders. 'The point for us is not to build the Organisation with a big 'O',' said Cohn Bendit, 'but to facilitate the creation of a multitude of centres of insurrection.'[138] 'Self-management [*autogestion*], direct management, the words don't matter. But we must not let capitalism give way to a rigid socialism.'[139] He feared that the spontaneous movement might be hijacked by the Communist party, but cited the Charter of Amiens as evidence that 'pre-1914 French syndicalism alone proves that workers can go beyond what Lenin called trade-union consciousness in the trade-union sphere itself'.[140] At some point, spontaneity had to give way to organisation, but Cohn Bendit shied away from it.

Only after the event did he look for inspiration for the self-organisation of the working classes, to the Paris Commune, the Russian revolutions, the Spanish Revolution, the German councils' movement of 1918 and the Italian factory committees of 1920.[141] Likewise, he believed fervently in direct action and resisted the recuperation of the movement by political parties. 'My personal view is that the revolutionary strategy has no need to take account of votes,' he wrote. 'Direct action in the factories and streets is what changes situations, not some electoral majority. . . . The simple fact of a left-wing government in power would not solve the problems created by capitalism.'[142]

Trade unions and political parties were nevertheless doing their best to take control of the spontaneous movement of students and workers. In this sense, they behaved no differently than had their predecessors faced by any other spontaneous uprising. As in 1936 and 1947, the Communist party and the CGT were anxious to dampen the anarchy and force the movement into trade-union and political channels. The CFDT and the PSU were the most imaginative in their reactions, and the established anarchist movement was the most perplexed.

The CGT was reluctant to cede pride of place to the students, and on 20 May attacked the 'incredible pretension' of the students' union to lead the mass struggle.[143] The CGT leader Georges Séguy refused to shake Cohn Bendit's hand on the demonstration of 13 May and, after the latter was banned from France, refused to have anything more to do with the organisations of students and lecturers. The CGT's main concern was to direct the industrial action into trade union channels, limit working-class demands to the classic ones of pay increases, better conditions and trade union recognition, and to press for negotiations with employers and the government. On 20 May Séguy told Renault car workers that the CFDT's demand for 'autogestion' and 'workers' control' were 'empty concepts' and negotiations were undertaken on 25–7 May which resulted in the Grenelle agreements.[144] After that CGT members were instructed to return for work.[145]

The Communist party, like the CGT, was accused at the time of betraying the Revolution. The spontaneous movement was in fact as much a threat to the Marxist ideology and Stalinist structures of the PCF as it was to the Gaullist régime. The PCF had no means of communicating with students, whom it regarded as bourgeois children being trained to serve the bourgeois state. Moreover, the ideology of class struggle warned it not to be deceived by an apparent conflict of generations because 'every question is a question of class and not a question of age'.[146] A somewhat skeletal Union of Communist Students (UECF) was constantly watched for signs of Maoism and Trotskyism, and Trotskyist militants such as Alain Krivine were expelled from the UECF congress in 1965. Formed into the Jeunesse Communiste Révolutionnaire they took a dim view of Cohn Bendit and his friends. 'The spontaneous mass movement is a fantastic source of steam', wrote Krivine, 'which is likely to disperse unless there is a piston capable of making it effective. That piston is the organisation, which must exist prior to the movement.'[147] The Trotskyists, though they played an important part in the demonstrations of May 68, never gained control of the movement.

The Communist party's attitude to the student movement was summed up in George Marchais' description of Cohn Bendit as a 'German anarchist'.[148] It refused to accept that the student movement had triggered off the strikes and factory occupations; rather it was argued that the proletarian movement had autonomous causes, such as the growth of capitalist monopoly and technocracy. The PCF warned that 'gauchistes' succeeded only in divorcing the student population from the masses, and urged that if they wanted to demonstrate they should do it alongside the working class. It feared what it called an 'insurrectional strike' and supported the CGT's strategy of negotiation to secure the 'legitimate demands' of the workers. Above all, it was concerned to blame as much as possible on the personal régime of General de Gaulle and to guide the mass movement into political action to the advantage of the party itself. The PCF general secretary Waldeck Rochet said on *France Inter* on 18 May that the time had come to 'plan the formation of a popular government of democratic union'.[149] On 27–8 May he opened negotiations with François Mitterrand on the composition of that government, but Mitterrand's promise of 'at least one' ministry was not enough for the Communists. The PCF was more than happy at de Gaulle's dissolution of the National Assembly and calling of parliamentary elections on 30 May. Sartre went as far as to say that 'the PC found itself in a position of objective complicity with de Gaulle: they did each other a service by both demanding elections'.[150] Now the spontaneous movement was rudderless as the politicians chased after the spoils.

The attitude of the CFDT and the PSU was quite different. The CFDT was quick to respond to requests for help from UNEF and immediately saw parallels between the student's demands for participation and democratisation in the universities, and those being demanded by workers in industrial relations.[151] A key document of its *Bureau confédéral*, drafted by Albert Detraz, on 16 May 1968 demanded that 'industrial and administrative monarchy should be replaced by democratic structures on the basis of *autogestion*'.[152] The concept of *autogestion* appeared to be the home at which *spontanéisme* could rest. Detraz was also keen to place it in anarchist context. 'Everyone agrees in recognising Proudhon as the father of *autogestion*, as the inspiration of self-management thought.' He went on to quote the Geneva congress of the First International, the Commune's decree of 16 April 1871 and the Charter of Amiens as other precursors of *autogestion*.[153] Jacques Julliard, another CFDT leader, seized the moment for a major historical reassessment of Fernand Pelloutier. 'Why should labour history', he asked, 'not have its legendary heroes and historic anniversaries?'[154] However, moderates in the union were concerned to point out that *autogestion* did not mean libertarian revolution and class struggle but was compatible with class collaboration and *cogestion* with management.[155] A similar debate was joined between those, like Detraz and Julliard, who adhered to the classic doctrine of the autonomy of the labour movement and those like Edmond Maire who believed in a common strategy of trade-union activity and political action, in consultation with sympathetic parties.[156]

The PSU was the party with the greatest affinity to the CFDT. It was close to the student movement, indeed, Jacques Sauvageot, the president of the student's union, was in fact a member of the party. Conversely, many students from the left-wing *groupuscules* joined the PSU in the hopes of converting it into a truly revolutionary party.[157] The mass meeting at Charléty stadium on 27 May, organised by the students and the PSU, attracted a large although unofficial representation of the CFDT, which was not happy with the Grenelle agreements, was prepared to break with the CGT and PCF (which boycotted the rally) and align itself behind the political initiative of the PSU.[158] Politically, the triumph of the PSU was to produce Mendès-France at the Charléty rally, though he declined to speak. The next day, in what seemed to be a power vacuum, Mendès-France appeared with Mitterrand at a press conference, and while the latter declared himself a candidate for the presidency of the Republic, Mendès-France agreed to serve as prime minister should he be required.

We should now return to the perspective of official anarchists and anarcho-syndicalists on the events of 1968. The Fédération Anarchiste was happy that the black flags of the anarchists had been prominent in the 13 May demonstration and that anarchists had been involved in factory occupations, especially at Nantes. But May 1968 was a vast libertarian explosion that burst beyond the organisation and ideology of the Fédération Anarchiste, much to the consternation of its high priest, Maurice Joyeux, who had been converted to anarchism in 1927 at the time of riots against the execution of the Italian-Americans Sacco and Vanzetti.[159] Joyeux illustrated the way in which the anarchist movement had become rigid and doctrinaire in its attempt to keep its ideological heroes free from pollution, and sectarian in its bid to save its own organisation. He had no time for the eclecticism of 'this revolutionary, questioning, iconoclastic youth which read Breton, Camus and Boris Vian, sang Prévert, Brassens and Ferré, and demanded more liberty vis-à-vis the party, the family and sexual morality'.[160] In particular, he was anxious about the way in which Marxism was appropriating anarchist ideas to form a hybrid libertarian Communism. The Fédération Anarchiste had lost control of *Le Libertaire* to libertarian Communists, and in 1968 was quick to accuse the anarchist students of Nanterre and Paris of mixing their own cocktail of anarchist and Marxist ideas, under the influence of Marxist lecturers and intellectuals who were trying to revive a dying credo by appropriating Bakunin. He launched a periodical, *La Rue*, named after a publication of Jules Vallès, which he used to defend the 'monstres sacrés' of anarchism against misappropriation by the Marxists.[161] Among those whose memory was kept pure were Bakunin, to whom an issue of *La Rue* was devoted in 1976 on the centenary of his death, and James

Guillaume, whose *Idées sur l'Organisation syndicale* of 1876, republished by Monatte in 1921, was published once again by the Fédération Anarchiste in 1979.[162]

Joyeux further accused the students of the 'infantile disorder' of rejecting anarchist elders and organisations and forming 'a clan, a pressure-group . . . which is divorced from the population and in particular by their milieu from the workers'.[163] An attempt was made to strengthen anarchist organisation at the International Congress of Anarchist Federations at Carrara in August 1968. A delegation of student anarchists led by Danny Cohn Bendit was kept out of the conference by Carrara miners serving as bouncers, although one evening was set aside for an exchange of views. Cohn Bendit had the measure of the official anarchists. He attacked the conference for 'turning its back on spontaneity which, in our view, is the key to the Revolution. . . . It is not by closing yourselves off, as you are doing, by claiming exclusive rights, by pursuing the eternal debate between Bakunin and Marx that you will advance the cause of the Revolution.'[164] The Fédération Anarchiste was indeed in danger of going the same way as other once-revolutionary movements, of becoming a sect and putting its own organisation and ideology before what Cohn Bendit lovingly called 'the Revolution'.

The cost of the preservation of ideological purity and organisational independence at the expense of everything else was also seen in the battle fought by Joyeux against the appropriation of the notion of *autogestion* by trade unions and political parties, in particular the CFDT and the PSU. The concept of *autogestion* was one of the most powerful thrown up by the events of 1968. Joyeux insisted that it should be used in the Proudhonian sense of workers' control in a classless, stateless society. Quite simply, he argued, '*autogestion* does not precede social revolution, it follows it'.[165] Twelve years later he reiterated the point, denouncing the way it had been used and abused not only by the CFDT and PSU but also by the PS, and even the PCF.

> *Autogestion* is the complement and the means of egalitarian socialism. Applied to an inegalitarian society *autogestion* is none other than participation of the slave in the exploitation the master inflicts on him . . . *autogestion* is not a production incentive or a production technique but the structural framework into which to fit socialism, true socialism, not that of Marx but that of Proudhon.[166]

This insistence that *autogestion* was incompatible with class collaboration, political action and the state itself was taken up by the Alliance Syndicaliste Révolutionnaire et Anarcho-Syndicaliste, which was formed in June 1969 by a federation of *La Révolution prolétarienne*, the CNT and the Anarcho-Syndicalist Union, which was based on the Fernand-Pelloutier group at Nantes. It attempted to prise away from the base of the labour movement workers who wanted 'the rehabilitation of labour unionism that has been divided and distorted by politicians trying to colonise it and led astray into class collaboration by reformists who are part of the establishment'.[167] It failed to make much of an impression on the major trade-union confederations, doing worse than the revolutionary syndicalists in 1921, let alone the Allemanists in 1894, and its response was to take refuge in a time-honoured traditions. Its national conference at Limoges in January 1971 asserted, 'We claim the herit-age of the militants of the First International, of the Commune, of the revolu-tionary pre-1914 CGT, of the combatants of the soviets in 1917–21, of the anarcho-syndicalist militants of revolutionary Spain in 1936, of the workers' councils in Hungary and those forming today in Poland.'[168]

The failure of anarchists and anarcho-syndicalists to make a significant impression on the labour movement after 1968 is largely explained by the purism of their ideology on matters of working-class separatism and political action. More flexible, and more successful by far, was the CFDT, which adopted the notion of *autogestion*, but adapted it to the possibilities of demo-cratic socialism. The 1970 congress of the CFDT decided that *autogestion* should be inserted within the framework of class struggle, but that this did not imply a 'workers' revolt'.[169] It stood for industrial democracy within a socialised society, and was distinct from nationalisation and planning which reinforced the power of the state. When the Left began to reorganise itself after 1971, the CFDT leader Edmond Maire distanced himself from the common programme of the parties of the Left and promoted a Union des forces populaires, some-what on the model of 1936. But the CFDT did not ignore the value of political action, which was considered the obvious way to achieve improvements for organised labour. Hence, it supported the parties of the Left in 1973 and 1978 and the candidatures of Mitterrand in 1974 and 1981. CFDT leaders accepted government posts after 1981, but the union campaigned to remove the state from the back of civil society, increasing the autonomy of labour organisations and individuals. Edmond Maire began to talk of the *société contractuelle* with a *pouvoir contractuelle* to counterbalance the *pouvoir politique* of the state.[170] It took up Proudhon's basic ideas of autonomy and federation, but accepted that the state would have to continue with limited powers as an arbitrating force. In this way, the substance of *autogestion* was preserved but freed from a doctrinaire interpretation that served only to alienate the mass of workers integrated into democratic society and the mixed economy.

That anarchists should dismiss the labour movement as conservative and unfit to appreciate their philosophies was nothing new: the strain of individu-alistic anarchism always ran alongside those anarchists who sought to penetrate and convert the labour movement. But anarchists who remained outside the labour movement tended to elaborate anti-authoritarianism on a global scale, arguing that the oppression suffered by workers was only one form of oppres-sion, and that the emancipation of the workers would be insufficient to eman-cipate humanity. Their recurrent concern was state-power and its most glaring manifestation, militarism. In the wake of 1968, a new dimension of state-power was provided by the nuclear problem. The question of nuclear weapons posed by France's independent deterrent was compounded by her switch to nuclear power in 1974 following the world oil crisis. This stimulated the emergence of the ecology movement, promoted largely by veterans of May 68, such as Daniel Cohn Bendit and Brice Lalonde. As Alan Touraine put it, 'the militants of political ecology are above all the children of May'.[171] The convergence of military and ecological questions provided an ideal bridge for anarchists to move into the ecology movement. Whether the organised anarchist movement would prove flexible enough to follow the children of May and incorporate ecologism into anarchism remained to be seen.

There were some favourable signs. The Fernand-Pelloutier group at Nantes, disillusioned by trade-union bureaucracy, which supported rather than challenged capitalism, changed the title of its broadsheet in December 1973 from *L'Anarcho-Syndicaliste* to *L'Anarcho*, signifying a more global approach to the problem of oppression. It welcomed the fact that 'the anti-nuclear struggle now joins the political libertarian struggle against centralisation and militarisation' and took inspiration from 'the convergence of ecological concerns and anti-authoritarian aspirations'.[172] Similarly, an extraordinary congress of the Fédération Anarchiste in November 1977 concluded that a society based on nuclear power would be 'police-run and centralist' and invented a new green-anarchist vision of 'the global *autogestion* of resources and the egalitarian and federalist sharing of production'.[173]

Just as anarchism was initially able to incorporate ecologism, so the ecology movement initially used the direct action methods of anarchism. On 31 July 1977 a crowd of sixty to eighty thousand demonstrated at Creys-Malville, near Grenoble, against the projected construction of a nuclear super-reactor. The authorities turned out in force and the demonstrators suffered numerous casualties. As a consequence, ecologists formed an Ecolo 78 front with a view to contesting elections. Some anarchists were prepared to ignore their maxim, 'élections, pièges à cons', and supported ecologists in the 1978 legislative elections.[174] But as the ecology movement grew from a protest movement into a parliamentary party or parties, anarchists became more sceptical. The movement was taken over by the politicians of the 1980s as the labour movement had been by the politicians of the 1880s. One branch of the Greens—les Verts—drifted away from socialism and indeed from the Left in general. 'Go and vote Antoine Waechter for capitalism with a human face!', joked anarchists when the leader of the Green party stood in the presidental elections of 1988.[175] During the European election campaign of 1989, ecologists were dismissed as 'the new managers (cleaner? wiser?) of capitalism'.[176] Another branch, the Génération écologie party of Brice Lalonde, a former Socialist environment minister, founded in 1990, was even less to the anarchists' taste. Little more than an extension of the Socialist party, its main aim was to recover Green votes for the presidential majority.[177]

Anarchists became disillusioned with both the labour and ecology movements because they were seen to compromise with capitalism, political action and the state. Their own libertarianism, which should have been so open-ended and inventive about challenging the state, shrank by a rigid adherence to the strategy of direct action which lost them allies and opportunities. And yet in the 1980s there was a recurrence of direct action of the individualistic kind, as shocking as that which gripped France in the 1890s, and which served to discredit such august institutions as the Fédération Anarchiste.

Between 1980 and 1986 a series of attacks took place on government ministries, the headquarters of industrial corporations, political parties, media offices and even the Préfecture de Police. They were organised by a group called Action Directe, set up in 1979 which, in order to finance their enterprises, resorted to bank hold-ups. The victims of periodic shoot-outs included a security guard and two high-ranking gendarmes.[178] André Olivier, the mastermind of the Lyon branch of the group, had espoused Maoist ideas in 1968 during a spell in La Santé prison for trafficking military secrets. In 1976 he met three members of the terrorist Groupes d'action révolutionnaire internationale (GARI), which had been founded to stop Franco's executions of his political opponents. A teacher at a Lyon lycée, Olivier was in a position to convert pupils to his cause. The most willing of these was Max Frérot, the son of a small businessman, who learned about explosives during military service in a parachute regiment, and demonstrated at Creys-Malville in the summer of 1977. Olivier was captured in 1986, Frérot the following year. Eighteen members of the Lyon branch of the Action Directe group went on trial in 1989. It was not easy to claim a respectable heritage for them. A defendant of Action Directe cited Ravachol, who turned the tables on the 'unjust, corrupt and immoral' society which, by 'sowing wretchedness harvests hatred and creates criminals'.[179] If Olivier was Ravachol then Max Frérot was Émile Henry, since Frérot considered bank clerks to be lackeys of capitalism and legitimate targets of attack in the same way that Henry viewed restaurant diners. The Rhône Assize Court condemned Olivier and Frérot to life imprisonment in June 1989. The Fédération Anarchiste was embarrassed. It could not endorse them, for fear of association with their crimes. On the other hand, it had to accept that it shared the libertarian goals of Action Directe, for fear of having nothing left to stand for.

> No, the militants of Action Directe do not belong to us, whatever their libertarian origins might once have been. But what their destruction represents is the triumph of a state that we also intend to destroy.[180]

Anarchism still stood for opposition to the state, and this would always provide a standard for criticism and material for a libertarian utopia. But torn between a refusal of electoral politics and a refusal of direct action in terrorist form, while retaining a disillusion with trade-unionism and ecology, the way forward seemed limited.

CHAPTER 7

Bridging the Revolution?

The Revolution divided the French people between Left and Right, revolution and counter-revolution. But while these divisions were underlined by those revolutionaries who had a vested interest in delegitimising the Right and excluding it from power, those on the Right in general tried to escape from the political ghetto in which they were placed. One solution was to accept some of the principles of the Revolution, such as civil equality, a constitution, if necessary the republic, in order to gain access to the political class and to power. This was the liberal solution, which was discussed in Chapter One. There was, however, an alternative solution, adopted by those on the Right who felt displaced by the new political class and its liberal institutions. This was to adopt the rhetoric of revolution and to reach out for a popular base with which to sweep the political class aside. The Right successively attempted to build bridges to republicans, radicals, socialists and syndicalists in pursuit of a popular base. This tactic of the Right has been called the *politique du pire* or alliance of the extremes against the centre.

The difficulty for those on the Right who adopted this tactic was to frame a political culture that could link elements both of the Right and of the Left against their common enemy, the political class. Broadly speaking, two alternative political cultures were elaborated. The first was that of a popular monarchy, in which the king was imagined as the father of his people and guarantor of their interests. Revolutionary concepts such as the sovereignty of the people and the social contract were adapted to strengthen this image. It was argued that the King was the representative of the Nation, and required full power to counterbalance parliamentary politicians, who were accused of perverting the national will. The second political culture centred on the concept of the nation rather than on that of the monarchy. It took up the argument that the political class perverted rather than represented the national will, and then held it responsible for a series of other crimes against the nation. It was accused of representing the forces of capitalism, which sacrificed the honest workers of society to private profit. And it was accused of representing cosmopolitan interests, such as those of Jews, Freemasons and foreigners, against the inter-

298

ests of the French nation. This culture was elaborated not only by dissidents of the Right but also by dissidents of the Left who characterised Marxism as German and Jewish and sought to define a specifically French or national socialism. How far they were able to make common cause is the subject of this chapter.

The Popular Monarchy

In Anatole France's novel, *Monsieur Bergeret à Paris* (1901), Joseph Lacrisse, a romantic young royalist, plans a coup d'état that will coincide with the retrial of Captain Dreyfus at Rennes and return the royalists to power. His plans receive short shrift from Henri Léon, a royalist far longer in the tooth, who warns of the ingratitude of princes, even should a restoration succeed.

> Conspirators are not greatly appreciated at Court. . . . The *ralliés* will themselves form a third of our political personnel and get to the till before us. . . . But what the *ralliés* receive will be a fraction of what the faithful republicans who go over at the last minute will get. . . . Have you never heard of Talleyrand and Fouché? . . . It was not an émigré but a regicide who was appointed minister of police by Louis XVIII in 1815. . . . Do I have to teach you the ABC of restorations?[1]

For Henri Léon the interests of royalists had been quite adequately protected by the conservative republican ministry of Jules Méline which fell at the beginning of the Dreyfus affair, and royalists were ill-advised to indulge in conspiratorial politics. The question of régime was quite secondary.

The analysis of Anatole France, satirical though it was, expressed a commonplace of French politics: that the judicious of the Right rallied to the régime of the day and did not make a virtue of lost causes. But this *ralliement* to the existing régime in pursuit of power and profit served only to drive those excluded from it either to counter-revolution or to some sort of alliance with revolutionaries who opposed those of their number who now enjoyed the benefits of power. This attempt to form alternative alliances was evident during the Revolution, at the Restoration in 1815, under the July Monarchy and during the Boulangist episode under the Third Republic. But to forge a political culture that could attract both the dissident Right and the dissident Left was no easy task.

When the Estates-General was summoned to Versailles in 1789, the majority of the nobility was intent on protecting their privileges as the second order against any more despotic claims by the king and his ministers. But the achievement of the Third Estate, forcing the merger of the chambers of the three orders into one National Assembly of equal citizens, which they claimed represented the sovereign people and was entitled to draft a new constitution, forced many nobles to rethink their position. Some, like Lafayette, accepted the new developments, others, like Cazalès and the comte d'Antraigues, did not. Their position was that the National Assembly, dominated by the leaders of the Third Estate and certain liberal nobles, now exercised a despotism infinitely worse than anything ever exercised by the crown. Since political discourse now revolved around such concepts as popular sovereignty and the social contract, they abandoned divine right and hereditary monarchy, and constructed an idealised version of a popular monarchy, established fourteen centuries earlier by a contract between king and people. According to this view, the national will was most recently established in the *cahiers de doléances* sent to the king by the people when they elected their deputies to the Estates General. But the Assembly had seen fit to appropriate the sovereignty of the people, claiming as its own the acts of the people, and was violating the ancient contract by recasting the constitution and ultimately abolishing the monarchy.[2]

The comte d'Antraigues, elected deputy for the nobility of Villeneuve-de-Berg in the Vivarais, was so horrified by the growing despotism of the National Assembly that he emigrated early in 1790. 'If one had to choose between two scourges,' he wrote, 'the tyranny of a king would be preferable to the tyranny of 1,200 deputies, sovereigns for a day by virtue of the law.'[3] D'Antraigues became involved with the émigré princes and pursued their plan to provoke a counter-revolutionary uprising in south-eastern France. When this failed he set about trying to prevent the establishment of a constitutional monarchy, that served to the dominance of the wealthy bourgeoisie, by a *politique du pire*. Understanding that convinced royalists like himself and democrats had a common interest in sabotaging the constitutional monarchy, he established secret links with the Jacobin Club and its affiliates. When the Constitution was established and the Legislative Assembly elected, d'Antraigues corresponded with the Girondins, particularly with Jérôme Pétion, the mayor of Paris, since they also opposed the constitutional monarchy. Rabaut Saint-Étienne denounced 'revolutionary aristocrats' who 'would prefer the Republic to a constitutional king decked out like Louis XVI and his wife'.[4] D'Antraigues himself relished the epithet 'Robespierre of the aristocrats' and admitted, 'People accuse me of saying, "Let France perish rather than its ancient constitution."'[5]

It was in fact almost impossible to link revolutionaries and counter-revolutionaries in any real sense in the heat of the Revolution. But this did not prevent those in power constantly imagining conspiracies of Right and Left designed to bring them down. Thus when the Montagnards came to power and were challenged by the sans-culottes, they accused them of plotting with counter-revolutionaries. When Robespierre wanted to terminate the sans-culotte de-Christianising campaign, which admittedly was driving Catholics to counter-revolution, he announced that 'atheism is aristocratic . . . the only fanaticism we have left to fear is that of immoral people, paid by foreign courts to stir up fanaticism'.[6] When the Hébertists, who tried to launch the sans-culottes against the Montagnards, went on trial in 1794, the grand inquisitor Fouquier-Tinville screamed at them. 'Have you not planned how you would pass off a king, a dictator, a tyrant? Vile traitors, you must die, your execution can wait no longer.'[7]

The restoration of the monarchy in 1814 and 1815 saw precisely the same division in the royalist camp between those who desired it only on a constitutional basis, and thus obliged Louis XVIII to endorse the Charter of 1814, and those who opposed all compromise with revolutionary principles and the recruitment of servants of the Empire now to serve the monarchy. This second view was held by ultra-royalists who fought a rearguard action in the Midi after the king's flight in 1815, drawing volunteers from the ranks of the people, and who after Waterloo massacred supporters of the Revolution and Empire during the so-called White Terror.[8] The ultra-royalists secured a landslide majority in the elections of August 1815 to the so-called Chambre Introuvable, but the ungrateful monarchy steered a middle course with moderate ministers and dissolved the Chamber after a year. A protest was made in a scathing pamphlet by the writer and former émigré Chateaubriand, who denounced minsterial despotism and accused the monarchy of employing Bonapartist men who pursued revolutionary measures. He wanted a traditional alliance of the throne and liberty, though he did not at this stage develop his perspective on the popular monarchy.[9] For the moment, moreover, ultras expressed their opposition to the constitutional monarchy within the parliamentary system: in the Isère in 1819, they elected the abbé Grégoire, former deputy of the Convention and reputed regicide, rather than let a constitutional royalist pass; and in December 1821 they allied with the Left in the Chamber to topple the ministry of Richelieu.[10]

In his pamphlet of 1816, Chateaubriand was already suspicious of a faction or party that wanted to change the dynasty, take the tricolour flag, impose even more stringent conditions than were imposed on Louis XVIII, and appoint even more servants of the Empire.[11] When this came about in July 1830 he let fly with another stinging pamphlet, which now took up the argument expressed by Cazalès and d'Antraigues before him, that politicians had confiscated sovereignty from the people, where it lay, given the crown to whom they wanted and stitched up the settlement that suited them best. The notion of popular sovereignty under which this deal was carried out was turned against the political class and used to revive the idea of a monarchy resting genuinely on popular consent. Chateaubriand argued that the popular sovereignty flouted by the politicians must be respected, and called for a genuine consultation of the people, convened in a national congress. Like d'Antraigues, he said that anything was preferable to constitutional monarchy, offspring of the union of monarchy and revolution. 'For myself', he said, 'a republican by nature, a monarchist by reason, and a bourbonist by honour, if I could not have kept the legitimate monarchy I would have been happier with a democracy than with a bastard monarchy granted by God knows whom.'[12]

Those in power under the July Monarchy knew their enemies, and feared the construction of a 'carlo-republican alliance' against the régime. In June 1832 the police unearthed a Société Gauloise which allegedly articulated the 'monstrous union' between legitimists and republicans and was active in the Paris insurrection occasioned by the funeral of General Lamarque.[13] There was in fact little to substantiate fears of a joint insurrection. Insurrections in the period 1832–4 tended to be either legitimist or republican, and, where there was collusion, as the régime settled down, it tended to be parliamentary. Thus in the elections of 1837, the republican Arago was elected at Perpignan with legitimist votes while the legitimist tribune Berryer was elected at Marseille with republican ones. In January 1839, moreover, the ministry of the middle-of-the-road comte Molé was overthrown by a parliamentary coalition of republicans and legitimists which provoked new elections and a governmental crisis.[14]

It order fully to activate the concept of the popular monarchy, it was necessary for royalists to take up the cause of universal suffrage proposed by the republicans and in particular to seize hold of the idea of a referendum on the régime. The trail pointed by Chateaubriand was blazed under the July Monarchy by the abbé de Genoude, editor of the legitimist *Gazette de France*, who aligned himself with republican advocates of universal suffrage in the name of the sovereignty of the people as the best way to break the political class's stranglehold on power. Genoude welcomed the concession of universal suffrage in 1848, and argued that 'with the *appel au peuple* for the constitution of the government, we shall have a leader elected by everyone'.[15] But the populists were confronted by moderate royalists who were prepared to do a deal with conservative republicans, accept the Republic as the régime that divided them least to forge a party of order, tie the hands of the newly elected president and abolish universal suffrage. In this way, power would continue to be monopolised by the political class.

The abbé de Genoude died in 1849 but his crusade was taken up by Henri de La Rochejacquelein, grandson of the famous Vendean leader and representative of the Morbihan in the Legislative Assembly. In March 1850 La Rochejacquelein told the Assembly that the proclamation of the Republic by the provisional government on 24 February 1848 had been as much a confiscation of power as those of 1814 and 1830, since there had been no consultation of the people. He proposed that the people should be polled as to whether they wanted a republic or a monarchy; if they wanted a monarchy a constituent assembly would be elected to settle the details.[16] The argument was based on the concept of *Droit national*, elaborated by Henri de Lourdoueix, the new editor of the *Gazette de France*. Rather than base monarchy on divine hereditary right, it argued that sovereignty had always been vested in the people. However, from the time the people had lifted Clovis onto their shields fourteen centuries earlier they had seen fit to delegate their executive authority to a ruling dynasty for as long as that dynasty lasted. According to this reading of history, successive estates-general were deemed to have been elected by universal suffrage and to have ratified this delegation of power. In 1789 the 'national delegation', or pact between king and people, had been renewed, but it had been violated in 1792, when the monarchy was overthrown, and again in 1814, 1830 and 1848; the time had come formally to renew it.[17] Outside parliament a growing *Droit national* movement took shape, with its own clubs and press, particularly in the Midi.[18] Moreover, the espousal of the principle of universal suffrage made possible a new phase of co-operation between the extreme Right and an extreme Left of radical republicans. The law of 31 May 1850 which abrogated universal suffrage drove the 'Montagne blanche' of 'flour-dredged Jacobins' into the arms of the 'Montagne rouge' against the political class in a common struggle to restore universal suffrage.[19]

The line between the political class and the populists ran not between republicans and royalists or even between Orleanists and Legitimists, but through the middle of the Legitimist camp. Conservative Legitimists were shocked by the ideology and practice of the *Droit national* movement, and managed to extract a ruling from the comte de Chambord in the summer of 1850 denouncing the *appel au peuple* doctrine on the grounds that it negated the principle of hereditary monarchy.[20] While endorsing the principle of heredity, Chambord kept up the rhetoric of the popular monarchy with the *Letter to Workers* in 1865. This announced that 'the monarchy has always been the patron of the working classes' and that it must 'do for the moral and material prosperity of the working classes what it did it former times for the emancipation of the towns'.[21] Unfortunately Chambord failed to see that he had to choose between restoration by popular power and restoration by parliamentary means. If he excluded the populist route he could hope for restoration only at the hands of parliament, as in 1814 and 1830. Elections to the National Assembly in 1871 returned a royalist majority, but most Legitimists as well as all Orleanists wanted a parliamentary monarchy. By insisting on something verging on absolute monarchy, Chambord alienated his parliamentary supporters and destroyed the alternative route to power.[22]

The comte de Chambord died in 1883, leaving the Orleanist comte de Paris as pretender. But the possibility of a parliamentary restoration evaporated with the loss of the royalist majority in the first elections to the Chamber of Deputies in 1876, and the steady decline of royalist support in the elections of 1877, 1881 and 1885. In September 1887 the comte de Paris broke out of the royalism of notables that served him no longer and made a bid for restoration by popular power. He published a manifesto urging that the people be consulted, by a constituent assembly or plebiscite, on whether they wanted a restoration of the monarchy. This was to follow the lead of *Droit national* legitimists, though Jules Ferry was quick to wave the Bonapartist spectre, accusing the comte of 'pulling on the old boots of Napoleon III'.[23]

For this change of tactic, however, a popular basis of support was required. To secure a majority in either a constituent assembly or a plebiscite royalists would have to make common cause with a popular movement that was as hostile to the parliamentary republic as they were. The Blanquists, many of who were former Communards and saw the parliamentary republic as the enemy of the people, went on the rampage with the Ligue des Patriotes in November–December 1887 to prevent Jules Ferry, who epitomised that Republic, from being elected its president. Henri Rochefort, editor of *L'Intransigeant*, acted as a link between Boulanger and former Communards and Blanquists such Emile Eudes, Ernest Granger, Ernest Roche and Édouard Vaillant. At the other end of the political spectrum, the royalist baron de Mackau developed the advantages of Boulangism for the comte de Paris. He argued that Boulangism could transform royalism from a movement of chiefs without Indians into a genuine populist enterprise. Boulangism would allow royalism to extend its electorate beyond traditional royalist fiefs to constituencies dominated by Opportunists, where there was a substantial vote of malcontent republicans and even socialists to be harnessed. This vote could never be appropriated by naked royalism, but Boulangism would serve to camouflage from the left hand what the right hand was doing.[24]

Boulangism was a complex phenomenon, and has already been analysed as a manifestation of Bonapartism.[25] It can also be seen, however, as another episode of populist royalism, which managed indirectly to tap some of the extreme left-wing elements in the nation. Large amounts of money were poured into the movement by such royalists as the flamboyant duchesse d'Uzès, although this was not revealed in the press until the summer of 1890.[26] The Blanquists acquired an extensive popular support in Paris by their support for the building workers' strike in July 1888, and this they delivered to General Boulanger in January 1889 to ensure his triumph in the Paris by-election.[27] In the legislative elections of October 1889, Granger and Roche were elected on the Boulangist list promoted by Rochefort respectively in the seventeenth and nineteenth *arrondissements* of Paris. But at this point the polarisation between Left and Right began to harden. Socialists who had been prepared to vote for Boulanger in order to attack the parliamentary republic or because the socialist camp still lacked definition, now began to suspect that Boulanger was a man of the Right. In the twentieth *arrondissement* Vaillant ran his own man against Rochefort, even though this meant letting in an Opportunist. After the sudden death of the Blanquist leader Eudes in August 1889, Blanquism tore itself apart. The battle for the leadership between Granger and Édouard Vaillant took the form of a dispute over whether the movement should endorse Rochefort and Boulangism, or redefine itself as revolutionary socialism, in the authentic spirit of the Commune, and realign with Jules Guesde and the Parti Ouvrier.[28] Each branch now went its separate way: Vaillant and Guesde towards international socialism, Granger and Rochefort towards a national socialism which was to be a further stage of populism, and pitched battles were fought over Blanqui's grave in the Père Lachaise cemetery as Blanquism was claimed for both Left and Right.

Anti-Semitism

In spite of some Boulangist successes, the legislative elections of October 1889 marked another victory for the parliamentary Republic. Rochefort's verdict in *L'Intransigeant* was lapidary: 'Le Triomphe de la Juiverie'. The Rothschild dynasty had not only given three million francs to Constans, the Opportunist minister of the interior, but had also brought in thirty-five thousand Jews from Romania and had them naturalised at once in order to swell the Opportunist vote.[29] 'We now know', Rochefort jested, 'that the initials R.F. inscribed on public monuments stand not for *République française* but in fact for *Rothschild frères.*'[30]

The significance of the eruption of political anti-Semitism after the Boulanger affair cannot be underestimated. In the first place, it recognised that a parliamentary majority could no longer be rallied around monarchism, and that the nation should replace the monarchy as the focus of loyalty of all those who opposed the political class of the Republic. Of course, the monarchy had always been built up as a national institution, but to confine nationalism within the bounds of monarchism was now felt to be too restrictive. Second, the nation was now given an exclusive rather than an inclusive definition. Even in 1789, the threat had been made that if the nobility did not agree to renounce their privileges and join the National Assembly, the nation would be constituted without and in spite of them. But the concept of the nation in 1789 was deemed to include all French citizens, equal under the law. The nation of 1889 was held to exclude certain categories not deemed worthy of French citizenship, in particular the Jews; indeed it was largely through anti-Semitism that it was now defined. Third, anti-Semitism was built up as an ideology that could genuinely bridge the revolutionary divide, not just to permit a *politique du pire* of dissident intellectuals, but to achieve a genuine mass base for the Right. For anti-Semitism in France originated on the Left rather than the Right, as a 'socialism of fools'. Through anti-Semitism, the Right could develop a social dimension for its nationalism, and hope to undermine the revolutionary international socialism that acquired its own definition after the Boulanger affair and began to challenge for power.

The left-wing critique of Judaism started with usury and identified it with a finance-capitalism that had taken off in the nineteenth century and was characterised by the growing influence of banks and the stock-market in commerce and industry. High interest rates, speculative booms and slumps, the ruin of small businesses, the growth of monopoly and the pauperisation of the proletariat were attributed to the Jews. The key text, *Les Juifs, rois de l'époque. Histoire de la féodalité financière* (1845), by Alphonse de Toussenel, a pupil of Fourier, went into a third edition in 1886. It was echoed by *Les Rois de la République* (1883), by Auguste Chirac, who also ran a series of articles on speculation in Malon's *Revue socialiste* in 1885–7. Meanwhile, the Blanquist ideologue Gustave Tridon, who had rehabiltated the Hébertists before the

Paris Commune, published *Du Molochisme juif* in 1884.[31] It was to this anti-Semitism of the Left that Rochefort turned in the election campaign of 1893 to build a broad electoral coalition of 'all those who, whatever their past, are determined to institute the social Republic on the ruins of the Opportunist Republic'.[32] He gathered Boulangist Blanquists, Guesdist socialists, independent socialists and radical-socialists to the cause and clarified their common goal as 'political purge and social emancipation'.[33] This linking of a socialist programme with a purge of the body politic, with the implication that purifying the nation would also redeem society, was to be at the heart of the developing populist rhetoric.

At the same time that anti-Semitism was taken up by the Left, it was developed on the Right in a bid to find a wide popular base for its nationalist position. Édouard Drumont, whose father had been a *quarante-huitard* and once employed Henri Rochefort at the Paris Hôtel de Ville, was himself an admirer of the Empire and subsequently of the monarchy.[34] His best-selling *La France juive* (1886) rehearsed the conventional left-wing arguments about financial feudalism, but claimed to expose the hand of the Jew in a multitude of ways that threatened Catholic, conservative France or, rather, an ideal construction of it. In this way, he interpreted antisemitism for the benefit of the Right.[35] The Jews were said to have controlled the masonic lodges which plotted the French Revolution. Through their control of the press they manipulated the politicians of the Third Republic; Gambetta in particular was their man. In return for their backing, they demanded a campaign of de-Christianisation: the divorce law sponsored by Naquet, and Camille Sée's law promoting the secular state education of girls, were cited as part of a plan to destroy the Catholic family in France.[36] Drumont's method was to proclaim France decadent, to demonise the Jews as responsible for all France's ills, and to prescribe their expulsion that France might become whole again.[37]

Though the individualistic, capitalistic, liberal and secular world identified with the Jews was criticised in the name of an organic, Christian, hierarchical, rural Arcadia, Drumont nevertheless argued that to deal with the Jewish question was also to deal with the social question. The simplest form of the argument was that poverty could be alleviated by confiscating five billion frances of Jewish capital. On a more subtle level, Drumont's populism claimed to defend the plain but honest citizen against the evils of money and intelligence that were corrupting the nation. Drumont's audience, unlike that of the socialists, was not restricted to the industrial proletariat. He also made a deliberate bid to challenge international socialists for popular support. In an extraordinary gesture for a man of the Right he expressed sympathy for the cause of the Paris Commune, and even praised its leaders, distinguishing between the leaders of working-class origin such as Benoît Malon and the bourgeois intellectuals. 'In the Commune it was the bourgeois element that was particularly ferocious,' he wrote, citing the likes of Delescluze, Rigault and Ferré. 'The popular element in the midst of this terrible crisis remained human, that is to say, French.'[38] Drumont also endeavoured to make capital out of the massacre of Fourmies in 1891. While the socialists presented it as a renewal of the class struggle, Drumont presented it as a plot against the French proletariat by the Jews. The Kaiser, he argued, was keen to purchase Lebel rifles but only after they had been tested on European as well as Asian bodies. The prefect of the Nord department, and the sub-prefect of Avesnes, in which Fourmies was situated, were happy to oblige by setting the French against each other, and were both Jews.[39]

Socialist leaders were undoubtedly concerned by the threat anti-Semitism posed to their support. Benoît Malon did not return the compliments of Drumont. Reviewing *La France juive* in *La Revue socialiste*, Malon characterised Drumont as 'the *enfant terrible* of the clerical party', more interested in waging a religious than an economic war against the Jews, ridiculed the scheme to redistribute Jewish wealth, and stated that the proletariat and the petty bourgeoisie were oppressed not only by Jewish capital but by capitalism as a whole.[40] The argument that capitalism could not by explained by the Jewish question became standard in the socialist camp, but the attraction of anti-Semitism to the working masses could not easily be dispelled. This was made especially clear during the Dreyfus affair. The trial of Emile Zola, who challenged the verdict of the military court in his article *J'Accuse*, sparked off a wave of anti-Semitic riots in metropolitan France and Algeria.[41] Left-wing anti-Semites like Henri Rochefort rode on the wave. He ran a hate campaign against the leading Dreyfusard Joseph Reinach, whom he nicknamed 'Boule de Juif'. Sentenced to five days' imprisonment for defamation, Rochefort was escorted to the prison of Sainte-Pélagie by a vast crowd led by 'the Blanquist batallion'.[42] The Blanquist and former Boulangist Ernest Roche intervened in the Chamber of Deputies to defend the army 'on behalf of the nationalist French socialists'.[43]

The swell of anti-Semitic and nationalist opinion greatly embarrassed socialists who considered themselves to be representatives of the international proletariat. In the run-up to the legislative elections due in May 1898, to admit Dreyfusism was electoral suicide. Charles Péguy tried to win over socialist leaders to the Dreyfusard cause but was cold-shouldered by Millerand, and discovered that Viviani was 'anti-Semitic in Algeria and a so-called socialist in the fifth *arrondissement*', where he was standing.[44] The official line of socialists from Millerand and Viviani to Jaurès, Guesde and Vaillant was that the Dreyfus affair was a struggle for power between two elements of the bourgeoisie, Jewish and the clerical, and was of no interest to the proletariat.[45] Socialists like Guesde and Jaurès, who let slip Dreyfusard opinions, lost their seats in the elections of 1898. By contrast, twenty-two anti-Semitic deputies were returned, including Drumont at Algiers.[46]

Anti-Semitism was found on the Left as well as on the Right, but politicians who adopted it tended to drift to the Right. Maurice Barrès is a case in point. When Barrès stood as a Boulangist candidate at Nancy in 1889, his manager

was a Blanquist journalist and his propaganda, while condemning the Opportunists as 'the Jews' party', announced, 'We are still the sacred *canaille* of
1789, 1830 and 1848.'[47] He affected a certain anarchism and in 1891 visited
the anarchist Jean Grave in prison to interview him.[48] After his defeat in
the elections of 1893, Barrès took over the editorship of the *Cocarde* newspaper in order to challenge the oligarchy of stuffy republicans now supported by Orleanist *ralliés*. Its columns were open to anarcho-syndicalists
like Fernand Pelloutier as well as to Charles Maurras, the future Action
Française leader. It sought to develop a distinctive French socialism which was
not baldly materialistic as it conceived German-Jewish Marxism to be, but
laid claim to a certain spiritual dimension that was deemed to be peculiarly
French.[49]

Steadily, however, nationalism began to take precedence over socialism in
Barrès' concerns. When he stood for parliament again (unsuccessfully) in 1898,
he linked socialism and nationalism through protectionism. His 'Nancy programme' demanded restrictions on immigration to protect French labour from
unemployment, higher tariffs against foreign imports, the control of international finance-capitalism and restrictions on naturalised citizens entering public
service.[50] This hostility to naturalised citizens, particularly German-Jewish
ones, was given expression in his portrayal of the Frankfurt-born banker
Jacques de Reinach. In this novels *Les Déracinés* and *Leurs Figures*, de Reinach
is seen to use his money-power and press interests to control the Opportunist
Republic for his own ends; his nephew, Joseph de Reinach, edits Gambetta's
mouthpiece *La République française*.[51] But justice is seen to be done when,
exposed by the Panama scandal, Jacques de Reinach takes his own life. Increasingly, Barrès became obsessed by the defence of the fabric of the nation
against insidious foreign influences. He saw the Dreyfusards as 'enemies
within' who, by demoralising the army, were responsible for the humiliation of
Fashoda.[52] The fate of one Jewish army officer could not have precedence over
the right of the French nation to survive. When the Dreyfusards in the end
forced Dreyfus' retrial, Barrès simply concluded, 'That Dreyfus is capable of
treachery I conclude from his race.'[53]

At the end of 1898, Barrès wrote that the Dreyfus affair was not a question
of *raison d'Etat*, which went out with the monarchy. 'Today,' he continued, 'to
tell the truth, there is no reason or power but in the nation itself.'[54] It is true that
the nationalist movement established the nation fairly and squarely as an alternative focus of allegiance to the republican government of the day, while
accepting the republican régime. But monarchism was not dead, and indeed
underwent a revival as a result of the Dreyfus affair. This may be seen by
considering the Jeunesses Royalistes, the Ligue Antisémitique Française, and
Action Française.

After the Boulanger fiasco, many royalists felt that it was time to come to
terms with the Republic and to attempt to replace radical and radical-socialist
coalitions by a Tory coalition of royalists and moderate republicans. This was

effectively realised under the ministry of Jules Méline (1896–8). 'With Méline we had everything,' reminisced Anatole France's fictional royalist, Henri Léon, 'we had the government, the magistracy, the administration, the police. Oh, happy times! Méline led the dance. Nationalists, monarchists, antisemites, plebiscitarians, we danced in unison to his village violin.'[55] This *Ralliement* to the Republic was not popular, however, with the young bloods of the Jeunesse Royaliste. Their leader, Eugène Godefroy, favoured direct action to establish a 'national monarchy'. 'It is time, Sirs,' Godefroy told a royalist banquet in 1896, 'to show the working masses, fooled by socialist utopias . . . that only the monarchy is strong enough to protect their rights against all oppression.'[56] The defeat of the Méline government in the elections of May 1898 destroyed the argument of the moderate royalists, and partisans òf direct action and a popular base regained influence with the pretender, the duc d'Orléans. One idea, which came to nothing, was to infiltrate Déroulède's Ligue des Patriotes. The more conservative Ligue de la Patrie Française, founded in January 1899, was more amenable to royalist influence. More outrageous, but more successful, was the attempt to harness the Ligue Antisémitique Française, which had been set up in 1897 by Jules Guérin, a bankrupt businessman, and initially had the blessing of Édouard Drumont. The core of Guérin's shock-troops was provided by butchers from the abattoirs of La Villette in north-east Paris. They had been active during the anti-Zola riots, and provided a delegation which accompanied Guérin in January 1899 when he went to Brussels to meet the pretender. The duc d'Orléans made a gesture to the anti-Semites in his San Remo declaration of February 1899 when he denounced 'anonymous and restless fortunes', and promised to 'protect the national genius'.[57] Guérin went into action alongside Déroulède at the funeral of President Faure on 23 February 1899, but met only disaster. The government of republican defence ordered his arrest in August 1899, and he and his men held out for six weeks in their new headquarters in the rue Chabrol, which had been paid for out of royalist funds.[58]

The main source of royalist revival came, nevertheless, from outside the traditional royalist movement, in the form of the Action Française movement of Charles Maurras. A Comité de l'Action Française was founded in March 1898 by Maurice Pujo, a writer whom later Maurras accused of 'sentimental anarchism', and by a schoolmaster, Henri Vaugeois. Describing the latter as 'the great-nephew of a member of the Convention, long believed to have been a regicide', Maurras nevertheless pointed out, 'we wanted to rally sons of Jacobins as well as sons of Chouans'.[59] Many Action Française supporters were indeed radicals who refused to follow the rest of the Left into the Dreyfusard camp. The movement was not in the least monarchist until Maurras joined it in the summer of 1899. Maurras himself confessed, 'I was not born a royalist.' His father had died in 1874 a supporter of the Republic of M. Thiers, although his mother's grandfather, a sea captain, had sailed under the Orleanist prince de Joinville.[60]

Maurras claimed that his royalism was not sentimental but rational. The Republic had demonstrated its international insignificance at Fashoda, and only a restoration of the monarchy could make France a great power once again. The total confusion into which the nationalists were thrown by the suicide of Colonel Henry in August 1899, which effectively signalled the innocence of Dreyfus, allowed Maurras to step in and proclaim that nationalism was not just an alternative to monarchism, it logically implied monarchism. The nationalism established by the monarchy would be both exclusive and popular. The monarchy would exercise a brief dictatorship, to punish the corrupt leaders of democracy, but them alone. He recalled that

> After the Commune, thousands of workers were shot, while the leaders were allowed to escape; a King of France would have punished the leaders mercilessly, but he would have spared the people.[61]

Maurras developed his theory in these two directions. On the one hand, the monarchy would purge the nation of the foreign bodies that were corrupting it. In 1941, under the Vichy régime, he praised Drumont for inventing the slogan, 'La France aux Français', which was then realised in the Statut des Juifs, excluding Jews from public life, and in the confiscation of their property.[62] In 1903 Maurras extended his sights from the Jews to the 'four confederate states'—Jews, Protestants, Freemasons and foreigners—who controlled the Republic, betrayed it to their cosmopolitan interests, and would be purged by the monarchy. In *L'Avenir de l'Intelligence* (1905), he reasoned that France had been run by intellectuals since the Enlightenment, and that since the mid-nineteenth century the written word had fallen under the control of the money-power and turned against the nation; he concluded that intellectuals needed to be freed from the tyranny of money, to undergo a moral reformation, and ally with the healthiest elements of the nation to regenerate it.[63]

Conversely, the monarchy was held out as the only force capable of restoring the working classes to their rightful place in society. The Republic was attacked as the instrument of the bourgeoisie which systematically refused workers the right to organise and broke strikes. The comte de Chambord's *Letter to Workers* was cited in defence of the monarchy's support for workers' associations.[64] When the Clemenceau government brutally suppressed the building workers' strike in 1908, Maurras announced, 'the bourgeoisie does not understand the labour question'; 'there can be no social peace in the Republic, and social reform is impossible without the king'.[65]

There was evidence of collusion between Action Française and the labour movement, on the ground and not only in Maurras' mind. Georges Bernanos recounted that he was one of the Camelots du Roi (the young activists of Action Française) thrown into La Santé prison with striking navvies at the time of the building workers' strike. Far from tearing each other apart, they had shared their food and 'sang together *Long live Henri V* and the *Internationale* in turn'.[66] Pujo told a similar story that in La Santé on 1 May 1909, which was both

Labour Day and St Philip's Day, Camelots and trade unionists drank to each others' causes.[67] But what happened in prison cells did not necessarily reflect events outside. On the one hand, the position of Action Française was complicated by its relationship with the pretender and his advisers, whom nominally they represented. The 'Court' in its Spanish exile, reacted sharply to what it saw as the revolutionary activities of Action Française, such as the incident in 1910 when a Camelot du Roi slapped the prime minister, Briand, across the face.[68] Squeezed between censure from above and insubordination from below, Maurras tended to err on the side of order and legality. On the other hand, though intellectuals linked to the labour movement were attracted by the idea of collusion with the extreme Right, the depth and durability of this collusion always remained problematic. The extent of this relationship can be gauged by a study of what might be called national syndicalism.

National Syndicalism

The Dreyfus affair was more than a question of miscarriage of justice; it involved a major political realignment, baptised the 'Dreyfusian revolution' by Georges Sorel in 1909, which brought to power a broad political class from moderate republicans to radicals and socialists. To prevent fracture, it constructed a political culture of the defence of revolutionary principles and the Republic, anticlericalism, Dreyfusism, and the shelving of most social legislation. In this way, though Jean Jaurès acquired a great deal of influence in the corridors of power, so little was done in practical terms for the masses that parliamentary socialists began to lose their grip on the labour movement. The movement began to assert its independence from the Socialist party, and turned away from political action to direct action in the form of the general strike.[69]

Intellectuals involved with the development of anarcho-syndicalism in the labour movement, though on the extreme left of the political spectrum, opened the door to the influence of the Right. For their criticisms were levelled not only against capitalism but also against the democratic and parliamentary system which, they claimed, as a result of the Dreyfusian revolution, had fallen into the hands of a clique. This vulnerability of syndicalism to appropriation by nationalism can be traced in the pages of *Le Mouvement socialiste*. Its editor, Hubert Lagardelle, was a former Guesdist, who sided with Dreyfusism against Guesde but then reacted against governmental socialism in the name of revolutionary syndicalism.[70] In July 1906 he published an article by Robert Louzon entitled 'The bankruptcy of Dreyfusism of the Triumph of the Jewish party'. This repeated the socialist orthodoxy of 1898 that the Dreyfus affair had been a battle between the Jewish bourgeoisie and the clerical bourgeoisie and was of no concern to the proletariat. But it concluded that the 'Jewish party' had now come to power and should be regarded as the enemy.[71]

More significant was George Sorel's *Reflexions on Violence*, which was published by Lagardelle's review between January and July 1906, and came out as a book in 1908. This work can be read in the first place as a contribution to a debate within Marxism. Sorel denounced what he called parliamentary or official socialism, which dispensed revolutionary rhetoric to the workers while selling tranquillity to the conservatives.[72] It restored the doctrine of class struggle to the centre of the analysis and argued that socialist politicians and intellectuals were actually seeking to stifle it. However, rejecting the Marxist view that ideas were only reflections of reality and had no purchase on them, he argued that the general strike had a mythic power, like the Reformation or Revolution, that could stimulate action. The myth of the general strike, generated as a series of powerful images by the ongoing class struggle, would drive the proletarian masses—without any intercession from socialist politicians or intellectuals—to undertake social revolution.[73] There was, however, a second reading that went beyond an apology of revolutionary syndicalism. Sorel likened the general strike to a Napoleonic battle, an act of war that was noble and honourable (unlike bourgeois violence which was bitter and vengeful), and insisted that contemporary decadence could be blown away by proletarian violence and new, heroic values created.[74] What emerged here was that Sorel's concerns were basically moral, that he held bourgeois parliamentary society responsible for the decadence of contemporary civilisation, and looked to creative violence as a means of regeneration. This creative violence he saw currently demonstrated by the proletariat, but the turning point of his argument was that if creative violence were to come from another source, that might also need to be cultivated as the source of regeneration.[75]

The possibility of a convergence of syndicalist and nationalist interests was pursued in the first instance not by Georges Sorel but by two of his disciples, Georges Valois and Édouard Berth. Valois, brought up in the cult of the Republic, turned to anarchism, moved in the orbit of Fernand Pelloutier, Jean Grave and Sébastien Faure, and in 1898 was introduced to Sorel, whom he considered a mentor. He became a Dreyfusard, but was then disgusted by the exploitation of the affair by the politicians. Two events took him in the direction of authoritarianism: military service in 1900, which ill-health forced him to quit, and a visit as a private tutor to Russia, where he was impressed by Tsarism.[76] In 1906 he published *L'Homme qui vient*, in which he stated that civilisation was based on work, and work on 'the man with the whip'; moreover, he claimed, 'war remains the nobility of nations, for only their strength in battle prevents men from returning to the animal state'.[77] Valois joined Action Française and set about trying to build a popular basis for royalism. 'Two young organisations', he wrote in 1907, 'are in parallel pursuing the same goal . . . the destruction of the republican and democratic régime. They are Action Française and the General Confederation of Labour.'[78] He was convinced that the labour movement would look to the monarchy not only because the monarchy stood above classes and arbitrated between them, but because 'the king is our liberator. He will free us from foreigners and politicians, idle bourgeois and the humiliating supervision of pedagogues.'[79]

Édouard Berth, for his part, was similarly repelled by the corrupt bourgeois-democratic-intellectual order that had been consecrated by the Dreyfus affair and by what he saw as the state socialism of the Marxists. He passed through anarcho-syndicalism and did not share Valois' authoritarian instincts. 'Workers, organised in production teams,' he wrote in 1908, 'can continue the achievement of capitalism without needing its supervision or discipline.'[80] But like Sorel he was obsessed by decadence and saw organised labour as a vehicle of redemption. 'There are only two nobilities,' he asserted, 'that of the sword and that of labour', and in the same way he likened the general strike to war: 'It is on those modern battlefields that are the scene of strikes that workers conquer their titles of nobility and found the new order.'[81] In the analyses of both Valois and Berth, the social and the national messages were thus elided.

Sorel's fascination by the creative violence of the proletariat was borne out by the wave of strikes that gripped France between 1906 and 1908. Subsequently, however, they died away, and anarchist influence in the trade union movement was displaced by that of reformists. In addition the movement was brought closer under the control of the Socialist party and effectively integrated into the republican establishment now headed by Aristide Briand. Sorel could attribute this discipline only to the tentacles of the masonic system.[82] In addition, he was becoming increasingly uneasy about the internationalism, antimilitarism and even pacifism of the labour movement. In 1908, looking for a movement that could challenge 'the most complete moral anarchy that this country has known perhaps for more than half a century', he broke with Lagardelle and *Le Mouvement socialiste* and turned to Action Française.[83] He reasoned,

> I am not a prophet; I don't know whether Maurras will bring the king back to France. That is not what interests me about him. What interests me is that he draws himself up in front of the dull, reactionary bourgeoisie, shaming them for having been defeated and trying to give them a doctrine.[84]

In July 1909, congratulating Maurras on the second edition of the *Enquête sur la Monarchie*, he was even more positive, agreeing that only the traditional monarchy was equipped to solve the serious problems facing France.[85]

The attraction of left-wing intellectuals to monarchism sketched in the outlines of a national syndicalism. Two conditions, however, had to be fulfilled before it could be possible to talk of a serious alliance: first, that the labour movement was effectively seduced by monarchism; and, second, that the intellectuals who flirted with monarchism genuinely left their left-wing reflexes behind them.

On the first point it is clear that the desertion of left-wing intellectuals like Sorel, Valois and Berth shocked the Left and was not followed by the labour movement *en masse*. Lagardelle riposted that 'all the high culture of M. Maurras would not prove the complicity of syndicalism and the monarchy', and that though Sorel and Berth had left, 'two swallows do not make a sum-mer'.[86] The only element of the labour movement to waver was the municipal workers' union of Émile Janvion, a former anarchist who criticised the increas-ing subordination of the unions to what he condemned as the Radical-masonic-Jewish establishment.[87] One of his collaborators on his newspaper *Terre Libre*, founded in 1907, was the royalist Marius Riquier. But when questioned by Valois for his enquiry, *Le Révolution sociale et le roi*, Janvion answered that he could not imagine a monarchy, like any régime, without its politicians and exploiters, and argued that the main concern of workers was not monarchy or republic but the socialisation of the means of production.[88] Syndicalists were critical of the way in which the revolutionary heritage was used by the govern-ment to draw socialists and the trade-union movement into the establishment, which is why they were open to seduction by the Right. But they also believed that if the politicians betrayed the true principles of revolution, then it was up to the labour movement to espouse them, and for this reason they could have no interest in monarchism, which seemed to be quite incompatible with social revolution.

The *rapprochement* between syndicalists and monarchists was therefore lim-ited to a small group of intellectuals. At the end of 1911, Édouard Berth joined with Georges Valois and young royalists such as Henri Lagrange and Marius Riquier to found the Cercle Proudhon. Their manifesto condemned democ-racy, which had permitted the uncontrolled development of capitalism, both of which undermined 'the nation, family and morality by substituting laws of gold for laws of blood'. To build a political culture that would embody the values of both Left and Right, they adopted the name of Proudhon to patronise the group, hoping that this would remind the labour movement that they had been warned against following Marxist intellectuals and politicians. Proudhon was held up as the embodiment of French socialism, in opposition to Marxism, which was German and Jewish. Next he was presented as the antithesis of the intellectual: rustic, plain, honest, the salt of the French earth. There was a little in his career—his humble origins in Besançon, a deep moralism, antifeminism and even anti-Semitism—to make him vulnerable to this sort of reinterpreta-tion. But on this narrow base Proudhon was recreated as a patriot, a militarist, and a Catholic. Maurras described him as 'that valiant Frenchman from the Marches of Burgundy'.[89] His 'Gallic, peasant and martial heritage' was pro-claimed. Lastly, though he was not a Christian he was said to have had 'a Christian *moral tone*', a 'latent, Old-France Christianity . . . the Christianity of this Most Christian France'. Pierre-Joseph Proudhon was thus repackaged as a male Joan of Arc, 'the peasant from Lorraine'.[90]

The significance of the Cercle Proudhon, even in intellectual circles, should not be overestimated. There was a good deal of tension between monarchists over forty, such as Maurras, and young activists like Henri Lagrange, twenty-six years his junior. Neither did Maurras want in any way to cede the initiative to Georges Valois. The Cercle Proudhon was essentially the work of dissident members of Action Française.[91] On the other side of the divide, though Sorel was honoured as a inspiration by the Cercle Proudhon, it would not be true to say, as Zeev Sternhell has done, that he approved the nationalist-syndicalist synthesis of the Cercle Proudhon, let alone that he followed obediently in the trail of Maurras' ideas.[92] 'Thinking about the Cercle Proudhon last night,' he told Berth, 'I became convinced that the enterprise is condemned to have not the slightest success.'[93] He flirted with monarchism because of the mythic force of Maurras' doctrine to shake the bourgeoisie out of its apathy, but he objected to the appropriation of the name of Proudhon by the Right, not least because it failed completely to take account of Proudhon's anti-authoritarianism. 'The Action Française,' he wrote in the same letter to Berth, 'subordinating everything to politics . . . demonstrates its obvious hostility to the current of ideas from which one has to judge Proudhon.'[94]

The fragile alliance of syndicalism and nationalism represented by the Cercle Proudhon did not survive the Great War. Some of its members, such as Henri Lagrange, were killed at the Front. More seriously, the separation so dear to the Cercle of proletarian and military values on one side of the equation and democratic, bourgeois, intellectual and internationalist values on the other, was totally reversed by events. The bourgeois democracies demonstrated that they could be as patriotic and militaristic as more aristocratic and authoritarian powers. The majority of the labour movement was integrated into the patriotic and military effort, but underwent a process of *embourgeoisement* in the process. The minority of the labour movement rediscovered revolutionism, but also antimilitarism and defeatism.

Sorel, Valois and Berth had looked to Action Française as a force to recreate heroic values, but they were left with no illusions after its transformation in the Great War. It joined the Union sacrée in 1914, and in the election campaign of 1919, fearful of revolutionary ripples spreading to France from Russia, ran on a Bloc National ticket with other right-wing groups, characterised by chauvinism, clericalism and social conservativism.[95] The capitulation of the extreme Right meant that the effects of the war in France were entirely anti-revolutionary: plutocracy and parliamentary democracy were strengthened, and the same compromised politicians were back in the saddle. Sorel and his disciples were adamant in their hostility to bourgeois democracy and the political class; they rejected Action Française's conservatism and parliamentarism; their only options were a return to revolution as class struggle and to the values of the proletariat, or an investigation of the new doctrine of fascism, but on condition that it did not capitulate to plutocracy and social conservatism.

Sorel welcomed the Russian Revolution. 'I cling to the hope of a socialist renaissance based on the activity of the Bolsheviks', he told the anarcho-syndicalist Paul Delesalle.[96] Of course, the Russian Revolution was susceptible of all kinds of construction in its early days and Sorel praised it while returning to the cult of Proudhon. 'Nothing is more essential for the future of the proletariat than to initiate it in the teachings of Proudhon', he stated in

1919.[97] This was emphatically not the Proudhon of the Cercle, for Sorel dedicated his thoughts to Paul and Léonie Delesalle, describing himself as 'an old man who persists like Proudhon in remaining a disinterested servant of the proletariat'.[98] At the end of his life, he showed an interest in Italian fascism. He was flattered that Mussolini might have read his works and declared him to be as a great a political genius as Lenin, for the former had 'invented something that is not in my books: the union of the national and the social, which I studied but never developed'.[99] At the same time, however, Sorel told Delesalle that he suspected that fascism was an instrument to destroy socialism, and reflected mournfully that 'Europe is without doubt destined to experience a new *Thermidoreanism*'.[100]

Far from succumbing to fascism, then, Sorel remained faithful to the proletariat so long as the proletariat remained faithful to class struggle and revolution. Édouard Berth was equally disillusioned by the 'war between states' which had only reinforced plutocracy and democracy, and drawn Action Française into social defence and parliamentarism, with Léon Daudet elected deputy for Paris. He interpreted the Russian Revolution as the realisation of the dreams of Marx and Sorel about class war and the general strike, and the source of socialism's revival. Proclaiming 'we are today what we were yesterday', he threw himself into Communism.[101] At this point, his path crossed with that of Pierre Monatte, who also believed that the labour movement would flourish under Communism. Disillusioned after the death of Lenin, Berth joined Monatte's review *Révolution prolétarienne*. Like Sorel, he rediscovered Proudhon, and argued against the Marxists that far from being reactionary, nationalist and petty-bourgeois, Proudhon was committed to 'revolution first', internationalism and class struggle.[102]

The progress of Georges Valois was more complicated. He remained within the orbit of Action Française after the war, but became increasingly disillusioned by its shift to conservatism. He felt that the victory of the Republic in the Great War, to the strains of the *Marseillaise*, had destroyed the thesis of Action Française that nationalism implied monarchism.[103] He nevertheless continued to press Action Française for a social programme and in 1922 obtained its approval for an Estates-General of Production. This would re-enact the events of 1789, but this time to found an 'État syndical', with an integral syndicalism binding workers and employers to ensure social justice and the harmony of the nation.[104] The defeat of the Right in the election of 1924 put paid to this scheme ever being realised. Valois, who had visited Mussolini's Italy in 1923, decided that the time had come to organise veterans and producers, finding them in the Socialist and Communist camps if necessary, in order to break the back of parliamentarism and plutocracy. He opened his campaign in Périgueux, where he had the good will of the Communist mayor Marcel Delagrange, urging the troops, 'Let's make the Revolution together.'[105] This fraternisation with Communists precipitated the final break with Maurras and Action Française. But Valois soon found another mantle. Recalling that

Maurice Barrès' '*Cocarde*, which was written with republicans, royalists and socialists, was the preface to our work', he launched *Le Nouveau Siècle* as its successor and recruitied Barrès' son, Philippe, to work on it.[106]

Initially the social dimension of Valois' movement was dictated by his nationalism. To sweep away the old political class and its financial backers, Valois proclaimed 'the law that saved France and civilisation on the banks of the Marne: the law of national fraternity, stirred by the spirit of heroism, acting under the command of a leader, for the greatness of the Fatherland'.[107] In November 1925 he founded the Faisceau des Combattants et Producteurs to establish 'a national state . . . above parties and classes'.[108] The formula was clear to Valois: 'Nationalism + Socialism = Fascism'.[109] There was a danger that the national project would swamp that of social transformation, and indeed serve as a vehicle of social defence. The problem was underlined by the fact that the main provider of funds for the Faisceau was the millionaire perfumer Coty, who was unhappy about most of its revolutionary pronouncements. Had Coty had his way the Faisceau would have become more conservative. But Valois was adamant that big business would not take over French fascism as it had taken over Italian fascism. Valois' revolutionism, like that of Berth and Sorel, was not to be stifled. Valois argued that fascism was 'precisely in the current of the movement of 1789' before it was taken over by bourgeois parliamentarism; it was 'on the lines of Blanquist and Proudhonian French socialism'.[110]

Valois' attacks on plutocracy became increasingly violent. In 1928 he finally broke with Coty and *Le Nouveau Siècle* ceased publication. He adopted the pacifism of the Left and dedicated a new book to Édouard Berth, in whose steps he was now following.[111] From 1926, he told Marcel Déat in 1933, 'I had only one thought: to move as quickly as possible, with our Left, to make common cause with socialism.'[112] His reaction to the events of 6 February 1934 was to try once more to organise an 'État syndical'. To win over Jouhaux and the CGT he announced that 'without any obligation to the Right I find myself on the Left with the revolutionary faith I had when I was twenty-five years old'.[113] However, Valois had dallied too long with monarchism and fascism to be able to regain the confidence of the Left. His application in December 1935 to join the SFIO was rejected and he was accused by the *Révolution prolétarienne* of responsibility for the assassination of Jaurès.[114] But he had also burned his bridges with the Right. Imprisoned under the Vichy régime, he told fellow prisoner Pierre Mendès-France that his arrest had been ordered by Maurras.[115] Isolated, he was briefly active in the Resistance movement in Savoy, and he died in February 1945 in the concentration camp of Bergen-Belsen.

Even the career of Hubert Lagardelle, who sailed very close to fascism, did not lose its revolutionary syndicalist origins. He had denounced attempts to demonstrate that syndicalism and monarchism were compatible and broke with of Sorel and Berth over their flirtation with the Right. He developed plans for 'the increasing syndicability of French society', and his involvement in the development of the Midi-Pyrénées region on behalf of the government during and after the war caused him to reflect on how his syndicalism could be dovetailed with a federal system for communes and regions.[116] He was regarded by Mussolini along with Sorel as one of the theoreticians of fascism and this was exploited by the French government, sending him on a mission to Rome in 1933–7 to keep Italy away from the embrace of Hitler. In 1942–3 Lagardelle was appointed minister of labour in the Laval government and presided over the deportation of French labour under the Service du Travail Obligatoire. For this he was sentenced to hard labour for life in 1946. But in spite of his political misjudgments he remained faithful to his syndicalist thinking. He tried to revise Vichy's rather truncated Charte du Travail in the direction of the Etat syndical, but was frustrated by both employers and labour, which wanted to keep their hands free. Moreover, in his journalistic work he returned more and more to the inspiration of Proudhon. At a time when Proudhon's heritage was being used and abused, he pointed to him as the force behind the French trade-union movement at the turn of the century, including Pelloutier and himself, urging that 'socialists, of whatever feather they are, must not forget that Proudhon remains one of the great visionaries of a world without capitalism and without proletariat'.[117] Like all Sorel's disciples and Sorel himself, he returned in the end to Proudhon's bosom.

National Socialism

Between the wars, political cultures in France had to take account of two events, the Great War and the Russian Revolution. The Right, which had been such a powerful source of opposition to the bourgeois, parliamentary Republic, was now much more integrated with it, since the Republic had so amply demonstrated its nationalism and social conservatism. The liberal tendency on the Right triumphed over the extremist tendency. Its main organisation, the Fédération Républicaine, functioned within the parliamentary process. This state of affairs was rocked by only two factors. First, outside parliamentary parties like the Fédération Républicaine, but connected with them, there were extra-parliamentary movements, and influence tended to shift to the latter if the Left gained power in the Republic. Second, there was a conflict of generations between those who had experienced the Great War, and those who had not. The youth were in general far more impatient than mature politicians with the parliamentary Republic and the political class that ran it, and constantly spoke of the need for revolution.

The effect of the Russian Revolution on the Left was both to fragment and to strengthen it. It divided the Left into two internationalist parties, the PCF and the SFIO, which in some ways was drawn further to the Left by competition for support with the Communists. But it failed to displace the Radical party, which strengthened its position as the natural party of government in the inter-war period, combining revolutionary principles with a vigorous anti-

Communism. The younger generation on the Left as on the right, had no time for the Radical bosses and other representatives of the political class. But many were repelled also by international Communism. When, after 1934, the parties of the Left, Communists, Socialists and Radicals, joined forces in the Popular Front, some of the younger generation combined their revolutionary opposition to the political class and their nationalist opposition to Communism in a new kind of fascism of the Left. But the very success of the Popular Front, successfully monopolising the electoral territory on the Left, forced the fascists of the Left to go to the Right in search of votes. Nevertheless, in order to deflect accusations of being on the Right, they tended to mask their drift to the Right by the reinvention of their left-wing credentials, whether Jacobin or socialist.

So long as the French Right in the shape of the Bloc National demonstrated that it could win elections and wield power there was no call for an extra-parliamentary movement of the Right. All this changed in 1924 when the Cartel des Gauches of Radicals supported by Socialists was elected to office and conservatives feared that barriers against Communism were now drastically weakened. The Fédération Républicaine, while continuing to act as a parliamentary party, established links with extra-parliamentary leagues which it used as instruments of propaganda and sometimes of action. The most important of these were the Jeunesses Patriotes and the Croix de Feu.[118]

The Jeunesses Patriotes were the youth wing of the Ligue des Patriotes, which had been founded by Paul Déroulède and presided over between 1914 and his death in 1923 by Maurice Barrès. It was revived after the electoral disaster of 1924 by General de Castelnau, who at the same time launched the Fédération Nationale Catholique.[119] 'To the international revolution that threatens us,' he declared, 'let us oppose French resistance. Let us unite, organise, act.'[120] What was action for Castelnau was, however, inaction for Pierre Taittinger, president of the Jeunesses Patriotes, also formed in 1924. He had been president of the Bonapartist Union de la Jeunesse Plébiscitaire de la Seine before the war, and after a brilliant military career was elected in 1919 as a Bonapartist in Charente-Inférieure on the Bloc National ticket. It was not enough, he argued, for the Ligue to 'celebrate patriotic anniversaries or simply to make a few speeches against policies the country does not want', if the Jeunesses were not to lose angry young men to the Faisceau or Action Française.[121] For Taittinger, action meant breaking up Communist meetings and celebrating the five 'martyrs' ambushed and killed in the rue Damrémont on 23 April 1925. He wanted an offensive not only against 'active and bloody anarchism: Communism', but also against 'passive and latent anarchism: the Cartel régime'.[122] He considered the parliamentary system and its beneficiaries, the political class, to be totally discredited. Parliament should be suspended for a few months by an emergency 'government of new men' who would revise the constitution. In tones which echoed those of the Jacobin dictatorship, he warned, 'This is the price of public safety.'[123] What he proposed for the constitution was summed up in two elements, 'Authority. A Leader'. Its fine print read very like the constitution of the Year VIII that inaugurated the Consulate. This was perhaps not surprising, given Taittinger's Bonapartist background.[124] He groped after a social programme to distinguish the Jeunesses Patriotes from the classic Right, but did little better than come up with the slogan 'Social Nationalism'. In general this meant replacing class conflict by 'class collabora-tion . . . national concord'.[125] When concrete proposals were required for the elections of 1932 nothing more was advanced than financial responsibility, the encouragement of saving and the reduction of the cost of living.[126] Priority given to the nation and the meagreness of its social programme (social nationalism, not national socialism) kept the Jeunesses Patriotes squarely on the Right.

The ideology of the Croix de Feu was even more explicitly national. Founded in 1927, taken over in 1931 by Colonel de La Rocque, it was formed, as the name implied, from veterans who had been decorated for gallantry during the Great War. Later it admitted veterans who had not been decorated and, from 1933, Volontaires Nationaux who were too young to have fought in the trenches. The Croix de Feu were angry that the war had been fought and won only to return the political generation of 1900, that of the Dreyfusard revolution, to power. This anti-Dreyfusism was developed as anti-Semitism, with opposition to 'the parasitism of intermediaries and speculators . . . poison-ing the best qualities of our hard-working, thrifty, provident race' expressed in the language of Drumont.[127] Against those evils, La Roque saw it as his task to mobilise the forces which represented national honour. 'Our intangible and unique tie', he said, 'is the cult of the Fatherland and the love of French order, together with our common nobility of combat.'[128] Since the Croix de Feu were a movement rather than a party, he saw no need to define doctrine more closely.

Events, however, forced La Rocque to clarify his position and his strategy. On 6 February 1934 angry crowds laid siege to the Chamber of Deputies in Paris and tried to invade it. [Fig. 24] Parliamentary institutions came quite literally within an ace of destruction. That night was the baptism of fire of a whole generation to whom the Great War was history, and yet who learned for themselves that the politicians of the Third Republic were not equal to saving France in an increasingly dangerous world. That night, La Rocque's troops marched and counter-marched but did nothing to help topple the régime. He claimed to have shouted 'Forward, grenadiers of Brumaire'; if he did, his men did not act accordingly.[129] A few years later, accusations were made that he failed to act because he was in the pay of the former premier Tardieu. What is certain is that La Rocque was under pressure after 6 February 1934, particu-larly from young Volontaires Nationaux like Pierre Pucheu, to define a pro-gramme with a national-socialist content, and to challenge the Republic decisively. La Rocque delivered on neither count, and the following year the young hotheads left the movement. What La Rocque provided in his manifesto

Fig. 24.   Riots of 6 February 1934 (Roger-Viollet)

Service public was an analysis of a number of social evils including the decline
of the family, social conflict and the immigration of Central European Jews.
'Greco–Latin civilisation', he wrote, 'is incompatible with domination by barbarians, and cannot withstand the invasion of parasites and mercenaries without degenerating.'[130] To deal with them, he argued, 'We must first of all restore
public morality, the authority of the state, and the French mystique.' The
components of that *mystique* were precisely those which would be propagated
by Vichy: 'Travail, Famille, Patrie'. Somehow La Rocque felt that patriotism
rightly understood would provide the cure for all France's ills.

> We have kept contact with all the martyrs of the French Passion, and in this
> way we have enabled the national *mystique* to gush forth again, rich in spirit,
> heroism, sacrifice and vigour, as in the time of Joan of Arc, of Fontenoy, of
> Valmy, of Montmirail, of Verdun.[131]

Those who expected a right-wing revolution to come from the Croix de Feu
were wasting their time. It claimed not only to be more patriotic than the
government, but also to be more republican. The Great War, after all, had
saved the Republic as well as France. In June 1936, when the movement was
dissolved, along with the other extra-parliamentary leagues, by the Popular

Front government, the Croix de Feu was refounded as a political party, the Parti Social Français (PSF). This was in no sense a fascist party. La Rocque espoused legalism and set about campaigning to achieve a parliamentary majority for his party in the general election due in 1940. He had to win over conservative opinion hitherto represented by the Fédération Républicaine and the Alliance Démocratique. But he also had to win over opinion represented in 1936 by Popular Front parties increasingly unhappy with the influence of the Communists within that coalition. On the one hand, he attacked the classic parties of the Right as 'sectarian fossils' who were threatened by the PSF's dynamism.[132] On the other, he was concerned to 'affirm our frankly republican views . . . to demonstrate that we are more republican than the Radicals'.[133] The strategy was to denounce the Radical leadership as dangerous, incompetent or useless and to prise away its supporters. In 1937 La Rocque claimed that forty per cent of PSF membership came from parties supporting the Popular Front.[134] However, across a series of by-elections in 1937–9 the PSF found Radical opinion a good deal harder to make inroads into than conservative opinion, particularly after Daladier stole La Rocque's thunder by attacking the Communists and breaking up the Popular Front. The PSF was lodged fairly firmly on the Right, while remaining trapped in a legalism, republicanism and even parliamentarism that was incompatible with any 'fascist' critique of the régime.

While the Jeunesses Patriotes and the Croix de Feu never succeeded in breaking free of the conservative Right, a new generation of militants of Action Française made another attempt to combine nationalism and socialism and forge a genuine movement of the revolutionary Right. As with the Croix de Feu, crisis was precipitated by the events of 6 February 1934. That night Maurras had not even got as far as the streets, remaining in the newspaper's offices. The monarchism of the court, which was given a fresh lease of life by the delegation of considerable authority by the duc de Guise, pretender since 1926, to his son Henri, comte de Paris, in 1934, remained hostile to violent actions committed on its behalf. But this did nothing to contain the impatience of the young generation of royalists within Action Française, who were keen to attack the Third Republic and its ageing politicians. The Camelots of the sixteenth *arrondissement* of Paris, who had been in the thick of the action that night, led by a former *polytechnicien* Eugène Deloncle, denounced the inactivity of the Action Française and were expelled from the movement. They took their revenge by beating up Léon Blum at the funeral of the historian Jacques Bainville on 13 Febuary 1936, which provoked the government immediately to dissolve Action Française. Deloncle and his friends set up a Comité Secret d'Action Révolutionnaire, commonly known as the Cagoule, which tried to establish links with anti-Communist officers in the French army, with the intention of sparking off a preventive coup. Disregarded by the army, they took to acts of terrorism, exploding bombs outside the offices of employers' organisations on 16 September 1937 in the hope that they would be taken as

Communist attacks and throw the army and *patronat* into their camp. Maurras denounced 'the ridiculous oaths of a would-be white or grey masonic order, which might well have links with the masonry of the reds', smearing the terrorists with the allegation of practising the *politique du pire*.[135]

More significant ideologically were a young graduate of the Sorbonne, born in 1906, Jean-Pierre Maxence, and three graduates of the École Normale Supérieure, all born in 1909: Thierry Maulnier, Maurice Bardèche and Robert Brasillach. They had seen action on 6 February 1934 but at the offices of Action Française found not leadership but Maurras talking about symbolist poets.[136] Maxence and Maulnier welcomed 6 February as 'the first demonstration of national energy witnessed since the war', which for a moment united young dissidents of both Left and Right, 'the sons of those shot at the Mur [des Fédérés] and the sons of those shot at Quiberon' [a royalist landing in 1795]. Having tasted blood they called for insurrection against 'our régime paralysed by corruption and senility' to push through a 'national revolution'.[137] While Maurras was safely out of the way in 1937, serving a prison term, Thierry Maulnier seized the opportunity to launch his own review. It was entitled *L'Insurgé*, a provocatively revolutionary echo of Jules Vallès' autobiographical work centering on the Paris Commune, and included references to Drumont's appeal to the working-class rebels of the Commune, *La Fin d'un Monde*. The message was violent and socialist, but also argued that only a national revolution against the Third Republic would inaugurate social justice. 'The exploited and disinherited classes will not be able to conquer their material and moral place in the nation without the backing of a power sufficiently strong, new and free to crack resistance and impose its arbitration', wrote Maulnier. And he concluded, 'the only legitimate revolution is national; the only legitimate nationalism today is revolutionary'.[138]

The national socialist message was developed by Robert Brasillach, who had a literary column on *Action Française* from 1931 and in 1936 was brought onto the team of a review which grew up under its auspices, *Je suis partout*.[139] Brasillach criticised conservative nationalists for sacrificing the need to incorporate the mass of workers into the national community to the obsession with social defence. When confronted by the Communist takeover of the CGT, however, he looked for inspiration to the anti-Marxist syndicalists of the pre-war era, 'Sorel, Lagardelle, Pelloutier, Pouget, Delesalle and many others' to construct a specifically French socialism to withstand Communism.[140] This French socialism was defined not only against Communists but against Jews. The pitch of its anti-Semitism was heightened in April 1938, when Léon Blum's second cabinet included a number of Jews. This anti-Semitism was the key to a shift from socialism to nationalism, incorporating the anti-Semitism of the Left by adding populist figures such as Drumont to the list of collective heroes, and claiming that thinkers who were contested by both Left and Right were precursors of fascism. 'Certainly, there are much more than prefascist 'gleams' in Drumont, Péguy, Proudhon and Sorel', he said in

July 1938, and then rubbed his hands, pointing out that 'it is not entirely in vain that the initiator of fascism [Sorel] was one of the pupils of the old Jew', Marx.[141]

Brasillach's anti-Semitism reached fever-pitch during the Munich crisis, when he argued that the government was full of Jews, Communists and their agents, who were dragging France into a needless war with Germany.[142] Under the Occupation he perfected his analysis, upgrading Maurras' 'four confederate states' into the 'seven Internationals against peace', the Communist, Socialist, Jewish, Catholic, Protestant, Masonic and Financial.[143] At the same time, seeking to define an authentic French fascism that would draw together Déat and Doriot, he again claimed the authority of Péguy and Sorel.[144] Sorel had been vulnerable, since his love-match with Mussolini, to claims that he invented fascism, but to appropriate the memory of Péguy who had broken with him in 1910 over the latter's flirtation with the Right, and had pantheonised the Jewish Dreyfusard Bernard-Lazare in *Notre Jeunesse*—required an expert manipulation of collective memory. Unfortunately, Charles Péguy's own son Marcel had written a book which opened the way to Péguy's recuperation by the Right; Brasillach was delighted in his review of it to welcome Péguy as 'a French national-socialist'.[145]

The brandishing of names previously associated with the Left was intended to indicate that national socialism was indeed socialist and to build a bridge between Right and Left. In the years around 1930, there was a good deal of discontent with the politicians of the Third Republic among a whole generation of 'non-conformists of the thirties', and distinctions between Left and Right became blurred.[146] But the events of 6 February 1934 created a repolarisation of politics between Left and Right. The parties and movements of the Left gathered in an anti-fascist coalition and, as we have seen, turned to the rhetoric of the French Revolution for legitimation, while delegitimising fascism as a movement of the Right. Nonconformists on the Left were placed in a difficult position. If they joined the anti-fascist coalition, they both acknowledged the leadership of politicians they had recently been attacking for incompetence, corruption and being too old, and were obliged to link arms with Communists who were the driving force behind that coalition. Those who remained nonconformists preserved their revolutionary, radical or socialist principles in order to continue their attacks on the politicians they so despised. But they combined this with a nationalist position, denouncing international Communists and their fellow travellers as a greater threat than fascists. To sanction this development, they often resorted to the rhetoric of Jacobinism, which they constructed as revolutionary and nationalist, at the same time as the Communists were using Jacobinism to justify their claims to lead the Popular Front. The main problem the nonconformists faced, however, was that the Popular Front was highly successful. It monopolised and closed off the electorate of the Left and forced the dissidents to move to the Right in search of support. Thus, though the writer Drieu de la Rochelle commented that 'fascism has always started on the Left', it rarely finished up there.[147] In the end the divisions constructed in the name of the French Revolution drove it to the Right.

The events of 6 February were as traumatic for the youth on the Left wing of politics as for that on the Right. Although the riots were directed against the political class which the Radical party dominated, there were young activists in the Radical movement angered that the riots seemed to have changed nothing. Bertrand de Jouvenel resigned from the Radical party and founded a paper aptly called *La Lutte des Jeunes*. One of its contributors, proud to have been on the place de la Concorde on 6 February, expostulated, 'All that blood to get where? To see Herriot and Tardieu back in power?'[148] *La Lutte des Jeunes* argued that the cosy self-interest of the 'République des camarades' should be subordinated to the general interest and acknowledge the sovereignty of the Nation with which it had lost contact.

Gaston Bergery was another Radical who resigned from the party, in 1933. He had been an adviser to Herriot but was alienated by Herriot's wheeler-dealing with other parties to stay in power and rhetorical attacks on the 'mur d'argent' while in fact doing nothing to check the influence of finance-capital in national affairs. After his resignation, Bergery attempted to unite Radical and Socialist voters in a Front Commun, dedicated to a second French re-volution to destroy the financial powers that held the Nation in thrall. He presented himself for re-election in his seat, but was defeated by a Communist, and his anti-Communism became more pronounced when it seemed that the Franco-Soviet pact of 1935 would drag France into a Soviet war. This risk became explicit when the Popular Front took power. To undermine Blum he called for a 'truly French socialism' and a 'rallying for national safety', which provoked accusations that he was a 'fascist of the Left'.[149] The language that he used was in fact transparently Jacobin. 'The entire Nation is oppressed by factions', he argued. 'Government must derive from the will of the people, but be given sufficient authority to enforce the will of the people against those factions.'[150] What was required, quite simply, was a 'Government of Public Safety'.[151]

Even more open in his appeal to Jacobinism than Gaston Bergery was Marcel Déat, who left the SFIO in 1933. Just as Bergery blamed the Radical leadership for putting their party's desire for power above the national interest, so Déat blamed the SFIO leadership for putting their party's desire for doctrinal purity above the national interest. From his *Perspectives socialistes* of 1930, which was published by Georges Valois, Déat subjected socialist doctrines to a funda-mental revision. He believed that the proletariat was too narrow an electoral base for the Socialist party, and that it should seek to win over the *classes moyennes* before they were won over by fascism. He criticised capitalism less as an exploitative system than as an anarchic system, which did as much damage to the middle- and lower-middle classes as it did to the working classes. Socialists should be prepared to accept power, not to destroy capitalism, but to direct and manage it in the national interest. This would be a national revo-

lution, taking place within the framework of the French state. Socialists would
be called upon to abandon internationalism for socialism in one country.[152]

Blum's response to Déat's views at the Paris congress of the SFIO in July
1933 was unambiguous: 'I am horrified.' Déat and his neo-socialists were
expelled from the party and founded a breakaway Parti Socialiste de France.
They adopted the motto 'Order, Authority, Nation', and placed themselves
under the patronage of Jean Jaurès. This was a further slap in the face for Blum,
who considered that he was himself the inheritor of the authentic tradition of
Jaurès. Lucien Rebatet, a journalist of *Je suis partout*, later praised Déat for
being 'one of the first to break the bridges between Jewish socialism and French
socialism'.[153] In the short term, however, it was Blum's 'Jewish' socialism that
triumphed. In the general election of May 1936, the SFIO became the largest
party and Blum premier, while Déat lost his seat to a Communist. Like
Bergery, Déat responded by appealing over the heads of the established parties,
launching a Rassemblement populaire that would include 'the quasi-totality of
the nation'.[154] But, like Bergery, he found that the grip of the Popular Front
parties on the electorate of the Left was unassailable, and when he managed to
return to parliament as a result of a by-election in Angoulême, it was thanks to
a candidate of La Rocque's Parti Social Français standing down.

In the confusion of July 1940 at Vichy, Déat won over Bergery to his scheme
of a 'parti unique' or single fascist party but he was unable to sell it to Marshal
Pétain, who would have no truck with such revolutionary ideas.[155] Though the
Third Republic and its parliamentary institutions were destroyed, those who
benefited were the conservative, Maurassian Right, not the revolutionaries.
Déat fell back in high dudgeon on Paris, where he set up a party of his own, the
Rassemblement National Populaire (January 1941), with the approval of
the German authorities. One of its components in the first half of 1941 was the
Cagoule of Eugène Deloncle, now revived under the label Mouvement Social
Révolutionnaire, who were equally displeased by the triumph of the
Maurassians. The main basis of its support, however, was provided by anti-
Communist trade unionists such as Georges Dumoulin of the Miners' Federation. The ideology developed by Déat at the RNP congress of June 1941
remained decidedly revolutionary. Déat ridiculed the Révolution Nationale
of the Vichy government, claiming, 'you can't have a revolution without
revolutionaries'. He also stated that the gerontocracy at Vichy was standing in
the way of true Franco-German collaboration. 'A conservative France cannot
truly collaborate,' he said, 'and a France that truly collaborates cannot remain
conservative.'[156]

To justify revolutionary collaboration, and to sell it to his supporters in the
labour movement, Déat turned to the revolutionary and socialist tradition. He
sought to demonstrate that his form of national socialism was in the tradition of
Jaurès, and beyond him, of Rousseau and Robespierre as well. Jaurès was both
a patriot and an internationalist, and whereas the SFIO in London formed a
Groupe Jean-Jaurès to express their hostility to the German Occupation, Déat

presented Jaurès as a passionate believer in Franco–German reconciliation to support his vision of a Europe of harmonious national socialist states.[157] Turning to Robespierre, Déat told an RNP congress in 1943 that he could not have been a national socialist because France in his time was a pre-industrial society. Instead, he was a national democrat and true precursor of the RNP, since 'the French Revolution tended towards national democratism as we now tend towards national socialism'. Moreover, whereas the Girondins were 'liberal bourgeois' who were responsible for the 'liberal and bourgeois deviation' of the French Revolution, Robespierre and his own mentor, Rousseau, stood not for parliamentary majorities but for the notion of the General Will which might be articulated by the Jacobin party, a forerunner of the 'parti unique', a Committee of Public Safety, or a dictator.[158] By a judicious rewriting of history, Déat placed his movement and his goals in the authentic tradition of the French Revolution. However, this did not mean that he was able to win over a significant following from the Left, as the French became increasingly polarised between collaborators and Resistants.

The most significant fascist movement to emerge on the Left was however a spin-off of the Communist party rather than the Radical party or of the SFIO. As with the previous breakaways, the trigger was provided by a dispute over political alignments. In this case, Jacques Doriot, Communist deputy-mayor of the Paris suburb of Saint-Denis, was a step ahead of the Comintern in calling after the events of 6 February for an end to the 'class against class' policy which ruled out co-operation with Socialists and for a policy of unity of action with Socialists against the fascist threat. The Comintern line, endorsed by Thorez and the PCF, was that bourgeois democracy and fascism were both forms of the dictatorship of capital, and that 'between the plague and cholera there is no choice'.[159] Behind this dispute over tactics, however, was a deeper unease felt by Doriot about the subordination of the PCF to the dictates of Moscow. This became intolerable when the Comintern was reduced to being merely the instrument of the strategic interests of the Soviet Union. The Franco–Soviet alliance of May 1935 threatened to return Europe to the system of power-blocs that had existed before 1914, and to make France the tool of an imperialist war fought by the Soviet Union against Germany. 'France will not be a country of slaves' was the blunt title of a collection of Doriot's newspaper articles in his aptly named *Émancipation* in 1936. Expelled from the party Doriot resigned as mayor of Saint-Denis, was re-elected with three-quarters of the vote, and set about shaping a 'national communist' movement the heart of which would be his own fief of Saint-Denis.[160]

With municipal elections due again in May 1935, and facing the danger of defeat by the Communists, Doriot made overtures to the SFIO as if the Congress of Tours had never happened, under the slogan, 'one class, one union, one party'. This he reinforced in the run-up to the elections by hosting at Saint-Denis the first exhibition to be devoted to the Paris Commune, a gesture that the city of Paris itself was still too fearful to risk.[161] On 14 July 1935 he kept his options open by marching in the procession that marked the inauguration of the Rassemblement populaire. The problem that he faced, however, was that having broken from the PCF he found the hunting-grounds of the Left monopolised by the parties of the Left. In the legislative elections of 1936, he held onto his seat at Saint-Denis by a mere seven hundred votes, beating off the challenge of the Communist with socialist support only with the help of right-wing votes. Doriot's appeal became increasingly national, decreasingly social. At a mass-meeting in Saint-Denis on 28 June 1936, he launched his own party, the Parti Populaire Français, interpreted by one of his lieutenants as 'an attempt to rally the deep forces of the nation, over and above classes, on the move towards socialism and greatness'.[162] At the first congress of the PPF in November 1936, Doriot took up the slogan, 'France first', and adopted the flag that had flown at the Fête de la Fédération in 1790.[163] Pierre Drieu de la Rochelle, who had joined *L'Émancipation nationale* as a journalist, dedicated a series of articles to Doriot as a force for national unity:

> Beneath the sign
> of Joan of Arc who arose alone and said: no,
> of Henri of Navarre, who reconciled,
> of Richelieu, who built,
> of Danton, who proclaimed the fatherland in danger,
> of Clemenceau, who freed the country from enemies and allies.[164]

In spite of the references to national unity, however, Doriot's path to the Left was blocked and he was forced, if he were break out of Saint-Denis, to make common cause with the parties of the Right. On 7 May 1937, at another mass-meeting in the Vélodrome d'Hiver, he launched the Front de la Liberté, a sort of mirror-image of the Popular Front. He won over the Fédération Républicaine and Pierre Taittinger's Parti Républicain National et Social, which had once been the Jeunesses Patriotes, but de La Rocque's Parti Social Français, which dreamed of an electoral majority in its own right, kept its distance.[165] Shortly afterwards, the government dismissed Doriot from his mayoral office, and in a by-election held in June 1937, he and his supporters were crushed by the Communists. Now there was no way back. On 8 May 1938 the PPF laid a wreath at the statue of Joan of Arc along with other right–wing organisations, and a month later Doriot spoke on the same platform as Charles Maurras.[166]

After the collapse of France in 1940, Doriot's traditionalism peaked with his reputation as 'l'homme du Maréchal' in Paris. Since the Germans were backing Déat in Paris, he secured the patronage of Vichy. The only revolutionary sign of his movement now was the title of the edition of his newspaper in the occupied zone, *Le Cri du Peuple*, once used by Jules Vallès. In order to make the flagging PPF attractive to the Germans, he made the newspaper the vehicle of violent anti-Semitism, including breaking up Jewish shops and synagogues, and helping with the mass arrest of Jews in Paris on 16 July 1942.[167] Likewise, he funnelled the energies of the PPF into the Légion des Volontaires Françaises contre le Bolchevisme which fought in German uniforms on the Eastern Front against the Soviet Union. The PPF tried to seize power in November 1942, when the Allies invaded North Africa and the Germans invaded the southern zone, but the Germans decided to stick with Laval, and Doriot was marginalised, sent back to the Eastern Front, and was not even included when Déat and Darnand, the head of the Milice, were brought into power in 1944. After the withdrawal of the German occupant and the collapse of its puppet government, the last remnants of French national socialism—a few thousand French Volontaires contre le Bolchevisme, Miliciens, and French Waffen SS formed into the SS Brigade Charlemagne—reached the end of the road early in 1945, encircled by the Red Army in Pomerania.[168]

The New Right

Whereas after the First World War the French Right was effectively integrated into the parliamentary Republic, after the Second World War it was virtually excluded from national life. French fascists and representatives of the Vichy state were accused of collaboration and war crimes, demonised by association with the extermination of the Jews, and suffered trial, execution, or imprisonment, the confiscation of their property and national degradation. Those who wanted to exclude were now excluded. Charles Maurras, led from the dock in January 1945, shouted, 'It is the revenge of Dreyfus.'[169]

Those who suffered were only a fraction of those connected with Vichy and collaboration, but it was the intention of the head of the new provisional government, Charles de Gaulle, to end the Franco–French civil war as quickly as possible, and this required drawing a veil over the immediate past. At the same time, those who had triumphed in the Liberation were keen to rewrite the history of France. The terms nationalist and socialist that had been appropriated by fascists were now recovered by the victors: nationalism now stood for the liberation of the French *patrie* from the German occupant and Vichy, while socialism was to be achieved by the returning parties of the Left within the framework of the democratic Republic.

For a long time after the war, fascism was taboo and the Right was discredited. Those deputies and senators who had voted *pleins pouvoirs* to Pétain on 10 July 1940 were disqualified and replaced by a new generation of politicians who were associated or associated themselves with the Resistance. Parties such as the RPF and MRP, while shifting to the Right, gained their legitimacy from the Resistance. Those connected with Vichy, who eventually returned to politics, tended to call themselves Independents. When Action Française reappeared it called itself Rénovation Française and its weekly *Aspects de la France*. Maurice Bardèche, colleague and brother-in-law of Robert Brasillach, who was shot on 6 February 1945, was asked by François Mauriac whether he now admitted that he had been wrong. Bardèche began a long campaign to recover a collective memory of the extreme Right that could open the way to a reshaping of fascist culture. In an open letter to Mauriac in 1947 he denounced 'the reign of lies' that flourished under the Liberation's monopoly of the interpretation of events. He attacked the myth whereby the Resistance had defeated Germany, calling it 'an act of rebellion' against legally constituted authorities, powerless without the Allied invasions, and counted its cost at 80,000 lives against a mere 17,000 victims of the Terror. The Liberation, concluded Bardèche, far from liberating French soil, ensured that the Communist domination of Europe also extended to France.[170] The following year Bardèche received a year's imprisonment for arguing in *Nuremberg ou la Terre promise* that the Nuremberg court had no right to punish men who were obedient servants of a legitimate state, and denying the existence of the Holocaust.

In the decade after the war there were only fragmentary fascist movements, small, illegal, constantly harassed by the authorities and changing their names, and harking back to inter-war or wartime fascism rather than marking a new departure.[171] One example was the movement or movements of René Binet. Binet had begun his political career in the Communist Youth, but he soon parted company with them. Expelled in 1934, he became a Trotskyist. Captured by the Germans in 1940, he ended the war in the SS Brigade Charlemagne. His organisation, the Parti républicain d'unité populaire (1946), was a response to the feeling that the Liberation had only brought new occupants and that a movement was needed to liberate France first, then Europe, from 'Mongols, Negroes and Jews'.[172] Binet opposed both what he called the Red Front and political reaction, and boasted to his supporters, 'You will rediscover the authentic traditions of European and particularly French socialism. . . . You will be the true successors of Proudhon, Blanqui and Sorel.'[173] When Binet's party became the Mouvement socialiste d'unité française in 1948, it called for a 'strong and French, national and socialist Republic'. Binet now claimed the heritage of Blanqui, adopting the Blanquist slogan 'Bread and Liberty' and the motto, 'He who wields the sword shall eat'.[174] But his claims to socialism only provided a justification for his nationalism. By equating feudalism with Aryanism, capitalism with Judaism, he was able to argue that capitalism had been imported into France by the 'men of inferior race', along with 'the lie of equality' and cosmopolitanism, and that therefore what was required was a 'racist socialism' to recover wealth and power for the nation.[175] This nonsense acknowledged a debt to Gobineau but was situated within a long tradition of French anti-Semitism.

The political class of the Fourth Republic survived, relatively unscathed by attacks from the Right, until the collapse of the French Empire in Indochina and its struggle for survival in North Africa. It then came under attack for incompetence, or treachery, or both in a climate which recalled that of the Dreyfus affair. Crisis in the Empire was paralleled by a crisis in French society and the rise of a populist movement led by Pierre Poujade, which protested against high taxes and high interest rates, and attacked politicians, bureaucrats, big business and intellectuals in the name of social justice.[176] It was a movement of small fry against powerful interests, of those who had shed blood in one, even two, world wars against those who had profited from war, of the *pays réel* against the *pays légal*. It was a movement of which Drumont or Barrès would have been proud, but which lacked a Drumont or a Barrès with the necessary political acumen to lead it.

Jean-Marie Le Pen was one individual who already demonstrated the ability to exploit both the imperial and the social crisis. As a nationalist student, he had campaigned for the Pétainist Union des Nationaux Indépendants et Républicains in the 1951 elections. He then abandoned his studies and enrolled as a paratrooper, arriving in Vietnam just after the catastrophe of Dien Bien Phu. He returned in 1955 with his comrade Demarquet and put himself at the service of Pierre Poujade. Of his performance at Rennes, Poujade said, 'He knew absolutely nothing about what I was doing. But he made a frenzied speech. He compared me to Joan of Arc, to Bayard, to Duguesclin, and received a thunderous reception. . . . Two months later they were deputies.'[177] Le Pen's skill was to reawaken feelings that had been expressed in another crisis, in April 1938. On that occasion Léon Blum, requesting *pleins pouvoirs* for his government, had been subjected in the Chamber to shouts of 'A Bas le Juif' and 'La France aux Français'. When the Socialist minister Marx Dormoy riposted that 'un juif vaut bien un Breton', a row was unleashed in the press and on the streets, acclaiming Bretons as the salt of the earth, the home of national heroes like Duguesclin and Dugay-Trouin, a people who had sacrificed 400,000 of their sons in the Great War, to Jewish losses amounting to only 1,689. When Le Pen was elected in 1956 the press exclaimed, 'Enfin un Breton!'[178] Le Pen rejoined his paratroop regiment and saw action at Suez, then confronted the Algerian insurrection, where he was allegedly involved in torture. Back in the Chamber he singled out Mendès-France, whose ministry had enjoyed Communist support and who had been the architect of French decolonisation, for attack. He projected onto Mendès-France all the anti-Semitic rancour that had greeted him as a young colleague of Léon Blum, in the Blum government of 1938. 'You fail to understand', railed Le Pen, 'that you cristallise, in your person, a certain repulsiveness, patriotically and almost personally.'[179] Le Pen was emerging as the true heir of Drumont.

The most important nationalist movement thrown up by the Algerian war was Jeune Nation. It was founded by two contemporaries of Le Pen, Pierre and Jacques Sidos, the sons of an official of Darnand's Milice who was executed at the Liberation. The militants of Jeune Nation modelled themselves on the heroes of 6 February 1934, and from 6 February 1954 held rallies annually on the place de la Concorde. They were joined in 1956 by Dominique Venner, a student whose father had been active in Doriot's PPF, and who injected a certain intellectual rigour into the movement. Inspiration was drawn from Brasillach (the anniversary of whose death also fell on 6 February), Drieu de la

Rochelle, and Hubert Lagardelle, to whom fulsome tribute was paid when he died in 1958.[180] The aim of Jeune Nation, according to its statutes, was 'to restore France to her place as a great nation by establishing the *popular state* and completing a second French revolution according to the principles of authority, responsibility and hierarchy'.[181] Its tactics were direct action, and it was so heavily involved in the events of 13 May 1958 that de Gaulle ordered its dissolution.

The demonstrators in Algiers and Paris on 13 May 1958 (Le Pen and Demarquet in their parachutists' berets were photographed at the front of the demonstration on the Champs-Elysées) and the army which demanded the return to power of de Gaulle were acting to save French Algeria. They suffered an acute sense of betrayal when it became increasingly clear that de Gaulle and the politicians who surrounded him were not prepared to sacrifice everything to keep Algeria French. Counter-revolutionary movements sprang up, with many of which, incidentally, Jeune Nation militants had contacts. First, there was a mass movement of *pieds-noirs* and nationalists which culminated in the 'week of barricades' in Algiers in January 1960. Second, there was a putsch by the generals led by General Raoul Salan, who felt they had been double-crossed by de Gaulle. Third, a wave of terrorism swept Algeria and metropolitan France, undertaken by the Organisation Armée Secrète (OAS), founded in 1961 and including both military and civilian personnel. Fourth, de Gaulle himself was the victim of an assassination attempt at Petit-Clamart outside Paris in 1962.

These movements were diverse and ill-co-ordinated. They lacked any coherent collective memory and therefore any clear political culture. Three activists may be selected to gain a sense of the worlds in which they operated. Robert Martel, organiser of the *pied-noir* Mouvement Populaire du 13 mai, believed in the divine mission of France and the popular monarchy, and failed to see why the French Revolution had not drawn the king and his people even closer together. His Catholic royalism earned him the nickname, 'Chouan of the Mitidja'.[182] Jean-Marie Curutchet, the son of a naval officer, was brought up in Algiers when it was the capital of Free France. For him Algeria was the base from which metropolitan France was liberated in 1944. As a young officer, he was involved in the generals' putsch of April 1961. Discovered, he decided to desert and founded a secret group, the Organisation Algérie-Révolution, which later fused with the OAS. Its charter was both nationalistic and revolutionary, but in the Jacobin tradition laid claim to by fascists from the Left in the 1930s. It called for a 'strong state' to revolutionise France and preserve her greatness, and drew inspiration from Robespierre, Saint-Just, Napoleon and Clemenceau.[183]

While Curutchet was sentenced to life imprisonment, Jean Bastien-Thiry, architect of the Petit-Clamart attack, was executed. A Lorrainer, the son and grandson of army officers who had served in Algeria, and graduate of the École Polytechnique, he became involved in the development of advanced aircraft and guided missiles. He complained in anonymous articles that the general staff was dominated by Communists, who commissioned useless jets from the Jewish industrialist Marcel Bloch, alias Dassault, because Dassault and Rothschild provided financial support for the Gaullist régime.[184] He told the court martial that he and his men were 'neither fascists nor factious, but nationalist Frenchmen, French of stock or French of heart'. He accused de Gaulle not only of breaking his promises over Algeria but of undermining French solidarity and honour in such as way as to make it 'an easy prey to Communist and materialist subversion'.[185] Bastien-Thiry was last in the tradition of *ultras*, vigilant of any compromise of political authority with revolution, self-appointed guardians of the honour and integrity of France, vassals who would overthrow their lord for betraying the cause.[186] But his culture was Barrésian (replacing his mother, who had died giving birth, by the nation of blood and soil), while the sense of decadence and the fear of Jews and Communists conspiring against the nation were reflexes that went back to Drumont and Maurras.

If one problem facing the extreme Right was the fragmentation of its collective memory, another was its inability to come to terms with the term fascism and the instant delegitimation it imposed. After 1960, there was something of a return of confidence and coherence. After the dissolution of Jeune Nation, Dominique Venner and other nationalist militants turned their attention to university students, to counter the left-wing UNEF which supported negotiation with the Algerian rebels. Venner founded the Fédération d'Étudiants Nationalistes and masterminded their *Manifesto of the Class of 60*. This re-established a link with the young martyr of fascism, Robert Brasillach, in two senses. First, it was a reply to his *Letter to a soldier of the class of 60*, written in Fresnes prison to his nephew, the son of Maurice Bardèche. Second, the ideas expressed in the manifesto of June 1960, and republished in *Cahiers universitaires* in 1962, virtually mirrored the views set out by Maurice Bardèche in his key text, *What is Fascism?*, published in 1961. Bardèche sought to free fascism from association with the Holocaust, arguing that fascism as a political system was no more guilty of exterminating the Jews than nuclear physics was guilty of Hiroshima, and using Hiroshima to point out that western democracies and Stalin's Russia were as guilty of war crimes as the Nazis.[187] He held that the key characteristic of fascism was a will to defend one's own race. This will was expressed by an élite which had more deeply than others the instinct of the survival of the race, and its task was to set up an authoritarian state to ensure that no harm came to the nation.[188] The manifesto rejected the idea of the equality of races, warned of the threat to white civilisation of coloured peoples in revolt, incited by Communism, and postulated the need for a 'revolutionary élite drawn from the people' to 'establish authority' in a 'rigidly hierarchised' state in order to 'defend the French ethnic group'.[189]

Inspired by Brasillach, the nationalist students set themselves the task of returning to the classic exponents of French nationalism, and their *Cahiers* ran in-depth articles on Barrès (whose centenary was celebrated in 1962), Maurras and Drumont. Venner developed this bid to give intellectual authority and coherence to the nationalists in the monthly review *Europe-Action*, launched in 1963 and enjoying a particular popularity in the universities of southern France. 'You don't make history by looking in the rear-view mirror,' he announced; but, on the other hand, 'there can be no Revolution without doctrine.'[190] The nationalists were very much confined to the extreme Right of the political spectrum, but, in an attempt to attract support from the disillusioned Left, the names of Proudhon and Sorel were added to the cult figures Barrès, Maurras and Drumont. Moreover, to reappropriate 'the Paris Commune which Marxists have stolen' a young colonel who escaped from the besieged city of Metz in 1870 to continue the fight in Paris, only to be executed by the Versaillais, was rediscovered.[191]

Politically, *Europe-Action* threw its weight behind the challenge for the French presidency in 1965 of Tixier-Vignancour, a formal official of Vichy whose legal defence had saved General Salan from the firing squad. However, Tixier won only five per cent of the votes, and the nationalists did even worse in the legislative elections of 1967, when they scored less than three per cent. *Europe-Action* disappeared from view and was replaced early in 1968 by a think-tank called GRECE, the Groupement de Recherche et d'Études pour la Civilisation Européenne, and its review, *La Nouvelle École*.[192] Dominique Venner was among its founders but its key figure was undoubtedly the philosopher Alain de Benoist. *La Nouvelle École* mounted a full-frontal attack not only on Marxist thought and the revolutionary credo but on the whole Judaeo-Christian tradition. Its twin bugbears were universalism and equality. It refined the theory of racial inequality being developed by the nationalists in the light of the findings of modern biology and particularly genetics, and argued that progess required constant struggle between races and the empowerment of élites. Both Communism and Americanism looked back to the Declaration of the Rights of Man, but ultimately Jesus was to blame for the doctrines of universalism and equality. GRECE therefore considered the high point of European civilisation to be pre-Christian, that of the Celts, Teutons and Vikings, and cultivated an admiration for noblities and military élites from the Samurai to the Waffen SS.[193] Though self-consciously intellectual in its approach, GRECE acquired a popular outlet in *Figaro-Magazine*, whose editorials by Louis Pauwels between 1977 and 1980 were hardly more than retranscriptions of texts by Alain de Benoist, in an attempt to pull Giscard d'Estaing from the centre-ground of French politics over to the Right.[194]

Though the new generation of nationalists tried to impose some coherence on the extreme Right, this proved impossible, not least because of the violent shaking of the political cocktail by the events of 1968. In ways reminiscent of the 1930s a new generation of activists, politicised by May 1968 as their predecessors had been politicised by February 1934, began to challenge the older generation of nationalists. At stake was both a struggle for power and the question of seeking common ground with activists of the Left, even a popular base.

Nowhere were these conflicts clearer than in Action Française. The rigidity of the movement was characterised by the dynastic succession of Maurice Pujo to his son Pierre, editor of *Aspects de la France* from 1966. In 1968 the paper was devoted to celebrating the centenary of Maurras' birth. It was convinced in May 1968 that France was 'on the edge of Communist revolution' and, as the crisis died away, it called for 'an intellectual, moral and political revolution', in the style of Maurras, if not one on the streets.[195] There was, however, a generation of young royalists, based on the student paper *A.F. Université* for whom the events of May 1968 came as an inspiration. They were impressed by the collusion of student and labour movements that made the events so powerful and, far from opposing *contestation*, argued that the régime had to be questioned and opposed. Accused by the right-wing press of 'Mao-Maurrassism' and unable to open the higher échelons of the organisation to new ideas, the young royalists left in 1971 to form the Nouvelle Action Française.[196]

'We have to leave to their peaceful preoccupations the conservatives who react with only a dumb horror to our plans of redemptive revolution', announced the first number of *La Nouvelle Action Française*. 'We must appeal to those active French . . . who can imagine something other that what exists.'[197] They looked to the youth who had been stirred up by the events of 1968 but had not found a home, and were anxious to check both the racist 'Nouvelle École' and the fascist Ordre Nouveau, to be considered presently. They argued that the working classes should be fully integrated into the nation and were prepared to side with the trade union movement against their employers. Although they had broken with the old reactionaries of Rénovation Française, Bertrand Renouvin and Gérard Leclerc, the young leaders of Nouvelle Action Française, did not reject the authority of Maurras. Rather they claimed that Maurras, like the God of 1968, was not a conservative. 'Maurras had nothing of the conservative,' stated Renouvin. On the contrary, he advocated 'a "redemptive revolution" to destroy the republican state and establish a monarchy which would be the basis of radical social change'. The revolution, he added, was to be undertaken not by the élite of society but by the *pays réel*, and by 'Jacobins as well as sons of Chouans'.[198]

Leclerc, the political editor of NAF, rediscovered the links between Camelots du Roi and trade unionists that had been forged in La Santé prison and described by Bernanos and Maurice Pujo. Similarly, he read Henri Massis on the young prodigy Henri Lagrange. Leclerc unearthed Maurras' hatred of plutocracy in *L'Avenir de l'Intelligence* and constructed him as a friend of the proletariat who had chaired the first meeting of the Cercle Proudhon.[199] 'For this reason', he concluded, 'Maurras' posterity must recuperate May 68 which belongs to it as of right.'[200] The young royalists carried their ideas into practice. Renouvin stood in the presidential elections of 1974, declaring that 'the French Revolution must be repeated'. Just as the nobility had been forced to surrender their feudal privileges in 1789, now 'the state has to be freed of economic and financial feudalism'.[201] He stood again in the presidential elections of 1981, but withdrew after the first ballot and urged his supporters to vote for François Mitterrand, because Giscard 'had systematically established the dictatorship of a clan and wanted to subject society as a whole to the tyranny of money'.[202]

Another nationalist movement to emerge from the events of 1968 was Occident. It had broken away from *Europe-Action* in 1964 and fell under the influence of the extremist François Duprat. Duprat subscribed to the strategy of direct action, and waged war on Communists, Trotskyists, Maoists and anarchists, in the streets and on the campuses. Occident attacked *gauchistes* at Nanterre University on 2 May 1968 and the following day at the Sorbonne. But Duprat was hostile to the Gaullist régime too, and Occident took part in the night of the barricades on 10–11 May, lest it find itself doing the dirty work of the régime and the classic Right.[203] He feared that his movement, driven out of the Latin Quarter, marching and counter-marching in the *beaux quartiers* would be as ineffective as Colonel de La Rocque's Croix de Feu.[204]

After the dissolution of Occident in November 1968, Duprat opted for an unambiguous revolutionary nationalist strategy. In 1970 he founded Ordre Nouveau, which declared that it wanted nothing to do with the old quarrels of the reactionary Right, from Dreyfus to 1934, Vichy and the Algerian war. It wanted to appeal to revolutionaries, those of the Left included, not to 'relics' or 'maladjusted nostalgics'.[205] Ordre Nouveau declared that 'Europe will be nationalist or it will not be', by which was meant an alliance of nationalist states, each preserving the culture of a Shakespeare, a Racine, a Cervantes, a Dante, a Goethe or a Pushkin. It established close links with other extreme nationalist parties in Europe and attacked both President Pompidou's 'Europe of technocrats' and the anti-German chauvinism of Action Française.[206] Its affinities were not with conservative nationalists but with the collaborationists of the Second World War, with Robert Brasillach, Lucien Rebatet and Maurice Bardèche.[207] But its totally intransigent stance and insistence on direct action led it nowhere. Ordre Nouveau was itself banned in June 1973 and fragmented. Duprat continued on his extremist path and founded the Groupe Nationalistes-Révolutionnaires, which went as far as to praise the Waffen SS and deny the Holocaust, before he was blown up by a car bomb in 1978.

Until 1981 a host of problems stood in the way of the emergence of a revolutionary movement of the extreme Right: fragmentation, the lack of a popular base, ideological incoherence and above all the taboo on any movement or culture that smacked of fascism. After 1981 there emerged a movement that seemed to conquer all those difficulties, and establish a powerful and threatening presence in French politics: the Front National.

The Front National was founded under the presidency of Jean-Marie Le Pen in 1972. As its title implied, it sought to build a coalition of all nationalist groups. Initially it did poorly, losing some who went to campaign for Giscard d'Estaing in the presidential elections of 1974 as the Faire Front organisation, and unable to control the revolutionary nationalists of François Duprat. Le Pen himself scored less than one per cent of the vote in the presidential elections of 1974 and 1981. But the triumph of the Left in the 1981 elections dramatically changed the fortunes of the Front National. Not only, it could be argued, was France a prey to a Marxist coalition, but the impotence of the classic Right was also exposed. All kinds of nationalists, reactionaries, Catholic integrists of Bernard Antony's Christianity-Solidarity movement, and deserters from the Giscardian and Gaullist camps now came to swell the ranks of the Front National, and the broad coalition began to take on consistency.

Le Pen forswore the direct action of the revolutionary nationalists and committed himself to legalism and parliamentarism in order to build up a mass base. After 1981 its popularity increased steadily. In March 1983 he won 11 per cent of the vote in the twentieth *arrondissement* of Paris, where Henri Rochefort had run for parliament in 1889. In the European elections of 1984 the Front National again won 11 per cent of the vote and had ten deputies elected. In the legislative elections of 1986, thirty-five deputies were elected on just under 10 per cent of the poll. And in the first round of the 1988 presidential elections Le Pen himself attracted 14 per cent of the vote. The Front National score slipped back to 11 per cent in the European elections of 1989 but returned to 14 per cent in the regional elections of 1992.

By entering the parliamentary arena, Le Pen ran the risk of being absorbed by the traditional parties of the Right, as had happened to nationalist movements after the Great War. He prevented this largely by the sharpness of his global vision of the problems facing French society and the solutions that needed to be found. There was little in his ideology that could not be found in the pages of Drumont, Barrès and Maurras. But Le Pen had no need to pay homage to these masters in any scholastic way. For Franch in the 1980s was in the same position as France in the 1880s when Drumont and company began their political careers: a nation fallen from great-power status, subjected to a wave of immigration, governed by a political class whose competence was open to question.

This at least was the construction put on events by Le Pen. The *leit-motif* of his argument, echoing that of Drumont, was the decadence into which France had fallen. He attacked the decline of French patriotism, and the decline of the French family through sexual promiscuity, contraception and abortion. At the same time, the population explosion of the Third World was breaking on France in waves of immigration. Le Pen placed immigration at the centre of his analysis, but he sidestepped the accusation of racism by treating it as a sociological problem, responsible for urban congestion, dirt, crime, insecurity, unemployment, AIDS, and high taxes to pay for immigrants' social security benefits and health care.[208] He demonstrated a pressing concern for social ills, while preserving the simplicity of the racist argument.

This decadence for Le Pen was not an evitable process but the fruit of conspiracy. Resonating with the four confederate states of Maurras, he declared, 'Four superpowers are colonising France, the Marxist, the masonic, the Jewish, and the Protestant, symbolised by the four ministers Fiterman, Hernu, Badinter and Rocard.'[209] Communist 'submariners' were to be found everywhere, in the parties, unions, bureaucracy and mass media. But not only the Left was guilty. After Communism, Le Pen denounced socialism, socialo-liberalism and liberalism. 'I always knew', he said, 'that the victory of Communism was made possible only by the moral disarmament, even more than by the material disarmament, of the West.'[210] 'Socialism does nothing but place its boots in the footprints of the previous régime.'[211] 'La classe politicienne' of both Left and Right was to be blamed for the 'socialism of the providential state' and its 'bureaucratico-financial yoke' which supported 'social parasites and social-security scroungers'.[212]

To save the French nation, the country would have to be purged of all those who were not properly French. 'La France aux Français' of Drumont became 'Les Français d'abord'. Here Le Pen was careful to avoid statements of racial superiority or inferiority which would be seized upon by the opposition to discredit him as a fascist. His language owed more to Barrès than to Gobineau. As a Breton and an ex-soldier, he stated that French nationality was conferred not by a document but by blood and soil. 'The Fatherland is the land of our fathers, the soil cleared and defended by them.' 'The foreigner . . . can be integrated into the Fatherland only by a sacrificial act: the spilling of his blood.'[213] Similarly, his racism was expressed in terms of geographical identity, not biological hierarchy, in terms of natural preference and loyalty, which appealed to the French feeling for the family and the *pays*.

I prefer my daughters to my nieces, my nieces to my neighbours . . . I am French and prefer the French. I feel that I am linked to the rest of the world, to the rest of the universe, by ties which are ordered hierarchically. Concentric in some way. There is a cameo of nuances that starts with myself, with my family, and extends to my commune, to my workplace community, to my communal, provincial or national community.[214]

In this way Le Pen not only managed to shake off the taboo previously imposed by such sentiments, he forced immigration to the top of the political agenda and obliged other parties to follow suit if they were not to lose support to him.

Le Pen combined the ideological baggage of the 1880s with the organisational flair of the 1930s. For he was far from being only a commentator or publicist. His movement has been compared to Colonel de La Rocque's Croix de Feu, and also (by the ever-vigilant camp dedicated to the memory of La Rocque) to Jacques Doriot's PPF.[215] In truth, Le Pen probably owed something to both La Rocque and Doriot while improving on their records. Le Pen's robust, plebeian style and gift for organisation matched that of 'le grand Jacques', and he shared Doriot's oratorical skills. He did well in the working-class quarters of Paris, its suburbs, and great cities dense with immigrants such as Marseille where Doriotism had been strong, but whereas Doriot had taken a

Communist following with him into the PPF, Le Pen's support in Communist strongholds was less a transfer of Communist votes than an anti-Communist vote.[216] Again, whereas Doriot had found it difficult to break out of his Communist bastion of Saint-Denis to win over the Right, and to win over the Right without losing control of Saint-Denis, Le Pen acquired a broad national base, although he was less strong in the traditional conservative west of France than La Rocque's PSF had been.

Above all, Le Pen was a master of the coalition. He established a firm base in the right-wing press by recruiting François Brigneau, the doyen of right-wing journalists, to his mouthpiece *National hebdo* and winning the support of Jean Madiran's *Présent*, the daily of the Catholic Right. On 1 May 1988 he used the clergy of Bernard Antony's Christianity-Solidarity movement for a mass of 150,000 in the Tuileries Gardens, followed by the singing of 'Catholiques et Français toujours'.[217] But by detaching his homage to Joan of Arc from the second Sunday in May, favoured by the traditionalists, and holding it on Labour Day, 1 May, Le Pen sought to demonstrate that the social question was a national question and to attract workers from other May Day rallies. Thus on 1 May 1989 at the Palais-Royal, to shouts of 'Du travail pour les Français', Le Pen argued that 'the biggest rally of French workers' was that of 'the popular, social and national Right'.[218] He was happy to take part in celebrating the bicentenary of the French Revolution—'Pourquoi pas?'—since, like Barrès, he held that the Revolution was a part of France's national heritage. But he declared that 14 July marked the 'fête de la nation' of 1790 rather than the storming of the Bastille, and refused to give much prominence to the cult of the Revolution, given the presence of counter-revolutionaries in his coalition.[219]

Le Pen was more successful than many in bridging the legacy of the Revolution. Many leaders of the Right before him adopted the left-wing rhetoric of the Revolution, defining themselves against the conservatism of the Right in order to win a popular base. But in general they failed to win over those who subscribed to the principles of the Revolution, so closely did these define, bind and legitimate the Left. Likewise, some leaders of the Left flirted with the national ideology of the Right and attempted to adapt cult figures such as Proudhon to the defence of a nationalist position. But they were largely unsuccessful in detaching Proudhon from those who claimed him to endorse the class struggle and hostility to the state. In the last resort, those who had a vested interest in using the Revolution to point up the opposition between Left and Right in French political culture always had the better of those who wanted to forge a new political culture by bridging it.

Conclusion

The purpose of this study has been to examine the formation of a cluster of political cultures, in the sense of the values and ideals that define, bind together and legitimate political communities, and to explore the contribution of collective memory to the shaping of those cultures. It has been my contention that there is no single French collective memory but parallel and competing collective memories, and that the past is constructed not as fact but as myth, to serve the interest of a particular community. That said, I have examined three different facets of the collective construction of the past. First, I have looked at the way in which political communities have striven to achieve acceptance of their own particular interpretation of the past as universal and objective, and to suppress other interpretations of events which might deprive them of legitimacy. Those rival interpretations represented a past from which they were anxious to escape, but which their enemies were determined should haunt them. Second, I have looked at the way in which rival political communities have seized on the same figure or event, and presented them in entirely different fashions in order to establish the legitimacy of their own cause. Third, I have looked at the way in which collective memories have been modified in the light of events, which have either permitted the political communities they served to secure a new legitimacy, or resulted in that legitimacy being eroded.

On the first point, what stood between a political community and a universal acceptance of its view of the past was an alternative past, constructed by its enemies, which threatened to deprive it of legitimacy. Revolutionaries drew legitimacy from the principles of 1789, but their enemies strove constantly to use the Terror of 1793 to discredit them. In return, revolutionaries lost no chance to accuse conservatives, Catholics and regionalists of standing for the institutions of the Ancien Régime, monarchy, feudalism, fanaticism and privilege. Bonapartists were accused of betraying liberty, the Republic, the Revolution itself, while anarchists were dismissed by their Jacobin and Marxist rivals of bourgeois leanings and of tolerating reactionary régimes. Federalists and regionalists were attacked not only as reactionaries but also as separatists

340

who wanted to destory the One and Indivisible France. Those who sought to promote a sense of greatness in the French nation were confronted by memories of defeat and national humiliation, and a reluctance to shoulder the obligations of greatness.

The task for each political community was to shake off the nightmares of the past and to campaign for the widest possible acceptance of its own more favourable version of events. This was not always as straightforward as might be desirable, because the demands of legitimacy were often at odds with those of a distinctive identity. Revolutionaries tried as a general rule to distance themselves from the curse of the Terror, but within the revolutionary camp at any moment there were struggles between moderates and radicals, and the radicals were torn between the wish to put the Terror behind them and the need to define themselves by reference to the more radical events and personalities of the Revolution, or to later manifestations of the revolutionary process—the June Days, the Paris Commune, 1917—which generally revived memories of the Terror. Against them, the Right was pulled on the one hand between the need to accept the principles of 1789 if it were to join the political class, or the need to adopt the rhetoric of revolution if it were to establish a popular base against the political class and, on the other, to the desire to magnify the Vendée as a harmonious *ancien régime* community in order to discredit the Revolution which they characterised as conspiracy, violence and anarchy.

For Bonapartists to succeed they had to establish that they respected the Republic and put aside dynastic ambitions, that they honoured the Revolution while seeking to end the Franco–French civil war, even that while strengthening the state they preserved liberty. Anarchists had to rival the revolutionary credentials of Jacobins and Marxists while asserting the primacy of their anti-authoritarian heroes and moments. Both Catholics and anticlericals had to demonstrate that they were on the side of liberty against uniformity and persecution, even while one was standing by the authority of the Church, the other by the authority of the state. For federalists and regionalists the task was to demonstrate their republican and democratic credentials, and to show that their strategy aimed to promote, not weaken, the unity of France, while at the same time constructing a regional identity. Finally, the champions of French greatness learned to draw victory from the jaws of defeat, grasping that national solidarity was best forged at a time of national mourning, and that victory tended to increase rather than to diminish national lethargy.

This leads to a consideration of the second point, that of competition between different political communities to privilege their own interpretation of a historical event or figure contested between them. Proudhon, for example, was celebrated by the anarchist Left as the embodiment of their anti-authoritarian ideals. He was also the subject of a challenge by the Right which sought to gain a popular base by appropriating his memory, but at the same time presented him as a rustic, Catholic patriot and militarist, a sort of masculine Joan of Arc.

This bid failed, not least because Sorel, Berth and Lagardelle, who flirted with the Right, could not abandon the anti-authoritarian image of Proudhon they had learned in their anarchist days.

More successful was the attempt of the Right to interpret Joan of Arc to their own benefit. The Left struggled to present her as a female version of the soldier of the Year II, a model that reached its high point at the Liberation. The Right, however, were keen to gain acceptance by the Republic of Joan as a Catholic and national heroine. This they achieved briefly after the Great War, but a national identity at one and the same time Catholic, patriotic and republican proved too difficult to sustain. Joan lost her universal appeal to become the preserve of the extreme Right, both monarchist and LePenist. The Left reverted to its own brand of revolutionary nationalism, incarnate in the myth of the soldiers of the Year II, a citizen army to defend the home of liberty, and to spread the gospel of liberty to oppressed peoples.

Like Joan of Arc, Napoleon also became a focus of national identity after the Great War, but his hour of glory was even shorter. The black legend of Napoleon the warmonger and dictator remained too potent for the republican political class. The official cult of Napoleon was not revived by Charles de Gaulle, lest it provoke unwanted comparisons of his designs with Bonapartism. What remains is the popular legend of the man in the cocked hat, sustained by a certain tendency among the educated classes, but purged of its revolutionary implications.

The third point was that collective memories were not set in stone but were reworked by political communities in the light of events in order to give them a new sheen of legitimacy. Alternatively, events might provide the opportunity for a rival political community to attack that legitimacy. So, for example, the coup d'état of Louis-Napoleon, according to Victor Hugo, provoked a revaluation of Napoleon Bonaparte's coup of *brumaire* which until then had been seen as just another of the coups that had marked the Directorial régime. On the other hand, the search for peace within a reorganised Europe in the eras of Locarno, Rome and Maastricht provided an attentive audience for those who sought to recast Napoleon as the pioneer of a federal Europe.

In a similar way, the Terror undermined those who championed a Jacobin model of republicanism for most of the nineteenth century. The Bolshevik Revolution, however, caused Jacobinism to be reconsidered by revolutionaries in a more favourable light as a precursor of Bolshevism, while at the same time Bolshevism was well received by revolutionaries in France as the heir and continuator of Jacobinism. At the same time, it is true to say that any manifestation of revolution with a small 'r' provoked anxieties about revolution with a capital 'R'. Thus the revolutions of 1871, 1917 and 1981 gave credence to those who wished to argue that the Revolution of 1789 was conspiratorial and violent, and that the Vendée represented the last stand of the natural, pious and hierarchical order of the Ancien Régime.

The Second World War made into common currency the language of liberation, totalitarianism and genocide. Revolution was rehabilitated as liberation, but so also was anticlericalism, Catholicism and Protestantism. Anticlericals and Catholics appropriated the terms totalitarian and genocide in order to discredit their opponents, while Protestants, who had long been embarrassed by the Camisard revolt, looked on it in a more positive way in the light of the Maquis. Regionalists, discredited by the espousal of regionalism by the Pétain government, were able to revive their cause partly by linking it to the Resistance, partly by setting in the context of moves towards European unity sublimated disputes between France and Germany, and partly by appropriating the language of colonial oppression and decolonisation during the period of the break-up of the French overseas empire. Fascism was totally discredited by association with collaboration, Nazism and the Holocaust, and attempts to portray the Liberation as worse than the Terror made little impact on the official myth. The revival of the extreme Right under Le Pen was made possible largely by an avoidance of the discourse of fascism and a reversion to the French conservative discourse of Drumont, Barrès and Maurras.

But what of the future? More than two hundred years after the French Revolution, can it be sustained that French political life continues according to the same rules, is still trapped in an obsession with the past? It will be said that ideology is dead, even or especially on the Left, which for so long was the bearer of revolutionary ideology, and that politics is now a matter of management, particularly of the economy. It will be said that the French have a short memory, and that in a materialistic age history holds less and less significance. It will be argued that history is now a matter for professional historians, who progressively are establishing a documented and footnoted account of history which can command universal consensus. It will be said, finally, that the world is changing so fast and in such novel ways that familiar historical signposts can longer show the way. Briefly, it will be asserted that arguments that were obvious in 1889, and may just have held good in 1989, will cease to have any relevance by the turn of the twenty-first century.

To which I shall reply, first, that the Socialist party has undoubtedly lost its way since it ceased to claim the values of Jaurès for its own, while the Gaullist party has begun to revive the Bonapartist myth for its cause. Second, that the taste for commemorating anniversaries has not faded and so long as anniversaries are celebrated past struggles, past achievements and past heroes will be dredged up to define, publicise and legitimate political cultures. The Bicentenary of the French Revolution was followed in 1990 by celebrations of the centenary of de Gaulle and the fiftieth anniversary of the appeal of 18 June. If the fiftieth anniversary of the *débâcle* of 1940 was more muted, and if celebrations of the founding of the Republic in 1992 and of the Jacobin dictatorship in 1993 are more difficult, that serves only to illustrate the point that some events, far from being eminently forgettable, are so painful and so traumatic that attempts are made to repress them, attempts which, given their power and the interest of some parties in commemorating them or using them to deprive their enemies of legitimacy, are doomed to failure. Third, it is not possible to envisage the writing of a universal and objective history. But this does not prevent each political community, in order to underpin its cause, from campaigning to have its own particular version of events or presentation of a cult figure accepted as universal and objective. Finally, changing perspectives and changing vocabulary have not insulated political communities from their past. Rather they have prompted a reshaping of their collective memory, in order to preserve or regain legitimacy, lest that vital element conferred by the past be lost to them for good.

Notes

Introduction

1. Jacques Le Goff and Pierre Nora, eds, *Faire de l'Histoire* (3 vols, Paris, Gallimard, 1974).
2. Paris, Hachette, 1898. Translated as *Introduction to the Study of History* (London, Duckworth, 1898).
3. *Ibid.*, 1.
4. *Ibid.*, 206, 211.
5. *Ibid.*, 216. See also, Charles Seignobos, *La Méthode historique appliquée aux sciences sociales* (Paris, Alcan, 1901), 281–2, 298–312, and Paul Ricoeur, *The Contribution of French Historiography to the Theory of History* (Zaharoff lecture, 1978–9, Oxford, Clarendon Press, 1980), 8–9.
6. Madeleine Rebérioux, 'Jaurès et la Révolution française', *AHRF* 38 no. 2 (1966), 171–95; *Jaurès, historien de la Révolution française* (Castres, Centre national et Musée Jean-Jaurès, 1989).
7. James Friguglietti, *Albert Mathiez, historien révolutionnaire, 1874–1932* (Paris, Société des Études robespierristes, 1974); Georges Lefebvre, 'L'Oeuvre historique d'Albert Mathiez', *AHRF* 9, (1932), 193–210; Albert Soboul, 'Georges Lefebvre (1874–1959), historien de la Révolu-tion française', in *Comprendre la Révolution* (Paris, Maspéro, 1981); Richard Cobb, 'Georges Lefebvre', *Past and Present* (18), Nov. 1960, 52–65.
8. See the tributes to Soboul in *AHRF* 250, (Oct.–Dec. 1982) and Richard Cobb, 'Albert Marius Soboul. A Tribute', *People and Places* (Oxford, Oxford University Press, 1985), 46–92.
9. Engels, *Socialism Utopian and Scientific*, in Marx and Engels, *Selected Works in One Volume* (London, Lawrence and Wishart, 1968), 395.
10. Jean Jaurès, *Histoire socialiste de la Révolution française*, I (Paris, Jules Rouff, 1901), 8.
11. See Bloch's review of *La Grande Peur*, *Annales d'Histoire économique et sociale* (5), 1933, 301–4.
12. Albert Soboul, 'Sentiment religieux et cultes populaires pendant la Révolution. Saintes patriotes et martyrs de la liberté', *AHRF* 29 (1957), 193–213.
13. Marx, *The Eighteenth Brumaire of Louis Bonaparte*, in *Selected Works in One Volume*, 96.
14. François Simiand, 'Méthode historique et science sociale', *Revue de Synthèse*, 1903, reprinted in *Annales ESC* 15/1, (Jan.–Feb. 1960), 83–119.
15. Georges Livet, 'Lucien Febvre et Strasbourg', in C.-O. Carbonell and Georges Livet, *Au Berceau des Annales* (Presses de l'Institut d'Études politiques de Toulouse, 1983), 52.
16. Marc Bloch, *The Historian's Craft* (Manchester, Manchester University Press, 1954), 63.

17. Fernand Braudel, *On History* (London, Weidenfeld and Nicolson, 1980), 3–5, 25–54. See also Peter Burke, *The French Historical Revolution. The Annales School, 1929–89* (Cambridge, Polity Press, 1990).

18. *Annales ESC*, 43/2 (March–April 1988), 291.

19. *Annales ESC*, 44/6 (Nov.–Dec. 1989), 1319.

20. Lawrence Wylie, *Village in the Vaucluse* (Cambridge, Mass., Harvard University Press, 1957).

21. Stanley Hoffmann, 'Paradoxes of the French Political Community', in *France: Change and Tradition* (London, Gollancz, 1963), 1–117.

22. Charles, Louise and Richard Tilly, *The Rebellious Century, 1830–1930* (London, Dent, 1975); Charles Tilly, *The Contentious French* (Cambridge, Mass., The Belknap Press of Harvard University Press, 1986).

23. Claude Duneton, *Parler Croquant* (Paris, Seuil, 1973), 19–26, 178–81.

24. See, for example, Emile Guillaumin, *La Vie d'un Simple* [1904] (Paris, Stock, 1943), 258–60.

25. *The Rebellious Century*, 60. See the stinging critique by Tony Judt, 'A Clown in regal purple: Social history and the historians', *History Workshop* (7), 1979, 66–94.

26. Eugen Weber, 'The Second Republic, politics and the Peasant', *French Historical Studies* (11/4), Fall 1980, 521–50, and '*Comment la politique vint aux paysans*: A Second Look at Peasant Politicization', *American Historical Review* (87/2), April 1982, 357–89, both reprinted in *My France. Politics, Culture, Myth* (Cambridge, Mass., The Belknap Press of Harvard University Press, 1991), 137–88.

27. Eugen Weber, 'The Nineteenth-century Fallout', in Geoffrey Best, ed., *The Permanent Revolution: the French Revolution and its Legacy, 1789–1989* (London, Fontana, 1988), 162.

28. Alfred Cobban, *The Myth of the French Revolution* (London, H.K., Lewis, 1955), reprinted in *Aspects of the French Revolution* (1968; Paladin, 1971), 90–112.

29. Quoted by C. V. Wedgwood, 'Alfred Cobban (1901–1968), in J. F. Bosher, ed., *French Government and Society, 1500–1850. Essays in memory of Alfred Cobban* (London, Athlone Press, 1973), xiii.

30. Richard Cobb, *Reactions to the French Revolution* (Oxford, Oxford University Press, 1972), is probably the best introduction to his method.

31. Simon Schama, *Citizens. A Chronicle of the French Revolution* (London, Penguin, 1989), xiv.

32. *Ibid.*, xv.

33. Theodore Zeldin, *France, 1848–1945* II (Oxford, Clarendon Press, 1977), 1156.

34. *Idem.*

35. *Ibid.*, 1157.

36. *Ibid.*, 1173.

37. For a major contribution by the Fondation nationale des Sciences politiques, see René Rémond, ed., *Pour une Histoire politique* (Paris, Seuil, 1988).

38. See for example Bernard Cohn, 'History and anthropology: the state of play', *Comparative Studies in Society and History* 22 (1980), 198–221, and 'Anthropology and History in the 1980s', *Journal of Interdisciplinary History* 12 (1981), 227–52, both reprinted in *An Anthropologist among the Historians and Other Essays* (Delhi, Oxford University Press, 1990), esp. pp. 40, 43–4, 61–4, 67–70.

39. Keith M. Baker, *The French Revolution and the Creation of Modern Political Culture I. The Political Culture of the Old Régime* (Oxford, Pergamon, 1987), xii. See also Baker, *Inventing the French Revolution* (Cambridge, Cambridge University Press, 1990), 4–5.

40. Maurice Halbwachs, *La Mémoire collective* (Paris, Presses Universitaires de France, 1950, 2nd edn, 1968), translated as *The Collective Memory* (New York, Harper and Row, 1980). See also the perceptive study of

Halbwachs by Gérard Namer, *Mémoire et Société* (Paris, Méridiens et Klincksieck, 1987).

41. Halbwachs, 57.
42. *Ibid.*, 113.
43. Maurice Agulhon, 'La "statuomanie" et l'histoire', *Ethnologie française* (8, 2/3) Mar.–Sept. 1978, 145–72, reprinted in *Histoire vagabonde* (Paris, Gallimard, 1988), I, 137–85; Daniel Sherman, *Worthy Monuments. Art Museums and the Politics of Culture in Nineteenth-century France* (Cambridge, Mass., Harvard University Press, 1989); Avner Ben-Amos, *Moulding the National Memory: State Funerals in Modern France* (forthcoming, Oxford University Press).
44. Pierre Nora, ed., *Les Lieux de Mémoire* (Paris, Gallimard), I, *La République* (1984), II (1–3) *La Nation* (1986), III (1–3) *La France* (1992).
45. See Steven Englund's review of Nora's project, 'The Ghost of the Nation Past', *JMH* 64 (1992), 299–320.
46. Philippe Joutard, *La Légende des Camisards. Une sensibilité au passé* (Paris, Gallimard, 1977), J.-C. Martin, *La Vendée de la Mémoire* (Paris, Seuil, 1989).
47. Broadcast of 17 June 1941, in Pétain, *Actes et Ecrits* (Paris, Flammarion, 1974), 551–2.

Chapter 1: Revolution

1. *Le Monde*, 22 June 1989.
2. *Le Monde*, 11 July 1989.
3. Flysheet of the Association Toussaint-Louverture. [Toussaint Louverture led a slave revolt in the French colony of Saint-Domingo in 1793]
4. *Le Monde*, 11 July 1989.
5. *Le Monde*, 15 Dec. 1988.
6. Pierre Pujo, *La Monarchie Aujourd'hui. Une nouvelle enquête* (Paris, Editions France-Empire, 1988), 315, 317–23.
7. Translated as *Interpreting the French Revolution* (Cambridge Paris, Cambridge University Press/Maison des Sciences de l'Homme, 1981).
8. *Ibid.*, 10.
9. In debate with Pierre Chaunu and Régis Debray, TF1, 3 May 1989. *Le Nouvel Observateur* 4–10 May 1989, 14.
10. Daniel Bensaïd, *Moi, la Révolution. Remembrances d'une Bicentenaire indigne* (Paris, Gallimard, 1989), cap. 1.
11. Antoine Casanova and Claude Mazauric, *Vive la Révolution* (Paris, Messidor/Editions sociales, 1989), 205.
12. Max Gallo, *Lettre ouverte à Maximilien Robespierre sur les nouveaux muscadins* (Paris, Albin Michel, 1986), 20–7.
13. Régis Debray, *Que vive la République* (Paris, Odile Jacob, 1989), 28, 81, 124.
14. Bensaïd, *op. cit.*, 234.
15. Pierre Chaunu, *Le Grand Déclassement. A Propos d'une Commémoration* (Paris, Robert Laffont, 1989).
16. Reynald Secher, *Le Génocide franco-français. La Vendée-Vengé* (Paris, Presses Universitaires de France, 1986).
17. *L'Anti-89* no. 22, July 1989.
18. Philippe de Villiers, *Lettre ouverte aux coupeurs de têtes et aux menteurs du Bicentenaire* (Paris, Albin Michel, 1989), 57.
19. Pujo, *op. cit.*, 302–4.
20. *Le Point* no. 749 (26 Jan.–1 Feb. 1987), 34.
21. Édouard Herriot, *Hommage à la Révolution* (Paris, Fasquelle, 1939), 13.
22. *L'Oeuvre*, 15 July 1939. In general see Pascal Ory, 'La Commémoration révolutionnaire en 1939', in René Rémond and Janine Bourdin, *La France et les Français en 1938–1939* (Paris, FNSP 1978), and the file in AN AB XIX 3054.
23. Léon Daudet, *Deux Idoles sanguinaires. La Révolution et son fils Bonaparte* (Paris, Albin Michel, 1939), 9–10.

24. *Je suis partout*, 30 June 1939.
25. Jacques Duclos, *Mémoires, II. 1935–1939* (Paris, Fayard 1969), 368–71; Maurice Thorez, *La France de la Révolution, 1788–1938* (La Brochure populaire, July 1938).
26. Speech at Ivry-sur-Seine, 13 April 1939, in *Oeuvres*, Livre 4e, tome 17e (Paris, Editions sociales, 1957) 142–4.
27. *L'Humanité*, 26 June 1939.
28. *L'Humanité*, 15 July 1939.
29. The journal was called *La Révolution française* from 1881 to 1887, and edited by Sadi Carnot, until it was taken over by more radical elements.
30. *La République française*, 6 May 1889.
31. *La République française*, 15 July 1889.
32. On the Centenary in general, see Pascal Ory, 'Le Centenaire de la Révolution française', in Pierre Nora, ed., *Les Lieux de Mémoire I. La République* (Paris, Gallimard, 1984), 523–60; Marc Angenot, *Le Centenaire de la Révolution, 1889* (Paris, La Documentation française, 1989).
33. BHVP, MS 1424, Ferry to Chassin, 9 Aug. 1889.
34. *Revue des Deux Mondes*, 1 May 1889, 229.
35. Michael Walzer, *Regicide and Revolution. Speeches at the trial of Louis XVI* (Cambridge, Cambridge University Press, 1974), 176.
36. For a brilliant analysis of the family model of the Revolution, see Lynn Hunt, *The Family Romance of the French Revolution* (London, Routledge, 1992).
37. Paul Lacombe, 'Les noms des rues à Paris sous la Révolution', *Revue de la Révolution* (7), 1886, 232; Daniel Milo, 'Les noms des rues', in Pierre Nora, ed., *Les Lieux de Mémoire II. La Nation* vol. 3 (Paris, 1986), 283–315. See also Mona Ozouf, 'La Révolution française et l'idée de l'homme nouveau', in Colin Lucas, ed., *The Political Culture of the French Revolution* (Oxford, Pergamon, 1988), 213–32, and in Ozouf, *L'Homme régénéré. Essais sur la*

Révolution française (Paris, Gallimard, 1989), 116–57.
38. Mona Ozouf, 'Le Panthéon', in Nora, *Les Lieux de Mémoire*, I, 139–166.
39. Mona Ozouf, *La Fête révolutionnaire* (Paris, Gallimard, 1976), 202.
40. Maximilien Robespierre, 'Discours sur la Constitution', 10 May 1793, *Oeuvres complètes*, IX (Paris, Presses Universitaires de France, 1958), 497. See also Ferenc Feher, *The Frozen Revolution. An Essay on Jacobinism* (Cambridge, Cambridge University Press/Paris, Maison des Sciences de l'Homme, 1987), 57–67, and Lucien Jaume, *Le Discours jacobin de la démocratie* (Paris, Fayard, 1989), 12–18.
41. Robespierre, speech of 17 *pluviôse* An II/5 Feb. 1794, in *Oeuvres complètes* X (Paris, Presses Universitaires de France, 1967), 357.
42. Rivarol, *Extraits du Journal politique et national*, in *Oeuvres complètes* (Paris, Collin, 1808), vol. IV. See also, William James Murray, *The Right Wing Press in the French Revolution* (Woodbridge, Boydell Press for the Royal Historical Society, 1986), 240–61, and Jean Lessay, *Rivarol, le Français par excellence* (Paris, Librairie académique Perrin, 1989).
43. Abbé Barruel, *Mémoires pour servir à l'Histoire du Jacobinisme* (5 vols, Hamburg, 1803), I, v.
44. Louis de Bonald, *Théorie du Pouvoir politique et religieuse dans la Société civile* (Constance, 3 vols, 1796), I, 285.
45. Proclamation of Louis XVIII at Verona, 15 Feb. 1796, in P. J. Buchez and P. C. Roux, *Histoire parlementaire de la Révolution française*, vol. 37 (Paris, Paulin, 1838, 186–7).
46. J. Lafolie, *Mémoires historiques relatifs à la fonte et à l'élévation de la statue equestre de Henri IV* (Paris, 1819), 219–20, 240–6.
47. Adophe Chenu, *Les Chevaliers de la République rouge* (Paris, Giraud & Dagneau, 1851), 9.

48. Maxime du Camp, *Les Convulsions de Paris* (Paris, 1878), I, 65–74.

49. Henri Wallon, *Histoire du Tribunal révolutionnaire de Paris* (6 vols, Paris, Hachette, 1880–82), vii, xi.

50. Hippolyte Taine, *Les Origines de la France contemporaine. La Révolution 1. L'Anarchie spontanée* (Paris, Hachette, 1878), 279.

51. *Idem, La Révolution 2. La Conquête jacobine* (1881), 471.

52. Augustin Cochin, *L'Esprit du Jacobinisme* (Paris, Plon, 1921, Presses Universitaires de France, 1979).

53. Pierre Gaxotte, *La Révolution française* (Paris, Fayard, 1928), 323.

54. John Sweets, *Choices in Vichy France. The French under Nazi Occupation* (Oxford, Oxford University Press, 1986), 34.

55. Dominique Rossignol, *Histoire de la Propagande en France de 1940 à 1944. L'Utopie Pétain* (Paris, Presses Universitaires de France, 1991), 118–19.

56. *Ibid.*, 77–105.

57. Robert Brasillach, 'Chénier', in *Ecrits à Fresnes* (Paris, 1967), 471.

58. Jean-Clément Martin, *La Vendée et la France* (Paris, Seuil, 1987), 200.

59. Marquise de La Rochejacquelein, *Mémoires* (4th edn, Paris, Michaud, 1817), 42–8.

60. Martin, *La vendée de la Mémoire*, 62, 90, 114.

61. Abbé de Genoude, *Vie de Jacques Cathelineau* (1821); Martin, 68.

62. Martin, *op. cit.*, 68.

63. Mgr Pie, *Eloge funèbre de Madame la Marquise de La Rochejacquelein* (Poitiers, 1857), 13.

64. Martin, *op. cit.*, 71.

65. Robert Tombs, 'Paris and the rural hordes: an exploration of myth and reality in the French civil war of 1870', *Historical Journal* 29/4 (1986), 795–808; General Cathelineau, *Le Corps Cathelineau pendant la guerre de 1870–1871* (2 vols, Paris, Amyot, 1871).

66. J.-C. Martin, 'La Vendée dans la mémoire des droites', in Jean-

François Sirinelli, *Histoire des Droites en France I. Politique* (Paris, Gallimard, 1992), 459; Cathelineau, *Noblesse oblige. Les Mauges, Vendée angevine* (Amiens, 1883), 12, 16.

67. Martin, *La Vendée de la Mémoire*, 129, 143–5.

68. *L'Action Française*, 26 July 1926.

69. *Le Souvenir vendéen*, no.1, June 1933, 5; J.-C. Martin, *op. cit.*, 197–9.

70. *Ibid.*, 199–200.

71. *La Croix*, 18 April 1950, article by abbé Brunellière.

72. *Le Figaro*, 17 July 1950.

73. *Ultra*, 15 June–15 July 1983.

74. Jules Michelet, *Histoire de la Révolution française* (2nd edn, Paris, 1869), III, 477; IV, 465–6.

75. Robespierre, speech in Convention, 7 Dec. 1793, in *Oeuvres* X (Paris, Presses Universitaires de France, 1967), 292–3.

76. Raymonde Monnier, 'Le Culte de Bara en l'an II', *AHRF*, 52 (1980), 321–37; F. Wartelle, 'Bara, Viala. Le Thème de l'enfance héroïque dans les manuels scolaires (IIIe République), *AHRF*, 52 (1980), 365–89.

77. Quoted by Bronislaw Baczko, *Comment sortir de la Terreur. Thermidor et la Révolution* (Paris, Gallimard, 1989), 169.

78. Madame de Staël, *Réflexions sur la paix intérieure* in *Oeuvres complètes* (Paris, 1820), 155.

79. Benjamin Constant, *De la force du gouvernement actuelle la France et de la nécessité de s'y rallier* (Paris, 1796).

80. Adolphe Thiers, *Histoire de la Révolution française* (Paris, 1823–7), I, 122, 136, 197, 308, II, 3–8, III, 34–5, 384, 435, IV, 301.

81. Lafayette, *Mémoires* (Paris, 1838), VI, 411.

82. *Le National*, 2 Aug. 1830.

83. *Le National*, 31 July 1830.

84. *Le National*, 6 Aug. 1830.

85. Jean-Claude Caron, 'La Société des Amis du Peuple', *Romantisme*, 28–9 (1980), 169–79.

86. Joseph Benoit, *Confessions d'un prolétaire* (Paris, Éditions sociales, 1968), 53.

87. *Le Réformateur*, 11 Jan. 1835. See also Georges Duveau, *Raspail* (Paris, 1948).

88. Michelet, *Histoire de la Révolution française* (Paris, 2nd edn, 1868), I, 4, 8.

89. Lamartine, *Histoire des Girondins* (8 vols, Paris, Furne, 1847), VI, 189; VII, 59–60; VIII, 380. See also William Fortescue, 'Poetry, Politics and Publicity, and the Writing of History: Lamartine's *Histoire des Girondins* (1847)', *European History Quarterly*, 17 (1987), 259–84.

90. Victor Hugo, *A ses concitoyens* (Paris, 1848).

91. F. V. Raspail, *Remerciements* in *Discours du citoyen Ledru-Rollin prononcé au banquet du Châtelet, 22 Sept. 1849* (Paris, 1849), 19.

92. Adolphe Thiers, speech of 13 Feb. 1850, *Discours parlementaires* VIII (Paris, Calmann Lévy, 1880), 609.

93. Thiers, speech of 24 May 1850, *Discours parlementaires*, IX (Paris, Calmann Lévy, 1880), 40; Bury and Robert Tombs, *Thiers, 1797–1887. A Political Life* (London, Allen and Unwin, 1986), 126.

94. Victor Hugo, *Actes et paroles. Avant l'exil, 1841–1851* (3rd edn, Paris, Michel Lévy, 1875), 330.

95. Louis Blanc, *Histoire de la Révolution française* VIII (Paris, 1856), 472–4; IX (Paris, 1857), 491–504; X (Paris, 1858), 5, 463; XI (Paris, 1861), 151.

96. Edgar Quinet, *La Révolution* (Paris, 1865), II, 182–3.

97. *Le Temps*, 6 and 30 Jan. 1866, cited in François Furet, *La Gauche et la Révolution au milieu du XIXe siècle* (Paris, Hachette, 1986), 204, 207. Furet and the revisionist school have held up Quinet as a model liberal historian.

98. Anecdote of President Grévy, 25 April 1883, cited in Bernard Lavergne, *Les Deux présidences de Jules Grévy, 1879–1887* (Paris, Librairie Fischbacher, 1966), 137–8.

99. Thiers, speech of 13 Nov. 1872, *Journal Officiel de la République Française*, 14 Nov. 1872, 6981.

100. Victor Hugo, *Quatre-Vingt-Treize* (Paris, Hetzel, s.d.), II, 245, 250.

101. See for example his speech at Angers, 7 April 1872, in Léon Gambetta, *Discours et plaidoyers politiques* II (Paris, Charpentier, 1881), 226–47.

102. Jean T. Joughin, *The Paris Commune in French Politics, 1871–1880* (Baltimore, Johns Hopkins, 1955).

103. *La République française*, 13 June 1877.

104. Odile Rudelle, *La République absolue 1870–1889* (Paris, Gallimard, 1982) offers a brilliant analysis of this point.

105. *La République française*, 2–3 July 1878.

106. *La République française*, 12 July 1880. Rosamonde Sanson, *Les 14 juillet. Fête et conscience nationale, 1789–1975* (Paris, Flammarion, 1976).

107. Charles-Ange Laisant, *La Politique radicale en 1885* (Paris, 1885), 84.

108. AN F1cI 169.

109. Ville de Paris, *Concours pour l'érection d'un monument à Danton* (Paris, Imprimerie Chaix, 1890).

110. *Journal Officiel. Chambre des Députés. Débats parlementaires*, 29 Jan. 1891, 155–6.

111. *Journal Officiel. Sénat Débats parlementaires*, 6 Feb. 1891, 59.

112. *Le Figaro*, 8 Jan. 1893.

113. Maxime Lecomte, *Les Ralliés. Histoire d'un parti. 1886–1898* (Paris, Flammarion, 1898), 233.

114. Jean-Thomas Nordmann, *Histoire des radicaux, 1820–1973* (Paris, La Table Ronde, 1974), 20.

115. Édouard Herriot, *Pourquoi je suis radical-socialiste* (Paris, Imprimeré nouvelle, 1928), 49.

116. Romain Rolland, *Théâtre de la Révolution* (Paris, Ollendorf, 1920).

117. For an eye-witness account see Charles Péguy, 'Le "Triomphe de la République"', in *Oeuvres en prose complètes* I (Paris, Gallimard, 1987, 299–318.

118. Jean-Thomas Nordmann, *op. cit.*, 124.

119. Alphonse Aulard, *Histoire politique de la Révolution française* (3rd edn, Paris, Colin, 1905), v, 350–2, 358,

367, 495.

120. *Le Bloc*, 26 May 1901.
121. Albert Mathiez, *La Question sociale pendant la Révolution française* (Paris, Cornély, 1905).
122. Mathiez, 'La Corruption parlementaire sous la Terreur', *Annales révolutionnaires* 5/2 (Mar.–April 1912), 157–77; *Annales révolutionnaires*, 6/3 (1913), 462.
123. Jules Vallès, *L'Insurgé* [1886] (Paris, Garnier-Flammarion, 1970), 124.
124. See Chassin's correspondence with Charras in BHVP MS 1417, and his autobiographical novel, 'Félicien, ou souvenirs d'un étudiant de 48', serialised in *Le Rappel*, 22 Aug. 1885–Jan.1886, in MS 1395; H. Monin, 'Deux historiens de la Révolution. Edgar Quinet et Charles–Louis Chassin', *Revue historique de la Révolution* (1), 1910.
125. *Le Cri du Peuple*, 25 Feb. 1870.
126. Jules Vallès, *L'Insurgé* [1886] (Paris, Garnier-Flammarion, 1970), 124.
127. Louis Jacob, *Hébert. Le Père Duchesne. Chef des sans-culottes* (Paris, Gallimard, 1960).
128. Gustave Tridon, *Les Hébertistes* (Paris, 1864), 12–13.
129. Jean Dubois, *Le Vocabulaire politique et sociale en France de 1869 à 1872* (Thesis, Paris, 1962), 315, 363.
130. Guesde to Marx, March–April 1879, cited by Claude Willard, *Le Mouvement socialiste en France, 1883–1905. Les Guesdistes* (Paris, Editions sociales, 1965), 18.
131. *L'Égalité*, 2nd series, 18 March 1880.
132. *L'Égalité*, 14 July 1880. See also Jacques Girault, 'Les Guesdistes, la deuxième *Égalité et* la Commune', in Jacques Rougerie, *Jalons pour une Histoire de la Commune* (Assen, van Gorcum, 1973), 421–30.
133. Patrick Hutton, *The Cult of the Revolutionary Tradition. The Blanquists in French Politics, 1864–1893* (Berkeley and Los Angeles, University of California Press, 1981).
134. Manifesto of 14 July 1899, cited by Willard, *op. cit.*, 423–4.
135. *La Petite République socialiste*, 21–22 Nov. 1899.
136. Speech of Jaurès, 7 June 1898, *La Petite République*, 9 June 1898.
137. Jules Guesde and Jean Jaurès, *Les Deux Méthodes. Conférence, Lille, 1900* (2nd edn, Paris, 1925), 9–10.
138. *Congrès général des organisations socialistes françaises tenu à Paris du 3 au 8 décembre, 1899* (Paris, 1900), 176. See also Alain Bergounioux, 'Socialisme et République avant 1914', in Serge Berstein and Odile Rudelle, *Le Modèle républicain* (Paris, Presses Universitaires de France, 1992), 117–28.
139. Madeleine Rebérioux, 'Le Mur des Fédérés', in Pierre Nora, ed., *Les Lieux de Mémoire*, I, 619–49.
140. Jaurès, speech of 17 Oct. 1908, in Parti Socialiste (SFIO), *5e Congrès national tenu à Toulouse les 15, 16, 17 et 18 octobre 1908* (Paris, 1908). See also the volume by Louis Dubreuilh in Jaurès' *Histoire socialiste, 1789–1900*, XI (Paris, Rouff, 1908), 249–496.
141. Mathiez, *Le Bolchévisme et le Jacobinisme* (Paris, Librairie du Parti socialiste et de L'Humanité, 1920), 3–4.
142. *Ibid.*, 22.
143. *Marcel Cachin vous parle* (Paris, Editions sociales, 1959), 15.
144. *L'Humanité*, 30 Aug. 1920.
145. *L'Humanité*, 8 Sept. 1920. L.-O. Frossard, *De Jaurès à Lénine* (Paris, Editions de la Nouvelle Revue Socialiste, 1930), 116. Frossard accompanied Cachin to Russia and joined the PCF but returned to the SFIO in 1923.
146. *L'Humanité*, 21 Aug. 1920.
147. Annie Kriegel, *Le Congrès de Tours, 1920* (Paris, Gallimard-Julliard, 1964), 52–62.
148. Léon Blum, *L'Oeuvre III.1, 1914–28* (Paris, Albin Michel, 1972), 3–7.
149. *Ibid.*, 110–12. Speech at Congrès national extraordinaire of SFIO, 21 April 1919.
150. Parti Socialiste (SFIO), *18e Congrès national tenu à Tours, 25–30 décembre 1920* (Paris, 1921), 256–69. See also

Kriegel, *op. cit.*, 99–136.

151. *Congrès de Tours*, 253.

152. *Ibid.*, 269.

153. *Le Populaire*, 2 Aug. 1922, in Léon Blum, *L'Oeuvre* III.1 (Paris, Albin Michel, 1972), 251.

154. *L'Humanité*, 30 May 1921; *L'Internationale*, 1 June 1921.

155. *Le Populaire*, 22 May 1921, cited in Blum, *L'Oeuvre* III.1, 216–17.

156. Maurice Agulhon, 'Une Contribution au souvenir de Jean Jaurès: les monuments en places publiques', *Histoire vagabonde* (Paris, Gallimard, 1988), I, 186–204.

157. Nicole Racine and Louis Bodin, *Le Parti communiste pendant l'entre-deux guerres* (Paris, Armand Colin, 1972), 214.

158. *L'Humanité*, 29 July 1934.

159. *L'Humanité*, 20 May 1935.

160. Interpellation of Flandin government by Thorez, 13 Nov. 1934, quoted by Racine and Bodin, *op. cit.*, 229.

161. *Ibid.*, 233–4; *L'Oeuvre*, 15 July 1935.

162. Parti Radical, *32e Congrès tenu à Paris, 24–7 octobre 1935*, 412.

163. Interview with Jean Kress in *L'avant-garde*, Feb. 1937, cited by Raymond Lefevre, *Cinéma et Révolution* (Paris, Edilig, 1988), 85. See also Chantal Thomas, '*La Marseillaise* de Jean Renoir: naissance d'un chant', in J.-C. Bonnet and P. Roger, *La Légende de la Révolution au XXe siècle* (Paris, Flammarion, 1988), 116–38.

164. Jacques Duclos, *Mémoires II. 1935–1939* (Paris, Fayard, 1969), 368–71.

165. *L'Humanité clandestine, 1939–1944*, ed. Germaine Willard (Paris, Editions sociales/Institut Maurice Thorez, 1975), I, 451.

166. *Le Père Duchesne* [BN Réserve G 1470 (294)], no. 1, April 1942.

167. *L'Humanité clandestine, II*, 48.

168. Annie Kriegel, 'Le Parti Communiste, la Résistance, la Libération', in *Communismes au miroir français* (Paris, Gallimard, 1974), 170–3.

169. Jacques Duclos, speech of 27 Dec. 1944, in *Batailles pour la République* (Paris, Editions sociales, 1947).

170. Maurice Thorez, *Une Politique française: Renaissance, Démocratie, Unité. Xe Congrès national du PCF, 26–30 juin 1945*, 52. André Marty, *Pour une Assemblée constituante souveraine, Xe Congrès national du PCF, 26–30 juin 1945*.

171. *The Times*, 18 Nov. 1946.

172. *L'Humanité*, 16 May 1958, 13 July and 1 Oct. 1962.

173. Jacques Duclos, *Vive l'Unité de la Classe ouvrière de France, Xe Congrès national du PCF, 26–30 juin 1945*, 5–6.

174. Léon Blum, address to 37th Congress of SFIO, 11–15 Aug. 1945, in *L'Oeuvre, VI, 1945–47* (Paris, Albin Michel, 1958), 100–1.

175. Vincent Auriol, 'Projet de Mémorandum du Parti socialiste (SFIO) sur l'unité ouvrière' (Typescript, 16pp., OURS C6 69 BD).

176. Parti Socialiste (SFIO), *Les Décisions du congrès national extraordinaire, 9–12 Nov. 1944* (Paris, 1944).

177. Jérôme Jaffré, 'Guy Mollet et la conquête de la SFIO en 1946', in Bernard Ménager, ed., *Guy Mollet, un camarade en République* (Presses universitaires de Lille, 1987).

178. SFIO, *Congrès national extraordinaire, Puteaux, 14–15 Jan. 1956*, 360.

179. Guy Mollet, *13 mai 1958–13 mai 1962* (Paris, Plon, 1962).

180. Édouard Depreux, *Renouvellement du socialisme* (Paris, Calmann-Lévy, 1960), 29, 80–1.

181. Quoted in Édouard Depreux, *Souvenirs d'un militant* (Paris, Fayard, 1972), 504–5.

182. Pierre Mendès-France to Depreux, 21 Sept. 1958, in Mendès-France, *Oeuvres complètes, IV. Pour une République moderne* (Paris, Gallimard, 1987), 538.

183. Depreux, *Renouvellement*, 162–3, 167.

184. François Mitterrand, *Ma Part de Vérité* (Paris, Fayard, 1969), 39.

185. Charles Hernu, *Priorité à gauche* (Paris, Denoël, 1969).

186. *Le Populaire de Paris*, 15–16 July

1969.
187. On all this see D. S. Bell and Byron Criddle, *The French Socialist Party. The Emergence of a Party of Government* (Oxford, Clarendon Press, 2nd edn, 1988).
187. François Mitterrand, *La Rose au poing* (Paris, Flammarion, 1973), 28–9, 43, 145–6.
188. Preface to Michel Bataille, *Demain, Jaurès* (Paris, Editions Pygmalion, 1977), 12.
189. Pierre Favier and Michel Martin-Rolland, *La Décennie Mitterrand I. Les Ruptures* (Paris, Seuil, 1990), 59–60.
190. *Le Quotidien de Paris*, 24–25 Oct. 1981.
191. Émile Waldeck-Rochet, *Les événements de mai–juin 1968. Leurs enseignements. Rapport présenté au comité central, Nanterre, 8–9 juillet 1968*, 18.
192. Manifeste du Comité central du PCF (Champigny-sur-Marne, 5–6 déc. 1968), *Pour une Démocratie avancée. Pour une France socialiste.*
193. Georges Marchais, interviewed on France-Inter, 20 Jan. 1976, cited by Annie Kriegel, *Un autre Communisme* (Paris, Hachette, 1977), 55.
194. Marchais on Grand Jury RTL-Le Monde, 15 Oct. 1989, in *Le Monde*, 17 Oct. 1989.
195. Marchais at the Club de la Presse Europe-1, 12 Nov. 1989, in *Le Monde*, 14 Nov. 1989.
196. Parti Communiste Français, *Construire le socialisme aux couleurs de la France. Rapport et résolutions du 24e congrès du PCF, fév. 1982* (Paris, Éditions sociales, 1982).
197. Georges Marchais, 'Nous sommes à l'heure de choix cruciaux', *Rapport au Comité central, 18–20 Jan. 1984.*
198. Georges Marchais, *Démocratie* (Messidor/Éditions sociales, 1990), part 4; 14.

Chapter 2: Bonapartism

1. *Le Monde*, 17–18 and 19 June 1990.
2. François Choisel, *Bonapartisme et Gaullisme* (Paris, Albatros, 1987), ex-pertly aligns texts by Napoleon III and de Gaulle. But, on his own admission, he looks only at the similarities between the two, does not examine the discourse of their political opponents, and offers no analysis of Bonapartism between 1870 and 1940, or after 1969.
3. Comte de Las Cases, *Le Mémorial de Sainte-Hélène* (London, 1823), II (ii), 348.
4. Frédéric Masson, *Le Sacre et le couronnement de Napoléon* (Paris, 1908), 192. References to the Republic vanished with the imperial decree from Tilsit in 1807.
5. *Catéchisme à l'usage de toutes les églises de l'Empire français* (Paris, Mame, 1811), 56–7.
6. Bonaparte to Talleyrand, 19 Sept. 1797, *Correspondance* t. III, no. 2223, cited by Frédéric Bluche, *Le Bonapartisme. Aux origines de la Droite autoritaire, 1800–1850* (Paris, Nouvelles Éditions Latines, 1980), 22.
7. *Mémorial de Sainte-Hélène*, I (ii), 337–8.
8. Frédéric Bluche, *Le Plébiscite des Cent-Jours* (Geneva, Droz, 1974).
9. *Mémorial de Sainte-Hélène*, I(i), 354–5.
10. Bonaparte to comte de Paris, 7 Sept. 1800, in *Correspondance*, VI (Paris, Imprimerie impériale, 1860), 574.
11. A.C. Thibaudeau, *Mémoires sur le Consulat* (Paris, 1827), 244.
12. *Ibid.*, 10–11.
13. Moreau described himself as a 'frère d'armes' at his trial. *Discours prononcé au tribunal criminel spécial du département de la Seine* (1804), 2.
14. *Mémorial de Saint-Hélène*, I (i), 354–5, 369.
15. Emile Le Gallo, *Les Cent-Jours* (Paris, 1924), 79–96; Léon Radiguet, *L'Acte additionnel* (Caen, 1911), 78–80.
16. *Mémorial de Sainte-Hélène*, I(ii), 334–6. This passage was lifted from Constant's *Mémoires sur les Cent Jours*, second part, letter II, which Napoleon was able to consult on St Helena.
17. R.S. Alexander, *Bonapartism and the*

Revolutionary Tradition in France. The Fédérés of 1815 (Cambridge, Cambridge University Press, 1991), 70–77, 87, 94, 106, 116, 160–1, 197–207. See also his 'The *Fédérés* of Dijon in 1815', *Historical Journal* 30, no. 2 (1987), 367–90.

18. Louis Fontanes, *Parallèle entre César, Cromwell, Monck et Bonaparte* (Paris, 1802), 11.

19. F. De Persigny, *Relation de l'entreprise du Prince Louis-Napoléon Bonaparte* (Stuttgart, 1838), 37–8.

20. Louis-Napoleon Bonaparte, *Des Idées napoléoniennes* (Paris, Paulin, 1839), 1.

21. *Rêveries politiques* [1832] in *Oeuvres de Napoléon III* I (Paris, 1854), 381–2.

22. *Des Idées napoléoniennes*, 44–6, 49.

23. *Ibid.*, 14–15.

24. *Rêveries politiques*, 378–9.

25. *Considérations politiques et militaires sur la Suisse* [1833], in *Oeuvres* II (Paris, 1854), 336.

26. André-Jean Tudesq, *L'Election présidentielle de Louis-Napoléon Bonaparte, 10 décembre 1848* (Paris, Colin/Kiosque, 1965).

27. Karl Marx, *The Eighteenth Brumaire of Louis-Bonaparte*, in Marx and Engels, *Selected Works in One Volume* (London, Lawrence and Wishart, 1968), 170–1.

28. *L'Extinction du paupérisme* in *Oeuvres de Napoléon III*, II (Paris, 1854), 122.

29. P.-J. Proudhon, *Napoléon III* (2nd edn, Paris, 1900), 188–9.

30. *La Fraternité*, 8 June 1848, cited by H. Forestier, 'Le mouvement bonapartiste dans l'Yonne', *Annales de Bourgogne*, 21 (1949), 120.

31. Hubert Juin, *Victor Hugo, 1844–1870* (Paris, Flammarion, 1984), 235.

32. See, for example, Maurice Agulhon, *The Republican Experiment, 1848–1852* (Cambridge, Cambridge University Press, 1983), 149–65; Ted Margadant, *The French Peasants in Revolt. The Insurrection of 1851* (Princeton University Press, 1979); James McMillan, *Napoleon III* (Harlow, Longman, 1991), 47–8; Pe-

ter McPhee, *The Politics of Rural Life. Political Mobilization in the French Countryside, 1846–1852* (Oxford, Clarendon Press, 1992), 227–259.

33. Choisel, *op.cit.*, 325; Bernard Ménager, *Les Napoléons du Peuple* (Paris, Aubier, 1988), 112; Alain Corbin, *Le Village des Cannibales* (Paris, Aubier, 1990).

34. Ménager, *op. cit.*, 115.

35. *L'Aigle républicain*, no. 1, cited by Robert-Pimienta, *La Propagande bonapartiste en 1848* (Paris, 1911), 53.

36. Proudhon, *op. cit.*, 200.

37. Tudesq, *op. cit.*, 223, 232.

38. *Ibid.*, 186.

39. Duc de Persigny, *Mémoires* (Paris, Plon, 1896), 7–8.

40. Speech at Sens, 9 Sept. 1849, *Oeuvres de Napoléon III*, III (Paris, 1856), 108.

41. Preamble to constitution, 14 Jan. 1852, in *Oeuvres* III, 288.

42. *Lettres de M. Guizot à sa famille et à ses amis* (Paris, 1884), 328.

43. Jacques Gouault, *Comment la France est devenue républicaine* (Paris, 1954), 25.

44. *Le Pays*, 23 Oct. and 3 Nov. 1871.

45. Maurice Flory, 'L'Appel au peuple napoléonien', *Revue internationale d'histoire politique et constitutionnelle* (new series, II, 1952), 215–22.

46. *Le Pays*, 17 Mar. 1874.

47. On Cassagnac, see Karen Offen, 'The Political Career of Paul de Cassagnac' (Stanford, Ph.D. thesis, 1971).

48. John Rothney, *Bonapartism after Sedan* (Cornell University Press, 1969), 259.

49. Georges Lachaud, *Les Bonapartistes et la République* (Paris, 1877), 32.

50. *L'Appel au Peuple*, 15 Feb. 1883.

51. *L'Autorité*, 25 Feb. 1886.

52. Speech of M. Lenglé, reported in *La Presse*, 22 Nov. 1888, in APP Ba 62.

53. Odile Rudelle, *La République absolue, 1870–1889* (Paris, Sorbonne, 1982), 230.

54. APP Ba 62, police reports of 27 May,

6 June, 21 July, 15 Aug. 1888.

55. William Irvine, *The Boulanger Affair Reconsidered. Royalism, Boulangism and the Origins of the Radical Right in France* (Oxford, Oxford University Press, 1989), 125–56. See also below, p. 304.

56. H. Galli, *Paul Déroulède raconté par lui-même* (Paris, 1900), 128.

57. Defence at Assize Court of the Seine, 29–31 May 1899, in Paul Déroulède, *Qui vive? France, quand même. Notes et discours, 1883–1910* (Paris, Bloud, 1910), 229.

58. APP Ba 1340, police reports, 18 Dec. 1900, 12 Feb. 1901.

59. Speech at the Manège Saint-Paul, 30 Nov. 1905, *Le Drapeau républicain plébiscitaire*, 2 Dec. 1905.

60. *L'Autorité*, 26 Aug. 1900.

61. *L'Autorité*, 6 Dec. 1903.

62. *L'Autorité*, 10 Dec. 1903.

63. *La Volonté nationale*, 17 June 1911.

64. *La Boute-Selle*, 12 Dec. 1897.

65. Paul de Cassagnac, *Faites une constitution ou faites un chef* (Paris, Les Editions de France, 1933), 102.

66. AN F7 13232, 'Notre Doctrine'. presented to second congress of the Jeunesses Patriotes, 30 Nov.–2 Dec. 1928. See below, p. 319–20.

67. *L'Action française*, 3 May 1926.

68. See, for example, Paul Reynaud, *Au Coeur de la Mêlée, 1930–1945* (Paris, Flammarion, 1951), 914.

69. See below, p. 144.

70. Gustave Hervé, *La République autoritaire* (Paris, 1926), 26–7.

71. *La Victoire*, 25 Jan. 1935.

72. *La Victoire*, 15 Feb. 1935, taken up in *C'est Pétain qu' il nous faut*, (Paris, 1935), 11–13.

73. *C'est Pétain qu' il nous faut!* 69–70.

74. *Le Procès de Maréchal Pétain* (Paris, Albin Michel, 1945), 244, 331.

75. Mauriac, article in *Le Figaro*, 3 July 1940, in *Oeuvres complètes* XI (Paris, Fayard, 1952), 310.

76. Charles de Gaulle, broadcast of 19 June 1940, *Discours et messages*, I (Paris, Plon, 1970), 4.

77. *Ibid.*, 62. Broadcast of 23 Jan. 1941.

78. Félix Gouin to Léon Blum, Oct.

1942, cited by Daniel Mayer, *Les Socialistes dans la Résistance* (Paris, Presses Universitaires de France, 1968), 206–7, and Jean Pierre-Bloch, *De Gaulle ou le temps des mépris* (Paris, La Table Ronde, 1969), 78.

79. Odile Rudelle, *Mai 58. De Gaulle et la République* (Paris, Plon, 1988), 284.

80. *Ibid.*, 472. Speech of 9 Nov. 1944.

81. Charles de Gaulle, speech of 15 Nov. 1941, *Discours et messages*, I, 137.

82. *Ibid.*, 432. Speech of 25 July 1944.

83. *Ibid.*, 441. Broadcast of 29 Aug. 1944.

84. Remarks of 20 June 1948, 29 Mar. 1949 and 12 April 1950 in *Discours et messages*, II, 200, 281 and 360; article by Colonel 'Rémy' in *Carrefour*, 11 April 1950; Henry Rousso, *Le Syndrôme de Vichy, 1944–198 . . .* (Paris, Seuil, 1987), 45–7.

85. Jacquier-Bruère [pseud. of Michel Debré], *Refaire la France* (Paris, Plon, 1945), 122.

86. Michel Debré, *Trois Républiques pour une France. Mémoires I* (Paris, Albin Michel, 1984), 393–6.

87. *Journal Officiel. Assemblée consultative provisoire. Débats parlementaires, 1945*, 1563. Speech of Marcel Plaisant, 27 July 1945.

88. Charles de Gaulle, speech of 12 Sept. 1948, in *Discours et messages II. 1946–58*, 203–4.

89. *La Victoire. Hebdomadaire de la République autoritaire, socialiste et plébiscitaire*, reappeared after ten years on 10 June 1951. See the open letter of Cassagnac to de Gaulle, 18 May 1952.

90. Charles de Gaulle, speech of 6 May 1953, *Discours et messages* II, 582.

91. Charles de Gaulle, *Discours et messages III, 1958–1962* (Paris, Plon, 1970), 3.

92. *L'Humanité*, 16 May 1958.

93. Guy Mollet, letter to a Belgian comrade, 29 May 1958, in Mollet, *13 mai 1958–13 mai 1962* (Paris, Plon, 1962), 10–11.

94. Laurent Greilsamer, *Hubert Beuve-Méry* (Paris, Fayard, 1990), 510–11.

95. Mendès-France, speech of 20 May, in *Oeuvres complètes IV. Pour une*

République moderne, 1955–62 (Paris, Gallimard, 1987), 415.

96. *Discours et Messages III*, 5.
97. See the brilliant analysis of Odile Rudelle, *Mai 58. De Gaulle et la République* (Paris, Plon, 1988). Also, René Rémond, *Le Retour de de Gaulle* (Paris, Éditions complexes, 1987).
98. Maurice Duverger, *Demain la République* (Paris, Julliard, 1958), 8–9, 35; *La Ve République et le Régime présidentiel* (Paris, Fayard, 1961), 107–8.
99. *Le Populaire de Paris*, 4 and 25 Oct. 1962.
100. Speech of Thorez, 29 Sept. 1962, in *L'Humanité*, 2 Oct. 1962.
101. Article by Christian Pineau in *Le Populaire de Paris*, 22 Oct. 1962.
102. Alfred Fabre-Luce, *Le Couronnement du Prince* (Paris, La Table Ronde, 1964); Philippe Tesson, *De Gaulle Ier. La Révolution manquée* (Paris, 1965).
103. Charles de Gaulle, broadcast of 29 Jan. 1960, *Discours et messages III*, 166.
104. Broadcast of 17 Dec. 1965, in *Discours et messages IV* (Paris, Plon, 1970), 443.
105. Press conference of 19 May 1958 in *Discours et messages III*, 10. Press conference of 31 Jan. 1964 in *Discours et messages IV*, 167–8.
106. Press conference of 28 Oct. 1966, in *Discours et messages V* (Paris, Plon, 1970), 116.
107. Broadcast of 30 May in *Discours et messages V*, 292.
108. Valéry Giscard d'Estaing, *Démocratie française* (Paris, Fayard, 1976), 154–5.
109. *Le Monde*, 2 July 1981, cited by Olivier Duhamel, 'The Fifth Republic under François Mitterrand. Evolution and Perspectives', in Stanley Hoffmann, ed., *The Mitterrand Experiment* (Cambridge, Polity Press, 1987), 143.
110. Cited by Alistair Cole, 'La France unie? François Mitterrand', in John

Gaffney, ed., *The French Presidential Elections of 1988* (Aldershot, Dartmouth, 1989), 87.
111. Jacques Chirac on A2 'L'Heure de vérité', 7 April 1988, cited in *Le Monde*, 9 April 1988.
112. *Le Monde*, 7 Feb., 13 Mar. 1991.
113. Philippe Séguin, *Louis-Napoléon le Grand* (Paris, Grasset, 1990), 63–5.
114. *Le Souvenir Napoléonien*, 373 (Oct. 1990), 37–41.
115. Jacques Trullard, *La Résurrection de Napoléon. Statue érigée par M.M. Noisot, grenadier de l'Ile de l'Elbe, et Rude, statuaire, à Fixin (Côte d'Or)* (Dijon, 1847), 16.
116. Jean Tulard, *Napoléon. Le mythe du sauveur* (Paris, Fayard, 1977), 83–5. Translated by T. Waugh as *Napoleon. The Myth of the Saviour* (London, Methuen, 1985).
117. Arsène Alexandre, *Histoire de la peinture militaire en France* (Paris, Renouard, 1889).
118. Madame de Staël, *Considérations sur les principaux événements de la Révolution française* (Paris, 1818), II, 260.
119. *Bulletin de la Grande Armée, An XIV*.
120. Marie-Louise Bivier, *Le Paris de Napoléon* (Paris, Plon, 1963).
121. See above, p. 23.
122. Bernard Ménager, *Les Napoléons du Peuple*, 16–33.
123. See Georges Lote, 'La Mort de Napoléon et l'opinion bonapartiste en 1821', *Revue des Études napoléoniennes*, 31, (July–Dec. 1930); A. Tudesq, 'La Légende napoléonienne en France en 1848', *Revue historique* (218), 1957; J. Lucas-Dubreton, *Le Culte de Napoléon, 1815–1848* (Paris, Albin Michel, 1960).
124. Albert Cim, *Le Chansonnier Emile Debraux, roi de la goguette, 1796–1831* (Paris, Flammarion, 1910).
125. Jean Touchard, *La Gloire de Béranger* (Paris, A. Colin, 1968), I, 261.
126. F. L'Homme, *Charlet* (Paris, Allison et Cie, 1892), 54.
127. Auguste Barthélemy and Joseph

Méry, *Napoléon en Egypte* (3rd edn, Paris, Dupont ed Cie, 1828), 5, 53.

128. Ménager, *op. cit.*, 74, 77, 80; Alexander, *op. cit.*, 153–4, 183–7, 278–9; Touchard, *op. cit.*, 417.

129. Chateaubriand, *De Buonaparte et des Bourbons* [April 1814] (Paris, Pauvert, 1961).

130. Madame de Staël, *op. cit.*, 253.

131. Benjamin Constant, *De l'esprit de conquête et de l'usurpation* [April 1814], in *Oeuvres* (Pléiade, 1957), 1031–2. *Journal des Débats*, 19 Mar. 1815, in Benjamin Constant, *Recueil d'articles, 1795–1817*, ed. Ephraïm Harpaz (Geneva, Droz, 1978), 150.

132. Hubert Juin, *Victor Hugo, I 1802–1843* (Paris, Flammarion, 1980), 245, 264.

133. Balzac, *Le Médecin de campagne* [1833], in *La Comédie humaine* IX (Paris, Gallimard, 1978), 529. See also Maurice Descotes, *La Légende de Napoléon et les Ecrivains français* (Paris, Minard, 1967), 225–67.

134. Hector Giacomelli, *Raffet. Son oeuvre lithographique et ses eaux-fortes* (Paris, 1862).

135. Henry Jouin, *Histoire et description de la Colonne de la Grande Armée, place Vendôme* (Paris, Plon, 1879).

136. François Guizot, *Mémoires pour servir à l'histoire de mon temps, VI* (Paris, 1864), 22. On this episode, see also Jean Bourguignon, *Le Retour des cendres* (Paris, Plon, 1941); J. Lucas-Dubreton, *op. cit.*, Jean Vidalenc, 'L'opinion publique en Normandie et le retour des restes de Napoléon en décembre 1840', in *Mélanges offerts à C.-H. Pouthas* (Paris, 1973).

137. A. de Granier de Cassagnac, *Souvenirs du Second Empire* (Paris, 1879), I, 65.

138. Report by the prefect of Bas-Rhin, cited by Ménager, *op. cit.*, 117.

139. Bourguignon, *op. cit.*, 237.

140. General Niox, *Napoléon et les Invalides* (Paris, Delagrave, 1911).

141. Speech of 24 May 1850, in *Discours parlementaires*, IX (Paris, 1880), 41.

142. Thiers, *Histoire du Consulat et de l'Empire* XX (Paris, Paulin, 1862), 795–6.

143. *Ibid.*, XX, 296–7.

144. Victor Hugo, 'Discours de réception à l'Académie française', 2 June 1841, *Actes et paroles. Avant l'exil, 1841–1851* (3rd edn, Paris, Lévy, 1875).

145. Hugo, *Napoléon le Petit* (London, 1852), 37.

146. Letter of 20 May 1861, quoted in Hubert Juin, *Victor Hugo, 1844–1870* (Paris, 1984), 456.

147. Lt.-Col. Charras, *Histoire de la Campagne de 1815. Waterloo* (3rd edn, Brussels, J. Hetzel, 1858), 417.

148. Edgar Quinet, *Histoire de la Campagne de 1815* (Paris, 1862), 16–17.

149. Jean-Pierre Rioux, *Erckmann et Chatrian ou le Trait d'union* (Paris, Gallimard, 1989), 15.

150. Erckmann-Chatrian, *Histoire d'un Conscrit de 1813* (Paris, Hetzel, 1864), 269.

151. *Le Cri du Peuple*, 24 Feb. 1871.

152. *Le Père Duchesne*, 25 germinal Year 79.

153. Léon Gambetta, speech of 1 June 1874, in *Discours et plaidoyers politiques*, 4 (Paris, Charpentier, 1881), 149.

154. Jules Ferry, speech at Saint-Dié, 2 Oct. 1887, in *Discours et opinions*, 7 (Paris, 1898), 95–6.

155. Jules Ferry, unfinished article of 1890 for the *North American Review*, published in *Revue de Paris*, 1 July 1897, in *Discours et opinions* 7 (Paris, 1898), 171.

156. AN Flcl 169, Conseil municipal de Paris, 17 June 1885.

157. H. Taine, 'Napoléon Bonaparte', *Revue des Deux Mondes* 79 (15 Feb. 1887), 721–52; 80 (1 Mar. 1887), 5–48. Compare with the analysis in *Les Origines de la France contemporaine* (IX), *Le Régime moderne*, I (26th edn, Paris, 1911), 17–19, 25, 207, 213, 219–20.

158. For a contemporary appreciation of this development see Francis Mag-

nard, 'La Résurrection d'une légende', *La Revue de Paris*, Feb.–Mar. 1894, 89–111.

159. *Le Figaro*, 28 Oct. 1893.
160. *Le Figaro*, 16 Mar. 1900.
161. See, for example, Georges d'Esparbès, *La Légende de l'Aigle* (Paris, Dentu, 1893).
162. Maurice Barrès, *Les Déracinés* [1897] (Paris, Plon, Livre de Poche, 1972), 233.
163. *Mémoires de général baron de Marbot* (3 vols, Paris, 1891), II, 217.
164. *Les Cahiers du Capitaine Coignet* (Hachette, Livre de Poche, 1968).
165. *Mémoires de M. de Bourrienne sur Napoléon, le Directoire, le Consulat, l'Empire et la Restauration* (new edn, Garnier frères, 1899).
166. Gourgaud, *Mémoires pour servir à l'histoire de France sous Napoléon, écrits à Saint-Hélène* (2 vols, Paris, Firmin Didot & Bossange, 1823); *Sainte-Hélène. Journal inédite de 1815 à 1818* (2 vols, Paris, Flammarion, 1899).
167. Henry Houssaye, *1814* (Paris, Perrin, 1888), *1815* (3 vols, 1893–1905).
168. Albert Vandal, *Napoléon et Alexandre Ier. L'Alliance russe sous le Premier Empire* (3 vols, Paris, Plon, 1891–6).
169. Frédéric Masson, *Napoléon inconnu. Papiers inédits, 1786–1793* (2 vols, Paris, Ollendorff, 1895); *Napoléon et sa Famille* (VIII, 3e edn, Paris, Ollendorff, 1907), xxxiv.
170. Emile Zola, 'Lettre à la France', 6 Jan. 1898, in *La Vérité en marche* (Paris, Charpentier, 1901), 63–4.
171. Henry Houssaye, 'Napoléon le Grand, par Victor Hugo', *Bulletin du Bibliophile* (1902), 97–105.
172. Charles Péguy, 'Notre Patrie', *Cahiers de la Quinzaine*, VIIe series, 3e cahier, 17 Oct. 1905, 52–8.
173. *Revue des Études napoléoniennes*, 10th year, no. 1, Oct. 1921, 175.
174. *L'Oeuvre*, 6 May 1921.
175. *Revue des Études napoléoniennes*, loc. cit.
176. *L'Humanité*, 5 May 1921.
177. Elie Faure, *Napoléon* (Paris, 1921), 158–9, 189.

178. Jacques Bainville, *Histoire de France* (Paris, Fayard, 1924), 396.
179. *Napoléon, vu par Abel Gance* (Paris, Plon, 1927), 391.
180. All this information is contained in the *Bulletin de l'Institut Napoléon*, no. 1. Jan. 1934–1936.
181. Charles Maurras, *Jeanne d'Arc, Louis XIV, Napoléon* (Paris, Flammarion, 1937), 220.
182. Octave Aubry, *L'Aiglon, des Tuileries aux Invalides* (Paris, Flammarion, 1941); Jean Bourguignon, *Le Retour des cendres* (Paris, Plon, 1941).
183. Jean Lacouture, *De Gaulle, the Rebel, 1890–1944* (London, Collins Harvill, 1990), 8.
184. Charles de Gaulle, lecture notes of 1921 in *Lettres, Notes et Carnets, 1919–juin 1940* (Paris, Plon, 1980), 117–18.
185. Speech of 5 April 1941 in de Gaulle, *Lettres, Notes et Carnets, juin 1940–juillet 1941* (Paris, Plon, 1981), 289.
186. See below, p. 129.
187. Charles de Gaulle, *Mémoires de Guerre, II. L'Unité, 1942–1944* (Paris, Plon, 1956), 313; Philip G. Cerny, *The Politics of Grandeur. Ideological Aspects of de Gaulle's Foreign Policy* (Cambridge, Cambridge University Press, 1980), 19.
188. Charles de Gaulle, *Lettres, Notes et Carnets, mai 1969–novembre 1970. Compléments de 1908 à 1968* (Paris, Plon, 1988), 173–82.
189. André Malraux, *Les Chênes qu'on abat* (Paris, Gallimard, 1971), 104.
190. *Ibid.*, 109, 111.
191. *Ibid.*, 110.
192. *Ibid.*, 52.
193. *Le Monde*, 16 Aug. 1969.
194. I am grateful to Liam Smith for this reference.
195. 'Le Héros, la Légende et l'Histoire', *L'Humanité*, 13 Aug. 1969. This text is virtually identical to the conclusion of an article of the same name in *La Pensée*, 143 (Feb. 1969), 61.
196. *Revue de l'Institut Napoléon*, no. 151, 1988/2, 5.
197. *Le Souvenir napoléonien*, 202 (April 1965); Sybille Mignon, 'Cinquante

années de Souvenir Napoléon', *Le Souvenir napoléonien*, 364 (April 1989).

198. *Le Souvenir napoléonien*, 365 (June 1989).

Chapter 3: Grandeur

1. Charles de Gaulle, *Mémoires de Guerre I. l'Appel, 1940–1942* (Paris, Plon, 1954), 1.
2. *Le Monde*, 20 May 1989.
3. Général Trochu, *L'Armée Française en 1867* (Paris, Amyot, 1867), 18.
4. Quoted by Jacques Godechot, *Les Constitutions de la France depuis 1789* (Paris, Flammarion, 1979), 65
5. M.-J. Chénier, 'La mort du général Hoche', *Oeuvres*, III, (Paris, 1826) 187–8.
6. Stan Scott, 'Napoleon's sacral kingship', *Australian Journal of French Studies* (12, no. 2), 1975, 199.
7. Norman Hampson, 'The French Revolution and the nationalisation of honour', in M. R. D. Foot, ed., *War and Society* (London, Paul Eleck, 1973), 199–212.
8. Letter to Marquis d'Osmond, ambassador in London, 28 May 1818, in *Lettres du duc de Richelieu au marquis d'Osmond, 1816–1818* (Paris, Gallimard, 1939), 192.
9. Speech to Chamber of Deputies, 15 Jan. 1840, in Thomas-Robert Bugeaud, *Par l'Épée et par la charrue* (Paris, Presses Universitaires de France, 1948), 66.
10. Thomas-Robert Bugeaud, *L'Algérie. Des moyens de conserver et d'utiliser cette conquête* (Paris, Dentu, 1842), 27.
11. Maurice Agulhon, 'La "statuomanie" et l'histoire', *L'Ethnologie française* 8 (Mar.–Sept. 1978), 147–8, 153–4.
12. Thomas W. Gaehtgens, *Versailles. De la Résidence royale au musée historique* (Paris, Albin Michel, 1984). His essay in Pierre Nora, ed., *Les Lieux de Mémoire. II. La Nation. 3* (Paris, Gallimard, 1986) covers much the same ground.
13. *Le National*, 4, 7 and 8 Oct. 1840.
14. Edgar Quinet, *Histoire de mes Idées*, in *Oeuvres complètes* X (Paris, Pagnerre, 1858), 104.
15. Quinet, 'Avertissement à la monarchie de 1830' [1831], in *Oeuvres complètes* VI (1857), 165.
16. Quinet, '1815 et 1840' [September 1840], in *Oeuvres complètes* X (1858), 13, 18.
17. Quinet, 'Avertissement au pays' [1841], in *Oeuvres complètes* X, 37–8, 42, 51.
18. Tocqueville, *De la Démocratie en Amérique* [1835] (Paris, Garnier-Flammarion, 1981) I, 314.
19. Lamartine's circular of 2 Mar. 1848, in Comité national du centenaire de 1848, *Documents diplomatiques du gouvernement provisoire et de la commission du pouvoir exécutif*, I (Paris, Imprimerie nationale, 1953), 8, 10–11.
20. Garnier-Pagès, *Histoire de la Révolution de 1848*, IX (Paris, Pagnerre, 1869), 186–7.
21. Speech of 16 April 1849 in Ledru-Rollin, *Discours et écrits divers* (Paris, Germer Baillière, 1879), II, 288.
22. Napoléon III, *Oeuvres III* (Paris, Plon, 1856), 388, 431. Speeches of 12 July 1854 and 29 Dec. 1855.
23. Order of the day to the Army of Italy, 12 May 1859, in Napoleon III, *Oeuvres V* (Paris, Plon/Amyot, 1869), 81.
24. *Ibid.*, 89. Proclamation to the Army of Italy, 12 July 1859.
25. Speeches of Ollivier and Thiers, 15 July 1870 in *Journal Officiel de l'Empire français*, 16 July 1870, 1260–1.
26. Stéphane Audoin-Rouzeau, *1870. La France dans la Guerre* (Paris, Armand Colin, 1989), 47.
27. Arthur de Gobineau, *Ce qui est arrivé à la France en 1870* [written Nov. 1870–June 1871], (Paris, Klincksieck, 1970), 125.
28. Gambetta, speech at Tours, 1 Dec. 1870, in *Télégrammes militaires de M. Léon Gambetta, 9 Oct. 1870–6 Feb.*

1871 (Paris, 1871), 71.

29. Ernest Renan, *La Réforme intellectuelle et morale de la France* [1871], in *Oeuvres complètes* I (Paris, Calmann-Lévy, 1947), 338, 379.

30. Trochu, *op. cit.*, 18.

31. Paul Déroulède, *Chants du Soldat* (2nd edn, Paris, Michel Lévy, 1872), 5–6.

32. *Le Drapeau*, 23 May 1885, reprinted in Paul Déroulède, *Le Livre de la Ligue des Patriotes* (Paris, 1887), 180–1.

33. Charles de Freycinet, *Souvenirs, 1878–1893* (New York, Da Capo Press, 1973), 268–9.

34. Ernest Renan, *Qu'est-ce qu'une nation?* Lecture given in the Sorbonne, 11 Mar. 1882, *Oeuvres complètes* I, 904.

35. APP Ba 1340. The calendar can be reconstituted from this police file of the Ligue des Patriotes between 1890 and 1907.

36. *Le Drapeau*, 17 Dec. 1883, reprinted in Paul Déroulède, *Le Livre de la Ligue des Patriotes* (Paris, 1887), 86–7.

37. Ernest Lavisse, *Souvenirs* (Paris, Calmann-Lévy, 1912), 281–2.

38. *Idem*, *La Première année d'histoire de France* (Paris, Colin, 1876), 3–4, 33. See also Pierre Nora, 'Ernest Lavisse. Son rôle dans la formation du sentiment national', *Revue historique*, 228 (1962), 73–106, republished as 'Lavisse, instituteur national', in Nora, ed., *Les Lieux de Mémoire* I, 247–89.

39. 'Correspondance d'Albert Sorel, 1870–1871', in *Revue des Deux Mondes*, 15 Dec. 1912, 1 Jan. 1913.

40. Albert Sorel, *De l'origine des traditions nationales dans la politique extérieure de la France* (Paris, Picard, 1882) serves as a good introduction to the mammoth *L'Europe et la Révolution française* (8 vols, Paris, Plon, 1885–1904).

41. Arthur Chuquet, *Les Guerres de la Révolution* (11 vols, Paris, Cerf, 1886–96).

42. Gabriel Hanotaux, *Mon Temps. I. De*

L'Empire à la République (Paris, Plon, 1933), 250, 319, 330.

43. *Idem, Histoire du Cardinal Richelieu* I (Paris, Firmin Didot, 1893), vii.

44. Charles Maurras, *Au Signe de Flore* (Paris, 1931), 51.

45. *Idem, Une Campagne royaliste au 'Figaro'* [1901–2], in *Enquête sur la Monarchie* (Paris, Nouvelle Librairie Nationale, 1925), 496–7.

46. See above, p. 76 and below, p. 309.

47. *Enquête sur la Monarchie*, 135, and Barrès/Maurras, *La République ou le Roi. Correspondance inédite, 1888–1923* (Paris, Plon, 1970), 297.

48. Zeev Sternhell, *Maurice Barrès et le nationalisme français* (Paris, Colin, 1972), 350.

49. Charles Maurras, *Kiel et Tanger, 1895–1905. La République française devant l'Europe* (2nd edn, Paris, Nouvelle Librairie Nationale, 1914), cii. He quotes the article by Sembat in *Le Courrier européen*, 3 April 1913.

50. Charles Péguy, 'L'Argent suite', *Cahiers de la Quinzaine* (9), 22 April 1913, republished in *Oeuvres complètes* (Paris, Nouvelle Revue Française, 1932), 128.

51. Maurice Barrès, *Chronique de la Grande Guerre, 1914–1920* (Paris, Plon, 1968), 132.

52. *Ibid.*, 138.

53. Arthur Chuquet, *De Valmy à la Marne* (Paris, Fontemoing, 1915), 33–4.

54. Maurice Barrès, *L'Appel du Rhin* (Paris, Société littéraire de France, 1919), 26, 53–4.

55. Paul Tirard, *La France sur le Rhin. Douze années d'occupation rhénane* (Paris, Plon, 1930), 9–12. Tirard was French high commissioner in the Rhineland.

56. Raymond Recouly, *Le Mémorial de Foch. Mes entretiens avec le Maréchal* (Paris, Les Editions de France, 1929), 183.

57. Georges Clemenceau, *Grandeur et misères d'une victoire* (Paris, Plon, 1930), 106–7.

58 Antoine Prost, 'Les Monuments aux morts', in Pierre Nora, ed., *Les Lieux*

de Mémoire I, 200–13.

59. *Idem*, 'Verdun', in Nora, ed., *Les Lieux de Mémoire* II. *La Nation*, 3 (Paris, Gallimard, 1986); *Le Populaire*, 12, 13 and 14 July 1936.

60. Philippe Pétain, *Actes et Écrits* (Paris, Flammarion, 1974), 451.

61. *Ibid.*, 457.

62. *Ibid.*, 459. Broadcast by Pétain to the Empire, 3 Sept. 1940. Charles-Robert Ageron, 'Vichy, les Français et l'Empire, 1940–1942', in Jean-Pierre Azéma and François Bédarida, eds, *Le Régime de Vichy et les Français* (Paris, Fayard, 1992), 122–34.

63. Pétain, text read to council of ministers, 16 June 1940, in *Actes et Écrits*, 448.

64. *Ibid.*, 451. Broadcast of 23 June 1940.

65. Charles de Gaulle, *Discours et messages*, I (Paris, Plon, 1970), 7.

66. *Ibid.*, 12.

67. *Ibid.*, 37.

68. *Ibid.*, 492, 494.

69. Letter to General Denvers, 2 Jan. 1945, in General de Lattre de Tassigny, *Histoire de la première armée française, Rhin et Danube* (Paris, Plon, 1949), 349–50, and also in Jean de Lattre, *Ne Pas Subir. Écrits, 1914–1952* (Paris, Plon, 1984), 310.

70. General de Langlade *et al.*, *Libération de Strasbourg* (Strasbourg, Editions des Dernières Nouvelles, 1948, 57–60. The inauguration ceremony was on 23 November 1945, first anniversary of the liberation of the city.

71. Charles de Gaulle, broadcast of 5 Feb. 1945 in *Discours et messages*, I, 518.

72. *Ordre du jour*, 24 April 1945, in De Lattre de Tassigny, *Histoire*, 564.

73. Charles de Gaulle, *Le Fil de l'Épée* [1932] (2nd edn, Paris, Berger-Levrault, 1944), 28–9.

74. Charles de Gaulle, broadcast of 10 Dec. 1945 in *Discours et messages*, I, 656.

75. Charles de Gaulle, *Mémoires de Guerre*. II. *Le salut, 1944–1946* (Paris, Plon, 1959), 390.

76. Charles de Gaulle, press conference of 12 Nov. 1947, in *Discours et messages*, II, 158.

77. Press conference, 14 Jan. 1963, *Discours et messages*, III, 71.

78. Speech at the Kremlin, 20 June 1966 in *Discours et messages*, V, 43.

79. Julius W. Friend, *Seven Years in France. François Mitterrand and the Unintended Revolution, 1981–1988* (Boulder, Colorado, Westview Press, 1989), 198.

80. See also below, p. 151.

81. Pierre Lagaillarde, *'On a triché avec l'honneur'* (Paris, La Table Ronde, 1961), 138.

82. Jacques Soustelle, *L'Espérance trahie, 1958–1961* (Paris, Editions de l'Alma, 1962), 261.

83. Charles de Gaulle, press conference, 5 Sept. 1961, *Discours et messages*, III (Paris, Plon, 1970), 339.

84. *Idem*, speech at Phnom Penh, 1 Sept. 1966, *Discours et messages*, IV (Paris, Plon, 1970), 76.

85. *Ibid.*, 200. Charles de Gaulle, speech in Guadeloupe, 20 Mar. 1964.

86. Jacques Adda and Marie-Claude Smouts, *La France face au Sud. Le Miroir brisé* (Paris, Editions Karthala, 1989), 11–14.

87. Charles de Gaulle, speech of 9 June 1948 in *Discours et messages*, II, 191.

88. Speech at Milan, 23 June 1959, in *Discours et messages*, III, 131.

89. *Ibid.*, 433. Speech at Elysée, 3 July 1962.

90. Georges Pompidou, *Entretiens et Discours, 1968–1974* (Paris, Plon, 1975), II, 127.

91. *Le Monde*, 28 July 1989.

92. *Le Monde*, 1 Dec. 1989. Interview of Mitterrand at Athens, 29 Nov. 1989.

93. *Le Monde*, 26 Oct. 1989. Speech of Mitterrand to Parliament of Strasbourg, 25 Oct. 1989.

94. *Le Monde*, 1 Dec. 1989.

95. *Le Point*, no. 899, 17 Dec. 1989, 61.

96. André Malraux, *Les Chênes qu'on abat* (Paris, Gallimard, 1971), 23, 46.

97. Speech of 2 Jan. 1792, in H. Morse Stephens, *Principal Speeches of the Statesmen and Orators of the French*

Revolution (Oxford, Clarendon Press, 1892) II, 311, 318–319.

98. Speech of 2 September 1792 in *ibid.*, II, 170.

99. The composition of the revolutionary armies has been examined by Jean-Paul Bertaud, *La Révolution armée. Les Soldats-citoyens et la Révolution française* (Paris, Robert Laffont, 1979); John A. Lynn, *The Bayonets of the Republic. Revolution and Tactics in the Army of Revolutionary France, 1791–1794* (Urbana and Chicago: University of Illinois Press, 1984); and Hew Strachan, 'The Nation-in-Arms', in Geoffrey Best, ed., *The Permanent Revolution. The French Revolution and its Legacy, 1789–1989* (London, Fontana, 1988).

100. See above, p. 113.

101. Jacques Godechot, *La Grande Nation* (2nd edn, Paris, Aubier, 1983), 75–6.

102. *Idem, Constitutions*, 91.

103. *Chants et Chansons populaires de la France* (Paris, 1843).

104. Tzvetan Todorov, *Nous et les Autres. La Réflexion française sur la Diversité humaine* (Paris, Seuil, 1989), 39–43, 215, is very suggestive on this question. See also Eric Cahm, 'French Socialist Theories of the Nation to 1889', in Eric Cahm and Vladimir Claude Fisera, eds, *Socialism and Nationalism* II (Nottingham, Spokesman, 1979), 2–3.

105. Alan Forrest, *Conscripts and Deserters. The Army and French Society during the Revolution and Empire* (New York and Oxford, Oxford University Press, 1988), 188–92, 211–12.

106. Paddy Griffith, *Military Thought in the French Army, 1815–1851* (Manchester, Manchester University Press, 1989), 7–9; Richard Holmes, *The Road to Sedan, 1866–1870* (London, Royal Historical Society, 1984), 87–9, 145.

107. Pierre Guiral and Raoul Brunon, eds, *Aspects de la vie politique et militaire en France à travers la correspondance reçue par le maréchal Pélissier, 1828–*

1864 (Paris, Bibliothéque Nationale, 1968), 42–53.

108. Jules Michelet, *Introduction à l'Histoire universelle* in *Oeuvres complètes*, ed. Paul Viallaneix, II (Paris, Flammarion, 1972), 227, 249.

109. *Idem, Le Peuple* (Paris, Marcel Didier, 1946), 247.

110. *Idem, Histoire de la Révolution française* (2nd edn, Paris, Librairie Internationale, 1869), III, 463, 465.

111. W. H. C. Smith, 'Napoleon III and the *politique des nationalités*', paper given to the conference of the Society for the Study of French History, 31 March 1992.

112. *Le Temps*, 14 June 1867, quoted by Jean Casevitz, *Une Loi manquée: la loi Niel (1866–1868). L'Armée française à la veille de la guerre de 1870* (Rennes, 1960), 45.

113. *Ibid.*, 107. Jules Simon in Chamber of Deputies, 19 Dec. 1867.

114. Stéphane Audoin-Rouzeau, *1870. La France dans la Guerre* (Paris, Armand Colin, 1989), 51, police report of 16 July 1870.

115. Victor Hugo, 'Aux Français', 17 Sept. 1870, *Actes et écrits, 1870–1872* (Paris, Michel Lévy, 1872), 15.

116. Edgar Quinet, Paris, 21 Sept. 1870, *Le Siège de Paris et la défense nationale* in *Oeuvres complètes*, 24 (Paris, 1880), 8.

117. J. P. T. Bury, *Gambetta and National Defence: a Republican Dictatorship in France* (London, 1936), 125.

118. Address of 9 Oct. 1870. *Télégrammes militaires de M. Léon Gambetta* (Paris, 1871), 19–20. The requisition decree was dated 4 Nov.

119. Jacques Rougerie, 'L'AIT et le mouvement ouvrier à Paris', in *Jalons pour une histoire de la Commune* (Assen, van Gorcum, 1973), 16–17.

120. *Affaire de la capitulation de Metz. Procès Bazaine* (Paris, Moniteur universelle, 1873), 195–6.

121. Evidence given to National Assembly, 14 June 1871, *Journal Officiel de la République française*, 15 June 1871, 1364, 1367.

122. *La Patrie en Danger*, 25 Nov. 1870.

123. Charles Rihs, *La Commune de Paris* (Paris, Seuil, 1973), 58.

124. Speech of 8 June 1872, quoted by Richard D. Challener, *The French Theory of the Nation-in-Arms, 1866–1939* (New York, Columbia University Press, 1955), 39–40; Jean-Claude Jauffret, *Parlement, Gouvernement, Commandement. L'Armée de Métier sous la 3e République, 1871–1914* (2 vols, Vincennes, Service Historique de l'Armée de Terre), I, 153, 225–6, 296–303, 341.

125. Edgar Quinet, *La République. Conditions de la Régénération de la France* (Paris, Dentu, 1872), 63.

126. *Marcel Cachin vous parle* (Paris, Editions sociales, 1959), 15.

127. Louis Lecoin, *De Prison en prison* (Paris, édité par l'auteur, 1947), 47.

128. Paul Louis, *Le Colonialisme* (Paris, Société nouvelle de librairie et d'édition-Librairie Georges Bellais, 1905), 41.

129. François Bédarida, 'L'Armée et la République. Les opinions politiques des officiers français', *Revue historique* 232 (1964), 119–64.

130. Paul-Marie de la Gorce, *La République et son armée* (Paris, Fayard, 1963), 30; Jauffret, *op. cit.*, I, 411–14.

131. Lucien Descaves, *Sous-offs. Roman militaire* (36th edn, Paris, Tresse & Stock, 1892).

132. Jean Maitron, *Le Mouvement anarchiste en France* (Paris, Maspéro, 1975), I, 371 note.

133. *La Guerre sociale*, 6–12 May 1914.

134. Speech at Marseille, 25 May 1893 in *Oeuvres* III (Paris, Rieder, 1931), 144–5.

135. Jean Jaurès, *Histoire socialiste de la Révolution française* II (Paris, Editions sociales, 1970), 183–4, 233–7.

136. Speech at Tivoli-Vauxhall, 7 Sept. 1907, in *Oeuvres* V (Paris, 1933), 128. This speech contains most of the ideas later developed in his *Armée nouvelle* of 1910.

137. Jean Rabaut, *L'Antimilitarisme en France, 1870–1975* (Paris, Hachette, 1975), 106. On socialists and the war,

see also Roland Stromberg, *Redemption by War. The Intellectuals and 1914* (Lawrence, The Regents Press of Kansas, 1982), 107–36.

138. AN F7 13371, report on CGT conference, 15 Aug. 1915. See also, Nicholas Papayanis, *Alphonse Merrheim. The Emergence of Reformism in Revolutionary Syndicalism, 1871–1925* (Dordrecht, Nijhoff, 1985).

139. Guy Pedroncini, *1917. Les Mutineries de l'armée française* (Paris, PUF, 1967), 282. Franchet, 30 May 1917.

140. *Ibid.*, 233–9, 288–90.

141. Stéphane Audoin-Rouzeau, 'The national sentiment of soldiers during the Great War', in Robert Tombs, ed., *Nationhood and Nationalism in France from Boulangism to the Great War* (London, HarperCollins Academic, 1991), 94–5.

142. *La Vague*, 19 Dec. 1918, quoted by André Marty, *La Révolte de la Mer noire* II (Paris, Bureau d'Éditions de Diffusion et de publicité, 1929), 36–7.

143. See also Jacques Raphaël-Leygues and J. L. Barré, *Les Mutins de la Mer noir* (Paris, Plon, 1981).

144. Speech in Chamber, 24 Mar. 1919, in *Marcel Cachin vous parle*, 65.

145. *L'Humanité*, 10 July 1925.

146. Jacques Doriot and André Marty, *Un an de terreur et de lutte révolutionnaire en Indochine* (Paris, Parti Communiste, 1931); *L'Humanité*, 19 June 1931.

147. Maurice Thorez, *France Today and the People's Front* (London, Gollancz, 1936), 180.

148. André Marty, *Avec l'Espagne, pour nos libertés et la paix!* (Paris, Parti Communiste, 1936), 13.

149. *L'Humanité clandestine, 1939–1944*, ed. Germaine Willard (Paris, Editions sociales/Institut Maurice Thorez, 1975), I, 51. Special no. Oct. 1939. 'A bas la guerre impérialiste!'

150. *Le Populaire*, 3 Sept. 1939.

151. Georges Michon, *Robespierre et la Guerre révolutionnaire, 1791–1792* (Paris, Marcel Rivière, 1937), 7; Nor-

man Ingram, *The Politics of Dissent. Pacifism in France, 1919–1939* (Oxford, Clarendon Press, 1991), 189.

152. *L'Intransigeant*, 11 Sept. 1939, quoted by Jean-Louis Crémieux-Brilhac, *Les Français de l'An 40 I. La Guerre, oui ou non?* (Paris, Gallimard, 1990), 276, n. 1.

153. *L'Humanité clandestine* I, 200, no. 60, July 1940; I, 204, no. 62, 17 July 1940.

154. Marc Bloch, *L'Étrange Défaite* (Paris, Editions Franc-Tireur, 1944), 131. This was written July–Sept. 1940.

155. *Procès de Riom. Déposition de M. Daladier* (s.l.n.d.), 11.

156. *L'Humanité clandestine* I, 451, 14 July 1941.

157. Speech of 11 Mar. 1942, 'Le Prison et le procès', in *L'Oeuvre* V, 323–4.

158. *L'Humanité clandestine* II, 114, no. 181, 25 Sept. 1942.

159. Claudy Delattre, 'L'attitude communiste à travers *L'Humanité clandestine* pendant l'occupation allemande', *Le Mouvement social* (74), 1971. The tract of Oct. or Nov. 1943 was published in *Cahiers du Communisme*, 1er trimestre 1944, 69–76, and inserted unnumbered between nos 60 (7 July) and 61 (13 July) of *L'Humanité clandestine*.

160. Speech of 1 April 1942 in *Discours et messages*, I, 180.

161. Paul Isoart, 'Les Aspects politiques, constitutionnelles et administratifs des recommendations', in Institut Charles-de-Gaulle/IHTP, *Brazzaville, Janvier-Février 1944. Aux Sources de la Décolonisation* (Paris, Plon, 1988), 80–9.

162. Godechot, *Constitutions*, 390.

163. *Le Monde*, 21 April 1956, cited by Jean-François Sirinelli, 'Guerre d'Algérie, guerre des pétitions? Quelques jalons', in J.-P. Rioux and J.-F. Sirinelli, eds, *La Guerre d'Algérie et les Intellectuels Français*, Cahiers de l'Institut d'Histoire du Temps Présent, 10 (Nov. 1988), 189–90.

164. *Ibid.*, 191. *Le Monde*, 23 May 1956. These paragraphs rely heavily on the excellent contributions to this collection.

165. Speech of 17 June 1956, quoted by Jean-Pierre Vittori, *Nous les appelés d'Algérie* (Paris, Stock, 1977), 57–8.

166. Maurice Thorez, *Pour un avenir de Progrès social, de paix et de grandeur social*, report of the Comité central to XIVe Congress of the PCF, Le Havre, 18–21 July 1956, 12; Jeannine Verdès-Leroux, 'La Guerre d'Algérie dans la trajectoire des intellectuels communistes', in Rioux and Sirinelli, *op. cit.*, 211–23; Danièle Joly, *The French Communist Party and the Algerian War* (Basingstoke, Macmillan, 1991), 47, 102–8, 117–21.

167. OURS, SFIO, *48e Congrès national, Lille, 28 juin–1 juillet 1956* (typescript), 230.

168. Édouard Depreux, *Souvenirs d'un militant* (Paris, Fayard, 1972), 449.

169. Maurice Maschino, *Le Refus* (new edn, Paris, Maspéro, 1960), 121–3. See also, Claude Liazu, 'Intellectuels du Tiers Monde et Intellectuels français: les années algériennes des Editions Maspéro', in Rioux and Sirinelli, *op. cit.*, 106–12.

170. Quoted by Vittori, *op. cit.*, 286–8.

171. Jacques Adda and Marie-Claude Smouts, *La France face au Sud. Le Miroir brisé*, (Paris, Editions Karthala, 1989), 10.

172. Gilbert Zoppi, 'Jeanne d'Arc et les républicains', in Jacques Viard, ed., *L'Esprit républicain*, Colloque d'Orléans, 4–5 Sept. 1970 (Paris, Klincksieck, 1972), 314, n. 8. Between 1835 and 1881 there were only 13 editions.

173. Voltaire, *La Pucelle d'Orléans*, in *Oeuvres complètes* II (Paris, Firmin-Didot, 1876), 388.

174. Voltaire, article 'Jeanne d'Arc' in *Dictionnaire philosophique, Oeuvres complètes* VII (Paris, 1876), 746–8; see also Egide Jeanné, *L'Image de la Pucelle d'Orléans dans la Littérature historique française depuis Vol-*

taire (Liège, Vaillant-Carmanne, 1935), 11–12, 15–16, 23; Jeroom Vercruysse, 'Jeanne d'Arc au siècle des Lumières', *Studies on Voltaire and the Eighteenth Century*, XC (Banbury, Voltaire Foundation, 1972), 1701–4.

175. Jules Quicherat, *Procès de condemnation et de réhabilitation de Jeanne d'Arc* (5 vols, Paris, Renouard, 1841–9).

176. Michelet, *Histoire de la France* V (Paris, Hachette, 1841), 71–2, 90.

177. Henri Martin, *Histoire de France. Nouvelle édition* VII (Paris, Furne, 1844), 68–9, 101, 127, 128.

178. Gerd Krumeich, *Jeanne d'Arc in der Geschichte* (Sigmaringen, Thorbecke, 1989), 34–6.

179. H. Herluison, *Les Panégyristes de Jeanne d'Arc* (2nd edn, Orléans, Herluison, 1870).

180. Mgr Dupanloup, *Seconde panégyrique de Jeanne d'Arc . . . le 8 mai 1869* (Orléans, Jacob, 1869), 44.

181. Krumeich, *op. cit.*, 176–80; Krumeich, 'Joan of Arc between left and right', in Robert Tombs, ed., *Nationhood and Nationalism in France from Boulanger to the Great War* (London, HarperCollins Academic, 1991), 69. See also Jean-Marie Goulemot and Eric Walter, 'Les Centenaires de Voltaire et de Rousseau', in P. Nora, ed., *Les Lieux de Mémoire*, I, 381–420, and Philippe Contamine, 'Jeanne d'Arc dans la mémoire des droites', in Jean-François Sirinelli, *Histoire des Droites en France* (Gallimard, 1992), II, 408–9.

182. Joseph Fabre, *Jeanne d'Arc. Libératrice de la France* (Paris, Delgrave, 1883), 272.

183. Henri Wallon, *Discours sur le contre-projet de M. M. Ranc, etc., Sénat, 8 juin 1894* (Paris, Imprimerie des Journaux officiels, 1894), 14.

184. Rosamonde Sanson, 'La "Fête de Jeanne d'Arc" en 1894. Controverse et célébration', *RHMC* 20 (1973), 455.

185. R. P. Feuillette, *Panégyrique de Jeanne d'Arc, prononcé à Notre Dame . . . le 22 avril 1894* (Paris, Quelquejeu, 1894); M. Chesnelong, *Jeanne d'Arc et la vocation chrétienne de la France* (lecture at Nancy, 17 May 1894, Paris, Levé, 1894).

186. Anatole France, *Vie de Jeanne d'Arc* (2 vols, Paris, Calmann-Lévy, 1908), I, Preface, xxxvii, xli, lvi–lvii, lxviii–lxix, II, 178–9, 465.

187. Amédée Thalamas, *Jeanne d'Arc. L'histoire et la légende* (Paris, Paclot, 1904), 10, 41, 52.

188. Maurice Pujo, *Les Camelots du Roi* (Paris, Flammarion, 1933), 163.

189. Paul Déroulède, *Hommage à Jeanne d'Arc. Discours prononcé à Orléans le 8 mai 1909, au banquet de la Ligue des Patriotes* (Paris, Bloud, 1909), 2.

190. Charles Péguy, *Jeanne d'Arc* [1897] in *Oeuvres poétiques complètes* (Paris, Gallimard, 1975).

191. *Action française*, 1 Mar. 1910; Eric Cahm, *Péguy et le nationalisme français* (Paris, Cahiers de l'Amitié Charles Péguy, 25, 1972), 151–61.

192. Charles Péguy, *Notre Jeunesse* (Paris, Gallimard, 1957), 242.

193. Alain, *Propos* (Gallimard, 1970), II, 255. 17 June 1912. Cited by Krumeich, *Jeanne d'Arc*, 215, and 'Joan of Arc', 72.

194. Maurice Barrès, article of 22 Dec. 1914, in *Autour de Jeanne d'Arc* (Paris, Champion, 1916), 44–5.

195. *Ibid.*, 70, article of 14 May 1915.

196. *Ibid.*, 46, article of 22 Dec. 1914.

197. Mgr Baudrillart, *Jeanne la Libératrice. Panégyrique prononcé à Notre-Dame de Paris le 16 mai 1915* (Paris, Beauchesne, 1915), 30–1.

198. Alfred Baudrillart, *Jeanne. L'Honneur du peuple français. Panégyrique prononcé dans la cathédrale d'Orléans, le 8 mai 1923* (Orléans, Marron, 1923), 5.

199. Gabriel Hanotaux, 'La Canonisation de Jeanne d'Arc', *Revue des Deux Mondes*, 15 Aug. 1920, 681, 691.

200. Letter of Pétain, 15 May 1932 in *Mémorial des Fêtes du Ve Centenaire de Jeanne d'Arc, Rouen 23 mai–31 mai 1931* (Rouen, Wolf, 1932).

201. *Action Française*, 12 May 1929.

Maurras used essentially the same wording in further instalments of his campaign, *Méditations sur la politique de Jeanne d'Arc* (Paris, Editions du Cadran, 1931), 19; which in turn appeared virtually unchanged in *Jeanne d'Arc, Louis XIV et Napoléon* (Paris, Flammarion, 1937), 25–90.

202. *L'Humanité*, 10 May 1936, 9 May 1937. See Francis J. Murphy, *Communists and Catholics in France, 1936–1939. The Politics of the Outstretched Hand* (Gainesville, University of Florida Press, 1989), 20, 87.

203. Victor Giraud, *Vie de Jeanne d'Arc* (Avignon, Aubanel, 1941), 26, note.

204. Marc Ferro, *Pétain* (Paris, Fayard, 1987), 312.

205. État français. Ministère de l'Information, *Instructions pour l'organisation de la manifestation Jeunesse, Foi, Volonté à l'occasion de la fête de Jeanne d'Arc, 10 mai 1942*, 6–7.

206. Pétain, *Actes et Écrits*, 231–2.

207. Paul Claudel, *Jeanne d'Arc au Bûcher* (Paris, Gallimard, 1939).

208. Gabriel Jacobs, 'The Rôle of Joan of Arc on the Stage of Occupied Paris', in Roderick Kedward and Roger Austin, *Vichy France and the Resistance. Culture and Ideology* (London, Croom Helm, 1985), 115–18; Serge Addad, 'Peut-on parler de "Théâtre Résistant"?', *RHMC*, XXXVII (Jan.–Mar. 1990), 136–46.

209. *L'Humanité clandestine* II (Paris, 1975), no. 161, 8 May 1942.

210. Jean Anouilh, *L'Alouette* (London, Methuen, 1956), 70.

211. *Etudes cinématographiques*, 18–19 (3e trimestre, 1962), 90, 94–5.

212. Mgr Cazaux [bishop of Luçon], *Panégyrique prononcé à la cathédrale Sainte-Croix d'Orléans, le 8 mai 1945* (Orléans, Pigelet, 1945); Mgr Chappoulie [archbishop of Angers], *Panégyrique de Sainte Jeanne d'Arc prononcé le 8 mai 1953 à Orléans* (Orléans, Éditions de l'Ouest, 1953).

213. *Libération*, 10 May 1982.

214. *Présent*, 2–3 May 1989.

215. Peter Novick, *The Resistance versus Vichy. The Purge of Collaborators in* *Vichy France* (London, Chatto and Windus, 1968), 198.

Chapter 4:   Regionalism

1. Jean-Sylvain Bailly, *Mémoires* (Paris, Levrault, Schoell & Cie, 1804), I, 204.

2. Lafayette, *Mémoires, correspondance et manuscrits*, vol. 3 (Paris, Fournier, 1837), 7–8.

3. Roland Debbasch, *Le Principe révolutionnaire d'Unité et d'Indivisibilité de la République* (Paris-Aix, Economica-P.U. d'Aix-Marseille, 1988), 124–5.

4. Pierre Goubert, *L'Ancien Régime* II. *Les Pouvoirs* (Paris, Armand Colin, 1973), caps 1,3,4.4.5.

5. Maurice Bordes, *D'Étigny et l'administration de l'Intendance d'Auch, 1751–1767* (2 vols, Auch, 1957), 957–8, 965; *idem*, ed., *Histoire de la Gascogne des origines à nos jours* (Roanne, Horvath, 1977), 157–8.

6. Albert Soboul, 'De l'Ancien Régime à la Révolution: problème régional et réalités sociales', in Christian Gras and Georges Livet, eds, *Régions et régionalisme en France du dix–huitième siècle à nos jours* (Paris, Presses Universitaires de France, 1977), 26. See also Alan Forrest, 'Regionalism and Counter-Revolution in France', in Colin Lucas, ed., *Rewriting French History* (Oxford, Clarendon Press, 1991), 157.

7. Soboul, *op. cit.*, 27–8. I am grateful to Peter Sahlins for underlining this point to me in conversation.

8. P. Charpenne, *Histoire des Réunions temporaires d'Avignon et du Comtat Venaissin à la France* (2 vols, Paris, 1886); Albert Mathiez, *Rome et le Clergé français sous la Constituante* (Paris, 1911); Henri Dubled, *Histoire du Comtat Venaissin* (Carpentras, 1981).

9. Bertrand Barère, *Rapport et projet de décret . . . sur les idiômes étrangers, et l'enseignement de la langue française*, 8 pluviôse An II [27 Jan. 1794], 8.

10. Abbé Grégoire, 'Sur la nécessité et

les moyens d'anéantir le patois et d'universaliser l'usage de la langue française', in Michel de Certeau, Dominique Julia, Jacques Revel, *Une Politique de la Langue: la Révolution française et le patois* (Paris, Gallimard, 1975), 301–9.

11. Protest of 13 Feb. 1791, cited by Paul Serant, *La Bretagne et la France* (Paris, Fayard, 1971), 379. See also Maurice Hutt, *Chouannerie and Counter-Revolution. Puisaye, the Princes and the British Government in the 1790s* (2 vols, Cambridge, Cambridge University Press, 1983), 364–6, 440–6.

12. Jacques-François Talvis de Faverney to Leopold II, 27 May 1791, cited by Maurice Gresset, 'Les Francs-Comtois entre la France et l'Empire', in *Régions et régionalisme en France du XVIIIe siècle à nos jours* (Paris, 1977), 87. See also Bernard Grosperrin, *L'Influence française et le sentiment national français en Franche-Comté. De la Conquête à la Révolution, 1674–1789* (Besançon, Annales littéraires de l'Université de Besançon, 1967).

13. Scey-Montbéliard to Schwartzenberg, n.d., but early Dec. 1813, in Francis Borry, *La Franche-Comté en 1814* (Paris-Nancy, Berger-Levrault, 1912), 13.

14. Nicholas Richardson, *The French Prefectoral Corps, 1814–1830* (Cambridge, Cambridge University Press, 1966), 68.

15. Debbasch, *op. cit.*, 197–8.

16. Quoted by Odilon Barrot, *Études contemporaines. De la Centralisation et de ses effets* (Paris, 1861), 16.

17. *La Revue provinciale*, 15 Sept. 1848, 7.

18. *Ibid.*, 15 Nov. 1848, 165.

19. *Idem*, 202–5; Kergolay to Tocqueville, 7 July and 22 Aug. 1856, in Tocqueville, *Oeuvres complètes*, 13 (Paris, Gallimard, 1977), 299–301, 306; Gobineau to Tocqueville, 29 Nov. 1856, in Tocqueville, *Oeuvres complètes*, 9 (Paris, Gallimard, 1959), 272–4.

20. Alexis de Tocqueville, *L'Ancien Régime et la Révolution, Oeuvres complètes* II (Paris, Gallimard, 1952), 91–6, 106–14, 139–46.

21. Bernard Le Clère and Vincent Wright, *Les Préfets du Second Empire* (Paris, FNSP/Armand Colin, 1973).

22. Montalembert, speech of 30 Aug. 1849 in *Oeuvres III. Discours III* (Paris, Lecoffre, 1860), 237.

23. *Annales Franc-Comtoises*, 31 Jan. 1864, 3.

24. *Annales du Comité flamand de France* I (1853), 1–2.

25. *Ibid.*, 117, letter of Jean-Joseph Carlier to Coussemaker, 25 May 1853.

26. Jacques-Louis Hénon, *Discours sur l'administration municipale de Paris et de Lyon*, 11 Feb. 1863 (Paris, 1863), 3.

27. Comité de Nancy, *Un Projet de décentralisation* (Nancy, 1865), 2, 11, 15, 65.

28. B. Basdevant-Gaudemet, *La Commission de Décentralisation de 1870* (Paris, Presses Universitaires de France, 1973), 48.

29. Basdevant-Gaudemet, 59–60, 82–4. See also Émilien Constant, 'Émile Ollivier et la décentralisation administrative sous le Second Émpire', in Anne Troisier de Diaz, ed., *Regards sur Émile Ollivier* (Paris, Publications de la Sorbonne, 1985), 183–90.

30. Louis M. Greenberg, *Sisters of Liberty. Marseille, Lyon, Paris and the reaction to the Centralized State, 1868–1871* (Cambridge, Mass., Harvard University Press, 1971), 175–80; Jeanne Gaillard, *Communes de province, communes de Paris* (Paris, Flammarion, 1971), 33–8.

31. Charles Rihs, *La Commune de Paris 1871* (Paris, Seuil, 1973), 162–76; Eugene Schulkind, ed., *The Paris Commune of 1871* (London, Cape, 1972), 151.

32. *La Solidarité* [Geneva], 12 April 1871, in James Guillaume, *l'Internationale. Documents et Souvenirs, 1864–1878* II (Paris, 1907), 143. On Guillaume, see also below, pp.

268–9.

33. Arthur Ranc, *De Bordeaux à Versailles. L'Assemblée de 1871 et la République* (Paris, Decaux & Dreyfous, n.d.), 27, 48.

34. Maurice Bourjol, *Les Institutions régionales de 1789 à nos jours* (Paris, Berger-Levrault, 1969), 113.

35. Henri Wallon, *La Révolution du 31 mai et le Fédéralisme en 1793, ou la France vaincue par la Commune de Paris* (2 vols, Paris, Hachette, 1886), I, i, iv; II, 433.

36. Bourjol, *op. cit.*, 138–41.

37. *La Dépêche*, 8 April 1904, cited in Joseph Paul-Boncour and Charles Maurras, *Un Débat nouveau sur la République et la Décentralisation* (Toulouse, Société provinciale d'édition, 1905), 121.

38. Paul Deschanel, *La Décentralisation* (Paris-Nancy, Berger-Levrault, 1895), 43.

39. Paul-Boncour in *La Renaissance latine*, 15 July 1903, reprinted in J. Paul-Boncour and Charles Maurras, eds, *op. cit.*, 27.

40. *Ibid.*, 104, reprinted from *Le Temps*, 28 July 1903.

41. Maurice Barrès, *Assainissement et Fédéralisme. Discours prononcé à Bordeaux le 29 juin 1895* (Paris, *La Revue socialiste*, 1895), 7–8.

42. *Idem, Mes Cahiers* II, 93–4, June 1896; *Les Déracinés* [1897, Livre de Poche, 1972], 178–34, 267–94; *Leurs Figures* continues the story of the financial corruption of the Republic.

43. *Idem, Mes Cahiers* II, 109, early 1899.

44. This argument was put most succinctly in *La Terre et les Morts*, a lecture given to the Ligue de la Patrie française on 10 Mar. 1899 (Paris, 1899), 9–26. It informs *L'Appel au Soldat* (1900), in which the Moselle valley and its 'âmes additionnés' [Livre de Poche, 1975, 254] are the key influences, and *Scènes et Doctrines du Nationalisme* (1902).

45. Charles Maurras, *Au Signe de Flore* (Paris, 1931), 32.

46. *Idem, L'Étang de Berre* (Paris, Champion, 1915), 196. On Mistral, see below, pp. 208–9.

47. Maurras, *L'Étang de Berre*, 127–31.

48. *Idem, L'Idée de la Décentralisation* (Paris, 1898), 8, 42.

49. Article by Maurras in *Gazette de France*, 30 June–1 July 1903, reprinted in J. Paul-Boncour and Charles Maurras, *op. cit.*, 85.

50. J. Charles-Brun, *Le Régionalisme* (Paris, Bloud, 1911), 277–80.

51. P. Vidal de la Blache, 'Régions françaises', *Revue de Paris*, 17e année, no. 24, 15 Dec. 1910, 821–49.

52. Jean Hennessy, *Régions de France (1911–1916)* (Paris-Zürich, Crès, 1916), 35. Speech of 6 April 1913.

53. *Ibid.*, 207–11.

54. Hennessy, *Réorganisation administrative de la France* (Paris-Nancy, Berger-Levrault, 1923), 158–63.

55. Henri Hauser, *Le Problème du Régionalisme* (Paris, Presses Universitaires de France, 1924), 90–2.

56. A.D. Nord, 2V 76, sub-prefect of Hazebrouck to prefect of Nord, 16 Oct. 1882.

57. Interview to *Candide*, 13 Nov. 1940, in *Actes et Écrits*, 523.

58. *Ibid.*, 526. Declaration of 8 Dec. 1940.

59. P.-J. Proudhon, *Du Principe fédératif, avec introduction et notes par Charles-Brun, secrétaire-général de la Société Proudhon* (Paris, Bossard, 1921), 14–15, 23–6, 36–7; Jean Hennessy and Jean Charles-Brun, *Le Principe fédératif, leçons faites au Collège libre des sciences sociales* (Paris, Alcan, 1940), esp. lectures of 4 and 14 Dec. 1939, 43–4, 141–51.

60. Michèle Cointet, *Le Conseil national de Vichy. Vie politique et réforme de l'Etat en régime autoritaire, 1940–1944* (Paris, Aux Amateurs du Livre, 1989), 211–16.

61. Sonia Mazey and Vincent Wright, 'Les préfets' in Jean-Pierre Azéma and François Bédarida, *Le Régime de Vichy et les Français* (Paris, Fayard, 1992), 267.

62. Pierre Barral, 'Idéal et pratique du régionalisme dans le régime de Vi-

chy', *Revue française de science politique* xxiv, no. 5 (Oct. 1974), 936.

63. Charles-Brun, *Le Régionalisme. Cahiers de Formation politique* no. 14 (Vichy, 1944), 41.

64. Speech to École des cadres de Chazeron, 12–14 Aug. 1943, quoted by Christian Faure, *Le Projet culturel de Vichy* (Paris-Lyon, CNRS/PU Lyon, 1989), 104.

65. Tixier to *commissaires*, 22 Sept. 1944, cited by Charles-Louis Foulon, *Le Pouvoir en province à la Libération. Les Commissaires de la République, 1943–46* (FNSP/Colin, 1975), 239.

66. *Ibid.*, 255–6.

67. Jean-François Gravier, *Régions et Nation* (Paris, Presses Universitaires de France, 1942), 62.

68. Jean-François Gravier, *Paris et le Désert français* (Paris, Le Portulan, 1947), 18.

69. *Idem, Régions et Nation*, 63.

70. *La Fédération*, no. 48 (Jan. 1949), 23–5.

71. Gravier, *Paris et le Désert français*, 250–3; (2nd edn, Flammarion, 1958), 145.

72. CELIB, *Programme d'Action régionale pour la Bretagne* (CELIB, 1956).

73. Olivier Guichard, *Aménager la France* (Paris, Laffont-Gonthier, 1965), 199.

74. P. Camous, 'La genèse du projet gouvernemental', and B. Pouyet, 'La région selon le projet de loi référendaire du 27 avril 1969', in Institut d' Études politiques de l'Université de Sciences Sociales de Grenoble, *La Réforme régionale et le référendum du 27 avril 1969* (Paris, Cujas, 1970).

75. J.-F. Gravier, *Paris et le Désert français en 1972* (Paris, Flammarion, 1972), 140.

76. Jean-Jacques and Michèle Dayries, *La Régionalisation* (Paris, Presses Universitaires de France, *Que sais-je?*, 2nd edn, 1982), 43ff.

77. Guy Héraud, *L'Europe des Ethnies* (Paris, Presses de l'Europe, 1963).

78. Pope John XXIII, *La Paix sur la Terre. Pacem in terris. Encyclical, 11 April 1963* (Paris, Centurion, 1963), 76–7.

79. ARC, *Autonomia. Pour que vive le peuple corse* (Bastia, *Arritti*, 1974), 135.

80. Pierre Favier and Michel Martin-Rolland, *La Décennie Mitterrand I. Les Ruptures* (Paris, Seuil, 1990), 150.

81. Georges Gontcharoff and Serge Milano, *Décentralisation. I Nouveaux pouvoirs, nouveaux enjeux* (Paris, ADELS-Syros, 1983), 13. In general, see Vivien A. Schmidt, *Democratizing France. The Political and Administrative History of Decentralization* (Cambridge, Cambridge University Press, 1990), esp. 105–20, 144–9.

82. Quoted by Jean Touchard, *La Gauche en France depuis 1900* (Paris, Seuil, 1977), 105–6.

83. Favier and Martin-Rolland, 145.

84. *Ibid.*, 147.

85. *Le Monde*, 24 March 1992.

86. A letter of Louise Dietrich to her brother in May 1792 suggests that she arranged Rouget's piece and that it was first sung by her husband, but the legend, immortalised by the painting of Pils for the Salon of 1849 will not have it so. Philippe Dollinger, *Documents de l'Histoire de l'Alsace* (Toulouse, Privat, 1972), 340–1; Michel Vovelle, 'La Marseillaise', in Pierre Nora, ed., *Les Lieux de Mémoire* I, 88–90.

87. Philippe Husser, *Un Instituteur alsacien. Entre la France et l'Allemagne, 1914–1951* (Paris, Hachette, 1989), 403.

88. F. L'Huillier, ed., *L'Alsace en 1870–1871* (Strasbourg, Faculté des Lettres, 1971), 376.

89. Jean-Marie Mayeur, *Autonomie et politique en Alsace. La Constitution de 1911* (Paris, Colin, 1970); Dan P. Silverman, *Reluctant Union: Alsace-Lorraine and Imperial Germany* (Pennsylvania State University, 1972).

90. Hansi, *Histoire de l'Alsace racontée aux Petits Enfants d'Alsace et de la*

France (Paris, Herscher, 1983), 2.

91. Alphonse Daudet, *Contes de Lundi* (Paris, Flammarion, 1984), 30.

92. L'Huillier, *op. cit.*, 52–4.

93. Mona Ozouf, 'L'Alsace-Lorraine, mode d'emploi. La question d'Alsace-Lorraine dans le *Manuel général*, 1871–1914', in *L'Ecole de la France* (Paris, Gallimard, 1984), 225–6.

94. AN F1cI 170, Minister of the Interior to J. Sansboeuf, 7 June 1905.

95. Maurice Barrès, *Les Lézardes sur la Maison* (3rd edn, Paris, Sansot, 1904), 20–2, 52–8.

96. *Idem, Au Service de l'Allemagne* [1905] in *L'Oeuvre* (Paris, 1966), 53, 61–4.

97. Barrès, *Colette Baudoche* (Paris, 1909), 231–8, 245, 250–2.

98. Barrès, *Les Bastions de l'Est. Le Génie du Rhin* (Paris, 1921), 209–10.

99. John Horne, '"Lost Sisters" or Enemy Within? France, Alsace-Lorraine, and the Alsatian-Lorrainers during the First World War', paper given to the Past and Present Conference, 'European Frontiers and Boundaries in the Nineteenth and Twentieth Centuries' (St Catherine's College, Oxford, 25–26 June 1992), 9–12.

100. Philippe Husser, *op. cit.*, 50, diary entry of 29 Sept. 1914.

101. Alan Kramer, '"Wackes"—the Enemy Within? Germany, Alsace-Lorraine and the Alsace-Lorrainers during the First World War', Past the Present Conference, *op. cit.*, *passim*.

102. Husser, *op. cit.*, 166, entry of 10 July 1919.

103. AN F7 13395, Mgr Ruch to the Ligue catholique, 22 June 1924.

104. AN F7 13395, *Die Zukunft*, 9 May 1925; Appeal to all Alsatians and Lorrainers of the Heimatbund, 5 June 1926.

105. AN F7 13397, record of the trial, 2 May 1928.

106. *Le Procès du complot autonomiste de Colmar, 1–24 mai 1928* (Colmar, Alsatia, 1928), 206.

107. Philip Bankwitz, *Alsatian Autonomist Leaders, 1919–1947* (Lawrence, Regents Press of Kansas, 1978), 32–3.

108. *Ibid.*, 67–70.

109. Émile Baas, *Situation de l'Alsace* (Strasbourg, Le Roux, 1946), 131.

110. Husser, *op. cit.*, 386, entry of 1 Jan. 1942.

111. Patrick Schaeffer, *L'Alsace et l'Allemagne de 1945 à 1949* (Metz, Centre de Recherches, Relations Internationales, 1976), 28–9.

112. Baas, *op. cit.*, 130, 140.

113. Frédéric Hoffet, *Psychanalyse de l'Alsace* (Paris, Flammarion, 1951), 120.

114. J.-M. Mayeur, 'Laïcité et question scolaire en Alsace et Moselle, 1944–63', in René Rémond, ed., *Forces religieuses et attitudes politiques*, Colloque de Strasbourg 1963 (Paris, 1965), 239–49; Pierre Maugué, *Le Particularisme alsacien, 1918–1967* (Paris, Presses d'Europe, 1970).

115. For example, the Mouvement Régionaliste d'Alsace-Lorraine, launched in 1970, with its paper, *Elsa*, and the more left-wing Mouvement EL-Front Autonomiste, with its *Le Nouvel Alsacien*, in 1976. See Eugene Philipps, *L'Alsace face à son destin. La Crise d'Identité* (Strasbourg, Société d'Edition de la Basse-Alsace, 1978).

116. *Rot un Wis*, July 1975, May 1982.

117. Théophile-Malo La Tour d'Auvergne, *Origines gauloises, celles des plus anciens peuples de l'Europe* (Paris, Quillau, Year V), vi–vii, 28, 182, 210.

118. *Mèmoires de l'Académie celtique*, I (1807), 67–8.

119. La Villemarqué, *Barzas-Breiz. Chants populaires de la Bretagne* (Paris, 1839), lxviii–lxix.

120. *Vie et Oeuvres de Mgr Joseph-Marie Graveran, évêque de Quimper et de Léon* (Paris, Vivès, 1870), II, 422.

121. Association bretonne, *Premier congrès agricole tenu à Vannes, 20–24 septembre 1843. Compte-rendu et procès-verbaux* (Nantes, 1843).

122. Jean-Yves Guiomar, *Le Bretonisme. Les historiens bretons au XIXe siècle* (Mayenne, Société d'Histoire et d'Archéologie de Bretagne, 1987), 115–73.

123. *Ibid.*, 188.

124. *Ibid.*, 247.

125. *Bulletin de l'Union Régionaliste Bretonne. Congrès de Morlaix, Vannes, Guingamp, Quimperlé, 1898–1901* (Saint-Brieuc, 1902).

126. *Bulletin de l'Union Régionaliste Bretonne. Congrès de Gourin, 1904* (Redon, 1905), 31.

127. *Bulletin de la Fédération Régionaliste de Bretagne*, I (1911–12), 3–4.

128. Marquis de l'Estourbeillon, *Le Régionalisme et la France de Demain* (Vannes, Imprimerie de Commerce, 1918), 17.

129. Henri Hauser, *Le Problème du Régionalisme* (Paris, Presses Universitaires de France, 1924), 82.

130. AN F17 9125/5, letter of Breton bishops to Catholic parents, Oct. 1913.

131. Henri Poisson, *L'Abbé Jean-Marie Perrot, fondateur de Bleun-Brug, 1877–1943* (Rennes, Plihon, 1955), 88–9.

132. Perrot to bishop of Quimper, 19 Sept. 1926, quoted in Poisson, 100.

133. Olier Mordrel, *Breiz Atao ou Histoire et Actualité du Nationalisme breton* (Paris, A. Moreau, 1973); Alain Déniel, *Le Mouvement breton* (Paris, Maspéro, 1976).

134. Anna Youénon, *Fransez Debauvais de Breiz-Atao et les siens* (Rennes, 1974–8), I, 58. (Anna Youénon married Debauvais in 1929.)

135. AN F7 13244, *Appel à la Jeunesse de Bretagne*, Feb. 1922.

136. Déniel, *op. cit.*, 343–6.

137. *Ibid.*, 149.

138. Michel Denis, 'Mouvement breton et fascisme. Signification de l'échec du second "emsav"', in C. Gras and G. Livet, *Régions et Régionalisme en France du dix-huitième siècle à nos jours* (Paris, Presses Universitaires de France, 1977), 492–502.

139. *L'Heure bretonne*, 21 July 1940; Déniel, 222–6; Yann Fouéré, *La Bretagne écartelée, 1938–48* (Paris, Nouvelles Éditions Latines, 1962), 55.

140. Déniel, *op. cit.*, 201, 236–9; Denis, 497.

141. Fouéré, *op. cit.*, 65.

142. Déniel, *op. cit.*, 282.

143. Yvonnig Gicquel, *Le Comité Consultatif de Bretagne* (Rennes, Simon, 1961).

144. *L'Heure bretonne*, 17 Oct. 1942, cited by Déniel, 283–4.

145. *Ibid.*, 304; Poisson, *op. cit.*, 248.

146. Yann Fouéré, lecture of 16 May 1956, *De la Bretagne à la France et à l'Europe* (Lorient, 1958), 25.

147. Mouvement pour l'Organisation de la Bretagne, *Cent et une questions et réponses sur le MOB, ses buts, sa position* (supplement to *l'Avenir*, no. 35, 1961).

148. Union Démocratique Bretonne, *Bretagne-Colonie* (Rennes, UDB, 1972), 88.

149. Olier Mordrel, *La Voie bretonne. Radiographie de l'Emsav* (Quimper, Nature et Bretagne, 1975), 36.

150. Michel Nicolas, *Le Séparatisme en Bretagne* (Brasparts, Editions Beltan, 1986), 44.

151. Paul Sérant, *La Bretagne et la France* (Paris, Fayard, 1971), 419.

152. FLB 72, *Procès de la Bretagne* (Editions Lelenn, 1973), 89.

153. Yann Fouéré, *En Prison pour le FLB* (Paris, Nouvelles Editions Latines, 1977).

154. *Idem, Les Droits que les autres ont . . . mais que nous n'avons pas. Les Cahiers de L'Avenir de la Bretagne* nos 6&7 (Quimper, Editions Nature et Bretagne, 1979).

155. *L'Avenir de la Bretagne*, 20 Jan. 1982, 25 April–25 May 1982.

156. *L'Avenir de la Bretagne*, 25 June–25 Sept. 1982.

157. *L'Avenir de la Bretagne*, Dec. 1989.

158. *L'Avenir de la Bretagne*, Nov. 1991, Jan. 1992.

159. *L'Avenir de la Bretagne*, Nov. 1991, Mar. 1992, April 1992.

160. Frédéric Mistral, *Mes Origines.*

Mémoires et Récits [1906] (Paris, Plon, 1937), 142.

161. Mistral to Tavan, 28 Nov. 1870, cited by Claude Mesliand, 'Le Félibrige, la République, et l'idée de décentralisation, 1870–1892,' in *La Décentralisation*, Colloque d'Aix-en-Provence, 1961 (Gap, 1964), 126–7.

162. Gérard Cholvy, 'Régionalisme et clergé catholique au XIXe siècle,' in *Régions et Régionalisme*, 197.

163. Mistral, *Le Félibrige et l'Empire du Soleil. Causerie faite au cercle artistique de Marseille, le 25 novembre 1882* (Montpellier, 1883), 7.

164. *Idem, Discours de Santo Estello*, 15 Aug. 1888 (Avignon, Roumanille, 1888).

165. *Idem, Discours pour l'ouverture des Jeux Floraux de Montpellier, 1878* (Avignon, n.d.), 7–11.

166. Maurras, *Enquête sur la Monarchie* [1990] (Paris, Nouvelle Librairie Internationale, 1925), 44–51, 88–96; Jean Charles-Brun, *Le Régionalisme* (Paris, Bloud, 1911), 277–80. See above, pp. 180–1.

167. Louis-Xavier de Ricard, *Le Fédéralisme* (Paris, Sandoz and Fischbacher, 1877), vi.

168. *Ibid.*, 184.

169. Ricard to Mistral, 9 Mar. 1876, in Jean-Marie Carbasse, *Louis-Xavier de Ricard. Félibre rouge* (Editions Mireille Lacave, 1977), 130–1.

170. *Ibid.*, 144, 24 Jan. 1878.

171. *Ibid.*, 151. Ricard to Mistral, 20 May 1879.

172. *Ibid.*, 99, *La Dépêche*, 4 July 1892.

173. Félix Napo, *1907: La Révolte des Vignerons* (Toulouse, Privat, 1971), 63–4.

174. Maurice Agulhon, 'Conscience nationale et conscience régionale en France de 1815 à nos jours,' in *Histoire vagabonde* (Paris, Gallimard, 1988), II, 150. Agulhon cites the winegrowers' revolt, unsympathetically, as evidence of 'la faiblesse des consciences régionales ou, pour prendre le point de vue inverse, le succès de l'acculturation nationale.'

175. Philippe Pétain, Declaration of 8 Dec. 1940, in *Actes et Écrits*, 526.

176. *Cahiers du Sud. Le Génie d'Oc et l'Homme méditerranéen*, Feb. 1943 (re-ed. Marseille, Rivages, 1981), 112. Similarly Jean Cassou, who was involved in the largely socialist *Libérer et Fédérer* movement at Toulouse, where he later became *commissaire de la République*, appealed to the Albigensian past to inspire the Resistance with an insurrectionary Occitanism. See Clare Jenkins, '"Un Régionalisme rouge ou un Régionalisme blanc?" Regionalism, National Revolution and Liberation in Toulouse, 1940–1944' (Ph.D. thesis, Warwick University, 1992), 235–6, 261–2.

177. Robert Lafont, *Mistral, ou l'illusion* (Paris, Plon, 1954), 144.

178. Alain Alcouffe, Pierre Lagarde, Robert Lafont, *Pour l'Occitanie* (Toulouse, Privat, 1979), 5, 166.

179. Robert Lafont, *La Révolution régionaliste* (Paris, Gallimard, 1967), 19.

180. Robert Lafont, *Décoloniser la France. Les régions face à l'Europe* (Paris, Gallimard, 1971), 65, 287.

181. Comité Occitan d'Etudes et d'Action, *Le Petit Livre de l'Occitanie* (Saint-Pons, 1971), 161.

182. *Pour l'Occitanie*, 189.

183. *Petit Livre de l'Occitanie*, 163.

184. *Poble d'Oc. Jeune Languedoc*, 10 (15 Jan. 1973), 11 (1 Mar. 1973); Poble d'Oc, *Schéma pour une Révolution occitane* (Spécial *Poble d'Oc*), nos 19–20 (Le Cres, 1975), 17, 28, 46, 91, 133.

185. François Fontane, *Ethnisme. Vers un nationalisme humaniste* [1961] (2nd edn, Bagnols-sur-Cèze, Librairie Occitane, 1975), 34.

186. *Ibid.*, 59.

187. François Fontan, *Orientation politique du Nationalisme occitan* (Bagnols-sur-Cèze, Librairie Occitane, 1970), 9.

Chapter 5: Catholicism

1. Léon Gambetta, speech of 16

Nov. 1871, D*iscours et plaidoyers politiques* II (Paris, Charpentier, 1881), 178.

2. Edgar Quinet, *L'Enseignement du Peuple* [1849] in *Oeuvres complètes 11* (Paris, Pagnerre, 1870), 13, 25–6.

3. *Idem, La Révolution* (Paris, 1865), II, 157, 165–6.

4. Victor Hugo, *Discours à propos de la discussion de la loi Falloux à la Chambre des Députés, le 15 janvier 1850*, 3–6.

5. A. Dessoye, *Jean Macé et la Fondation de la Ligue de l'Enseignement* (Paris, Marpon et Flammarion, 1883).

6. *Centenaire de Voltaire. Fête oratoire présidée par Victor Hugo, le 30 mai 1878* (Paris, Dentu, 1878), 66.

7. Paul Bert, speech at Coulanges-sur-Yonne, 15 Aug. 1880, *Leçons, Discours et Conférences* (Paris, Charpentier, 1881), 450.

8. Jules Ferry, speech of 23 Dec, 1880, in *Discours et opinions* IV (1896), 126.

9. A. Lanfrey, 'Église et monde ouvrier. Les congréganistes et leurs écoles à Montceau-les-mines, 1875–1903, *Cahiers d'histoire* 23 (1978), 51–71.

10. *Conseil municipal de Paris. Procès-verbaux. 1885. Premier semestre* (Paris, Impprimerie nationale, 1885), session of 12 June 1885, 784.

11. Ferry, speech of 21 Dec. 1888, in *Discours et Opinions* VII (Paris, 1898), 129.

12. Le Père Didon, *L'Esprit militaire dans une nation. Discours prononcé à la distribution des prix des écoles Albert-le-Grand et Laplace, le 19 juillet 1898* (Paris, Mersch, 1898), 16, 19.

13. *La Dépêche de Toulouse*, 25 July 1898, cited by René Rémond, *L'Anticléricalisme en France de 1815 à nos jours* (Paris Fayard, 1976), 201–2.

14. Waldeck-Rousseau, speech of 11 April 1900, in *La Défense républicaine* (Paris, Fasquelle, 1902), 82.

15. Émile Combes, *Mon Ministère* (Paris, Plon, 1956), 88–96.

16. AN F1cI 170, Fédération internationale de la Libre-Pensée-section

Française to Paris municipal council, 1904.

17. Parti socialiste (SFIO), *XXXIIe Congrès national, Mulhouse, 9–12 Juin 1935*, speech of Naegelen (Bas-Rhin), 473–4.

18. André Lorulot, *Ma vie, mes idées* (Les Amis d'André Lorulot, 1973).

19. *Idem, La Grande Trahison de 1940* (Herblay, L'Idée libre, 1945), 136.

20. *La Calotte*, Oct. 1945.

21. *Parti Socialiste (SFIO). Les Décisions du Congrès national extraordinaire, 9–12 november 1944*, 11.

22. *Journal Officiel. Débats de l'Assemblée consultative provisoire*, 28 Mar. 1945, 837, 839.

23. *L'Humanité*, 8–9 April 1946.

24. Prosper Alfaric, *De la Foi à la Raison* (Paris, Union rationaliste, 1955).

25. Victor Hugo, *Pages choisies sur l'école*, ed. Prosper Alfaric (Strasbourg, Bibliothèque Jean Macé, 1935), 18–30.

26. Prosper Alfaric, 'Pourquoi je suis laïque', *Cahiers laïques* 7 (Jan.–Feb. 1952), 15, 16.

27. *Idem*, 'La querelle de la liberté de l'enseignement', *Cahiers laïques* (1), Jan.–Feb. 1951, 3, 9.

28. *Le Monde*, 2 Oct. 1951.

29. Duclos, speech in Senate, 29 Dec. 1959, cited in François Billoux, Georges Cogniot, Jacques Duclos, *Avec l'Ecole laïque* (Paris, Presses Universitaires de France, 1960), 34.

30. Georges Cogniot, *Pour l'Union dans la Bataille laïque* [speech at La Roche-sur-Yon, 3 June 1959] (Paris, PCF, 1959), 3–4.

31. Georges Cogniot, speech in Senate, 29 Dec. 1959, cited in Billoux *et al.*, *op. cit.*, 22.

32. *Le Monde*, 21 June, 1960; Jean Cornec, *La Laïcité* (Paris, Sudel, 1965), 320.

33. Letter of François Mitterrand, 1 May 1981, quoted by Alain Savary, *En toute liberté* (Paris, Hachette, 1985), 16.

34. Savary, *op. cit.*, 113–14.

35. *La Calotte*, Jan. 1984.

36. *La Calotte*, Feb. 1984.

37. Savary, *op. cit.*, 153, 164.
38. *Extract from the Manifesto of the Association of 15 August 1789*, sent to the author by the Association, 10 rued' Édimbourg, 75008 Paris.
39. Joseph de Maistre, *Considératons sur la France* (London, 1797), 1, 76.
40. Joseph de Maistre, *Les Soirées de Saint-Pétersbourg, ou entretiens sur le gouvernement temporel de la Providence* (Paris-Lyon, 1822), I, 39–40. See also, Fernand Baldensperger, *Le Mouvement des idées dans l'émigration française, 1789–1815* (Paris, 1924/ New York, 1968), II, 88–93; and Richard A. Lebrun, *Joseph de Maistre. An Intellectual Militant* (Kingston and Montreal, McGill-Queen's University Press, 1988).
41. de Maistre, *Soirées* II, 285.
42. Louis Veuillot, article of 14 Aug. 1870, in *Paris pendant les deux sièges* (2nd edn, Paris, Victor Palmé, 1872), I, 13–14.
43. *Ibid.*, II, 401. Article of 27 May 1871. See also Claude Digeon, *La Crise allemande de la pensée française, 1870–1914* (Paris, Presses Universitaires de France, 1959), 119–20; John Roberts, *The Paris Commune from the Right* (English Historical Review, supplement 6, London, Longman, 1973), 9–10, 12–13.
44. *Le Patriote des Pyrénées*, quoted by Jacques Duchesne, *Les Catholiques français sous l'Occupation* (Paris, Grasset, 1965), 29. See also Pierre Laborie, *L'Opinion française sous Vichy* (Paris, Seuil, 1990), 225–8.
45. Pétain, *Actes et Ecrits* (Paris, Flammarion, 1974), 453.
46. Jacques Duquesne, *op. cit.*, 46.
47. *L'Émancipation nationale*, 14 Dec. 1941, cited by Duquesne, 170.
48. Mgr Freppel, *Lettre à M. Gambetta* (Angers, Briand et Hervé, 1878), 4–5, 6.
49. Mgr Freppel, *La Révolution française. A propos du centenaire de 1789* (Paris, Roger et Chernoviz, 1889), 53–4.
50. Speech of 11 April 1900 in Waldeck-Rousseau, *La Défense républicaine* (Paris, Fasquelle, 1902), 82, 84. See above, p. 219.
51. Albert de Mun, *Les Responsabilités de M. Waldeck-Rousseau* (Paris, 1902).
52. Parti républicain, radical et radical-socialiste, *21e Congrès tenu à Boulogne-sur-mer, 16–19 Oct. 1924*, quoted in speech by Jean Montigny, 126.
53. *L'Écho de Paris*, 31 Oct. 1924.
54. *Journal Officiel. Débats de l'Assemblée nationale constituante*, 779, speech of Teitgen, 14 Mar. 1946.
55. *La Croix*, 25 April, 1950; René Rémond, 'Laïcité et question scolaire dans la vie politique française sous la IVe République', in *La Laïcité* (Aix-Marseille, Centre de Sciences politiques de l'Institut d'études juridiques de Nice, 1960), 398.
56. Mgr Perrin, *Directives catholiques en matière scolaire* (Paris, Fédération nationale d'Action catholique, 1953), 34–5.
57. *Le Monde*, 5 June 1984.
58. *La Croix*, 26 June 1984.
59. *Ibid.*, 26 June 1984.
60. *Le Monde*, 24–5 June 1985.
61. *Le Monde*, 8 Dec. 1989. Marat's body was in fact removed from the Panthéon in 1795.
62. *Le Monde*, 16–17 July 1989.
63. Abbé Grégoire, *Mémoires* (Paris, 1837), I, 88.
64. Bernard Plongeron, *L'Abbé Grégoire ou l'Arche de la Fraternité* (Paris, Letouzey et Ané, 1989).
65. *Résurrection du Souvenir de l'Abbé Grégoire, promoteur de la lutte contre l'esclavage et le racisme* (Paris-Lunéville, 1956).
66. Grégoire's *Essai sur la Regénération physique, morale et politique des juifs* was re-published by Flammarion in 1988. See also Robert Badinter, *Libres et Égaux. L'Émancipation des Juifs sous la Révolution française, 1789–1791* (Paris, Fayard, 1989).
67. On this typology of Catholic positions, see Jean-Marie Mayeur, 'Catholicisme intransigeant, Catholicisme social, démocratie chrétienne', *Annales ESC* 27 (1972), 483–99. See

also Emile Poulat, *Eglise contre bourgeoisie* (Paris, Casterman, 1977).

68. Lamennais, *De la Religion considérée dans ses rapports avec l'ordre politique et civil*, [1825] in *Oeuvres complètes* VII (Paris, 1836–7), 146.

69. *L'Avenir*, prospectus, 20 Aug., 7 Sept. 1830.

70. Letter of Lacordaire, 6 Oct. 1833, cited by Montalembert, *Le Père Lacordaire* [1862] in *Oeuvres polémiques* III (Paris, Lecoffre, 1868), 432.

71. Lamennais, *Paroles d'un croyant* [1833], in *Oeuvres complètes* XI (Paris, 1836), 84.

72. Lamennais to the archbishop of Paris, 29 April 1834, cited in M.J. and Louis Guillou, *La Condemnation de Lamennais* (Paris, Beauchesne, 1982), 457.

73. Lamennais, *Le Livre du Peuple* (Paris, 1838), 189.

74. *L'Ère Nouvelle*, 23 April, 1848. See also Jean-Baptiste Duroselle, *Les Débuts du Catholicisme social en France, 1822–1870* (Paris, 1951).

75. *L'Ère nouvelle*, 1 May 1848.

76. *Ibid.*, 16 Oct. 1848. See also Claude Bressolette, *L'Abbé Maret. Le Combat d'un Théologien pour une Démocratie chrétienne, 1830–1851* (Paris, Beauchesne, 1977), 459–508.

77 Frédéric Ozanam, *Les Origines du socialisme* (Paris, 1848), 4.

78 Article in *L'Ami de la religion*, 21 Oct. 1848, in Montalembert, *Oeuvres IV: Oeuvres polémiques et diverses* I (Paris, Lecoffre, 1860), 500–1. See also, Marcel Prélot and F. Gallouédec Genuys, *Le Libéralisme catholique* (Paris, Colin, 1969), and Jacques Gadille and J.-M. Mayeur, 'Les milieux catholiques libéraux en France', in *Les Catholiques libéraux au XIXe siècle* (Grenoble, 1974).

79. Letter to Cavour, 22 Oct. 1860 in Montalembert, *Oeuvres V: Oeuvres polémiques et diverses* II (Paris, 1860), 655–6.

80. Speech of 8 September 1878, in Albert de Mun, *Discours I. Questions sociales* (Paris, Poussielgue, 1888), 299–300.

81. *Idem*, speech of 16 November 1878, cited in *Ma vocation sociale* (1908), 182–3.

82. Benjamin Martin, 'The Creation of the Action libérale populaire', *French Historical Studies*, 9 (1976), 660–89, and *idem, Count Albert de Mun. Paladin of the Third Republic* (Chapel Hill, University of North Carolina Press, 1978).

83. Jean-Marie Mayeur, *Un Prêtre démocrate: l'abbé Lemire, 1853–1928* (Paris, Casterman, 1968), 106–38.

84. Suzanne Berger, *Peasants against Politics* (Cambridge, Mass., Harvard University Press, 1972), 46–7; Caroline Ford, *Creating the Nation in Provincial France. Religion and Political Identity in Brittany* (Princeton, New Jersey, Princeton University Press, 1993), 127–33.

85. *La Justice sociale*, 22 July 1893.

86. Jean-Marie Mayeur, 'Les congrès nationaux de la 'Démocratie chrétienne' à Lyon, 1896, 1897, 1898', *RHMC* 9, (1962), 181, 203–6, reprinted in *Catholicisme social et Démocratie chrétienne* (Paris, Cerf, 1986), 165–6, 188–92.

87. *Le Petit Démocrate de Saint-Denis et de la région*, 8 Dec. 1912.

88. Auguste Cavalier, *Les Rouges Chrétiens* (Paris, Bossard, 1929).

89. Jean-Claude Delbreil, *Centrisme et Démocratie-Chrétienne en France. Le Parti Démocrate Populaire des Origines au MRP, 1919–1946* (Paris, Publications de la Sorbonne, 1990), 95–129, 103–4, 149–52, 139–41, 189, 233, 313.

90. Francisque Gay, *Pour un Rassemblement des forces démocratiques d'inspiration chrétienne* (Paris, chez l'auteur, 1935), 40, 45, 59–61. See also, Françoise Mayeur, *L'Aube. Étude d'un journal d'opinion* (Paris, Colin, 1966).

91. *L'Aube*, 20 Jan. 1932.

92. *L'Aube*, 9 June 1936.

93. MRP, *2e Congrès national, Paris, 13–16 décembre 1945*.

94. Jean-Marie Mayeur, *Des Partis catholiques à la démocratie chrétienne*

(1980), 162.

95. Robert Buron, *La Mayenne et Moi. De la Démocratie Chrétienne au Socialisme* (Paris, Cana, 1978).

96. Speech of 1 Feb. 1903, in Marc Sangnier, *Discours, I. 1891–1906* (Paris, Bloud, 1910), 139; and speech of 22 May 1904, in *ibid.*, 266–7.

97. Robert Cornilleau, *De Waldeck-Rousseau à Poincaré* (Paris, Spes, 1926), 199.

98. Debate with Guesde at Roubaix, 9 Mar. 1905, in *Discours*, I, 360.

99. Speech of 5 April 1908, in Sangnier, *Discours* II (Paris, Bloud, 1910), 252.

100. Charles Maurras, *Le Dilemme de Marc Sangnier* [1906], and *Politique religieuse* [1912], in *L'Oeuvre II. Démocratie religieuse* (Paris, Nouvelle Librairie internationale, 1925); Michael Sutton, *Nationalism, Positivism and Catholicism. The Politics of Charles Maurras and French Catholics, 1890–1914* (Cambridge, Cambridge University Press 1982), 78–9, 96–100.

101. Letter of Pius X to French bishops, 25 Aug. 1910, quoted by Maurras, *L'Oeuvre* II, 167.

102. *La Jeune République*, 26 Dec. 1920.

103. *La Jeune République*, 21 Nov. 1924.

104. Paul Christophe, *1936. Les Catholiques et le Front populaire* (Paris, Desclée, 1979).

105. *Esprit.* 1ère année, no. 6, 1 Mar. 1933. See also Michel Winock, *Histoire politique de la revue 'Esprit', 1930–1950* (Paris, Seuil, 1975), 70–6.

106. *Esprit*, May 1933, column of *Troisième Force*, quoted in P. Mounier-Leclercq ed., *Mounier et sa génération. Lettres, carnets et inédits* (Paris, Seuil, 1956), 125–6, and Jean-Marie Domenach, *Emmanuel Mounier* (Seuil, 1972), 60. Mounier collaborated for some time with Georges Izard of *Troisième Force*.

107. Francis J. Murphy, *Communists and Catholics in France, 1936–1939. The Politics of the Outstretched Hand* (Gainesville, University of Florida Press, 1989), 79.

108. *Mounier et sa génération*, 288.

109. Bernard Comte, 'Emmanuel Mounier devant Vichy et la Révolution nationale en 1940–41', *Revue d'Histoire de l'Église de France* (1985), 253–79, and *Une Utopie combattante. L'École des Cadres d'Uriage, 1940–1942* (Paris, Fayard, 1991), 104–12, 180–6, 380–6.

110. Marcel Péguy, *Le Destin de Charles Péguy* (Paris, Perrin, 1941), 254.

111. *Esprit*, 14e année, no. 12, 1 Feb. 1946, 166, 181. Winock, *op. cit.*, 248–66.

112. Henri Perrin, *Journal d'un prêtre ouvrier en Allemagne* (2nd edn, Paris, Seuil, 1945), 229.

113. *Itinéraire d'Henri Perrin, prêtre ouvrier* (Paris, Seuil, 1958), 168. See also Émile Poulat, *Naissance des Prêtres-Ouvriers* (Paris, Casterman, 1965), and Oscar L. Arnal, *Priests in Working-Class Blue. The History of the Worker-Priests, 1943–1954* (New York/Mahwah, Paulist Press, 1986).

114. *Témoignage chrétien*, 12 Feb. 1954.

115. Marcel Prélot, *Le Catholicisme libérale* (Paris, Colin, 1969), 8; Société des sciences historiques et naturelles de Semur-en-Auxois, *Centenaire de Montalembert, 20 Aug. 1970* (Dijon, 1971).

116. Mgr Francis Marty, Letter to curés, 22 May 1968, cited by Robert Serrou, *Dieu n'est pas conservateur* (Paris, Robert Laffont, 1968), 201–2.

117. *Pax Christi*, 10–11, (Epiphany and Easter 1950), 69.

118. Jean Marial, *Au Commencement. Rappel de Quelques Principes et Notions* (Salon-de-Provence, Les Editions du Verbe, 1946), 141. The title-page bears the words 'Pour le triomphe du Christ-Roi par Marie Reine du Ciel et Reine de France.'

119. *Itinéraires*, Feb. 1964, in Jean Madiran, *Éditoriaux et critiques* I (Paris, Dominique Martin Morin, 1983), 231–2, 234–5.

120. Lecture of 1969, in Mgr Marcel Lefebvre, *Un Évêque parle. Écrits et*

Allocations I, 1963–1973 (Paris, Dominique Martin Morin, 1977), 106.

121. Sermon at Lille, 29 Aug. 1976, in *Ecrits et Allocations II. 1975–6* (1977), 108, 110.

122. *Présent*, Nov. 1976.

123. *National Hebdo*, 21 June 1984.

124. Charles Maurras, *La Démocratie religieuse* (re-ed. Jean Madiran, Paris, Nouvelles Éditions Latines, 1978).

125. *Présent*, 15 June 1988.

126. Jean Madiran, open letter to the Pope, 1 Aug. 1988, in his *Itinéraires*, nos 325–6 (July–Oct. 1988), 14.

127. André Siegfried, 'Le Groupe protestant cévenol', in Marc Boegner and André Siegfied, eds, *Protestantisme français* (Paris, Plon, 1945).

128. Antoine Court, *Histoire des Troubles des Cévennes ou de la guerre des Camisards* [1760] (new edn, 3 vols, Alès, J. Martin, 1819), xiv–xv. I am heavily indebted to the brilliant study of Philippe Joutard, *La Légende des Camisards. Une sensibilité au passé* (Paris, Gallimard, 1977) for the following paragraphs.

129. Napoléon Peyrat, *Histoire des Pasteurs du Désert depuis la Révocation de l'Édit de Nantes jusqu'à la Révolution française, 1685–1789* (2 vols, Paris/Vienne, 1842).

130. Jules Michelet, *Histoire de France*, 14 (Paris, Chamerot, 1860), 226, 228.

131. Michelet, *op. cit.*, vol. 13, 434–5.

132. *Bulletin de la Société de l'Histoire du Protestantisme français* (32), 1883, 433–6.

133. Ariste Viguié, *La Fête religieuse des Églises reformées des Cévennes à Font-morte* (Paris, Fischbacher, 1887), 16.

134. *Bulletin de la Société d'Histoire du Protestantisme français*, 3e série (6), 1887, 447.

135. Raoul Allier, *Voltaire et Calas. Une erreur judiciaire au XVIIIe siècle* (Paris, Stock, 1898), 43, 48–9.

136. Ernest Renauld, *Le Péril protestant* (Paris, 1899); Pierre Froment, *La Trahison protestante* (Paris, 1899); Maurras, 'Les Monods peints par

eux-mêmes', *Action française*, 1 and 15 Oct. 1899, I Jan. 1900; Jean Baubérot, 'L'Antiprotestantisme politique à la fin du XIXe siècle', *Revue d'histoire et de philosophie des religions* 52 (1972), 449–84: 53 (1973), 177–221.

137. *La République des Cévennes*, 17 May 1902.

138. Speech of Frank Puaux, 24 Sept. 1911, in *Inauguration du Musée du Désert, en Cévennes* (SHPF, 1912), 19, 26.

139. *Bulletin de la Société d'histoire du Protestantisme français* (60) 1911, 474.

140. Maurice Barrès, *Les Diverses Familles Spirituelles de la France* [1917] (Paris, 1930), 42, 44, 47–9.

141. *Le Semeur* (37e année, no 9), 15 July 1935.

142. André Chamson, *Trois Discours 'au Désert', 1935, 1954, 1958* (Paris, 1959), 15.

143. Philippe Joutard, Jacques Poujol, Patrick Cabanel, *Cévennes, Terre de Refuge, 1940–1944* (Presses du Languedoc/Club cévenol, 1987), 252.

144. André Ducasse, *La Guerre des Camisards. La Résistance huguenote sous Louis XIV* (Paris, Hachette, 1946), 245. See also Roderick Kedward, 'The Maquis and the Culture of the Outlaw', in Kedward and Roger Austin, eds, *Vichy France and the Resistance* (London and Sydney, Croom Helm, 1985), 244–9, and Janet Teissier du Cros, *Divided Loyalties. A Scotswoman in Occupied France* (Edinburgh, Canongate Press, 1992).

145. Roland de Pury, *Journal de Cellule* (Paris, Editions 'Je sers', 1944), 85.

146. André Philip, *La Résistance française. Ses fondaments juridiques et moraux* (New Delhi, Bureau d'information de la France Combattante, s.d. but early 1943), 6.

147. André Chamson, *Trois Discours 'Au Désert', 1935–1954–1958* (Paris, 1959), 27–8, 33–4.

148. *Idem, La Superbe* (Paris, Plon, 1967),

xiv.

149. *Idem, La Tour de Constance* (Paris, Plon, 1970), 556–7.

150. On Protestants in the Midi in the revolutionary period, see Gwynn Lewis, *The Second Vendée. Continuity and Counter-revolution in the department of the Gard* (Oxford, Clarendon Press, 1978).

151. Quoted by Charles H. Pouthas, *La Jeunesse de Guizot, 1787–1814* (Paris, Félix Alcan, 1936), 8.

152. François Guizot, *Mémoires pour servir à l'histoire de mon temps* I (2nd edn, Paris, Michel Lévy, 1858), 4.

153. Pierre Rosanvallon, *Le Moment Guizot* (Paris, Gallimard, 1985), 205–12, fails to draw any conclusions about Guizot's historical writings from his personal experiences. See also in general, Douglas Johnson, *Guizot: Aspects of French History, 1787–1874* (London/Toronto, 1963).

154. *Mémoires*, 109–10.

155. *Ibid.*, 311.

156. *Ibid.*, II (1859), 19, 26.

157. Odilon Barrot, *Mémoires posthumes* I (Paris, Charpentier, 1875), 547–8.

158. Pierre Guiral, *Prévost-Paradol (1827–1870). Pensée et action d'un libéral sous le Second Empire* (Paris, Presses Universitaires de France, 1955), 207; Henri Cordey, *Edmond de Pressensé et son temps, 1824–1891* (Lausanne, Bridel, 1916).

159. Michel Richard, 'Les ministres protestants du cabinet Waddington', in *Les Protestants dans les débuts de la Troisième République*, Actes du Colloque, 3–6 octobre 1978 (*Bulletin de la Société d'histoire du Protestantisme français*, 1979), 199–226.

160. Speech at Nantes, Sept. 1878, in Charles de Freycinet, *Souvenirs, 1878–1893* (New York, Da Capo Press, 1973), 26–7.

161. Cordey, *op. cit.*, 477.

162. Fallot to Pressensé, 25 Nov. 1889, cited by Jean Baubérot, *Le Retour des Huguenots* (Paris, Cerf/Labor et Fides, 1985), 125.

163. *L'Espoir du monde. Organe du*

Socialisme chrétien, 1908.

164. *L'Avant-garde. Journal populaire du Christianisme social*, articles by Dr P. Antonin, 1 Aug. 1930, 1 May 1932.

165. Loïc Philip, *André Philip* (Paris, Beauchesne, 1988).

166. *La Terre Nouvelle*, no. 3, Sept. 1928.

167. Gaston Doumergue, speech of 21 April 1934, in *Discours à la nation française* (Paris, Denoël et Steele, 1934), 37–8. See also Pierre Lafue, *Gaston Doumergue* (Paris, Plon, 1933).

168. Interview to *Le Monde*, 13 April 1965, cited by Colette Ysmal, *Defferre parle* (Paris, FNSP/Centre d'Étude de la vie politique française, 1966), 42.

169. Gaston Defferre, *Un nouvel horizon* (Paris, Gallimard, 1965), 19, 22. See Georges Marion, *Gaston Defferre* (Paris, Albin Michel, 1989).

170. Jean Baubérot, *Le Protestantisme doit-il mourir?* (Paris, Seuil, 1988), 171–86.

171. Caton, *Comment aider Mitterrand à sauver le Capitalisme en France* (Paris, Albin Michel, 1989), 78.

Chapter 6:   Anarchism

1. Benoît Malon, *La Troisième Défaite du Prolétariat Français* (Neuchâtel, 1871).

2. See, for example, Gareth Stedman Jones, 'Rethinking Chartism', in *Languages of Class. Studies in English Working-Class History, 1832–1982* (Cambridge, Cambridge University Press, 1982), 96–104; Tony Judt, *Marxism and the French Left. Studies on Labour and Politics in France, 1830–1981* (Oxford, Clarendon Press, 1986), 60–80; William H. Sewell, 'Uneven Development, the Autonomy of Politics and the Dockworkers of Nineteenth-Century Marseille', *American History Review*, 93/3 (June 1988), 604–37; Dick Geary, ed., *Labour and Socialist Movements in Europe before 1914* (New York, Munich, Oxford, Berg,

1989), 4; Gérard Noiriel, *Workers in French Society in the Nineteenth and Twentieth Centuries* (Berg, 1990), 64–5.

3. *L'Artisan. Journal de la classe ouvrière*, 22 Sept. 1830. See also William H. Sewell, *Work and Revolution in France. The Language of Labour from the Old Régime to 1848* (Cambridge, Cambridge University Press, 1980), 195–8.

4. See above, p. 34.

5. Sewell, *Work*, 201–18; Judt, *op. cit.*, 52–5.

6. Eugène Fournière, *Le Règne de Louis-Philippe*, vol. 8 of Jaurès' *Histoire socialiste* (Paris, n. d.), 156.

7. *L'Écho de la Fabrique*, 4 Dec. 1831.

8. Joseph Benoît, *Confessions d'un Prolétaire* (Paris, Éditions sociales, 1968), 53.

9. Robert J. Bezucha, *The Lyon Uprising of 1834* (Cambridge, Mass., Harvard University Press, 1974).

10. Louis Blanc, *L'Organisation du Travail* (4th edn, Paris, Cauville Frères, 1845), 7.

11. *L'Atelier*, Sept. 1840.

12. P.-J. Proudhon, *Les Confessions d'un révolutionnaire* [October 1849], in *Oeuvres complètes*, 7 (Paris, Rivière, 1929), 167–9.

13. *Le Peuple*, 8–15 Nov. 1848.

14. Proudhon, *Napoléon III* (2nd edn, Paris, 1900), 184.

15. *Idem*, *L'Idée générale de la Révolution au XIXe siècle* [July 1851], in *Oeuvres complètes*, 2 (Paris, Marcel Rivière, 1924), 301.

16. *Idem*, *Du Principe fédératif, Oeuvres complètes*, 19 (Paris, Marcel Rivière, 1959), pp. 315–31.

17. Proudhon to Paris workers, 8 March 1864, quoted by Daniel Guérin, *Ni Dieu ni maître. Anthologie historique du mouvement anarchiste* (Lausanne, 1969), 151.

18. *Idem*, *De la capacité politique des classes ouvrières*, in *Oeuvres complètes*, 3, (Paris, Rivière, 1924), 90.

19. *Ibid.*, 112, 125.

20. Albert Richard, 'Les Débuts du parti socialiste français', *Revue politique et parlementaire* (11), 1897, 71.

21. Marx to L. Kugelmann, 9 Oct. 1866, published in *Neue Zeit*, 12 April 1902 and again by James Guillaume, *L'Internationale. Documents et Souvenirs. (1864–1878)*, I (Paris, Société Nouvelle de Librairie et d'Édition/ Librarie Georges Bellais, 1905), 26.

22. Benoît Malon, *op. cit.*, 138.

23. Jean-Baptiste Dumay, *Mémoires d'un militant ouvrier du Creusot, 1841–1905* (Paris, Maspéro, 1976), 117–28; Fernand L'Huillier, *La Lutte ouvrière à la fin du Second Empire* (Paris, Colin, 1957), 47, 50, 53, 74.

24. Jacques Rougerie, 'L'AIT et le mouvement ouvrier à Paris pendant les événements de 1870–1', in Rougerie, *Jalons pour une Histoire de la Commune de Paris* (Assen, van Gorcum, 1973), 8–10.

25. H. Tolain, *L'Internationale. Discours prononcé à l'Assemblée Nationale, séances des 4 et 13 mars 1872* (Paris, 1872), 32. Tolain gives a figure of 15 or 17.

26. Rougerie, *op. cit.*, 51.

27. *Ibid.*, 59.

28. *La Solidarité*, 12 April 1871, in James Guillaume, *L'Internationale. Documents et Souvenirs (1864–1878)*, II (Paris, Rivière, 1907), 143.

29. Eugene Schulkind, ed., *The Paris Commune of 1871. The View from the Left* (London, Cape, 1972), 163–5, 136; Bernard H. Moss, *The Origins of the French Labour Movement* (Berkely, Los Angeles and London, University of California Press, 1976), 61.

30. Rihs, *La Commune de Paris 1871* (Paris, Seuil, 1973), 162–76; Schulkind, *op. cit.*, 151.

31. Jean Allemane, *Mémoires d'un Communard. Des barricades au bagne* (Paris, n. d.), 63.

32. Jean Dubois, *Le Vocabulaire politique et sociale en France de 1869 à 1872* (Paris, 1962), 105, and Jacques Rougerie, *Paris libre 1871* (Paris, 1871), 160.

33. Guillaume, *op. cit.*, II, 240.

34. *Bulletin de la Fédération jurassienne de l'Association internationale des travail-*

leurs (Milan, Fetrinelli reprints), nos 17–18.

35. Guillaume, *op. cit.*, IV, 1910, 276.

36. Jean Grave, *Le Mouvement libertaire sous la Troisième République. Souvenirs d'un Révolté* (Paris, 1930), 1–13.

37. Paul Brousse, *Le Suffrage universel et le Problème de la Souveraineté du Peuple* (Geneva, 1874), 48.

38. Manifesto by Brousse for Fédération française de l'Internationale, Oct. 1877, in Guillaume, *op. cit.*, IV, 282.

39. Speech of Bellèle, 3 Feb. 1878, in *Séances du Congrès ouvrier en France. Deuxième session, tenue à Lyon du 28 janvier au 8 février 1878* (Lyon, 1878; Paris, Hachette 1976), 281.

40. Guillaume, *op. cit.*, IV, 118.

41. *Séances, 1878*, 335. Speech of Ballivet, 3 Feb. 1878.

42. Guillaume, *op. cit.*, IV, 312.

43. Jean Lombard, speech of 20 Oct. 1879, in *Séances du Congrès ouvrier de France. Troisième session tenue à Marseille du 20 au 31 octobre 1879* (Marseille, 1879; Paris, Hachette 1975), 41.

44. *L'Égalité*, 31 Mar. 1880, cited by Peter Schöttler, 'Politique syndicale ou lutte des classes: notes sur le syndicalisme apolitique des Bourses de Travail', *Le Mouvement social* 116 (1981), 16–17.

45. Marx to Sorge, 5 Nov. 1880, cited by James Guillaume, *op. cit.*, IV, v–vi.

46. David Stafford, *From Anarchism to Reformism* (London, Weidenfeld and Nicholson, 1971), 139.

47. Parti ouvrier socialiste français, *Cinquième congrès national tenu à Reims du 30 octobre au 6 novembre 1881* (Paris, 1881; Paris, Hachette, 1975), 14, 55–7.

48. Paul Brousse, speech of 25 Sept. 1882, in Parti ouvrier socialiste révolutionnaire français, *Compte rendu du sixième congrès national tenu à Saint-Étienne, du 25 au 31 septembre 1882* (Paris, 1885; Paris, Hachette, 1975), 87, 89.

49. *Le Prolétaire*, 30 Sept. 1882.

50. Jean Allemane, speech of 17 June 1888, in *Compte rendu du neuvième Congrès régional de l'Union fédérative du Centre, tenu à Paris du 17 au 26 juin 1888* (Paris, 1888; Paris, Hachette, 1975), 32.

51. Michel Winock, 'La Scission de Châtellerault et la naissance du parti allemaniste, 1890–1', *Le Mouvement social* 75 (April–June 1971), 33–62; Maurice Charnay, *Les Allemanistes* (Paris, 1912); and Michel Winock, 'Jean Allemane: une fidélité critique', in Jacques Rougerie, *Jalons pour une Histoire de la Commune* (Paris, 1973), 379.

52. *La Vie et l'oeuvre de Sébastien Faure* (Paris-Brussels, Editions Pensée et Action, 1961).

53. Christine de Goustine, *Pouget. Les Matins noirs du syndicalisme* (Paris, 1972).

54. Jean Maitron, *Le Mouvement anarchiste en France* I (Paris, Maspéro, 1975), 252.

55. *Ibid.*, 236.

56. Maurice Dommanget, *Histoire du Premier Mai* (Paris, 1953), 87–99; James Joll, *The Second International* (London, Weidenfeld and Nicolson, 1956), 48–55.

57. Peter Schöttler, *Naissance des Bourses du travail. Un Appareil idéologique d'État à la Fin du XIXe siècle* (Paris, Presses Universitaires de France, 1985).

58. Parti ouvrier socialiste révolutionnaire, *Compte rendu du dixième congrès national tenu à paris, du 21 au 29 juin 1891* (Paris, 1892; Paris, Hachette, 1975), 101.

59. Jacques Julliard, *Fernand Pelloutier et les origines du syndicalisme d'action directe* (Paris, Seuil, 1971).

60. *Ibid.*, 323–9.

61. Fernand Pelloutier, 'L'Anarchisme et les syndicats ouvriers', *Les Temps nouveaux*, 2–8 Nov. 1895.

62. [Paul Delesalle], *Les Révolutionnaires au Congrès de Londres. Conférences anarchistes*. Publications des *Temps nouveaux* no. 4 (Paris, 1896), in *Le Congrès de Londres devant la presse* (Geneva, Minkoff Reprint, 1980),

517–37. See also, Jean Maitron, *Paul Delesalle. Un Anarchiste de la Belle Epoque* (Paris, Fayard, 1985).

63. Fernand Pelloutier, 'Lettre aux anarchistes', in *Le Congrès général du Parti socialiste français, 3–8 décembre 1899* (Paris, 1900).

64. *Les Temps nouveaux*, 23–29 Mar. 1901.

65. CGT, *Congrès national corporatif, tenu à Bourges du 12 au 20 septembre 1904* (Bourges, 1904), 216.

66. *La Voix de Peuple*, 25 Sept.–2 Oct. 1904.

67. *Les Temps nouveaux*, 2 Dec. 1905.

68. Henri Ghesquière, *Le Travailleur*, 28 April 1906, cited by Robert Baker, 'Socialism in the Nord, 1880–1914. A Regional view of the French socialist movement', *International Review of Social history* (12), 1967, 369.

69. Parti socialiste (SFIO), *Troisième congrès national tenu* à Limoges, 1–4 Novembre 1906 (Paris, s.d.; 1975), 160–1.

70. Eugène Fournière, *Les Théories socialistes au XIXe siècle de Babeuf à Proudhon* (Paris, Alcan, 1904), 377–8.

71. Édouard Droz, *P.-J. Proudhon* (Paris, 1909), 34, 91–2. This view was criticised by Lucien Febvre, 'Une question d'influence: Proudhon et le syndicalisme des années 1900–1914', *Revue de Synthèse historique* (XIX/2), 1909, 179–93, reprinted in *Pour une Histoire à part entière* (Paris, SEVPEN, 1962), 772–86. On this, see the excellent study by Annie Kriegel, 'Le Syndicalisme révolutionnaire et Proudhon', in *Le Pain et les Roses* (Paris, Presses Universitaires de France, 1968), 33–50.

72. *Les Temps nouveaux*, 27 Oct. 1906.

73. Pierre Monatte, speech of 28 August 1907, *Congrès anarchiste, tenu à Amsterdam, août 1907* (Paris, La Publication sociale, 1908), 64–5. See also, James Joll, *The Anarchists* (London, 1964), 204–5.

74. IFHS 14 AS 53ter, Guillaume to Pouget, 1 Dec. 1909.

75. IFHS 14 AS 246a, Maxime Leroy, 'survivant de la jurassienne', article in *La Grande Revue*, 10 Sept. 1912, 161–6.

76. Obituary by Charles Albert, *La Feuille. Socialiste, syndicaliste, révolutionnaire*, 30 Nov. 1916.

77. Guillaume, *op. cit.*, IV, vii.

78. IFHS 14 AS 246a, Guillaume to Monatte, 15 May 1913.

79. IFHS 14 AS 246a, Guillaume to Monatte, 9 Oct. 1909, 23 April and 15 May 1913; no. 87 of *La Vie ouvrière*, 5 May 1913 was totally dedicated to 'un oublié', Eugène Varlin; the enduring anarchist interest in Varlin is confirmed by Paul Delesalle's review of the Saint-Denis exhibition of the Commune, *La Révolution proletarienne*, April 1935, and IFHS 14 AS 12.

80. Michel Bakounine, *Oeuvres* II (Paris, Stock, 1907; 1980).

81. *La Vie ouvrière*, (112), 20 May 1914.

82. IFHS 14 AS 246a, Guillaume to Monatte, 9 April 1911; *La Vie ouvrière* 46–47, (20 Aug.–5 Sept. 1911), 311.

83. Jean-Jacques Fiechter, *Le Socialisme français: de l'affaire Dreyfus à la Grande Guerre* (Paris, Droz, 1965), 207.

84. Louis Lecoin, *De Prison en Prison* (Paris, Édité par l'auteur, 1947), 79.

85. *Le Libertaire*, 15 June 1919.

86. René Michaud, *J'avais vingt ans. Un jeune ouvrier au début du siècle* (Paris, Syros, 1983), 108.

87. *Ibid.*, 141.

88. *Ibid.*, 124.

89. Capitaine Jacques Sadoul, letter of 6/19 January 1918, in *Notes sur la Révolution bolchévique* (Paris, Éditions de la Sirène, 1919), 199–200.

90. Georges Gurvitch, 'Proudhon et Marx', in *L'Actualité de Proudhon*, Colloque des 24–25 novembre 1965 (Brussels, 1967), 96.

91. Annie Kriegel, *Aux Origines du Communisme Français, 1914–1920* (Paris-La Haye, Mouton, 1964), I, 128–9, 287–8, 312–13.

92. Christian Gras, *Alfred Rosmer et le Mouvement révolutionnaire international* (Paris, Maspéro, 1971), 138;

Pierre Monatte, article of 27 Feb. 1917, in 'Réflexions sur l'Avenir syndicale', *Les Cahiers du Travail, 1re série, 9e cahier* (Paris, Editions de la Bibliothèque du Travail, 1921), 15.

93. *Les Cahiers du Travail. 1re série, 2e cahier. Un coup d'oeil en arrière* (Paris, 1921), 37.

94. Robert Louzon, 'Guesde avait-il raison?', *La Vie ouvrière* 18 (27 August 1919).

95. *La Vie ouvrière*, 23 July 1919.

96. Pierre Lémont, 'Le Procès du complot', in *La Vie ouvrière*, 25 Feb. 1921.

97. CGT, *XXIIe Congrès national corporatif, tenu à Lille du 25 au 30 juillet 1921* (Villeneuve-Saint-Georges, 1921), 267, 275.

98. *Ibid.*, 271.

99. *Ibid.*, 268, 278. See also, Pierre Monatte, *Trois scissions syndicales* (Paris, 1958), 159–63.

100. James Guillaume, *Idée sur l'Organisation Syndicale, Les Cahiers du Travail* (Ire série, 8e cahier, 15 June 1921).

101. IFHS 14 AS 246b, minutes of private meeting of ISR bureau and the French delegation, 13 Aug. 1921.

102. Trotsky to Monatte, 13 July 1921, quoted by Jean Maitron and Colette Chambelland, eds, *Syndicalisme révolutionnaire et Communisme. Les Archives de Pierre Monatte* (Paris, 1968), 297.

103. *La Vie ouvrière*, 22 July 1921.

104. IFHS 14 AS 246b, Losovsky, secretary-general of the ISR, to Monatte, Jan. 1922.

105. CGTU, *Congrès national extraordinaire, tenu à Bourges, du 12 au 17 novembre 1923* (Paris, n.d.), 46.

106. IFHS 14 AS 246b, Losovsky to Monatte, 7 May 1924. Monatte to Zinoviev, 16 June 1924.

107. Letter of 22 Nov. 1924, in P. Monatte, A. Rosmer, V. Delagarde, *Lettres aux membres du Parti communiste* (Paris, 1924), 11–12.

108. CGTU, *Compte-rendu sténographique des débats du premier congrès national corporatif, tenu à la Bourse du travail de Saint-Étienne, du 26 juin au 2 juillet 1922*, 409.

109. Charter of Lyon, 1–2 Nov. 1926, in *Le Combat syndicaliste*, Dec. 1926 and Pierre Besnard, *L'Ethique du Syndicalisme* (Paris, 1938), 139.

110. *Le Combat syndicaliste*, 1 Mar. 1928; Pierre Besnard, *Les Syndicats ouvriers et la Révolution sociale* (Paris, 1930), 23, 343.

111. Albert Cane to Pierre Besnard, *Le Libertaire*, 28 Feb. 1936.

112. *La Révolution prolétarienne* 217 (25 Feb. 1936), 51.

113. Speech of Chambelland, 3 Mar. 1936, CGT, *Congrès national de l'unité, Toulouse*, 91.

114. Jacques Girault, *Benoît Frachon. Communiste et Syndicaliste* (Paris, FNSP, 1989), 166–8.

115. IFHS 14 AS 53ter has the manuscripts of Delesalle's original articles; *La Vie ouvrière*, 15 and 22 May, 19 and 26 June 1936 contain the articles finally published. Delesalle subsequently published his own collection as *Paris sous la Commune. Documents et souvenirs inédits* (Paris, 1937). On the Commune exhibition, see *La Révolution prolétarienne*, April 1935.

116. *La Révolution prolétarienne* (242), 10 Mar. 1937, 493–5.

117. *Le Libertaire*, 5, 12, 26 June 1936, 7 Aug. 1936.

118. Pierre Besnard, *L'Ethique du Syndicalisme* (Paris, 1938), 42.

119. *La Révolution prolétarienne* 224 (10 June 1936), 145.

120. *Ibid.*, 233 (25 Oct. 1936), 320–3, article by Robert Louzon.

121. Bernard Georges, 'La CGT et le gouvernement Léon Blum', *Le Mouvement social* 54 (1966), 57.

122. Jacques Duclos, *Mémoires* II, 1935–9 (Paris, Fayard, 1969), 155.

123. Burnett Bolloten, *Grand Camouflage: the Spanish Civil War and Revolution, 1936–39* (New York, Praeger, 1961, 1968); *The Spanish Revolution. The Left and the Struggle for Power during the Civil War* (Chapel Hill, University of N. Carolina Press, 1979), and

The Spanish Civil War. Revolution and Counter-Revolution (Hemel Hempstead, Harvester Wheatsheaf, 1991) offer an excellent accounts of this anarchist revolution.

124. *Le Libertaire*, 31 July 1936.

125. David Berry, 'The Other Popular Front: French Anarchism and the Front révolutionnaire', in Martin Alexander and Helen Graham, *The French and Spanish Popular Fronts. Comparative Perspectives* (Cambridge, Cambridge University Press, 1989). I am most grateful to David Berry for letting me see a draft of his thesis, which expounds these issues with great skill.

126. *Le Libertaire*, 9 April and Sept. 1945.

127. *Le Libertaire*, 20 Sept. 1945.

128. *L'Action syndicaliste*, April 1945, 1 June 1946.

129. Pierre Monatte, *Où va la CGT? Lettre d'un ancien à quelques jeunes syndiqués sans galons* (Paris, 1946), 20–1. This letter was reprinted in *Trois scissions syndicales* (Paris, 1958), 18–51.

130. Idem, *Un Secrétaire confédérale parle. Deuxième lettre d'un ancien à quelques jeunes syndiqués sans galons*, in *Révolution prolétarienne*, April 1947, and *Trois scissions syndicales*, 52–68.

131. *Le Libertaire*, 27 Nov. 1947.

132. *La Révolution prolétarienne*, Nov. 1947, reprinted in *Trois scissions syndicales*, 176–7.

133. Pierre Monatte, 'Souvenirs sur le Congrès d'Amiens', *Actualité de l'Histoire*, Oct. 1956, reprinted in *Trois scissions syndicales*, 137.

134. J. Sauvageot, A. Geismar, D. Cohn-Bendit, J.-P. Duteil, *La Révolte étudiante. Les animateurs parlent* (Paris, Seuil, 1968), 62.

135. Henri Lefebvre, *L'Irruption de Nanterre au sommet* (Paris, Anthropos, 1968), 120, 123.

136. Alain Touraine, *Le Mouvement de mai ou le Communisme utopique* (Paris, Seuil, 1968), 11.

137. Juliette Minces, *Un Ouvrier parle* (Paris, Seuil, 1969), 52. See also, Sabine Erbès-Seguin, 'Le Déclenchement des grèves de mai: spontanéité des masses et le rôle des syndicats', *Sociologie du Travail* (2) 1970, 177–89.

138. Daniel Cohn Bendit, *Le Gauchisme. Remède à la maladie sénile du Communisme* (Paris, 1968), 269–70.

139. Sauvageot, *et al., op. cit.*, 63.

140 Cohn Bendit, 233.

141. *Ibid.*, 15–16; postscript.

142. Sauvageot, *et al., op. cit.*, 64–5.

143. Alain Monchablon, 'L' UNEF et mai 1968', Colloque 'Acteurs et terrains du mouvement social de mai 1968, 24–25 novembre 1988' (Paris, FNSP–CEVIPOF), 7.

144. André Barjonet, *La Révolution trahie de 1968* (Paris, 1968). Barjonet resigned from his CGT post on 23 May.

145. René Mouriaux, 'Le mai de la CGT', in Colloque 'Acteurs et terrains du mouvement social de mai 1968'.

146. Roland Leroy to the 17th congress of the PCF, 15 May 1964, *L'Humanité*, 16 May 1964.

147. Alain Krivine, *Questions sur la Révolution. Entretiens avec Roland Biard* (Paris, Stock, 1973), 149–50.

148. *L'Humanité*, 3 May 1968.

149. Danielle Tartakowsky, 'Le PCF en mai–juin 1968', in Colloque 'Acteurs et terrains du mouvement social de mai 1968', 7. See also, Waldeck-Rochet, *Les Enseignements de mai–juin 1968* (Paris, Editions sociales, 1968).

150. J.-P. Sartre, *Les Communistes ont peur de la Révolution* (Paris, 1968), 10–11.

151. Editorial of André Jeanson, *Syndicalisme*, 16 May 1968.

152. Frank Georgi, 'La CFDT en mai–juin 1968', in Colloque 'Acteurs et terrains du mouvement social de mai 1968', 10.

153. Edmond Maire, Alfred Krumnow, Albert Detraz, *La CFDT et l'Autogestion* (Paris, Cerf, 1973), 70, 74.

154. Jacques Julliard, *op. cit.*, 10.

155. See the report of the 35th congress of the CFDT at Issy-les-Moulineaux, 6–10 May 1970, in *Syndicalisme*, 14

May 1970.

156. CFDT, *Les Documents fondamentaux pour comprendre l'évolution de la CFDT* (Paris, Seuil, 1971), 170–9.

157. Edouard Depreux, *Servitude et grandeur de la PSU* (Paris, Syros, 1974), 234.

158. Georgi, *op. cit.*, 16.

159. Maurice Joyeux, *Souvenirs d'un Anarchiste* (Paris, Editions du *Monde Libertaire*, 1986), 88–104.

160. Idem, *L'Anarchisme et la Révolte de la Jeunesse* (Paris, Casterman, 1970), 104.

161. *La Rue* 1, (May 1968), 17, attacked the 'l'anarchisation du marxisme' and 'la refonte doctrinale . . . pour sauver le marxisme' of Daniel Guérin, whose works included *Anarchisme* (Paris, Gallimard. Idées, 1965) and *Ni Dieu ni Maître. Anthologie historique du mouvement anarchiste* (1966).

162. *La Rue*, 22 (3rd and 4th terms, 1976).

163. *La Rue* 2 (2 Oct. 1968), 4–6.

164. *Le Monde*, 3 Sept. 1968, cited by Roland Biard, *Histoire du Mouvement anarchiste, 1945–1975* (Paris, Gallilée, 1976), 190.

165. *La Rue* (1st term, 1969), 20.

166. *La Rue* (29), 1981.

167. *Front libertaire*, Dec. 1970.

168. *Solidarité ouvrière*, April 1971.

169. Guy Groux and René Mouriaux, *La CFDT* (Paris, Economica, 1989), 133–5.

170. Edmond Maire, *CFDT-Aujourd'hui*, 83 (Jan. 1987), cited by Groux and Mouriaux, *op. cit.*, 239.

171. Alain Touraine, *et al.*, *La Prophétie anti-nucléaire* (Paris, Seuil, 1980), 32.

172. *l'Anarcho*, 152, Dec. 1975.

173. Motion on ecology passed by the extraordinary congress of the Fédération anarchiste, 11–13 Nov. 1977, in *Le Monde Libertaire*, Nov. 1977.

174. *L'Anarcho*, Feb.–Mar. 1978.

175. *Le Monde Libertaire*, 24 April 1988.

176. *Ibid.*, 11 May 1989.

177. Guillaume Saintenay, 'Les écologistes', in Dominique Chagnollaud, *L'État politique de la France. Année 1991* (Paris, Quai Voltaire, 1992),

108–9.

178. *Le Monde*, 25 July 1986, 31 Aug. 1988.

179. *Le Monde*, 30 June 1989.

180. *Le Monde libertaire*, 29 June 1989.

Chapter 7: Bridging the Revolution

1. Anatole France, *Monsieur Bergeret à Paris* [1901] (Paris, Calmann-Lévy/Livre de Poche, 1973), 131–3.

2. Jacques-Antoine-Marie de Cazalès, *Deffense de Louis Seize* (1792), 12–16, 25–9; Norman Hampson, *Prelude to Terror. The Constituent Assembly and the Failure of Consensus* (Oxford, Blackwell, 1988), 104, 109.

3. Comte d'Antraigues, *Quelle est la Situation de l'Assemblée Nationale?* (1790), 29, cited by Colin Duckworth, *The D'Antraigues Phenomenon. The Making and Breaking of a Revolutionary Royalist and Espionage Agent* (London, Unwin, 1986), 193.

4. Letter of 12 Oct. 1791, cited by Jacqueline Chaumié, *Le Réseau d'Antraigues et la contre-révolution, 1791–1793* (Paris, Plon, 1965), 106.

5. AN 419 AP 1. Comte d'Antraigues, *Copie d'un fragment intéressant de mes mémoires pendant les années 1789 jusqu'en 1799*, 124–5.

6. Maximilien Robespierre, speech in Jacobin Club, 1 *frimaire* an II/21 Nov. 1793, cited by John Hardman, *French Revolution Documents II. 1792–1795* (Oxford, Blackwell, 1973), 373.

7. Antoine Fouquier-Tinville, 4 *germinal* An II, cited by Henri Wallon, *Histoire du Tribunal révolutionnaire de Paris* III (Paris, Hachette, 1881), 64.

8. Baron de Vitrolles, *Mémoires et relations politiques* (Paris, 1884), III, 393; G. de Bertier de Sauvigny, *Le Comte Ferdinand de Bertier et l'Énigme de la Congrégation* (Paris, 1948); J. J. Oechslin, *Le Mouvement ultra-royaliste sous la Restauration* (Paris,

law thesis, 1960); Gwynn Lewis, *The Second Vendée* (Oxford, Clarendon Press, 1978), caps 5 and 6; Brian Fitzpatrick, *Catholic Royalism in the Department of the Gard, 1814–52* (Cambridge, Cambridge University Press, 1983), cap. 2

9. Chateaubriand, *De la Monarchie selon la Charte* (Paris, 1816), 7, 26, 43, 65, 70, 91.

10. Abbé H. Grégoire, *Mémoires* (Paris, 1837), 214, 235; Comte Molé, *Mémoires* IV (Paris, 1925), 447.

11. Chateaubriand, *De la Monarchie*, 65.

12. Chateaubriand, *De la Nouvelle proposition relative au banissement de Charles X et de sa Famille* (Paris, 1831), 26.

13. APP Aa 421, Prefect of Police to Procureur Général, copied to the Minister of War, 28 June 1832.

14. Count Molé, *Memoires* V, (Paris, 1930), 202–3, 223.

15. *La Gazette de France. Journal de l'Appel au Peuple*, 18 Aug. 1848.

16. H. de La Rochejacquelein, *Appel à la Nation. A mon pays. Dèfense de ma proposition* (Paris, 1850).

17. Henri de Lourdoueix, *Le Droit National* (Paris, 1851).

18. *L'Étoile du Gard. Catholicisme. Vote Universel. Appel au Peuple* (July 1849) became *L'Étoile du Gard et de l'Hérault* in May 1850 and *L'Étoile du Midi. Journal du Droit national et de l'Appel au Peuple*, covering the Gard, Hérault, Bouches-du-Rhône, Var and Vaucluse, in Nov. 1850.

19. Raymond Huard, 'Montagne rouge et Montagne blanche', in *Droite et Gauche de 1789 à nos jours* (Montpellier, 1975).

20. Pierre de Luz, *Henri V* (Paris, 1931), 184.

21. Comte de Chambord, *Lettre sur les Ouvriers*, 20 April 1865.

22. Comte de Falloux, *Mémoires d'un royaliste* II (Paris, 1888), 481–5; Marquis de Dreux-Brézé, *Notes et Souvenirs pour servir à l'histoire du parti royaliste, 1872–1883* (Paris, 1895), 83–4; Duc d'Audiffret-Pasquier, *La Maison de France et l'Assemblée Nationale. Souvenirs, 1871–1873* (Paris, 1938), 54–5.

23. Jules Ferry, *Discours et Opinions* VII (Paris, 1898), 82.

24. William D. Irvine, *The Boulanger Affair Reconsidered* (Oxford-New York, OUP, 1989), 126–7.

25. See above, pp. 74–5.

26. APP BA 974, police file on the funding of Boulangism; Mermeix, [pseud. of G. Terrail] *Les Coulisses du Boulangisme* (Paris, 1890); *Souvenirs de la Duchesse d'Uzès, née Mortemart* (Paris, 1939); Irvine, *op. cit.*, 96, 141.

27. Zeev Sternhell, *La Droite révolutionnaire, 1885–1914* (Paris, Seuil, 1978), 52–6; Patrick Hutton, 'The Rôle of the Blanquist party in left-wing politics in France, 1879–90', *Journal of Modern History* (46), July 1974, 277–95; Jacques Néré, 'Les Blanquistes au temps du Boulangisme', in Société d'Histoire de la Révolution de 1848 et des Révolutions du XIXe siècle, *Blanqui et les Blanquistes* (Paris, SEDES, 1986), 205–11.

28. APP BA 1515, police file on struggles within Blanquism; Wladimir Martel, *Mes Entretiens avec Granger, lieutenant de Blanqui* (Paris, 1939); Patrick Hutton, *The Cult of the Revolutionary Tradition. The Blanquists in French Politics, 1864–1893* (Berkeley and Los Angeles, University of California Press, 1981), 149–58.

29. *L'Intransigeant*, 15 Oct. 1889.

30. *L'Intransigeant*, 21 Oct. 1889.

31. Sternhell, *op. cit.*, 177–214.

32. Manifesto of 1893, quoted by Sternhell, *op. cit.*, 61.

33. *L'Intransigeant*, 21 Aug. 1893.

34. E. Beau de Loménie, *Édouard Drumont ou l'Anticapitalisme national* (Paris, Pauvert, 1968), 3.

35. Michel Winock, *Nationalisme, antisémitisme et fascisme en France* (Paris, Seuil, 1990), 121–7.

36. Édouard Drumont, *La France juive* (Paris, 123rd edn, 1886), I, 265, 408, 545, II 201–5, 454–5.

37. Winock, *op. cit.*, 103–16.

38. Édouard Drumont, *La Fin d'un*

Monde (Paris, Savine, 1889), 128.

39. *Idem, Le Secret de Fourmies* (Paris, Savine, 1892), 7–9, 80–4.

40. *La Revue socialiste* (18), July 1886, 505–14.

41. Sternhell, *op. cit.*, 231–6; Stephen Wilson, *Ideology and Experience. Antisemitism in France at the time of the Dreyfus Affair* (Farleigh Dickinson UP/Associated University Press, 1982), 13–15, 106–24.

42. *L'Intransigeant*, 22 Feb. 1898.

43. *L'Intransigeant*, 26 Jan. 1898.

44. Auguste Martin, 'Péguy et Millerand', *Feuillets mensuels* 78 (June 1960), 17, 23–4.

45. Manifesto of 19 January 1898, quoted in *L'Intransigeant*, 20 Jan. 1898.

46. Wilson, *op. cit*, 215.

47. Zeev Sternhell, *Maurice Barrès et le nationalisme français* (Paris, Colin, 1972), 153, 233.

48. Jean Grave, *Le Mouvement libertaire sous la Troisième République* (Paris, 1930), 82.

49. *La Cocarde*, 17 Sept. 1894, article on Malon; Sternhell, *Maurice Barrès*, 203–6.

50. Maurice Barrès, *Scènes et Doctrines du Nationalisme* (Paris, 1902), 437–8.

51. *Idem, Les Déracinés* (Paris, Plon/ Livre de Poche, 1972), 268–94.

52. *Idem, Scènes et Doctrines*, 371.

53. *Ibid.*, 152–3.

54. *Le Journal*, 9 Dec. 1898, cited in *ibid.*, 36.

55. Anatole France, *op. cit.*, 90, 92.

56. Eugène Godefroy, *Quelques années de politique royaliste* (Paris, Librairie nationale, 1900), 67.

57. Quoted by Yves Chiron, *La Vie de Charles Maurras* (Paris, Perrin, 1991), 154.

58. Haute Cour de Justice, *Affaire Buffet, Déroulède, Guérin et autres inculpés de complot. IV. Groupe antisémite* (Paris, 1899); Sternhell, *La Droite révolutionnaire*, 215–30; Maurice Larkin, '"La République en danger"? The pretenders, the army and Déroulède, 1898–1899', *English His-* *torical Review* (100), 1985; R. Texier, *Le Fol Été du Fort Chabrol* (Paris, France-Empire, 1990).

59. Charles Maurras, *Au Signe de Flore* (Paris, 1931), 92; *La Contre-Révolution spontanée* (Lyon, Lardanchet, 1943), 57.

60. *Au Signe de Flore*, 1. See also, Victor Nguyen, *Aux Origines de l'Action Française. Intelligence et politique à l'aube du XXe siècle* (Paris, Fayard, 1991), 115, 179.

61. Maurras, 'Dictateur et Roi' [Aug. 1899], in *Enquête sur la Monarchie* (Paris, Nouvelle Librairie Internationale, 1925), 448.

62. *Idem, La France seule* (Lyon, Lardanchet, 1941), 182–97.

63. *Idem, L'Avenir de l'Intelligence* (Paris, 1905).

64. *Enquête sur la Monarchie*, 58–9.

65. *L'Action Française*, 30 July, 1 Aug. 1908.

66. Georges Bernanos, *Les Grands Cimetières sous la Lune* (Paris, Plon, 1938), 48–9.

67. Maurice Pujo, *Les Camelots du Roi* (Paris, 1933), 233–6.

68. Eugen Weber, *L'Action Française* (Paris, Stock, 1962), 75–81.

69. See above, pp. 275–7.

70. Jeremy Jennings, *Syndicalism in France. A Study of Ideas* (Macmillan, 1990), 87–95.

71. Robert Louzon, 'La Faillite du Dreyfusisme ou le Triomphe du Parti juif', *Le Mouvement socialiste* (176), July 1906, 193–9. See also Sternhell, *Droite révolutionnaire*, 326–7.

72. Georges Sorel, *Réflexions sur la Violence* (1908), 87–8, 143–6.

73. *Ibid.*, 147–54, 169–72.

74. *Ibid.*, 80–1, 141–2, 211–12, 282–3, 329–30.

75. John Stanley, *The Sociology of Virtue. The Political and Social Theory of Georges Sorel* (Berkeley, Los Angeles, University of California, 1981), 221, 231, 314.

76. Yves Guchet, *Georges Valois. L'Action Française. Le Faisceau. La République syndicale* (Paris, Albatros,

1975) is the standard biography of Valois.

77. Georges Valois, *L'Homme qui vient. Philosophie de l'Autorité* (Paris, 3rd edn, 1910), 168.

78. *Idem, La Révolution sociale ou le Roi* [originally published in *Action Française* review, 15 Sept., 15 Oct., 15 Nov. 1907], in *La Monarchie et la classe ouvrière* (Paris, 1909), 4.

79. *Ibid.*, 54.

80. Édouard Berth, *Les Nouveaux Aspects du Socialisme* (Paris, 1908), 38.

81. *Ibid.*, 57, 62. See also Sternhell, *Droite révolutionnaire*, 344–6.

82. Sorel to Delesalle, 2 Nov. 1908, in Georges Sorel, *Lettres à Paul Delesalle, 1914–1921* (Paris, Grasset, 1947), 108–9; Sorel to Berth, 1 Dec. 1908, in *Cahiers Georges Sorel* (3), 1985, 146–7.

83. Sorel, *La Révolution Dreyfusienne* (Paris, 1909), 37.

84. *Idem*, 14 Nov. 1908, cited by Jean Variot, *Propos de Georges Sorel* (Paris, Gallimard, 1935), 27.

85. Sorel to Maurras, 6 July 1909, cited in Pierre Andreu, *Notre Maître, M. Sorel* (Paris, Grasset, 1953), 325–6; Paul Mazgaj, *The Action Française and Revolutionary Syndicalism* (Chapel Hill, 1979), 120.

86. Hubert Lagardelle, *Le Socialisme ouvrier* (Paris, 1911), xiv.

87. Paul Mazgaj, *op. cit.*, 105–6, 157–9.

88. Valois, *La Monarchie et la Classe ouvrière*, 228–30.

89. *Cahiers du Cercle Proudhon*, 17 Dec. 1911, 4.

90. *Cahiers du Cecle Proudhon*, 10 Jan. 1912, lecture by Jean Darville, 11, 21–2, 25. See also Sternhell, *Droite révolutionnaire*, 391–2.

91. Georges Valois, *L'Homme contre l'Argent. Souvenirs de Dix Ans, 1918–1928* (Paris, 1928), 61–2.

92. Zeev Sternhell, Mario Sznajder, Maia Asheri, *Naissance de l'Idéologie fasciste* (Paris, Fayard, 1989), 117, 120–1, 166. For a contrary view, see Jack Roth, *The Cult of Violence. Sorel and the Sorelians* (Berkeley, Los Angeles, University of California Press,

1980), 122, 126–7.

93. Sorel to Berth, 24 Dec. 1911, in *Cahiers Georges Sorel* (5), 1987, 168.

94. *Ibid.*

95. Weber, *L'Action Française*, 150–2.

96. Sorel to Delesalle, 26 Aug. 1918, in Georges Sorel, *Lettres à Paul Delesalle*, 169.

97. Sorel, *Matériaux d'une Théorie du prolétariat* (Paris, Marcel Rivière, 1919), 394.

98. Dedication of the *Matériaux*.

99. Jean Variot, *Propos de Georges Sorel* (Paris, Gallimard, 1935), 55–6.

100. Sorel to Delesalle, 19 Mar. and 9 April 1921, in *Letters to Paul Delesalle*, 215, 219.

101. Édouard Berth, *Guerre des États ou Guerre des Classes* (Paris, Marcel Rivière, 1924), 24.

102. *Idem*, 'Proudhon et Marx', *Clarté*, Nov. 1926, cited by Jules Levey, 'The Sorelian Syndicalists: Édouard Berth, Georges Valois, Hubert Lagardelle' (Ph.D., Columbia University, 1967), 237–8.

103. Georges Valois, *L'Homme contre l'Argent*, 18–19.

104. *Ibid.*, 24, 33, 41–2, 58, 71.

105. *Ibid.*, 127.

106. *Ibid.*, 184.

107. *Le Nouveau Siècle*, 26 Feb. 1925.

108. *Le Nouveau Siècle*, 12 Nov. 1925.

109. Georges Valois, *Le Fascisme* (Paris, Nouvelle Librairie Nationale, 1927), title of chapter 3.

110. *Ibid.*, 36, 28.

111. Georges Valois, *Guerre ou Révolution* (Paris, Librairie Valois, 1931), dedicated to Édouard Berth.

112. Georges Valois, *Lettre à Marcel Déat* [Aug.–Sept. 1933] in *Technique de la Révolution syndicale* (Paris, Editions Liberté, 1935), 25.

113. Georges Valois, *Lettre à Léon Jouhaux et aux dirigeants de la CGT* [Feb. 1935]. in *Technique de la Révolution syndicale* (Paris, 1935), 113.

114. Levey, *op. cit.*, 283–5.

115. *Ibid.*, 298–9.

116. Jennings, *op. cit.*, 112–13, 200–1, 209.

117. *La France socialiste*, 19 Feb. 1944.
118. William D. Irvine, 'French conservatives and the 'New Right' during the 1930s, *French Historical Studies* 8 (1974), 538–9; Irvine, *French Conservatism in Crisis. The Republican Federation of France during the 1930s* (Baton Rouge and London, Louisiana State UP, 1979), xix, 104–26.
119. See above, p. 231.
120. AN F 13231, General de Castelnau, *Appel à tous les Français*, Jan. 1925.
121. AN F7 13231, minutes of the Comité directeur of the Ligue des Patriotes, 28 Jan. 1926.
122. AN F7 13232, tract quoted in police report, 20 May 1926.
123. Pierre Taittinger, *Les Cahiers de la Jeune France* (Paris, Editions du *National*, 1926), 89.
124. AN F7 13232, 'Notre Doctrine', circulated for the second congress of Jeunesses Patriotes, 30 Nov.–2 Dec. 1928.
125. *Les Cahiers de la Jeune France*, 20.
126. *Le National*, 22 Nov. 1931.
127. *Le Flambeau*, 1 Oct. 1931.
128. *Ibid.*
129. Quoted by E. Beau de Loménie, *La Responsabilité des Dynasties bourgeoises* (Paris, Librairie Française, 1977), I, 31.
130. Lt. Col. de La Rocque, *Service public* (Paris, Grasset, 1934), 107.
131. *Ibid.*, 15, 28.
132. Irvine, *art. cit.*, 554; *French Conservatism*, 155.
133. G.A. Howlett, 'The Croix de Feu, the Parti Social Français and Colonel de La Rocque' (Oxford D. Phil. thesis, 1985), 362. From an undated document, 'Le PSF et les Radicaux' in AN 451 AP 120. For an alternative view, see William Irvine, 'Fascism and the strange case of the Croix de Feu', *JMH* 63 (1991), 271–95, and Robert Soucy, 'French Fascism and the Croix de Feu', *JCH* 26 (1991), 159–88.
134. *Le Petit Journal*, 14 July 1937.
135. Christian Bernadac, *Les Carnets secrets de la Cagoule* (Paris, 1977), 15. See also Georges Loustanau-Lacau,

Mémoires d'un Français rebelle, 1914–1948 (Paris, Robert Laffont, 1948), 112–14, 127.
136. Henri Massis, *Maurras et notre temps* (Paris-Geneva, La Palatine) II, 77. See also Lucien Rebatet, *Les Décombres* (Paris, Pauvert 1976), 30.
137. Robert Francis, Thierry Maulnier, J.-P. Maxence, *Demain la France* (Paris, Grasset, 1934), 11, 13, 10.
138. *L'Insurgé*, 13 Jan. 1937.
139. Pierre-Marie Dioudonnat, *Je suis partout, 1930–1944. Les maurrassiens devant la tentation fasciste* (Paris, La Table Ronde, 1973).
140. *Je suis partout*, 29 Aug. 1936.
141. *Je suis partout*, 8 July 1938.
142. *Je suis partout*, 30 Sept., 7 Oct. 1938.
143. *Je suit partout*, 25 Sept. 1942.
144. *Je suis partout*, 6 Nov. 1942.
145. *Je suis partout*, 24 Jan. 1942.
146. Jean-Louis Loubet del Bayle, *Les Non-conformistes des années trente* (Paris, Seuil, 1969).
147. *La Lutte des Jeunes*, 4 Mar. 1934.
148. *La Lutte des Jeunes*, 25 Feb. 1934.
149. Philippe Burrin, *La Dérive fasciste* (Paris, Seuil, 1986), 219, 236–7.
150. *La Flèche*, 14 Oct. 1938.
151. *La Flèche*, 21 Oct. 1938.
152. S. Grossman, 'L'Évolution de Marcel Déat', *RHDGM* 97 (1975); Alain Bergounioux, 'Le néo-socialisme. Marcel Déat: réformisme traditionnel ou esprit des années trente', *Revue historique* 260 (1978); Zeev Sternhell, *Ni Droite ni Gauche* (Paris, Seuil, 1983), 172–3, 193–4, 201.
153. Rebatet, *Les Décombres*, 589.
154. Burrin, *op. cit.*, 251.
155. J.-P. Cointet, 'Marcel Déat et le parti unique', *RHDGM* 91 (1973).
156. Marcel Déat, *Rassemblement national populaire. La Politique générale* (Paris, 1941), 10.
157. *La France socialiste*, 1 Nov. 1941; *L'Oeuvre*, 13 April 1942.
158. Marcel Déat, *Révolution française et Révolution allemande, 1793–1943*. Lecture at the Centre de Culture du RNP, 18 Dec. 1943 (Paris, 1943), 18, 5, 11. This is reiterated in his

Mémoires politiques (Paris, Denoël, 1989), 785–6.

159. Jean-Paul Brunet, *Jacques Doriot* (Paris, Balland, 1986), 150.

160. Dieter Wolf, *Doriot, du Communisme à la collaboration* (Paris, Fayard, 1969), 145.

161. Ville de Saint-Denis, *Exposition d'Art et d'Histoire. La Commune de Paris, 18 mars–28 mai 1871* (catalogue, 1935).

162. Victor Barthélemy, *Du Communisme au fascisme* (Paris, Albin Michel, 1978), 95.

163. Brunet, *op. cit.*, 261.

164. Drieu de la Rochelle, *Avec Doriot* (Paris, Gallimard, 1937).

165. Philippe Machefer, 'L'Union des Droites, le PSF et le Front de la Liberté, 1936–7', *RHMC* 17 (1970), 112–26.

166. *L'Émancipation nationale*, 13 May, 10 June 1938.

167. Brunet, 340–50.

168. Albert Merglen, 'Soldats français sous uniformes allemands. LVF et Waffen SS français', *RHDGM* 108 (1977), 71–84.

169. *Le Procès de Charles Maurras* (Paris, Albin Michel, 1946), 371.

170. Maurice Bardèche, *Lettre à François Mauriac* (Paris, La Pensée Libre, 1947), 12, 63, 73–80, 107, 112–13.

171. In general, see Joseph Algazy, *La Tentation néo-fasciste en France, 1945–1965* (Paris, Fayard, 1984); François Duprat, *Les Mouvements d'Extrême-Droite en France depuis 1944* (Paris, Albatros, 1972).

172. *Le Combattant européen*, 6 April 1946.

173. *Le Combattant européen*, 6 April 1946.

174. *L'Unité*, 13 Nov. 1948.

175. René Binet, *Théorie du Racisme* (chez l'auteur, 1950), 7–17, 23, 28.

176. Stanley Hoffmann, *Le Mouvement Poujade* (Paris, FNSP, 1956).

177. Quoted by Alain Rollat, *Les Hommes de l'Extrême Droite* (Paris, Calmann-Lévy, 1984), 14.

178. Pierre Birnbaum, *Un Myth politique: la République juive, de Léon Blum à Pierre Mendès-France* (Paris, Fayard, 1988), 154–5, 338.

179. Speech of 11 Feb. 1958, cited by Rollat, *op. cit.*, 32.

180. *Jeune Nation*, 30 Aug.–12 Sept. 1958, 4–7 Oct. 1958.

181. Algazy, *op. cit.*, 118.

182. Claude Mouton, *La Contre-révolution en Algérie* (Chiré-en-Montreuil, Diffusion de la Pensée Française, 1972), 27.

183. Jean-Marie Curutchet, *Je veux la tourmente* (Paris, Robert Laffont), 1973, 270.

184. Jean Bastien-Thiry, *Sa Vie. Ses Écrits. Témoignages* (Paris, Albatros, 1973), 94–5.

185. *Ibid.*, 120, 133.

186. Richard Cobb, 'The counter-revolutionary tradition', in *A Second Identity* (Oxford, OUP, 1969), 181–2.

187. Maurice Bardèche, *Qu'est-ce le Fascisme?* (Paris, Les Sept Couleurs, 1961), 53, 179.

188. *Ibid.*, 164–5, 174, 183.

189. *Cahiers universitaires*, 9–10 (Sept.–Oct. 1962), 9–10.

190. *Europe-Action*, 1 (Jan. 1963), 7–8; 5, (May 1963), 36.

191. *Ibid.*, 2 (1963), 55.

192. Anne-Marie Duranton-Crabol, *Visages de la Nouvelle Droite. Le GRECE et son histoire* (Paris, FNSP, 1988).

193. *Nouvelle Ecole* 1 (Feb.–Mar. 1968–), and Alain de Benoist, *Vu de Droite* (Paris, Copernic, 1977). Dominique Venner edited a series on *Corps d'élite*, edited by Balland, with volumes on the Samurai, Marines, SS, etc.

194. Natalie Krikorian, 'Européanisme, nationalisme, libéralisme dans les éditoriaux de Louis Pauwels (*Figaro-Magazine*, 1977–1984)', *Mots* 12 (1986), 172.

195. *Aspects de la France*, 13 and 30 May 1968.

196. *Minute*, 12–18 May 1971. It also ventured 'une AF hippy, ou tout comme'.

197. *La Nouvelle Action Française*, 26 April 1971.

198. Bertrand Renouvin, *Le Projet*

royaliste (Paris, 1973), 23, 26, 132.

199. Gérard Leclerc, *Un autre Maurras* (Paris, 1974), 11–13, 18.

200. *Ibid.*, 21.

201. *La Nouvelle Action française*, 23 April 1974.

202. *Royaliste*, 23 April–6 May 1981.

203. François Duprat, *op. cit.*, 158.

204. François Duprat, *Les Journées de mai 1968. Les dessous d'une révolution* (Paris, Nouvelles Editions Latines, 1968), 159.

205. *Pour un Ordre nouveau* 1 (July–Aug. 1971).

206. *Ibid.*, 10 (April 1972).

207. *Pour un Ordre nouveau*, (Feb. 1972, 15 Sept.–15 Oct. 1972, Jan. 1973).

208. Jean-Marie Le Pen, *Les Français d'abord* (Paris, Carrère-Michel Laffon, 1984), 106–21. See also Birgitta Orfali, *L'Adhésion au Front national* (Paris, Kime, 1990).

209. Speech at la Mutualité, Paris, 16 Oct. 1983, quoted by Edwy Plenel and Alain Rollat, *L'Effet Le Pen* (Paris, La Découverte, 1984), 11.

210. *Les Français d'abord*, 24.

211. Plenel and Rollat, *op. cit.*, 41.

212. *Les Français d'abord*, 13, 133, 138.

213. *Ibid.*, 74–5.

214. *Ibid.*, 239. See also the analysis of Pierre-André Taguieff, 'L'identité nationale saisie par les logiques du racisme', *Mots* (12), Mar. 1986, 91–128, and Taguieff, 'La métaphysique de Jean-Marie Le Pen', in Nonna Mayer and Pascal Perrineau, *Le Front national à Découvert* (Paris, FNSP, 1989), 173–94.

215. Serge Berstein, *Libération*, 26 April 1988; Jacques Nobécourt, *Le Monde*, 9 May 1988; Pierre Milza, 'Le Front national, droit extrême', in Jean-François Sirinelli, ed., *Histoire des Droites en France* (Paris, Gallimard, 1992) I, 726–7.

216. François Platone and Henri Rey, 'Le FN en terre communiste', in Nonna Mayer and Pascal Perrineau, *op. cit.*, 268–83.

217. *Présent*, 2–3 May 1988.

218. *Présent*, 2–3 May 1989.

219. Pierre-André Taguieff, 'Un programme "révolutionnaire"?' in Mayer and Perrineau, *op. cit.*, 197–9.

Bibliography

Adda, Jacques and Smouts, Marie-Claude, *La France face au Sud. Le Miroir brisé* (Paris, Editions Karthala, 1989).

Addad, Serge, 'Peut-on parler de "Théâtre Résistant"?' *RHMC*, XXXVII (Jan.–Mar. 1990), 136–46.

Agulhon, Maurice, 'Conscience nationale et conscience régionale en France de 1815 à nos jours', in *Histoire vagabonde* II (Paris, Gallimard, 1988).

Agulhon, Maurice, 'Une Contribution au souvenir de Jean Jaurès: les monuments en places publiques', in *Histoire vagabonde* I (Paris, Gallimard, 1988), 186–204.

Agulhon, Maurice, 'La "statuomanie" et l'histoire', *Ethnologie française* (8, 2/3) Mar.–Sept. 1978, 145–72, reprinted in *Histoire vagabonde* I (Paris, Gallimard, 1988), 137–85.

Alcouffe, Alain, Lagarde, Pierre, Lafont, Robert, *Pour Occitanie* (Toulouse, Privat, 1979).

Alexandre, Arsène, *Histoire de la peinture militaire en France* (Paris, Renouard, 1889).

Alexander, R.S., 'The *Fédérés* of Dijon in 1815', *Historical Journal* 30, no. 2 (1987), 367–90.

Alexander, R.S., *Bonapartism and the Revolutionary Tradition in France. The Fédérés of 1815* (Cambridge, Cambridge University Press, 1991).

Algazy, Joseph, *La Tentation néo-fasciste en France, 1945–1965* (Paris, Fayard, 1984).

Andreu, Pierre, *Notre Maître, M. Sorel* (Paris, Grasset, 1953).

Angenot, Marc, *Le Centenaire de la Révolution, 1889* (Paris, La Documentation française, 1939).

Anouilh, Jean, *L'Alouette* (London, Methuen, 1956).

Arnal, Oscar L., *Priests in Working-Class Blue. The History of the Worker-Priests, 1943–1954* (New York/Mahwah, Paulist Press, 1986).

Aubry, Octave, *L'Aiglon, des Tuileries aux Invalides* (Paris, Flammarion, 1941).

Audoin-Rouzeau, Stéphane, *1870. La France dans la Guerre* (Paris, Armand Colin, 1989).

Aulard, Alphonse, *Histoire politique de la Révolution française* (3rd edn, Paris, Armand Colin, 1905).

Azéma, Jean-Pierre and Bédarida, François, eds, *Le Régime de Vichy et les Français* (Paris, Fayard, 1992).

Baas, Emile, *Situation de l'Alsace* (Strasbourg, Le Roux, 1946).

Baczko, Bronislaw, *Comment sortir de la Terreur. Thermidor et la Révolution* (Paris, Gallimard, 1989), 169.

Balzac, Honoré de, *Le Médecin de campagne* [1833], in *La Comédie humaine* IX (Paris, Gallimard, 1978).

391

Bankwitz, Philip, *Alsatian Autonomist Leaders, 1919–1947* (Lawrence, Regents Press of Kansas, 1978).

Bardèche, Maurice, *Lettre à François Mauriac* (Paris, La Pensée Libre, 1947).

Bardèche, Maurice, *Qu'est-ce le Fascisme?* (Paris, Les Sept Couleurs, 1961).

Barjonet, André, *La Révolution trahie de 1968* (Paris, John Didier, 1968).

Barrès, Maurice, *L'Appel du Rhin* (Paris, Société littéraire de France, 1919).

Barrès, Maurice, *Assainissement et Fédéralisme. Discours prononcé à Bordeaux le 29 juin 1895* (Paris, La Revue socialiste, 1895).

Barrès, Maurice, *Autour de Jeanne d'Arc* (Paris, Champion, 1916).

Barrès, Maurice, *Les Bastions de l'Est. Au Service de l'Allemagne* [1905] in *L'Oeuvre* (Paris, 1966).

Barrès, Maurice, *Les Bastions de l'Est. Colette Baudoche* (Paris, Société d'Edition et de Publications. Librairie Féix Juven, 1909).

Barrès, Maurice, *Les Bastions de l'Est. Le Génie du Rhin* (Paris, Plon, 1921).

Barrès, Maurice, *Chronique de la Grande Guerre, 1914–1920* (Paris, Plon, 1968).

Barrès, Maurice, *Les Diverses Familles Spirituelles de la France* [1917] (Paris, Plon, 1930).

Barrès, Maurice, *Les Lézardes sur la Maison* (3rd end, Paris, Sansot, 1904).

Barrès, Maurice and Maurras, Charles, *La République ou le Roi. Correspondance inédite, 1888–1923* (Paris, Plon, 1970).

Barruel, Abbé, *Mémoires pour servir à l'Histoire du Jacobinisme* (5 vols, Hamburg, 1803).

Barthélemy, Victor, *Du Communisme au Fascisme* (Paris, Albin Michel, 1978).

Basdevant-Gaudemet, B., *La Commission de Décentralisation de 1870* (Paris, Presses Universitaires de France, 1973).

Bastien-Thiry, Jean, *Sa Vie. Ses Écrits. Témoignages* (Paris, Albatros, 1973).

Bataille, Michel, *Demain, Jaurès* (Paris, Editions Pygmalion, 1977).

Baubérot, Jean, 'L'Antiprotestantisme politique à la fin du XIXe siècle', *Revue d'histoire et de philosophie des religions* 52 (1972), 449–84: 53 (1973), 177–221.

Beau de Loménie, E., *Édouard Drumont ou l'Anticapitalisme national* (Paris, Pauvert, 1968).

Ben-Amos, Avner, *Moulding the National Memory: State Funerals in Modern France* (forthcoming 1994, Oxford University Press).

Bensaïd, Daniel, *Moi, la Révolution. Remembrances d'un Bicentenaire indigne* (Paris, Gallimard, 1989).

Berger, Suzanne, *Peasants against Politics* (Cambridge, Mass., Harvard University Press, 1972).

Bernanos, Georges, *Les Grands Cimetières sous la Lune* (Paris, Plon, 1938).

Berry, David, 'The Other Popular Front: French Anarchism and the Front révolutionnaire', in Martin Alexander and Helen Graham, *The French and Spanish Popular Fronts. Comparative Perspectives* (Cambridge, Cambridge University Press, 1989).

Berth, Édouard, *Guerre des États ou Guerre des Classes* (Paris, Marcel Rivière, 1924).

Berth, Édouard, *Les Nouveaux Aspects du Socialisme* (Paris, 1908).

Biard, Roland, *Histoire du Mouvement anarchiste, 1945–1975* (Paris, Gallilée, 1976).

Birnbaum, Pierre, *Un Myth politique: la République juive, de Léon Blum à Pierre Mendès-France* (Paris, Fayard, 1988).

Blanc, Louis, *Histoire de la Révolution française* (Paris, 12 vols, Langlois et Leclerq, 1847–62).

Bloch, Marc, *L'Étrange Défaite* (Paris, Éditions Franc-Tireur, 1944).

Bluche, Frédéric, *Le Plébiscite des Cent-Jours* (Geneva, Droz, 1974).

Bluche, Frédéric, *Le Bonapartisme. Aux origines de la Droite autoritaire, 1800–1850* (Paris, Nouvelles Editions Latines, 1980).

Bonald, Louis de, *Théorie du Pouvoir politique et religieuse dans la Société civile* (Constance 3 vols, 1796).

Bonaparte, Louis-Napoleon, *Des Idées napoléoniennes* (Paris, Paulin, 1839).

Bourguignon, Jean, *Le Retour des Cendres* (Paris, Plon, 1941).

Bourjol, Maurice, *Les Institutions régionales de 1789 à nos jours* (Paris, Berger-Levrault, 1969).

Brunet, Jean-Paul, *Jacques Doriot* (Paris, Balland, 1986).

Burrin, Philippe, *La Dérive fasciste* (Paris, Seuil, 1986).

Bury, J. P. T. and Tombs, Robert, *Thiers, 1797–1877. A Political Life* (London, Allen and Unwin, 1986).

Cahiers du Sud. Le Génie d'Oc et l'Homme méditerranéen (reed. Marseille, Rivages, 1981).

Carbasse, Jean-Marie, *Louis-Xavier de Ricard. Félibre rouge* (Editions Mireille Lacave, 1977).

Casanova, Antoine and Mazauric, Claude, *Vive la Révolution* (Paris, Messidor/Éditions sociales, 1989).

Centenaire de Voltaire. Fête oratoire présidée par Victor Hugo, le 30 mai 1878 (Paris, Dentu, 1878).

Cerny, Philip G., *The Politics of Grandeur. Ideological Aspects of de Gaulle's Foreign Policy* (Cambridge, Cambridge University Press, 1980).

Challener, Richard D., *The French Theory of the Nation-in-Arms, 1866–1939* (New York, Columbia University Press, 1955).

Chamson, André, *Trois Discours 'au Désert', 1935, 1954, 1958* (Paris, 1959).

Charles-Brun, Jean, *Le Régionalisme* (Paris, Bloud, 1911).

Charles-Brun, Jean, *Le Régionalisme. Cahiers de Formation politique* no. 14 (Vichy, 1944).

Charnay, Maurice, *Les Allemanistes* (Paris, M. Rivière, 1912).

Charras, Lt.-Col. J.-B., *Histoire de la Campagne de 1815. Waterloo* (3rd edn, Brussels, J. Hetzel, 1858).

Chateaubriand, François-René de, *De Buonaparte et des Bourbons* [April 1814] (Paris, Pauvert, 1961).

Chateaubriand, François-René de, *De la Monarchie selon la Charte* (Paris, 1816).

Chaumié, Jacqueline, *Le Réseau d'Antraigues et la Contre-révolution, 1791–1793* (Paris, Plon, 1965).

Chaunu, Pierre, *Le Grand Déclassement. A Propos d'une Commémoration* (Paris, Robert Laffont, 1989).

Choisel, François, *Bonapartisme et Gaullisme* (Paris, Albatros, 1987).

Christophe, Paul, *1936. Les Catholiques et le Front populaire.* (Paris, Desclée, 1979).

Chuquet, Arthur, *Les Guerres de la Révolution* (11 vols, Paris, Cerf, 1886–96).

Chuquet, Arthur, *De Valmy à la Marne* (Paris, Fontemoing, 1915).

Cim, Albert, *Le Chansonnier Émile Debraux, roi de la goguette, 1796–1831* (Paris, Flammarion, 1910).

Claudel, Paul, *Jeanne d'Arc au Bûcher* (Paris, Gallimard, 1939).

Cobb, Richard, *A Second Identity* (Oxford, Oxford University Press, 1969).

Cochin, Augustin, *L'Esprit du Jacobinisme* (Paris, Plon, 1921, Presses Universitaires de France, 1979).

Cohn, Bernard, *An Anthropologist among the Historians and Other Essays* (Delhi, Oxford University Press, 1990).

Cohn Bendit, Daniel, *Le Gauchisme. Remède à la maladie sénile du Communisme* (Paris, Seuil, 1968).

Combes, Émile, *Mon Ministère* (Paris, Plon, 1956).

Comte, Bernard, *Une Utopie combattante. L'École des Cadres d'Uriage, 1940–1942* (Paris, Fayard, 1991).

Constant, Benjamin, *De l'Esprit de Conquête et de l'Usurpation* [April 1814], in *Oeuvres* (Paris, Pléiade, 1957).

Constant, Benjamin, *De la Force du Gouvernement actuelle la France et de la Nécessité de s'y Rallier* (Paris, 1796).

Constant, Benjamin, *Recueil d'articles, 1795–1817*, ed. Ephraïm Harpaz (Geneva, Droz, 1978).

Corbin, Alain, *Le Village des Cannibales* (Paris, Aubier, 1990).

Curutchet, Jean-Marie, *Je veux la tourmente* (Paris, Robert Laffont, 1973).

Daudet, Alphonse, *Contes de Lundi* (Paris, Flammarion, 1984).

Daudet, Léon, *Deux Idoles sanguinaires. La Révolution et son fils Bonaparte* (Paris, Albin Michel, 1939).

Déat, Marcel, *Mémoires politiques* (Paris, Denoel, 1989).

Debbasch, Roland, *Le Principe révolutionnaire d'Unité et d'Indivisibilité de la République* (Paris-Aix, Economica-PU d'Aix-Marseille, 1988).

Debray, Régis, *Que vive la République* (Paris, Odile Jacob, 1989).

Debré, Michel, *Refaire la France* (Paris, Plon, 1945).

Debré, Michel, *Trois Républiques pour une France. Mémoires* I (Paris, Albin Michel, 1984).

Defferre, Gaston, *Un Nouvel Horizon* (Paris, Gallimard, 1965).

Delbreil, Jean-Claude, *Centrisme et Démocratie-Chrétienne en France. Le Parti Démocrate Populaire des Origines au MRP, 1919–1946* (Paris, Publications de la Sorbonne, 1990).

Déniel, Alain, *Le Mouvement breton* (Paris, Maspéro, 1976).

Denis, Michel, 'Mouvement breton et fascisme. Signification de l'échec du second "emsav"', in C. Gras and G. Livet, *Régions et Régionalisme en France du dix-huitième siècle à nos jours* (Paris, Presses Universitaires de France, 1977).

Depreux, Édouard, *Renouvellement du socialisme* (Paris, Calmann-Lévy, 1960).

Depreux, Édouard, *Servitude et grandeur de la PSU* (Paris, Syros, 1974).

Depreux, Édouard, *Souvenirs d'un militant* (Paris, Fayard, 1972).

Déroulède, Paul, *Le Livre de la Ligue des Patriotes* (Paris, 1887).

Déroulède, Paul, *Qui vive? France, quand même. Notes et discours, 1883–1910* (Paris, Bloud, 1910).

Descotes, Maurice, *La Légende de Napoléon et les Ecrivains français* (Paris, Minard, 1967).

Dessoye, A. *Jean Macé et la Fondation de la Ligue de l'Enseignement* (Paris, Marpon et Flammarion, 1883).

Dioudonnat, Pierre-Marie, *Je suis partout, 1930–1944. Les Maurrassiens devant la Tentation fasciste* (Paris, La Table Ronde, 1973).

Domenach, Jean-Marie, *Emmanuel Mounier* (Paris, Seuil, 1972).

Doumergue, Gaston, *Discours à la nation française* (Paris, Denoël et Steele, 1934).

Drieu de la Rochelle, Pierre, *Avec Doriot* (Paris, Gallimard, 1937).

Droz, Édouard, *P.-J. Proudhon* (Paris, Pages Libres, 1909).

Drumont, Édouard, *La Fin d'un Monde* (Paris, Savine, 1889).

Drumont, Édouard, *La France juive* (Paris, Marpon et Flammarion, 123rd edn, 1886).

Drumont, Édouard, *Le Secret de Fourmies* (Paris, Savine, 1892).

Dubois, Jean, *Le Vocabulaire politique et sociale en France de 1869 à 1872* (Paris, 1962), 315, 363.

Duckworth, Colin, *The D'Antraigues Phenomenon. The Making and Breaking of a Revolutionary Royalist and Espionage Agent* (London, Unwin, 1986).

Duprat, François, *Les Journées de mai 1968. Les Dessous d'une Révolution* (Paris, Nouvelles Editions Latines, 1968).

Duprat, François, *Les Mouvements d'Extrême-Droite en France depuis 1944* (Paris, Albatros, 1972).

Duranton-Crabol, Anne-Marie, *Visages de la Nouvelle Droite. Le GRECE et son histoire* (Paris, FNSP, 1988).

Erckmann-Chatrian, *Histoire d'un Conscrit de 1813* (Paris, Hetzel, 1864).

Faure, Elie, *Napoléon* (Paris, Crès, 1921).

Febvre, Lucien, 'Une question d'influence: Proudhon et le syndicalisme des années 1900–1914', *Revue de Synthèse historique* (XIX/2), 1909, 179–93, reprinted in *Pour une Histoire à part entière* (Paris, SEVPEN, 1962), 772–86.

Flory, Maurice, 'L'Appel au peuple napoléonien', *Revue internationale d'histoire politique et constitutionnelle* (new series, II, 1952), 215–222.

Forestier, H., 'Le mouvement bonapartiste dans l'Yonne', *Annales de Bourgogne*, 21 (1949).

Ford, Caroline, *Creating the Nation in Provincial France. Religion and Political Identity in Brittany* (Princeton, New Jersey, Princeton University Press, 1993).

Fortescue, William, 'Poetry, Politics and Publicity, and the Writing of History: Lamartine's *Histoire des Girondins* (1847), *European History Quarterly*, 17 (1987), 259–84.

Fouéré, Yann, *De la Bretagne à la France et à l'Europe* (Lorient, 1958).

Fouéré, Yann, *Les Droits que les autres ont . . . mais que nous n'avons pas. Les Cahiers de L'Avenir de la Bretagne, nos 6 & 7* (Quimper, Éditions Nature et Bretagne, 1979).

Fouéré, Yann, *En Prison pour le FLB* (Paris, Nouvelles Éditions Latines, 1977).

Fournière, Eugène, *Les Théories socialistes au XIXe siècle de Babeuf à Proudhon* (Paris, Alcan, 1904).

France, Anatole, *Monsieur Bergeret à Paris* (Paris, Calmann-Lévy, 1973).

France, Anatole, *Vie de Jeanne d'Arc* (2 vols, Paris, Calmann-Lévy, 1908).

Francis, Robert, Maulnier, Thierry, Maxence, J.-P., *Demain la France* (Paris, Grasset, 1934).

Front de Libération de la Bretagne 72, *Procès de la Bretagne* (Editions Lelenn, 1973).

Furet, François, *La Gauche et la Révolution au milieu du XIXe siècle* (Paris, Hachette, 1986).

Furet, François, *Interpreting the French Revolution* (Cambridge/Paris, Cambridge University Press/Maison des Sciences de l'Homme, 1981).

Furet, François, and Ozouf, Mona, *A Critical Dictionary of the Frenh Revolution* (tr. Arthur Goldhammer, The Belknap Press of Harvard University Press, 1989).

Gadille, Jacques and Mayeur, J.-M., 'Les milieux catholiques libéraux en France', in *Les Catholiques libéraux au XIXe siècle* (Grenoble, 1974).

Gaehtgens, Thomas W., *Versailles. De la Résidence royale au musée historique* (Paris, Albin Michel, 1984).

Gaffney, John, ed., *The French Presidential Elections of 1988* (Aldershot, Dartmouth, 1989).

Galli, H., *Paul Déroulède raconté par lui-même* (Paris, 1900).

Gallo, Max, *Lettre ouverte à Maximilien Robespierre sur les nouveaux muscadins* (Paris, Albin Michel, 1986).

Gaulle, Charles de, *Le Fil de l'Épée* [1932] (2nd edn, Paris, Berger-Levrault, 1944).

Gaulle, Charles de, *Lettres, Notes et Carnets, 1919–juin 1940* (Paris, Plon, 1980).

Gaulle, Charles de, *Lettres, Notes et Carnets, mai 1969–novembre 1970. Compléments de 1908 à 1968* (Paris, Plon, 1988).

Gaulle, Charles de, *Mémoires de Guerre* I. *L'Appel, 1940–1942* (Paris, Plon, 1954).

Gaulle, Charles de, *Mémoires de Guerre* II. *L'Unité, 1942–1944* (Paris, Plon, 1956).

Gaulle, Charles de, *Mémoires de Guerre* III. *Le Salut, 1944–1946* (Paris, Plon, 1959).

Gaxotte, Pierre, *La Révolution française* (Paris, Fayard, 1928).

Giacomelli, Hector, *Raffet. Son oeuvre lithographique et ses eaux-fortes* (Paris, 1862).

Gicquel, Yvonnig, *Le Comité Consultatif de Bretagne* (Rennes, Simon, 1961).

Girault, Jacques, 'Les Guesdistes, la Deuxième Egalité et la Commune', in Rougerie, Jacques, *Jalons pour une Histoire de la Commune* (Assen, van Gorcum, 1973), 421–30.

Giscard d'Estaing, Valéry, *Démocratie française* (Paris, Fayard, 1976).

Godechot, Jacques, *Les Constitutions de France depuis 1789* (Paris, Flammarion, 1979).

Godechot, Jacques, *La Grande Nation* (2nd edn, Paris, Aubier, 1983).

Goulemot, Jean-Marie and Walter, Eric, 'Les Centenaires de Voltaire et de Rousseau', in P. Nora, ed., *Les Lieux de Mémoire*, I (Paris, Gallimard, 1984), 381–420.

Gras, Christian, *Alfred Rosmer et le Mouvement Révolutionnaire international* (Paris, Maspéro, 1971).

Gras, Christian and Livet, Georges, eds, *Régions et régionalisme en France du dix-huitème siècle à nos jours* (Paris, Presses Universitaires de France, 1977).

Grave, Jean, *Le Mouvement libertaire sous la Troisième République. Souvenirs d'un Révolté* (Paris, 1930).

Gravier, Jean-François, *Paris et le Désert français* (Paris, Le Portulan, 1947).

Greenberg, Louis, *Sisters of Liberty. Marseille, Lyon and the Return to a Centralized State* (Cambridge, Mass., Harvard University Press, 1971).

Groux, Guy and Mouriaux, René, *La CFDT* (Paris, Economica, 1989).

Guchet, Yves, *Georges Valois. L'Action Française. Le Faisceau. La République syndicale* (Paris, Albatros, 1975).

Guérin, Daniel, *Ni Dieu ni maître. Anthologie historique du mouvement anarchiste* (Lausanne, La Cité, 1969).

Guillaume, James, *L'Internationale. Documents et Souvenirs. (1864–1878)* 2 vols (Paris, Société Nouvelle de Librairie et d'Edition/Librarie Georges Bellais, 1905–7).

Guiomar, Jean-Yves, *Le Bretonisme. Les historiens bretons au XIXe siècle* (Mayenne, Société d'Histoire et d'Archéologie de Bretagne, 1987).

Guizot, François, *Mémoires pour servir à l'histoire de mon temps* I (2nd edn, Paris, Michel Lévy, 1858).

Gurvitch, Georges, 'Proudhon et Marx', in *L'Actualité de Proudhon*, Colloque des 24–5 novembre 1965 (Brussels, Institut de Sociologie de l'université libre, 1967).

Halbwachs, Maurice, *La Mémoire collective* (Paris, PUF, 1950, 2nd end, 1968), translated as *The Collective Memory* (Harper and Row, 1980).

Hampson, Norman, 'The French Revolution and the nationalisation of honour', in M. R. D. Foot, ed., *War and Society* (London, Paul Eleck, 1973), 199–212.

Hanotaux, Gabriel, *Histoire du Cardinal Richelieu* I (Paris, Firmin Didot, 1893).

Hanotaux, Gabriel, *Mon Temps. 1. De L'Empire à La République* (Paris, Plon, 1933).

Hansi, *Histoire de l'Alsace racontée aux Petits Enfants d'Alsace et de la France* (Paris, Herscher, 1983).

Hennessy, Jean and Charles-Brun, Jean, *Le Principe fédératif, leçons faites au Collège libre des sciences sociales* (Paris, Alcan, 1940).

Herriot, Édouard, *Hommage à la Révolution* (Paris, Fasquelle, 1939).

Hervé, Gustave, *La République autoritaire* (Paris, Librarie de la Victoire, 1926).

Hervé, Gustave, *C'est Pétain qu' il nous faut* (Paris, Éditions de la Victoire, 1935).

Hoffet, Frédéric, *Psychanalyse de l'Alsace* (Paris, Flammarion, 1951).

Hoffmann, Stanley, *France: Change and Tradition* (London, Gollancz, 1963).

Hoffmann, Stanley, ed., *The Mitterrand Experiment* (Cambridge, Polity Press, 1987).

Hoffmann, Stanley, *Le Mouvement Poujade* (Paris, FNSP, 1956).

Houssaye, Henry, *1814* (Paris, Perrin, 1888).

Houssaye, Henry, 'Napoléon le Grand, par Victor Hugo', *Bulletin du Bibliophile* (1902), 97–105.

Howlett, G. A., 'The Croix de Feu, the Parti Social Français and Colonel de La Rocque' (Oxford D.Phil. thesis, 1985).

Hugo, Victor, 'Discours de réception à l'Académie française', 2 June 1841, in *Actes et paroles. Avant l'exil, 1841–1851* (3rd edn, Paris, Lévy, 1875).

Hugo, Victor, *Napoléon le Petit* (London, Jeffs, 1852).

Hugo, Victor, *Quatre-Vingt-Treize* (Paris, Hetzel, n.d.).

Hunt, Lynn, *Politics, Class and Culture in the French Revolution* (London, Macmillan, 1986).

Hunt, Lynn, *The Family Romance of the French Revolution* (London, Routledge, 1992).

Husser, Philippe, *Un Instituteur alsacien. Entre la France et l'Allemagne, 1914–1951* (Paris, Hachette, 1989).

Hutton, Patrick, *The Cult of the Revolutionary Tradition. The Blanquists in French Politics, 1864–1893* (Berkeley and Los Angeles, University of California Press, 1981).

Irvine, William D., *The Boulanger Affair Reconsidered. Royalism, Boulangism and the Origins of the Radical Right in France* (Oxford, Oxford University Press, 1989).

Irvine, William D., 'Fascism and the strange case of the Croix de Feu', *JMH* 63.2 (1991) 271–95.

Irvine, William D., 'French conservatives and the "New Right" during the 1930s', *French Historical Studies* 8 (1974).

Irvine, William D., *French Conservatism in Crisis. The Republican Federation of France during the 1930s* (Baton Rouge and London, Louisiana State University Press, 1979), xix, 104–26.

Jacobs, Gabriel, 'The Rôle of Joan of Arc on the Stage of Occupied Paris', in Kedward, Roderick and Austin, Roger, *Vichy France and the Resistance. Culture and Ideology* (London, Croom Helm, 1985).

Jaurès, Jean, *Histoire socialiste de la Révolution française* (7 vols, Paris, Editions sociales, 1968–73).

Jeanné, Egide, *L'Image de la Pucelle d'Orléans dans la Littérature historique française depuis Voltaire* (Liège, Vaillant-Carmanne, 1935).

Jenkins, Clare, '"Un Régionalisme rouge ou un Régionalisme blanc?" Regionalism, National Revolution and Liberation in Toulouse, 1940–46' (University of Warwick, Ph.D. thesis, 1992).

Jennings, Jeremy, *Syndicalism in France. A Study of Ideas* (Basingstoke, Macmillan, 1990).

Johnson, Douglas, *Guizot: Aspects of French history, 1787–1874* (London/Toronto, Routledge and Kegan Paul/University of Toronto Press, 1963).

Joll, James, *The Anarchists* (London, Eyre and Spottiswoode, 1964).

Joll, James, *The Second International* (London, Weidenfeld and Nicolson, 1956).

Joly, Danièle, *The French Communist Party and the Algerian War* (Basingstoke, Macmillan, 1991).

Joughin, Jean T., *The Paris Commune in French Politics, 1871–1880* (Baltimore, Johns Hopkins, 1955).

Jouin, Henry, *Histoire et description de la colonne de la Grande Armée, place Vendôme* (Paris, Plon, 1879).

Joutard, Philippe, *La Légende des Camisards. Une sensibilité au passé* (Paris, Gallimard, 1977).

Joutard, Philippe, Poujol, Jacques, Cabanel, Patrick, *Cévennes, Terre de Refuge, 1940– 1944* (Montpellier, Presses du Languedoc/Club cévenol, 1987).

Joyeux, Maurice, *L'Anarchisme et la Révolte de la Jeunesse* (Paris, Casterman, 1970).

Joyeux, Maurice, *Souvenirs d'un Anarchiste* (Paris, Éditions du *Monde Libertaire*, 1986).

Judt, Tony, *Marxism and the French Left. Studies on Labour and Politics in France, 1830–1981* (Oxford, Clarendon Press, 1986).

Juin, Hubert, *Victor Hugo, I 1802–1843* (Paris, Flammarion, 1980).

Julliard, Jacques, *Fernand Pelloutier et les origines du syndicalisme d'action directe* (Paris, Seuil, 1971).

Kriegel, Annie, *Un autre Communisme* (Paris, Hachette, 1977).

Kriegel, Annie, *Le Congrès de Tours, 1920* (Paris, Gallimard-Julliard, 1964).

Kriegel, Annie, *Aux Origines du Communime Français, 1914–1920* (Paris-La Haye, Mouton, 1964).

Kriegel, Annie, 'Le Parti Communiste, la Résistance, la Libération', in *Communismes au miroir français* (Paris, Gallimard, 1974).

Kriegel, Annie, 'Le Syndicalisme révolutionnaire et Proudhon', in *Le Pain et les Roses* (Paris, Presses Universitaires de France, 1968), 33–50.

Krivine, Alain, *Questions sur la Révolution. Entretiens avec Roland Biard* (Paris, Stock, 1973).

Krumeich, Gerd, *Jeanne d'Arc in der Geschiche* (Sigmaringen, Thorbecke, 1989).

Jean Lacouture, *De Gaulle* (2 vols, trans. Patrick O'Brian, London, Collins Harvill, 1990).

Lafolie, J., *Mémoires historiques relatifs à la fonte et à l'élevation de la statue equestre de Henri IV* (Paris, 1819).

Lafont, Robert, *Décoloniser la France. Les régions face à l'Europe* (Paris, Gallimard, 1971).

Lafont, Robert, *Mistral, ou l'illusion* (Paris, Plon, 1954).

Lafont, Robert, *La Révolution régionaliste* (Paris, Gallimard, 1967).

Lagaillarde, Pierre, '*On a triché avec l'honneur*' (Paris, La Table Ronde, 1961).

Lamartine, Alphonse de, *Histoire des Girondins* (8 vols, Paris, Furne, 1847).

La Rochejacquelein, Henri de, *Appel à la Nation. A mon Pays. Défense de ma proposition* (Paris, 1850).

La Rochejacquelein, Marquise de, *Mémoires* (4th edn, Paris, Michaud, 1817).

La Rocque, Lt.-Col. de, *Service public* (Paris, Grasset, 1934).

Las Cases, Comte E. de, *Le Mémorial de Sainte-Hélène* (Paris, *chez l'auteur*, 1823).

Lattre de Tassigny, Jean de, *Histoire de la première armée française, Rhin et Danube* (Paris, Plon, 1949).

Lattre de Tassigny, Jean de, *Ne Pas Subir. Écrits, 1914–1952* (Paris, Plon, 1984).

La Villemarqué, Hersart de, *Barzaz-Breiz. Chants populaires de la Bretagne* (Paris, Charpentier, 1839).

Lebrun, Richard A., *Joseph de Maistre. An Intellectual Militant* (Kingston and Montreal, McGill-Queen's University Press, 1988).

Leclerc, Gérard, *Un autre Maurras* (Paris, Institut de politique nationale, 1974).

Lecoin, Louis, *De Prison en Prison* (Paris, Édité par l'auteur, 1947).

Lefebvre, Henri, *L'Irruption de Nanterre au sommet* (Paris, Anthropos, 1968).

Lefebvre, Mgr Marcel, *Un Evêque parle. Écrits et Allocations I, 1963–1973. II. 1975–6* (Paris, Dominique Martin Morin, 1977).

Le Pen, Jean-Marie, *Les Français d'abord* (Paris, Carrère-Michel Laffon, 1984).

Levey, Jules, 'The Sorelian Syndicalists: Édouard Berth, Georges Valois, Hubert Lagardelle' (New York, University of Columbia, Ph.D. thesis, 1967).

L'Homme, F., *Charlet*, (Paris, Allison et Cie, 1892).

L'Huillier, F., ed., *L'Alsace en 1870–1871* (Strasbourg, Faculté des Lettres, 1971).

Lorulot, André, *Ma vie, mes idées* (Les Amis d'André Lorulot, 1973).

Lote, Georges, 'La Mort de Napoléon et l'opinion bonapartiste en 1821', *Revue des Études napoléoniennes*, 31, (July–Dec. 1930).

Loubet del Bayle, Jean-Louis, *Les Non-Conformistes des années trente* (Paris, Seuil, 1969).

Lourdoueix, Henri de, *Le Droit National* (Paris, 1851).

Lucas-Dubreton, J., *Le Culte de Napoléon, 1815–1848* (Paris, Albin Michel, 1960).

Magnard, Francis, 'La Résurrection d'une légende', *La Revue de Paris*, (Feb.–Mar. 1894), 89–111.

Maire, Edmond, Krumnow, Alfred, Detraz, Albert, *La CFDT et l'Autogestion* (Paris, Cerf, 1973).

Maistre, Joseph de, *Considérations sur la France* [1797] (Paris, La Société Typographique, 1814).

Maistre, Joseph de, *Les Soirées de Saint-Pétersbourg, ou entretiens sur le gouvernement temporel de la Providence* (Paris-Lyon, Librairie Grecque Latine et Française, 1822).

Maitron, Jean, *Le Mouvement anarchiste en France* (2 vols, Paris, Maspéro, 1975).

Maitron, Jean, *Paul Delesalle. Un Anarchiste de la Belle Époque* (Paris, Fayard, 1985).

Maitron, Jean and Chambelland, Colette, eds, *Syndicalisme révolutionnaire et Communisme. Les Archives de Pierre Monatte* (Paris, Maspéro, 1968).

Malon, Benoît, *La Troisième Défaite du Prolétariat français* (Neuchâtel, 1871).

Malraux, André, *Les Chênes qu'on abat* (Paris, Gallimard, 1971).

Marchais, Georges, *Démocratie* (Messidor/Éditions sociales, 1990).

Marion, Georges, *Gaston Defferre* (Paris, Albin Michel, 1989).

Martin, Benjamin, *Count Albert de Mun. Paladin of the Third Republic* (Chapel Hill, University of North Carolina Press, 1978).

Martin, Jean-Clément, *La Vendée et la France* (Paris, Seuil, 1987).

Martin, Jean-Clément, *La Vendée de la Mémoire* (Paris, Seuil, 1989).

Marx, Karl, *The Eighteenth Brumaire of Louis-Bonaparte*, in Marx and Engels, *Selected Works in One Volume* (London, Lawrence and Wishart, 1968).

Maschino, Maurice, *Les Refus* (new edn, Paris, Maspéro, 1960).

Massis, Henri, *Maurras et notre temps* (Paris-Geneva, La Palatine, 1961).

Mathiez, Albert, *Le Bolchévisme et le Jacobinisme* (Paris, Librairie du Parti socialiste et de *L'Humanité*, 1920).

Mathiez, Albert, 'La Corruption parlementaire sous la Terreur', *Annales révolutionnaires* 5/2 (Mar.–April 1912).

Maugué, Pierre, *Le Particularisme alsacien, 1918–1967* (Paris, Presses d'Europe, 1970).

Maurras, Charles, *L'Avenir de l'Intelligence* (Paris, Fontemoing, 1905).

Maurras, Charles, *Une Campagne royaliste au 'Figaro'* [1901–2], in *Enquête sur la Monarchie* (Paris, Nouvelle Librairie Nationale, 1925).

Maurras, Charles, *La Contre-Révolution spontanée* (Lyon, Lardanchet, 1943).

Maurras, Charles, *Le Dilemme de Marc Sangnier* [1906], and *Politique religieuse* [1912], in *L'Oeuvre II. Démocratie religieuse* (Paris, Nouvelle Librairie Internationale, 1925).

Maurras, Charles, *Enquête sur la Monarchie* (Paris, Nouvelle Librairie Internationale, 1925).

Maurras, Charles, *L'Étang de Berre* (Paris, Champion, 1915).

Maurras, Charles, *La France seule* (Lyon, Lardanchet, 1941).

Maurras, Charles, *L'Idée de la Décentralisation* (Paris, 1898).

Maurras, Charles, *Jeanne d'Arc, Louis XIV et Napoléon* (Paris, Flammarion, 1937).

Maurras, Charles, *Kiel et Tanger, 1895–1905. La République française devant l'Europe* (2nd edn, Paris, Nouvelle Librairie Internationale, 1914).

Maurras, Charles, *Au Signe de Flore* (Paris, Ouvres représentatives, 1931).

Mayeur, Françoise, *L'Aube. Étude d'un journal d'opinion* (Paris, Armand Colin, 1966).

Mayeur, Jean-Marie, *Autonomie et politique en Alsace. La Constitution de 1911* (Paris, Armand Colin, 1970).

Mayeur, Jean-Marie, 'Catholicisme intransigeant, Catholicisme social, démocratie chrétienne', *Annales ESC* 27 (1972), 483–99.

Mayeur, Jean-Marie, 'Les congrès nationaux de la "Démocratie chrétienne" à Lyon, 1896, 1897, 1898', *RHMC* 9, (1962), reprinted in *Catholicisme social et Démocratie chrétienne* (Paris, Cerf, 1986).

Mayeur, Jean-Marie, 'Laïcité et question scolaire en Alsace et Moselle, 1944–63', in Rémond, René, ed., *Forces religieuses et attitudes politiques*, Colloque de Strasbourg 1963 (Strasbourg, 1965), 239–49.

Mayeur, Jean-Marie, *Des Partis catholiques à la démocratie chrétienne* (Paris, Armand Colin, 1980).

Mayeur, Jean-Marie, *Un Prêtre démocrate: l'abbé Lemire, 1853–1928* (Paris, Casterman, 1968).

Mazgaj, Paul, *The Action Française and Revolutionary Syndicalism* (Chapel Hill, 1979).

Ménager, Bernard, *Les Napoléons du Peuple* (Paris, Aubier, 1988).

Mendès-France, Pierre, *Oeuvres complètes IV. Pour une République moderne, 1955–62* (Paris, Gallimard, 1987).

Mesliand, Claude, 'Le Félibrige, la République, et l'idée de décentralisation, 1870–1892', in *La Décentralisation*, Colloque d'Aix-en-Provence, 1961 (Gap, 1964).

Meyer, Nonna, and Perrineau, Pascal, *Le Front national à Découvert* (FNSP, 1989).

Michaud, René, *J'avais vingt ans. Un jeune ouvrier au début du siècle* (Paris, Syros, 1983).

Michelet, Jules, *Histoire de la Révolution française* (2nd edn, Paris, Librairie Internationale, 1869).

Michelet, Jules, *Histoire de France* V (Paris, Hachette, 1841).

Michelet, Jules, *Histoire de France*, XIV (Paris, Chamerot, 1860).

Michelet, Jules, *Introduction à l'Histoire universelle* in *Oeuvres complètes*, ed. Paul Viallaneix, II (Paris, Flammarion, 1972).

Michelet, Jules, *Le Peuple* (Paris, Marcel Didier, 1946).

Mignon, Sybille, 'Cinquante années de Souvenir Napoléon', *Le Souvenir napoléonien*, 364 (April 1989).

Mistral, Frédéric, *Mes Origines. Mémoires et Récits* [1906] (Paris, Plon, 1937).

Mitterrand, François, *Ma Part de Vérité* (Paris, Fayard, 1969).

Mitterrand, François, *La Rose au poing* (Paris, Flammarion, 1973).

Mollet, Guy, *13 mai 1958–13 mai 1962* (Paris, Plon, 1962).

Monatte, Pierre, *Trois scissions syndicales* (Paris, 1958).

Monnier, Raymonde, 'Le Culte de Bara en l'an II', *AHRF*, 52 (1980), 321–37.

Mordrel, Olier, *Breiz Atao ou Histoire et Actualité du Nationalisme breton* (Paris, A. Moreau, 1973).

Mordrel, Olier, *La Voie bretonne. Radiographie de l'Emsav* (Quimper, Nature et Bretagne, 1975).

Namer, Gérard, *Mémoire et Société* (Paris, Méridiens et Klincksieck, 1987).

Napo, Félix, *1907: La Révolte des Vignerons* (Toulouse, Privat, 1971).

Napoleon III, *Oeuvres* (I–III, V) (Paris, Plon, 1854–6, 1869).

Napoléon, vu par Abel Gance (Paris, Plon, 1927).

Nguyen, Victor, *Aux Origines de l'Action Française. Intelligence et politique à l'aube du XXe siècle* (Paris, Fayard, 1991).

Nicolas, Michel, *Le Séparatisme en Bretagne* (Brasparts, Editions Beltan, 1986).

Nora, Pierre, 'Ernest Lavisse. Son rôle dans la formation du sentiment national', *Revue historique*, 228 (1962), 73–106. Republished as 'Lavisse, instituteur national', in Nora, ed., *Les Lieux de Mémoire* I, 247–89.

Nora, Pierre, ed., *Les Lieux de Mémoire* (Paris, Gallimard) I *La République* (1984), II (1–3) *La Nation* (1986), III (I–III), *Les France* (1992).

Offen, Karen, 'The Political Career of Paul de Cassagnac' (Stanford, University of California Ph.D. thesis, 1971).

Orfali, Birgitta, *L'Adhésion au Front national* (Paris, Kime, 1990).

Ory, Pascal, 'Le Centenaire de la Révolution française', in Pierre Nora, *Les Lieux de Mémoire* I. *La République* (Paris, Gallimard, 1984), 523–60.

Ory, Pascal, 'La Commémoration révolutionnaire en 1939', in René Rémond and Janine Bourdin, *La France et les Français en 1938–1939* (Paris, FNSP, 1978).

Ozouf, Mona, 'Alsace-Lorraine mode d'emploi. La question d'Alsace-Lorraine dans le *Manuel général*, 1871–1914', in *L'École de la France* (Paris, Gallimard, 1984).

Ozouf, Mona, *La Fête révolutionnaire* (Paris, Gallimard, 1976). Translated as *Festivals and the French Revolution* (Cambridge, Mass., Harvard University Press, 1988).

Ozouf, Mona, *L'Homme régénéré. Essais sur la Révolution Française* (Paris, Gallimard, 1989).

Ozouf, Mona, 'Le Panthéon', in Nora, *Les Lieux de Mémoire* I, 139–166.

Paul-Boncour, Joseph and Maurras, Charles, *Un Débat nouveau sur la République et la Décentralisation* (Toulouse, Société provinciale d'édition, 1905).

Pedroncini, Guy, *1917. Les Mutineries de l'armée française* (Paris, Presses Universitaires de France, 1967).

Péguy, Charles, 'L'Argent suite', *Cahiers de la Quinzaine* (9), 22 April 1913, republished in *Oeuvres complètes* (Paris, Nouvelle Revue Française, 1932).

Péguy, Charles, *Jeanne d'Arc* [1897] in *Oeuvres poétiques complètes* (Paris, Gallimard, 1975).

Péguy, Charles, 'Le Mystère de la Charité de Jeanne d'Arc', in *Oeuvres poétiques complètes* (Paris, Gallimard, 1975).

Péguy, Charles, 'Notre Patrie', *Cahiers de la Quinzaine*, VIIe series, 3e cahier, 17 Oct., 1905.

Péguy, Charles, 'Le "Triomphe de la République"', in *Oeuvres en prose complètes* I (Paris, Gallimard, 1987), 299–318.

Péguy, Marcel, *Le Destin de Charles Péguy* (Paris, Perrin, 1941).

Pelloutier, Fernand, 'Lettre aux anarchistes', in *Le Congrès général du Parti socialiste français, 3–8 décembre 1899* (Paris, 1900).

Perrin, Henri, *Itinéraire d'Henri Perrin, prêtre ouvrier* (Paris, Seuil, 1958).

Perrin, Henri, *Journal d'un prêtre ouvrier en Allemagne* (2nd edn, Paris, Seuil, 1945).

Pétain, Philippe, *Actes et Ecrits* (Paris, Flammarion, 1974).

Peyrat, Napoléon, *Histoire des Pasteurs du Désert depuis la Révocation de l'Édit de Nantes jusqu'à la Révolution française, 1685–1789* (2 vols, Paris-Vienne, 1842).

Philip, Loïc, *André Philip* (Paris, Beauchesne, 1988).

Plenel, Edwy and Rollat, Alain, *L'Effet le Pen* (Paris, La Découverte, 1984).

Plongeron, Bernard, *L'Abbé Grégoire ou l'Arche de la Fraternité* (Paris, Letouzey et Ané, 1989).

Poisson, Henri, *L'Abbé Jean-Marie Perrot, fondateur de Bleun-Brug, 1877–1943* (Rennes, Plihon, 1955).

Pompidou, Georges, *Entretiens et Discours, 1968–1974* (Paris, Plon, 1975).

Poulat, Émile, *Église contre bourgeoisie* (Paris, Casterman, 1977).

Poulat, Émile, *Naissance des Prêtres-Ouvriers* (Paris, Casterman, 1965).

Pouthas, Charles H., *La Jeunesse de Guizot, 1787–1814* (Paris, Félix Alcan, 1936).

Prélot, Marcel, *Le Catholicisme libérale* (Paris, Armand Colin, 1969).

Prélot, Marcel and Gallouédec Genuys, F., *Le Libéralisme catholique* (Paris, Armand Colin, 1969).

Le Procès de Charles Maurras (Paris, Albin Michel, 1946).

Le Procès du complot autonomiste de Colmar, 1–24 mai 1928 (Colmar, *Alsatia*, 1928).

Prost, Antoine, 'Les Monuments aux morts', in Pierre Nora, ed., *Les Lieux de Mémoire* I, 200–13.

Prost, Antoine, 'Verdun', in Pierre Nora, ed., *Les Lieux de Mémoire* II (3).

Proudhon, P.-J., *De la Capacité politique des classes ouvrières*, in *Oeuvres complètes*, 3 (Paris, Rivière, 1924).

Proudhon, P.-J., *Les Confessions d'un révolutionnaire* [October 1849], in *Oeuvres complètes*, 7 (Paris, Rivière, 1929).

Proudhon, P.-J., *L'Idée générale de la Révolution au XIXe siècle* in *Oeuvres complètes*, 2 (Paris, Marcel Rivière, 1924).

Proudhon, P.-J., *Napoléon III* (2nd edn, Paris, 1900).

Pujo, Pierre, *La Monarchie Aujourd'hui. Une nouvelle enquête* (Paris, Editions France-Empire, 1988).

Quinet, Edgar, *L'Enseignement du Peuple*, *Oeuvres complètes* (Paris, Pagnerre, 1870).

Quinet, Edgar, *Histoire de la Campagne de 1815* (Paris, 1862).

Quinet, Edgar, *Oeuvres complètes* VI, X, XI (Paris, Pagnerre, 1857, 1858, 1870).

Quinet, Edgar, *La Révolution* (Paris, A. Lacroix, Verboeckhoven et Cie, 1865).

Rabaut, Jean, *L'Antimilitarisme en France, 1870–1975* (Paris, Hachette, 1975).

Rebatet, Lucien, *Les Décombres* (Paris, Pauvert, 1976).

Rebérioux, Madeleine, 'Jaurès et la Révolution française', *AHRF* 38 (1966), 171–95.

Rebérioux, Madeleine, 'Le Mur des Fédérés', in Pierre Nora, ed., *Les Lieux de Mémoire* I, 619–49.

Renan, Ernest, *Oeuvres complètes* I (Paris, Calmann-Lévy, 1947).

Rémond, René, *L'Anticléricalisme en France de 1815 à nos jours* (Paris, Fayard, 1976).

Rémond, René, ed., *Pour une Histoire politique* (Paris, Seuil, 1988).

Renouvin, Bertrand, *Le Projet royaliste* (Paris, Institut de politique nationale, 1973).

Ricard, Louis-Xavier de, *Le Fédéralisme* (Paris, Sandoz and Fischbacher, 1877).

Richard, Michel, 'Les ministres protestants du cabinet Waddington', in *Les Protestants dans les débuts de la Troisième République*, Actes du Colloque 3–6 octobre 1978 (*Bulletin de la Société de l'histoire du Protestantisme français*, 1979), 199–226.

Rioux, J.-P., *Erckmann et Chatrian ou le Trait d'union* (Paris, Gallimard, 1989).

Rioux, J.-P. and Sirinelli, J.-F. eds, *La Guerre d'Algérie et les Intellectuels*

Français, Cahiers de l'Institut d'Histoire du Temps Présent, 10 (Nov. 1988).

Roberts, John, *The Paris Commune from the Right* (*EHR*, supp. 6, London, Longman, 1973).

Rollat, Alain, *Les Hommes de l'Extrême Droite* (Paris, Calmann-Lévy, 1984).

Rosanvallon, Pierre, *Le Moment Guizot* (Paris, Gallimard, 1985).

Roth, Jack, *The Cult of Violence. Sorel and the Sorelians* (Berkeley, Los Angeles, University of California Press, 1980).

Rothney, John, *Bonapartism after Sedan* (Ithaca, New York, Cornell University Press, 1969).

Rougerie, Jacques, *Jalons pour une Histoire de la Commune de Paris* (Assen, van Gorcum, 1973).

Rousso, Henri, *Le Syndrôme de Vichy, 1944–198 . . .* (Paris, Seuil, 1987). Translated as *The Vichy Syndrome: History and Memory in France since 1944* (Cambridge, Mass., Harvard University Press, 1991).

Rudelle, Odile, *Mai 58. De Gaulle et la République* (Paris, Plon, 1988).

Rudelle, Odile, *La République absolu, 1870–1889* (Paris, Gallimard, 1982).

Sadoul, Jacques, *Notes sur la Révolution bolchévique* (Paris, Éditions de la Sirène, 1919).

Sanson, Rosamonde, 'La Fête de Jeanne d'Arc' en 1894. Controverse et célébration', *RHMC* 20 (1973).

Sanson, Rosamonde, *Les 14 juillet. Fête et conscience nationale, 1789–1975* (Paris, Flammarion, 1976).

Sartre, J.-P., *Les Communistes ont peur de la Révolution* (Paris, John Didier, 1968).

Sauvegeot, J., Geismar, A., Cohn-Bendit, D., Duteil, J.-P., *La Révolte étudiante. Les animateurs parlent* (Paris, Seuil, 1968).

Savary, Alain, *En Toute liberté* (Paris, Hachette, 1985).

Schmidt, Vivien A., *Democratizing France. The Political and Administrative History of Decentralization* (Cambridge, Cambridge University Press, 1990).

Schöttler, Peter, *Naissance des Bourses du travail. Un Appareil idéologique d'Etat à la Fin du XIXe siècle* (Paris, PUF, 1985).

Schöttler, Peter, 'Politique syndicale ou lutte des classes: notes sur le syndicalisme apolitique des Bourses de Travail', *Le Mouvement social* 116 (1981).

Secher, Reynald, *Le Génocide franco-français. La Vendée-Vengé* (Paris, Presses Universitaires de France, 1986).

Séguin, Philippe, *Louis-Napoléon le Grand* (Paris, Grasset, 1990).

Sérant, Paul, *La Bretagne et la France* (Paris, Fayard, 1971).

Serrou, Robert, *Dieu n'est pas conservateur* (Paris, Robert Laffont, 1968).

Sewell, William H., *Work and Revolution in France. The Language of Labour from the Old Régime to 1848* (Cambridge, Cambridge University Press, 1980).

Silverman, Dan P., *Reluctant Union: Alsace-Lorraine and Imperial Germany* (Pennsylvania State University, 1972).

Sirinelli, Jean-François, *Histoire des Droites en France I. Politique II. Culture III. Sensibilités* (Paris, Gallimard, 1992).

Sorel, Albert, *L'Europe et la Révolution française* (8 vols, Paris, 1885–1904).

Sorel, Georges, *Lettres à Paul Delesalle* (Paris, Grasset, 1947).

Sorel, Georges, *Matéraux d'une Théorie du prolétariat* (Paris, Marcel Rivière, 1919).

Sorel, Georges, *Réflexions sur la Violence* (Paris, Pages Libres, 1908).

Sorel, Georges, *La Révolution Dreyfusienne* (Paris, Rivière, 1909).

Soucy, Robert, 'French fascism and the Croix de Feu', *JCH* 26 (1991), 159–88.

Soustelle, Jacques, *L'Espérance trahie, 1958–1961* (Paris, Editions de l'Alma, 1962).

Staël, Madame de, *Considérations sur les principaux événements de la Révolution française* (Paris, 1818).

Staël, Madame de, *Réflexions sur la paix intérieure* in *Oeuvres complètes* (Paris, 1820).

Stafford, David, *From Anarchism to Reformism. A Study of the political activities of Paul Brousse within the First International and the French socialist movement* (London, Weidenfeld and Nicholson, 1971).

Stanley, John, *The Sociology of Virtue. The Political and Social Theory of Georges Sorel* (Berkeley, Los Angeles, University of California, 1981).

Sternhell, Zeev, *La Droite révolutionnaire, 1885–1914* (Paris, Seuil, 1978).

Sternhell, Zeev, *Maurice Barrès et le nationalisme français* (Paris, Armand Colin, 1972).

Sternhell, Zeev, *Ni Droite ni Gauche* (Paris, Seuil, 1983).

Sternhell, Zeev, Sznajder, Mario, Asheri, Maia, *Naissance de l'Idéologie fasciste* (Paris, Fayard, 1989).

Sutton, Michael, *Nationalism, Positivism and Catholicism. The Politics of Charles Maurras and French Catholics, 1890–1914* (Cambridge, Cambridge University Press, 1982).

Taine, H., *Les Origines de la France contemporaine. La Révolution 1. L'Anarchie spontanée 2. La Conquête jacobine* (Paris, Hachette, 1878, 1881).

Taine, H., *Les Origines de la France contemporaine* (V), *Le Régime moderne*, I (Paris, Hachette, 1891).

Taine, H., 'Napoléon Bonaparte', *Revue des Deux Mondes* 79 (15 Feb. 1887), 721–52, 80 (1 Mar. 1887) 5–48.

Taittinger, Pierre, *Les Cahiers de la Jeune France* (Paris, Éditions du National, 1926).

Thalamas, Amédée, *Jeanne d'Arc. L'histoire et la légende* (Paris, Paclot, 1904).

Thibaudeau, A.C., *Mémoires sur le Consulat* (Paris, 1827).

Thiers, Adolphe, *Histoire de la Révolution française* (Paris, Lecointe et Durey, 1823–7).

Thiers, Adolphe, *Histoire du Consulat et de l'Empire* (21 vols, Paris, Paulin, 1845–69).

Thomas, Chantal, '*La Marseillaise* de Jean Renoir: naissance d'un chant', in J.-C. Bonnet and P. Roger, *La Légende de la Révolution au XXe siècle* (Paris, Flammarion, 1988), 116–38.

Tombs, Robert, ed., *Nationhood and Nationalism in France from Boulangism to the Great War* (London, HarperCollins Academic, 1991).

Todorov, Tzvetan, *Nous et les Autres. La Réflexion française sur la Diversité humaine* (Paris, Seuil, 1989).

Touchard, Jean, *La Gloire de Béranger* (Paris, Armand Colin, 1968).

Touraine, Alain, *Le Mouvement de mai ou le Communisme utopique* (Paris, Seuil, 1968).

Touraine, Alain, *et al.*, *La Prophétie anti-nucléaire* (Paris, Seuil, 1980).

Tridon, Gustave, *Les Hébertistes* (Paris, 1864).

Tudesq, André-Jean, *L'Élection présidentielle de Louis-Napoléon Bonaparte, 10 décembre 1848* (Paris, Colin/Kiosque, 1965).

Tudesq, André-Jean, 'La Légende napoléonienne en France en 1848', *Revue historique* (218), 1957.

Tulard, Jean, *Napoléon. Le mythe du sauveur* (Paris, Fayard, 1977). Translated by T. Waugh as *Napoleon. The Myth of the Saviour* (London, Methuen, 1985).

Vallès, Jules, *L'Insurgé* [1886] (Paris, Garnier-Flammarion, 1970).

Valois, Georges, *Le Fascisme* (Paris, Nouvelle Librairie Nationale, 1927).

Valois, Georges, *Guerre ou Révolution* (Paris, Librairie Valois, 1931).

Valois, Georges, *L'Homme contre l'Argent. Souvenirs de Dix Ans, 1918–1928* (Paris, Librairie Valois, 1928).

Valois, Georges, *L'Homme qui vient. Philosophie de l'Autorité* (Paris, Nouvelle Libraire Nationale, 3rd edn, 1910).

Valois, Georges, *La Révolution sociale ou le Roi* in *La Monarchie et la Classe ouvrière* (Paris, Action Française, 1909).

Vandal, Albert, Napoléon et Alexandre 1er. *L'Alliance russe sous le Premier Empire* (3 vols, Paris, Plon, 1891–6).

Variot, Jean, *Propos de Georges Sorel* (Paris, Gallimard, 1935).

Vercruysse, Jeroom, 'Jeanne d'Arc au siècle des Lumières', *Studies on Voltaire and the Eighteenth Century*, XC (Banbury, Voltaire Foundation, 1972).

Vidalenc, Jean, 'L'opinion publique en Normandie et le retour des restes de Napoléon en décembre 1840', in *Mélanges offerts à C.-H. Pouthas* (Paris, Publications de la Sorbonne, 1973).

Villiers, Philippe de, *Lettre ouverte aux coupeurs de têtes et aux menteurs du Bicentenaire* (Paris, Albin Michel, 1989).

Voltaire, 'Jeanne d'Arc' in *Dictionnaire philosophique, Oeuvres complètes* VII (Paris, 1876).

Voltaire, *La Pucelle d'Orléans*, in *Oeuvres complètes* II (Paris, Firmin-Didot, 1876).

Vovelle, Michel, 'La Marseillaise', in Pierre Nora, ed., *Les Lieux de Mémoire* I, 88–90.

Waldeck-Rochet, Émile, *Les Enseignements de mai–juin 1968* (Paris, Editions sociales, 1968).

Waldeck-Rousseau, René, *La Défense républicaine* (Paris, Fasquelle, 1902).

Wallon, Henri, *Histoire du Tribunal révolutionnaire de Paris* (6 vols, Paris, Hachette, 1880–2), vii, xi.

Wallon, Henri, *La Révolution du 31 mai et le Fédéralisme en 1793, ou la France vaincue par la Commune de Paris* (2 vols, Paris, Hachette, 1886).

Wartelle, F., 'Bara, Viala. Le Thème de l'enface héroïque dans les manuels scolaires (IIIe République), *AHRF*, 52 (1980), 365–89.

Weber, Eugen, *L'Action Française* (Paris, Stock, 1962).

Weber, Eugen, *My France. Politics, Culture, Myth* (Cambridge, Mass., The Belknap Press of Harvard University Press, 1991).

Winock, Michel, *Histoire politique de la revue 'Esprit', 1930–1950* (Paris, Seuil, 1975).

Winock, Michel, 'Jean Allemane: une fidélité critique', in Jacques Rougerie, *Jalons pour une Histoire de la Commune* (Assen, van Gorcam, 1973).

Winock, Michel, *Nationalisme, antisémitisme et fascisme en France* (Paris, Seuil, 1990).

Winock, Michel, 'La Scission de Châtellerault et la naissance du parti allemaniste, 1890–1', *Le Mouvement social* 75 (April–June 1971), 33–62.

Wolf, Dieter, *Doriot, du Communisme à la collaboration* (Paris, Fayard, 1969).

Ysmal, Colette, *Defferre parle* (Paris, ENSP/Centre d'Étude de la Vie politique française, 1966).

Zoppi, Gilbert, 'Jeanne d'Arc et les républicains', in Jacques Viard, ed., *L'Esprit républicain*, Colloque d'Orléans, 4–5 Sept. 1970 (Paris, Klincksieck, 1972).

Index